THE CAMBRIDGE HIST·

AUSTRALIA

*

VOLUME I

Indigenous and Colonial Australia

Volume 1 of *The Cambridge History of Australia* explores Australia's history from ancient times through to Federation in 1901. It begins with an archaeological examination of the continent's Indigenous history, which dates back 50,000 years. This volume examines the first European encounters with Australia and its Indigenous people, and the subsequent colonisation of the land by the British in the late eighteenth century, providing insight into the realities of a convict society and how this shaped the nation's development.

Part I traces the dynamic growth in Australia's economy, demography and industry throughout the nineteenth century, as it moved towards a system of liberal democracy and one of the most defining events in its history: the Federation of the colonies in 1901. Part II offers a deeper investigation of key topics, such as relations between Indigenous people and settlers, and Australia's colonial identity. It also covers the economy, science and technology, law and literature.

This volume is informed by a geographic sensibility: land emerges as a central theme in Australian history, shaping its political, legal and social past; and the authors examine regional and Australian–Pacific ideas of history and identity.

ALISON BASHFORD is Vere Harmsworth Professor of Imperial and Naval History, University of Cambridge.

STUART MACINTYRE is a Professorial Fellow in the School of Historical and Philosophical Studies at the University of Melbourne, Australia.

Praise for *The Cambridge History of Australia*

'*The Cambridge History of Australia* provides so much more than a chronology of events... here are two volumes filled with wisdom that will inform those who make the choices for the future... Alison Bashford and Stuart Macintyre, in their work as editors, have brought together a diversity of intelligent voices and presented them in a consistent and engaging manner which invites us to pursue further reading. There is something for all of us: teachers, researchers, students and curious laymen who wish to engage in and celebrate our shared story.'

The Honourable Dame Quentin Bryce AD CVO, former Governor-General of the Commonwealth of Australia

'This impressive work includes contributions from 67 historians, a veritable Who's Who of Australian history, and covers the nation's past from its earliest people to the ways we live now.'

Anna Clark, *Sydney Morning Herald*

'Lucid, balanced, innovative and comprehensive, this book shows Australian historians at their best. At a turning-point in the national experience, Australians have a right to expect such a book as this, a report card on the long-term progress of their country.'

Emeritus Professor Alan Atkinson

THE CAMBRIDGE
HISTORY OF
AUSTRALIA

*

VOLUME 1
Indigenous and Colonial Australia

*

Edited by
ALISON BASHFORD
and
STUART MACINTYRE

CAMBRIDGE
UNIVERSITY PRESS

Contents

Contents

Contents

Abbreviations

AAAS	Australasian Association for the Advancement of Science (later ANZAAS)
ABS	Australian Bureau of Statistics
AGPS	Australian Government Printing Service
ANU	Australian National University
ASN	Australasian Steam Navigation Company
BHP	Broken Hill Proprietary
BPA	Board for the Protection of Aborigines
CMS	Church Missionary Society
CO	Colonial Office
CSR	Colonial Sugar Refinery
GDP	gross domestic product
GPS	Great Public School
HMSO	Her Majesty's Stationery Office
LMS	London Missionary Society
MP	member of parliament
NAEE	North Australian Exploring Expedition
NSW	New South Wales
NT	Northern Territory
NZ	New Zealand
OECD	Organisation for Economic Co-operation and Development
OSL	optically stimulated luminescence
P&O	Peninsular & Oriental Steam Navigation Company
Qld	Queensland
SA	South Australia
SLV	State Library of Victoria
TNA	The National Archives, United Kingdom
UCLA	University of California Los Angeles
UNSW	University of New South Wales
UQP	University of Queensland Press
UWA	University of Western Australia
VDL	Van Diemen's Land
Vic.	Victoria
WA	Western Australia
WCTU	Woman's Christian Temperance Union
years BP	(radiocarbon years) before present

Maps

Figures

Tables

Notes on contributors

TRACEY BANIVANUA MAR is Senior Lecturer in History at La Trobe University, and researches colonial and transnational indigenous histories.

ALISON BASHFORD is Vere Harmsworth Professor of Imperial and Naval History at the University of Cambridge, and specialises in the history of science and medicine.

MELISSA BELLANTA is Australian Research Council Postdoctoral Fellow at the University of Queensland, and writes on Australian popular culture and gender.

EMMA CHRISTOPHER is Australian Research Fellow at the University of Sydney, researching slave and convict transportation in West Africa, the Atlantic and Australia.

ANN CURTHOYS is Australian Research Council Professorial Fellow in History at the University of Sydney, and has published widely on race and Australian identity.

ROBERT DIXON is Professor of Australian Literature at the University of Sydney and has published widely on Australian literature, postcolonialism, photography and early cinema.

PENELOPE EDMONDS is Australian Research Council Future Fellow at the University of Tasmania and works on comparative settler frontiers and race relations.

MARK FINNANE is Australian Research Council Professorial Fellow at Griffith University, where he researches Australian policing and law.

LISA FORD is Senior Lecturer in History at the University of New South Wales, where her research focuses on legal histories of sovereignty.

LIONEL FROST is Associate Professor in Economics at Monash University with specialist interests in urbanism and regional development in Australia.

JOHN GASCOIGNE is Scientia Professor of History at the University of New South Wales, and his research chiefly focuses on exploration, science and religion during the Enlightenment.

ANDREA GAYNOR is Professor of History at the University of Western Australia and specialises in environmental history.

DAVID GOODMAN is Associate Professor in History at the University of Melbourne, and his research interests include American history and the Australian gold rushes.

JEANETTE HOORN is Professor of Visual Cultures at the University of Melbourne, where she researches orientalism, gender and modernity in early twentieth-century film, travel writing and painting.

Contributors

JULIA HORNE is the University Historian and Senior Research Fellow at the University of Sydney, and writes on the history of higher education, philanthropy and nineteenth-century travel.

HELEN IRVING is Professor of Law at the University of Sydney, and specialises in constitutional law and history.

GRACE KARSKENS is Associate Professor of History at the University of New South Wales, and researches colonial and urban history, focusing especially on Sydney.

REBECCA KIPPEN is Australian Research Council Future Fellow at the University of Melbourne's Centre for Health and Society, specialising in historical demography.

SHINO KONISHI is Research Fellow in Indigenous History at the Australian National University, writing on eighteenth-century encounters between Europeans and Indigenous Australians.

MARILYN LAKE is Australian Research Council Professorial Fellow and Professor of History at the University of Melbourne, and writes on the national and transnational histories of politics and nation.

JANET McCALMAN is Professor in the Centre for Health and Society at the University of Melbourne, specialising in social history, family history and historical demography.

CINDY McCREERY is Senior Lecturer in British and European History at the University of Sydney. Her research interests encompass British visual culture and maritime history.

STUART MACINTYRE is a Professorial Fellow in the School of Historical and Philosophical Studies at the University of Melbourne, and has written widely on Australian national, political and labour history.

KIRSTEN McKENZIE is Associate Professor in Australian history at the University of Sydney, where she focuses on status and politics in the British Empire.

SARA MAROSKE is Research Associate of the Royal Botanic Gardens Melbourne and editor of the Mueller Correspondence Project.

HAMISH MAXWELL-STEWART is Associate Professor in history at the University of Tasmania, and specialises in the history of convict transportation.

JESSIE MITCHELL has published on Australian colonial missionary and political history, while working as a research associate at the University of Sydney.

MARIA NUGENT is Research Fellow in Indigenous History at the Australian National University, where she works on Aboriginal historical memory in Australia.

ANNE O'BRIEN is Associate Professor at the University of New South Wales, where she researches histories of religion, spirituality, gender and welfare.

SUE O'CONNOR is Laureate Fellow of Archaeology at the Australian National University, and specialises in the archaeology of Southeast Asia and Australia.

DAVID ANDREW ROBERTS is Senior Lecturer at the University of New England, and conducts research into convict and settler history in Australia.

PENNY RUSSELL is Professor of History at the University of Sydney, and specialises in histories of gender, status and manners.

SEAN SCALMER is Associate Professor at the University of Melbourne, where he researches social and political movements in Australia.

Contributors

DERYCK M. SCHREUDER is an imperial historian, and was previously Challis Professor of History at the University of Sydney before becoming vice-chancellor of the universities of Western Sydney and Western Australia.

GEOFFREY SHERINGTON is Emeritus Professor at the University of Sydney, and has published extensively on histories of education and immigration.

PETER VETH is Winthrop Professor of Archaeology at the University of Western Australia, and specialises in the evolution of global desert societies and rock art.

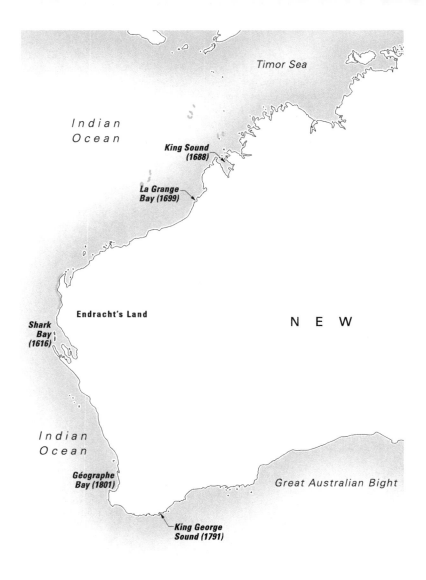

Timor Sea

Indian Ocean

King Sound (1688)

La Grange Bay (1699)

N E W

Endracht's Land

Shark Bay (1616)

Indian Ocean

Géographe Bay (1801)

Great Australian Bight

King George Sound (1791)

Southern Ocean

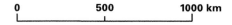

0   500   1000 km

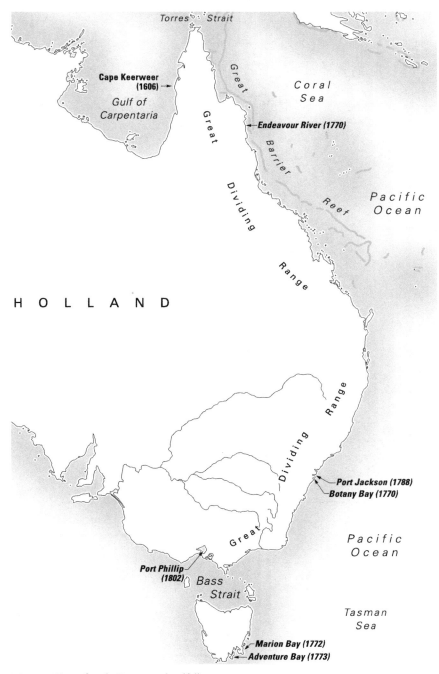

Torres Strait

Cape Keerweer
(1606) →

Gulf of
Carpentaria

Coral
Sea

Great

Great

Endeavour River (1770)

Barrier

Reef

Pacific
Ocean

Dividing

Range

H O L L A N D

Dividing Range

Great

Port Jackson (1788)
Botany Bay (1770)

Pacific
Ocean

Port Phillip
(1802)

Bass
Strait

Tasman
Sea

Marion Bay (1772)
Adventure Bay (1773)

Map 0.1 Sites of early European landfall

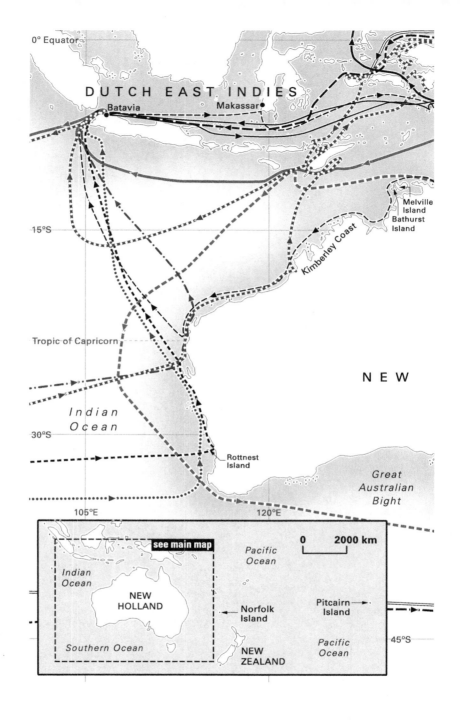

0° Equator

DUTCH EAST INDIES

Batavia   Makassar

15°S

Melville
Island
Bathurst
Island

Kimberley Coast

Tropic of Capricorn

NEW

Indian
Ocean

30°S

Rottnest
Island

Great
Australian
Bight

105°E   120°E

see main map

Pacific
Ocean

0   2000 km

Indian
Ocean

NEW
HOLLAND

Norfolk
Island

Pitcairn
Island

Southern Ocean

NEW
ZEALAND

Pacific
Ocean

45°S

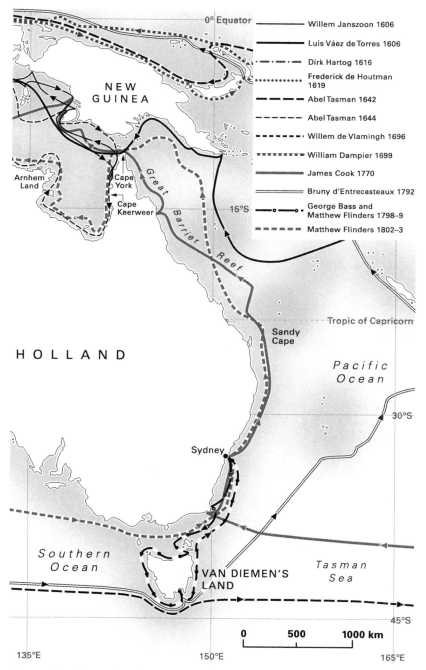

0° Equator

	Willem Janszoon 1606
	Luis Váez de Torres 1606
	Dirk Hartog 1616
	Frederick de Houtman 1619
	Abel Tasman 1642
	Abel Tasman 1644
	Willem de Vlamingh 1696
	William Dampier 1699
	James Cook 1770
	Bruny d'Entrecasteaux 1792
	George Bass and Matthew Flinders 1798–9
	Matthew Flinders 1802–3

NEW GUINEA

Arnhem Land

Cape York

Cape Keerweer

Great Barrier Reef

15°S

Tropic of Capricorn

Sandy Cape

HOLLAND

Pacific Ocean

30°S

Sydney

Southern Ocean

Tasman Sea

VAN DIEMEN'S LAND

45°S

0   500   1000 km

135°E   150°E   165°E

Map 0.2 Maritime exploration, 1606–1803

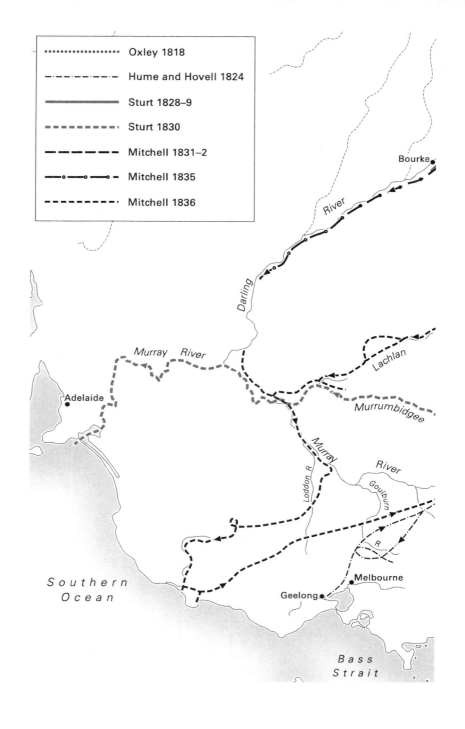

••••••••••••••	Oxley 1818
–·–·–·–·–·–	Hume and Hovell 1824
—————	Sturt 1828–9
– – – – – – –	Sturt 1830
– – – – –	Mitchell 1831–2
–o–o–o–	Mitchell 1835
– – – – – –	Mitchell 1836

Bourke

Darling River

Murray River

Lachlan

Adelaide

Murrumbidgee

Murray River

Loddon R

Goulburn

R

Melbourne

Geelong

Southern Ocean

Bass Strait

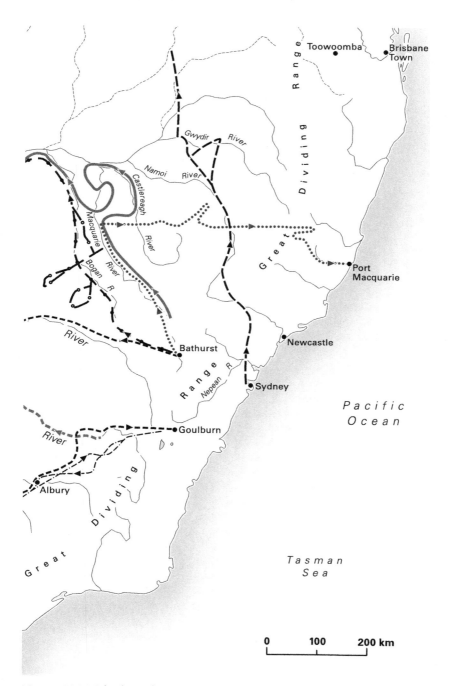

Map 0.3 Major inland expeditions, south-east Australia, 1818–36

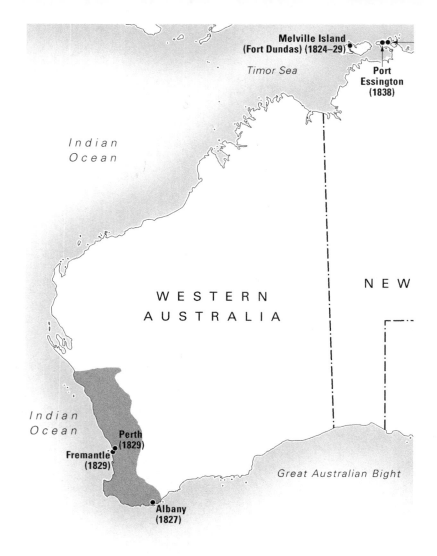

Melville Island
(Fort Dundas) (1824–29)

Timor Sea

Port
Essington
(1838)

*Indian
Ocean*

WESTERN
AUSTRALIA

NEW

*Indian
Ocean*

Perth
(1829)

Fremantle
(1829)

Great Australian Bight

Albany
(1827)

*Southern
Ocean*

0   500 km

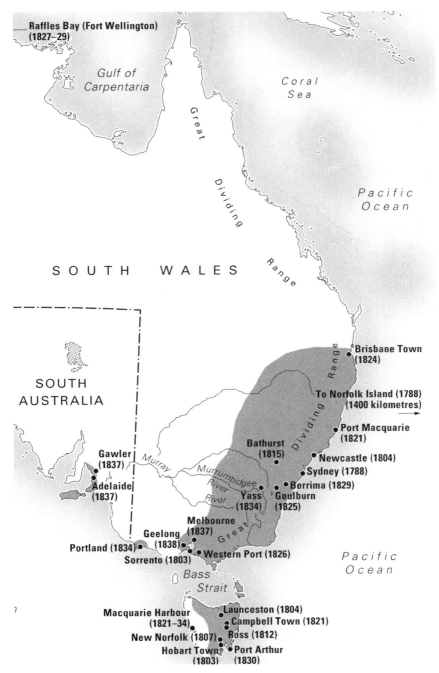

Map 0.4 The Australian colonies showing colonial occupation, c. 1838

Timor Sea

DARWIN

*Indian
Ocean*

Kimberley
District

Broome

Pilbara District

W E S T E R N
A U S T R A L I A

Alice
Springs

S O U T H

*Indian
Ocean*

Kalgoorlie
Coolgardie

PERTH

Great Australian Bight

Albany

Southern

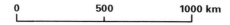

0   500   1000 km

Map 0.5 The Australian colonies, c. 1895

Preface

The history of Australia is the past of a continent and a Commonwealth, of ancient and modern times, Indigenous people and settlers. The *Cambridge History of Australia* captures the expertise of 67 historians, across generations and fields of knowledge, to present a fresh account of the nation's past. Volume I, *Indigenous and Colonial Australia*, deals with Australia's history to 1901, when the colonies federated. The result of that Federation was the first new nation of the twentieth century. Volume II, *The Commonwealth of Australia*, encompasses Australian history as it has unfolded since 1901.

These volumes succeed a limited number of multi-authored antecedents, which form a telling historical sequence. On one view, the new *Cambridge History of Australia* follows the inter-war *Cambridge History of the British Empire*. Part One of Volume VII dealt with Australia, Part Two with New Zealand. Formally adviser to the three British editors of the eight-volume series, Ernest Scott of the University of Melbourne commissioned chapters from the fledgling Australian historical profession to produce a history that revealed the successful British settlement of Australia and the growth of a country coming to appreciate 'the responsibilities as well as the privileges which nationhood involves'.[1] Published in 1933, the book was used widely for two decades.

It was succeeded in 1955 by a new collaborative history edited by Gordon Greenwood of the University of Queensland, which was sponsored by the committee responsible for celebrating the 50th anniversary of the Australian Commonwealth in 1951. Its title, *Australia: A Social and Political History*, signalled a reorientation away from the *Cambridge History*'s emphasis on exploration, settlement and constitutional development, and towards the growth

---

1 J. Holland Rose, A.P. Newton and E.A. Benians, with Ernest Scott (eds), *The Cambridge History of the British Empire*, vol. VII, part 1, *Australia* (Cambridge University Press, 1933), p. 624.

of a distinctive society. Greenwood assembled younger practitioners in the emergent field of Australian history with the expectation that they could guide the student and provide the 'layman' with 'an intelligent understanding of the development of his own society'.[2]

Greenwood's history passed through eleven printings before it was superseded in 1974 by *A New History of Australia*, edited by Frank Crowley.[3] This, too, was organised in a sequence of periods chosen to 'highlight the significant events and turning points in Australia's development'; it was conceived as a general history, drawing on the substantial body of research produced in the previous decades to integrate social and economic history with government and politics. Both the Greenwood and Crowley volumes spoke to the mood of confidence in the post-war decades of rising prosperity and also to the growing diversity of Australian society.

The Australian volume of the *Cambridge History of the British Empire* was reissued in 1988, with a new introduction by Geoffrey Bolton – published, if not always read, as a period piece. That was the Bicentenary year, 200 years after Governor Arthur Phillip came ashore from his First Fleet at Sydney Cove in 1788. It was not surprising that the once-authoritative Cambridge history attracted little attention during the appearance in this year of shelves of national, nationalist and anti-nationalist history writing. It had emphasised the British origins of a burgeoning nationhood, whereas in 1988 the Australian government wanted to celebrate a far more diverse nation and withheld support from a private re-enactment of the voyage of the First Fleet. The Bicentenary was marked by uncertainty over the place of Indigenous Australians in the national story and heated debate over the legacy of the past. Neither the Greenwood nor the Crowley volume served the new mood of self-questioning.

The direct antecedents to the new *Cambridge History of Australia* were the ambitious collaborative works of 1988. Much of the historical profession was drawn into the preparation of *Australians: A Historical Library*, by far the largest historical project then or since. It consisted of five multi-authored volumes that dealt with slices of Australian history at 50-year intervals: *Australians to 1788, Australians 1838, 1888, 1938* and *Australians after 1938*. It also comprised five reference volumes: an historical atlas, a dictionary, a chronology, a guide to sources and a volume of historical statistics. The 'slicing' methodology adopted for all but the first and last of the five non-reference volumes, in

---

2 Gordon Greenwood (ed.), *Australia: A Social and Political History* (Sydney: Angus & Robertson, 1955), p. v.
3 F.K. Crowley (ed.), *A New History of Australia* (Melbourne: Heinemann, 1974).

which a cross-section of Australian society in particular years could be considered deeply, was designed to counter the narrative organisation of prior histories and to draw specialist fields of scholarship into an integrated whole.

Australians: A Historical Library employed high production standards and made extensive use of illustrations and graphical devices, as well as paying close attention to accessible prose designed to reach a popular audience. Along with many other Bicentennial publications and an extensive program of commemorative events, it foregrounded the politics of history in a settler colonial nation and stimulated historical debate in public and scholarly forums. Australian public life has been all the better for it. History was brought to the notice of an audience both more inclusive and more engaged than Greenwood's 'laymen', and with an intensity that perhaps would have surprised the post-war generation. Two hundred years of British colonisation was an anniversary simultaneously celebrated, criticised and debated as 50 years of national Federation had not been.

That the past held new significance for the present was evident on the shores of Sydney Harbour, where Indigenous activists and supporters protested 'Australia Day' as 'Invasion Day' on 26 January 1988. It was also evident in the history profession as *Australians: A Historical Library* was countered by four volumes written and edited by dissident historians as *A People's History of Australia*.[4] That was followed by a further collaborative endeavour of national reassessment, perhaps unique in the genre of national histories anywhere. *Creating a Nation* was written by four leading feminist historians as a new interpretation in which the entire national story was recast with gender to the fore.[5] The 1988 volumes, the people's history and the feminist history were all responses to a lack of confidence in earlier sequential narratives.

First published in 2013, the *Cambridge History of Australia* has the virtue of not coinciding with any official commemoration. In 1813 Sydney's Blue Mountains were crossed by Blaxland, Lawson and Wentworth, a staple of an earlier national history, and in 1913 came the less-remembered naming of the new national capital of Canberra. But perhaps the key anniversary that marks this major venture in Australian collaborative history is its publication 25 years after the Bicentenary. It includes a number of eminent historians

4 Verity Burgmann and Jenny Lee (eds), *A People's History of Australia since 1788*. 4 vols: *Making a Life; Staining the Wattle; A Most Valuable Acquisition; Constructing a Culture* (Melbourne: McPhee Gribble, 1988).
5 Patricia Grimshaw, Ann McGrath, Marilyn Lake and Marian Quartly, *Creating a Nation* (Melbourne: McPhee Gribble, 1994).

who played a prominent role in the Bicentennial ventures – but it involves more historians who were taught by them. It is thus a national history shaped by a new generation. It carries neither the celebration nor the stark critique of Australian nationalism that characterised the Bicentenary. It incorporates much of the postcolonial, cultural and feminist scholarship that has strongly shaped historical awareness, knowledge and methodology. At the same time, it has been conceived, discussed and written well after the cultural turn in history writing that privileged theory over investigative research, language over experience.

The histories edited by Greenwood and Crowley marked the growth of the Australian history profession and of Australian history as a field of research. Whereas the earlier *Cambridge History of the British Empire* contained chapters written by economists, lawyers, a geographer and a literary scholar, not all of them working in universities and several based overseas, the post-war histories relied almost entirely on the work being done in local history departments. That self-sufficiency allowed the contributors to delineate more confidently the stages of national development around which they organised their histories, and to highlight in their chapters the growing body of specialised research. Since then, however, the disciplinary boundaries have shifted as scholars working in cognate disciplines have turned to Australian history, historians have drawn on these disciplines in turn, and new fields of knowledge have emerged. While most of the contributors to this *Cambridge History of Australia* are historians, it includes chapters written by practitioners of archaeology, political science, economic, educational and literary history, environmental, gender and Indigenous studies. Part of its purpose is to bring these different ways of understanding the past into conversation.

The *Cambridge History of Australia* stands apart from previous collaborative works, in part because it is a national history written in global times. It is the work of a generation of historians for whom national history now means a combination of encounters located in time and place and the large-scale patterns that transcend national boundaries. While such a global outlook itself is not new – indeed, it is perhaps more longstanding in Australian history than elsewhere – it is now informed by new ways of exploring the relations between the global and the local. Australia's place in global history is reinterpreted after race, after Empire and after postcolonialism.

Part I of each volume of the *Cambridge History* presents Australia's history in a sequential summary of the important events and changes over stretches of time that range from one to two or three decades. Some decades have received concentrated attention, since they saw major turns or accelerations in Australia: the 1850s gold rush; the formative political and social develop-ments of the 1890s; and 1939–49, bringing together Australia's involvement in World War 2 and the great post-war reconstruction, for example.

Part II of each volume cuts a different way. Recognising the limitations of telling a national history through a chronological narrative alone, it 'slices' Australian history, not vertically by time as in *Australians: A Historical Library*, but horizontally by theme. In these chapters contributors assess the whole period covered by that volume in the light of a particular aspect (such as reli-gion), an historical phenomenon (such as environmental transformations), a particular category of analysis (such as gender) or a geographical dimension (for example, Australia and the Asia-Pacific region). It is in these chapters that change over time is most evident.

Such thematic interpretation of the past is one of the lasting effects of a robust critical tradition in Australian historiography. It stems from intellectual exchange with other disciplines, as well as transnational approaches to telling national stories. Australian history has been recast in the light of new comparative histories that locate it not just within the context of the British Empire, but also with respect to North American history, Chinese history and the history of the Pacific and Southeast Asia. In the process, core business in Australian history has been revised.

Authors have been asked to write beyond their own interpretative positions, to present and explain key trends and events, and, where debate has been significant, to explain to the reader the contours and implications of the changing historiography. There is no uniform voice, but there is consistency of scope and scale. None of these chapters are simply essays displaying an author's specialism. They are all more than that, and the list of further reading at the end of each volume directs the reader to the key works in the authors' fields. In addition to the design of each volume as a coherent whole, contributors had the opportunity to consider their own chapters in the light of the others, and to discuss questions of treatment, nomenclature and coverage.

Australian readers will recognise how strongly the past shapes the present, from the commemoration of wars fought on foreign soil to the 'history wars' fought over frontier violence; and from the recuperation of local history to the integration of migrant histories that graft onto Australian life the past of other places. The contributors have not shied from the contested nature of such uses of the past but neither have they allowed their own sympathies to prevail over the obligations of historical scholarship. International read-ers, untroubled by the fault lines of domestic sensibilities, will appreciate a treatment that attends to the distinctive features of Australian history.

The preparation of these volumes has been a collaboration enjoyed with many colleagues. Particular thanks go to David Armitage, Richard Broome, Anne Clarke, Ann Curthoys, Graeme Davison, John Hirst, Rebecca Kippen, Cindy McCreery and Tim Rowse. Frank Bongiorno provided invaluable advice as we brought the project to conclusion. For research assistance we are grateful to Hannah Forsyth, Chris Holdridge, Sean Cosgrove and Tiarne Barratt. Three meetings were held with contributors, to develop and refine chapters, in Launceston, Sydney and Adelaide. They were made possible by the generosity of the Harvard Committee on Australian Studies, the universities of Sydney and Melbourne, and the Australian Historical Association.

Alison Bashford, Sydney
Stuart Macintyre, Melbourne

Introduction

ALISON BASHFORD AND STUART MACINTYRE

Australia's history has unfolded on vastly different scales, temporal and geographical. It has a human history in 'deep time' – an Indigenous history of perhaps 50,000 years – that continues to the present. This temporal expanse confounds both the conventional chronology of human history, measured in far shorter periods, and the geological eras to which deep time normally refers. It is sometimes comprehended by Aboriginal Australians not as a past at all, but as what has become known as the 'Dreaming', in which 'before' and 'after' are indistinct.[1]

Modern Australian history, by contrast, is foreshortened. The colonisation and settlement of the Australian continent by the British took place as part of economic and population growth that marked the eighteenth and nineteenth centuries out from any preceding period in world history. Colonial Australia was a product of the late Enlightenment and of the age of revolutions that hit its stride – for better and for worse – in a century of accelerating agricultural, industrial and demographic change.

Australian history has also unfolded on geographic scales that are both global and local. On one hand, the human past has taken place on a large and geologically old island. In this way, Australian 'national' history doubles as the history of one of the planet's continents. The island's location in the southern hemisphere partly explains its foreshortened modern history. From the early seventeenth century Portuguese and Spanish ships accidentally encountered, and sometimes actively explored, the west coast on journeys elsewhere, and the Dutch journeyed along the far south-east coast. In the process Van Diemen's Land was named and, for two centuries, the continent was known by the English as New Holland. At about the same time, fishing and trading expeditions by Southeast Asians began, and gradually turned

---

1 Deborah Bird Rose, 'Hard Times: An Australian Study', in Klaus Neumann, Nicholas Thomas and Hilary Ericksen (eds), *Quicksands: Foundational Histories in Australia and Aotearoa New Zealand* (Sydney: UNSW Press, 1999), pp. 2–19.

into seasonal visits, beginning a centuries-long regional connection between communities along and within the Torres Strait and present-day Indonesia.

Australia's eighteenth-century history is deeply connected to the British and French exploration of the Pacific. Behind this was an Enlightenment-inspired desire for knowledge of the natural and human world, strategic ambitions in an era of European wars that extended to their overseas empires, and commercial forces that increasingly linked Pacific, Atlantic and Indian Ocean trade. In all three regions convicts, settlers and slaves were moved across the seas. Out of that history, in one small cove on the south-east of the Australian continent, British colonisation and settlement began. Even there and then, at the beginning of 1788, connections and encounters were simultaneously local and global. Aboriginal people and British officers and convicts watched one another warily, their histories meeting.[2] And, to the surprise of all, two French ships entered and anchored in Botany Bay, their officers and crew exchanged compliments with their British counterparts and six weeks later sailed on.

First encounters between cultures took place over many generations as the Australian frontier moved inland from coastal settlements. Europeans tended to produce long accounts of these meetings.[3] But in what ways, and through what knowledge, do we assess and make claims about Aboriginal experience of such encounters – and, even more difficult, Aboriginal history before them? How is Australian 'prehistory' to be incorporated into Australian national history? Through colonial history is one answer, as empirically correct as it is politically challenging. Another is through material culture, the analysis of which is the work of archaeologists. In the opening chapter to this volume, archaeological knowledge is set out, telling Australian 'deep time' history through environmental changes and analysis of remaining material culture, from ancient human occupation to the mid-1600s. This chapter summarises the current archaeological consensus about human migration into and within the continent, across great climate changes and different environments that prompted technological developments. Surviving traces of material culture tell us a lot. And for more recent times, there is much more than mere traces. Extensive rock art sites in the Northern Territory depict the visiting 'Macassan' fishing boats, for example. Life-scale humans and animals were engraved into the sandstone on which Sydney is built, common enough to form part of many Sydney residents' awareness of Aboriginal history. In

2 Maria Nugent, *Botany Bay: Where Histories Meet* (Sydney: Allen & Unwin, 2005).
3 Shino Konishi, *The Aboriginal Male in the Enlightenment World* (London: Pickering & Chatto, 2012).

addition to such graphic communication – there was no written language through which pre-contact Aboriginal people told their past – history was communicated orally. Part of this storytelling concerned the occasional visits of seaborne strangers. Some of these accounts appear in the second chapter, offering a different mode through which Indigenous history is brought into the present.

One way or another, almost everything about the history of the Australian colonies was about land. Late-eighteenth and early nineteenth-century convicts who would never have been landowners had they stayed in England, Scotland, Wales or Ireland, were granted, bought and sometimes just took land in the new colonial world after serving their sentences. Property laws and policies regulating the control and then release of crown land into private hands were attempts to bring to order what was sometimes an extra-legal, ad hoc occupation. This was the case from the earliest decades in New South Wales and Van Diemen's Land right up to the 1830s, when pastoralists 'squatted' on large runs of crown land. Whole new colonial ventures – the colony of South Australia in particular – were executed on pre-planned visions of land settlement, ownership and use that would promote suitable forms of sociability. Pressure for land reform remained a constant political conversation between different interest groups throughout the century.

An early generation of Australian historians documented this history of land and the regulation of its tenancy, use and ownership. There was an emphasis on exploring and pioneering, after which scholars turned to analyse the struggle to wrest control from powerful large landholders known as 'squatters' as a principal theme in colonial politics and economic development. Historical and economic geographers contributed their own accounts of colonial land and agricultural practice.[4] This was one of the intellectual trajectories that produced a later generation of environmental historians who have productively combined the history of science with the history of settler societies.[5]

---

4 D.W. Meinig, *On The Margins of the Good Earth: The South Australian Wheat Frontier, 1869–1884* (Adelaide: Rigby, 1970); J.M. Powell, *The Public Lands of Australia Felix: Settlement and Land Appraisal in Victoria, 1834–91* (Oxford University Press, 1970). And later, social and cultural histories of land: Sharon Morgan, *Land Settlement in Early Tasmania: Creating an Antipodean England* (Cambridge University Press, 1992); Richard Waterhouse, *The Vision Splendid: A Social and Cultural History of Rural Australia* (Perth: Curtin University Books, 2005).

5 Tom Griffiths, *Hunters and Collectors: The Antiquarian Imagination in Australia* (Cambridge University Press, 1996); Tom Griffiths and Libby Robin (eds), *Ecology and Empire: Environmental History of Settler Societies* (Melbourne University Press, 1997); Tim Bonyhady, *The Colonial Earth* (Melbourne: Miegunyah Press, 2000).

As in many contexts, evolving property law determined access to crown land and adjudicated between the competing claims of private holders. But in a settler colony more was at stake. Land raised the prior question of sovereignty: the state's claim to that territory in the first place. Earlier studies of land-taking and land reform have been rethought extensively in connection with the political and legal history of dispossession. That Britain initially claimed portions of the continent and then the whole continent – James Cook's claim of territory from Possession Island in 1770, Arthur Phillip's proclamation of sovereignty of the eastern half in 1788 and Charles Fremantle's declaration of possession of the western part of New Holland in 1829 – used to be taught as part of the natural order of things. This understanding of acquisition has not been held for many decades now. In its place is a new awareness of the substantial and protracted legal discussion over the nature and very possibility of those claims.[6] The claim to land was by no means clear or straightforward for historical actors at the time, especially during the 1830s, when pastoral expansion brought a major geographic reach into new territories of Aboriginal people. Land has been firmly reinstated as a subject of historical inquiry with a new Indigenous perspective. If 'colonial' Australian history used to signal a period, now it unmistakably signals the process of colonisation itself. It is no coincidence that Australian historians have been at the forefront internationally of analysis of the phenomenon of settler colonialism.[7]

Indigenous and settler relations across the century are the subject of a dedicated thematic chapter, and are explained in chapters on law, environmental transformations, population and health, and religion. The multiple means by which Aboriginal people defended land, moved into or were expelled from colonial social and legal systems; the ways in which they participated in or were kept out of a growing economy; the episodes of violence and attempts at conciliation – each of these aspects is examined, taking account of historical scholarship that traces the continuous history of Indigenous and settler

6 Henry Reynolds, *The Law of the Land* (Melbourne: Penguin, 1987); Lisa Ford, *Settler Sovereignty: Jurisdiction and Indigenous People in America and Australia, 1788–1836* (Cambridge, MA: Harvard University Press, 2010).

7 Julie Evans, Patricia Grimshaw, David Phillips and Shurlee Swain, *Equal Subjects, Unequal Rights: Indigenous Peoples in British Settler Colonies, 1830–1910* (Manchester University Press, 2003); Bain Attwood, 'Settler Histories and Indigenous Pasts: New Zealand and Australia', in Axel Schneider and Daniel Woolf (eds), *The Oxford History of Historical Writing*, vol. 5 (Oxford University Press, 2011), pp. 594–614; Heather Douglas and Mark Finnane, *Indigenous Crime and Settler Law: White Sovereignty after Empire* (Basingstoke: Palgrave Macmillan, 2012).

relations throughout the century and beyond.[8] While a broad pattern is evident, the possibilities and experiences were determined by the specific laws and policies of each colony. The fact that the colonies were independent of one another in legal and political terms is perhaps nowhere more significant than it is with respect to the management of Indigenous Australians. They often found themselves caught between jurisdictions, in ways that settler Australians also sometimes did, but rarely where the stakes were so high.

If land is central to Australian political, legal and social history, so, too, the sea that separates the continent from elsewhere is a major theme of recent spatially informed histories. Geoffrey Blainey suggested in the 1960s how distance shaped Australian history,[9] but now connection and proximity claim as much attention. Notwithstanding the famous statement by Australia's first prime minister, Edmund Barton, that '[f]or the first time in history, we have a nation for a continent and a continent for a nation',[10] Australian colonial historians have become less interested in the progressive formation of the continent-nation and more interested in a historical perspective that looks outwards from Australian shores to its immediate global region.

Although such a view can be overstated, some coastal settlements were more connected to other colonial outposts altogether – Port Darwin and Singapore, New South Wales and New Zealand, for example – than to some of the colonies that eventually federated to become Australia. Indeed, rather than seeking antecedents to a 'national' history, some colonial historians now emphasise the legal distinctions between colonies, and even 'patriotic' cultural attachment to one colony over another.

The island continent of Australia has a most interesting part to play in the new 'oceanic' histories. If 'Australia' was the term that Matthew Flinders promoted early as the name for the continent, 'Australasia' was also commonly used, incorporating New Zealand as well as many Pacific islands that later became British crown colonies or protectorates: Fiji, Norfolk Island, the Gilbert and Ellice Islands, Pitcairn Islands and New Guinea.[11] They

---

8 Bain Attwood and S.G. Foster (eds), *Frontier Conflict: The Australian Experience* (Canberra: National Museum of Australia, 2003); Richard Broome, *Aboriginal Australians: A History Since 1788*, rev. edn (Sydney: Allen & Unwin, 2010); Lyndall Ryan, *Tasmanian Aborigines: A History Since 1803* (Sydney: Allen & Unwin, 2012).

9 Geoffrey Blainey, *The Tyranny of Distance: How Distance Shaped Australia's History* (Melbourne: Sun Books, 1966).

10 Edmund Barton, speech at Annandale, *Sydney Morning Herald*, 8 April 1898.

11 For the development of the term 'Australasia' see Philippa Mein Smith and Peter Hempenstall, 'Rediscovering the Tasman World', in Philippa Mein Smith, Peter Hempenstall and Shaun Goldfinch, *Remaking the Tasman World* (Christchurch: University of Canterbury Press, 2008), pp. 13–30.

were linked to the Australian colonies as parts of the British Empire, and through missions, trade and commerce. In passing administrative moments, they moved into and out of Australian jurisdiction. Such a Pacific view of Australian history is not new: the 1933 *Cambridge History of the British Empire* devoted two chapters to it, 'The Exploration of the Pacific' and 'The Western Pacific, 1788–1885'. As Benians noted in the latter, during the 1820s courts in New South Wales and Van Diemen's Land were empowered to rule on offences committed by British subjects across the Pacific, not least since convicts were escaping in that direction.[12]

The imperial perspective that shaped that generation's scholarly interest is now just one part of the Australian-Pacific story. More recently, coastal China and the west coast of North America have also been incorporated into Australia's transpacific history.[13] As contributors note here, during the gold-rush decade of the 1850s and before the opening of the Panama Canal, it was easier to travel from California to Melbourne than it was from California to New York. Over the nineteenth century the Pacific was the site of a great circuit of Chinese labour and commerce, and after the 1851 gold rush the Australian colonies were key destinations. This defined a great deal of subsequent colonial history, and indeed Australian national history after 1901. Australia's colonial history was also linked directly to the Pacific region through the Islander labour trade that facilitated the Queensland sugar cane economy from the mid-1860s. The presence of these Islanders is at once part of the history of the Australian labour movement and the history of race in the Pacific. It is also part of the history of Australia's own imperial ambitions. While the idea of an 'Asia-Pacific region' was a product of the later twentieth century, its colonial origins and dynamics lie here.

There has been considerable interest in the north coast of Australia, not from the vantage point of the south-eastern metropolis, or even from the administrative standpoint of South Australia (it was the Northern Territory of South Australia from 1863 to 1911), but rather as a region linked by trade and culture with Singapore, the Dutch East Indies and the Torres

---

12 E.A. Benians, 'The Western Pacific, 1788–1885' in J. Holland Rose, A.P. Newton, E.A. Benians, with Ernest Scott (eds) *The Cambridge History of the British Empire*, vol. VII, part I, *Australia* (Cambridge University Press, 1933), pp. 325–64.

13 For example, Ian Tyrrell, *True Gardens of the Gods: Californian-Australian Environmental Reform, 1860–1930* (Berkeley: University of California Press, 1999); Penelope Edmonds, *Urbanizing Frontiers: Indigenous Peoples and Settlers in 19th-Century Pacific Rim Cities* (Vancouver: University of British Columbia Press, 2010); Marilyn Lake, 'Chinese Colonists Assert Their "Common Human Rights": Cosmopolitanism as Subject and Method of History', *Journal of World History*, 21, 3 (2010): 375–92.

Strait islands. The Torres Strait is in some ways the southern hemisphere's Mediterranean, a 'middle sea' that connected as much as separated the British settlements of Port Darwin and Singapore, as well as those of the Dutch and Portuguese empires. Here, on one view, is the long history of relations between Australians, Indonesians and Chinese people.[14] Similarly, the connections between colonial Australian history and the Indian Ocean have attracted recent analysis.[15] In a maritime world, and especially after the opening of the Suez Canal, the west coast on the Indian Ocean was the first Australian port of call for ships from Britain and Europe. Their route took them to India and Ceylon along the way, an intercolonial journey that brought mainly Europeans, but also some South Asians. In such ways, the oceans and the margins of colonial Australia have been incorporated into the historical account, accompanying longstanding analyses of interior explorations, transcontinental expeditions and vain searches for inland seas. Australian historians are now looking outwards as well as inwards, just as their historical actors did, to the Pacific Ocean and the Indian Ocean, and across the Torres Strait and Timor Sea.

In these ways the *Cambridge History of Australia*, Volume 1, is shaped by a distinct geographic sensibility. It is a world geography in which London no longer functions as the reference point it once was. This affects both nationalist histories that determinedly ignore London, and imperialist histories that see everything converging on the imperial metropolis. Even so, it remains a defining fact of Australian colonial history that New South Wales, Tasmania, Victoria, South Australia, Western Australia and Queensland were each part of the British Empire, and developed within a nineteenth-century 'Greater Britain'. How these imperial ventures became self-governing polities, and how a distinctive settler colonial nationalism bore political fruit at the end of the century, is part of the history of Britain and also constitutes the history of Australia. British imperial politics and procedures were shaped by the Australian experience, first in its administration of the faraway colonies and then in letting them go. How should self-government best proceed in the nineteenth century after the disastrous American War of the eighteenth? What was 'free trade' inside this imperial economic system? Were Indigenous people British subjects or not? Such questions are longstanding,

14 Regina Ganter with Julia Martínez and Gary Lee, *Mixed Relations: Asian–Aboriginal Contact in North Australia* (Perth: UWA Press, 2006), pp. 122–39.
15 Heather Goodall, Devleena Ghosh and Lindi R. Todd, 'Jumping Ship – Skirting Empire: Indians, Aborigines and Australians across the Indian Ocean', *Transforming Cultures eJournal*, 3, 1 (2008): 44–74.

broached by the first generation of Australian academic historians and by political historians of the British Empire since.[16] The Australian case has been taken up strongly within discussion of the 'British world',[17] and as part of a 'new imperial history' with its close conceptual links to feminist and transnational history.[18]

Just why the British decided to send convicts to Botany Bay in particular is perhaps Australian historiography's most enduring question; one that has always foregrounded the movement of people, goods and ideas. Historians once understood it largely in terms of a 'turn to the east' after the American War, and debated various strategic and commercial reasons for colonising the south-west Pacific. Revisionist histories, including the chapter here, place it within a global history of convict transportation and slavery, linking activity on the African continent to the American and European.[19] This is followed by a chapter that explores the social history of that unlikely new society over its first few decades. Historical analysis of the convict experience, of ordinary men's and women's social exchanges, leisure and messy day-to-day negotiations comes after decades of more policy oriented scholarship that concentrated on the policies followed by governors, and the changing systems through which they managed their convict charges and, sometimes with greater difficulty, their officers. The place of the Australian convict system in the history of penology has received considerable attention as well, with close analysis of the penitentiaries and the experiments in carceral punishment, as well as the more typical practice of assigning convicts to free settlers and setting them to work as part of households and farming ventures, or using them as labourers on public works. Convict

16 For example, John M. Ward, *Colonial Self-Government: The British Experience, 1759–1856* (London: Macmillan, 1976); Luke Trainor, *British Imperialism and Australian Nationalism: Manipulation, Conflict, and Compromise in the Late Nineteenth Century* (Cambridge University Press, 1994).

17 Carl Bridge and Kent Fedorowich (eds), *The British World: Diaspora, Culture, and Identity* (London: Frank Cass, 2003); Kate Darian-Smith, Patricia Grimshaw and Stuart Macintyre (eds), *Britishness Abroad: Transnational Movements and Imperial Cultures* (Melbourne University Press, 2007).

18 Ann Curthoys and Marilyn Lake (eds), *Connected Worlds: History in Transnational Perspective* (Canberra: ANU E Press, 2005); Zoë Laidlaw, *Colonial Connections 1815–45: Patronage, the Information Revolution and Colonial Government* (Manchester University Press, 2005). See also Ann Curthoys, 'Identity Crisis: Colonialism, Nation, and Gender in Australian History', *Gender and History*, 5, 2 (1993): 165–76.

19 For example, Ged Martin (ed.), *The Founding of Australia: The Argument about Australia's Origins* (Sydney: Hale & Iremonger, 1978); Emma Christopher, *A Merciless Place: The Lost Story of Britain's Convict Disaster in Africa and How it Led to the Settlement of Australia* (Sydney: Allen & Unwin, 2010); Alan Frost, *Botany Bay: The Real Story* (Melbourne: Black Inc., 2011).

labour was central to commercial enterprise in the economic history of early Australia.[20]

The great social fault-line of early colonial society was between felon and free. This lingered even into the twentieth century, when convict origins were perceived as shameful elements in a family history (and convict-free origins the great source of South Australian pride). Tracing convict genealogies is now a pastime eagerly pursued. Yet the founding convict population did not, it turns out, leave an especially significant demographic legacy. The population growth in Australia from the initial 1,300 Europeans to around 4 million in 1901 was mainly due to the natural increase of free settlers on the one hand, and the large immigrations of the gold rush on the other.

The original penal system did leave a massive political legacy. The welfare of the convict population was state business from the beginning, and this meant that some of the major politico-legal questions of the nineteenth century were at the heart of Australian history: freedom, punishment, improvement, reform. It was a society created not just in the light of a late-Enlightenment science, but also in the crucible of modern political thought about the nature of individual rights, punishment and legal systems. This is why, for example, Jeremy Bentham's prolific output includes *Panopticon versus New South Wales, or, The panopticon penitentiary system, and the penal colonization system, compared*.[21] More or less at the same time and as a kind of antipodean response, the native-born politician William Charles Wentworth, a Cambridge-educated lawyer and son of a convict mother, pitched his bids for 'Australasia' – 'a new Britannia in another world' – in terms of anti-transportation, free emigration, elected assemblies, freedom of the press and trial by jury.[22]

Not a few of the convicts were themselves deeply schooled in just such aspirations, having been transported for political offences. They included the early 'Scottish martyrs' primed in the liberty, equality and fraternity of the French Republic. Tolpuddle martyrs, Chartists, Irish republicans and rebels from British North America all made up the mix of convict and emancipist

---

20 Kirsty Reid, *Gender, Crime and Empire: Convicts, Settlers and the State in Early Colonial Australia* (Manchester University Press, 2007); Hamish Maxwell-Stewart, *Closing Hell's Gates: The Death of a Convict Station* (Sydney: Allen & Unwin, 2008); Grace Karskens, *The Colony: A History of Early Sydney* (Sydney: Allen & Unwin, 2009).

21 Jeremy Bentham, *Panopticon versus New South Wales, or, The panopticon penitentiary system and the penal colonization system, compared* (London: Wilks and Taylor, 1812).

22 William Charles Wentworth, *Australasia: A Poem Written for the Chancellor's Medal at the Cambridge Commencement, July 1823*, ed. G.A. Wilkes (Sydney University Press, 1982).

populations, working and politicking alongside the majority of convicts who were transported for theft.

The process by which liberal democracy was institutionalised in nineteenth-century Australia is an internationally significant one, and has engaged Australia's leading historians for many decades.[23] After responsible government was granted, electoral reform unfolded to dimensions that would have left Wentworth bewildered had he lived long enough to see his imagined free 'Australasia' turn into the Commonwealth of Australia in 1901. He might have been able to understand the contest of free trade and protection that formed the political dividing line at the end of the century. But the world's first labour government in Queensland in 1899 (albeit a minority government that held power for one week) and the enfranchisement of women in South Australia in 1894 were not part of his New Britannia.

Movements to end transportation and allow self-government were well established by the 1840s. The process of self-government was invited by Britain itself but the form it took was largely determined by colonial politics. This was the work of a local, if deeply divided elite, including the wealthy 'emancipists' who sought controls over the new legislatures (that materialised differently in each colony) and a limited franchise. But there were radical democratic pressures in play as well. Chartist demands, strengthened by political activity on the goldfields over the 1850s, were realised rapidly: manhood suffrage was quickly introduced in several of the colonies, the secret ballot was instituted, the eight-hour day embraced, and the first labour member of parliament was elected as early as 1859 in Victoria.

Accompanying this trend towards democratic inclusion was a deliberate exclusion of others. It was Victoria and California – both gold-defined societies – that simultaneously implemented the earliest immigration-restriction acts, initially directed at Chinese gold seekers, merchants and labourers. In the Victorian case, regulations made entry into colonial territory increasingly difficult for Chinese, and later Indian and other 'coloured aliens'. These restrictions have been seen as formative of Australian society over the last half of the nineteenth century. Older histories of crude colonial racism have been extended in histories that investigate the active engagement of Chinese

23 J.B. Hirst, *The Strange Birth of Colonial Democracy: New South Wales 1848–1884* (Sydney: Allen & Unwin, 1988); Stuart Macintyre, *A Colonial Liberalism: The Lost World of Three Victorian Visionaries* (Oxford University Press, 1991); Alan Atkinson, *The Europeans in Australia, A History. Volume 2, Democracy* (Oxford University Press, 2004); Peter Cochrane, *Colonial Ambition: Foundations of Australian Democracy* (Melbourne University Press, 2006); Ann Curthoys (ed.), 'Indigenous People and Settler Self Government', special issue, *Journal of Colonialism and Colonial History*, 13, 1 (2012): online.

merchants especially in the assertion of 'rights'.[24] Others tell the histories of people who slipped through and around the growing racial and labour regulations: individuals who contributed to the history of coastal and rural Australia over the nineteenth century. What became known late in the century as 'white Australia' was sometimes and in some places more myth than practice.[25] At the same time, the regulations designed to restrict Chinese entry that began in Victoria were revived and strengthened, especially after an 1888 conference at which the premiers agreed to uniform legislation. Often enough these laws encountered the resistance of the Colonial Office, but in the process Britain's own *Aliens Act* of 1905 was shaped in the likeness of its own colonies.[26]

The wealth generated by gold, immigration and foreign investment created a society with one of the highest standards of living in the world. The gold-rush years and what Australian historians have come to call the 'long boom' – from the 1860s to the end of the 1880s – have generated many local histories, especially of Melbourne and Victoria but also comparative studies, especially with similar economic patterns on the west coast of the North America.[27] During the long boom cities grew, primary produce was exported, electoral reform and institutions of civil society were consolidated and trade unions sorted out their procedures, scope and memberships. For Australian historians, this period was one in which urban and suburban forms that would be recognisable in the twentieth century were laid out: the visible patterns of the cities, transportation and communications, the invisible patterns that governed social engagement, family formation and leisure, and institutional patterns that materialised as public and secular educational institutions, schools and universities became the business of colonial government.

Everything was tested in the Depression of the 1890s. This iconic decade has received a vast amount of historical assessment and reassessment, and

---

24 John Fitzgerald, *Big White Lie: Chinese Australians in White Australia* (Sydney: UNSW Press, 2007); Marilyn Lake and Henry Reynolds, *Drawing the Global Colour Line: White Men's Countries and the Question of Racial Equality* (Melbourne University Press, 2008).

25 Heather Goodall, 'Digging Deeper: Ground Tanks and the Elusive Indian Archipelago', in Alan Mayne (ed.), *Beyond the Black Stump: Histories of Outback Australia* (Adelaide: Wakefield Press, 2008), pp. 129–60; Ann Curthoys, 'Expulsion, Exodus and Exile in White Australian Historical Mythology', *Journal of Australian Studies*, 61 (1999): 1–18.

26 Alison Bashford and Catie Gilchrist, 'The Colonial History of the 1905 Aliens Act', *Journal of Imperial and Commonwealth History*, 40, 3 (2012): 409–37.

27 Lionel Frost, *The New Urban Frontier: Urbanisation and City-building in Australasia and the American West* (Sydney: UNSW Press, 1991); David Goodman, *Gold Seeking: Victoria and California in the 1850s* (Sydney: Allen & Unwin, 1994).

not just from economic historians.[28] It gave rise to a series of large-scale strikes, part of the canon of Australian labour historiography. There was also an upsurge in nationalist cultural activity that has drawn attention from art historians, literary and cultural historians.[29] A generation of organised women entered the political scene over the 1890s with a clear sense of how apparently private matters were properly the business of the public sphere. Parliament should therefore expand to include women's representation directly, it was argued. Women's exclusion from political participation and representation, and the sexual and gendered politics of both liberalism and socialism were on the table.

This coincided with important conversations about the nature of any new 'Australia' that would result from the federation of the colonies. Over the 1890s, the possibility of a federal Australia – initially a federated Australasia including New Zealand – became a probability and then a formality, as Queen Victoria assented to a compact designed by popularly elected delegates and accepted by a vote of the people. Older histories documented how various interest groups influenced constitutional design and the results of the referendums in the various colonies: why people voted as they did. Newer histories have restored awareness of citizenship and popular aspirations for nationhood.[30] But the road to Federation in 1901 was not laid out in advance; it might have led nowhere, and it might have stopped at the border of Western Australia.

If five of the colonies voted for Federation in the referendum of 1899, it was Western Australia that held out until the eleventh hour, not agreeing until 1900. There is a certain exceptionalism about Western Australian history that complicates the standard chronology drawn from the eastern colonies. For this reason, two narrative chapters here stretch the chronology of Part I, extending across the continent and across time to deal with events in the west that had taken place in the east decades earlier. In Western Australia there was a major gold rush in the late 1880s, not the 1850s. This meant that when the other colonies were suffering from a flight

28 Most significantly, N.G. Butlin, *Investment in Australian Economic Development 1861–1900* (Canberra: Department of Economic History, Research School of Social Sciences, ANU, 1972).

29 John Docker, *The Nervous Nineties: Australian Cultural Life in the 1890s* (Oxford University Press, 1991); Melissa Bellanta, *Larrikins: A History* (Brisbane: UQP, 2012).

30 John Hirst, *The Sentimental Nation: The Making of the Australian Commonwealth* (Oxford University Press, 2000); Helen Irving (ed.), *A Woman's Constitution? Gender and History in the Australian Commonwealth* (Sydney: Hale & Iremonger, 1996); Helen Irving, *To Constitute a Nation: A Cultural History of Australia's Constitution* (Cambridge University Press, 1997).

of capital in the Depression of the 1890s, Western Australia attracted foreign investors while providing a livelihood to thousands from the east. The history of convict transportation is different, too: it started there just as the anti-transportation leagues achieved success in New South Wales, Tasmania and Victoria. Similarly, if five of the six colonies secured self-government over the 1850s, it was delayed in the west until the 1890s. It is well known that responsible self-government in Western Australia was finally granted after accepting the Colonial Office's conditions for Aboriginal 'protection'. Here, in a revisionist chapter, the links between management of Aboriginal people and bids for responsible government are shown to have existed in the 1850s in the eastern colonies as well.

The two volumes of the *Cambridge History of Australia* take Federation in 1901 as the pivot for Australian history. But this foregrounds a particular political history of the colonies as they became the nation. It is a chronology that lets some turn-of-the-century events fall inadvertently through the cracks of periodisation: the Anglo-Boer War, for example, to which Australians were sent and served. The national and political periodisation cuts right down the middle of what in other fields of historical scholarship form a distinct period, from the later nineteenth century to the world wars. There are in fact many histories in Australia – and many Australian historians – that work across the nineteenth and twentieth centuries, especially in social, environmental, health and cultural history. It is important to recall that all of the major public cultural and political figures of Australia's first few national decades were born, schooled and shaped in the 1860s–90s; sometimes they were immigrants themselves, sometimes they were the children of immigrants, connected in living memory to the transportation and anti-transportation era of Australian colonial history. There was even one ex-convict who served briefly in the first federal parliament.

The nineteenth century saw unprecedented change across the world, but this was surely greater in Australia than on any other continent. At the beginning of the century, tiny outposts of the maritime British Empire sought to work out a new society. Aboriginal people on the continent outnumbered the British, despite the decline from disease, and most were unaware and untroubled by the strange events on the coasts. By the end of the century, major cities and a middle-sized economy had been built and the whole continent had been claimed. But even that was not as secure and settled as is sometimes presumed. *Indigenous and Colonial Australia* follows the history of the continent from ancient times to the point at which the colonies were poised to become the Commonwealth of Australia.

PART I

★

I

The past 50,000 years:
an archaeological view

PETER VETH AND SUE O'CONNOR

The 'beginnings' of Australian history are always difficult to determine. In addition to Indigenous systems of knowledge with their own epistemologies, understanding ancient Australia involves the disciplines of archaeology, anthropology and linguistics, as well as history. These disciplines developed out of earlier forms of knowledge whereby European explorers, settlers, naturalists, ethnologists, antiquarians and collectors sought to ascertain the Australian past.

In the absence of written records, archaeologists have played a leading role in reconstructing this past. Initially relying on the stratified sequence of excavated material to produce a relative chronology of cultural change, from the 1950s they were able to employ new methods of dating their discoveries – first radio-carbon dating and later electron spin resonance and luminescence methods. During the 1950s it was commonly believed that people had occupied Australia no earlier than 10,000 years ago, during the last Ice Age, and it was only in 1962 that radiocarbon dates exceeded 10,000 years. The earliest known occupation stretched to 20,000 years ago by 1965, 30,000 years by 1969 and 40,000 by 1973.

Within this enlarged chronology, a rapid occupation was posited along with a narrative of adaptation to diverse environments and growing technological sophistication. These findings coincided with demands of Aboriginal and Torres Strait Islander people for self-determination and a growing non-Indigenous appreciation of Indigenous cultures. The common view that Australia had only an abbreviated history gave way to a new awareness of a deep past. Popular interest was served by surveys such as *The Prehistory of Australia* (1969) by the pioneer archaeologist John Mulvaney, and Josephine Flood's *The Archaeology of the Dreamtime* (1983).[1] Some historians sought to explore the implications of this extended human occupation, among them Geoffrey Blainey in *The Triumph of the Nomads* (1975) and Noel

---

1 D.J. Mulvaney, *The Prehistory of Australia* (London: Thames & Hudson, 1969); Josephine Flood, *Archaeology of the Dreamtime: The Story of Prehistoric Australia and its People*, 6th edn (Adelaide: J.B. Publishing, 2004).

Butlin in *Economics and the Dreamtime* (1993).[2] Yet the increasingly technical nature of archaeology has forged new partnerships with natural history and environmental sciences. This chapter presents a picture of the results: an archaeological view of Aboriginal Australia's 50,000-year history.

Migrations

Modern humans left Africa approximately 70,000 years ago. They reached Sahul (the landmass that comprised Australia, New Guinea and the Aru Islands – part of present-day Indonesia) at the eastern end of this diaspora before 50,000 years ago.[3] This was an impressive accomplishment since it required a series of substantial water crossings out of sight of land, crossing through Wallacea, which encompasses the islands of the Lesser Sundas including Flores and Timor (Map 1.1). With the exception of Flores, the archaeological evidence left is indisputably the product of human behaviour.[4]

There has been considerable debate about the route that humans took to reach Australia and the timing of first landfall. A southern route through the Lesser Sunda islands with landfall on the expanded north-west shelf of Australia has usually been preferred, as it would have involved shorter water crossings between larger islands (Map 1.1).[5] Others have favoured a northern route from Borneo to Sulawesi, through northern Maluku and into West Papua, or alternatively through Buru, Ceram and on to the Sunda shelf near the Aru Islands. Morwood and van Oosterzee have argued that maritime migration from Sulawesi to Sahul bypassed the Lesser Sunda islands

2 Geoffrey Blainey, *Triumph of the Nomads: A History of Ancient Australia* (Melbourne: Macmillan, 1975); N.G. Butlin, *Economics and the Dreamtime: A Hypothetical History* (Cambridge University Press, 1993).

3 Peter Hiscock, *Archaeology of Ancient Australia* (New York: Routledge, 2008).

4 Jane Balme et al., 'Symbolic Behaviour and the Peopling of the Southern Arc Route to Australia', *Quaternary International*, 202, 1–2 (2009): 59–68; Sue O'Connor and Barry Fankhauser, 'Art at 40,000 BP? One Step Closer: an Ochre Covered Rock from Carpenter's Gap Shelter 1, Kimberley Region, Western Australia', in Atholl Anderson, Ian Lilley and Sue O'Connor (eds), *Histories of Old Ages: Essays in Honour of Rhys Jones* (Canberra: Pandanus Books, 2001), pp. 287–300; Peter Veth et al., 'The Role of Information Exchange in the Colonization of Sahul', in Robert Whallon, William A. Lovis and Robert K. Hitchcock (eds), *Information and its Role in Hunter-Gatherer Bands* (Los Angeles: The Costen Institute of Archaeology Press, 2011), pp. 203–20.

5 Joseph Birdsell, 'The Recalibration of a Paradigm for the First Peopling of Greater Australia', in J. Allen, J. Golson and R. Jones (eds), *Sunda and Sahul: Prehistoric Studies in Southeast Asia, Melanesia and Australia* (London: Academic Press, 1977), pp. 113–67; Butlin, *Economics and the Dreamtime*; Sue O'Connor, 'Revisiting the Past: Changing Interpretations of Pleistocene Settlement, Subsistence, and Demography in Northern Australia', in Ian Lilley (ed.), *Archaeology of Oceania: Australia and the Pacific Islands* (Oxford: Blackwell, 2006), pp. 29–47.

altogether.[6] While this theory might account for the late persistence of *Homo floresiensis* in Flores, it is incompatible with the overwhelming evidence for human presence in this region 42,000 years ago.[7] Whichever route people took, they clearly spread rapidly through this island region.[8]

The oldest sites found so far are in Arnhem Land, in the north of the continent. These sites are close to the present coast but would have been a significant distance inland at the time of first occupation. Dates of between 65,000 BP and 50,000 BP have been obtained for sediments in association with the lowest stone artefacts recovered (Map 1.1).[9] Sites in the inland arid zone such as at Lake Gregory (*Parnkupirti*) have been dated to between 50,000 and 45,000 BP.[10] Using the radiocarbon technique that dates charcoal and other organic remains, dates in the order of 50,000–45,000 cal BP have been obtained for sites in both northern and southern Australia.[11] A spectacular limestone cave in the extreme south-west of Western Australia, Devil's Lair, currently has the oldest radiocarbon date for occupation, approximately 47,000 BP.[12]

The place of first occupation on the expanded northern coastline of Sahul is now submerged and thus the precise time of human arrival will never be known. There is general consensus, however, that as sites with ages of between approximately 50,000 and 40,000 BP have been recovered from all regions of Sahul, occupation probably occurred somewhere on the northern coastline between 60,000 and 50,000 years ago.[13]

6 Mike Morwood and Penny van Oosterzee, *The Discovery of the Hobbit: The Scientific Breakthrough that Changed the Face of Human History* (Sydney: Random House, 2007).

7 M.J. Morwood et al., 'Archaeology and Age of a New Hominin from Flores in Eastern Indonesia', *Nature*, 431, 7012 (2004): 1087–91.

8 Adam Brumm and Mark W. Moore, 'Symbolic Revolutions and the Australian Archaeological Record', *Cambridge Archaeological Journal*, 15, 2 (2005): 157–75; Sue O'Connor et al., 'Cave Archaeology and Sampling Issues in the Tropics: A Case Study from Lene Hara Cave, a 42,000 Year Old Occupation Site in East Timor, Island Southeast Asia', *Australian Archaeology*, 71 (2010): 29–40.

9 Rockshelter sites Malakunanja and Nauwalabila 1 (see Map 1.1). These dates are based on the optically stimulated luminescence (OSL) method. Cal BP (years before 1950) are used to here to denote calendar years; years BP and BP are used to denote radiocarbon years before present.

10 Peter Veth et al., 'Excavations at Parnkupirti, Lake Gregory, Great Sandy Desert: OSL Ages for Occupation before the Last Glacial Maximum', *Australian Archaeology*, 69 (2009): 1–10.

11 Jane Balme, 'Excavations Revealing 40,000 Years of Occupation at Mimbi Caves, South Central Kimberley, Western Australia', *Australian Archaeology*, 51 (2000): 1–5; Sue O'Connor, 'Carpenter's Gap Rockshelter 1: 40,000 Years of Aboriginal Occupation in the Napier Ranges, Kimberley, W.A.', *Australian Archaeology*, 40 (1995): 58–9; O'Connor, 'Revisiting the Past'.

12 Chris S.M. Turney et al., 'Early Human Occupation at Devil's Lair, Southwestern Australia 50,000 Years Ago', *Quaternary Research*, 55, 1 (2001): 3–13.

13 Hiscock, *Archaeology of Ancient Australia*, p. 44; Sue O'Connor and John Chappell, 'Colonization and Coastal Subsistence in Australia and Papua New Guinea: Different

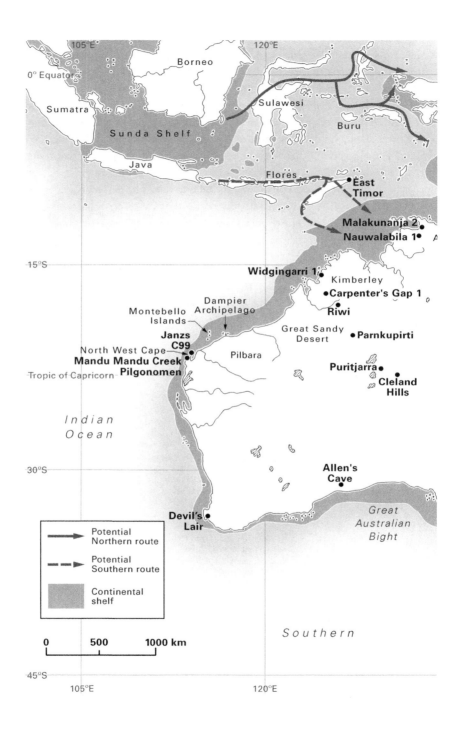

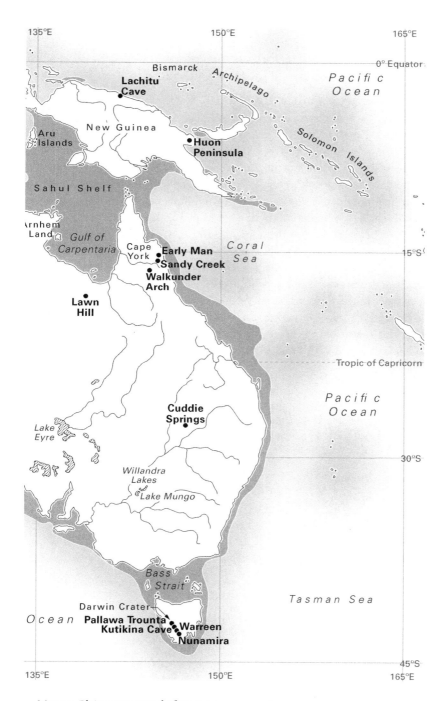

Map 1.1 Pleistocene sites (before 10,000 years ago)

Models for continental spread
and the megafauna debate

Since the first people to land on Greater Australia were island dwellers and arrived by watercraft, it is not surprising that some early models of Australia's occupation stressed the need for a major, early phase of maritime subsistence, followed by coastal dispersion.[14] Others have argued that the Pleistocene coastlines would have been precipitous and inhospitable compared with today's shorelines, and that the early occupants would have quickly abandoned the coast: all environmental niches would have been occupied relatively rapidly.[15] Many species of plants (tubers, corms and fruits) would have been familiar to the arriving groups and likely formed staples in their diet from the start.[16] This is supported by the evidence from the oldest sites in Papua New Guinea (Map 1.1) dated to between 49,000 and 36,000 BP, which contain large waisted axes thought to have been hafted and used to clear patches in the forest canopy.[17]

Environmental reconstructions suggest that while conditions would have been colder than today, other factors may have promoted early movement inland. Hiscock and Wallis make the case that:

> In many regions it is likely that up until 45,000 years ago – and perhaps to 30,000 years ago in some locations – the availability of fresh surface water would have been at least as good, if not better, than during the Holocene…
> The greater relative availability and predictability of resources…would have facilitated exploration and exploitation of these unique interior landscapes.[18]

Timing, Different Modes?', in Christophe Sand (ed.), *Pacific Archaeology: Assessments and Prospects* (Nouméa: Département Archéologie, Service des Musées et du Patrimoine de Nouvelle-Calédonie, 2003), pp. 17–32; Sean Ulm, 'Coastal Foragers on Southern Shores: Marine Resource Use in Northeast Australia since the Late Pleistocene', in Nuno F. Bicho, Jonathan A. Haws and Loren G. Davis (eds), *Trekking the Shore: Changing Coastlines and the Antiquity of Coastal Settlement* (New York: Springer, 2011), pp. 441–61.

14 Sandra Bowdler, 'The Coastal Colonisation of Australia', in Allen et al. (eds), *Sunda and Sahul*, pp. 205–46.

15 Rhys Jones, 'The Fifth Continent: Problems Concerning the Human Colonization of Australia', *Annual Review of Anthropology*, 8 (1979): 445–66. The Pleistocene period extends from 2 million to c.10,000 years ago, when the Holocene epoch begins.

16 Sylvia J. Hallam, *Fire and Hearth: A Study of Aboriginal Usage and European Usurpation in South-Western Australia* (Canberra: Australian Institute of Aboriginal Studies, 1975).

17 Glenn R. Summerhayes et al., 'Human Adaptation and Plant Use in Highland New Guinea 49,000 to 44,000 Years Ago', *Science*, 330, 6000 (2010): 78–81.

18 Peter Hiscock and Lynley A. Wallis, 'Pleistocene Settlement of Deserts from an Australian Perspective', in Peter Veth, Mike Smith and Peter Hiscock (eds), *Desert Peoples: Archaeological Perspectives* (Oxford: Blackwell, 2005), pp. 34–57.

These recent environmental reconstructions, coupled with the patterning of radiocarbon dates and economic evidence from numerous archaeological sites, support a very early movement of people into well-watered inland regions. In northern Australia specialised tools such as polished axes and hatchets were made in order to fashion a range of wooden tools from Australian hardwoods. By 39,000 BP the alpine highlands of Tasmania were settled, at the southern extremity of the Pleistocene continent. Sites show that the transitional grassland/forest landscapes in these upland regions were profitable hunting grounds for marsupial fauna.[19] These human groups were flexible, innovative and able to move into, and exploit, vastly different environments.

Since Pleistocene coastal sites are now submerged, the testing of these competing models has always been problematic. Over the past two decades, however, one region where the continental shelf comes close to the present coastline has been explored. This is the Northwest Cape and Montebello Islands of north-west Western Australia, which provide a unique opportunity for insights into Pleistocene coastal land use (Map 1.1). Rock shelter sites on this limestone system would always have been proximal to the Pleistocene coastline and have produced occupation records extending back some 40,000 years. The fauna in these sites include both marine and terrestrial species. From very early on people enjoyed a wide variety in their diet.[20]

It is known that over 60 species of animals that lived in Australia in the middle to late Pleistocene did not survive to the Holocene. Most of these animals were large to gigantic marsupials, birds and reptiles, and are thus often referred to as the Australian megafauna.[21] Some of these animals looked similar to extant species, such as the giant kangaroos (*Macropus rufus* and *Macropus gigantus titan*), and were in fact ancestors of today's red and grey kangaroos. Others, like the quadrupeds *Palorchestes* and *Diprotodon*, *Zygomaturus* and the marsupial carnivore *Thylacaleo*, have no modern equivalents. There was also a giant flightless bird known as *Genyornis*, much larger than the current emu

19 Richard Cosgrove, 'Forty-Two Degrees South: The Archaeology of Late Pleistocene Tasmania', *Journal of World Prehistory*, 13, 4 (1999): 357–402.
20 Sue O'Connor and Peter Veth (eds), *East of Wallace's Line: Studies of Past and Present Maritime Cultures of the Indo-Pacific Region* (Rotterdam: A.A. Balkema, 2000); Peter Veth et al., *The Archaeology of Montebello Islands, North-West Australia: Late Quaternary Foragers on an Arid Coastline* (Oxford: Archaeopress, 2007).
21 Judith Field et al., 'Chronological Overlap between Humans and Megafaua in Sahul (Pleistocene Australia – New Guinea): A Review of the Evidence', *Earth-Science Reviews*, 89, 3–4 (2008): 97–115; Timothy F. Flannery, 'Debating Extinction', *Science*, 283, 5399 (1999): 182–3.

and a varanid that was larger than the Komodo dragon. The largest of the megafauna, (*Diprotodon optatum*), was a four-legged browser that inhabited the inland savannah and weighed over 2,500 kilograms, equivalent to the modern rhinoceros and hippopotamus.[22]

The timing of these extinctions and whether they were in any way linked with the arrival of humans has been hotly debated.[23] One camp argues that the elimination of these large fauna followed rapidly on human arrival and dispersal throughout Sahul.[24] Another contends that rather than catastrophic extinctions wrought by human hunting pressure and firing practices, the extinctions occurred gradually over a 10–20,000-year period and were largely the result of a long phase of drying and associated environmental change. This trend may have been coupled with changes brought about by Indigenous firing.[25] Between these two positions, some believe that climate change, acting in concert with the arrival of humans and their practice of firing the vegetation, may have put additional stress on populations of these large species, which were already in decline due to increasing aridity.

Early economics and Pleistocene regionalisation

Human groups not only occupied radically different environments in a relatively short period of time, they also began to develop signature regional traits. These are inferred from differences in tool production (for example, edge-ground axes in the north); long-distance exchange networks (witnessed in the movement of ochre); complex funerary practices (such as at Lake Mungo at the Willandra Lakes); and different group-identifying behaviours, which have been inferred from varying art styles thought to date to the Pleistocene period. A common theme in most earlier interpretations

---

22 Stephen Wroe et al., 'The Size of the Largest Marsupial and Why It Matters', *Proceedings of the Royal Society of London B: Biological Sciences*, 271 (2004): S34-S36; Stephen Wroe et al., 'An Alternative Method for Predicting Body Mass: The Case of the Pleistocene Marsupial Lion', *Paleobiology*, 29, 3 (2003): 403–11.

23 Rainer Grün et al., 'ESR and U-Series Analyses of Faunal Material from Cuddie Springs, NSW, Australia: Implications for the Timing of the Extinction of the Australian Megafauna', *Quaternary Science Reviews*, 29, 5–6 (2010): 596–610.

24 Richard G. Roberts et al., 'New Ages for the Last Australian Megafauna: Continent-wide Extinction about 46,000 Years Ago', *Science* 292 (2001): 1888–92; Chris S.M. Turney, 'Late Surviving Megafauna in Tasmania, Australia, Implicate Human Involvement in Their Extinction', *Proceedings of the National Academy of Sciences of the United States of America*, 105 (2008): 12150–3.

25 Wroe et al., 'The Size of the Largest Marsupial'; Field et al., 'Chronological Overlap between Humans and Megafauna', pp. 97–115.

was that such practices evolved from simple to complex over time, a process intensifying during the past several thousand years. This unidirectional and evolutionary narrative has not been borne out in more recent systematic studies of many Pleistocene-aged sites.[26]

The early pan-continental 'core tool and scraper' tradition based on early analyses of the dominant artefacts from Lake Mungo soon expanded into regional characterisations of different stone-tool production systems and dominant tool types across Australia.[27] Examples include edge-ground axes from northern Australia, more than 35,000 years old, to similarly aged thumbnail scrapers from southern Tasmania and seed-grinding bases and mortars.[28] Early sites often contain generalised flake and flake-tool assemblages (tools made on stone struck from parent cores and then used or further modified) that appear to be largely determined by the nature of the raw materials locally available, and the distance groups had to travel to replenish supplies. Steep-edged scrapers (made on thick flakes with one or more edges retouched/stepped) and flat-edged scrapers (with fine oblique retouch) are ubiquitous, although they do not comprise a high proportion of all artefacts. Many 'scraper' forms were clearly a product of the degree to which flake tools were retouched and used – this changing their shape over their useful lives.[29]

Lumps of faceted ochre, grindstones on which ochre has been ground and slabs smeared with ochrous pigment date back to c. 42,000 years ago, from sites in the south-west Kimberley and from a burial site in Lake Mungo, from excavations in Arnhem Land and from excavations dated more than 32,000 BP from central Australia.[30] It is assumed that ochres were

26 Hiscock, *Archaeology of Ancient Australia*, pp. 102–10.
27 J. M. Bowler et al., 'Pleistocene Human Remains from Australia: A Living Site and Human Cremation from Lake Mungo, Western New South Wales', *World Archaeology*, 2, 1 (1970): 39–60.
28 Jean-Michel Geneste et al., 'Earliest Evidence for Ground-Edge Axes: 35,400 +/- 410 Cal BP from Jawoyn Country, Arnhem Land', *Australian Archaeology*, 71 (2010): 66–9; Sue O'Connor and Peter Veth, 'Revisiting the Past: Changing Interpretations of Pleistocene Settlement Subsistence and Demography', in Lilley (ed.), *Archaeology of Oceania* pp. 29–47; Richard Fullagar and Judith Field, 'Pleistocene Seed Grinding Implements from the Australian Arid Zone', *Antiquity*, 71, 272 (1997): 300–7; Paul Gorecki et al., 'The Morphology, Function and Antiquity of Australian Grinding Implements', *Archaeology in Oceania*, 32, 2 (1997): 141–50.
29 Peter Hiscock and Val Attenbrow, *Australia's Eastern Regional Sequence Revisited: Technology and Change at Capertee 3* (Oxford: Archaeopress, 2005).
30 O'Connor and Fankhauser, 'Art at 40,000 BP?'; Richard G. Roberts et al., 'The Human Colonisation of Australia: Optical Dates of 53,000 and 60,000 Years Bracket Human Arrival at Deaf Adder Gorge, Northern Territory', *Quaternary Science Reviews*, 13,

used in the earliest pigment art, likely part of the repertoire of Indigenous Australians.[31]

Shell beads were important signals of early human behaviour in Africa and the Levantine. These items of personal adornment and identity have now been recovered in Australasia as well. Two key sites lie on the edge of the deserts of north-west Australia and have yielded 'strands' of 22 cone shells older than 32,000 BP and ten tusk shells dated to approximately 30,000 BP.[32] Such regionally distinct personal wear is seen to have helped in mediating interactions within and between groups. Long-distance exchange can be inferred from artefacts that lie well outside their supply zone and can be sourced accurately. The oldest comes from a burial site in the Willandra Lakes, more than 40,000 years old, 250 kilometres distant from the closest source of ochre in the Barrier Range. Ochre as old as 32,000 BP was transported 125 kilometres to central Australia (the site of Puritjarra), while ochres from north-western Australia (Mandu Mandu Creek Rockshelter) were transported over 300 kilometres as early as 25,000 BP. Pearl, baler and tusk shell were moved up to 500 kilometres from as early as 30,000 BP.

Complex tools require the use of other tools for their production, or multiple production steps, and are found in the earliest assemblages. The multi-purpose edge-ground axes, often with pecking and abrasion to facilitate hafting, appear from 35,000 BP. Early north-west Kimberley paintings include figures with boomerangs, spears with hafted barbs, dilly bags and other organic paraphernalia. Fibre and nets are implicated in watercraft crossings and fishing before 40,000 BP in Australia.[33]

Reliable dating of the earliest rock art is still in its infancy. However, it is generally believed that art assemblages from at least four areas plausibly date to the Pleistocene and that some of this body of art was produced before the Last Glacial Maximum.[34] Examples come from the Kimberley, including

---

5–7 (1994): 575–83; M.A. Smith et al., 'The Changing Provenance of Red Ochre at Puritjarra Rock Shelter, Central Australia: Late Pleistocene to Present', *Proceedings of the Prehistoric Society*, 64 (1998): 274–92.

31 Veth et al., *The Role of Information Exchange*, pp. 203–20.

32 See Map 1.1; Jane Balme and Kate Morse, 'Shell Beads and Social Behaviour in Pleistocene Australia', *Antiquity*, 80, 310 (2006): 799–811.

33 Balme et al., 'Symbolic Behaviour', pp. 59–68.

34 Jo McDonald, 'Archaic Faces to Headdresses: The Changing Role of Rock Art across the Arid Zone', in Veth et al., *Desert Peoples*, pp. 116–41; M.J. Morwood, *Visions from the Past: The Archaeology of Australian Aboriginal Art* (Sydney: Allen & Unwin, 2002); Ken J. Mulvaney, 'Murujuga Mami-Dampier Petroglyphs: Shadows in the Landscape Echoes across Time', PhD Thesis, University of New England, 2010; Sue O'Connor et al., 'Faces of the Ancestors Revealed: Discovery and Dating

depictions of an extinct carnivore (*Thylacoleo carnifex*) and a Gwion Gwion (previously labelled Bradshaw) style figure with a multi-barbed spear.[35] Four phases in Arnhem Land art include early weapon-wielding motifs, part human and animal, and extinct fauna.[36] Cape York art is inferred to date from at least 32,600 BP, while it has been argued that four of the six phases of art production on the Dampier Archipelago of north-west Australia precede the rise in the sea level, dated to circa 8,000 BP.[37] A highly conspicuous component of the earliest engraving tradition found here and across much of arid Australia includes the Archaic Face associated with complex geometric designs and zoomorphs.[38] Some researchers believe that even the apparently oldest engravings and pigment art probably date only from the terminal Pleistocene period. Others favour the view that art was practised from the time of earliest occupation and that proving this will simply be a matter of deploying more refined techniques of sampling and dating.[39]

Societies in transition

About 30,000 years ago global climates and environments experienced a dramatic shift, marked most conspicuously by a rapid build up of glacial ice in the northern hemisphere and an associated, sharp fall in global sea level.[40] While the northern hemisphere's Ice Age story is well known,

of a Pleistocene-Aged Petroglyph in Lene Hara Cave, East Timor', *Antiquity*, 84 (2010): 649–65; Andrée Rosenfeld et al., *Early Man in North Queensland*. Vol. 6, Terra Australis (Canberra: Department of Prehistory, ANU, 1981).

35 Kim Akerman and Tim Willing, 'An Ancient Rock Painting of a Marsupial Lion, Thylacoleo Carnifex, from the Kimberley, Western Australia', *Antiquity*, 83, 319 (2009): online.

36 George Chaloupka, 'Chronological Sequence of Arnhem Land Plateau Rock Art', in Rhys Jones (ed.), *Archaeological Research in Kakadu National Park* (Canberra: ANU Press, 1985), pp. 269–80.

37 Alan Watchman, 'Wargata Mina to Gunbilmurrung: The Direct Dating of Australian Rock Art', in Anderson et al. (eds), *Histories of Old Ages*, pp. 313–25.

38 Jo McDonald and Peter Veth, 'Rock-Art of the Western Desert and Pilbara: Pigment Dates Provide New Perspectives on the Role of Art in the Australian Arid Zone', *Australian Aboriginal Studies*, 1 (2008): 4–21; Jo McDonald and Peter Veth, 'L'iconographie du desert occidental d'Australie', *Diogène*, 231 (2010): 9–27; Josephine J. McDonald and Peter Veth, 'Information Exchange Amongst Hunter-Gatherers of the Western Desert of Australia', in Whallon et al. (eds), *The Role of Information in Hunter-Gatherer Band Adaptations*, pp. 221–4.

39 Maxime Aubert, 'A Review of Rock Art Dating in the Kimberley, Western Australia', *Journal of Archaeological Science*, 39, 3 (2012): 573–7.

40 Kurt Lambeck and John Chappell, 'Sea Level Change through the Last Glacial Cycle', *Science*, 292, 5517 (2001): 679–86.

the southern hemisphere's environmental transformations were just as dramatic. High-altitude parts of the southern Alps and Tasmania were ice-covered during the height of this climate phase, which peaked between approximately 22,000 and 18,000 years ago. Australian deserts experienced some of the greatest and most variable changes during this time.[41] Australian deserts are not uniform, however, and the impact of these environmental transformations was variable. While deserts were thought to have been barriers to human occupation until the Holocene, with many analogues to the Great Basin of the United States,[42] sites of human occupation in the order of 40,000 BP, pre-dating glacial aridity, are now well established in Australia.[43]

There are now eight sites that would have been located within the expanded arid core of Australia before and during the Last Glacial Maximum. The oldest is *Parnkupirti*, located on a tributary of the once mega-lake of Lake Gregory in the south-eastern Kimberley, and dated from 50,000 BP to 45,000 BP. Lake Gregory itself would have once been a very large freshwater lake fed by the Kimberley ranges to the north and containing shellfish, fish, water fowl and fauna such as emu and macropods. Other sites in the Kimberly are dated to 45,000 BP, while Puritjarra Rockshelter at the western edge of the central Australian ranges shows evidence for occupation around 40,000 BP. On the Nullarbor Plain to the south, Allen's Cave has an optically stimulated luminescence (OSL) date of 40,000 years, while the earliest occupations at Lake Mungo to the east are estimated by OSL to lie in the range of 50,000–46,000 years ago. To the north-east, Cuddie Springs dates to 38,500 years ago, while a shelter near Lawn Hill in Queensland has a radiocarbon determination of 41,500 BP (Map 1.1).[44]

Conditions were generally more favourable, meaning that people were not entering the daunting and ostensibly 'dangerous' landscapes lamented by early European explorers. In what has been described as the 'desert transformation model', groups first adapted to more benign climates and then made changes in their settlement behaviour, technology, economy, diet and material culture to accommodate significant changes in the landscape.[45]

---

41 Peter M. Veth, *Islands in the Interior: The Dynamics of Prehistoric Adaptations within the Arid Zone of Australia* (Ann Arbor: University of Michigan Press, 1993).
42 Richard A. Gould, 'Subsistence Behaviour Among the Western Desert Aborigines of Australia', *Oceania*, 39, 4 (1969): 253–74.
43 Veth et al., 'Excavations at Parnkupirti', pp. 1–10.
44 Hiscock and Wallis, 'Pleistocene Settlement of Deserts from an Australian Perspective', pp. 34–57.
45 Ibid.

The last glacial cycle intensified rapidly after 45,000 years ago. By 30,000 years ago sea levels dropped by almost 50 metres in 1,000 years, exposing the continental shelf; the monsoon was the least effective it had been for over 100,000 years and temperatures plummeted in the south-east by as much as 9 degrees celsius.[46] Some groups consolidated occupation and their territories around productive and well-watered refuges,[47] while interior lowlands such as the dunefields became devegetated, lakes dried up and surface waters became scarce. While desert occupation persisted, the onset of climatic amelioration after 17,000 BP and especially wetter conditions generally by 14,000 BP suggests occupation of the entire arid zone. The Australian deserts have therefore witnessed some of the most dynamic responses by humans to a major change in landscape caused by climate change.

Sea-level rise and the emergence of coastal and island societies

With global water locked up in the caps of the poles between 21,000 and 19,000 years ago, the sea level was as much as 123 metres lower than it is today. North-east Australia was connected to New Guinea across the Torres Strait, and Tasmania was joined to south-eastern Australia, forming a landmass that was more than a quarter larger than today. From about 19,000 years ago global temperatures increased and the sea level rose accordingly. The effects around the Australian coastline would have been dramatic and particularly so in the northern regions, where the continental shelf was wide and of a low gradient.[48] There were periods of major inundation of land due to sea-level rise in the terminal Pleistocene, when land was consumed so rapidly that the changes in shoreline would have been perceptible during a human lifespan. Indigenous people living on the broad coastal plain during this time would have experienced loss of territory and resources.[49] Between approximately 40,000 and 12,200 years ago an enormous freshwater lake, Lake Carpentaria, dominated

46 Kurt Lambeck, Yusuke Yokoyama and Tony Purcell, 'Into and out of the Last Glacial Maximum', *Quarternary Science Reviews*, 21, 1–3 (2002): 343–60.

47 Peter Hiscock, 'Prehistoric Settlement Patterns and Artefact Manufacture at Lawn Hill, Northwest Queensland', PhD thesis, University of Queensland, 1988.

48 Rhys Jones, 'Man as an Element of a Continental Fauna: The Case of the Sundering of the Bassian Bridge', in Allen et al. (eds), *Sunda and Sahul*, pp. 317–86; Sean Ulm, 'Coastal Foragers on Southern Shores', in Bicho et al. (eds), *Trekking the Shore*, p. 444.

49 John Mulvaney and Johan Kamminga, *Prehistory of Australia* (Sydney: Allen & Unwin, 1999), p. 121.

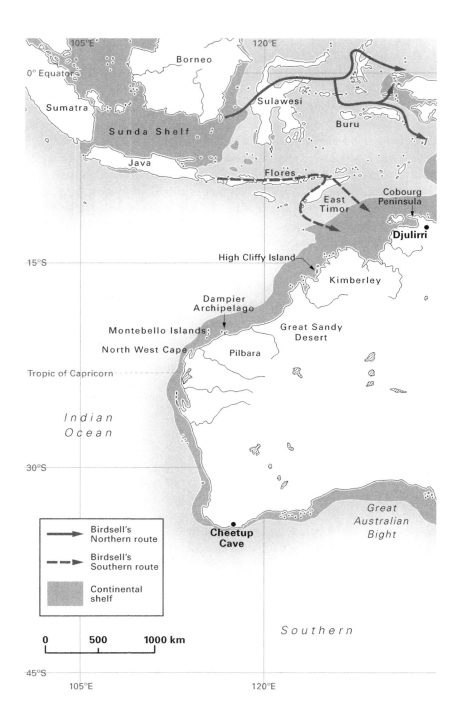

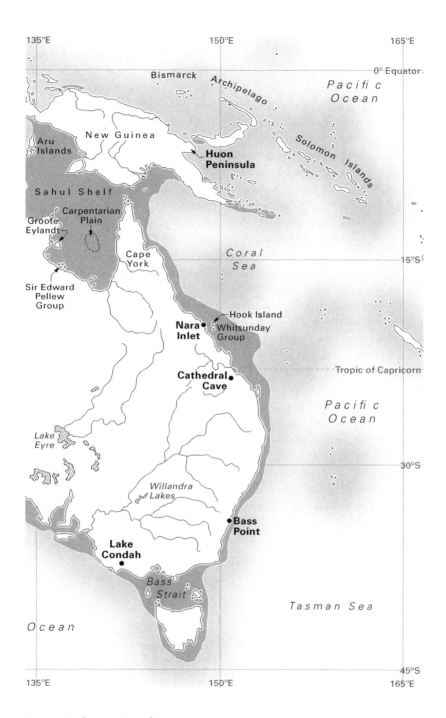

Map 1.2 Holocene sites (after 10,000 years ago)

the low-lying country between present-day New Guinea and north-west Queensland. At its maximum extent 14,000 years ago it was approximately 190,000 square kilometres in size and no doubt provided an important wetland resource in the tropics. By 10,000 BP the lake was gone – flooded by the rising seas that cut off New Guinea from Australia. Between approximately 8,000 and 6,000 years ago the many thousands of islands that exist today in Torres Strait and around the coastline of Australia were formed for the first time.

Tasmania is one of most important islands formed with the rise in sea level after the last Ice Age. While Bass Strait flooded some 14,000 years ago, Tasmania was occupied as early as 39,000 to 37,000 years ago. This early occupation of glacial uplands was globally significant, given its extreme southern latitude.[50] Important debates emerged in the 1970s about the effects of the 'isolation' of people after the sea rose to turn Tasmania into a large island, positing social and economic decline.[51] As archaeologists critically examined these questions over the following decades, the only apparent examples of cultural 'losses' included the cessation of fishing and bone-tool use between 4,000 and 3,700 years ago.[52] While the prohibition on eating fish was originally portrayed as maladaptive, it more probably resulted from a significant switch in the choice of key marine species on which people relied. As climate and vegetation changed in the mid-Holocene, Tasmanian Aboriginal people's use of, and residence within, interior lands increased significantly. Fish, which had been caught with stone traps earlier on, appear to have been deliberately replaced by abalone and crayfish, as coastal staples. A new division of labour saw women diving for abalone and crayfish, as they were at the time of European contact.[53] The archaeological evidence shows an increase in shell midden sites over the last 3,000 years; and there was an expansion of territory, including the re-colonisation of abandoned islands off the Tasmanian coast, and probably an increase in population before contact.[54] This pattern profiles the efflorescence of Tasmanian Aboriginal societies over the past several millennia – the very opposite of the previous 'devolution' argument.

---

50 Cosgrove, 'Forty-Two Degrees South', pp. 357–402.
51 Jones, 'Man as an Element of a Continental Fauna', pp. 318–86.
52 Hiscock, *Archaeology of Ancient Australia*, pp. 136–8.
53 Robin Sim, 'Why the Tasmanians Stopped Eating Fish: Evidence for Late Holocene Expansion in Resource Exploitation Strategies', in Jay Hall and Ian McNiven (eds), *Australian Coastal Archaeology* (Canberra: ANU Press, 1999), pp. 263–9.
54 Sandra Bowdler, 'Tasmanian Aborigines in the Hunter Islands in the Holocene: Island Resource Use and Seasonality', in Geoff Bailey and John Parkington (eds), *The Archaeology of Prehistoric Coastlines* (Cambridge University Press, 1988), pp. 42–52; Colin Pardoe, 'Isolation and Evolution in Tasmania', *Current Anthropology*, 32, 1 (1991): 1–21; Hiscock, *Archaeology of Ancient Australia*, pp. 143–4.

A number of major changes have been detected throughout Australia in the mid to late Holocene coastal record, following sea-level stabilisation (Map 1.2). Primary among these changes is the widespread use of offshore islands, evident in the creation of coastal shell middens and other sites containing records of marine subsistence dating from approximately 8,000 to 6,000 BP and more recently. New types of coastal sites appear (such as large, single-species shell mounds) and there is evidence for the use of maritime technology such as fish traps and specialised fishing equipment such as hooks and watercraft. In a few areas where the continental shelf is steep the use of coastal resources is registered from early in the Holocene and some of these sites continued in use throughout the Holocene, allowing an assessment of change over a 10,000 to 7,000-year period, such as from the south-west Kimberley (Map 1.1).[55] In other regions, such as Northwest Cape and the Pilbara coastline, a range of open shell middens appear from 8,000 BP onward and together provide a picture of Holocene coastal exploitation.

Most offshore islands were incorporated into a coastal seasonal round only in the past few thousand years. Hook Island in the Whitsunday group of islands off the east coast is an exception, and there are no doubt others. This rocky continental island is adjacent to deep water and would never have been far from the coast throughout the final stages of the marine transgression. Hook Island (Map 1.2) was first occupied about 8,000 years ago when it was joined to Whitsunday Island, forming a large peninsula connected to the mainland; it was cut off about 500 years ago. Unlike most Australian near-shore islands, however, it continued to be used after this time and contains marine resources, including turtle, dugong fish and rocky shore shellfish throughout the entire 8,000-year sequence.[56]

A rock shelter on Badu Island in the Torres Strait (located between Cape York and Papua New Guinea) was also first occupied around 8,000 years ago, when it was still connected to the Australian mainland. Badu appears to have been abandoned after it was cut off by rising seas about 6,000 years ago.[57] The first phase of occupation of the Torres Strait islands began about 4,000 years

---

55 Sue O'Connor, *30,000 Years of Aboriginal Occupation: Kimberley, Northwest Australia*. Vol. 14, Terra Australis (Canberra: Research School of Pacific and Asian Studies, ANU, 1999).

56 Bryce Barker, *The Sea People: Late Holocene Maritime Specialisation in the Whitsunday Islands, Central Queensland*. Vol. 20 Terra Australis (Canberra: Research School of Pacific and Asian Studies, ANU, 2004).

57 David Bruno et al., 'Badu 15 and the Papuan-Austronesian Settlement of Torres Strait', *Archaeology in Oceania*, 39, 2 (2004): 65–78.

ago.[58] One site registers small quantities of shell, fish, turtle and dugong at this time.[59] Another, on Pulu Island in western Torres Strait, contains small amounts of fish and turtle bone from about 3,800 years ago.[60]

Sites on the remote Montebello Islands, on the north-west coast of Australia, contain dense middens and a wide range of marine resources, including turtle, crocodile and fish remains dating between approximately 8,500 and 7,500 years ago; these indicate the increased proximity of a greater range of marine habitats as the sea level rose. However, these sites also contain diverse terrestrial sand-plain animals such as wallaby, bettong, bandicoots, bilby, possum, snake and lizards, showing the exploitation of both limestone plateau habitats as well as the now-submerged sand plain that formed the coastal hinterland of the enlarged island.[61] Rather than providing a picture of marine specialisation, the faunal remains in these shelters evoke generalised and broadly based hunting-gathering and foraging behaviour using all available resources from all habitats. Again, on the north-west coast, Kimberley sites indicate the incorporation of coastal resources as sea level comes closer.[62] Sites at Northwest Cape show a recent increase in turtle and an expanded use of marine resources.[63]

On the mainland Pilbara coast of the north-west and on the small inshore islands of the Dampier Archipelago, shelters with midden deposits, shell mounds and linear middens also include a wide range of marine and terrestrial faunal remains.[64] The dates obtained indicate that coastal resources were exploited from the time the sea approached the outer islands of the archipelago, between approximately 8,500 and 7,000 years ago. The analysis of data from these different regions shows that maritime competencies and subsistence behaviours were probably always present, and that when sea level rose and maritime resources became accessible, they become an important component of people's secular and ceremonial lives.

---

58 Ian J. McNiven, 'Torres Strait Islanders: The 9000-Year History of a Maritime People', in *The Torres Strait Islands* (Brisbane: Queensland Art Gallery, 2011), pp. 211–19.
59 See Map 1.1. Occupation at Badu 15 recommenced circa 3,500 years ago.
60 Ian J. McNiven et al., 'Mask Cave', *Archaeology in Oceania*, 41, 2 (2006): 49–81.
61 Veth et al., *Archaeology of Montebello Islands*.
62 O'Connor, *30,000 Years of Aboriginal Occupation*, p. 92.
63 Kate Morse, 'Shell Beads from Mandu Mandu Creek Rock-Shelter, Cape Range Peninsula, Western Australia, Dated before 30,000 B.P', *Antiquity*, 67, 267 (1993): 877–83.
64 Genevieve Clune, 'Abydos: An Archaeological Investigation of Holocene Adaptations on the Pilbara Coast, Northwestern Australia', PhD thesis, University of Western Australia, 2002.

On both the east and west coasts of Australia there appears to be a significant increase in the numbers of sites and intensity of site use after about 4,000 BP.[65] Large shell mounds began to appear in northern Australia at approximately 4,000 BP and are distributed along the Australian coastline from the Pilbara region of Western Australia to far north Queensland. On the Western Australian coast the large mounds are comprised almost exclusively of a single species of cockle. In most areas the highest densities and largest of these shell mounds are dated between circa 2,500 and 1,000 BP. The appearance of these at times enormous mounds has been linked to an elaboration in social complexity and ceremonial behaviours.[66] Others have explained this phenomenon in terms of environmental change, or attributed it to sampling issues[67] or preservation factors that reduce the survival of older sites. Similarly, while large earth mounds also first appeared around 4,000 years ago, they occurred in profusion after approximately 2,000 years ago along the margins of newly formed freshwater wetlands of Arnhem Land.[68] The importance of fish and freshwater turtles, whose bones are found in these earth mounds, is reflected in the painted rock art from this period.

After 2,500 years ago there was widespread use of the Torres Strait Islands. Many more sites were occupied, and there was a significant increase in quantity of marine resources deposited. It seems likely that Torres Strait was permanently occupied from this time, probably marking the origin of the distinctive marine-oriented Torres Strait cultural complex that was observed at the time of European contact.[69] After 700 years ago villages appear in the archaeological record and the first evidence for the construction of ritual structures made from dugong and other marine remains similar to those observed ethnographically also appear.[70]

---

65 Barker, *The Sea People*; Sean Ulm, 'Investigations Towards a Late Holocene Archaeology of Aboriginal Lifeways on the Southern Curtis Coast, Australia', PhD thesis, University of Queensland, 2004.

66 Barker, *The Sea People*.

67 Ulm, 'Investigations Towards a Late Holocene Archaeology of Aboriginal Lifeways'.

68 Sally Brockwell et al., 'Radiocarbon Dates from the Top End: A Cultural Chronology for the Northern Territory Coastal Plains', *Australian Aboriginal Studies*, 1 (2009): 54–76.

69 Anthony J. Barham, 'Late Holocene Maritime Societies in the Torres Strait Islands, Northern Australia – Cultural Arrival or Cultural Emergence?' in O'Connor and Veth (eds), *East of Wallace's Line*, pp. 223–314.

70 Ian J. McNiven and Ricky Feldman, 'Ritually Orchestrated Seascapes: Hunting Magic and Dugong Bone Mounds in Torres Strait, NE Australia', *Cambridge Archaeological Journal*, 13, 2 (2003): 169–94.

Changes in the Holocene

Following the Last Glacial Maximum the climate ameliorated. The Holocene was not a homogeneous period for Aboriginal cultures of Australia, however. Sea levels rose to assume their current levels by approximately 6,500 years ago; wetter conditions then occurred in many areas, followed by intensification of the El Niño/La Niña Southern Oscillation by approximately 4,000 BP. There was a proliferation of stone-tool, plant-processing and landscape-modification technologies, art and economic modes of production. This was clearly a time of dynamism.

Argument for 'cumulative advancement' in peoples' skills and increasing proficiency in using specific resources during the Holocene culminated in a phenomenon over the past several thousand years that has been labelled 'social intensification'. However, this narrative has not always been borne out by a critical assessment of the archaeological data.[71] The intensification paradigm held that intergroup dynamics at large gatherings needed to be underwritten with new infrastructure exploiting specific species of foods, combined with their more efficient production. While symbolic, technological, social and exchange behaviours were undoubtedly changing, and in some cases becoming more complex, there is much to suggest that 'intensive' resource management existed before the past several thousand years. A few examples will illustrate this proposition.

Extensive, stone-walled fish traps and races designed to capture eels and fish have been recorded in western Victoria. These are up to 6 metres in height and operated largely during major floods over the past 2,000 years. Channels measuring over 3 kilometres in length to drain into swamps have been recorded, and these were used to flush eels and fish into the traps and to assist in the growth of food plants such as bracken.[72] Dating the traps has been challenging; however, a team of archaeologists and traditional owners recently carried out dating of channel in-fill sediments associated with an elaborate freshwater fish-trap complex at Lake Condah, in western Victoria. An early phase of basalt removal to create a channel has sediments that contain stone artefacts and charcoal dated to approximately 6,600 cal BP. After a hiatus, basalt blocks were added to the sides of the channel to create multi-tiered walls within the past 600–800 years. This recent work

---

71 Harry Lourandos, *Continent of Hunter-Gatherers: New Perspectives in Australian Prehistory* (Cambridge University Press, 1997).
72 Harry Lourandos, 'Aboriginal Settlement and Land Use in South Western Victoria: A Report of Current Fieldwork', *The Artefact*, 1, 4 (1976): 174–93.

shows that such elaborate fish trapping and the aquaculture system were not part of a process of intensification *per se,* but an earlier infrastructure innovation that was probably repeated when the hydrological regime was amenable to this kind of harvesting. Importantly, the Lake Condah site represents one of the world's oldest known fish traps.[73] Similarly, mounds found over the volcanic plains of south-east Victoria have been portrayed as representing the emergence of 'village' sites with wooden structures, 'garden areas' facilitating the growth of the daisy yam and the systematic exploitation of wetlands. While they likely represent more sedentary occupation sites, their appearance with wetter conditions and higher lake levels of the late Holocene is as much a response to, as a product of, inundation of lowlands.

Another example is the use of Cycad seeds (*Macrozamia moreii*), which was argued to have supported ceremonies in north-east Australia for over 4,000 years.[74] Because the fresh seeds are poisonous and they appeared to be in large quantities in the Cathedral Cave site, it was argued the Cycad stands were burnt or managed in order to increase yield, that the seeds were leached to render them edible and that they supported ritually mediated groupings of people. Remarkably, at Cheetup Cave in south-western Australia, on the other side of the continent, *Macrozamia* seeds were also excavated from a preparation pit and dated to 15,680 BP.[75] Further analysis showing the low rate at which seeds were discarded and the fact that most were probably detoxified – because they were not fresh when prepared – means that they did not necessarily underwrite large gatherings of people. They could well, however, have been part of a broad-spectrum suite of plant foods that in combination supported gatherings of various sizes.[76] The use of Cycads, then, has an antiquity stretching back to the Pleistocene and cannot be implicated within a neat package for recent social intensification. It is very likely that changes in climate and environment provided the conditions for significant changes in Aboriginal social and economic organisation, and occurred during the Holocene (such as the appearance of wetlands in Arnhem Land only

---

73 Ian McNiven, 'Dating Aboriginal Stone-Walled Fishtraps at Lake Condah, Southeast Australia', *Journal of Archaeological Science*, 39 (2012): 268–86.

74 J.M. Beaton, 'Cathedral Cave: A Rockshelter in Carnarvon Gorge, Queensland', *Queensland Archaeological Research*, 8 (1991): 33–84.

75 Moya Smith, 'Revisiting Pleistocene *Macrozamia*', *Australian Archaeology*, 42 (1996): 52–3.

76 Brit Asmussen, 'Dangerous Harvest Revisited: Taphonomy, Methodology and Intensification in the Central Queensland Highlands, Australia', PhD thesis, ANU, 2005.

within the past 2,000 years). People could not exploit eels in the Victorian wetlands or barramundi from billabongs in the Northern Territory if they did not exist.

While it was argued previously that many stone-tool types, attendant ideas about their production and use, and the dingo were brought into Australia from approximately 4,000 years ago,[77] the current consensus is that most stone-tool technologies, ways of processing plants, modes of hunting Australian fauna and portraying secular and sacred themes in art were uniquely Australian developments. Only the dingo was an introduction. Three tools formed part of what were labelled 'hafted' implements of the Australian small-tool tradition. These are backed artefacts, having a long, sharp edge opposite a blunted one (with many variations in shape); bifacial points, with invasive flaking on both sides and straight to converging edges, and tula adzes characterised by robust, large platform flakes. Careful analysis of sites and data show that these different tools appeared at very different times. Backed artefacts are now dated to approximately 10,000 years ago in New South Wales and as early as 16,000 years ago in the Gulf of Carpentaria.[78] Bifacial points have been dated to approximately 8,000 years ago in Arnhem Land, while the oldest tula adze dates to less than 4,000 years ago.[79] The proposition that some of these small tools were introduced as a package circa 5,000–4,000 years ago from Southeast Asia is not consistent with present archaeological evidence. Backed artefacts occur largely within the lower two-thirds of the continent; bifacial points occur only in Arnhem Land and the Kimberley (the Top End) and tula adzes are mainly found within the arid and semi-arid zones. While these artefacts were certainly multi-functional, many were likely hafted with thermoplastic compounds (such as spinifex resin). Backed artefacts thus served as spear barbs, knives, scrapers and vegetable processors. Points (both unifacial and bifacial) certainly served as armatures as well as engravers, scrapers and plant-processing tools. Tula adzes, while uniquely equipped to serve as hard wood 'chisels', could also be deployed to fashion, maintain and engrave

---

77 Sandra Bowdler, 'Hunters in the Highlands: Aboriginal Adaptations in the Eastern Australian Uplands', *Archaeology in Oceania*, 16, 2 (1981): 99–111.

78 Peter Hiscock and Val Attenbrow, 'Early Holocene Backed Artefacts from Australia', *Archaeology in Oceania*, 33, 2 (1998): 49–62; Michael J. Slack et al., 'New Pleistocene Ages for Backed Artefact Technology in Australia', *Archaeology in Oceania*, 39, 3 (2004): 131–7.

79 Peter Hiscock, 'Blunt and to the Point: Changing Technological Strategies in Holocene Australia', in Lilley (ed.), *Archaeology of Oceania*, pp. 69–95; Peter Veth, Peter Hiscock and Alan Williams, 'Are Tulas and ENSO Linked in Australia?', *Australian Archaeology* 72 (2011): 7–14.

a wide range of artefacts as well as to process plant and animal foods. The portability, longevity and multi-functionality of these tools and their ability to be rejuvenated and retouched to extend their working life presumably made them both desirable and adaptively advantageous. Diffusionist models for the introduction or spread of backed artefacts, bifacial points and the tula adze have had to be replaced by models that look at adaptation, style, function and regional variations – which were probably determined to differing degrees by social mechanisms.

Northern contacts

The northern Australian shores have been witness to many visits by voyagers from Southeast Asia and even the Pacific islands to the east, but few such contacts are documented archaeologically. The dingo appeared in Australia sometime between 4,500 and 4,000 years ago and was almost certainly introduced, translocated by people as a domestic animal.[80] At approximately the same time, the Tasmanian Tiger, or Thylacine, became extinct, thought to have been a casualty of competition from the dingo.

There is evidence in the archaeological and rock art record of contact of a more intensive type with peoples from outside Australia in the late Holocene period. This evidence includes changes in the size and content of shell middens, an increase in hunting large marine game such as dugong and turtles, and the appearance of new artefact types such as shellfish hooks, and later metal harpoons. There is copious painted art depicting Southeast Asian watercraft, animals, weapons and utilitarian objects. There are also stone arrangements echoing features of Southeast Asian boats and, later still, campsites and processing sites associated with the *trepang* industry, which contain pottery and other Southeast Asian metal artefacts.

It is now well established that fish hooks first appeared in northern Australia about 1,200 years ago and were used widely along much of the northern, north-eastern and south-eastern coasts of Australia by 1,000 years ago.[81] They are often found with small stone files. The distribution and chronology of shell hooks indicates that they were introduced from outside Australia,

---

80 Hiscock, *Archaeology of Ancient Australia*, p. 148.
81 Val Attenbrow, 'Aboriginal Fishing in Port Jackson, and the Introduction of Shell Fish-Hooks to Coastal New South Wales, Australia', in Daniel Lunney et al. (eds), *The Natural History of Sydney* (Sydney: Royal Zoological Society of New South Wales, 2010), pp. 16–34.

possibly from Torres Strait, or even from the east by early Polynesian voyagers. There is a gap in their distribution of 1,000 kilometres between the Keppel Islands in Queensland and Port Stephen in New South Wales, and they do not extend west of Western Port in Victoria. At the Bass Point site in New South Wales the appearance of shell hooks coincided with changes in the size and species of fish and shellfish in the midden.[82] These appear to indicate a change in the gendered division of labour: fishing had previously been done by men using spears and was then taken up by women, who had less time for collecting shell fish. Although we know that historically it was men who used spears and women who used the hook and line, subsequent research at other sites on the New South Wales coast creates an even more complex picture of gender divisions.[83]

From at least the mid-1600s until 1907, fishing fleets from present-day Indonesia sailed to the northern coast of Australia in search of edible *trepang* – also known as *bêche de mer*, or sea cucumber – which had a high value in the Chinese markets. These mariners made regular visits to the Northern Territory coast.[84] While they came predominantly from Macassar in southern Sulawesi, some also sailed from other parts of the Indonesian archipelago, including the islands of Timor, Roti and Aru. They collected other products of value as well, including Hawksbill sea turtle shell and pearl shell, pearls, sandalwood and even minerals, some of which found their way into a much larger trade network that included the Maluku islands (Moluccas) and West Papua.[85] Local Aboriginal groups stockpiled these products in anticipation of the so-called 'Macassan' return the following season. The *trepang* had to be dried and smoked, and the Macassans made large camps on protected areas of the coastline, within which they constructed their tripots, smokehouses and living quarters.

The regularity and duration of the Macassan visits allowed the establishment of social and trade relationships. The period of contact was brief in terms of the history of occupation of Australia, but it had a major effect, being recorded in Indigenous oral traditions, ceremonies, stone arrangements and rock and bark paintings. Many hundreds of images of *praus* (boats),

82 Sandra Bowdler, 'Hook, Line, and Dilly Bag: An Interpretation of an Australian Coastal Shell Midden', *Mankind*, 10, 4 (1976): 248–58.
83 Attenbrow, 'Aboriginal Fishing', p. 30.
84 C.C. Macknight, *The Voyage to Marege': Macassan Trepangers in Northern Australia* (Melbourne University Press, 1976).
85 Anne Clarke and Ursula Frederick, 'Closing the Distance: Interpreting Cross-Cultural Engagements Through Indigenous Rock Art', in Lilley (ed.), *Archaeology of Oceania*, pp. 116–33.

other items of material culture and scenes relating to Macassan visitation can be found in the rock shelters on Groote Eylandt, along the Arnhem Land coastline and in the Edward Pellew Islands, Queensland.[86] One image of a Southeast Asian *prau* from Djiliri rock shelter in western Arnhem Land has recently been dated to before 1664 in the current era (CE).[87]

It has been also suggested that the Macassan presence had a significant effect on Aboriginal settlement patterns, exchange networks, mobility and subsistence.[88] A comparative study of midden sites before and after Macassan contact on the Cobourg Peninsula in Arnhem Land concluded that the post-contact middens were substantially larger and contained a wider variety of exotic artefacts and remains of large marine fauna.[89] This was explained by the adoption of new technology brought by the Macassans, specifically dugout canoes and the detachable metal harpoon head, which enabled more effective hunting of turtle and dugong. The use of the harpoon might have had a similar effect on the Kimberley coast of Western Australia: the turtle bones in the Widgingarri and High Cliffy shelters (Maps 1.1 and 1.2) mostly date to the past 500 years. While there is evidence for use of newly formed islands after sea-level rise (which finished approximately 6,500 years ago) from before 3,000 years ago, there appears to have been an increase in island use immediately preceding European contact in the 1600s. The ability to capture marine animals more reliably might have allowed people to occupy permanently even very small islands for the first time. Some islands are less than one kilometre square in area but contain the remains of dozens of stone 'house' bases. Inside the stone walls are grinding stones with rust residues on them, resulting from the sharpening of metal harpoon heads.

Archaeology provides unique windows into human–social–landscape relationships, from both the perspective of deep-time narratives covering the past 50,000 years through to the recent contact with outsiders. It is often the dynamism and details of these cultural and physical configura-tions – and their at times breathtaking antiquity and cyclical nature – that

---

86 Anne Clarke, 'Time, Tradition and Transformation: The Negotiation of Intercultural Encounters on Groote Eylandt, Northern Australia', in Robin Torrence and Anne Clarke (eds), *The Archaeology of Difference: Negotiating Cross-Cultural Engagements in Oceania* (London: Routledge, 2000), pp. 142–81.

87 Paul S.C. Taçon et al., 'A Minimum Age for Early Depictions of Southeast Asian Praus in the Rock Art of Arnhem Land, Northern Territory', *Australian Archaeology*, 71 (2010): 1–10.

88 Clarke and Frederick, 'Closing the Distance'.

89 Scott Mitchell, 'Culture Contact and Indigenous Economies on the Cobourg Peninsula, Northwestern Arnhem Land', PhD thesis, Northern Territory University, 1994.

gives valency to the view, held strongly by Aboriginal people, that this is the world's oldest continuous culture. It is likely one of the most resilient cultures, precisely because of its adaptability, dynamism and the inherent competencies held by people from the very beginnings of Australian history

2

Newcomers, c. 1600–1800

SHINO KONISHI AND MARIA NUGENT

The history of Aboriginal people in Australia spans tens of thousands of years; the history of newcomers to their shores is much shorter. The first known arrivals began in the early 1600s, although were probably preceded by seafarers and fishermen, their visits unrecorded, from islands along the continent's north coast. Visits from European voyagers were part of a broader history of gradually expanding knowledge of the southern hemisphere. At the frontiers of maritime exploration in the fifteenth, sixteenth and seventeenth centuries were the Portuguese, Spanish and Dutch. In 1488 the Portuguese navigator Bartolomeu Dias had rounded the Cape of Good Hope, proving there was ocean south of Africa and in 1498 his countryman Vasco de Gama reached the west coast of India. By 1520 the Spanish navigator, Ferdinand Magellan, had determined that the Pacific Ocean, extending from Patagonia to East Asia, was connected to the Atlantic Ocean.[1] Throughout the sixteenth century, the Spanish drew ever closer to Australia as they searched for the fabled *terra australis*, a hypothesised continent that often appeared on early-modern maps of the world. These explorers' attempts were launched mainly from the west coast of South America, from where they reached the Solomon Islands in 1567. In 1605 the expedition led by Pedro Fernandes de Queirós left Peru with hopes of finding the Great South Land and claiming it for Spain. While unsuccessful, the expedition's second in command, Luís Vaez de Torres, sailed through the strait (which now carries his name) that separates New Guinea from the northern Australian coastline. Throughout this period, the Dutch were also active in the region, having entered the Asian spice trade by launching commercial voyages to Banten (Bantam, Java). They consolidated their regional presence when they established the United East India Company or *Verenigde Oostindische* (VOC) in 1602. The Dutch claim the honour of

---

1 Michael Pearson, *Great Southern Land: The Maritime Exploration of Terra Australis* (Canberra: Department of Environment and Heritage, 2005), p. 3.

making the first known European landfall in 1606. From this moment onwards, newcomers arrived continuously, if sporadically (see maps 0.1 and 0.2).

Between the early seventeenth and early nineteenth centuries Europeans – including French and British merchants, privateers, explorers and surveyors as well as Macassan fishermen from the Indonesian archipelago – all crossed into Indigenous people's country around the coastlines of Australia. These visits were both deliberate and accidental. Many came in search of trade goods such as spices, gold and *trepang*, while others were determined to discover new lands and contribute to the mapping of the still largely uncharted southern oceans. The less fortunate were shipwrecked on the continent's coasts and reefs.

The history of European and Asian contact with Australia before British colonisation in the late-eighteenth century has generated a large literature. It tends to emphasise the expansion of Europe into Southeast Asia and the Pacific, and the exploration and mapping of the Australian continent's coastline, which is typically presented as leading to British colonisation. Newcomers' perspectives predominate. Yet there are other ways to understand this history. More recent interpretations have reconstituted the two-sided nature of meetings between newcomers and the Indigenous people they encountered, in an effort to understand how each perceived the other.[2] That perspective frames this history less as an expansion of Europe than as an incursion of European and Asian newcomers into Indigenous people's country.

The newcomers' reactions to this unknown land and its inhabitants were mixed. Those with mercantile interests were often disappointed by their failure to find trade goods and resources as they gazed upon the flat and sandy shores of Australia's northern and western coasts. Seventeenth-century European traders were frustrated by Aboriginal people's lack of material resources and, on occasion, their refusal to labour for them, dismissing them as mere savages. Later visitors, keen to make navigational and scientific discoveries, were by contrast entranced by the green and fertile vistas they observed on the continent's south-east region. In the eighteenth century, explorers' perceptions of the people they observed were tempered by European notions of the 'noble savage', through which they expected to encounter 'natural man'. Typically, the eighteenth-century explorers had

2 Anne Salmond, *The Trial of the Cannibal Dog: Captain Cook in the South Seas* (London: Allen Lane, 2003); Nicholas Thomas, *Discoveries: The Voyages of Captain Cook* (London: Allen Lane, 2003); Greg Dening, *Islands and Beaches: Discourse on a Silent Land, Marquesas, 1774–1880* (Melbourne University Press, 1980).

longer sojourns with Aboriginal people than their seventeenth-century counterparts, and more intricate interactions; sometimes hostile, sometimes friendly, yet almost always perplexing. Not only were 'natives' and newcomers in want of a common language, they were ignorant about each other's culture and mores.

The newcomers did not realise that the Aboriginal men, and sometimes women and children, they encountered belonged to any of approximately 250 language groups comprising 500 clans that populated the continent. While some gradually recognised that Indigenous people at different locations spoke distinct languages, the visitors were unaware of the continent's linguistic richness and variety. They were similarly ignorant of the social, cultural and legal compositions of each clan. To the European eye, these Aboriginal people possessed no religion and no laws, and were simply organised into family units. Such a view contributed to the eventual wholesale dispossession of Indigenous people from their land by British settlers. European visitors did not realise that each clan possessed numerous Dreaming stories that related how the land was traversed and marked by the ancestral beings who created the landforms, people, animals, plants and celestial stars. They did not appreciate that the experiences of these ancestral beings, and often the consequences of their actions, formed the basis for kinship systems, laws and ways of caring for and connecting to country, nor that their exploits and travails were commemorated through song, dance and complex rituals.[3]

Understanding how Indigenous people perceived the outsiders they encountered is a difficult task, not least because they did not use writing. Hence there are no written accounts documenting their side of cross-cultural encounters, against which written European accounts can be tested. This problem is compounded because the European records, written and pictorial, are coloured by misunderstandings, false assumptions and prejudices. Indigenous people's perceptions of outsiders were expressed in a variety of forms other than writing: oral stories, dances, songs, art and ritual. Some of these Indigenous records of encounters have survived to the present, such as rock art images of ships, and can be used in an effort to interpret Indigenous people's impressions of outsiders.

In addition, Aboriginal people across Australia have told stories about contact with newcomers, often featuring a stranger who arrives from the sea and disrupts existing ways of life. Although such stories might centre upon a

3 Tony Swain, *A Place for Strangers: Towards a History of Australian Aboriginal Being* (Cambridge University Press, 1993).

well-known European explorer, such as Captain James Cook, they are usually an amalgamation and condensation of various contact experiences and events. In this way, they are a means for accounting for changes in Aboriginal people's lives resulting from the incursion of outsiders, rather than an accurate record of a particular contact event.[4] Nevertheless, they provide some insight into Aboriginal people's perceptions and explanations of outsiders and their influence.

As a general principle, Indigenous people's responses to the newcomers who crossed into their country from the sea can be understood as attempts to deal with uninvited strangers.[5] In a continent inhabited by numerous groups with different dialects and defined territories, Indigenous people were already well accustomed to dealing with outsiders, so when the seaborne strangers who are the subject of this chapter entered Indigenous people's country, they entered a world in which protocols governing relations with newcomers were already highly developed. Only rarely did Europeans understand this to be so.

The Dutch

Well, before, there were no White people; and this was before Mr Richter – sorry, before Giblett. He came later.

First there were previously those…Dutchmen who came, to Cape Keerweer there.

It's 'Thewena' actually, the proper name, not 'Cape Keerweer'.

It's Thewena there, that river mouth.

Many boats were there, which the Dutchmen had built.

They built a house.

They (the Aboriginals) did not yet understand things, no, not our colour.

The poor things used to kill each other, used to spear each other with spears.

And it was at their country that the (Dutchmen) had arrived.

They were still fighting, still spearing each other with spears.

*And then **they** arrived.*

If (the Dutchmen) had behaved properly, (the Aboriginals) would not have killed them.

Jack Spear Karntin (born c. 1905)[6]

---

4 Chris Healy, 'Captain Cook: Between Black and White', in Margo Neale and Sylvia Kleinert (eds), *Oxford Companion to Aboriginal Art and Culture* (Oxford University Press, 2000), p. 93.

5 Sylvia J. Hallam, 'A View From the Other Side of the Western Frontier: or "I met a man who wasn't there…"', *Aboriginal History*, 7, 2 (1983): 134–56.

6 Extract from a translation of story told by Jack Spear Karntin (born c. 1905) recorded at Wathanhiina (Peret Outstation) via Aurukun, Queensland, December 1976, in Luise

The first newcomers to Australia were Dutch explorers and traders employed by the VOC, which was established in 1602 to consolidate the Netherlands' commercial interests in Asia's spice trade. VOC vessels travelled regularly between Amsterdam and Ambon or Batavia in present-day Indonesia, and some travelled further eastward in search of new trade opportunities. In 1606 the VOC sent the *Duyfken*, commanded by Willem Janszoon, to investigate the 'rumours of trade opportunities and gold in the uncharted waters lying to the southeast of the Spice Islands'.[7] After coasting along New Guinea's southern shores, Janszoon's crew became the first Europeans to land in Australia when they unwittingly crossed the Torres Strait and charted the west coast of Cape York. Instead of finding the fabled *Isla del Oro* that the Spanish claimed had beaches sprinkled with gold, all that the Dutch saw as they sailed along the cape near present-day Weipa was a charmless, barren wasteland, sparsely wooded with low-lying bush and 'little oily trees'. Despite the unappealing aspect of the shore, Janszoon was still eager to land and 'intreate' with the locals.

Sailing down the coast the Dutch arrived at a promontory that they named Cape Keerweer, and here, as the Dutch name suggests, they turned around again and entered a cove that they named Fly Bay (now Albatross Bay). Janszoon then sent a boat to explore an unnamed waterway (Wenlock River), where his sailors were attacked by a group of Aboriginal men, and one of the VOC men was killed by a fatal spear wound. Janszoon failed to find any trade opportunities. All the Dutch discovered about this new land was that it was inhabited by 'wild, cruel, black and barbarous men who killed some of our sailors'.[8]

Later VOC expeditions were issued with instructions to 'never go ashore or into the interior unless well-armed, trusting no one, however innocent the natives may be in appearance, and with whatever kindness they may seem to receive you'.[9] The Aboriginal people, in turn, learned about the 'fatal effect' of the Dutch 'muskets' and, according to Jan Carstenszoon, captain of the VOC vessels *Arnhem* and *Pera* that visited Cape York in 1623, to treat newcomers as 'enemies'. Dutch explorers also kidnapped local people, in hopes of putting captives to 'useful purpose', which the anthropologist Peter Sutton

---

Hercus and Peter Sutton (eds), *This Is What Happened: Historical Narratives by Aborigines* (Canberra: Australian Institute of Aboriginal Studies, 1986), p. 99.

7 William Eisler, *The Furthest Shore: Images of Terra Australis from the Middle Ages to Captain Cook* (Cambridge University Press, 1995), p. 69.

8 Günter Schilder, *Australia Unveiled: The Share of the Dutch Navigators in the Discovery of Australia*, trans. Olaf Richter (Amsterdam: Theatrum Orbis Terrarum Ltd, 1976), p. 50.

9 J.E. Heeres, *The Part Borne by the Dutch in the Discovery of Australia, 1606–1756* (London: Luzac, 1899), pp. 20–1.

argues was to 'serve as guides on return visits'.[10] Carstenszoon was the first to execute this strategy in Australia. When the *Pera* landed on the western side of Cape York in 1623, the Dutch 'seized one of the blacks by a string which he wore round his neck, and carried him off to the pinnace'. A few weeks later the practice was repeated with Carstenszoon himself seizing one 'round the waist, while at the same time a quartermaster put a noose round his neck'.[11] It is not known what became of these men who were 'put in irons' and taken back to Ambon 'as curiosities'.[12]

As well as charting Australia's north coast, the Dutch also surveyed the expansive west coast. In 1616 Dirk Hartog was the first to land on that coast after arriving at Shark Bay in the *Eendracht*, and sailing north along a stretch that he named Eendracht's Land. The VOC landings on the west coast resulted from a new and faster route across the Indian Ocean devised by Henderick Brouwer in 1611, which took advantage of the westerly winds at southern latitudes, the 'roaring forties'.[13] This brought VOC vessels closer to Australia, and since a chronometer that allowed an accurate measure of longitude was not invented until the mid-eighteenth century, many that failed to deviate north towards Batavia at the right moment landed around Shark Bay or the Abrolhos Islands (named after the Dutch phrase 'keep your eyes open'). Consequently, throughout the seventeenth century a number of vessels were wrecked off the western coast, with some survivors finding their way back to Batavia and Ambon.

Few Dutch mariners encountered Aboriginal people during their brief stays. Willem de Vlamingh, who named and explored the Swan River and Rottnest Island near today's Perth, saw many signs of people – their huts, smoke from their fires – and, according to later French explorers, 'gigantic human footprints' suggesting that the unseen Aboriginal people were giants.[14] It has also been conjectured that some Dutch survivors of shipwrecks on the west coast might have been adopted into local Aboriginal clans. Rupert Gerritsen, for example, argues that the Nhanda language spoken south of

10 Ibid., p. 41; Peter Sutton, 'Stories about Feeling: Dutch–Australian Contact in Cape York Peninsula, 1606–1756', in Peter Veth et al. (eds), *Strangers on the Shore: Early Coastal Contacts in Australia* (Canberra: National Museum of Australia, 2008), p. 45.
11 Ibid., pp. 36, 40.
12 Colin Sheehan, 'Strangers and Servants in the Company: The United East India Company and the Dutch Voyages to Australia', in Veth et al. (eds), *Strangers on the Shore*, p. 27.
13 Schilder, *Australia Unveiled*, p. 57.
14 Shino Konishi, '"Inhabited by a race of formidable giants": French Explorers, Aborigines, and the Endurance of the Fantastic in the Great South Land, 1803', *Australian Humanities Review*, 44 (2008): 13.

Shark Bay includes Dutch sounds. However, this theory has been dismissed by the linguist Juliette Blevins, who notes that the apparent similarity is a consequence of errors in the early orthography of the Nhanda language.[15] Even the VOC's Abel Janszoon Tasman, who charted both the south-east coast of the eponymous Tasmania, which he named Van Diemen's Land after the then governor-general of Batavia in 1642, as well as the north coast of the continent two years later, had no face-to-face contact with Aboriginal people. Upon stepping ashore at Van Diemen's Land, Tasman's men found a 'level land covered with greenery', which they assumed was 'not planted, but growing naturally', and thought they heard human voices which 'resemble[ed] a trumpet or a little gong'. Noticing that the trees were notched with 'steps five feet apart', they surmised that the inhabitants 'must be very big' or else climb the trees by some other means.[16] On his 1644 voyage to the Gulf of Carpentaria Tasman did encounter Aboriginal people, but reported only that he 'found nothing profitable' there except 'poor naked people walking along the beaches, without rice or many fruits, [who were] very poor and bad-tempered in many places'.[17] After Tasman's journeys, however, the Dutch had a more complete image of Australia's northern, western and south-eastern Tasmanian coasts, and their subsequent maps named the continent *Nova Hollandia* (New Holland).[18]

William Dampier

The most extensive contact with Aboriginal people in the seventeenth century was made by the English buccaneer William Dampier, who twice visited Australia's north-west coast and recorded one of the most influential descriptions of Aboriginal people. In the 1680s he joined two privateering expeditions to raid Spanish possessions, first in South America and the Pacific and then in the East Indies, that brought him close to New Holland. In January 1688 he landed at King Sound. Here, Dampier met with local Aboriginal people on numerous occasions and even attempted to use them as water carriers,

15 Rupert Gerritsen, *And Their Ghosts May Be Heard* (Fremantle Arts Press, 1994), ch. 8; Juliette Blevins, 'A Dutch Influence on Nhanda? Wanyjidaga Innga!', *Australian Aboriginal Studies*, 1 (1998): 43–6.

16 Edward Duyker (ed.), *The Discovery of Tasmania: Journal Extracts from the Expeditions of Abel Janszoon Tasman and Marc-Joseph Marion-Dufresne 1642 & 1772* (Hobart: St David's Park Publishing, 1992), p. 13.

17 Günter Schilder, 'New Holland: The Dutch Discoveries', in Glyndwr Williams and Alan Frost (eds), *Terra Australis to Australia* (Oxford University Press, 1988), p. 103.

18 Eisler, *The Furthest Shore*, p. 96.

without much success. Dampier dismissed them as 'the miserablest People in the World', for they 'have no houses', appeared not to 'worship any thing', failed to till the soil or pasture livestock, and did not possess any iron or 'any other sort of metal'. He also criticised their physical appearance, observing that they had 'Great Brows', 'bottle-noses, pretty full lips', not 'one graceful feature in their faces', and that 'The Colour of the Skins, both of their Faces and the rest of their Body is Coal-black like that of the Negroes of Guinea'.[19]

After the success of his published journal, A New Voyage Round the World (1697), Dampier was commissioned by the British Admiralty to explore the then-unknown east coast of New Holland. Returning in 1699, he landed further south at La Grange Bay, and again met with Aboriginal people, though this time relations were hostile. As the English dug for water a small group of Aboriginal people observed them from a distance and, when one man approached, Dampier went towards him making 'all the Signs of Peace and Friendship' he could. However, the man ran away and the others refused to come any nearer to the strangers. Dampier was determined to 'catch one of them' in order to 'learn where they got their fresh water', so assembled a small party to find the 'natives'. Upon seeing a group of ten or twelve, the English party gave chase and when the fastest runner caught up with the men they 'fac'd about and fought him' with their 'Wooden Lances'. Dampier fired his gun at the Aboriginal men in order to scare them away, but the men 'toss[ed] up their Hands, and crying *Pooh, Pooh, Pooh*', ran 'afresh with great Noise' towards Dampier, so he shot one of them. Dampier's runner escaped, and the English, being 'very sorry for what had happen'd already', returned to the ship while the Aboriginal men carried away their 'wounded Companion'.[20] Dampier did not meet any other Aboriginal people, though did describe one man's physical appearance, assuming that his body paint marked him out as 'the chief of them, and a kind of Prince or Captain'.[21] After his stay at La Grange Bay Dampier sailed to Timor and the islands north of New Guinea, before problems with the rotting HMS *Roebuck* forced him to abandon his mission to investigate New Holland's east coast. Although his descriptions of Aboriginal people were relatively brief, they were read widely and informed the expectations of later voyagers to Australian waters.

19 William Dampier, A New Voyage Round the World: The Journal of an English Buccaneer, ed. Mark Beken [1697] (London: Hummingbird Press, 1998), pp. 218–19.
20 William Dampier, A Voyage to New Holland, &c., in the year 1699 (London: James Knapston, 1703), pp. 144–7.
21 Ibid., pp. 147–8.

Macassan *trepangers*

This story is about the Macassans long ago.
I know we lived together, the old men, all my fathers, uncles and others and the
Macassans. We lived at Amakalyuwakba.
They collected trepang. We ate 'birrida', rice, 'dirdirra', sugar, 'kalukwa', coconut,
we ate rice. We ate rice which they called 'birrida', and what do you call it, cocoa.
They collected trepang.
A lot of us Aboriginals lived together, women and men.
Time went by, they went on collecting trepang, and then Mamariga *blew this way*
and over to its country, to the Macassans' country.
The Macassans went away and stayed over there and then Barra *began to blow*
across this way.
The boats arrived once more in our country, over at Amakalyuwakba.
We camped at Bajuwini, the Macassans' camp, at Kwurrilili, over here at
Lembakwurridi, over there at Arrikburnamanja, at Akwamburrkba, at the
Macassan camp at Amakarjirrakba and at Yarranya.
That was all.
We used to get tomahawks, knives and material. That's all.

Charlie Galiyawa Wurramarrba (c. 1893–1978)[22]

While not inspiring Dutch mercantile interest, the north and north-west coasts of the continent were sites for occasional, and later seasonal, visits from fleets of 'Macassan' *praus* (or *perahus*) harvesting *trepang*.[23] The term 'Macassan', as it is used in Australian scholarship, references the main port of origin and return, the city of Makassar in south Sulawesi, and by extension is used to describe crews of diverse ethnic composition.[24]

Monsoonal winds carried the fleets from Makassar some 2,000 kilometres to the coast of Arnhem Land (known as *Marege'* to the *trepangers*), or to the Kimberley coast (or *Kai Jawa*) further to the west, in November and December each year. As one elderly Yolngu man told the anthropologist Lloyd Warner in the 1930s, 'when the first lightning came the Macassar man came, too'.[25] A fleet would consist of 50 or more vessels, and its journey would

22 Extract from a translation of story told by Charlie Galiyawa Wurramarrba (born c. 1893, died 1978) recorded at Angurugu, Groote Eylandt, c. 1969, in Hercus and Sutton (eds), *This Is What Happened*, p. 119.

23 See Campbell Macknight, 'The View from Marege': Australian Knowledge of Makassar and the Impact of the Trepang Industry across Two Centuries', *Aboriginal History*, 35 (2011): 129.

24 Campbell Macknight explains it is not what the people called themselves. Their own term was '"Mangkasara"; in Bugis, it is *Mangkasa'*; the most usual form in Malay or Indonesian is *Makassar* or *Mengkasar*"', see Macknight, 'The View from Marege'', p. 129.

25 W. Lloyd Warner, 'Malay Influence on the Aboriginal Cultures of North-Eastern Arnhem Land', *Oceania*, 2 (1931–32): 479.

take somewhere between ten and fifteen days.[26] In 1803, when the explorer Matthew Flinders came across six *praus* in the Gulf of Carpentaria, their captain, Pobassoo, told him 60 *praus* were working the coast that season.[27] Each carried a crew of about 30 men. The fleet would break into small groups and work between four and six locations along the coast before making the return trip home in April with the south-east trade winds. The encounter in 1803 between a European expedition of exploration and a small fleet of Asian fishing boats has been described as a 'symbolic moment in Australian history', because 'for centuries European and Asian nations had been potential arbiters of the fate of Australia's Indigenous population'.[28] It would be British colonisation that ultimately prevailed.

It is unclear precisely when regular *trepang*-collecting voyages to northern Australia began. Initial studies suggested between 1650 and 1750, and there is certainly evidence for intermittent contact in this period. Archaeologists now confidently date an image of a *prau* at the Djulirri rock art site in Arnhem Land to 1664,[29] and the earliest known reference in Dutch records dates to 1754, when a report to the directors of the Dutch East India Company noted that

> The Southland which is in the Southeast of Timor not far from thence, is made now and then from Timor and Makassar, but produces so far [as] we know nothing but trepang, being dried jelly-fish, and wax.[30]

Yet the establishment of a regular, seasonal trade in northern Australia began later than this. Recent research into the *trepang* industry as it operated from its base in Makassar shows that increased quantities of *trepang* entered Asian markets in the 1770s and 1780s, and northern Australia is considered its most likely source.[31] On this evidence, Campbell Macknight has recently proposed around 1780 as a probable date for the foundation of the industry in a

---

26 John Mulvaney and Johan Kamminga, *Prehistory of Australia* (Sydney: Allen & Unwin, 1999), p. 410.

27 Matthew Flinders, *A Voyage to Terra Australis: Undertaken for the Purpose of Completing the Discovery of that Vast Country, and Prosecuted in the Years 1801, 1802, and 1803*, 2 vols and atlas (Pall Mall: G. and W. Nicol, 1814), vol. 2, pp. 229–30.

28 Mulvaney and Kamminga, *Prehistory of Australia*, p. 408.

29 Paul S.C. Taçon et al., 'A Minimum Age for Early Depictions of Southeast Asian Praus in the Rock Art of Arnhem Land, Northern Territory', *Australian Archaeology*, 71 (2010): 1–10.

30 Cited in C.C. Macknight, *The Voyage to Marege': Macassan Trepangers in Northern Australia* (Melbourne University Press, 1976), p. 95. The reference is probably to the Kimberley coast.

31 Gerrit Knaap and Heather Sutherland, *Monsoon Traders: Ships, Skippers and Commodities in Eighteenth-Century Makassar* (Leiden: KITLV Press, 2004), pp. 98–102.

formalised way along the Kimberley and Arnhem Land coasts.[32] This makes Macassan activity in northern Australia concurrent with British and French exploration on the east coast and in Van Diemen's Land, and coincidental also with British colonisation at Port Jackson in 1788, although the Macassan fishermen appear not to have been aware of this. When Flinders interviewed Pobassoo in 1803, he quizzed him on this point and found that 'they had no knowledge of any European settlement in this country; and on learning the name Port Jackson, the son of Pobassoo made a memorandum of it.'[33] By the time Flinders met with these fishermen, some had been regularly visiting the region for about 20 years.

The *trepangers* who seasonally entered Indigenous people's 'country', a concept that incorporates land and sea, were in notable respects unlike the European maritime explorers who were active around the Australian coastline in the same period. As fishermen in pursuit of a commodity, they had little interest in what lay beyond the littoral zone, where they dived for and processed their hauls. They had neither future designs on territory, nor ethnological interest in the local population. They were also unlike the British colonisers who began to arrive in eastern Australia from 1788, and who from the 1820s began fitfully to move into the north (when the *trepang* industry was still in operation), for they did not form permanent settlements, claim possession over the land or attempt to convert Indigenous people to their own religion. Even though their annual visits could last up to six months, the *trepangers* were not dependent on Indigenous people or local resources, as they brought rice and other staples with them. Not 'settlers' in the colonial sense, they nonetheless left a palpable imprint by digging wells, naming places and planting tamarind trees; their influence on Indigenous society was likewise notable.[34] Local groups acquired new technology, such as dugout canoes and steel axes, along with trade items such as pipes, cloth and tobacco, which were received in exchange for pearls, pearl shell and tortoise-shell. The influx of new material culture had an influence on Indigenous trade networks.[35]

Interactions between Aborigines and *trepangers* were multifaceted. Flinders' 1803 account reports violence. The *trepangers*, Flinders wrote, 'sometimes had skirmishes with the native inhabitants of the coast; Pobassoo himself had been formerly speared in the knee, and a man had

32 Macknight, 'The View from Marege'', p. 134.
33 Flinders, *A Voyage to Terra Australis*, vol. 2, p. 232.
34 Regina Ganter, 'Turning the Map Upside Down', *History Compass*, 4, 1 (2006): 28.
35 Scott Mitchell, 'Foreign Contact and Indigenous Exchange Networks on the Cobourg Peninsula, North-Western Arnhem Land', *Australian Aboriginal Studies*, 2 (1995): 44–8.

been slightly wounded since their arrival in this road'.[36] Some evidence indicates that certain groups, such as the Tiwi of the Bathurst and Melville Islands, were persistently hostile towards *trepangers,* but that aggression elsewhere was more circumstantial. In general, the *trepangers* had an interest in developing and maintaining reasonably good relations with Indigenous people. Occasionally individuals operated as 'go-betweens' and made 'payments' of desired material goods for access rights as well as labour and services. Inadequately or improperly negotiated transactions could be a source of conflict.[37] For their part, some Indigenous groups found ways to accommodate the *trepangers.* It has been suggested that Macassans could be assimilated into Indigenous society because the seasonality of the trade articulated with the patterns around which Indigenous people organised their own lives, allowing these visitors to be incorporated into a cyclical or seasonal calendar. They were regular and expected traders, not occasional visitors, like European explorers.

While Indigenous groups on the north and north-west coast had sustained exposure to outsiders prior to British colonisation, experience upon which they drew when dealing with future colonists, this was not the case for Indigenous people in the south-east of the continent. There, the interval between the first fleeting visits of European voyagers in the 1770s and the establishment of a British colonial settlement was devastatingly brief.

James Cook

The big ship came an' anchored out at Snapper Island. He put down a boat an' rowed up the river into Bateman's Bay. He landed on the shore of the river – the other side from where the church is now. When he landed, he gave the Kurris clothes, an' them big sea-biscuits. Terrible hard biscuits they was.

When they were pullin' away to go back to the ship, them wild Kurris were runnin' out of the scrub. They'd stripped right off again. They was throwin' the clothes an' biscuits back at Captain Cook as his men was pullin' away in the boat.

Percy Mumbulla (c. 1905–1991).[38]

The eighteenth century was the age of scientific voyaging, and James Cook's three expeditions to the Pacific between 1768 and 1779 epitomised this

---

36 Flinders, *A Voyage to Terra Australis,* vol. 2, pp. 231–2.

37 Peta Stephenson, *The Outsiders Within: Telling Australia's Indigenous–Asian Story* (Sydney: UNSW Press, 2007), p. 32.

38 Extract of story told by Percy Mumbulla (c. 1905, d. 1991) to Roland Robinson at Bodalla, NSW, c. 1950s, published in Roland Robinson, *The Shift of Sands: An Autobiography, 1952–62* (Melbourne: Macmillan, 1976), p. 96.

Enlightenment enterprise. Cook had wealthy patrons – the Admiralty and scientific societies – so he could afford to conduct more leisurely explorations than the earlier Dutch ventures, and pursue interests that would not necessarily return great financial reward. In this context, European interactions with, and descriptions of, Indigenous people became more fully developed and heterogeneous as 'advancements in knowledge' were incorporated into the goals of voyages of discovery. The crews of such expeditions included naturalists, botanists, zoologists, proto-anthropologists, artists and men familiar with various philosophical approaches to the study of humanity.[39] In some instances they also came to include Polynesian men. A Tahitian man, Aotourou, accompanied the French navigator Louis-Antoine de Bougainville back to Europe in the late 1760s. Two Polynesian men joined Cook's first voyage at Tahiti in 1769, although both died in Batavia before reaching Europe. Another participated in Cook's second voyage, eventually arriving in Europe in 1774 before departing on Cook's third voyage in 1776.

Between 1770 and 1803 more than 20 European expeditions landed on the continent, then still known as New Holland, but only a handful have had an enduring legacy on the history of culture contact. Prominent among them is James Cook's *Endeavour* voyage along the east coast in 1770, which included interactions with Indigenous people at Botany Bay (near present-day Sydney) and Endeavour River (near present-day Cooktown) on the far north coast. During his second voyage, Cook's companion ship, the *Adventure*, visited Van Diemen's Land (Tasmania) and Cook himself landed there briefly on his third and final voyage. Despite these later contacts, it is his first voyage on the *Endeavour* that was long considered to have inaugurated British history in Australia. His accounts of the country and people, as well as those of Joseph Banks, the naturalist on the *Endeavour*, contributed to the selection of Botany Bay as a site for a penal colony.

The *Endeavour* reached the east coast of New Holland in late April 1770, after the expedition had observed the transit of Venus in Tahiti and circumnavigated New Zealand. About four months were spent charting the coast from the first sighting of land at Point Hicks in the south to Torres Strait in the north, but landings were few and far between. Cook's charts helped to complete European cartographic knowledge about New Holland that had begun two centuries earlier with Dutch expeditions. Along the

---

39 D.J. Mulvaney, 'The Australian Aborigines, 1606–1929: Opinion and Fieldwork, Part 1', in J.J. Eastwood and F.B. Smith (eds), *Historical Studies: Selected Articles* (Melbourne University Press, 1964), p. 8.

way, the expedition added greatly to geographical, botanical and scientific knowledge.

Cook's interactions with Indigenous people were characterised by miscommunication and misunderstanding. At Botany Bay, the *Endeavour*'s first landing place, relations were initially strained. When two local men 'opposed' the landing party's advance to the shore, Cook eventually fired towards them, wounding one. This violent start to the voyagers' contact with Indigenous people foreclosed possibilities for closer interaction, which would have allowed the accumulation of greater and more accurate knowledge. As it was, for the following seven days that the *Endeavour* remained in the bay, the locals and newcomers merely co-existed, observing each other from a distance, and no 'connections' were formed.[40] Cook's observations were limited to material traces, such as shelters, watercraft, food, weapons and utensils. He was unimpressed by the canoes, which he described as the 'worst I think I ever saw'.[41] Completely closed to him, however, was the intangible world of religious, social and political life. As he explained it, '...we could know but little of their customs as we never were able to form any connections with them, they had not so much as touch'd the things we had left in their huts on purpose for them to take away'.[42]

The expedition was not prepared for the Indigenous people's disinclination to engage. The almost total absence of trade, which had been the conduit for contact in other places visited in the Pacific, is particularly striking. At Botany Bay, the local people showed little interest in the things that Cook and his men offered to them. The absence of trade troubled Cook. Not only did it limit means for interaction, but it also suggested something particular about Indigenous society. In eighteenth-century Enlightenment thought, 'traffick' indicated capacity for commerce, a marker of civilisation.[43] Although Cook was not able to observe it, the economy and practice of exchange, trade and gift giving was a highly complex and ritualised affair among Indigenous groups, structuring social relations and creating obligations of reciprocity. The reluctance to accept, or even touch, the outsiders' things could well

40 Maria Nugent, '"To Try to Form Some Connections with the Natives": Encounters between Captain Cook and Indigenous People at Botany Bay in 1770', *History Compass*, 6, 2 (2008): 469–87.

41 James Cook, *The Journals of Captain James Cook: The Voyage of the Endeavour, 1768–1771*, ed. J.C. Beaglehole, vol. 1 (Cambridge: Hakluyt Society, 1955), vp. 305.

42 Ibid., p. 312.

43 Bruce Buchan, 'Traffick of Empire: Trade, Treaty and *Terra Nullius* in Australia and North America, 1750–1800', *History Compass*, 5, 2 (2007): 386–405.

indicate caution about entering into relations with strangers, especially when such relations would necessarily involve reciprocity.[44]

Cook's and Banks' descriptions of Indigenous people on the east coast were also circumscribed because their encounters were brief and cursory; the explorers had little opportunity to observe Indigenous people within their own domestic settings and social spheres. Interactions generally occurred when Indigenous people, almost exclusively men (hardly any women were seen), approached the voyagers.[45] They tended to avoid interactions initiated by the strangers. Both Cook and Banks described many instances when Indigenous people withdrew upon their approach. It is also clear that Aboriginal people sought to contain and manage the outsiders' range of movement within their country. They 'resisted any unauthorised encroachment on their preserves'.[46] The British sailors often found themselves shadowed at a distance while they surveyed. On other occasions they would be observed by parties of armed men, who formed a barrier between the beach and the country behind them. Cook concluded: 'all they seem'd to want was for us to be gone'.[47]

Cross-cultural relations developed differently at Endeavour River on the far north coast, where the *Endeavour* was forced to remain for seven weeks for repairs after it had been wrecked on the Great Barrier Reef. Cook seems to have learnt from his earlier experience at Botany Bay: rather than initiate dealings, he kept his distance. When a small group of men made their presence known, Cook instructed his crew to ignore them. His newly acquired technique had the desired result. Some local men came aboard the ship and a short-lived period of close contact ensued. This time gifts were accepted, including an old shirt that Cook gave to a man, who returned the following day wearing it around his head.[48]

These were encounters between Indigenous people from different islands of the Pacific, as much as between Indigenous people and Europeans. Tupaia, the Ra'iatean man who had joined the voyage in Tahiti after forming a friendship with Banks, played an influential role. He had been a careful observer of Indigenous people at Botany Bay, and managed to get sufficiently close to produce a detailed illustration of three people fishing from two canoes.

44 D.J. Mulvaney, *Encounters in Place: Outsiders and Aboriginal Australians, 1606–1985* (Brisbane: UQP, 1989), p. 4.
45 Hallam, 'A View from the Other Side of the Western Frontier', p. 143.
46 Ibid., p. 150.
47 Cook, *Journals*, vol. 1, p. 306.
48 Ibid., p. 359.

At Endeavour River, Tupaia, unwittingly or perhaps knowingly, followed protocol. He convinced the local men to lay down their arms and to come and sit with him. This provided conditions for friendly interactions, enough ultimately for a portrait to be sketched, some names exchanged and a word list compiled.[49] Yet, a fragile friendliness soon turned sour over some turtles Cook's crew had caught.[50] The local men took umbrage when the sailors refused to allow them to take one, and responded by setting fire to the grass on the shore near the sailors' camp, which burnt a tent to the ground and a pig to death. In this instance, fire was deployed as a tool of defiance and deterrence.

Despite the absence of sustained interactions, Cook's and Banks' descriptions of Indigenous people, while speculative, are detailed and perceptive. Their observations and conclusions represented a radical revision of the ideas and impressions based primarily on Dampier's damning descriptions that had prevailed for decades. Much had changed in thought about other races in the period between Dampier and Cook.[51] Cook sailed in the aftermath of Rousseau, whose central philosophical tenet revolved around the idea that by nature humans are essentially good but that society corrupts them.[52] While European explorers before him had judged Indigenous people in New Holland harshly for the seeming absence of material goods, social hierarchy or permanent settlements, Cook was inclined to ascribe greater value to material, social and spiritual simplicity. And so, whereas Dampier had described Indigenous people in the north-west of the continent as the 'miserablest People in the World', Cook was moved to characterise those he encountered along the east coast in 1770 as 'far more happier than we Europeans'. He continued

> being wholy unacquainted not only with the superfluous but the necessary Conveniencies so much sought after in Europe, they are happy in not knowing the use of them. They live in a Tranquillity which is not disturb'd by the Inequality of Condition...they covet not Magnificent Houses, Household-stuff &c, they live in a warm and fine Climate and enjoy a very wholsome Air, so that they have very little need of Clothing...In short they seem'd to set no Value upon any thing we gave them, nor would they ever part with any thing of their own for any one article we could offer them...[53]

---

49 Glyndwr Williams, 'Reactions on Cook's Voyage', in Ian Donaldson and Tamsin Donaldson (eds), *Seeing the First Australians* (Sydney: Allen & Unwin, 1985), p. 39.
50 Thomas, *Discoveries*, p. 122.
51 Mulvaney, 'The Australian Aborigines, 1606–1929', p. 9.
52 Ibid., p. 8.
53 Cook, *Journals*, vol. 1, p. 399.

Cook challenged Dampier's 'contempt' for the New Hollanders and rejected his view that the Indigenous people were related to people in Africa or New Guinea.

Before quitting the east coast, Cook paused at an outer island, which he called Possession Island, to formally claim the territory over which he asserted rights as 'first discoverer', for King George III. This act was contrary to the Admiralty's Instructions with which Cook had sailed, which specified that he was to claim territory only with consent of Indigenous inhabitants.[54] The discrepancy between instruction and action has contributed to debates among Australian scholars, not only concerning Cook's reasoning when he assumed possession without consent, but also regarding the legal basis of subsequent British assertions of sovereignty over the territory. Most historians and legal scholars agree that British claims to Indigenous people's territory lies less with Cook's ceremony of possession in 1770, and more with the subsequent and bloody history of British occupation, conquest and settlement, in which the land was taken by force from its original owners.[55] Either way, Cook occupies a prominent place in Aboriginal people's historical imagination as the embodiment of a greedy land grabber and responsible for introducing immoral law.[56]

After his first voyage, James Cook never returned to the Australian main-land, but his two subsequent voyages both touched at Van Diemen's Land. In 1773 his companion ship, the *Adventure*, commanded by Tobias Furneaux, made landfall at Adventure Bay after becoming separated from Cook's *Resolution*. Like Tasman, they failed to see any Indigenous people during their very brief stay – only huts that Furneaux thought would 'hardly keep out a showr of rain'. Nor did the British see any Indigenous watercraft or metals of any kind, so they concluded that the unseen Aboriginal people were 'a very Ignorant and wretched set of people'.[57] Cook himself landed at Adventure Bay in 1777 during his third voyage, and on finally encountering a group of Aboriginal people had a relatively positive interaction. The surgeon William Anderson recorded detailed descriptions of their appearance, noting that their features were 'not at all disagreeable', while the expedition's artist John

---

54 Ibid., pp. cclxxiix-cclxxxiv.
55 Alan Atkinson, 'Conquest', in Deryck M. Schreuder and Stuart Ward (eds), *Australia's Empire* (Oxford University Press, 2008), pp. 33–53.
56 Deborah Bird Rose, 'The Saga of Captain Cook: Remembrance and Morality', in Bain Attwood and Fiona Magowan (eds), *Telling Stories: Indigenous History and Memory in Australia and New Zealand* (Sydney: Allen & Unwin, 2001), pp. 61–79.
57 Cook, *Journals*, vol. 3, p. 735.

Webber was able to draw an Aboriginal man's portrait.[58] In an apparently convivial atmosphere, Webber apparently showed his sketch to the man, for Anderson noted that the charcoal the Aboriginal people applied to their skins to protect themselves from insect bites left marks on the white paper.[59] Cook stayed at Adventure Bay only briefly, and it was not until French explorers visited Van Diemen's Land that newcomers had more extensive contacts with Aboriginal people.

The French

WOORRADY...Said he saw the French discovery ships and that the men had white collars on. Said that the white men when they first came cut the head of a man on a tree and children, that the natives never destroyed it and that it is still there at Recherche Bay. Natives call it WRAGEOWRAPPER, and when the children saw it they were frightened and ran away. Said when they saw the first ship coming at sea they were frightened, and said it was WRAGEOWRAPPER.
Conversation between Woorrady and George Augustus Robinson, 11 July 1831.[60]

Like the Dutch and British before them, the French sent ships to chart this still little-known land. Ten French expeditions arrived in Australia between the 1770s and 1830s, and like Cook with a scientific purpose, although with a greater emphasis on studying native peoples and cultures. Following Bougainville's romanticised depiction of Tahiti and the South Seas, the French were even more expectant of finding exemplars of 'natural man'. While some encounters with Aboriginal people seemed to give substance to Rousseau's characterisation of a state of nature as egalitarian and pacific, others did not. Following Cook's example, the French explorers also took the liberty of naming places they observed and visited, particularly in the western part of the continent, where many French names remain.

In March 1772, just two years after Cook's first voyage along the east coast, Marc-Joseph Marion-Dufresne's *Mascarin* and *Marquis de Castries* landed at Marion Bay in Van Diemen's Land, near Tasman's anchorage 130 years earlier, and where Cook would land five years later on his third voyage. The French ships were on their way to Tahiti to return their Tahitian companion,

---

58 Ibid., p. 785.
59 Ibid., pp. 785–6.
60 Conversation between Woorrady and George Augustus Robinson, 11 July 1831, published in N.J.B. Plomley (ed.), *Friendly Mission: The Tasmanian Journals and Papers of George Augustus Robinson, 1829–1834*, 2nd edn (Hobart: Quintus, 2008), p. 408.

Aotourou, who had accompanied Louis-Antoine de Bougainville to Europe, as well as to investigate the South Seas. Marion-Dufresne's men spent four days in Van Diemen's Land, and were the first Europeans to come face-to-face with Indigenous people there.

After anchoring at Marion Bay, the French approached the shore in three longboats. Upon seeing them, Aboriginal people lit a fire and watched their progress, shouting and gesturing at them as they neared. Marion-Dufresne evaluated the scene; judging that they seemed friendly enough, he had two sailors swim ashore naked and bearing gifts. The archaeologist John Mulvaney suggests that sending the men ashore naked meant they would emerge from the sea like 'natural man' and not frighten the Aboriginal people with their unfamiliar appearance.[61] At first the Aboriginal men greeted the sailors with enthusiasm and seemed to delight in their gifts of mirrors and necklaces. Marion-Dufresne's boat then landed, and although clothed, the captain was similarly welcomed. He was given a lit torch and in turn offered 'several pieces of cloth and some knives' and bread, although the Aboriginal people mainly seemed interested in the French weapons and clothes, 'especially the scarlet ones'.[62]

The French explorers imagined that they understood the Aboriginal protocols for receiving visitors. One of the officers recorded that Marion-Dufresne believed that to show he 'had come with pacific intentions' he should light a nearby small pile of wood with the firebrand he had been given. This was a mistake: lighting the fire seemed to symbolise a 'declaration of war', for the Aboriginal people immediately responded by hurling stones at the French explorers. Another officer offered a more prosaic explanation for the attack: the Aborigines were alarmed by the sight of the third French longboat approaching the shore. Irrespective of the cause, the French responded by firing, and killed at least one man.[63] This brief and violent encounter confirmed French prejudices that the people of Van Diemen's Land were, like those Dampier met at New Holland, 'the most miserable people of the world, and the human beings who approach closest to brute beasts', for they seemed to have 'no fixed abode in any one place'.[64] The dead man's appearance seemed similar to the Aboriginal people described by Dampier, leading the French to believe that Van Diemen's Land was a part of New Holland.

61 Mulvaney, *Encounters in Place*, p. 29.
62 Duyker, *Discovery of Tasmania*, p. 20.
63 Ibid., p. 25.
64 Ibid., p. 22.

Other French expeditions followed, but the expedition led by Antoine-Raymond-Joseph Bruny d'Entrecasteaux offers rich and unusually positive descriptions of Indigenous people. D'Entrecasteaux's expedition was supported by the *Société des observateurs de l'homme* and given instructions to 'investigate the customs and habits of the natives'. He visited south-east Van Diemen's Land in 1792 and again in 1793, depicting Indigenous people more positively than earlier European accounts, commensurate with d'Entrecasteaux's enthusiastic embrace of Rousseau's philosophy.[65] On the first visit, his expedition did not meet any Aboriginal people, but did find some burnt human remains, and erroneously concluded that the Indigenous people must be cannibals, before realising instead that they cremated their dead.[66] When the French returned in 1793 they finally encountered Aboriginal people and lamented that they could have been so mistaken about them.

On 8 February 1793 a small party set off by foot on a two-day overland excursion from Port D'Entrecasteaux.[67] When the French met a group of Aboriginal men, women and children, they were given an elaborate welcome and both sides greeted each other warmly. Sitting down together, they conversed through gestures and an Aboriginal man indicated that they had seen the French the previous night. The explorers concluded that since they were not killed in their sleep, the Aborigines must be a kind and gentle people.

Astounded by the Aboriginal men and women's affection for their children, the French admired the way they gently disciplined them after any 'trifling quarrels': D'Entrecasteaux believed that a 'primordial natural affection [was] alive in them', and exclaimed 'how much…civilised people' could 'learn from this school of nature!'[68] In this remote corner of the world the Europeans believed they had found Rousseau's noble savage, for the Aboriginal people they met offered 'strong proof in support of the idea which the immortal J.J. Rousseau has developed in his discourse on the origin of inequality of conditions'.[69] This is not to suggest that the French considered all Aboriginal mores praiseworthy. Seeing that the women were responsible for diving for shellfish, they assumed them to be oppressed drudges, unfairly burdened

65 Brian Plomley and Josiane Piard-Bernier (trans. and eds), *The General: The Visits of the Expedition Led by Bruny d'Entrecasteaux to Tasmanian Waters in 1792 and 1793* (Launceston: Queen Victoria Museum, 1993), p. 11.

66 Bruny d'Entrecasteaux, *Voyage to Australia & the Pacific, 1791–1793*, trans. and ed. Edward Duyker and Maryse Duyker (Melbourne University Press, 2001), p. 147.

67 Jacques de Labillardière, *An Account of a Voyage in search of La Pérouse… Translated from the French…* 2 vols (London: John Stockdale, 1800), vol. 2, pp. 29–30.

68 D'Entrecasteaux, *Voyage to Australia*, p. 142.

69 Plomley and Piard-Bernier (trans. and eds), *The General*, p. 302.

by the men.[70] They also noticed two men who each shared a fire with two women, and speculated that Aboriginal people practised polygamy.[71] After almost six weeks in Van Diemen's Land the *Recherche* and the *Esperance* followed Marion-Dufresne's lead, and departed for New Zealand.

In 1800 the French launched their most ambitious scientific expedition to the southern lands. Nicolas Baudin's *Géographe* and *Naturaliste* sailed around the continent from 1801 to 1803, amassing a vast array of floral and faunal specimens. The naturalists were given detailed instructions and were well versed in the latest ethnographic philosophies and methodologies. The expedition charted the west and south coasts of New Holland and spent five months in the British colony at Port Jackson, as well as almost three months in Van Diemen's Land, where the explorers made detailed ethnographic observations of the Aboriginal people they met.

Their first encounter with Aboriginal people was at Geographe Bay on the south-west of the continent, where they observed an old man fishing who shied away from the gifts they offered and fled their approach. They next met an Aboriginal man and woman, and again the man ran away before they could initiate any direct contact; the woman, noticeably pregnant, was transfixed with fear and collapsed on the ground, ignoring French attempts to befriend her by offering her some trinkets. Their third encounter at Geographe Bay was with a larger group of men armed with spears. Knowing that European explorers before them had too often resorted to gunfire in their encounters with unwelcoming Aboriginal people, Baudin's men chose on this occasion to retreat and avoid any bloodshed. These brief encounters with Aboriginal people did not make a positive impression on the French, though they remained relatively open-minded as they continued their exploration of the continent.[72]

In Van Diemen's Land, the verdant landscape and lofty mountains, unlike the flat and uninspiring environs of the west coast, heightened French expectations of finding an Arcadian paradise inhabited by noble savages. François Péron, the expedition's official chronicler, was impressed by the first Aboriginal man he saw, a physically dexterous and inquisitive young man who enthusiastically received the French strangers by marvelling at their clothes and eagerly inspecting their belongings. Soon after, the explorers

70 Ibid., p. 306.
71 Labillardière, *An Account of a Voyage*, vol. 2, p. 60.
72 Jean Fornasiero, Peter Monteath and John West-Sooby, *Encountering Terra Australis: The Australian Voyages of Nicolas Baudin and Matthew Flinders*, rev. edn (Adelaide: Wakefield Press, 2010), pp. 360–2.

encountered a friendly Aboriginal family who invited them to sit at their hearth, conversed with them by way of gestures, and joined in when the explorers decided to regale them with songs.[73]

Subsequent meetings did not remain so friendly. Perhaps the Aborigines tired of the Europeans' tendency to dole out 'triflings' while withholding their more desirable tools, weapons and favoured clothing, or the explorers' increasingly intrusive attempts to test Rousseau's contentious thesis that natural man was physically superior to civilised man either by wrestling them or testing their physical strength with a dynamometer. Most likely, the arrival of so many strangers en masse sparked suspicion and concern over their intentions and effect on resources. Péron himself speculated that the Aboriginal men must have considered the French 'treacherous strangers' who only wanted to test their physical strength 'so as to come afterwards and oppress [them] by the strongest means'.[74] Later encounters in Van Diemen's Land were marked by suspicion, physical threats from both sides, and the Aborigines' rejection of French gifts. In turn, the French reconceived Aboriginal people as innately treacherous, unattractive and physically weak. Thus, the French explorers' ethnographic descriptions of Indigenous people, like that of most newcomers', were often mediated by the nature of their encounters and the kinds of reception they received from the natives.[75]

Matthew Flinders

Shortly after Baudin set sail the English navigator Matthew Flinders embarked from England on an expedition to circumnavigate Australia in the HMS *Investigator*. He had served as a midshipman on the HMS *Reliance* and travelled to Port Jackson in 1795. Shortly afterwards he explored the Illawarra coast and in 1798 charted Bass Strait between Van Diemen's Land and the mainland. Impressed by his cartographic achievements, the Admiralty chose him to lead the expedition to map Australia's entire coastline. Setting off in 1801, Flinders had circumnavigated the continent by 1803. In April 1802, while charting the southern coast, he encountered the Baudin expedition, much to

---

73 François Péron, *Voyage of Discovery to the Southern Lands, Books I to III, Comprising Chapters I to XXI*, 2nd edn, 1824, trans. Christine Cornell (Adelaide: Friends of the State Library of South Australia, 2006), pp. 177–82.

74 N.J.B. Plomley, *The Baudin Expedition and the Tasmanian Aborigines, 1802* (Hobart: Blubber Head Press, 1983), pp. 89–90.

75 Bronwen Douglas, 'Seaborne Ethnography and the Natural History of Man', *Journal of Pacific History*, 38, 1 (2003): 3–27.

the surprise of both parties, and though they believed their nations were still at war, the captains had two meetings that were both amiable and civil.[76]

Flinders also met many Aboriginal people during his circumnavigation of the continent. Unlike other eighteenth-century explorers, he was accompanied by an Aboriginal guide, Bungaree, or 'Bongaree', his 'good-natured Indian from Port Jackson'. Bungaree was a Guringai man who had lived in the Broken Bay region before moving south to the settlement at Port Jackson. Having previously served on the *Norfolk*, he impressed Flinders with his 'good disposition and manly conduct'.[77] Flinders was delighted when Governor Phillip Gidley King authorised Bungaree to join the *Investigator*, for he knew the benefits of 'the presence of a native…in bringing about a friendly intercourse' with other Aboriginal people. King also permitted Nanbaree, an orphan who had lived in Port Jackson since boyhood and often acted as an interpreter, to accompany the expedition.[78]

While Flinders assumed that the guides would be able to assist in communicating with other Aboriginal people, he was surprised to find that the Indigenous languages were all 'wholly different'. Although Bungaree was rarely able to converse with the Aboriginal people they met, he did act as a conduit in facilitating exchanges.[79] When the *Investigator's* crew saw a group of Aboriginal people at Sandy Cape, near Hervey Bay in Queensland, Bungaree approached them as they retreated, shedding his clothes and laying down his weapons. As they did not understand his words, much to the amusement of Flinders, the 'poor fellow' then attempted to address them in 'broken English'. Despite Flinders' incredulity, the group accepted Bungaree's advances and eventually welcomed all of the English and accepted their gifts. Twenty of them even accompanied Flinders' men back to their boats, where, after a feast of porpoise blubber provided by the British, the naturalists were given two scoop nets used for fishing in exchange for some hatchets. Thanks to Bungaree, Flinders learned that the Sandy Cape Aboriginal people had a material culture very different from that of the Aboriginal people in Port Jackson even though, to English eyes, they appeared to be of the same people.[80]

However, at times Bungaree's connection to Flinders perplexed the Aboriginal people they encountered. At Caledon Bay Flinders was particularly

76 Fornasiero, Monteath and West-Sooby, *Encountering Terra Australis*, pp. 154–5.
77 Flinders, *A Voyage to Terra Australis*, vol. 2, p. 206; Flinders, *A Voyage to Terra Australis*, vol. 1, p. cxciv.
78 Flinders, *A Voyage to Terra Australis*, vol. 1, p. 235.
79 Flinders, *A Voyage to Terra Australis*, vol. 2, p. 205.
80 Ibid., p. 10.

vexed when the locals repeatedly stole his hatchets, so he decided to discipline them by holding hostage an adolescent boy named Woga until the stolen items were returned. The Caledon Bay people perhaps deemed Bungaree, a fellow Aboriginal man, especially culpable for they attempted to seize him in retaliation for the kidnap. The captive Woga certainly felt a closer affinity to Bungaree than the white strangers, and called to him for help as he was tied up, yet this does not seem to have been forthcoming.[81] In this case Bungaree's allegiance was to Flinders, having previously served with him on two expeditions. Nonetheless, Flinders released Woga after two days. This was no easy decision as he thought Woga could be 'of service' in providing information and facilitating future 'intercourse' with other natives. Yet Flinders worried about the implications the abduction might have for other explorers. He did not want them to suffer a hostile or violent reception from the Caledon Bay Aborigines as a 'consequence' of his actions.[82]

Flinders' circumnavigation of the continent between 1801 and 1803 marks a break in the history of maritime exploration in Australia. His major achievement was to chart the geographical limits of the island continent, proving that it was in fact one large landmass. He entitled his official account *A Voyage to Terra Australis*, but in the preface claimed he would have preferred to refer to the continent as Australia, a term 'more agreeable to the ear' and more in tune with the 'names of the other great portions of the earth'.[83] This was the name by which the nation and its territory would eventually become known.

*

While two centuries of newcomers to the continent ultimately resulted in a complete chart of its coastline, the knowledge accrued about Aboriginal people was far less comprehensive and authoritative. This was due in no small measure to the nature of the interactions with Indigenous people. Although many newcomers – whether in search of valuable resources, in pursuit of knowledge about the land and its inhabitants, or in hope of discovering new territory to claim – landed on Australian shores, their landfalls were, on the whole, occasional and fleeting. As a result, their dealings with Indigenous people can be described, at best, as idiosyncratic. Apart from Macassan fishermen, few voyagers made return trips to places they had previously visited or stayed for very long in one place. Newcomers' interactions with

81 Ibid., pp. 208–9.
82 Ibid., pp. 209–10.
83 Flinders, *A Voyage to Terra Australis*, vol. 1, p. iii.

Indigenous people were slight and not sustained. Rather than building upon experience, each encounter followed its own particular dynamic, shaped by a complex of factors. Not only contingent upon the immediate reactions of Indigenous people to seaborne strangers, these meetings were also shaped by the newcomers' own interests, expectations and motives, be it Dutch desire for trade, Macassan want of *trepang*, or the scientific, geographical and territorial interests that motivated French and British expeditions, and by their various methods for making contact, whether by gift-giving, shows of force or kidnapping.

European visitors were often unprepared for local people's responses to them. Their previous experience with indigenous people in other places in the region, such as New Zealand or New Guinea, did not always prove helpful. And they had little opportunity to learn from others who had preceded them. The information garnered by particular expeditions between the early seventeenth and early nineteenth centuries circulated in only limited ways, circumscribed by the nature of relations at different times between the various nations involved, as well as competing and guarded mercantile, defensive or territorial interests. In any case, it was not always possible to apply lessons learnt in one location to another. The diversity of Indigenous people across the continent meant that experience gained on the north-west coast, for instance, was not readily applicable to the south-east. And so, despite historical interpretations that have stressed either the destructive or the amicable nature of cross-cultural contact, it is almost impossible to generalise.

Yet for all its singularity, this two-century long history of newcomers was not without consequences. While most only had brief stays on isolated stretches of the extensive coastline, European explorers had a lasting legacy on Australia's history as they charted the continent, described its natural history, and ascribed names to its geographical features. While their descriptions of Aboriginal people were superficial and speculative, diverse and contradictory, ranging from the most miserable people on earth to exemplars of the noble savage, the explorers' accounts were to become the foundation upon which notions of Aboriginal people as primitive and lacking in laws, religion and agriculture, were based. Early explorer accounts made it possible for later colonists and settlers to imagine a land freely available and open to occupation and possession. Today these same accounts are being interpreted in new ways as Aboriginal people mine them for details about ancestors, country, material culture and practices, allowing them to reconnect with ways of life and being before the rupture brought about by colonisation.

3

Convict transportation in global context, c. 1700–88

EMMA CHRISTOPHER AND HAMISH MAXWELL-STEWART

On 18 January 1788 the Royal Navy's armed tender, *Supply*, sailed into a large estuarine inlet on the eastern seaboard of the continental mass of Australia. This was a place that British vessels had been to before. James Cook had visited in April 1770, naming it Sting Ray Harbour on account of the large number of fish of that species netted by the crew of the *Endeavour*. He later renamed the expanse of water Botany Bay – a reference to the haul of exotic plants garnered by Joseph Banks and Daniel Solander, the expedition's scientists. Yet it was the subsequent visit of the *Supply* that was to make Botany Bay a British household name. Over the following two days a collection of six blunt-nosed and round-bodied transport vessels slipped into the harbour, accompanied by three store ships and HMS *Sirius*. On board were officers, seamen and marines, plus 736 convicts.[1] This 'First Fleet' was a harbinger of things to come. Over the next 80 years it would be followed by a further 800 transports that would deliver a total of 160,000 convicts to Britain's Australian colonies.[2]

The announcement of the Botany Bay scheme in 1786 excited much comment in British newspapers. Many wanted to know more about the location and geography of the intended settlement. Was it closer to Cape Horn or the Cape of Good Hope, they asked?[3] In an attempt to cash in on the public's curiosity, newspaper editors printed extracts from Cook's account of

---

1 Charles Bateson, *The Convict Ships, 1787–1868* (Glasgow: Brown, Son & Ferguson, 1985), p. 115. The six transports were the *Alexander, Friendship, Scarborough, Charlotte, Prince of Wales* and *Lady Penrhyn*.

2 Stephen Nicholas and Peter R. Shergold, 'Transportation as Global Migration', in Stephen Nicholas (ed.), *Convict Workers: Reinterpreting Australia's Past* (Cambridge University Press, 1988), p. 30. In all 80,000 arrived in New South Wales 1788–1840, plus an additional 3,000 shipped to Moreton Bay and the Port Phillip District between 1846 and 1850. Van Diemen's Land (renamed Tasmania in 1856) received between 67 and 69,000 between 1803 and 1853, and Western Australia 9,000 between 1850 and 1868.

3 *Morning Chronicle and London Advertiser*, 30 September 1786.

New Holland while others offered charts for sale.[4] Enterprising quacks even hawked remedies for scurvy to officers about to embark.[5] To many, the distances involved seemed astonishing. One correspondent reported sarcastically that his proposal to establish 'a short Cut through the Centre of the Earth' had induced enthusiastic responses from 'several Royal Academies and Philosophical Societies'.[6] The scheme spawned many jokes. Notes at the theatre that read 'Bound to Botany Bay' were surreptitiously pinned to the backs of dashing blades, and caricatures of the first parliament of the 'Thief Colony' were offered for sale.[7] The proposed settlement sounded like a world turned upside down, geographically and socially. As one newspaper speculated, this was a place where a notorious liar might claim the role of future historiographer, a harlot might stand as maid of honour and a pirate serve as admiral.[8]

Despite the press attention, the idea of shipping convicts overseas was hardly new. The European expansion into the Atlantic used forced labour on an unprecedented scale.[9] The bulk of these unwilling migrants were slaves purchased in central and west Africa, but convicts and indentured servants made up a sizeable minority. Thus, over 200,000 indentured servants were shipped to Britain's American colonies in the seventeenth and eighteenth centuries.[10] Indenture was a form of assisted migration. The cost of a passage to the New World was equivalent to half the annual salary of an English artisan. In lieu of a fare, migrants commonly entered into an agreement with a contractor whereby they forfeited claim to wages for a number of years, effectively selling themselves.[11] Convict labour, in turn, was an involuntary variant of indenture. The state disposed of the body of the condemned by handing the prisoner over to a contractor for sale in the New World for the length of the sentence imposed upon him or her by a court. By such means

4 See, for example, *General Evening Post*, 28 September 1786; *Morning Post and Daily Advertiser*, 9 December 1786.
5 *Morning Chronicle and London Advertiser*, 9 January 1787.
6 *St James's Chronicle or the British Evening Post*, 5 December 1786.
7 *Public Advertiser*, 6 October 1786; *Morning Post and Daily Advertiser*, 26 December 1786.
8 *Public Advertiser*, 21 December 1786.
9 Peter Linebaugh and Marcus Rediker, *The Many-Headed Hydra: Sailors, Slaves, Commoners, and the Hidden History of the Revolutionary Atlantic* (Boston: Beacon Press, 2000), pp. 36–70.
10 Aaron S. Fogleman, 'From Slaves, Convicts, and Servants to Free Passengers: The Transformation of Immigration in the Era of the American Revolution', *Journal of American History*, 85, 1 (1998): 44.
11 Farley Grubb, 'The Transatlantic Market for British Convict Labor', *Journal of Economic History*, 60, 1 (2000): 103.

successive English, later British, administrations sought to temper domestic crime by the threat of forced labour overseas while simultaneously gambling that the hoes and axes wielded by exiled prisoners would stimulate colonial growth.[12]

It was thus not the presence of convicts on board the First Fleet that elicited surprise, but their destination. The ships under Governor Arthur Phillip's command did not sail west towards the plantations of the Atlantic, but south. Furthermore, once they had cleared the Cape of Good Hope they did not head for the Indian Ocean colonies administered by the East India Company. Instead, the First Fleet turned away from Empire towards the South Seas, using the roaring forties to propel it to a place that seemed absurdly remote to eighteenth-century newspaper readers. There were no planters short of labour at Botany Bay, or other colonial enterprises that might benefit from an injection of cheap penal labour, and it is this absence that made the enterprise appear novel, if not risky.

Historians have been baffled, also, by the manner in which Australia first came to be settled by Europeans. Over the years two broad interpretations have emerged. The majority position has sought to understand the decision to dispatch the First Fleet within the confines of the crisis of penal management that beset the Pitt administration following the loss of the American colonies. An alternative camp emerged towards the end of the nineteenth century, suggesting that wider imperial considerations played an important role in the selection of Botany Bay as a site of colonisation, an argument extended strongly by historians since.[13] This dispute has become one of the most enduring of all Australian historiographical debates. In order to understand the issues that have driven this longstanding exchange between historians it is necessary to take a closer look at the manner in which convict labour was deployed prior to 1787.

---

12 David Meredith and Deborah Oxley, 'Condemned to the Colonies: Penal Transportation as the Solution to Britain's Law and Order Problem', *Leidschrift*, 22, 1 (2007): 19–39.

13 E.C.K. Gonner, 'The Settlement of Australia', *English Historical Review*, 3, 12 (1888): 625–34; K.M. Dallas, *Trading Posts or Penal Colonies: The Commercial Significance of Cook's New Holland Route to the Pacific* (Hobart: Fullers, 1969); Geoffrey Blainey, *The Tyranny of Distance: How Distance Shaped Australia's History*, new edn (Sydney: Sun Books, 1983), pp. 18–39; Alan Frost, *Convicts and Empire: A Naval Question* (Oxford University Press, 1980); Alan Frost, *Botany Bay Mirages: Illusions of Australia's Convict Beginnings* (Melbourne University Press, 1994); Alan Frost, *The Global Reach of Empire: Britain's Maritime Expansion in the Indian and Pacific Oceans, 1764–1815* (Melbourne: Miegunyah Press, 2003); H.T. Fry, '"Cathay and the way thither": The Background to Botany Bay', in Ged Martin (ed.) *The Founding of Australia: The Argument about Australia's Origins* (Sydney: Hale & Iremonger, 1978), pp. 136–49.

In chains on the shores of the Atlantic

British courts had sentenced convicts to transportation since 1615, the majority being despatched to colonies in the New World. In the words of the original decree, those felons 'whoe for strength of bodie or other abilities shall be thought fitt to be ymploied in forraine discoveries' might be spared the gallows on condition of overseas service.[14]

At first a mere trickle was sent. The number of transported felons increased during the Interregnum (1649–60), although records were poorly kept and it is difficult to distinguish between prisoners of war, political exiles and those reprieved from the gallows. Most were sent to the Caribbean to work on tobacco plantations – indeed, to be 'shipped for the Barbadoes' became a euphemism for transportation.[15] By the mid-seventeenth century the connection between exile and forced labour had become firmly entrenched and around 6,000 felons were sold into colonial servitude between 1660 and 1717.

The Poor Unhappy Transported Felon's Sorrowful Account, a work that has late seventeenth-century roots, gives some sense of the process of transportation. Upon disembarkation in Virginia, the felons' hair was combed, their wigs straightened and faces shaved. Smartened up for auction, their limbs and teeth were examined by prospective buyers as though they were horses. Deprived of shoes and stockings, the convicts were then set to work hoeing tobacco alongside slaves imported from Africa.[16]

It is the reference to white and black bonded labour working together that suggests that this is an early account. The shift in the Caribbean from tobacco to sugar and coffee production was accompanied by a preference for African over European bonded labour. While the market for convicts in other American colonies remained buoyant, by the early eighteenth century it was rare for them to be worked alongside slaves. The majority of the estimated 50,000 felons shipped to the New World between 1718 and 1775 ended

---

14 A.E. Smith, *Colonists in Bondage: White Servitude and Convict Labour in America, 1607–1776* (Chapel Hill: University of North Carolina Press, 1947), p. 93. See also Don Jordan and Michael Walsh, *White Cargo: The Forgotten History of Britain's White Slaves in America* (New York University Press, 2008), p. 71.

15 See C.G. Pestana, *The English Atlantic in the Age of Revolution 1640–61* (Cambridge, MA: Harvard University Press, 2004), pp. 183–9; Margaret Sankey, *Jacobite Prisoners of the 1715 Rebellion: Preventing and Punishing Insurrection in Early Hanoverian Britain* (Aldershot: Ashgate, 2005), p. 56; J.D. Butler, 'British Convicts Shipped to American Colonies', *American Historical Review*, 2 (1896): 13–14; Hilary M. Beckles, *White Servitude and Black Slavery in Barbados, 1627–1715* (Knoxville: University of Tennessee Press, 1999).

16 James Revel, *Poor Unhappy Felon's Sorrowful Account of His Fourteen Years Transportation at Virginia in America* (London, 1767).

up in Virginia and Maryland, where they were employed as artisans, servants and farmhands.

As a system, convict transportation took its cue from the transatlantic trade in indentured labour – a process that enabled impoverished migrants to cover the costs of a New World passage. What distinguished penal exile from indenture was the length of the sentence imposed upon the felon; in other respects their legal status and rights were almost identical. Only a fraction of indentured servants signed contracts for more than seven years – the minimum length of time for which the services of convicts were sold.[17] For example, the average length of servitude for male felons landed in Baltimore between 1767 and 1775 was nine years, compared to just under four for indentured servants.[18] While their record of criminality made convicts less attractive to prospective buyers, such disadvantages could be offset by the additional years they were bound to serve.[19] In short, the length of a sentence to transportation was fixed, not for legal reasons, but in order to position convicts competitively within the transatlantic market in unfree labour.[20]

Over the course of the eighteenth century the issue of convict transportation became something of a transatlantic *cause célèbre*. For many Britons it marked the American colonies as a place beyond the pale. One member of the House of Commons quipped that as well as being the 'offspring' of British, French, Dutch and German settlers, the colonists were descended from 'innumerable Indians, Africans, and a multitude of felons'. 'Is it possible', he wondered aloud, 'to tell which are the most turbulent amongst such a mixture of people?'[21] The colonists fought back. Writing under the pseudonym 'Americanus', Benjamin Franklin accused his imperial masters of running roughshod over colonial interests:

These are some of thy Favours, BRITAIN! Thou art called our MOTHER COUNTRY; but what good *Mother* ever sent Thieves and *Villains* to

17 See David W. Galenson, 'British Servants and the Colonial Indenture System in the Eighteenth Century', *Journal of Southern History*, 44, 1 (1978): 52–5; Farley Grubb, 'The Auction of Redemptioner Servants, Philadelphia, 1771–1804: An Economic Analysis', *Journal of Economic History*, 48, 3 (1988): 596–603.
18 Grubb, 'The Transatlantic Market for British Convict Labor', p. 103.
19 Farley Grubb, 'The Market Evaluation of Criminality: Evidence from the Auction of British Convict Labor in America, 1767–1775', *American Economic Review*, 91, 1 (2001): 295–304.
20 Grubb, 'The Transatlantic Market for British Convict Labor', pp. 114–15.
21 As quoted in Gwenda Morgan and Peter Rushton, *Eighteenth-Century Criminal Transportation: The Formation of the Criminal Atlantic* (Basingstoke: Palgrave Macmillan, 2004), p. 147.

accompany her *Children*; to corrupt some with their infectious Vices, and murder the rest?[22]

Even after their Revolution, Americans remained sensitive to the issue. Thomas Jefferson was appalled to read a draft entry for the *Encyclopédie* that claimed that America was populated by three classes of people – servants, slaves and convicts.[23] It is perhaps not surprising that the new republic refused to accept future shipments of felons to corrupt their sons and debauch and pox their daughters.[24] The impact of the Revolution on transportation was abrupt. No convicts were sent to the Americas between 1777 and 1782 and, while a few were despatched from Ireland in the 1780s, the policy was soon abandoned as the convicts proved unsaleable.[25]

There were more prosaic reasons for this market failure than political sensibilities. Transportation had always been unpopular with free workers, as competition with cheap convict labour lowered colonial wage rates. In the years immediately preceding the Revolution, artisan, non-importation movements began to appear in American seaports.[26] At the same time, the falling cost of a transatlantic passage undercut the rationale for the wider indenture system. Increasingly, migrant workers were able to pay for their passage up front and were unsurprisingly less inclined to sign away labour rights in order to cover the costs of the New World journey. While transportation may have been curtailed by the Revolution, its demise was accompanied by the general decline, and ultimate cessation, of the whole North European transatlantic trade in indentured labour.[27] In other words, politics aside, the days of transportation to the American colonies were numbered.

Wartime measures

The outbreak of hostilities forced the British government to adopt the interim solution of housing convicts in old dismasted warships. The *Hulk Act* of 1776 was initially passed for just two years, although it quickly became

---

22 *Pennsylvania Gazette*, 11 April 1751.
23 Morgan and Rushton, *Eighteenth-Century Criminal Transportation*, pp. 151–2.
24 *Pennsylvania Gazette*, 9 May 1751.
25 Bob Reece, *The Origins of Irish Convict Transportation to New South Wales* (Basingstoke: Palgrave Macmillan, 2001).
26 S.V. Salinger, *To Serve Well and Faithfully: Labor and Indentured Servants in Pennsylvania, 1682–1800* (Cambridge University Press, 1987), pp. 148–65.
27 Charlotte Erickson, 'Why Did Contract Labour Not Work in the Nineteenth-Century United States?' in Shula Marks and Peter Richardson (eds), *International Labour Migration: Historical Perspectives* (London: Maurice Temple Smith, 1984), pp. 34–49.

clear that it would have to be extended. By February 1779 questions were raised in parliament about the capacity of the hulks to take more prisoners from the gaols, although this does not appear to have become a substantial concern until after the British defeat of 1783.[28] In the meantime those on board the floating prisons anchored in the Thames amused themselves by showering stones, insults and other detritus on the occupants of passing river craft.[29] The hulks, however, were always more dangerous for those who were secured within their frames, and the 'pestilential' fevers that regularly broke out within their wooden walls raised wider concerns. At one stage, plans were even made to sink the *Justicia* hulk in the Thames in order to protect the metropolis.[30]

Shore-based architectural solutions might have provided a better means of dealing with overcrowding and the threat of typhus that it brought in its wake. The British could have followed the Dutch route, expanding the number of workhouses, penitentiaries and other terrestrial places of punishment. With the exception of about 50 convicts transported to Surinam in the late-seventeenth century, the Dutch republic did not send its felons into exile, choosing instead to build a series of correctional institutions. While the English did construct houses of correction, these were mainly used to confine vagrants and petty offenders. Sentences were short – frequently less than a month (a stark contrast to the seven years or more for which transported felons were banished).[31] A parsimonious government baulked at the expense of expanding these in response to the American revolutionary crisis. For similar reasons it subsequently rejected Jeremy Bentham's proposal to erect a series of colour-coded, multi-storey circular penitentiaries to be painted white for debtors, blue for lesser offenders and black for 'lifers'.[32]

The felons incarcerated in the nation's hulks had their uses, and were put to work aiding the war effort.[33] One of their tasks was to load supplies onto ships. Shot drill, an exercise performed in prisons in the nineteenth century, had its origins in this kind of labour. As Binny and Mayhew described it in the 1860s, shot was moved from one side of the yard to the other through the successive hands of a chain of prisoners. When the pile at one end was

28 *Morning Post and Daily Advertiser*, 6 February 1779.
29 *Morning Chronicle and London Advertiser*, 25 June 1778.
30 *Gazetteer and New Daily Advertiser*, 24 February 1779.
31 Pieter Spierenburg, *The Prison Experience: Disciplinary Institutions and Their Inmates in Early Modern Europe* (Amsterdam University Press, 2007), pp. 41–68, 265.
32 Joan Kerr, 'Introduction', in James Kerr, *Out of Sight, Out of Mind: Australia's Places of Confinement* (Sydney: National Trust of Australia, 1988), pp. 1–10.
33 See Dallas, *Trading Posts or Penal Colonies*.

depleted the exercise was reversed. The two journalists concluded that it was 'impossible to imagine anything more *ingeniously useless*' than this utterly unproductive form of hard labour.[34] Yet in its original form the exercise had a practical use – it was employed to load shot onto men-of-war. Convicts also constructed coastal defences and helped to dredge shipping channels. These were all activities that took on a critical importance when the nation was at war.

During periods of hostility the number of convicts transported declined. Armed conflict increased shipping costs considerably. Not only was there the risk of capture, but the diminished supply of sailors as a result of increased naval recruitment drove up wages, making the movement of anything by sea more expensive. There were similar effects on land. During wars the number of unemployed fell, as did the crime rate. The relatively small number of sentences to transportation passed by courts meant that the government paid little attention to the transportation issue. Besides, the hulks made useful recruiting grounds for convict soldiers who could be deployed to the less desirable outposts of empire.

Between 1775 and 1776 a total of 746 felons were sent to garrison the island of Goree off the coast of Senegambia.[35] The experiment was repeated in 1780 when the Dutch entered the American Revolutionary War, threatening British slaving interests. The thirteen British forts located between Senegambia and Whydah were manned by just 554 disease-ridden troops. There was also a shortage of labourers and canoe men employed by the Company of Merchants trading out of Africa. Competition between Europeans was particularly fierce on the Gold Coast, where there were twelve forts in Dutch hands.

The European hold on these tiny enclaves was tenuous. As the Company admitted, 'it is necessary to keep black men of power in our pay that we may live at peace with the natives who would otherwise molest us, knowing we have not sufficient power to protect ourselves'.[36] In order to shore up defences two independent companies were formed out of 350 convicts reprieved on condition of overseas service. These were distributed among several forts, from the Island of Goree in Senegambia to Cape Coast Castle. A further 40 convicts were transported the following year on the *Den Keyser*, a slaving vessel hired for the occasion.

34 Henry Mayhew and John Binny, *The Criminal Prisons of London and Scenes of Prison Life* (London: Griffin Bohn and Company, 1862), pp. 308–9.
35 *General Advertiser*, 12 October 1786.
36 Wifred Oldham, *Britain's Convicts to the Colonies* (Sydney: Library of Australian History, 1990), pp. 65–8.

In this the British were merely following European practice. The Portuguese had long transported convicts (or *degredados* as they were known) to Africa. They were first used in the capture of the north African city of Ceuta in 1415, and had subsequently been employed to construct and man fortifications in west and central Africa.[37] This was a policy driven by the fearful reputation of the region. Death rates amongst Europeans in tropical Africa were so great that 50 per cent were expected to die within a year of arrival. As the popular rhyme would have it: 'Beware, beware the Bight of Benin, for one that comes out, there's forty go in'. It was thought to be 'morally just' that convicts should be sent to such zones in order to spare the lives of others.[38] Almost all British observers agreed, however, that the experiment with the independent companies was a complete disaster.

Some of those who survived the ravages of disease deserted to the Dutch, while others seized vessels or escaped into the interior. Those that remained traded their equipment, together with the fort fittings (they literally took the doors off their hinges), in return for alcohol supplied by west African dealers. In a desperate attempt to impose discipline, one was executed on the walls of the fort at Mori by being strapped to the muzzle of a cannon and eviscerated. Kenneth McKenzie, the officer who had ordered this bloody and unconventional punishment, was later himself put on trial. It was a high-profile case that served to publicise the utter failure of the exercise.[39]

The Company added its voice to the rising tide of protest. It was concerned that the deployment of convict labour would undermine European authority by demonstrating that whites could be enslaved as well as Africans – similar fears derailed an attempt in 1784–85 to send convicts to work alongside slaves in the British settlement at Honduras.[40] The Company was also worried, rightly as it turned out, that the actions of the convicts might undermine the local operation of the slave trade. Some west African middlemen refused to supply slaves to the Company after being swindled by the transportees.

Despite an unpromising start, the British persisted with the idea of sending convicts to west Africa. Unemployment rose sharply in 1783, following the demobilisation that accompanied the end of the American Revolutionary War. Crime rates soared and, as more sentences to transportation were

---

37 *Degredados* were also sent to Sao Tomé and Angola; see G. J. Bender, *Angola Under the Portuguese: The Myth and the Reality* (London: Heinemann, 1978), pp. 60–93.

38 A.G.L. Shaw, *Convicts and the Colonies* (London: Faber & Faber, 1971), p. 43.

39 Emma Christopher, *A Merciless Place: The Lost Story of Britain's Convict Disaster in Africa and How it Led to the Settlement of Australia* (Sydney: Allen & Unwin, 2010), pp. 201–5, 330.

40 Alan Frost, *Botany Bay: The Real Story* (Melbourne: Black Inc., 2011), pp. 99–102.

passed, the hulks became dangerously overcrowded. Under mounting pressure, the administration of William Pitt the Younger looked for solutions. The Treaty of Versailles, which formally brought the war to a close, gave the British exclusive rights to the Gambia River. In order to secure the territory it was proposed to send convicts to McCarthy Island (also called Lemain or Lemaine), about 320 kilometres inland from the river mouth. A further attraction was that shipping costs were likely to be low since the government could utilise the services of outward-bound slave vessels. A novel feature of the scheme was that the convicts were to be left to their own devices – in a departure from all previous transportation proposals, they would not be sold as unfree labour but rather left to fend for themselves. As such, it might be argued that the settlement provided no challenge to the increasingly racialised division of labour in the Atlantic world. In anticipation of the scheme the island was purchased from local chiefs for £1,000.[41]

Transportation to Africa had always proved unpopular. There was a mutiny among some of the convicts at Woolwich when a rumour spread that a ship had been secured to transport them there. The protest was only quelled after troops fired through the hulk gratings, killing three of the insurgents.[42] The discontent spread, infecting wider public opinion – typhus was not the only contagion that leaked out of the hulks. In the end the Gambia plan had to be abandoned. A 1785 parliamentary select committee chaired by Lord Beauchamp concluded that it would be tantamount to a death sentence, this despite recommendations that the prisoners be issued with cinchona, or Jesuit's bark, to protect them from the ravages of malaria.[43] The death rates associated with previous attempts to send convicts to west Africa had certainly been serious. It was reported, for example, that of 746 convict soldiers despatched there between 1755 and 1766, 344 had died, 271 had deserted and the fate of the remaining 141 was unknown.[44]

Curiously, the Beauchamp Committee at first made no recommendation of an alternative site to which convicts could be dispatched. As Beauchamp himself explained, this was because 'a particular circumstance' had 'rendered it improper' to do so. Alan Atkinson argues that the sticking point

41 Patrick Webb, 'Guests of the Crown: Convicts and Liberated Slaves on McCarthy Island, the Gambia', *Geographical Journal*, 160, 2 (1994): 136–42.
42 *General Evening Post*, 27 June 1786.
43 Emma Christopher, 'A "Disgrace to the very Colour": Perceptions of Blackness and Whiteness in the Founding of Sierra Leone and Botany Bay', *Journal of Colonialism and Colonial History*, 9, 3 (2008): online; Webb, 'Guests of the Crown', pp. 136–8.
44 *General Advertiser*, 12 October 1786; Mollie Gillen, 'The Botany Bay Decision, 1786: Convicts not Empire', *English Historical Review*, 97, 385 (1982): 754.

may well have been East India Company objections and, in his view, it is likely that the preferred option of the committee was New South Wales.[45] Later, Beauchamp issued a second report recommending Das Voltas Bay in present-day Namibia. Not only did this lie outside of the East India Company's charter, which stretched from the Cape of Good Hope to Cape Horn, but it was a proposal that aligned closely with one made in 1782 by Alexander Dalrymple, the Company's hydrographer. In his view Das Voltas Bay might provide the same benefits for the English East India Company that the settlement at Cape Town rendered to its Dutch counterpart.

A perceived benefit of the proposal was that East Indiamen often sailed light on the passage to the Orient and therefore might be induced to ship convicts on the cheap. The naval sloop *Nautilus* was despatched to survey the area, but returned in July 1786 with the disappointing news that this section of the African coast was barren, frequently fog-bound and devoid of a safe anchorage. Indeed, during the entire survey the vessel had failed to locate a source of fresh water or even see a tree. It was a place, declared the commander of the *Nautilus*, 'doomed to everlasting sterility'.[46] The news forced an immediate rethink. Just two weeks later the Pitt administration announced its intention to send convicts to Botany Bay.[47]

In chains on the shores of the Pacific

Many were amazed. It seemed as though the government, clutching at straws, had plumped for a risky, ill-conceived and potentially costly venture. The idea, however, had been percolating since 1779. It had first been proposed by Sir Joseph Banks, the naturalist who had accompanied Cook on his 1768–71 voyage, and who had suggested that 300 convicts be despatched to New Holland. The scheme had been resurrected in 1783. Botany Bay was touted as a place that possessed soils and a climate that would support a mixture of Atlantic and Asian plantation crops. Sugar cane, tea, coffee, silk, cotton, indigo, tobacco and flax might be cultivated there, it was suggested. When the *Nautilus* returned with the news that the Das Voltas region of Africa was utterly unsuitable for settlement, Botany Bay got the nod as the most viable of the remaining alternatives, although if Atkinson is right it might have been

45 Alan Atkinson, 'Whigs and Tories and Botany Bay', in Martin (ed.), *The Founding of Australia*, pp. 197–8.
46 Christopher, *A Merciless Place*, pp. 326–7.
47 Frost, *Botany Bay*, pp. 109–10, 193–4.

selected earlier if negotiations with the East India Company had progressed smoothly.[48]

The government did briefly investigate the costs of shipping convicts to India and in 1786 Madagascar was proposed as a possible destination. Neither of these options appears to have been seriously contemplated,[49] although there is no technical reason convicts could not have been sent to a destination in the Indian Ocean. If the East India Company had been willing to acquire the labour of British and Irish convicts, they could have been shipped without breaching monopoly rights. Such an arrangement would merely have mirrored the pre-1775 method of disposing of convicts by transferring property rights in the bodies of felons to shipping contractors.

Convict labour, however, was something that India House was not short of – it had plenty of felons who had been convicted in its own courts. The transportation of convicts from the Indian subcontinent had first been mooted in 1773 by the governor of Bengal, who had recommended sending them to the pepper plantations at Bencoolen in Sumatra. This plan was eventually put into action in 1787, the very year that the First Fleet set sail. It was a scheme that also coincided with the Company's decision to abandon slavery. The use of Indian convict labour had many advantages. It could be deployed on infrastructure projects, substituted for plantation labour or used to drive down free labour rates. While convicts were unfree, they were technically not slaves and this enabled the Company to benefit from the exploitation of its charges while simultaneously escaping any unwelcome associations with the politically odious practice of slaving.[50]

The East India Company drew up plans to send Indian convict labour to Prince of Wales Island (also known as Penang) in 1788, a settlement it had acquired two years earlier. The first convicts were disembarked there in 1790. By then convicts had also been used to help secure the Andaman Islands, although high death rates led to the abandonment of the settlement in 1796, with survivors transferred to Penang. Thus, while the East India Company

---

48 Christopher, *A Merciless Place*, pp. 329–33.
49 Ibid., pp. 313, 336.
50 Anand A. Yang, 'Indian Convict Workers in Southeast Asia in the Late Eighteenth and Early Nineteenth Centuries', *Journal of World History*, 14, 2 (2003): 182–91; Clare Anderson, 'The Politics of Convict Space: Indian Penal Settlements and the Andaman Islands', in Carolyn Strange and Alison Bashford (eds), *Isolation: Places and Practices of Exclusion* (London: Routledge, 2003), p. 40; Richard B. Allen, 'Suppressing a Nefarious Traffic: Britain and the Abolition of Slave Trading in India and the Western Indian Ocean, 1770–1830', *William and Mary Quarterly*, 66, 4 (2009): 873–94.

was not averse to using convict labour to secure strategic objectives, it had no need to acquire that labour from the British government. Indeed, there were very good reasons for it to distance itself from such a venture. Just as the Company of Merchants trading out of Africa had opposed the importation of felons to the forts and factories of the Gold Coast, so the East India Company feared that the introduction of European convict labour might undermine labour hierarchies based on race. In fact, the Company later used the British penal colonies in Australia to dispose of European convicts sentenced on the Indian subcontinent, while indigenous offenders were sent to company-run penal settlements.[51] The bifurcation of transportation flows on the basis of race is illustrative of the nature of the problem that the Pitt administration faced.

It was not so much the difficulty of finding a new penal colony that troubled the government as the lack of private-sector demand for British and Irish felons. Falling wages and rising prices, as much as political considerations, blocked North American markets, whereas the Caribbean and Africa were amply supplied with slaves. From the Malacca Straits to Honduras, British settlement was by the late-eighteenth century marked by the exploitations of peoples of colour.[52] One might even go as far as to say that New Holland was colonised by convict labour because the vast majority of those felons were white. If more had been dark-skinned the chances are that the government would have been able to sell them on the cheap to cut mahogany or sugar, plant pepper or cart stores in the heat of the tropics.

The thief colony

Some have argued that the Botany Bay decision was motivated by a desire to break with the penal practices of the past. Atkinson, for example, contends that the British settlement in New Holland was not planned as a place of coercion. Instead, he argues that the 'Thief Colony' had two virtues – its distance from Europe and the fact that it was considered useless. The convicts were intended to be peasants in a land of their own, prevented from

51 Clare Anderson, *Legible Bodies: Race, Criminality, and Colonialism in South Asia* (Oxford: Berg, 2004), pp. 1–2; Clare Anderson, '"Weel about and turn about and do jis so, Eb'ry time I weel about and jump Jim Crow": Dancing on the Margins of the Indian Ocean', in Sameetah Agha and Elizabeth Kolsky (eds), *Fringes of Empire: Peoples, Places, and Spaces in Colonial India* (Oxford University Press, 2009), pp. 169–87.
52 Fogleman, 'From Slaves, Convicts, and Servants to Free Passengers', pp. 43–76, and Ged Martin, 'The Alternative to Botany Bay', in Martin (ed.), *The Founding of Australia*, pp. 156–7.

returning from whence they had been banished by the watery wastes of the world's oceans.[53]

Joseph Banks first suggested Botany Bay as a penal destination to a House of Commons select committee in 1779. While other submissions had been confined to the shores of the Atlantic (the benefits of sending convicts to Gibraltar, Gambia, Florida and Georgia were all raised), Banks had spruiked the merits of New Holland. He had recommended that 200–300 convicts equipped with seeds, fishing equipment, arms and other basic supplies should be shipped there and left to fend for themselves. The suggestion had later been incorporated in the ill-fated Gambia proposal. Atkinson argues that the scheme appealed to those who were worried that the Hulk Act had led to an erosion of the rights of Englishmen. To many the sight of convicts labouring in irons implied that Britons could indeed be slaves. Botany Bay, on the other hand, would serve as a 'ragged but real commonwealth' to which malefactors could be safely exiled.[54]

The governance of the proposed colony was indeed the subject of much speculation between the announcement of the plan and the departure of the First Fleet. For the price of sixpence members of the public were invited to attend a meeting held at the Westminster Forum to debate the motion that the 'intended transportation of convicts to Botany Bay' was a disgrace 'to a civilized community'.[55] Yet rather than raising concerns about the extent to which a renewal of transportation might impose limits upon traditional English liberties, the majority of correspondents expressed concerns that the scheme would prove too lenient.

As the government's opponents pointed out, the idea of a penal colony free from coercion was an expensive way of giving malefactors a chance to start a new life. Those that committed an offence did so, it was argued, in the knowledge that if detected they would be removed to a country where their circumstances would be infinitely better than they were at present.[56] According to the London *Morning Herald*, the toast amongst the felons of Newgate was to 'Pitt and Botany Bay'. As the paper put it, 'Gratitude, as well as honor, is to be found amongst thieves!'[57] Concerns grew that the popularity of the scheme among the lower orders might increase, rather than

---

53 Alan Atkinson, *The Europeans in Australia: A History. Volume 1, The Beginning* (Oxford University Press, 1998), p. 58.
54 Ibid., pp. 50–1. See also Brian Fitzpatrick, *British Imperialism and Australia, 1783–1838: An Economic History of Australasia* (London: Allen & Unwin, 1939), p. 14.
55 *Morning Herald*, 2 October 1786.
56 Ibid., 27 November 1786.
57 Ibid., 11 November 1786.

decrease, the number of offenders.[58] Courts reacted accordingly and, when it was discovered that a soldier had stolen a hat in order to secure a free passage to Botany Bay, it was directed that he should be transported instead to Africa.[59]

One wit quipped that the settlement would help former offenders to mend their ways, as for several years there would not be a pocket worth picking.[60] Others feared that left to their own devices the new colonists would find pockets to pick elsewhere. The threat of piracy was a recurring theme. Having 'colonized America with gaol-birds and saints of the Newgate Calendar', one bemoaned, the government was about to repeat the experiment. 'If disease and the length of the voyage should spare them', he predicted they would turn their hand to terrorising 'every vessel they can master'.[61] Many thought that the 'most serious argument' against the plan was that Botany Bay 'would necessarily become a harbour of pirates' – a place which 'may prey on the trade of England, Spain and all the world'. As 'Philanthropos' put it, 'the spirit of rapine and villainy will be kept up amongst both the present and succeeding generations'. He was not alone in recommending that instead of being transported, the convicts should be executed or swapped for European sailors held captive on the Barbary Coast. Others thought that it was best to banish them underground to work in coalmines or sell them as slaves to the plantation economies of the Caribbean.[62]

In fact there is little evidence that the government seriously contemplated the establishment of an antipodean commonwealth of thieves. The Beauchamp Committee formed in 1785 to evaluate the Gambia proposal had been especially critical of the notion. It was of the Committee's 'decided Opinion' that the 'Idea of composing an Entire Colony of Male & Female Convicts, without any other Government or Control but what they may from Necessity be led to Establish for themselves can answer no good or rational purpose'. Indeed, the Committee recommended that if 'his Majesty think fit to establish a new Settlement for Enlarging the Commerce of his Subjects, the labour of these Convicts may be employed to the most useful Purposes'.[63]

58 *General Evening Post*, 16 December 1786.
59 *General Advertiser*, 18 December 1786.
60 Ibid., 24 October 1786.
61 *Public Advertiser*, 30 September 1786.
62 *Whitehall Evening Post*, 2 December 1786; *Morning Chronicle and London Advertiser*, 9 December 1786; *Morning Herald*, 7 February 1787.
63 For this point see Angus R. McGillivery, 'Seamen's Greens, and Imperial Designs at Port Jackson: A Maritime Perspective of British Settler Agriculture', *Agricultural History*, 78, 3 (2004): 261–88.

The government's supporters repeatedly sought to ram the point home. As one put it, New Holland was 'not a land flowing with milk and honey'. The laws of the future 'Thief Colony', it was reported, were to be of 'the most salutary nature' and were to be modelled on those 'adopted in the African settlements'.[64] By this they meant that the settlement would be governed according to military, rather than civil law – a proposition that may well have conjured up images of the blood-splattered walls of Fort Mori.

Those who argued that transportation would lead to an erosion of rights were more likely to bemoan the effects of the settlement on indigenous people. 'By what rule of justice', asked the *Morning Herald*, did the government 'dare to dispossess the natives of their property and authority?'[65] It was a perceptive question. While both the Gambia and Das Voltas Bay schemes included plans to purchase territory from the indigenous inhabitants, such stipulations were never part of the Botany Bay venture.[66]

Convicts or Empire?

The notion that convicts were to be 'dumped' on the shores of New Holland assumes that their labour would be of little utility. It also implies that no great hopes were held out for the future of the venture other than that the colony might prove to be self-supporting.[67] It was selected, in Mollie Gillen's words, because in August 1786 there was nowhere else to send convicted felons. If the British government had more expansive plans for the New Holland colony, she argues, it would not have continued to fill the settlement with subsequent drafts of convicts.[68] Most historians, in fact, who have examined the Botany Bay decision have concluded that the settlement was founded as a place to dispose of convicts rather than for reasons of Empire. Yet this is a conclusion that sits uneasily with the manner in which convict labour had been deployed historically.[69]

The use of convict labour to further wider imperial objectives has a long European history. The Portuguese used convict labour to construct forts and other infrastructure in both Africa and the New World. Indeed, one of the

---

64 *Public Advertiser*, 13 December 1786, and *Morning Post and Daily Advertiser*, 27 November 1786.
65 *Morning Herald*, 1 November 1786.
66 Stuart Banner, 'Why *Terra Nullius*? Anthropology and Property Law in Early Australia', *Law and History Review*, 23, 1 (2005): 98.
67 Atkinson, *The Europeans in Australia*, p. 58.
68 Gillen, 'The Botany Bay Decision', pp. 740–66.
69 For a summary of these arguments see Martin (ed.), *The Founding of Australia*.

reasons Captain Arthur Phillip was selected to command the First Fleet was that he had previously been employed by the Portuguese to transport convicts to Brazil.[70] The Spanish also made extensive use of convicts, especially to construct fortifications in tropical environments, where their labour was considered more expendable than the use of slaves, the latter being considerably more expensive to acquire.[71]

Before the advent of assisted migration programs in the mid-nineteenth century, the dangers associated with overseas colonisation meant that it was difficult to attract the necessary volume of working-class migrants to secure a colonial labour force. Those that did migrate aspired to escape waged labour by acquiring land. Thus, rather than stifling the development of the Australian colonies, convict labour forcibly deported from Britain, Ireland and other places in the Empire catalysed colonial development by supplying a source of cheap, coerced labour.[72] In the words of the Beauchamp Committee, the use of convict labour might play an important factor in establishing 'the Prosperity' of a future settlement.

A perceived benefit of the various schemes to transport convicts to west Africa was that shipping costs could be offset by hiring stowage space on outward-bound slavers. The Das Voltas Bay scheme was in part predicated on the possibility of striking a similar deal with the East India Company. Following the announcement of the Botany Bay decision it was widely reported that the Pitt administration had made an agreement with the East India Company to charter transport vessels at the 'small price' of £7 per tonne in the knowledge that the contractors could load up with tea at Canton for the return leg. As the *London Chronicle* put it, 'This makes a very considerable saving also to the Company, and by this mutual compact the new colony will be annually recruited with our convicts at a moderate expense to the nation'.[73]

Gillen argues that the proposal to cut costs by permitting transports to return laden with tea appears to have first been proposed three weeks after the scheme was initially announced.[74] It may well have been raised in relation to negotiation with the East India Company directors, some of whom

70 *London Chronicle*, 1 February 1787.
71 R. Pike, 'Penal Servitude in the Spanish Empire: Presidio Labor in the Eighteenth Century', *Hispanic American Historical Review*, 58, 1 (1978): 21–40.
72 Stephen Nicholas, 'The Convict Labour Market', in Nicholas (ed.), *Convict Workers*, pp. 111–26.
73 *London Chronicle*, 19 September 1786; *Morning Chronicle and London Advertiser* 20 September 1786; see also ibid., 20 October 1786.
74 Gillen, 'The Botany Bay Decision', p. 758.

saw the Botany Bay scheme 'as a direct violation of their charter'.[75] The Company's hydrographer, Alexander Dalrymple, went as far as to publish a pamphlet condemning the scheme. He proposed sending the convicts to Tristan de Cunha, an Atlantic island that lay outside of the area to which the Company had been given exclusive rights of trade and navigation.[76] Yet an agreement with the Company was signed in early December 1786 permitting the contractors to proceed from Botany Bay to China to bring back tea.[77] It was a deal that the government promoted in order to counter criticism that the scheme would prove too costly.[78]

Afterthought or not, it is tempting to read the negotiations with the East India Company as evidence that Pitt and his ministers embarked on the Botany Bay decision with wider strategic considerations in mind than locating a distant shore upon which to discharge the nation's criminal detritus. This was a line of thinking first elucidated by Gonner in 1888 and subsequently expanded by the historians Fry, Dallas, Blainey and Frost.[79]

As Fry points out, Alexander Dalrymple's 1782 'Memoir concerning the Passages to and from China' highlighted the threat that hostile Dutch action would pose to East India Company vessels attempting to negotiate the Malacca and Sunda straits. The same memoir flagged the possibility of utilising the passage south of Australia to maintain the China trade in times of conflict. Following the end of the Fourth Anglo Dutch War (1780–84), both the East India Company and the British government made use of convict labour to secure key bases on both of these routes (Penang and Botany Bay). Indeed, just seven days separated the annexation of Penang and the announcement of the Botany Bay decision. Yet this interpretation implies that the East India Company was closely involved with the decision to send convicts to New South Wales, whereas the evidence suggests that company reactions to the proposal were at best mixed. Alexander Dalrymple was one of Botany Bay's principal critics.[80]

Other historians have suggested that the First Fleet was despatched to secure naval stores. Botany Bay was founded when Britain was slipping from an age of wood into a future that would be powered by coal, but for all of that it was an era in which military might still rested on timber. A single 74-gun

---

75 *Morning Herald*, 11 October 1786.
76 Alexander Dalrymple, *A Serious Admonition to the Publick, on the Intended Thief-Colony at Botany Bay* (London: John Sewel, 1786).
77 *General Advertiser*, 8 December 1786.
78 *London Chronicle*, 23 November, 1786.
79 See note 13.
80 Fry, '"Cathay and the way thither"', pp. 136–49.

ship could consume over 3,000 mature trees. It was a staggering amount, and nurturing the nation's stock of forests was serious business.[81] Admirals were even known to carry acorns in their pockets to distribute through the estates of their hosts in order to propagate trees to build the ships of the future.[82]

The loss of the American colonies exacerbated domestic timber shortages. As well as supplying large quantities of oak, North America was an important source of pine for masts and spars. The problem could be partially solved by using the East India Company docks, but this required the constant shipping of naval stores from Europe. Cables, cordage and canvas could not be stored for long periods of time in tropical climates.[83] In the years when the British government was searching for an alternative destination to send convicts, the available stocks of timber in British Navy yards declined by 61 per cent. Conversely, the European trend was to construct ever-larger vessels. Between 1775 and 1790 the tonnage of warships increased by 46 per cent.[84]

The plan to establish the settlement at Botany Bay made reference to the utilisation of flax. It also provided instructions for the simultaneous colonisation of Norfolk Island, a place that Cook had identified as a potential source of naval stores. This 35-square-kilometre lump of volcanic rock, located 1,600 kilometres off the coast of New Holland, abounded with pines of an impressive size and *Phormium tenax,* a form of flax that produced much longer fibres than its European cousin.[85] The attempt to write Norfolk Island and its pines and flax into the Botany Bay proposal seems, however, to have been at best half-hearted. It is almost as though the Pitt administration tried to pad out the scheme with cordage, planks and sailcloth in order to furnish it with a degree of respectability. While the naval stores argument certainly featured prominently in the often-heated discussion that broke out in the London press following the announcement of the Botany Bay decision, this is usually read as a belated attempt by the supporters of the proposal to put a favourable gloss on the scheme.[86] As the *Public Advertiser* put it

It is the wish of Ministry to leave no portion of his Majesty's dominions unimproved. Whatever provisions or naval stores, or useful natural productions are to be found, or where factories can be established, or harbours formed with a view to the extension of trade and the encouragement of

81 James Dodds and James Moore, *Building the Wooden Fighting Ship* (London: Hutchinson, 1984), pp. 13–20.
82 Simon Schama, *Landscape and Memory* (London: Harper Perennial, 2004), p. 173.
83 Frost, *The Global Reach of Empire*, pp. 101–12
84 Ibid., pp. 269–71.
85 Ibid., pp. 279–80.
86 Alan Atkinson makes a similar point, 'Whigs and Tories', pp. 201–5.

manufactures, thither, unquestionably, the eyes of Government will be turned.[87]

Correspondents pointed out that the intended settlement was just a fortnight's sail from New Zealand, a place covered with timber 'of such an enormous size and height, that a single tree would be much too large for a mast of a first rate man of war'.[88] With an eye to the future, 'Nautilus' argued that the colony might 'afford abundance of excellent provisions for our *navy* in that part of the globe'.[89] Even the opponents of the government alluded to the naval stores argument. As an editorial in the *General Evening Post* put it, while it was 'thought that our East India possessions might have been supplied with many hemp and stores' from Botany Bay, on 'enquiry' it has been found 'highly impolitic to trust to so precarious a resource' – a discovery that had necessitated an expansion of the scheme to include the colonisation of Norfolk Island.[90]

Some have speculated that Botany Bay was established in order to facilitate new whaling and sealing ventures or to aid the opening up of Pacific commerce. The American Revolution severed more than the transatlantic trade in felons. The entry of the Spanish into the war also severely restricted British access to New World silver. Since silver was one of the few commodities that Qing China would accept in exchange for tea, silk and porcelain, the war had considerable implications for the East India Company. While opium from Bengal was substituted for silver in the long run, Russian, American and British traders attempted with some success in the 1780s to import sea-otter pelts.[91] As the *General Advertiser* put it, Botany Bay would facilitate access to furs from the 'Aleitian and Fox islands', an objective that would help to diminish 'the immense drain of silver' occasioned by the China trade.[92]

Others made broader claims for the utility of the settlement. 'New Holland', it was argued, was most happily situated 'for acquiring the various enriching articles of Eastern commerce'.[93] Far from being remote, newspaper correspondents argued that Botany Bay was strategically located. It was in sailing time roughly equidistant from the Cape of Good Hope, Madras, Canton, the Moluccas and Batavia. As such the place might form

---

87 *Public Advertiser,* 23 September 1786.
88 *General Advertiser,* 12 October 1786.
89 *Public Advertiser,* 28 September 1786.
90 *General Evening Post,* 2 December 1786.
91 Alicja Muszyński, *Cheap Wage Labour: Race and Gender in the Fisheries of British Columbia* (Montreal: McGill-Queen's University Press, 1996), p. 146.
92 *General Advertiser,* 13 October 1786; *General Evening Post,* 16 November 1786.
93 *Morning Chronicle and London Advertiser,* 21 November 1786.

an 'important object', when viewed 'with a *political eye*'.[94] Others saw it as a strategic base – a place where 'our ships' sailing 'in that quarter of globe, may receive refreshments in greater plenty'.[95] As the editor of the *Morning Chronicle* argued: 'is not impossible, nor even improbable', that the convict settlers of this remote colony 'may become useful to the empire'.[96] The sentiment was even committed to verse

> Let no one think much of a trifling expense,
> Who knows what may happen a hundred years hence!
> The loss of America what can repay?
> New colonies seek for at Botany Bay.[97]

David MacKay has argued that 'it requires some gifts of imagination to embody the foundation of the New South Wales colony into the substance of some wider imperial purpose'.[98] If so, then there was certainly no shortage of imagination in the 1780s. Yet while newspaper speculation may reveal much about the way in which the decision to send convicts to Botany Bay was rationalised, it is far less informative about the 'preliminary impulse' that led to the act of colonisation.[99] When the much-vaunted Norfolk Island pines proved rotten at the core and the flax (although impressive in size) impossible to work using European methods, the talk of naval stores was quickly dropped.[100] Over-exploitation also put an end to the trade in sea-otter pelts. The fast route to China idea also came undone. Although some of the transports that made up the First Fleet proceeded to Canton, the experiment appears not to have been repeated.

The Botany Bay venture was an entirely new form of undertaking and thus it is natural that the decision should have promoted public speculation. It is worth pausing, however, to reflect on the factors that drove the decision to send convicts to New Holland.[101] The decline in the Atlantic trade in indentured servants and the growing association between race and 'unfreedom' made it impossible to sell British and Irish convict labour to the private sector. This not only closed off markets in the Atlantic, but effectively

---

94 *General Advertiser*, 12 October 1786.
95 *London Chronicle*, 18 January 1787.
96 *Morning Chronicle and London Advertiser*, 3 October 1786 and 14 October 1786.
97 *Public Advertiser*, 23 November 1786.
98 D.L. Mackay, 'Direction and Purpose in British Imperial Policy, 1783–1801', *Historical Journal*, 17, 3 (1974): 487–501.
99 Michael Roe, 'Australia's Place in "the swing to the East" 1788–1810', in Martin (ed.), *The Founding of Australia*, p. 59.
100 Dallas, *Trading Posts or Penal Colonies*, p. 11; Frost, *The Global Reach of Empire*, pp. 279–80.
101 Martin, 'The Alternatives to Botany Bay', p. 153.

ruled out Indian Ocean destinations, too. Changing market conditions did not lead to changes in sentencing practices, however. The convicts on the First Fleet were encumbered with the same legal shackles that had been fashioned in order to position felons within the seventeenth and eighteenth-century market for transatlantic indentured servants. Far from being 'dumped' on a distant shore to be left to their own devices, the services of convicts remained the property of the British state for a minimum of seven years.[102]

What did the state do with that labour? The short answer was that it put a hoe into its hands. While it has become something of a tradition to paint early European attempts to cultivate the harsh and 'unyielding' antipodean landscape as a pathetic failure, the colonists achieved a number of notable successes. While south-eastern Australia may have been remote from the British Isles, its winter rains and Mediterranean-like climate meant that European crops could be cultivated there. The settlement's gardens produced the necessary foodstuffs to overcome the initial potentially serious difficulties associated with importing supplies from elsewhere.[103] Not only that, but in a few short years the convict settlement was able to provide fresh provisions to visiting vessels. As the Spanish botanist Luis Née put it in 1793 when he saw the cultivated fields around Parramatta: 'It delights the soul to contemplate the happy change of conduct in men who, if they had been harmful to their homeland, were today useful because of their application to work and because of the constant efforts by which they were transforming a rude, wild country into a pleasant garden'.[104] Greens may not have been the naval stores imagined by Blainey and Frost, but by the 1790s the British settlement in New Holland had clearly achieved an imperial objective of sorts. Like the intended settlement at Das Voltas Bay, it provided a harbour where vessels could be careened and resupplied, thus fulfilling at least one newspaper prediction. It did indeed become a place where 'our ships' sailing 'in that quarter of globe, may receive refreshments in greater plenty'.[105]

*

In February 1787, a few months before the First Fleet departed, a masquerade was held in the Pantheon, Oxford Street. This was one of the most

---

102 Hamish Maxwell-Stewart, 'Convict Transportation from Britain and Ireland 1615–1870', *History Compass*, 8, 11 (2010): 1221–42.
103 Grace Karskens, *The Colony: A History of Early Sydney* (Sydney: Allen & Unwin, 2009), pp. 98–157.
104 As quoted in McGillivery, 'Convict Settlers, Seamen's Greens, and Imperial Designs', p. 278.
105 Ibid., pp. 261–88; *London Chronicle*, 18 January 1787.

fashionable locations in London. Horace Walpole called it the 'most beautiful edifice in England', but it was always the great room with its dome modelled on the Hagia Sophia in Constantinople that was the principal drawcard.[106] The masquerade attracted a great number of 'fancy dressers'. Amongst the multitude of harlequins, nuns, friars, sailors and country bumpkins, two revellers stood out. One was dressed as a '*West-Indian negro girl*' who 'skipped about with great agility' while the other was decked out as the '*Bishop of Botany Bay*' – a costume designed to highlight the ambiguities that lay at the heart of Britain's latest imperial venture. Metaphorically, the two made a fitting couple.

Why did the Pitt administration affix its 'political eye' on Botany Bay? It is safe to say that those who made the decision thought the colony would result in strategic benefits, even if they were undecided about the precise nature of these. In order to realise those benefits it was necessary to disentangle transportation from its Atlantic roots. Like the two revellers who danced under the gilded dome of the Pantheon, convict labour had developed in partnership with other forms of unfreedom. The Botany Bay decision marked the moment when the couple parted – the dancing 'bishop' moving in one direction and the slave girl in another.[107] New Holland's greatest advantage was that it was a place where convicts could be sent to labour far removed from other colonial enterprises and, as such, it provided little by way of a challenge to pre-existing systems of exploitation based on race.

---

106 Michael Forsyth, *Buildings for Music: The Architect, The Musician and the Listener from the Seventeenth Century to the Present Day* (Cambridge University Press, 1985), p. 32
107 *Felix Farley's Bristol Journal*, 10 February 1787.

4

The early colonial presence, 1788–1822

GRACE KARSKENS

The arrival of the 'First Fleet' in Botany Bay in 1788 marked the birth of modern Australia. The governor, 550 officers and marines and 736 settler-convicts (188 women, 548 men, along with around 25 children of convicts) who came ashore in January and February that year were not the first settlers of the continent. But the settlement they founded at Sydney Cove was the starting point for early colonial expansion, and ultimately created the social and economic foundations of the nation.

This great migration also marked the beginning of what historian Alan Frost calls 'the most striking penal experiment in history'.[1] The settlers of 1788 were there to found an unusual colony: one designed explicitly for the reform and resettlement of convicts. The British government envisaged a subsistence agricultural colony that would transform felons into farmers. It was to be a new society, not a gaol. The long-term role of the colony was less clear, perhaps deliberately so. But at the outset Governor Phillip's Instructions were unambiguous: convicts would initially work on large public farms, growing 'food from a common industry' to replace the rations that would run out after two years. Once free, men were eligible for small land grants: 30 acres for a man, 20 more for a wife and ten for each child, with tools, seed grain and rations for two years. Women were integral to the scheme from the start, though as helpmeets rather than subjects in their own right. Men and women, reformed by hard, simple agricultural work, would eventually become small landowners.[2] Land was the lynchpin of the scheme. It would succour them, anchor them: it was the basis of a new society.

By contrast, Phillip had no instructions at all on urban development, nor any real economic plan, apart from some vague hopes of producing raw

---

1 Alan Frost, *Botany Bay: The Real Story* (Melbourne: Black Inc., 2011), p. 227.
2 Governor Phillip's Instructions, 25 April 1787, *Historical Records of Australia* (HRA), series I, vol. I, pp. 14–15; Marian Aveling, 'Imagining New South Wales as a Gendered Society, 1783–1821', *Australian Historical Studies*, 25, 98 (1992): 1–12.

materials for England. In fact, the colony was to be kept isolated, both in order to prevent convicts escaping and because of the East India Company's monopoly over trade in the region. Thus shipping, ship building and trade were banned. Officially, there were to be no consumer goods apart from the most basic necessities, to be provided by the British government. The logic was beautifully simple: with nowhere to run and no other sustenance, those who refused to work would starve.[3]

These formal instructions were given to the first five governors – Arthur Phillip, John Hunter, Philip Gidley King, William Bligh and Lachlan Macquarie – and this agrarian vision continued until 1825, when the policy of giving free grants to ex-convicts ended. Visions of social transformation through land-holding, small farming and agricultural work, partnered and promoted by government, would be powerful vectors in Australian history. So, too, would the tangled impulses to evade authority and live as one pleased, on the one hand, and to embrace authority, conditionally, on the other.[4]

The original scheme rested heavily on certain underlying assumptions about land, distance and peoples. James Cook and Joseph Banks described New South Wales as extensive, open, fertile and thus easily cultivated. It seemed too distant to allow convicts to return to England. The Aboriginal people were reportedly few, wandering nomads with no discernible rights to the land, and passive, weak and incurious besides. They apparently presented no obstacle, moral or physical, to annexing territory and establishing a colony.[5] As for the colonists themselves, the military was there for security, and the depraved convicts, cast into the wilderness, would have no option but to submit to their fate.

Each one of these assumptions turned out to be far too simplistic. New South Wales was not a land of open, boundless meadows – the sandstone soils of Sydney were unsuited to growing nutrient-hungry crops such as wheat and maize. Much of the country was covered in eucalypt forests. The Aboriginal people were numerous, and their warriors were fierce. The

---

3 Phillip's Instructions; Grace Karskens, *The Colony: A History of Early Sydney* (Sydney: Allen & Unwin, 2009), pp. 64–6.

4 Brian H. Fletcher, *Landed Enterprise and Penal Society: A History of Farming and Grazing in New South Wales before 1821* (Sydney University Press, 1976), p. 6; Richard Waterhouse, *The Vision Splendid: A Social and Cultural History of Rural Australia* (Perth: Fremantle Arts Press, 2005); Alan Atkinson, *The Europeans In Australia: A History. Volume 1, The Beginning*, (Oxford University Press, 1997), p. 116.

5 Atkinson, *The Europeans in Australia*, vol. 1, pp. 70–7; Alan Frost, 'New South Wales as *terra nullius*: The British Denial of Aboriginal Land Rights', *Australian Historical Studies*, 19, 77 (1981): 513–23; Karskens, *The Colony*, p. 111.

military officers sent out with the First Fleet had ambitions at odds with the penal–agricultural project. As for the convict majority, many of them saw the colony in much the same way that officers did: as a place to profit and to amass property. Some grabbed opportunities with both hands. Others had simpler ambitions: to make new families; to work, play and socialise as they pleased; to live free of all restriction. Still others dreamed only of escape. Ships represented their best hope. Distance was no deterrent.

The convicts

Between 1788 and 1868 around 160,000 convicts were sent to the Australian colonies, but only 27,000 of them arrived before 1822.[6] Convicts still tend to be dismissed either as brutes or abject victims, people who had no active role in the making of early Australia. Yet the social profiles and cultural identities of those first convict arrivals had profound effects on early colonial society, economy, demography and cultural life. It is difficult to generalise about such a large and diverse group. They came mainly from the various ranks of the eighteenth-century lower orders, and from many regions of England, Ireland, Scotland and Wales. Among them were Jewish convicts and African-Americans who had been slaves in the American colonies. There were forgers and political prisoners, tradespeople, unskilled and unlettered people, men and women, old and young.[7]

Most convicts were thieves, often convicted more than once. A large proportion came from urban centres, although the Irish, who made up roughly 25 per cent, tended to come from rural areas. The convicts had a slightly higher literacy rate than their contemporaries back home – about half the men could read and write. Thus early settler Australia combined an oral and strongly visual as well as a literate culture.[8] These men and women brought a large range of skills with them. Men who could build, cut timber, quarry, make bricks, farm, sail, fish and hunt, and who could organise and supervise other men, were most valued. The female convicts brought essential

---

6 B.H. Fletcher, 'Agriculture', in G.J. Abbott and N.B. Nairn (eds), *Economic Growth of Australia 1788–1821* (Melbourne University Press, 1978), p. 191.

7 Patrick O'Farrell, *The Irish in Australia: 1788 to the Present* (Sydney: UNSW Press, 1993); John S. Levi and George F.J. Bergman, *Australian Genesis: Jewish Convicts and Settlers, 1788–1860* (Melbourne University Press, 2002); Cassandra Pybus, *Black Founders: The Unknown Story of Australia's First Black Settlers* (Sydney: UNSW Press, 2006).

8 Stephen Nicholas and Peter R. Shergold, 'Convicts as Migrants', and 'Convicts as Workers', in Stephen Nicholas (ed.), *Convict Workers: Reinterpreting Australia's Past* (Cambridge University Press, 1988), pp. 43–61, 62–84; Atkinson, *The Europeans in Australia*, vol. 1, p. 6.

domestic skills, and they included needlewomen, nurses, dairywomen and farm workers.[9]

The early colonies were pre-industrial in culture and economy, powered by wind, water and the muscles of men and animals, not by coal and steam. Governors tried to impose clock time but people measured their days by sunrise and sunset, by tides and the arrival of ships. It was a world that entwined eighteenth-century consumerism, commercial activity and mobility with older communal habits. Poorer people still regarded access to common land as their right. Those drinking together drank from the same glass. They still thought of their societies as made up of interdependent ranks within the two great orders, the higher and lower. Relations were personal and face-to-face; contracts were often made by verbal agreement. Attitudes to sex, marriage and children and public behaviour were not much affected by modern ideas of respectability. As for racial attitudes, convicts were not humanitarians but their relations with Aboriginal people were marked by localised contacts, familiarity, friendships and shared enjoyment as well as exploitation and violence. Both higher and lower orders, and later Aboriginal people, enjoyed the riotous and disorderly pleasures of pre-industrial popular culture. The colonies were marked and made by opportunistic risk-taking, but the reverse side of this was a wellspring of fatalism and resignation to things beyond human control. This pre-industrial culture and world view, with its unruly energy, shaped the early colonial presence far more than silent subservience, endless toil and brutal punishments.[10]

Founding settlements and the first farming frontier

The ships of the First Fleet dropped anchor in Botany Bay, the country of the Gweagal and Kamaygal.[11] In that first El Niño summer a shortage of fresh water, as well as the lack of shelter for the ships, led Phillip to seek a more favourable site. He found it at Sydney Cove, a snug cove in Port Jackson to

---

9 Deborah Oxley, *Convict Maids: The Forced Migration of Women to Australia* (Cambridge University Press, 1996).

10 Grace Karskens, *The Rocks: Life in Early Sydney* (Melbourne University Press, 1997), pp. 7–12; Karskens, *The Colony*, 178–82, 356–65, 431, 443–6; Richard Waterhouse, *Private Pleasures, Public Leisure: A History of Australian Popular Culture Since 1788* (Melbourne: Longman, 1995), ch. 1; James Boyce, *Van Diemen's Land* (Melbourne: Black Inc., 2008), pp. 5–7; Alan Atkinson, *The Europeans in Australia: A History. Volume 2, Democracy* (Oxford University Press, 2004), pp. 22–3.

11 Val Attenbrow, *Sydney's Aboriginal Past: Investigating the Archaeological and Historical Records* (Sydney: UNSW Press, 2002), pp. 22–8.

the north, and moved his ships and people there. A good stream of fresh water flowed into the salt and, more importantly, there were no armed warriors standing on the shore or wading out to meet the boats. It must have been a striking absence. Phillip and the officers had been met by warriors in other bays, and had seen them shouting from cliff tops as the ships sailed into the harbour.

Port Jackson is the drowned valley of the Parramatta River, which drains the flat or undulating Cumberland Plain to the west. The plain is girdled by another river, the Hawkesbury-Nepean, and encircled by high sandstone plateaux. Located at the centre of what became the County of Cumberland, the Cumberland Plain was the locus of settlement during its first 30 years, the cradle of modern Australia and the cauldron of the first frontier wars.[12]

Sydney had a twin settlement. Soon after he landed, Phillip despatched a party of 22 convicts, seamen and others to Norfolk Island, 1,600 kilometres east-north-east of Sydney, under the command of Lieutenant (later Governor) Philip Gidley King. This twin-peaked, 35 square-kilometre volcanic island was discovered by Cook in 1774 and was then uninhabited, though settlers found traces of earlier people. While landings there were always hazardous in the absence of a harbour, the island's rich soils and abundant fresh water yielded good harvests of wheat and maize. The purpose of the settlement, its headquarters also called Sydney, was to secure the island as a British possession, as well as to investigate the potential of the flax found growing there for cloth-making. Within two years Norfolk Island supported 41 per cent of the colony's population and British officials wondered whether the whole colony might not have been better sited there.[13]

Meanwhile, back on the mainland, Phillip and his officers searched frenetically for arable soils. Their earliest treks through sandstone country northwards were disappointing, but within a month more open grassy country was seen up the Parramatta River, and by June 1788 they had found shale soils and open forest country 25 kilometres west of Sydney. Large public farms were established, first at Parramatta in 1788, and then at Toongabbie to the north-west; the latter involving enormous work in clearing the dense forests of turpentine, lillipilli and coachwood. Phillip's new, grid-patterned township was laid out at Parramatta in 1790, complete with neat rows of huts for the convicts, probably based on the planned villages that had appeared

12 Tim Flannery, *The Birth of Sydney* (Melbourne: Text, 1999), pp. 8–17.
13 Merval Hoare, *Norfolk Island: A Revised and Enlarged History, 1774–1998* (Rockhampton: Central Queensland University Press, 1999), pp. 1–13; Atkinson, *The Europeans in Australia*, vol. 1, p. 72.

on English estates in the 1770s and 1780s. Observers were confident that Parramatta would be the new headquarters of the colony, and that unruly Sydney would wither away.[14]

After successfully testing the viability of individual farming with the transported Cornish farmer James Ruse and his wife Elizabeth Perry, Phillip began to implement the greater plan.[15] Most of the expirees wanted to return to England and had no interest in becoming farmers, but after some bullying, bribery and persuasion, Phillip managed to establish the first groups in clusters of small farms around Parramatta. The ex-convicts received tools, seed and rations for a year and had huts built for them. They appear to have considered their grants as a contract rather than an indulgence.[16]

Phillip was a cautious and diligent man, and implemented his orders to the letter. The earliest farms were kept close and carefully monitored: tiny, ragged patches of wheat and maize in the vast forests of New South Wales. With the end of El Niño and the arrival of a more favourable climate, progress was steady. Stock was increasing slowly, fruits and vegetables were thriving and the colonists were healthy. On Norfolk Island, King established two small towns, supervised the building of a road and managed to oversee good harvests in spite of the depredations of rats, grubs and birds.[17]

These were hiatus years. The uncertainties of the first months were over and the great floods and droughts on the mainland were yet to come. The colonists were optimistic and lavished praise on the land's bounty and healthfulness. So Phillip was shocked to learn from people on the *Halcyon*, arriving in June 1792, that people in England believed the colony was starving, the land a barren desert and the whole experiment a disaster. The exaggerated and damning complaints from disgruntled military officers had done their work.[18] Phillip's departure from the colony later that year – unwell and perhaps demoralised – marked a turning point in the expansion of the farming

---

14 Karskens, *The Colony*, pp. 75–97.
15 Arthur Phillip, Journal, in John Hunter, *An Historical Journal of Events at Sydney and at Sea, 1787–1792* [1793] (Sydney: Angus & Robertson, 1968), pp. 300–1, 351; David Collins, *An Account of the English Colony in New South Wales*, vol. 1 [1798] (Adelaide: Libraries Board of South Australia, 1971), pp. 92–3, 158, 225.
16 Collins, *An Account*, vol. 1, p. 340; Watkin Tench, *A Complete Account of the Settlement at Port Jackson* [1793], published as *Sydney's First Four Years*, ed. L.F. Fitzhardinge (Sydney: Library of Australian History, 1979), pp. 250–9; Matthew Everingham, *The Everingham Letterbook* (Sydney: Anvil Press, 1985), p. 35.
17 Collins, *An Account*, vol. 1, pp. 243–4, 249, 320; Phillip, Journal (in Hunter), p. 340; Lynne McLoughlin, 'Landed Peasantry or Landed Gentry', in Graeme Aplin (ed.), *A Difficult Infant: Sydney Before Macquarie* (Sydney: UNSW Press, 1988), pp. 120–2.
18 Phillip to Dundas, 19 March 1792, HRA, vol. 1, pp. 340–1; Collins, *An Account*, vol. 1, p. 375.

frontier, relations with Aboriginal people, and new land-alienation practices, which resulted in officers becoming large landholders.

Hawkesbury settlement: the Nile of the colony

There was a dramatic breakout from Phillip's small, supervised constellation of farms (67 settlers in total) around Parramatta. The initiative was taken, not by government but by ex-convicts themselves. Early in 1794 a group of ex-convicts asked Acting Governor Grose to grant them land on the banks of the distant Hawkesbury River. Grose did not have much choice: they were already settled there. A band of men and women, most convicts who had served their sentences, led by James Ruse, had already taken the rich, lightly forested and open grassy river flats they called the Green Hills (now Pitt Town and Windsor).[19]

The reports from the river were electrifying. The soil was so rich it could grow almost anything with a minimum of labour. The Hawkesbury was soon dubbed the 'Nile of the colony'. Hundreds of people made their way out to the river, on foot or by water, in Australia's first land rush. Many seem to have taken land without any formal lease or grant, or with only verbal approval. By mid-1795 there were 400 white people living along the river. At the same time, the population of Norfolk Island began to decline – from a peak of 1,115 people in 1792, it fell to 875 in 1797, though it rose again to 1,078 in 1805.[20]

For governors, the settlement of the Hawkesbury was a relief: the colony's self-sufficiency in grain seemed in sight at last. But there were also concerns. The ex-convict settlers were creating an independent society, with no authority, no constables and no clergy. Judge Advocate David Collins wrote disapprovingly of the feckless Hawkesbury farmers, freed from hard labour by the bountiful river soils to drink, gamble and 'riot' as they pleased.[21] Instead of ensuring arduous lives, these rich soils left time for socialising and the pleasures of pre-industrial popular culture, the culture of resistance and opposition, of pleasure for its own sake, of bare-knuckle prize fights, horse

19 Collins, An Account, vol. 1, p. 249; Brian Fletcher, 'Grose, Paterson and the Settlement of the Hawkesbury 1794–1795', Journal of the Royal Australian Historical Society, 51, 4 (1965): 342–3; Karskens, The Colony, pp. 117–20.
20 Collins, An Account, vol. 1, pp. 406–7, 413; 'A Soldier's Letter', 13 December 1794, in F.M. Bladen (ed.), Historical Records of New South Wales [HRNSW] (Sydney: Government Printer, 1893), vol. 2, p. 817; Fletcher, 'Grose, Paterson and the Settlement of the Hawkesbury', 345–6; Fletcher, 'Agriculture', p. 195; Hoare, Norfolk Island, pp. 24–27, 31.
21 Collins, An Account, vol. 1, pp. 54, 338–9, 400.

races, dog fights and cock fights, as well as drinking, gambling and singing. All the early centres – Sydney, Parramatta, the Green Hills, Norfolk Island and, later, Van Diemen's Land and Melbourne – developed this type of popular culture in the early period. The Hawkesbury remained its vigorous bastion over much of the nineteenth century.[22]

Farming the colonial earth

Farming itself was for the main part small-scale and simple. These were hoe farmers, for hoes were the agricultural tools first sent out, three for each convict, probably in the hope that cultivation would be as arduous and slow as possible. It was a tool freighted with associations of slavery and subjection. Yet the ex-convict farmers inverted this meaning: given the shortages of skilled labour and beasts for ploughing, and the long, snaking gum-tree roots that stymied the ploughshares, these simple tools turned out to be the most appropriate and useful. Even unskilled workers could quickly learn to use the hoe; the public farms were training grounds in this respect, and hoe-farming became a tradition in Sydney, Norfolk Island and in Van Diemen's Land, now Tasmania, where another colony was founded in 1803. Ploughs did not become more common until the 1820s, and then only among the more ambitious and better-off settlers. These farmers also diversified their stock and crops, planted orchards and vegetables, and built more substantial houses.[23]

In the Sydney region, wheat was the grain insisted upon by convicts and soldiers for their bread, so it commanded the best prices and was the cash crop, sold to the Commissariat. On Norfolk Island both wheat and maize were flourishing in 1793 despite earlier problems, but wheat harvests began to fail from 1797 and farmers were discouraged from growing it.[24] Maize growing was another innovation. It flourished in roughly cleared, cultivated ground and became the staple food of the poorer rural classes. In New South Wales and on Norfolk Island, protein came from pigs, which were easily raised on small farms (in 1796 there were 887 people and an astounding 14,642 pigs on Norfolk Island and the adjacent Phillip Island). Maize did not grow

22 Waterhouse, *Private Pleasures, Public Leisure*, ch. 1; Karskens, *The Colony*, pp. 123–8; Boyce, *Van Diemen's Land*, pp. 126–44.

23 Alan Frost, *Botany Bay Mirages: Illusions of Australia's Convict Beginnings* (Melbourne University Press, 1994), pp. 132–3; Geoff Raby, *Making Rural Australia: An Economic History of Technical and Institutional Creativity, 1788–1860* (Oxford University Press, 1996), pp. 36–7; Fletcher, *Landed Enterprise and Penal Society*, p. 214.

24 Raby, *Making Rural Australia*, pp. 42–3, 53–57; Hoare, *Norfolk Island*, p. 26.

well in Van Diemen's Land, however, so wheat dominated the small farms there.[25]

The poorer farmers and tenants built cheap, flexible shelters from local materials. These were one or two-roomed huts built of wattle and daub (hence the popular name for acacias became 'wattle') or bark, and later the more substantial timber slabs, split from local hardwoods. By the 1810s the better off were building boxy farm houses with jerkinhead roofs, or the characteristic U-shaped farmhouse complex with drooping verandahs that became typical of Australian rural architecture. But among the poor and tenant farmers, bark huts were still as common on the Hawkesbury-Nepean in the 1860s as they were in the frontier areas.[26]

Expansion and abandonment

On Norfolk Island, some neat and sturdy limestone houses rose alongside the older wattle-and-daub and timber huts. There were schools, shops, an orphanage and, for a short time, a theatre. But despite King's continued advocacy, from 1803 the British government considered the settlement too distant and too costly, and wanted to establish its new strategic settlements on Van Diemen's Land. Here, colonisation was strangely reversed, its abandonment slow and unwilling. On hearing of the decision to abandon the island, the male settlers presented a petition, saying that they had wives, and children born on the island, and wished to stay on their cleared farms and in comfortable homes. They were now old men, and had no wish to start the whole pioneering process again. Nevertheless, the first groups of settlers sailed in 1804 and 1805 for new, larger farms promised them in Van Diemen's Land. But the last settlers did not depart the island until 1814, 26 years after it was founded. They burned down the buildings, and left the island to pigs, dogs and goats, and the enclosing forests. The new settlements in Van Diemen's Land were named Norfolk Plains and New Norfolk, but the settlers found it hard to start again, and the lieutenant-governors there were unable to fulfil the promises made to them. The Norfolk Islanders never

---

25 Raby, *Making Rural Australia*, pp. 45, 52ff; Jocelyn Powell, 'Early Hawkesbury River Settlement', in Jocelyn Powell and Lorraine Banks (eds), *Hawkesbury River History* (Sydney: Dharug and Lower Hawkesbury Historical Society, 1990), pp. 43–57; Hoare, *Norfolk Island*, pp. 25–6.

26 J.M. Freeland, *Architecture in Australia: A History* [1968] (Melbourne: Penguin, 1982), pp. 10–12; James Broadbent, *The Australian Colonial House* (Sydney: Hordern House, 1997), pp. 19, 23, 25, 103–9.

forgot their old island farms and 'years later spoke of the change with regret and sadness'.[27]

The life and death of Norfolk Island's first settlement reminds us that European colonisation in Australia was no simple, one-way story of founding followed by inevitable growth and permanence. It was an unstable, mutable process, dependent upon the local environments and emerging economies, and the vagaries of government edicts. Many successful settlements left a trail of failed attempts. During the first decade of the nineteenth century, the discovery of Bass Strait's rich resources of seals and whales, and fears of French incursions, led Governor King and the British government to establish a series of colonies further south, yet a number of these were abandoned. Sorrento, in Port Phillip Bay, where 308 convicts and a handful of free settlers arrived direct from England under the command of David Collins in 1803, soon failed for want of food and water, through scurvy and deaths, and because of Aboriginal hostility.[28] Collins moved the group to Sullivan's Cove (now Hobart) on the Derwent River. At Port Dalrymple in north-east Van Diemen's Land, there were multiple attempts to found settlements between 1804 and 1807. Problems with stock losses and crop failures led Lieutenant Governor William Paterson to remove the settlement further upstream to the site of Launceston in about 1807.[29]

The agricultural decades

During King's governorship (1800–06) the original policy of subsistence farming was revised, and the size of some of the land grants was increased to 80 acres or more in the hope of establishing more profitable farms.[30] Nevertheless, the practice of giving land to ex-convicts, as well as ex-soldiers and the few free settlers, continued in New South Wales and Van Diemen's Land. Hunter, King and Bligh all actively supported the small farmers. Macquarie, while he assisted and granted land to graziers and free settlers, also tried to help and encourage the small farmers and considered agriculture a higher activity than 'the lazy object of rearing of cattle'.[31]

27 Hoare, *Norfolk Island*, pp. 29–32; Kirsty Reid, *Gender, Crime and Empire: Convicts, Settlers and the State in Early Colonial Australia* (Manchester University Press, 2007), pp. 39–41; John West, *The History of Tasmania*, vol. 1 (Launceston: Henry Dowling, 1852), p. 38.
28 Alison Alexander, *Tasmania's Convicts* (Sydney: Allen & Unwin, 2010), pp. 5–13.
29 Diane Phillips, *An Eligible Situation: The Early History of George Town and Low Head* (Canberra: Karuda Press, 2004), pp. 7–14.
30 Atkinson, *The Europeans in Australia*, vol. 1, p. 218.
31 Fletcher, *Landed Enterprise and Penal Society*, pp. 6, 130–1; McLoughlin, 'Landed Peasantry', p. 132.

On the land, the years up to 1822 were the agricultural decades. Grain crops were the most valuable product, followed by stock. Cereal crops are estimated to have constituted 40 per cent of the colonies' gross domestic product, while pastoralism (still largely for meat and hides) contributed only 14 per cent in New South Wales and 19 per cent in Van Diemen's Land.[32] By 1804 the farmers were productive enough to feed the colony, though sudden population fluctuations, good years, droughts and the devastating floods caused gluts of grain in some years and shortages in others.[33]

Almost from the beginning, the original plan for independent cells of ex-convict families, each set permanently on its own small farm, broke down. Land grants were intended as 'indulgences', or favours, to be paid for in quit rents (rents due to the crown as payment for land grants). They were not to be sold. But grantees considered land grants as their private property, to sell or lease as they wished. Some of the original ex-convict grantees were forced by debt or poverty to sell; others wanted to cash in on their windfall, and still others simply tired of farming. Nevertheless, it appears that most of the land buyers were also ex-convicts. They were the backbone of agriculture during this period, for they grew the bulk of grains that fed the colony, even though they were working lands that averaged less than 10 acres each. At least by 1813, rural people outnumbered those living in Sydney by a thousand souls; by 1820 Sydney housed only a quarter of the colony's population.[34] Astonishingly, and against the odds, the original vision for the colony was realised in this period, though in ways and with costs the British government had not foreseen.

Outriders of civilisation

Beneath this chronicle of sanctioned land use lay another history, one which predated, constantly shadowed and became entwined with the official colony: the history of convict exploration and movement. One injunction governors felt strongly was the prevention of independent communities of wild, lawless banditti, as had occurred in some of the colonies of North America.[35] But soon after they landed in Sydney Cove in 1788, around half the convicts left. They made their way back to Botany Bay overland to try to board the French

32 Raby, *Making Rural Australia*, p. 22.
33 Fletcher, 'Agriculture', p. 195.
34 K.W. Robinson, 'Land', in Abbott and Nairn (eds), *Economic Growth of Australia*, pp. 87–8.
35 Peter Linebaugh and Marcus Rediker, *The Many Headed Hydra: Sailors, Slaves, Commoners and the Hidden History of the Revolutionary Atlantic* (London: Verso, 2000).

ships moored there, under the command of La Perouse. Rebuffed, many of them stayed out in the bush.[36] Historians and others often refer to the colonies as 'gaols' or 'prisons', but the settlements were not walled or barred. There was nothing to stop convicts, and soldiers and sailors, from walking off in search of food, collectables and sex, or setting out on exploratory journeys of their own. Some, like the fabled John Caesar, a Madagascan, took to the bush; he became Australia's first bushranger.[37] Others were gamekeepers, sent out by the governor and officers to shoot emu, wallabies and kangaroos for the table. These men soon developed relationships with Aboriginal hunters, to their mutual benefit, and learned the lie of the land far from the towns and farms. By 1794 New South Wales Corps officer John MacArthur could boast that his servants and hunting dogs killed an average of 300 pounds (136 kilograms) of wild game a week at Parramatta.[38] Dogs were essential for the chase, and they were settlers' constant companions, both on the farms and in the towns. Soon they were adopted by Aboriginal people as well. But hunting dogs also presented a security hazard. Convicts who possessed them could live independently in the bush, which is why the commandant at the Newcastle convict station (founded in 1804) ordered every dog in the area shot.[39]

A few convicts in both New South Wales and Van Diemen's Land went to live with Aboriginal people, though not many. The extraordinary John Wilson joined a group in the Hawkesbury River; he learned the language and underwent scarification. Wilson travelled further inland than anyone else in the early 1790s, at least to a radius of 125 but possibly 250 kilometres. Recruited and sent out in 1798 by Governor Hunter to prove that the Blue Mountains were impenetrable, he and two companions crossed them instead – fifteen years before the publicised crossing by pastoralists in 1813. The detailed written account kept of that journey was given to Governor Hunter but prudently 'lost'.[40]

There were many convicts reportedly living in the bush around the Cumberland Plain settlements in the early period – not bushmen like Wilson

36 Collins, *An Account*, vol. 1, pp. 5, 9, 15.
37 J.B. Hirst, *Convict Society and its Enemies: A History of Early New South Wales* (Sydney, Allen & Unwin, 1983), p. 69; Pybus, *Black Founders*, pp. 2–3, *passim*.
38 Sibella M. Onslow, *Some Early Records of the Macarthurs of Camden* (Adelaide: Rigby, 1975), pp. 44–6.
39 J.W. Turner (ed.), *Newcastle as a Convict Settlement: The Evidence Before J.T. Bigge in 1819–1821* (Newcastle: Newcastle Public Library, 1973), pp. 76, 95.
40 Chris Cunningham, *The Blue Mountains Rediscovered* (Sydney: Kangaroo Press, 1996), pp. 58–61, 78, ch. 4.

but supporting themselves by robbing settlers, by being fed and sheltered by friends, or by working for labour-starved farmers, especially on the Hawkesbury. Such men were the forerunners of generations of wanderers, hunters, escapees, rebels, hermits, squatters, timber getters, cattle duffers and bushrangers who moved constantly in the hinterlands, and who made discoveries and built up geographical familiarity well before the officials made their maps and wrote their journals. They fostered disorder, of course, but also exchange, trade and social networks of both loyalty and betrayal. They were the 'outriders of civilisation',[41] the carriers of information about the country beyond the horizon, the guides for official expeditions and tourists; they scouted new lands for pastoralists, too. Some stole cattle, which were customarily left to roam the bush, drove them inland and became squatters themselves.[42]

By the time settlements were founded in Van Diemen's Land from 1803, at least some of the colonists were already seasoned settlers. They knew how to build using local materials, which ground was best for agriculture and how to clear and farm most efficiently. They were familiar with Aboriginal people, and they were experienced hunters. In Van Diemen's Land this knowledge converged with the local environment to produce a distinctive economy based partly on hunting kangaroos with dogs. The grassy plains of the island's east coast teemed with kangaroos and wallabies, which were easier to bring down than the mainland species; in the absence of dingos they had no predators besides the slower thylacine. When stores ran low in 1805, Collins allowed the Commissariat to buy kangaroo meat: people were nourished by it and they wore clothes and shoes made of the hides. But this decision had a profound effect on the type of society that emerged. For around two decades, the economy allowed convicts and ex-convicts with hunting dogs to become 'masters of the hinterlands' and live independently in the bush, although most also had to rely on bushranging – that is, by robbery – to survive.[43] After Collins' sudden death in 1810, bushranging increased dramatically, partly protected by the bushrangers' links with pastoralists and others in authority, to the extent that bushrangers, most notably Michael Howe, challenged the very governance of Van Diemen's Land. But as

41 Deborah Rose, 'The Year Zero and the North Australian Frontier', in Deborah Bird Rose and Anne Clark (eds), *Tracking Knowledge in North Australian Landscapes* (Canberra: North Australia Research Unit, ANU, 1997), pp. 19–36.
42 Karskens, *The Colony*, pp. 280–309.
43 Lloyd Robson and Michael Roe, *A Short History of Tasmania* (Oxford University Press, 1997), p. 11; Boyce, *Van Diemen's Land*, chs 1–4.

in New South Wales, their freedoms and bravado were generally short-lived. Most bushrangers were caught and either hanged or transported to places of secondary punishment.[44]

Officers, civil servants and free settlers

Convicts, ex-convicts and their children dominated the population in the 1820s and they believed that the colonies had been intended for them. 'What business have [you] here in the prisoners colony?' asked a bushranger of a free settler in the late 1820s.[45] By 1821 they grew most of the colony's grain, owned over two-thirds of the land under cultivation, half the cattle and a third of the sheep in the colony. Yet this was no longer the convicts' colony in terms of outright land holding. Free settlers (including civil and military officers) who made up only 17 per cent of all landholders, held 57 per cent of the alienated land.[46] How had this come about?

Despite their initial disappointment at the rocky, sterile lands of Sydney Cove, the military officers of the first and later fleets soon changed their minds. Once the beautiful, open forest lands around Parramatta were discovered, they clamoured for land grants, lobbying Phillip to have the original policy – that land was only to be granted to ex-convicts and some marines – altered. Phillip obliged but permission did not arrive until January 1793, by which time he had left, and his successor Grose had already begun to grant land to brother officers. Grants of 100 acres (40.5 hectares) were made to both civil and military officers around Sydney and Parramatta. They were small compared to the vast later estates, but much larger than the 30-acre (12.1 hectare) farms of ex-convicts. By the early 1800s, areas of 1,000 and 1,500 acres (607 hectares) were granted to men, and some women, of 'substance'. The new landowners of 1792 were each assigned ten convicts, on full rations, to work their land. This was the birth of the assignment system, which became the most common experience for convicts still under sentence throughout the period of convict transportation.[47]

---

44 Reid, *Gender, Crime and Empire*, pp. 30–1; Hamish Maxwell-Stewart, 'The Bushrangers and the Convict System of Van Diemen's Land, 1803–1846', PhD thesis, University of Edinburgh, 1990, p. 218.

45 Alexander Harris, *Settlers and Convicts, or, Recollections of Sixteen Years' Labour in the Australian Backwoods* [1847] (Melbourne University Press, 1964), p. 34; Malcolm R. Sainty and Keith A. Johnson (eds), *Census of New South Wales, November 1828* (Sydney: Library of Australian History, 1986).

46 Fletcher, 'Agriculture', pp. 212–13.

47 Fletcher, *Landed Enterprise and Penal Society*, pp. 10–12, 57.

The officers set about planting crops with enthusiasm, but soon largely gave up cultivation in favour of trading in the early town, and experimenting with sheep breeding for fine wool, or grape-growing. On their estates closest to the towns they built comfortable, elegant homes and planted gardens.[48] Along with a few energetic free settlers they became graziers, their increasingly large estates located on the open forest lands of the Cumberland Plain. Many of the officers lived with convict mistresses and had children with them; some later married them. The next generation married one another and genteel free arrivals (though the convict 'taint' later became a serious concern for notable families such as the Wentworths). These intermarried families were like a net thrown across the Cumberland Plain, linking the large estates.[49]

The estates furthest from Sydney and Parramatta were usually occupied by ex-convict managers, overseers and convict workers, and not their owners. Sometimes Aboriginal people who had formed alliances with the landowners against other Aboriginal groups lived on these estates. Like the small farmers, the estate workers lived in huts and houses of bark and slabs. The estates were used mainly for grazing sheep and cattle for meat to feed the growing population. After an unpromising start, and with Governor King's careful nurturing, the colony's stock numbers increased rapidly. The last major government importation of cattle was in 1803, and there were enough by then for King to begin to distribute them to farmers as draught animals. The colonists were great meat eaters, preferring beef as the premium. Dairy products were also important, and hides had many practical uses.[50]

Some wool was exported to England, with good results, but the clip was as yet negligible, despite the confident predictions of the pastoralist and now former military officer, John Macarthur. The Macarthurs, along with Rev. Samuel Marsden and free settler and landowner Alexander Riley, were among the few who could afford to breed Spanish merinos for fine wool. Sheep breeding was a slow process: a long-term investment with no immediate profit, but one which would eventually shape the economic course of the colonies and the nation.

48 George Parsons, 'The Commercialisation of Honour: Early Australian Capitalism 1788–1809', in Aplin (ed.), *A Difficult Infant*, pp. 108–9; Barrie Dyster, *Servant & Master: Building and Running the Grand Houses of Sydney 1788–1850* (Sydney: UNSW Press, 1989), pp. 14–15.
49 Carol Liston, *Sarah Wentworth, Mistress of Vaucluse* (Sydney: NSW Historic Houses Trust, 1988); Karskens, *The Colony*, pp. 137–50, 208–212.
50 J.R. Thompson, 'Cattle and Cattlemen in Early New South Wales', PhD thesis, University of New South Wales, 1990, chs 1–6; Abbott, 'Pastoral Industry', p. 219.

Aboriginal people

Settlers knew the lands that they took or travelled through were already occupied by Aboriginal people. Convicts foraging and exploring from the earliest years had already encountered them; these encounters could be violent, brutal and fatal, or they could be friendly. For around two years, Aboriginal people largely avoided the settlement camp at Sydney Cove. But when settlers began to take larger areas of land for farms, sustained violence erupted. The settlers' farms were of necessity placed on the most fertile ground near watercourses. These were the lands most densely occupied by Aboriginal people. And the areas kept clear through Aboriginal fire regimes were like magnets for settlers. This was the beautiful country the white people admired, coveted and took first.[51]

While the British government knew that Aboriginal people occupied the land, and instructed Phillip to treat them with kindness, Aboriginal sovereignty and resistance were not foreseen or considered. Meanwhile settlers, from governor to convict, carried with them a sense of entitlement to take the land. Their ideas were based on the theories of John Locke, in which rights to property entailed mixing land with labour through building and cultivation. They also held assumptions about cultural superiority and the inevitable triumph of civilisation over 'savagery'. Officially, Aboriginal people became British subjects, protected by British law. In practice they had no such protection, though warriors who killed settlers sometimes escaped the noose because they were considered to be incapable of understanding British law.[52] In reality, though, it was a matter of attempting friendship, then negotiation and then war. Many settlers befriended Aboriginal people and shared their maize and meat with them: food was a kind of insurance. Nevertheless, the first frontier wars broke out on the Hawkesbury from 1794. When Aboriginal people took the maize for themselves, or harvested yams, or burned country, the settlers fired on them and revenge attacks multiplied.[53]

Acts of law turned to acts of war with the attacks and battles of the resistance fighter Pemulwuy and other leaders. Governor King was first to work out a solution by banishing all Aboriginal people from the settled areas, forbidding

---

51 Karskens, *The Colony*, chs 11–13; Bill Gammage, *The Biggest Estate on Earth: How Aborigines Made Australia* (Sydney: Allen & Unwin, 2011), ch. 5.

52 Frost, 'New South Wales as *terra nullius*'; Andrew Fitzmaurice, 'The Genealogy of Terra Nullius', *Australian Historical Studies*, 38, 129 (2007): 1–15; Bruce Kercher, *An Unruly Child: A History of Law in Australia* (Sydney: Allen & Unwin, 1995), pp. 4–5.

53 Karskens, *The Colony*, ch. 13.

settlers to have relations with them and demanding that they give up their resistance leaders. This strategy worked twice: first in 1802, when Pemulwuy was surrendered and killed; and then in 1805, when Aboriginal people met with Samuel Marsden near Prospect and gave up the names of six leaders.[54]

Governor Macquarie, who took office in 1810, seemed unaware of both the earlier frontier war and King's strategy. When new lands were opened to the south around Camden and Appin, the entire cycle started anew – first friendship and alliances, then raids and killings, followed by a massive military operation in 1816. This raid culminated in the massacre of at least fourteen men women and children on 17 April. Again, revenge killings of settlers were terrible. Macquarie eventually repeated King's successful strategy: he banished Aboriginal people but declared an amnesty, and instigated the great annual feasts for them at Parramatta. By the time he departed in 1822, he considered peace had been achieved. But soon violence broke out over the mountains on the new frontier at Bathurst.[55]

In Van Diemen's Land some of these patterns were repeated, although the long period of the dog and kangaroo economy between 1805 and around 1820 mitigated violent exchange. The co-existence of hunters, sheep and cattlemen, bushrangers and Aboriginal people on the grassy midlands resulted in a longer period of relatively peaceful relations. Violence was sporadic and localised, and there were instances of friendship and cooperation. In New South Wales, war broke out each time settlers moved into a new area, and was followed by accommodation, with surviving Aboriginal groups either retreating into as-yet uninvaded land, or 'sitting down' on large estates.[56]

Geographical reach

By 1820 explorers in New South Wales had reached the inland rivers on the western side of the Blue Mountains, the Macquarie, Cudgegong, Lachlan and Castlereagh rivers. They had seen the country to the north as far as the Hastings River and the New England Tableland and, to the south, Lake George, Lake Bathurst and the Murrumbidgee River. News of the fresh country fuelled great optimism for expansion and wealth, but in 1820 these were still largely Aboriginal lands. In New South Wales there were some tiny clusters of settlers in the Hunter Valley, at Bathurst and at the Illawarra to the

---

54 Ibid., pp. 487–8.
55 Ibid.; David Roberts, 'Bells Falls Massacre and Bathurst's History of Violence', *Australian Historical Studies*, 26, 105 (1995): 615–33.
56 Boyce, *Van Diemen's Land*, ch. 14; Karskens, *The Colony*, pp. 537–9.

south. But most of both cultivation and grazing remained on the Cumberland Plain, while urban development clustered in three substantial towns: Sydney, Parramatta and Windsor.[57] This region remained the locus of the colony, not because the settlers were 'hemmed in' by the Blue Mountains but because until around 1819 there was still sufficient land for them. Only when drought, pests and continuous grazing destroyed the pastures was there a need to look further afield. Hence the famous (though not the first) crossing of the Blue Mountains by stock owners Gregory Blaxland, William Lawson and a young William Charles Wentworth in 1813, during a drought. They searched primarily for more grass for stock, not more land for people.[58]

Settlement on the Cumberland Plain was consolidated as settlers moved into areas between the older settlements. The farms reached Wiseman's Ferry in the north and the foothills of the Kurrajong in the west. The farmers around Airds, Appin and down to Picton were the vanguard of expansion to the south and south-west in the 1820s, just as the Hawkesbury was the springboard for the settlement of the upper Hunter valley to the north, while the penal settlement at Newcastle created access to the lower Hunter.[59]

In Van Diemen's Land the pattern was similarly concentrated on the east coast. Again, settlers clustered at just two urban centres, Hobart and Launceston, while the open grasslands between them were occupied as small farms or vast commons. The island was circumnavigated in 1815–16 during a remarkable voyage in a whaleboat by a whaler, James Kelly, and four others.[60] In 1821 a penal station was established for convicts at Macquarie Harbour on the wild and isolated west coast, 'a bleak anchorage…at the back of a wind-blasted, rain-soaked shore'. In colonies that had proved highly permeable and mobile, Macquarie Harbour was intended, finally, as an inescapable hell at the ends of the Earth. It was a sign of things to come.[61]

Seaboard settlements

Despite Phillip's discouragement, shipping, trade and commerce expanded rapidly. The early colonists were a maritime people. Ships were like

57 D.N. Jeans, *An Historical Geography of New South Wales to 1901* (Sydney: Reed Education, 1972), pp. 38–40, ch. 6.
58 T.M. Perry, *Australia's First Frontier: The Spread of Settlement in New South Wales, 1788–1829* (Melbourne University Press, 1963), pp. 26–33.
59 Ibid., ch. 3.
60 Boyce, *Van Diemen's Land*, pp. 91–100.
61 Hamish Maxwell-Stewart, *Closing Hell's Gates: The Death of a Convict Station* (Sydney: Allen & Unwin, 2008), p. 2.

familiar friends and although ship building and boat building were banned, they emerged nonetheless in Sydney and on the Hawkesbury River, and became major early industries. Many people owned small boats and customarily moved about on water, and they transported supplies and produce by rivers and along the coastline between the great harbours of the Sydney region, Port Jackson and Broken Bay. Most of their early exploration was by water, too, and larger towns were established from the sea or at the heads of navigable rivers. They were all port towns to begin with, shaped around the shorelines and wharves, buildings facing the water, watching out over harbours, headlands, channels, tides and currents.[62]

In Sydney's earliest years shipboard practices, routines and discipline were transferred onto land. The first four governors were naval captains and their officers became the first civil servants. People were rationed weekly, like sailors, prepared their food at communal cooking places and messed in groups. They were punished like sailors, too: flogged and hanged. But the judicial terror of the navy was even more savage on land because, with no walls, wooden or otherwise, it was relatively easy to ignore rules and evade authority. Floggings were 'surprisingly few' but brutal. When planned Irish rebellions were discovered, the plotters were flogged and sent to Norfolk Island. King's 1803 attempt to quarantine Irish convicts at the isolated Castle Hill farm, north-west of Sydney, backfired: this concentration resulted in a major convict uprising. In March 1804 more than 300 rebels marched from Castle Hill to Parramatta, their leaders calling all men to join them in the struggle for 'Death or Liberty'. They intended to kill the elite, continue to Sydney, take a ship and sail back to Ireland. Instead, they were betrayed, forced to retreat and their leaders arrested, while pursuing troops shot and bayoneted those who tried to flee. Survivors were severely flogged and transported; the leaders were hanged and their bodies suspended in chains to rot near the places where they had massed. The increasingly savage floggings of the naval governors were not reduced until Governor Macquarie limited the number of lashes to 50, officially at least.[63]

The early colonists were always eager to show off the wonders of their ships to Aboriginal people. They considered the Aboriginal people's own bark *nowies* (canoes) the worst craft they had ever seen, but were amazed

62 Karskens, *The Rocks*, pp. 183–94; Karskens, *The Colony*, pp. 160–7; Tench, *A Complete Account of the Settlement at Port Jackson*, p. 245.
63 A.J. Gray, 'Social Life at Sydney Cove in 1788–1789', *Journal of the Royal Australian Historical Society*, 44 (1958): 381; Lynette Silver, *The Battle of Vinegar Hill: Australia's Irish Rebellion 1804* (Sydney: Doubleday, 1989), ch. 12.

by the Eora fisherwomen, who with their children on board paddled safely through terrifying surf. The *nowies* moved swiftly along the rivers, crossed harbours and hugged the coastlines, but could not take the Eora more than a few kilometres out to sea. Women dominated the harbours and fishing, but from 1791 young Aboriginal men boarded ships, learned to sail and voyaged beyond the horizon. They went to Norfolk Island, Nootka Sound, Hawai'i and Bengal, as well as joining sealing gangs at the Bass Strait islands. Two Eora men, Bennelong and Yemmerrawanie, sailed to London in 1792 with Arthur Phillip, the former returning in 1795 and the latter dying far from home. Returned sailors often became leaders and elders among their peoples. In 1802 Bungaree, later the famous leader and spokesman of a Sydney tribe, was the first Australian to circumnavigate the continent on HMS *Investigator* with Matthew Flinders.[64]

Phillip's choice of Sydney Cove as the site for the new colony had far-reaching and unforeseen outcomes. He dutifully deflected all newly arrived ships to the north shore, as instructed, and drew up a plan for a town without merchants' stores or workers' housing. Nevertheless, Sydney quickly became a thriving, polyglot port town, alive with people, ships and goods from all over the globe. Convict transports calling at Sydney continued to China, and from 1790 they began bringing consumer goods to the colony. After a supply route with India was opened in 1790, ships also began to arrive from Bombay and Calcutta with speculative cargoes of livestock, sugar, meat and rum. By the first decade of the nineteenth century, ships from the United States, the Cape of Good Hope, India and China, as well as whalers from the southern fisheries, called in numbers of between 23 and 33 a year. In 1802 the visiting Frenchman Francois Péron could marvel at 'this assemblage of grand operations, this constant movement of shipping'.[65]

But the labour-hungry ships were inimical to a penal colony because they offered escape routes for convicts, who as a result fetched up in Calcutta, the Dutch East Indies, Ceylon, South America, Mauritius, New Zealand, Fiji and other Pacific islands. The rate of escape grew in tandem with the port and led to ever-increasing regulation – with great inconvenience to ships' captains. By 1820 Sydney had the most extensive and complex

64 Keith Vincent Smith, *Mari Nawi: Aboriginal Odysseys* (Sydney: High Stakes Publishing, 2010); Karskens, *The Colony*, pp. 38–41, 403–8, 425–31.
65 Péron, cited in Graeme Aplin and George Parsons, 'Maritime Trade: Shipping and the Early Colonial Economy', in Aplin (ed.), *A Difficult Infant*, pp. 161–2; Alan Frost, 'The Growth of Settlement', in Bernard Smith and Alwyne Wheeler (eds), *The Art of the First Fleet & Other Early Australian Drawings* (New Haven: Yale University Press, 1988), p. 141.

port regulations in the British Empire.[66] The pattern was in some ways repeated in Hobart, also selected for its sheltered, deep-water harbour and fresh-water rivulet. The first tents and huts clung around the shoreline of Sullivan's Cove, and whaling ships of the southern fisheries, as well as those that hunted seasonally in the Derwent Estuary provided supplies, income and escape routes.[67]

Trade, commerce, industries and property

The enterprising colonists saw New South Wales not as an isolated agrarian penal colony, but in much the same way as other colonies of the Empire – a place of economic opportunity. Most of the military officers were adventurers seeking their fortunes rather than disinterested career men. As the only colonists who through their pay had access to sterling for foreign exchange, they were soon importing goods, including rum. Trading made them rich in these early years, and financed their fine houses and agricultural and pastoral experiments.[68]

The officers' codes of honour prevented them from engaging in retail trade, so they wholesaled goods to the smaller dealers, usually soldiers, convict servants or their convict mistresses. Soon emancipists like James Underwood, Simeon Lord and Mary Reibey were petitioning to be allowed to purchase goods straight off the ships. They too profited richly from trade, amassing property in town and farms on the plain, and building their own fashionable houses.[69]

Some convicts brought capital, goods and tools of their trade. As John Hirst points out, convicts in New South Wales were treated not according to their crimes, but according to their abilities and usefulness.[70] Those with skills and capital were free to set up shop or otherwise find their own way. The rest were told to turn up for their government work when the drums

66 Grace Karskens, '"This Spirit of Emigration": The Nature and Meanings of Escape in Early New South Wales', *Journal of Australian Colonial History*, 7 (2005): 1–34.
67 Susan Lawrence, *Whalers and Free Men: Life on Tasmania's Colonial Whaling Stations* (Melbourne: Australian Scholarly Press, 2006), pp. 1–14; Boyce, *Van Diemen's Land*, pp. 30–1, 47.
68 Parsons, 'The Commercialisation of Honour', pp. 102–119; Ross Fitzgerald and Mark Hearn, *Bligh, Macarthur and the Rum Rebellion* (Sydney: Kangaroo Press, 1988), p. 61.
69 Parsons, 'The Commercialism of Honour', pp. 102–119; D.R. Hainsworth, *The Sydney Traders: Simeon Lord and his Contemporaries, 1788–1821* (Melbourne: Cassell Australia, 1972), pp. 82–5, 128–56; Robert Irving (ed.), *The History & Design of the Australian House* (Oxford University Press, 1985), pp. 44–8.
70 Hirst, *Convict Society and its Enemies*, pp. 82–3.

beat the tap-too in the mornings.[71] Sydney thus grew less on an official plan than on these tides of ambitions, hopes and freedoms.

Convicts and ex-convicts purchased the traders' goods. They were consumers, familiar with comfort and fashion and the fruits of England's eighteenth-century commercial revolution and global trade. A great number of new mass-produced commodities such as tea, sugar, rum, glass, printed cotton, gilt buttons and buckles, fashionable hats, ceramic dinner sets and glass tumblers had already become part of their lives and expectations. All of these were highly desired goods in early Sydney and, as archaeological evidence confirms, convict and ex-convict householders bought and used them. The town was studded with warehouses and shops, all jockeying to be closest to the water, wharves and ships.[72]

This urban, consumer society had been enabled by three factors. First, convicts in New South Wales were not legally attainted as they would have been in England, so they could use the civil court to force their creditors to pay up, defend their property and establish businesses. And they were avid users of the early courts.[73] Moreover, the courts upheld women's rights to property, independent of their husbands. A number of enterprising convict and ex-convict women joined the ranks of early landholders, dealers and publicans as a result.[74] Outnumbered by men by about three to one, women could also take their pick of husbands, usually choosing older, skilled and better-off men. They were desperately desired, needed as partners for business or farming ventures, and for making new homes and families. But should a husband threaten or leave them, they and their children were guaranteed support by government rations. Paradoxically, men of all ranks often wrote of convict women as useless whores. These misogynistic outbursts seem to reflect a resentment of women's rights, protection and opportunities in the colony, as well as their lowly origins.[75]

While no money had been sent with the First Fleet, a lively and relatively sophisticated monetary system soon emerged, based on 'mutual

---

71 Karskens, *The Rocks*, pp. 159–60.
72 Grace Karskens, *Inside the Rocks: The Archaeology of a Neighbourhood* (Sydney: Hale & Iremonger, 1999), chs 1–2; Jane Elliott, 'Was There a Convict Dandy? Convict Consumer Interests in Sydney, 1788–1815', *Australian Historical Studies*, 26, 104 (1995): 373–92.
73 Bruce Kercher, *Debt, Seduction, and Other Disasters* (Sydney: Federation Press, 1996), pp. 1–2; Frank Decker, *The Emergence of Money in Convict New South Wales* (Marburg: Metropolis-Verlag, 2010), p. 185.
74 Atkinson, *The Europeans in Australia*, vol. 1, pp. 134, 137, 144; Kercher, *An Unruly Child*, pp. 49–51.
75 Karskens, *The Colony*, ch. 10; Kay Daniels, *Convict Women* (Sydney: Allen & Unwin, 1998).

obligations...book accounts, bills and notes', including promissory notes and, from 1809–10, small merchant's notes.[76] The vigorous private economy far outstripped the government economy in these early years. The emancipist trader Simeon Lord alone had running accounts with London brokers of £102,120 between 1804 and 1810. By comparison, Governor King drew bills on the British Treasury totalling £87,447 over his entire governorship (1800–06).[77]

Working convicts had money to spend because of the high demand for their labour. Those assigned to the various work gangs – cutting timber and stone, making bricks, building – insisted on task work, as opposed to a full day on the job. Once they had completed their tasks for the government, they could work for private masters. Labour was so short, and agriculture, building and production were so labour-intensive, that workers earned good wages (three shillings a day for unskilled work and five shillings a day for skilled, though women were paid much less), to spend as they pleased.[78]

Soon the Sydney traders were looking for an export commodity. The search for valuable raw materials that could be shipped back to Britain and defray the costs of the colony was also a persistent concern for governors. Given the maritime orientation of the early colonies, it is not surprising that the first successful export industries came not from the land but the sea. Seals were hunted for their fur, skins and oil in Dusky Bay in New Zealand and, from 1798, on the Furneaux Group of islands in Bass Strait. Independent settlements also emerged there. Sealers often stole Aboriginal women from mainland Van Diemen's Land, established small farms, hunted and lived independent of authority. In subsequent years, sealers moved to other islands in search of their prey, from the east coast of Van Diemen's Land, along the southern seaboard of continental Australia and over to King Georges Sound and the islands off Western Australia. In all these places they encountered Aboriginal people and made settlements years before official annexation.[79]

Whaling was also a significant industry, though it was more capital intensive than sealing, and was pursued largely by British companies in competition

---

76 Frank Decker, 'Bills, Notes and Money in Early New South Wales, 1788–1822', *Financial History Review*, 18, 1 (2011): 74; David Povey, 'Prosperity in New South Wales before 1810', Grad. Dip. thesis, University of New South Wales, 2010.

77 Hainsworth, *The Sydney Traders*, pp. 84–5.

78 Karskens, *The Rocks*, pp. 157, 158, 160–1, 164–5; Hirst, *Convict Society and its Enemies*, pp. 36–46.

79 Alan Frost, *The Global Reach of Empire: Britain's Maritime Expansion in the Indian and Pacific Oceans, 1764–1815* (Melbourne: Miegunyah Press, 2003), pp. 241, 308–9, 317; Boyce, *Van Diemen's Land*, pp. 15–19, 89–91.

with French and US companies. By 1791 convict transports went whaling after they left Port Jackson, despite the East India Company's monopoly. The protection of the whaling and sealing industries against incursion from other nations was another motive for the British settlement of Van Diemen's Land, with Hobart in the south developing as a whaling port, while the northern ports were associated with sealing.[80]

The final key factor in the emergence of seaboard settlements was the ready acquisition of urban land by convicts, ex-convicts and soldiers. Well into the 1820s, the vast majority held neither lease nor grant to their town property. They held it by 'naked possession', the legal term for this permissive occupancy – the lowest form of title. The practice was customary and accepted, and the colonists knew that long occupancy and improvements *did* in theory create rights to the land in law.[81]

This practice was established in the earliest months of settlement. Convicts, ordered to build huts, simply appropriated them and fenced in yards. Until and even after 1819, convicts were not locked up in gaols or barracks, but lived as lodgers with established householders. Officially, urban land remained Crown Land, but the de facto occupants nevertheless readily sold these allotments and buildings to others. By 1810 some people had occupied allotments for fifteen or twenty years. Insecurity of tenure did not discourage substantial building in Sydney, for residents considered themselves rightful owners, building solid, plain houses of stone and shingles.[82] This is why Sydney evolved organically, without much planning. It further explains how a private society and economy, and foundational ideas about private-property rights, were able to emerge so quickly. Phillip tried to keep land better controlled at Parramatta, but eventually 'naked possession' became the norm there, too. Most governors, despite their extensive powers, were loath to deprive townsfolk of what they had managed to make: homes, gardens and businesses.[83]

Phillip, Hunter and King all made a few town grants and leases to officers and emancipist traders, but when Bligh arrived as governor in 1806, around

---

80 Lawrence, *Whalers and Free Men*, p. 7; Boyce, *Van Diemen's Land*, p. 47.
81 Karskens, *The Rocks*, p. 28; Grace Karskens, 'Naked Possession: Building and the Politics of Legitimate Occupancy in Early New South Wales, Australia', in Carole Shammas (ed.), *Investing in the Early Modern Built Environment: Europeans, Asians, Settlers and Indigenous Societies* (Leiden: Brill Academic Publishers, 2012), pp. 325–57; T.E. Tomlins and T.C. Granger, *The Law Dictionary, Explaining the Rise, Progress, and Present State of the British Law* (London: J. and W.T. Clarke, 1835), entry for 'Title'.
82 Karskens, *Inside the Rocks*, ch. 1.
83 Karskens, 'Naked Possession'; Karskens, *The Colony*, pp. 71–82; 178–82.

85 per cent of the population occupied their property by naked possession. Both leaseholders and permissive occupants felt themselves under siege during his governorship, as he decided to wrest back control of Sydney and reassert the ownership of the Crown. Bligh cancelled leases, evicted occupants, including high-profile officers, and pulled down houses. The majority who occupied with no lease at all must have felt still more threatened. On 26 January 1808 Bligh was deposed by the officers and soldiers of the New South Wales Corp, led by Major George Johnston, with the apparent support of the townsfolk.[84] Fifty years later this event was dubbed the 'Rum Rebellion' in the mistaken belief that it was caused by Bligh's attempt to break the officers' monopoly on rum.[85] The rhetoric of the rebels both at the time and during Johnston's court martial was framed in the passionate language of rights to liberty and property, upon which the tyrant Bligh had trampled. With the arrival of Governor Macquarie, the colony's towns were finally fixed, not as space controlled by governors, even theoretically, but by private property holders.[86]

The age of the Macquaries, 1810–22

The arrival of Lachlan and Elizabeth Macquarie in 1810 marked a decade of consolidation, expansion and some grand embellishment for the colonies of New South Wales and Van Diemen's Land. Macquarie was the first military governor of the colony after four naval governors. He was sent to restore order after the overthrow of Bligh and brought his own regiment, the 73rd, with him. He and his talented wife, Elizabeth (née Campbell), shared a passion for fashionable architecture, art and landscapes, and considered themselves agents of taste and civilisation in what they expected would be an antipodean wilderness.[87]

What they found in Sydney surprised and inspired them. Despite major floods in 1809 that had once more jeopardised food supplies, Macquarie declared Sydney to be in good order, although he was taken aback by the primitiveness and poverty of the farming communities. He began to lay out

84 Alan Atkinson, 'Taking Possession: Sydney's First Householders', in Aplin (ed.), *A Difficult Infant*, pp. 72–90; Fitzgerald and Hearn, *Bligh, Macarthur and the Rum Rebellion*, pp. 79, 92,101–104.
85 W. Howitt, *Land, Labour, and Gold, or, Two Years in Victoria*, vol. 2 (London: Longman, Brown, Green and Longmans, 1855), p. 125.
86 Grace Karskens and Richard Waterhouse, '"Too Sacred to be Taken Away": Property, Liberty, Tyranny and the "Rum Rebellion"', *Journal of Australian Colonial History*, 12 (2010): 1–22.
87 James Broadbent and Joy Hughes (eds), *The Age of Macquarie* (Melbourne University Press, 1992), pp. 1–2; Atkinson, *The Europeans in Australia*, vol. 1, pp. 317–26.

new towns on high ground above the Hawkesbury floodplains and to make existing towns more orderly. Streets in Sydney were renamed, straightened, widened and levelled. Pigs, dogs and goats were confined. He laid out Hobart's present grid plan over the old cove-hugging settlement, and founded a new town on the George Town site at Port Dalrymple.[88] In Sydney, however, these orders were only partially successful, and the pre-industrial-style town persisted, so the Macquaries concentrated instead on new zones to the south, east and west. They drew upon the British Treasury and available convict labour to construct handsome classical or gothick public buildings in brick and stone, including convicts' and soldiers' barracks, a grand new hospital, a large orphanage, expensive stuccoed villas for civil servants, handsome churches and a great many ornamental structures. All of this building was listed by Macquarie as 'public works', and he continued his building program in defiance of orders to desist.[89]

Macquarie instigated other important reforms. He reorganised the Commissariat and colonial revenue. In 1816 he proclaimed sterling as the official colonial standard and he presided over the establishment of the Bank of New South Wales. He also granted well over half a million acres of Aboriginal land to settlers, especially on the new frontiers to the south of Sydney, and he ordered the construction of Cox's Road over the Blue Mountains in 1814–15. A rough and precipitous track, this was nevertheless the first official inland road.[90]

At the same time, Macquarie's period of office was tumultuous. The retail market collapsed in 1811–12, followed by a depression that ruined many of the early traders. Droughts, floods and caterpillar plagues continued to jeopardise the food supply and pasture for stock. The end of the Napoleonic wars in 1815 resulted in a dramatic rise in convict arrivals. In six years, the colony's population more than doubled, from 12,911 to 29,783. A labour shortage became a glut, and accommodation in the town was stretched to the limit. Macquarie dealt with the crisis by instigating his urban building program, and by building Sydney's first convict barracks near Hyde Park.[91]

Like every other governor, Macquarie made enemies among the officers and free settlers, especially for his liberal policies with regard to emancipists,

88 Karskens, *The Colony*, pp. 190–5, 226, 307.

89 Broadbent and Hughes (eds), *The Age of Macquarie*, chs 1, 5 and 12; Karskens, *The Colony*, ch. 7.

90 'Lachlan Macquarie', *Australian Dictionary of Biography*, vol. 2, pp. 187–95; Fletcher, *Landed Enterprise and Penal Society*, p.125; Grace Karskens, *Cox's Way: An Historical and Archaeological Study of Cox's Road* (Sydney: NSW Lands Department, 1988).

91 Karskens, *The Colony*, pp. 222–6.

whom he supported, invited to social events at Government House and appointed to key government positions. Himself risen from very humble beginnings, he was the last governor to believe that convicts and their descendants were the rightful inheritors of the colony. Enemies used his ever-more ambitious building projects as evidence of extravagance and waste. In 1819, the British government sent Commissioner John Thomas Bigge to review the colony and the effectiveness of transportation. Bigge was persuaded that the colony's future lay not with small farming by felons, but with grazing on large estates granted free to men of some fortune and worked by assigned convicts.[92] Bigge's report, published in 1823, after Macquarie's return to England, heralded the end of the convicts' colony, though the idea stayed alive in the minds of those first generations of settlers. The report was also a devastating critique of Macquarie's administration.[93]

Despite his occasional attacks on the rights of individuals, his penchant for renaming places after himself and his family, and his increasingly erratic and autocratic behaviour, Macquarie was the longest-serving and most popular governor of the early colonial period. He was fondly remembered for decades. This had less to do with his gentrifying projects than with his charisma, and his commitment to the colony as a *place*, the public good and the emancipist cause. The Macquaries saw that the colonists were themselves proud of the place they had made, despite the odds. They drew these feelings together, giving them voice and form through official artists Joseph Lycett and John Lewin, and poet Michael Massey Robinson. Macquarie was responsible for popularising the name 'Australia' for the continent, for fostering a sense of history and moment. From 1817 colonists celebrated 26 January as Anniversary Day under vice-regal patronage. So much of the couple's efforts and passions were poured into the place, to be shaped, improved, enhanced, to be invested with meanings as they understood them, to be cared for, celebrated and passed onto the generations that followed.[94]

Aboriginal people and urban life

Aboriginal people became urban dwellers very quickly. The coastal Eora were a notable presence in Sydney after November 1790, when the first group, led

92 Raby, *Making Rural Australia*, pp. 29–32, 66–7.
93 Ibid., pp. 227–8; John Thomas Bigge, *Report of the Commissioner of Inquiry on the Colony of New South Wales* [1823] (Adelaide: Library Board of South Australia, 1996).
94 Broadbent and Hughes (eds), *The Age of Macquarie*, chs 2, 7, 8; Atkinson, *The Europeans in Australia*, vol. 1, ch. 15.

by the famous cross-cultural envoy Bennelong, 'came in' at Phillip's repeated invitation. This breakthrough in race relations was achieved after a long process of kidnapping, retribution (Phillip himself took a spear in the shoulder), diplomacy and reconciliation. It was met with relief and delight by the British officers. Some of the younger Eora people lived with the Europeans, while older people included Sydney on their travel itineraries or camped on the outskirts. Bennelong's square brick house, built at his own request, stood on Sydney Cove's eastern headland, which would later take his name.[95]

Sydney continued to attract Aboriginal people over the succeeding decades. They were part of the social fabric of the town, and many became well-known Sydney identities. They sold fish and shellfish, and sometimes worked for whites in homes and pubs, guided exploratory and hunting parties, and gathered specimens for eager collectors. Their adaptations were matched by extraordinary cultural continuities. Apart from the warriors' adoption of jackets, they largely rejected clothing. They continued to cook and eat traditional foods alongside maize and bread. Families continued to camp in the open or build traditional shelters of bark and brush. Perhaps most importantly, Aboriginal people in Sydney continued to impose their own laws through the great contests, in which the accused stood trial by the spears of those they had wronged. They used the streets and public spaces of the town for this purpose, intermittently, until at least 1824.[96]

But Aboriginal presence in Sydney was inimical to the elegant and virtuous city of which the Macquaries dreamed. They had been accepted, or at least tolerated, in the motley pre-industrial town, but from the mid-1810s, they were increasingly made 'scapegoats for urban disorder'. The Macquaries attempted to shift them out of Sydney in 1815 and again in 1822. In 1816, after the Appin massacre, regulations were passed forbidding their contests. The contests continued nonetheless.[97]

Attitudes to Sydney's Aboriginal people hardened in the 1820s and 1830s. Visitors and new settlers created increasingly harsh and grotesque images of them. Once courted and welcomed, they were now considered a blight on Sydney, as they would be in later Australian cities. Many eventually withdrew,

95 Karskens, *The Colony*, pp. 386–401.
96 Ibid., ch. 12; Keith Vincent Smith, *King Bungaree: A Sydney Aborigine Meets the Great South Pacific Explorers, 1799–1830* (Sydney: Kangaroo Press, 1992), pp. 117–18; Grace Karskens, 'Red Coats, Blue Jacket, Black Skin: Aboriginal Men and Clothing in Early New South Wales', *Aboriginal History*, 35 (2011): 1–36; Lisa Ford, *Settler Sovereignty: Jurisdiction and Indigenous People in America and Australia, 1788–1836* (Cambridge, MA: Harvard University Press, 2010), pp. 75–9.
97 Coll Thrush, *Native Seattle: Histories from the Crossing-Over Place* (Seattle: University of Washington Press, 2007); *Sydney Gazette*, 4 May 1816.

finding refuge in the places beyond the settlers' gaze by the bays and beaches of Sydney Harbour and the coastline where fish and shellfish were available. Here, they continued social gatherings and ceremonial life, where these were still viable, and camped in the old way. But these retreats were in turn threatened by the arrival of increasing numbers of middle-class settlers, civil servants and professional men and their families from the 1820s. These new-comers ushered in a significant new phase in Australia's urban development: suburbanisation. They coveted the same waterfront lands that Aboriginal people still occupied. The villas and gardens forced them out once more.[98]

They continued to retreat to the peri-urban places shunned by whites, to public lands, commons and other reserves, to bushland and wetlands, places beyond the reach and view of roads and carriages. They became invisible people. Dispossession was not a single event in the Sydney region, but a cycle repeated continually as the city expanded into its hinterland.[99]

★

Cox's Road over the Blue Mountains, cut and opened in only six months, was more an impossibly steep goat track than a highway – and intention-ally so. How a road could simultaneously enable and discourage movement was one of those delicate balancing acts that early governors of New South Wales often had to perform. They were charged with both encouraging the colony's development, and restricting and controlling the movement of the population. The contradiction between penal colony and free society, and the fact that convicts were largely indistinguishable from free people, under-pinned these first 30-odd years, and continued to cause difficulties into the 1830s.

In one sense the governors were successful, for by 1822 official 'concen-trated' settlement was largely contained on the Cumberland Plain and the eastern side of Van Diemen's Land. At the same time, the presence of ships and the absence of gaol walls meant that governors were only ever partly suc-cessful in restricting movement. The restless counter-history of the colonies can be told in the determination of some convicts and ex-convicts to have their liberty: not liberty bestowed by political rights, but by evading captivity, laws and government altogether. They escaped on ships, made independent settlements beyond the pale of law, lived in the bush as hunters, sealers and bushrangers. In doing so, many of them also built Australia's first economies.

98 Karskens, 'Naked Possession'.
99 Heather Goodall and Allison Cadzow, *Rivers and Resilience: Aboriginal People on Sydney's George's River* (Sydney: UNSW Press, 2009).

But from the 1820s the men roaming wherever they wanted, unrestrained by government, were no longer lowly runaways, sealers and bushrangers, but squatters.[100]

The environmental experience essential to this expansion – how to read the country, hunt, forage, build, grow grain, manage stock – was learned in the first 30 years. Bush habits were long-lived. The same wattle-and-daub, timber-slab and shingle huts appeared on the site of Melbourne from 1835 as had first appeared in Sydney in 1788, set out in the same way, straggling irregularly along a track above the Yarra River. And the same sorts of people – those who had been convicts and their children – founded Melbourne, just as they had made all the settlements between 1788 and 1822. When free immigrants began to arrive in the older colonies from the 1820s, they found thriving towns, busy wharves and warehouses, substantial public buildings, shops, pubs, banks, houses and roads, all of which had been built over the first 30 years.

As the historian John Hirst pointed out, New South Wales was intended as a new society, not a prison, and that is what materialised. The early colonial period was marked by relative freedom for convicts, even those 'within the pale', which contrasts with the rising severity of the 1820s and 1830s. When transportation to New South Wales ended in 1840 'no legal or institutional changes were required', and when democracy was achieved in 1856, it was enabled by the existing 'social structure of a free society', and built upon the economic competence established in those earliest years.[101]

100 Richard Waterhouse, '"...A bastard offspring of tyranny under the guise of liberty": Liberty and Representative Government in Australia, 1788–1901', in Jack P. Greene (ed.), *Exclusionary Empire: English Liberty Overseas, 1600–1900* (Cambridge University Press, 2010), pp. 220–47.
101 John Hirst, *Freedom on the Fatal Shore: Australia's First Colony* (Melbourne: Black Inc., 2008), pp. viii, ix.

5

Expansion, 1820–50

LISA FORD AND DAVID ANDREW ROBERTS

The settlement of Australia on a continental scale was unimaginable in 1820. Yet by 1850 the continent had been transformed by Europeans and their domesticated animals, and the Australian colonies ranked, with other Anglophone settler societies, among the fastest growing economies in history. Rapid expansion in Australia was neither organic nor inevitable. It was contingent on ecological limits and global political and economic contexts, and was contested by imperial and colonial governments, by excluded settlers and, most of all, by Indigenous people.

Early expansion, 1822–27

In New South Wales, vital groundwork for expansion was laid during the administration of Governor Lachlan Macquarie (1810–21). First, at the end of the Napoleonic wars, Britain appeared to rediscover its convict colony; an influx of convict transports after 1815 increased the tiny local workforce dramatically. Second, there had been important geographic discoveries in the Macquarie era. Driven by overstocking, drought and caterpillar plagues, settlers had crossed the Cowpastures and moved south-west into the cooler climes of Bargo Brush and Sutton Forest, and then beyond, towards the foothills of the southern tablelands. Isolated pockets of coastal settlement had also proliferated, to the south on the Illawarra plains and north at Newcastle, where the colony's old penal settlement had grown into an industrial centre supporting around 1,000 prisoners. An overland route from the Hawkesbury River to the lower Hunter Valley, north of Newcastle, paved the way for expansion into what would soon be one of the colony's most productive agricultural districts. Most important, however, was the breaching of the Blue Mountains west of Sydney, that great physical and perceptual boundary that had long defined the colony's horizon. By 1818 a long, sinuous road had been carved across the sandstone ridges of the Great Dividing Range, descending onto the Bathurst plains where two great waterways, the Lachlan and Macquarie rivers, flowed enticingly inland. Even so, Governor Macquarie was more a consolidator than an expansionist. He concentrated land grants in the Cumberland Plain and restricted access to newly discovered regions; for the most part, grazing beyond the Cumberland was allowed only under temporary permit, and sentries were posted on the western road to prevent unauthorised access to the Bathurst plains. As a result, in 1821 roughly 94 per cent of the colony's population, 97 per cent of its cultivated land and over 70 per cent of its livestock remained within a 70-kilometre radius of Sydney.[1]

Macquarie's efforts did not go uncontested. A small coterie of elite or 'exclusive' settlers, combined with new immigrants, mobilised against the Governor's restrictive land policies, his autocratic government and his tolerance for emancipated convicts. They argued that land and convict labour should be reserved for respectable free people with capital to invest in colonial enterprises. Their emphasis on rural, pastoral pursuits tapped into the growing conviction among British reformers that town life was not conducive to the moral reform of convicts and that Macquarie's urbanised colony had become a haven for vice and profligacy.[2]

Their arguments bore fruit when, between June 1822 and February 1823, Commissioner John Thomas Bigge published his reports on the state of the colony and its institutions. The imperial government had directed Bigge to propose some means by which transportation to the colony might once again 'be rendered an Object of real Terror'.[3] At the same time, he was asked to find ways to reconcile convict punishment with the interests of the growing population of free immigrants, emancipists and the colonial-born. He forged a nexus between 'punishment and profit' by endorsing large-scale agriculture and pastoralism, fostered through an adjustment of English wool duties to stimulate trade, generous land grants to well-heeled free settlers, and the redistribution of convict labour from vice-ridden town to virtuous countryside.[4] Bigge also advocated the legal and political subordination of convicts and emancipists (or ex-convicts). Emancipists were to be excluded

---

1 T.M. Perry, *Australia's First Frontier: The Spread of Settlement in New South Wales, 1788–1829* (Melbourne University Press, 1963), pp. 130–2.

2 John Ritchie, *Punishment and Profit: The Reports of Commissioner John Bigge on the Colonies of New South Wales and Van Diemen's Land, 1822–1823; Their Origins, Nature and Significance* (Melbourne: Heinemann, 1970), pp. 1–30; John Hirst, *Freedom on the Fatal Shore: Australia's First Colony* (Melbourne: Black Inc., 2008), pp. 38, 79–81.

3 Bathurst to Bigge, 6 January 1819, *Historical Records of Australia* [HRA], series I, vol. 10, p. 7; Hirst, *Freedom on the Fatal Shore*, p. 80.

4 This is Ritchie's phrase, *Punishment and Profit*.

from public office, large land grants and patronage networks. Convicts were to be controlled with more administrative rigour, greater social isolation and fiercer regimes of exemplary punishment. Bigge also advocated the modest expansion of local political and legal institutions to temper the autocratic powers of government.

Reforms

Bigge's blueprint led to incremental but formative changes in the administration of the colony, all of which fostered rapid geographical expansion. Some of the most important reforms were institutional in nature. The *New South Wales Act* of 1823 established an appointed legislative council that gave local elites some small say in the administration of the colony. It also established the Supreme Court of New South Wales, which was armed with plenary jurisdiction and staffed by three judges. These institutions both effected and contested important changes in the colony, including the subordination of convicts, the simplification of commercial and land transactions, and exercise of jurisdiction over Indigenous people.[5]

The convict labour system was transformed in what has been described as a 'series of reversals' for convicts.[6] Before the Bigge report was received in the colony, Macquarie's successor, Governor Sir Thomas Brisbane (1821–25), anticipated some of its key recommendations.[7] He ordered that convicts be directed into private assignment up-country, removing them from the comforts and corruptions of town life. Convict mechanics, once reserved for ambitious but extravagant public work programs, were now hired out to settlers. From mid-1822, unassigned men, especially those who were weak, unskilled and intractable, were directed into 'falling gangs', clearing bushland for farming or grazing, or into expanded public agricultural stations where they were made to acquire some useful skills before their assignment to settlers. Under Brisbane's successor, Governor Ralph Darling (1825–31), 'falling gangs' were replaced with 'road gangs', thereby channelling thousands of convicts into the construction of the arteries that connected Sydney to the Hunter Valley in the north, to Goulburn in the south, and west to Bathurst.

---

5 Bruce Kercher, *An Unruly Child: A History of Law in Australia* (Sydney: Allen & Unwin, 1995), pp. 67–123.
6 Barrie Dyster, 'A Series of Reversals: Male Convicts in New South Wales 1821–1831', *The Push from the Bush*, 25 (1987): 18–36.
7 Brisbane to Bathurst, 30 August 1822, *HRA*, series I, vol. 10, p. 724.

Measures for tighter regulation and closer surveillance of the convict population complemented these reforms. These included more bureaucratic methods for monitoring and managing convict life and labour, especially in Van Diemen's Land, where the new lieutenant-governor, George Arthur (1824–36), orchestrated a pervasive system of scrutiny and supervision in which every convict was 'regularly and strictly accounted for...from the day of their landing until...their emancipation or death'.[8] Meanwhile, the powers of magistrates to punish convicts were supervised more closely by a growing coterie of stipendiary magistrates.[9] Responsibility for the administration of convicts in New South Wales was vested in the Colonial Secretary's Office, and in both colonies systems were established for keeping convict 'registers', compiling returns of fines and punishments, and collating and advertising lists of runaways. New regulations specified the minimum periods of service required before convicts were entitled to tickets-of-leave (a form of parole, allowing convicts to work for themselves), and tied early reprieve explicitly to collaboration in the policing of other convicts. Many convicts were inducted directly into the constabulary, particularly in Van Diemen's Land, which was divided into nine districts patrolled by a vastly expanded convict police force. The assignment system was regulated and formalised. In New South Wales an independent Assignment Board, and later the office of Assignment Commissioner, were established to obviate nepotism and patronage in the distribution of convict labour. Expanded bureaucracies also imposed new rules and record-keeping practices on private masters.

The system was made more coercive by the expansion of a network of new penal settlements. While for a time it was envisioned that all convicts transported to Australia might henceforth be kept completely separate from the established districts,[10] remote receptacles were established in the wake of the Bigge report to take convicts who could not be integrated into the colony's expanding economy. Exemplary centres of punishment and deterrence were established at the mouth of the Hastings River at Port Macquarie (in northern New South Wales) from 1823, in Moreton Bay (near Brisbane) from 1824, and from 1833 at Port Arthur (in south-eastern Tasmania). Most

---

8 Arthur to Bathurst, 3 July 1825, quoted in A.G.L. Shaw, *Convicts and the Colonies: A Study of Penal Transportation from Great Britain and Ireland to Australia and Other Parts of the British Empire* (London: Faber & Faber, 1966), p. 199.
9 Hilary Golder, *High and Responsible Office: A History of the New South Wales Magistracy* (Oxford University Press, 1991), pp. 35–8, 41–50; Stefan Petrow, 'Policing in a Penal Colony: Governor Arthur's Police System in Van Diemen's Land, 1826–1836', *Law and History Review*, 18, 2 (2000): 364.
10 Bathurst to Brisbane, 9 September 1822, *HRA*, series I, vol. 10, p. 791.

functioned as both penal settlements and colonial vanguards, paving 'the way for the free Settler, who could never venture so far amongst savage Tribes, until Government had preceded them'.[11] Local administrators also toyed with using penal stations as bastions of imperial competition. Short-lived forays into the northern coast of the continent at Melville Island (1824) and at Raffles Bay (1827) on the Cobourg Peninsula sought to counter Dutch control of the East Indies,[12] while outposts formed on the shores of Bass Strait at Western Port (east of Port Phillip) in 1826, and in Western Australia at King George Sound (Albany) in 1827, all displayed a British presence to the French.[13]

New technologies of subordination did not assure social order. The increasing severity of 'the system', the ruralisation of the convict workforce and inequitable convict distribution favouring large-scale, frontier enterprises over small farms, caused some of the most pressing social and political problems of the decade. For example, the relocation of some 1,000 convicts to the Bathurst region between 1822 and 1825 did not instil the anticipated docility and self-reflection, but rather sowed the seeds of serious discontent. Expansion without policing and social control generated an atmosphere of independence and mobility – a 'state of constant migration' as one observer put it – as men took to the roads that meandered back to the settled districts, or moved from station to station with little restraint or concern for the consequences.[14] Others hid on the fringes of the frontier, sustaining themselves by robbing travellers and outstations, or overcoming the new barriers to capital acquisition by finding vacant land and stocking it with (often stolen) cattle and sheep. Throughout the colony, men walked away from their employment, especially from the remote road gangs, and the behaviour of those seeking to avoid recapture grew increasingly desperate. Expansion so stretched the New South Wales government's resources and weakened the influence of central authority that the colonial state was forced to bolster its apparatus with extraordinary legislation such as the 'Harbouring' and

---

11 Brisbane to Horton, 24 March 1825, and 16 June 1825, *HRA*, series I, vol. 11, pp. 555, 649. See Bill Thorpe and Raymond Evans, 'Freedom and Unfreedom at Moreton Bay: The Structures and Relations of Secondary Punishment', in Barrie Dyster (ed.), *Beyond Convict Workers* (Sydney: Department of Economic History, University of New South Wales, 1996), pp. 64–82.

12 'Official Papers Relating to the Settlement of North Australia, 1823–1827', *HRA*, series III, vol. 5, pp. 737–824.

13 Arthur to Hay, 15 November 1826, *HRA*, series III, vol. 5, p. 434; Wetherall to Barrow, 7 November 1826, *HRA*, series III, vol. 5, p. 830. See Map 0.4.

14 Alexander Harris, *Settlers and Convicts, or, Recollections of Sixteen Years' Labour in the Australian Backwoods* [1847] (Melbourne University Press, 1964), p. 67.

'Bushranging' Acts (1825 and 1830) and through the formation in 1825 of a rapid-response military unit known as the Mounted Police.[15] In newly independent Van Diemen's Land, bushranging was at crisis levels even before the implementation of Bigge's reforms, leading Governor Arthur to institute the most coercive penal and policing system in early Australia.[16]

Changes in the land grant system were even more problematic. The Colonial Office and a succession of governors embraced Bigge's recommendation to concentrate land grants in the hands of moneyed elites, but they did not wholly accept his endorsement of pastoralism. Instead, policy makers in the 1820s sought to spread civilisation through agricultural 'improvement'. In some respects, theirs was a nostalgic vision: they sought to recreate a system that would tether landholders and labourers to land in a manner rapidly disappearing in post-enclosure Britain. In other respects, their concerns about pastoralism were linked with modern modes of imperialism. Pastoralism looked far too much to them like barbarism or savagery at a moment when pastoralists and hunter-gatherers were being dispossessed globally on the grounds that transient modes of subsistence created no valid legal claim to land.

Even before Bigge left the colony in 1821, Macquarie had started to link land grants to the possession of capital. In one of the first acts of his administration, Brisbane indexed convict assignment to the size of land grants, demanding that owners of more than 100 acres (40.5 hectares) maintain at least one convict at private expense. Large land grants required that gentlemen settlers cultivate their land, while very small grants to emancipists and tradesmen attempted to create pockets of intensive agricultural land use.[17] By favouring a pattern of large-scale ownership in New South Wales, these measures helped to reassert and refine the dominance of the colonial elite. Macquarie's system of issuing temporary de-pasturing permits to pastoralists was continued, however. Under Brisbane, new 'Tickets of Occupation' authorised increasingly land-hungry pastoralists to use unsurveyed land in remote corners of the colony on a temporary basis at no charge, causing further dispersion of settlement but without surrendering crown ownership.

The goals of new land policy were most clearly fulfilled in the rich alluvial plains of the Hunter Valley, to the north of Sydney. Surveying began

---

15 David Andrew Roberts, 'A "change of place": Illegal Movement on the Bathurst Frontier, 1822–1825', *Journal of Australian Colonial History*, 7 (2005): 97–122.

16 Petrow, 'Policing in a Penal Colony', p. 356.

17 Stephen H. Roberts, *History of Australian Land Settlement 1788–1920* [1924] (Melbourne: Macmillan, 1968), p. 39.

upriver from Newcastle in 1822. Within three years the most propitious river-frontages in the lower and middle Hunter were spoken for, and settlement was spreading further north into the Paterson and Williams river valleys, and north-west towards the base of the Liverpool Range. There, the wealthiest of the newly arrived gentlemen tilled and grazed some of the best agricultural lands in New South Wales, sending commodities back and forth via the Hunter River. The Valley quickly emerged as the colony's most significant and socially stratified area of settlement. By 1833 it ranked among the most densely populated agricultural regions, yet it had some of the highest numbers of convict workers, and the lowest numbers of emancipist landowners.[18]

In contrast, settlement inland beyond the Blue Mountains demonstrated the fragility of these new policies. Governor Brisbane granted some 100,000 acres (40,500 hectares) of land near Bathurst and issued around 200 tickets of occupation for remote and unsurveyed grazing runs, many of them to the long-established Cumberland settlers and their children. The environment placed expansion in this region outside the control of government. Less arable and far less accessible than the Hunter, the Bathurst region was ill suited to both agricultural cultivation and geographically confined pastoralism. Instead, the area emerged as the colony's primary sheep-grazing district. Rather than expanding existing grazing runs, pastoralists found it more practical to search further afield for natural grassland to feed their growing herds. Thus by the early 1820s some of the first stakeholders had small parties of men driving stock into extraordinarily remote pockets of land, along the Cudgegong and Talbragar rivers and toward the Warrumbungle Ranges in the west, for example. In this manner, settlement bypassed many less desirable locations and quickly extended beyond the modest boundaries envisaged by Brisbane's system of land grants, sales and tickets of occupation.[19]

The same forces encouraged and shaped expansion in other directions as well. The Hunter Valley became a conduit for settlers moving northward. By the mid-1820s routes had been marked through Pandora's Pass to the Liverpool Plains, and through Cunningham's Pass to the Darling Downs. In the south-west, while land long used under permissive occupancy was being surveyed and formally granted, pastoralists drove stock beyond to the Breadalbane and Goulburn Plains, around Lakes Bathurst and George,

18 Sandra J. Blair, 'The Revolt at Castle Forbes: A Catalyst to Emancipist Emigrant Confrontation', *Journal of the Royal Australian Historical Society*, 64, 2 (1978): 98–9.
19 J.M. Powell, *The Public Lands of Australia Felix: Settlement and Land Appraisal in Victoria 1834–91* (Oxford University Press, 1970), pp. 13–14.

on the 'Limestone Plains' (now the Australian Capital Territory), and on to the Murrumbidgee River. In 1824 the soldier and settler William Hovell accompanied the colonial-born adventurer Hamilton Hume south across the Murrumbidgee, Murray, Goulburn and Ovens rivers, eventually reaching Corio Bay in Port Phillip. Numerous tracts of agricultural and grazing lands were discovered, though at the time they seemed distant and inaccessible.

In Van Diemen's Land there was also a swell of interest in land from new immigrants. In 1823 1,000 land grants were issued, twice the number issued in the previous decade. In the years to 1831, another 1.5 million acres were granted and sold.[20] After the most fertile and accessible sites around Hobart and Launceston had been appropriated, settlement spread along the Tamar, North Esk and South Esk rivers in the north, the Derwent, Coal and Clyde rivers in the south, and in the midlands, around the growing villages of Perth, Oatlands and Brighton along the Elizabeth and Macquarie rivers. By 1835 land-hungry pastoralists had turned their attention to Port Phillip on the mainland, across the Bass Strait.

Squatters and the first boom

The turn to wool production in the early 1820s that underpinned much of this early growth built on metropolitan rather than local imperatives. A reduction of wool tariffs in Britain in 1823 brought an immediate surge in Australian wool exports, from 175,400 pounds to 400,000 (181,500 kilograms) per year.[21] New industrial production techniques required longer, stronger wool than English growers provided. British industrialists had been increasingly dependent on German wool, but after the Napoleonic wars ended they sought more stable supply in the British colonies. Opportunistic locals and new arrivals began to herd their sheep beyond the reach of surveyors and tickets of occupation. By 1825 uncontrolled pastoral expansion had become a central concern of government.[22]

The real turning point came in 1828. A parliamentary select committee into the British wool industry endorsed the quality of Australian fleece and precipitated the colonies' first export boom. By 1831 New South Wales and Van Diemen's Land were exporting 2.5 million pounds of wool.[23] By 1834

20 Sharon Morgan, *Land Settlement in Early Tasmania: Creating an Antipodean England* (Cambridge University Press, 1992), p. 22.
21 Stephen H. Roberts, *The Squatting Age in Australia, 1835–1847* [1935] (Melbourne University Press, 1964), p. 42.
22 Bathurst to Brisbane, 1 January 1825, HRA, series I, vol. 11, pp. 434–44.
23 Roberts, *The Squatting Age in Australia*, pp. 42–3.

New South Wales, Van Diemen's Land, South Australia and the Swan River colony were together exporting 13.5 million pounds (6.1 million kilograms) and were major suppliers of wool to Britain.[24] Whereas in 1830 the Australian colonies provided only 8.1 per cent of Britain's wool imports (and Germany 75.8 per cent), by 1850 the Australian colonies provided 47 per cent to Germany's 10.6 per cent.[25]

This export boom rested on geographical expansion on a scale that could not be contained by government; it marked the advent of the 'squatting age' in the Australian colonies. As their name suggests, squatters occupied land without the imprimatur of the state. It was a complex label to apply in a continent chiefly occupied and controlled by Indigenous people. The notion that someone could illegally occupy 'Crown Land' in Australia reflected an emerging consensus about the nature of Britain's claim to the continent. In a variety of cases spanning tax law and the killing of wandering cattle, lawyers began to claim that the British crown owned the continent in fee simple, wholly unencumbered by Indigenous title to land.[26] Thus while the men who marched beyond the settled frontiers of New South Wales with hungry quadrupeds took land and resources from Indigenous people, an emerging legal fiction asserted that they trespassed on the property of the British monarch.

Until the mid-1830s the term 'squatter' denoted a disreputable class; those without the means or respectability to acquire sufficient property through legal means.[27] Like their US equivalents, many of the first squatters were poor settlers, chiefly emancipists or ticket-of-leave men who illegally occupied land either to support themselves or to turn a quick profit.[28] They ran cattle in order to raise capital to purchase sheep.[29] Feral cattle were plentiful, and privately owned herds roamed unfenced and largely unprotected; easy targets for poor men locked out of land ownership in the 1820s. Cattle

---

24 Richard Waterhouse, *The Vision Splendid: A Social and Cultural History of Rural Australia* (Perth: Curtin University Books, 2005), p. 77.

25 Roberts, *The Squatting Age in Australia*, p. 45.

26 Lisa Ford, *Settler Sovereignty: Jurisdiction and Indigenous People in America and Australia, 1788–1836* (Cambridge, MA: Harvard University Press, 2010), p. 165.

27 For example, Alexander M'Leay (chairman), Council Committee on Police and Gaol Establishments, June–October 1835, cited in Roberts, *The Squatting Age in Australia*, pp. 54–64; Philip McMichael, *Settlers and the Agrarian Question: Foundations of Capitalism in Colonial Australia* (Cambridge University Press, 1984), p. 89; Kercher, *An Unruly Child*, p. 120; Roberts, *History of Australian Land Settlement*, p. 187.

28 Roberts, *The Squatting Age in Australia*, pp. 53–4; John Mack Faragher, *Sugar Creek: Life on the Illinois Prairie* (New Haven: Yale University Press, 1986), p. 181.

29 John Perkins and Jack Thompson, 'Cattle Theft, Primitive Capital Accumulation and Pastoral Expansion in Early New South Wales, 1800–1850', *Australian Historical Studies* 29, 3 (1998): 297.

were also easier to muster, were locally consumed and garnered more profit per beast than sheep.[30] Indeed cattle were vital to the growth of the colonial economy in this period because they lowered the price of food locally, feeding the growth of towns in the colony with a surfeit of cheap meat.[31]

With the local government refusing to grant or sell unsurveyed land, and clearly unable to police its peripheries effectively, respectable, moneyed settlers soon followed the lead of the thieves and vagabonds they despised. Unlike cattle, sheep required both capital and cheap land, so better connected or more well-to-do squatters gravitated to the booming global wool market. The fringes of settlement soon accommodated an array of immigrants, emancipists and colonial-born of varying degrees of wealth and status. As Rev. Haygarth commented in 1848, the 'Bush of Australia' became a place where 'men differing entirely in birth, education and habits, and in their whole mores and intellectual nature, [are] thrown into such contact [and] united by common interests'.[32]

Neither colony nor Empire sat idly by as their visions of order and their land revenues were gutted by illegal settlement. Legislators tried incentive, coercion and concession to control squatting in New South Wales between 1828 and 1846. Governor Darling first sought to control expansion by drawing an official frontier line; the 'limits of location' were first defined in 1826 and redrawn more definitively in 1829. Stretching from the Manning River in the north to the Moruya River in the south, with a western border running from the Murrumbidgee north to the Barwon River, the boundary line enclosed the 'settled districts', or the nineteen counties within which land could be legally granted, purchased or leased. It was chiefly intended to facilitate mapping and surveying, rather than to prevent further movement beyond the boundaries.[33] Nevertheless, this geographical limitation of land tenure made a potent legal and administrative boundary.[34] The *Crown Lands Encroachment Act* of 1833 went further, declaring that 'the unauthorized occupation' of land would not be 'considered as giving any legal title thereto' through adverse possession, or any other device of common law. The Act also gave the

---

30 Waterhouse, *The Vision Splendid*, pp. 81–2.
31 James Belich, *Replenishing the Earth: The Settler Revolution and the Rise of the Anglo-World, 1783–1939* (Oxford University Press, 2009), p. 277.
32 Henry William Haygarth, *Recollections of Bush Life in Australia, During a Residence of Eight Years in the Interior* (London: J. Murray, 1861), p. 22.
33 June Philipp, 'Wakefieldian Influence and NSW, 1830–1832', *Historical Studies Australia and New Zealand* 9, 34 (1960): 173–80.
34 Dennis Norman Jeans, 'Territorial Divisions and the Location of Towns in New South Wales, 1826–1842', *Australian Geographer*, 10, 4 (1967): 243–55.

governor of New South Wales powers to appoint Commissioners of Crown Lands as frontier magistrates to check the 'encroachment, intrusion and trespass' on crown lands.

In contrast, the so-called 'Ripon regulations' (issued by the Secretary of State to all settler colonies in 1831) made a grand attempt to entice settlers everywhere to purchase and settle on surveyed, agricultural land. Like the land-distribution policies they replaced, the Ripon regulations were intended to slow uncontrolled expansion in colonies such as New South Wales, and to achieve 'systematic' or 'concentrated' land settlement patterns to ensure 'civilised' society.[35] Their chief innovation was to end land grants throughout the Empire.[36] Henceforth, land was to be sold by auction and the proceeds used to fund emigration to the colonies. Auctions had a mandatory reserve of five shillings per acre. Crown lands within the limits of location could also be leased in 640-acre lots (259 hectares) for one year, for a minimum rent of £1 per annum. Following the principles of land settlement advocated by the influential Edward Gibbon Wakefield, the scheme sought to make land too expensive for poor emigrants, who would be forced instead to contribute to the scanty pool of colonial labour. The Ripon system remained in operation until 1840–41, although the minimum reserve for auction sales increased considerably over time and the system of leases was changed to one of annual licences.[37] It had considerable impact on the settlement of South Australia and New Zealand – both Wakefieldian enterprises – but did nothing to curb the growth of squatting in eastern Australia.

When both stick and carrot failed to restrain squatting, local and imperial legislators deployed incremental concessions to try to bring the squatters of greater New South Wales back within the reach of the law. Governor Richard Bourke's *Crown Land Unauthorised Occupation Act* of 1836 partially acceded to squatter demands for more security of tenure by creating a licensing system that allowed squatters to run as many animals as they desired across an unlimited extent of terrain for an annual fee of £10.[38] Governor George Gipps' *Crown Lands Unauthorised Occupation Act* of 1839

35 Kercher, *An Unruly Child*, p. 120; McMichael, *Settlers and the Agrarian Question*, pp. 79, 84–5.
36 See, for example, Commission of Governor Darling, HRA, series I, vol. 12, pp. 99–107.
37 A.R. Buck, *The Making of Australian Property Law* (Sydney: Federation Press, 2006), p. 74.
38 Michael Roe, *Quest for Authority in Eastern Australia, 1835–1851* (Melbourne University Press, 1965), p. 62. Cf. Rodney Harrison, *Shared Landscapes: Archaeologies of Attachment and the Pastoral Industry in New South Wales* (Sydney: UNSW Press, 2004), p. 25. Ben Boyd ran animals over 426,000 acres in return for his £10: Kercher, *An Unruly Child*, p. 121.

then identified eight squatting districts, gave the Commissioner of Crown Lands power to mediate boundary disputes and to remove licences for misconduct, and established a 'Border Police' to aid the commissioner and to control violence between squatters and Aboriginal people. Most importantly, the 1839 Act also protected licensees from encroachment by any other party engaged in 'the depasturing of stock'.[39] This right was augmented in the same year by the Supreme Court of New South Wales, which held that a licensed squatter could sue in trespass against everyone except the crown. The crown, however, could still sell squatting runs at will, without compensation for improvements. Despite this fundamental insecurity, squatters purchased and sold their runs and made permanent improvements to them.[40] And they continued to overrun the eastern half of the continent, occupying both Port Phillip District and the Darling Downs by 1840.

Concessions became more generous and more contentious in the 1840s for a number of reasons. First, the importance of pastoralism to imperial prosperity became painfully apparent during the severe global economic crisis of 1841–44. In the Australian colonies, easy British credit had led to extravagant land speculation in towns and agricultural districts, and had artificially inflated stock prices. When credit faltered during the drought of 1837–39, colonial economies crashed. Property, stock and wool prices plummeted, reducing land sales and drying up immigration funds. Many of the biggest pastoral stations collapsed into insolvency. But pastoralism also led the way to economic recovery. The collapse opened opportunities for emancipists, colonial-born settlers and a host of newly arrived investors to join the pastoral industry, further diversifying this class of colonial capitalist. Moreover, while wool was cheap in the Depression, new packing technologies enabled wool exports to grow and eventually to prosper, underpinning renewed prosperity in Australia and elsewhere.[41]

The British parliament responded by endorsing the governor's power to grant annual occupation licenses beyond the limits of location and by preventing the sale of licensed land by the crown for the term of the licence. However, the Act left many squatters unhappy because it reasserted London's

---

39 Kercher, *An Unruly Child*, p. 122.
40 *Scott v Dight* [1839] NSW Supreme Court 16, in *Sydney Gazette*, 25 March 1839. See generally, Henry Reynolds and Jamie Dalziel, 'Aborigines and Pastoral Leases: Imperial and Colonial Policy, 1826–1855', *UNSW Law Journal*, 19, 2 (1996): 346.
41 Roberts, *The Squatting Age in Australia*, pp. 186–213; McMichael, *Settlers and the Agrarian Question*, pp. 142–4.

control of the administration of land, outlawed freehold sales beyond the nineteen counties, and set a minimum price of £1 per acre at auction within the counties, effectively preventing them from purchasing their runs.[42] Indeed, the New South Wales Select Committee on Crown Land Grievances reported in 1844 that the £1 per acre price was encouraging squatting.[43]

Second, squatters became better organised from the late 1830s and formed new political connections. Key members of the squatting elite, including W.C. Wentworth and Archibald Boyd, were also active supporters of the rights of native-born settlers. Their objects included representative government and the liberal treatment of former convicts; both goals appealed to broad segments of the general public. The abolition of convict assignment, meanwhile, created new economic and political bonds between large pastoralists and small farmers seeking supplementary seasonal employment by shearing sheep. These new coalitions bore fruit when squatters won a dominant role in the partly elected legislature established by imperial legislation in 1842 (effective from 1843).[44] At the same time, squatters strengthened their political clout in England by forging ties with stakeholders in the wool importing, exporting, shipping and banking industries, and by sending an agent to London.[45]

Squatters demonstrated their influence in April 1844 when Governor Gipps passed new land regulations for the colony. The rules gave more rights to squatters even as they sought to redress the inequity of existing land regulations, which allowed the holding of multiple runs under a single licence and charged the same fee no matter how many animals were de-pastured on the land. Gipps' regulations stipulated that a licence covered a single run, not to exceed 20 square miles (51.8 square kilometres) or to hold more than 4,000 sheep. After five years' occupation, a squatter had a right of pre-emption to purchase up to 320 acres of his run, less the value of improvements. In exchange, the squatter would have undisturbed possession of the remainder of the licence for a further eight years, after which he could purchase another 320 acres, and so on indefinitely. However, if a squatter did not exercise his

42 Buck, *The Making of Australian Property Law*, p. 76; Reynolds and Dalziel, 'Aborigines and Pastoral Leases', p. 347.
43 'Select Committee on Crown Land Grievances', *Votes and Proceedings of the New South Wales Legislative Council*, 1844, vol. 2, pp. 1–4, quoted in Buck, *The Making of Australian Property Law*, p. 76.
44 See generally Roberts, *The Squatting Age in Australia*, pp. 214–62.
45 Buck, *The Making of Australian Property Law*, p. 80; Roberts, *The Squatting Age in Australia*, pp. 249–52.

option to purchase, any other person could buy the land so long as they paid the squatter for improvements.[46]

The reaction of squatters to Gipps' regulations illustrated their increasing political influence even as it alienated some erstwhile supporters.[47] While the right of pre-emption was not widely disputed, squatters protested against the prohibitive cost of buying their runs under the scheme.[48] Others were outraged about limits on size and holding capacity. They set about lobbying in London, sending petitions to the Queen, holding public meetings and forming the Pastoral Association and Melbourne's Mutual Protection Society.[49] With the help of British stakeholders, squatters convinced the British parliament that defeating Gipps' plan was vital to imperial interests.[50]

The result was the *Waste Lands Occupation Act* of 1846 (UK), followed by the Order in Council of 9 March 1847, which marked a turning point in land regulation. The Act allowed squatters to obtain a lease for pastoral purposes for 8 years (in intermediate districts) or 14 years (in 'unsettled' districts) with an annual rent of £10 for each station that could carry 4,000 sheep. The Act imposed an additional £2/10s for every additional 1,000 sheep held on the land. Tenants had an uncontested option to convert a minimum of 160 acres of their leasehold land to a fee simple interest for £1 per acre during the term of their lease, so long as those acres did not have an excessive length of water frontage. The crown retained the right of resumption; that is, the governor could grant or sell lands within the boundaries of a run or held under a crown lease if the public interest required it. This Act remained unchanged until 1859, when intermediate districts were reclassed as 'settled' districts. Otherwise, it remained in force in eastern Australia until the Nicholson *Land Act* of 1860 (Victoria) and the Robertson Land Acts of 1861 (New South Wales).[51] Using the device of leasehold, the Act succeeded, finally, in turning squatters into leaseholders and consolidating the pastoral monopoly, even as it brought squatters decisively back into the fold of the law. By the end of the

---

46 Roberts, *History of Australian Land Settlement*, p. 191; Reynolds and Dalziel, 'Aborigines and Pastoral Leases', pp. 347–8.

47 Alan Atkinson, 'Time, Place and Paternalism: Early Conservative Thinking in New South Wales', *Australian Historical Studies* 23, 90 (1988): 1–18; Terence H. Irving, 'The Idea of Responsible Government in New South Wales before 1856', *Historical Studies Australia and New Zealand* 11, 42 (1964): 194–9.

48 Roe, *Quest for Authority in Eastern Australia*, p. 69; Roberts, *History of Australian Land Settlement*, pp. 191–4.

49 Reynolds and Dalziel, 'Aborigines and Pastoral Leases', p. 348; Roe, *Quest for Authority in Eastern Australia*, p. 63.

50 Buck, *The Making of Australian Property Law*, p. 80.

51 Ibid., p. 80. Similar legislation was passed in South Australia in 1869, the *Waste Lands Amendment Act*, known as the 'Strangways Land Act'.

1840s some 70 million acres (28 million hectares) covering more or less the entire eastern third of the continent had been commandeered by fewer than 2,000 squatters, securing their economic and political dominance and setting the scene for the great struggles of the succeeding decades.[52]

Multiple beginnings

Conflict between squatters and government in eastern Australia is but one dimension of the expansion that occurred between 1820 and 1850. Indeed, whaling, not wool, dominated the region's exports into the 1830s, and wool still constituted only half of Australian exports in 1844. In this period comparatively modest demographic growth underwrote multiple expansions across the continent, producing several economically, socially and politically distinct colonial projects.

More people came to the Australian colonies after 1820 because sailing time and costs were dramatically reduced, the number of convict transportees increased and colonial and imperial governments began to provide financial assistance to poor immigrants. Even so, it still took 110 days of uncomfortable and unhealthy travel to get from Europe to the southern Pacific, so most emigrants headed for the United States and Canada instead. Australian colonies received some 200,000 immigrants from the United Kingdom between 1821 and 1850, while the United States received 2.45 million people, more than 60 per cent of them British, in the same period.[53]

The modest population increase in New South Wales was concentrated in towns. To the great inconvenience of pastoralists, most immigrants seemed 'naturally averse to go into the interior on any terms', having 'brought with them to the colony the habits and feelings of a town population'.[54] Immigrants ran urban businesses, speculated on suburban blocks, grew market produce and built infrastructure. Most importantly, they consumed goods and services, harnessing the tiny colonial settlements to the global economic cycles of boom and bust.[55] Growing centres also became sites of social division and refinement – a task that fell particularly to the growing

52 Roberts, *The Squatting Age in Australia*, pp. 362–3.
53 Robin F. Haines, *Emigration and the Labouring Poor: Australian Recruitment in Britain and Ireland, 1831–60* (Houndmills: Macmillan, 1997), p. 263; Julian L. Simon, 'Basic Data Concerning Immigration to the United States', *Annals of the American Academy of Political and Social Science*, 487, 1 (1986): 35.
54 *Australian*, 30 November 1843, p. 3.
55 Belich, *Replenishing the Earth*, pp. 182–206, 275–8.

population of women who policed social boundaries through dinner invitations and calling cards, and whose very comportment displayed either real rank or social aspiration.

Nevertheless, an insatiable demand for labour in the rural districts and high wages did draw thousands of immigrants into the bush. Many set up as independent workers, tradesmen and small capitalists, serving landed proprietors and their workers. Others developed moderate land and stock interests of their own. In this way the expansion and consolidation of Sydney was replicated in many small regional towns, which developed as administrative, commercial and logistical hubs. Even on the remote stations, there was consolidation and improvement. Towards the end of this period, women and children made their first appearances on pastoral runs as huts gave way to homesteads, with gardens, cellars, kitchens, drawing rooms and other accoutrements of respectability. On the long roads that connected the towns and stations, new villages were laid out for blacksmiths, saddlers, retailers and innkeepers to service the increasing traffic.[56]

In other parts of the region, new emigrants fed new colonial enterprises. The first grew out of a garrison established at King George Sound in 1826 to ward off imperial competitors from the western coast of the continent. It was followed in 1829 by an English settlement at the mouth of the Swan River, which became Australia's first convict-free, privatised colony. The product of arrangements between the Colonial Office and a syndicate of investors, the new colony was intended to transplant the best of British rural society; it was to be commanded by gentlemen of means and populated by yeoman farmers and industrious working families. The history of the Swan River to 1850, however, was one of early stagnation and then very modest growth. At the outset, the colony suffered from an eccentric land distribution system that placed most arable land in this arid and largely infertile expanse into the hands of negligent, absentee owners.[57] Governor Stirling introduced landholding restrictions in 1830, but the colony continued to be plagued by endemic food shortages, lack of capital and labour, and a lagging rural economy. The 'Glenelg Regulations' of 1837, which allowed original grantees to surrender portions of their land, combined with the strict enforcement of improvement restrictions from 1838 under the new Governor, John Hutt (brother of one of Wakefield's most prominent parliamentary allies), freed arable land and stimulated modest agricultural

---

56 Jeans, 'Territorial Divisions', pp. 243–55.
57 Roberts, *History of Australian Land Settlement*, pp. 48–51, 153–6, 207–9.

development.[58] Hutt also introduced annual de-pasturing licences in 1844, as part of a compromise between graziers, the executive and the Colonial Office, bringing another 1.5 million acres (607,000 hectares) into use by just 124 licensees.[59]

But agriculture and pastoralism developed slowly. By 1841 there were barely more than 40,000 sheep in the colony, with wool exports totalling a mere 3,000 pounds. Although there was some pastoral expansion into the south-west corner of the continent, it was observed with suspicion by a government anxious to minimise state expenditure on public works and policing.[60] As in New South Wales, other exports proved vital to the struggling economy, especially the lucrative whale and sealing trades. After the Depression of the early 1840s, the Swan River economy diversified further into tobacco and wine production, coal mining and harvesting sandalwood. Yet the colony remained utterly marginal, and a far less inviting prospect for British investment than the eastern colonies. Many of its founding families packed up and moved east. By 1850, despite an influx of assisted immigrants and some batches of juvenile criminals from Parkhurst penitentiary, the settler population had only reached 5,254, half of them children, and few willing to engage in isolated rural work. Graziers, constrained by aridity and labour shortages, had only spread some 300 kilometres from the coast.[61] Ironically, it took the importation of nearly 10,000 convicts into Western Australia from 1850 to 1868 to boost its small settler population.

The Port Phillip District was settled in a different way again. This region had long served as a maritime borderland, frequented by whalers, sailors and sealers from a variety of countries. While pastoralists from Britain, Sydney and even the Swan River expanded into the region after 1834, Port Phillip functioned largely as a pastoral frontier for land-starved Van Diemen's Land.[62] Concerted occupation followed after the Port Phillip Association (formed in Van Diemen's Land) signed its abortive Treaty with Kulin people

58 Pamela Statham, 'Swan River Colony 1829–1850', in C.T. Stannage (ed.), *A New History of Western Australia* (Perth: UWA Press, 1981), pp. 189–94.

59 B.K. de Garis, 'Political Tutelage 1829–1890', in Stannage (ed.), *A New History of Western Australia*, p. 319.

60 Geoffrey Bolton, *Land of Vision and Mirage: Western Australia Since 1826* (Perth: UWA Press, 2008), pp. 15, 18.

61 Statham, 'Swan River Colony 1829–1850', pp. 181, 190; Bolton, *Land of Vision and Mirage*, pp. 21–2; and see maps of settled districts in J.M.R. Cameron, *Ambition's Fire: The Agricultural Colonization of Pre-Convict Western Australia* (Perth: UWA Press, 1981), pp. xvi, 173.

62 A.G.L. Shaw, *A History of the Port Phillip District: Victoria before Separation* (Melbourne University Press, 1996), p. 59.

in 1835.[63] Despite the claims of proud Victorians that theirs was a free colony, some 20,000 escapees and emancipists travelled across Bass Strait. They were supplemented by hundreds of assigned convicts from Sydney and 1,500 'Pentonvillians' sent from Britain's new model prison in the 1840s.

If Port Phillip began as a Vandemonian enterprise, it quickly became the quintessence of the northern manias for sheep and for town building.[64] Steadily, from 1837 onward, a number of 'overlanders' made the trek south from Sydney and surrounds.[65] They brought with them huge numbers of stock, contributing to the natural growth of sheep from Van Diemen's Land.[66] 100,000 sheep inspected by Governor Bourke in early 1837 had grown to 300,000 by the following year.[67] Pastoralism was king until the gold rush of the 1850s: 'By the year 1848, there were five million sheep and nearly four hundred thousand head of cattle'.[68] This sudden ingress of pastoralists precipitated a great deal of Aboriginal–settler violence, which in turn opened the region to imperial scrutiny. The first Aboriginal Protector was appointed to police the Port Phillip District's frontiers, rather than the western and northern frontiers of New South Wales. The protectorate encompassed the area south of the Murray River and stretched from the grasslands bordering South Australia to the east coast.

Town-dwelling settlers followed squatters in unusual numbers. There were only 4,000 settlers by 1839; 6,000 by 1840, and most of them lived in Melbourne. However, by 1846 Melbourne was home to 10,954 people, Geelong had 1,370 occupants and 8,877 people inhabited their agricultural and pastoral hinterlands. By 1850 the region had 70,000 settlers – compared with 180,000 in the rest of the eastern mainland.[69] The relatively sudden influx of immigrants after 1835 combined with the ties to Van Diemen's Land and the huge distance between Sydney and Melbourne led locals to call for early independence from New South Wales.[70] This influx also laid foundations for

63 Bain Attwood, *Possession: Batman's Treaty and the Matter of History* (Melbourne: Miegunyah Press, 2009), pp. 13–39.
64 James Boyce, *1835: The Founding of Melbourne & the Conquest of Australia* (Melbourne: Black Inc., 2011), pp. 147–80.
65 For the overlanders, see Ralph V. Billis and Alfred Stephen Kenyon, *Pastures New: An Account of the Pastoral Occupation of Port Phillip* [1930] (Melbourne: Stockland Press, 1974), pp. 44–66.
66 Shaw, *A History of the Port Phillip District*, pp. 63–6; Lynnette J. Peel, *Rural Industry in the Port Phillip Region, 1835–1880* (Melbourne University Press, 1974), p. 28.
67 Shaw, *A History of the Port Phillip District*, pp. 69, 73, 85.
68 Billis and Kenyon, *Pastures New*, p. 110.
69 Peel, *Rural Industry in the Port Phillip Region*, p. 18.
70 Jessie Mitchell, '"The galling yoke of slavery": Race and Separation in Colonial Port Phillip', *Journal of Australian Studies*, 33, 2 (2009): 125–37.

Victoria's gold-driven demographic and economic explosions in the following decade.

In contrast, South Australia, formed in 1836, was always a deliberately separate colonial endeavour, distinct from the moral and geographical chaos of greater New South Wales. It was a company colony. The *South Australia Act* of 1834 divided the colony's administration between the Colonial Office and a Colonisation Commission that was answerable to 300 or so shareholders. Wakefield-inspired, 'systematic colonisation' was intended to foster an independent, self-financing colony, more productive and orderly in its settlement patterns than its neighbours, but also more moral and harmonious in its nature. Convicts were to be excluded. Land was to be sold at a fixed price and used to fund the emigration of an earnest, ambitious and devout workforce. The Colonisation Commission even committed to a measure of Aboriginal protection. Most importantly, religious, political and commercial freedoms were guaranteed.

The result, by 1850, was a thriving colony with a mixed agricultural, mineral and pastoral economy. Adelaide was laid out neatly and its hinterland surveyed and allotted to purchasers intending to cultivate the proceeds used to ship in around 12,000 assisted immigrants over the following several years. Conflict with Aboriginal people quickly reduced the Commission's promises of protection to fiction – a reversal that only served to facilitate colonial expansion.[71] The contribution to growth of the colony's commitment to religious pluralism and secular, liberal government is also unclear, though some German Lutherans clearly came to the colony because of its religious voluntarism.[72]

Early agricultural successes produced an early oversupply of grain and this, combined with the government's over-investment in infrastructure, nearly bankrupted the colony in the crisis of the early 1840s. However, it grew again after 1845. Sheep numbers reached over a million by 1850.[73] In 1845 there were 1,269 grain farmers producing 343,000 bushels of wheat; by 1851, this had doubled to 2,821 farmers and 681,000 bushels.[74] By this time the market in grain was more open and overproduction no longer a problem, while the proximity

71 Robert Foster and Amanda Nettelbeck, *Out of the Silence: The History and Memory of South Australia's Frontier Wars* (Adelaide: Wakefield Press, 2011).
72 Douglas Pike, *Paradise of Dissent: South Australia 1829–1857* (London: Longmans, Green, 1957), pp. 221–78.
73 Ibid., p. 324.
74 A. Grenfell Price, *The Foundation and Settlement of South Australia*, new edn (Adelaide: Library Board of Australia, 1973), pp. 226–9.

of the colony's farmers to the sea made the cost of transport manageable.[75] The colony also enjoyed a small but exciting mineral boom in copper ore, which dominated exports. Between 1845 and 1850 the value of wool exports totalled £719,000; wheat and breadstuffs accounted for £200,000. Over the same period, mineral exports totalled £1,550,000.[76] Copper not only made money, it attracted investment and fostered land speculation.[77] As a result, like Port Phillip, the South Australian population grew more rapidly than most. The population of the colony shot from 22,460 in 1845 to 63,700 in 1850.[78]

The most peculiar expansion of all occurred across the Tasman Sea. New Zealand was essentially 'an Australian frontier', a reminder that British expansion in the region was a maritime as well as a pastoral affair.[79] The North Island of New Zealand served as an increasingly busy stopover for whalers, sealers, missionaries, traders and timber harvesters in the second quarter of the nineteenth century, escaped convicts among them. Up to 150 ships visited the Bay of Islands yearly in the 1830s. Although people came from the United States, Britain and France, most expeditions were funded and staffed from Sydney.[80] Their increasing lawlessness prompted the appointment of a British Resident to New Zealand in 1832 and, by 1840, the British had convinced key Māori chiefs that British sovereignty over the islands was the sole means of controlling settlers and sojourners. New Zealand was briefly annexed to New South Wales in 1840, before becoming a separate Crown Colony in 1841 and securing self-government with the *New Zealand Constitution Act* of 1852. Like most settler projects in the region, New Zealand became an exporter of wool. However, its peculiar geography combined with well-articulated Māori land claims, missionary agitation, pre-colonial land purchases and the personal involvement of Wakefield, made New Zealand a very different colonial enterprise from the other Australasian colonies.

Colonial publics

In every Australian colony, this multiplicity of demographic, geographical and economic expansions created new and interrelated public spheres. They

---

75 Pike, *Paradise of Dissent*, p. 329; Price, *The Foundation and Settlement of South Australia*, pp. 232–5.
76 Pike, *Paradise of Dissent*, p. 324.
77 Ibid., pp. 301–4, 331–9.
78 Ibid., p. 517.
79 Keith Sinclair, *A History of New Zealand*, rev. edn (Auckland: Pelican, 1980), p. 34.
80 James Belich, *Making Peoples: A History of the New Zealanders, From Polynesian Settlement to the End of the Nineteenth Century* (Honolulu: University of Hawai'i Press, 2001), p. 131.

were characterised by robust freedom of expression. After New South Wales received its legislative council and first Supreme Court in 1823, two local barristers (including the future squatter W.C. Wentworth) began the colony's first non-government newspaper. *The Australian*, established in 1824, supported emancipist civil rights, jury trials and representative government, and was soon followed by the more radical *Monitor* in 1826, the patrician *Sydney Herald* in 1831 and a variety of journals, including a range of short-lived labour papers for working men in the 1840s. The Port Phillip District had two newspapers long before it had a separate government, South Australia had five newspapers by 1841, and Van Diemen's Land had eleven by 1854. Even the few thousand immigrants in Swan River Colony were served by one commercial paper and a government gazette by 1855.[81] Curiously, colonial newspapers enjoyed much broader freedoms than their equivalents in Britain.[82] Every paper had its own constituency, though editors changed political allegiances to reflect the shifting coalitions among squatters, agriculturalists, smallholders and labourers.[83]

Each public sphere responded in one way or another to the problem of convicts. One of the most pressing issues in the eastern colonies was whether or not emancipists could sit on colonial juries. Participation in a jury would signal resumption of their civil status.[84] Open juries, for some, exemplified the dystopian nature of the colony. For others, they were a building block of a reformed civil society. After a false start in 1824, when a loophole in the *New South Wales Act* allowed for their use in courts of Quarter Sessions, the colony gained civilian juries for criminal trials in 1833.[85] In Van Diemen's Land, trial by jury was resisted by Governor Arthur and Chief Justice John Lewes Pedder, and remained a fiercely contested matter long after the first Act to regulate juries was passed in 1830.[86]

Likewise, divisions over the fate of unfree labour became a central political issue in New South Wales and Van Diemen's Land in the 1830s. The marked

---

81 Alan Atkinson, *The Europeans in Australia: A History. Volume 2, Democracy* (Oxford University Press, 2004), pp. 214–15.

82 Kercher, *An Unruly Child*, p. 86.

83 For example, see the radical changes in the tone of the *Sydney Gazette* in the 1830s; Sandra Blair, 'The Convict Press: William Watt and the *Sydney Gazette* in the 1830s', *Push from the Bush* 5 (1979): 98–119.

84 Kirsten McKenzie, *Scandal in the Colonies: Sydney and Cape Town* (Melbourne University Press, 2004), pp. 51–6; Sandra Blair, 'The Felonry and the Free? Divisions in Colonial Society in the Penal Era', *Labour History*, 45 (1983): 1–16; Hirst, *Freedom on the Fatal Shore*, pp. 148–58.

85 See generally John Bennett, 'The Establishment of Jury Trial in New South Wales', *Sydney Law Review*, 3 (1961): 463–85.

86 Alex Low, 'Sir Alfred Stephen and the Jury Question in Van Diemen's Land', *University of Tasmania Law Review*, 21, 1 (2002): 79–119.

increase of assisted free immigrants after 1820 meant that many settlers had little more than the absence of the convict taint to commend them in business or labour. Concerns about the effect of convicts on colonial society and colonial reputations added local support to metropolitan calls to phase out convict assignment in 1837 and to end convict transportation to New South Wales in 1840. One of the first legislative acts of self-governing Van Diemen's Land in 1851 was also to vote against the continuation of convict transportation there.

The residual presence of convicts and ex-convicts in New South Wales and Van Diemen's Land in the 1840s and 1850s continued to generate anxieties about crime rates and moral pollution, not just in the former convict colonies but also in their new neighbours, South Australia and the Port Phillip District. Persistent attempts by the British government to revive convict transportation led to a growing inter-colonial campaign, with some even calling for complete separation from Britain.

Debates about civil liberties also echoed around the eastern seaboard. In New South Wales and Van Diemen's Land, government autocracy was so often discussed in the free press that governors Darling and Arthur brought numerous cases of criminal libel against local publishers. Newspapers in the settlement at Port Phillip should have had fewer infringements of liberty to complain about, yet they spilled ink protesting against their overbearing resident judge, the imperially imposed system of Aboriginal Protection and, increasingly, the tyranny of the Sydney government. Meanwhile, the fledgling free colony of South Australia was preoccupied by confessional rivalries, frontier conflict and its impending bankruptcy in the wake of the 1841–44 Depression. These disputes connected in complicated ways with calls for local, elected legislatures. A sea change in imperial policy in the 1840s led to the creation of a semi-elected and semi-appointed Legislative Council in New South Wales in 1843, and over the following decade, in South Australia, the Port Phillip District (now separated and renamed Victoria) and Van Diemen's Land (which changed its name to Tasmania in 1856). Fully elected legislatures based on almost universal male suffrage soon followed in every colony, except the slow growing Swan River Colony.

Indigenous people and expansion

Every aspect of expansion between 1820 and 1850 entailed the dispossession of Aboriginal people, first in New South Wales and Van Diemen's Land, and then on the pasture lands and arable portions of South Australia, Swan

River, Port Phillip, and to the north in Moreton Bay and the Darling Downs. Aboriginal dispossession was as multifaceted as the urban, rural and pastoral expansions that occasioned it. Yet, violence was only one means to the end of continental settlement. Expansion between 1820 and 1850 also rested on the quiet encroachment of legal institutions and legal ideologies that gave the imprimatur of law to the rapid, physical dispossession of Indigenous people.

The invasion of Australia between 1820 and 1850 came to rest on a radical assertion that Aboriginal Australians, who had occupied parts of the continent for up to 55,000 years, not only lacked proprietary interest in the land but also lacked recognisable law or political communities. The British did not arrive in Australia with the fully fledged notion that the continent was 'empty' and could be claimed *terra nullius*, as a land without sovereigns or owners.[87] In some respects this is surprising. The notion that hunter-gathering people lacked land rights and political community had been spread widely by John Locke's *Two Treatises of Government* (1689) and Emmerich de Vattel's *The Law of Nations* (1753). Yet neither the founding governor's instructions nor the first Charter of Justice for New South Wales specified the legal status and land rights of Australian Aboriginal people. Instead, the Colonial Office issued its early governors with instructions to 'conciliate' and protect the Aboriginal people but otherwise to leave them to their own devices. In the absence of formal treaties, the problems of Indigenous–settler relations were met through a combination of state-sponsored violence, cooperation and informal negotiation.

What became the doctrine of *terra nullius* was articulated in tandem with the geographical and demographic expansions of the second quarter of the nineteenth century. It began quietly in a series of legal opinions related to tax and feral animals. In the 1820s it spilled over into new exercises of criminal jurisdiction when Indigenous people were tried in colonial courts either for violence against settlers or for violence against other Aboriginal people (violence *inter se*).[88] In New South Wales and Van Diemen's Land, the first Indigenous Australians were tried for murdering settlers in 1823 and 1826, respectively. Both trials elicited considerable debate about whether Indigenous people could or should be tried in colonial courts. Governor

---

87 Contrast Stuart Banner, *Possessing the Pacific: Land, Settlers, and Indigenous People from Australia to Alaska* (Cambridge, MA: Harvard University Press, 2007), 13–46.

88 See David Andrew Roberts, '"They would speedily abandon the country to the newcomers": The Denial of Aboriginal Rights', in David Andrew Roberts and Martin Crotty (eds), *The Great Mistakes of Australian History* (Sydney: UNSW Press, 2006), pp. 14–31; Ford, *Settler Sovereignty*, pp. 27, 42–54.

Brisbane and Governor Arthur both deployed martial law to control frontier violence in the 1820s – martial law asserted that Aboriginal people were governed by British law at the same time as it authorised the use of military violence against them.[89] Older logics persisted, however. In 1825 the Secretary of State for the Colonies, Lord Bathurst, advised Governor Darling 'to oppose force by force', employing aggression 'in the same manner, as if they proceeded from subjects of any accredited State'.[90] In this state of ambivalence, authorities in New South Wales did not try seriously to control frontier violence with criminal law until 1835, when 20 Indigenous men from Brisbane Waters, to the north of Sydney, were tried for a range of crimes from petty theft to rape.

The assertion that Indigenous people had no laws or land rights derived more clearly from other episodes in expansion. One of the most notorious of these occurred in 1835, when the Port Phillip Association, formed in Van Diemen's Land, signed treaties with the Kulin people of Port Phillip, exchanging some trinkets for either access to or ownership of 600,000 acres of land. In doing so it asserted that Australian Aboriginal people had land rights to sell. Here, it borrowed from the repertoire of North American land speculators who, before the American Revolution, had negotiated private contracts with North American Indian tribes for the sale of land (many with the aid of fraudulent chiefs and alcohol). From 1763 the Empire outlawed these dealings, claiming that it alone had the sovereign capacity to buy land from Indians. When John Batman and his consortium signed the treaty in order to leverage a charter for a proprietary colony, Governor Bourke and the Colonial Office invoked this doctrine of pre-emption, declaring that 'every...treaty, bargain and contract with the Aboriginal Natives...or the possession, title or claim to any Lands...is void and of no effect against the rights of the Crown'.[91] Importantly, however, 'pre-emption' did not necessarily rest on British title to unsettled land, merely on its jurisdiction over British subjects in the colonies.[92] When the eminent jurist, Dr Stephen Lushington, pointed this out and noted that the British crown had engaged in 'no [consistent] act of ownership' of the Port Phillip territory, Imperial administrators were forced to confront the ambiguity of their claims to the continent of Australia: such an argument,

89 Ford, *Settler Sovereignty*, pp. 173–4.
90 Lord Bathurst to Governor Darling, quoted in Ford, *Settler Sovereignty*, p. 174.
91 Proclamation of Governor Bourke, 10 October 1835, The National Archives [TNA], CO 201/247.
92 Arguably sovereign title to land was conflated with 'pre-emption' only after *Johnson v McIntosh* 21 U.S. 543, 5 L.Ed. 681, 8 Wheat. 543 (1823).

after all, might 'apply with equal force to all the waste Lands in any other part of the Colony of New South Wales'.[93]

Arguments about the establishment of South Australia revealed more explicit contradictions in British understandings of Aboriginal legal status in Australia. While the proprietors of South Australia promised to protect Indigenous people against settler abuse, conversations between the South Australian Colonisation Commission and the Colonial Office demonstrated wildly different notions of what protection might entail. Although the 1834 *South Australian Colonisation Act* held the territory to be 'waste and unoccupied', correspondence from the Secretary of State, as well as the Letters Patent issued in February 1836, enjoined the Commissioners to ensure 'the rights of any Aboriginal native…to the actual occupation or enjoyment' of their land. The Commissioners argued in reply that settlement in Australia from the Swan River to Van Diemen's Land had proceeded on the basis that Australian land was 'waste and unoccupied', and that 'unlocated tribes have not arrived at that stage of social improvement, in which a proprietary right to the soil exists'. They argued that Indigenous welfare could only be protected in South Australia by colonial forbearance, not on the basis of Aboriginal rights to land.[94]

Ironically, it was urban violence that prompted the clearest articulations both of Britain's claim to Australian land and of its right to govern Australian Aboriginal people. Settler towns drew in large numbers seeking food, alcohol, cloth and tools, and hoping to meet with colonial officials and with each other. Intertribal and intratribal conflict was therefore a commonplace of colonial urban life around the continent – a commonplace that was not regulated by settler law before the decades of rapid expansion. When the first man was arrested and brought before a court for killing another Aboriginal person in the centre of Sydney in 1829, the Supreme Court refused to hear the case on the grounds that crimes between Indigenous people lay outside the purview of British law. In 1836 the Supreme Court came to a radically different conclusion in the case of Jack Congo Murrell. Citing Vattel, Judge William Burton claimed that British law governed Aboriginal people because they 'had not attained…a position in point of numbers and civilisation…as to be entitled to be recognised as so many sovereign states governed by laws of their own'.[95] He argued that because they did not till soil, hunter-gatherers could not own

93 Ford *Settler Sovereignty*, pp. 180–1.
94 Grey to Torrens, 15 December 1835, TNA CO 13/1; Torrens to Grey, December 1835, TNA CO 13/3.
95 Ford, *Settler Sovereignty*, p. 200.

land; nor could they form political communities or establish binding laws. So Britain could claim absolute ownership of Australia and exercise jurisdiction over everyone who lived there. Indeed, to recognise Indigenous law would be to establish a state within a state – an unacceptable challenge to this modern iteration of British sovereignty. Following the advice of the controversial missionary, Rev. Lancelot Threlkeld, Burton also reasoned that the only way to protect Indigenous people from themselves and from settlers was to bring them decisively under the protection of British law.

This logic of protection came to provide the dominant legal justification for Aboriginal dispossession,[96] but it only provided sporadic legal protection to Aboriginal people on new colonial frontiers. Private and state-sponsored violence remained the primary mode of dispossession hundreds of miles from the centres of colonial governance into the twentieth century, not least because it proved virtually impossible to convict settlers of crimes against Indigenous people. Attempts to legislate for the admission of Aboriginal evidence in British courts failed in New South Wales, Western Australia and South Australia. While 60 Europeans (mostly convicts) were tried for murdering Aboriginal people in New South Wales between 1788 and 1855, most escaped penalty.[97] In Port Phillip only six men faced the courts for the murder of Aboriginal people (in two separate trials in 1843 and 1845). All were acquitted by settler-dominated juries.[98] Even the celebrated conviction of the Myall Creek murderers in 1838 occurred only after the accused men had been tried twice. Moreover, convictions served only to prompt frontier settlers to exercise more discretion in frontier conflicts.

Even the notion that Aboriginal people should be tried for their crimes was openly questioned around Australia for decades after 1836. In Port Phillip in 1841, the bothersome Justice Willis rejected the New South Wales Supreme Court's decision in the Murrell case when considering the fate of the Aboriginal man 'Bonjon' (who murdered a countryman at Geelong in 1841). He decided that no 'express law...makes the Aborigines subject to our Colonial Code'. This urged New South Wales Governor Gipps to seek urgent and final clarification of the matter, and in 1842, the British government, without subjecting the question to legal advice, accepted the extinguishment of Aboriginal sovereignty as 'the Law of the Colony'.[99]

96 For example, *Milirrpum v Nabalco Pty Ltd* (1971), 17 *Federal Law Reports*, 141.
97 Barry Bridges 'The Aborigines and the Law: New South Wales 1788–1855', *Teaching History*, 4, 3 (1970): 40–70.
98 Susanne Davies, 'Aborigines, Murder and the Criminal Law in Early Port Phillip, 1841–1851', *Historical Studies*, 22, 88 (1987): 313–35.
99 Roberts, '"They would speedily abandon the country to the newcomers"', p. 26.

Similar ambivalence prevailed in the remote, convict-free colony of Western Australia, without reference to developments in the eastern colonies. There, the founding governor (Stirling) had previously proclaimed Aboriginal people to be equals of 'other of His Majesty's subjects'.[100] Cases of *inter se* violence brought before the local Court of Quarter Sessions tended to accept that Aboriginal people 'were adopted as British subjects',[101] and thus subject to both protection and prosecution. However, Governor Hutt rejected recommendations made to the British government by George Grey (former resident magistrate in King George Sound, Western Australia) that the protection of Aboriginal people required British law to override customary law.[102] Likewise, key decisions in the 1840s tended to draw a distinction between 'civilised and remote Aborigines' – exercising jurisdiction chiefly over the former.[103]

In South Australia, where Governor Hindmarsh's 1836 Proclamation promised to regard Indigenous people as 'entitled to the privileges of British Subjects', a succession of frontier atrocities challenged the modern logic of sovereignty. In 1840, after Aboriginal people murdered settlers shipwrecked on the remote Coorong, Supreme Court Judge Charles Cooper expressed doubts about the possibility of trying 'a wild and savage tribe...who have never submitted themselves to our dominion'. A police party sent out by Governor Gawler to execute 'summary justice' arrested two Aboriginal men and hanged them on the spot, unleashing a furore over the legality of the proceedings. The local advocate-general (drawing on different parts of Vattel) justified the execution on the grounds that South Australian Aboriginal people were not British subjects. They were entitled to protection only in circumstances where they had acquiesced to or integrated with British settlement. Again, the British law officers declared that Aboriginal people were British subjects, and therefore the Coorong executions were unlawful.[104]

Thus, haltingly, a new consensus emerged about the nature of British sovereignty in Australia. Long-established practices of land grants and sales

100 Stirling's Proclamation, 18 June 1829, in Stannage (ed.), *A New History of Western Australia*, p. 80.
101 See Ann Hunter, 'The Boundaries of Colonial Criminal Law in Relation to Inter-Aboriginal Conflict ("Inter Se Offences") in Western Australia in the 1830s–1840s', *Australian Journal of Legal History*, 8, 2 (2004): 215–36.
102 'Report upon the best means of promoting the civilisation of the aboriginal inhabitants of Australia', in George Grey, *Journals of Two Expeditions of Discovery in North-West and Western Australia*, vol. 2 (London: T. and W. Boone, 1841), pp. 373–88.
103 The key case here was *R v Wemar* 1842, in *Perth Gazette*, 8 January 1842.
104 S.D. Lendrum, 'The "Coorong Massacre": Martial Law and the Aborigines at First Settlement', *Adelaide Law Review*, 6, 1 (1977): 26–43.

came to rest on the notion that Indigenous people had no individual or corporate rights that survived British settlement. Aboriginal protection might be a duty of new settler colonies and Aboriginal people might be temporarily exempted from prosecution or protection under settler law, but these were increasingly understood as concessions made by settlers, not rights enjoyed by Aboriginal people. Assumptions about crown ownership of land governed Aboriginal–settler relations until 1992 and 1996, when the *Mabo* and *Wik* decisions acknowledged the existence of a weak native title over unalienated crown lands and pastoral leases. Some argue that the logic of legal protection still serves to limit the civil rights of Australian Aboriginal and Torres Strait Islander people. From the 1860s, protective regimes exercised broad and arbitrary control over Aboriginal life, limiting their freedom of movement, their right to work, and their capacity to marry. The combination of imperialism and humanitarianism underpinning legal arguments in the 1830s articulated into the coercive regimes of protection instituted in every colony in the late-nineteenth century. In the end, these regimes of control have been the longest lasting artefacts of Australian expansion before 1850.[105]

*

In 1818 Governor Lachlan Macquarie erected an obelisk in the heart of Sydney to mark the meeting point of a network of public roads connecting the colony's various settlements to its outermost stations and outposts. Thirty years later the scale of that project seemed laughable. Between 1820 and 1850 two small settlements around Sydney and Hobart transformed into a truly continental colonial enterprise. Pastoral entrepreneurs stretched geographical boundaries, expanded exports and fed towns. Colonies proliferated around the continent, some dependent on unfree labour, and others formed as havens for free farmers. Administrative and legal expansion controlled convict labour and aided settlers in the project of Aboriginal dispossession. Meanwhile, the growth of new, settler publics paved the way for the representative governments whose investment in economic growth transformed the Australian colonies into some of the most dynamic economies in history.

---

105 Anna Haebich, *Broken Circles: Fragmenting Indigenous Families 1800–2000* (Perth: Fremantle Arts Centre Press, 2000).

6

The advent of self-government, 1840s–90

ANN CURTHOYS AND JESSIE MITCHELL

Prior to British colonisation, Australia was populated by self-governing Aboriginal societies. Linked through kinship and trade, these societies, though sometimes hostile to one another, neither seized each other's land nor sought to exploit the labour of other groups. Their system of government was through transmission of ancestral law, kinship networks and power differences based largely on age and gender, and ceremonies and ritual.[1] If Aboriginal people were self-governing, the British who encountered them thought they lacked government altogether, an idea that was foundational to Britain's proclamation of their lands as settled colonies. Whereas British colonisers in other parts of the world usually had to recognise and negotiate with indigenous systems of government, in the Australian colonies they rarely did so.

This chapter examines the granting of a different system of self-government to most of the Australian colonies in the 1850s and to Western Australia in 1890. It is also concerned with its shadow-side: Aboriginal dispossession, loss of self-government and enforced dependence on colonial charity. Self-government was a complex matter for colonies such as New South Wales and Van Diemen's Land, given their origins as convict settlements. Over time, as the free proportion of the population increased and under pressure from the colonies, Britain had granted elements of what was known as 'representative government': a local parliament, called a legislative council, whose task was to represent 'the people' and make laws on a specified range of matters. While the early legislative councils were nominated and advisory, they grew in size, authority and representativeness as the proportion of elected members increased. Representation by itself, however, was not enough; what mattered was whether the governor (representing the crown) or parliament (representing the people) had control.

---

1 Ian Keen, *Aboriginal Economy and Society: Australia at the Threshold of Colonisation* (Oxford University Press, 2004), p. 389.

In the mid-nineteenth century, imperial and settler interests combined to produce a particular system known as 'responsible government'. Devised originally for the management of Britain's Canadian colonies, it became the means of granting Britain's settler colonies across the globe a measure of political independence while retaining them within the Empire, something Britain had been unable to do with the American colonies in the 1770s. Responsible government entailed the creation in each colony of two houses of parliament with extensive powers, limited only by continuing British control over matters of imperial interest and Britain's (rarely exercised) power of veto over legislation. This system of government was responsible in the same way that ministers in Britain were responsible to the parliament, and relied on its confidence in them for their tenure of office. The position of governor would remain as a link to the crown, but with executive government now comprised of ministers answerable to the elected parliament rather than the governor, the latter's powers were limited.

Australian historians of the origins of responsible government have not typically seen it as having any connection to the contemporaneous displacement and replacement of Aboriginal societies. They debate the relative importance of British and colonial initiative in devising and implementing the new system, the importance of the anti-transportation campaigns and the nature of class conflict within colonial society. Some see the institution of responsible government and thus the shift in power from Britain to the colonies as gradual, uneventful and almost inconsequential. Terry Irving, for example, has suggested there was 'no anti-imperial "struggle for responsible government" in the Australian colonies'; the conflict was rather about who should rule once responsible government had been achieved.[2] At the same time, histories of Aboriginal–settler relations rarely emphasise the transition from British to settler government; indeed, the change often passes unnoticed, although Henry Reynolds notes tellingly that with 'the decision in 1850 to grant the colonies of eastern Australia self-government, the Colonial Office prepared to surrender responsibility for the Aborigines to the very colonists whom they had frequently accused of trying to exterminate the tribes they encountered'.[3] This chapter suggests that the process and memory of dispossession did shape colonists' sense of what it meant to be self-governing Britons,

2 T.H. Irving, '1850–1870', in F.K. Crowley (ed.), *A New History of Australia* (Melbourne: Heinemann, 1974), p. 127.
3 Henry Reynolds, *An Indelible Stain? The Question of Genocide in Australia's History* (Melbourne: Viking, 2001), p. 99.

while the shift in power from centre to periphery was indeed significant to Aboriginal affairs.

The system of responsible government for the settler colonies was developed at a time when British displacement and dispossession of indigenous people was accelerating worldwide. Britons in the settler colonies were demanding political rights in a context in which the economic foundation of their own society was dependent on successful conquest of landscapes and people. Although the peaceful move to responsible government occurred at approximately the same time in five of the six Australian colonies, the process of replacing Aboriginal sovereignty with a new settler society was at a different stage in each; these different conjunctions helped create distinct political cultures. In Tasmania, when responsible government was instituted in 1856, frontier violence had concluded over 25 years earlier, government protection and civilising missions were almost over, and colonists generally expected the Aboriginal Tasmanians would soon be extinct. Across Bass Strait, Victoria had barely emerged from an unusually rapid process of dispossession and displacement, first through pastoralism, then gold and the mixed agricultural and commercial economy that followed. To Victoria's north, New South Wales had by 1856 been the site of Aboriginal social destruction and rapid depopulation for almost 60 years, and still had large northern districts (which would separate to form the new colony of Queensland in 1859) where frontier conflict raged. To Victoria's west, South Australia exhibited an odd hybrid of Christian charity, rule of law and frontier violence, while even further west, the vast territory of Western Australia, with its small settler population, intake of British convicts from 1850 to 1868 and continuing frontier violence, would not be considered fit for responsible government for another 30 years.

The imperial context

Both imperial and colonial thinking about government of the Australian colonies were profoundly affected by events in Britain's other colonies, especially the remaining British colonies in North America. Struggles for political control in Upper and Lower Canada had become so severe that there were unsuccessful armed rebellions in 1837 and 1838. Fearful of losing the rest of its North American colonies, the British government commissioned John Lambton, the first Earl of Durham, to take control as the new governor-general and to investigate the reasons for the political crisis. Durham's resulting *Report on the Affairs of British North America* (1839) recommended that Britain grant a larger measure of self-government to the colonists as a way of maintaining the North American colonies within the Empire and ensuring the continued flow of British immigrants there. Wishing to retain direct imperial control, the government initially rejected the recommendation. In response to continuing unrest and after further negotiation, however, the new Secretary of State for the Colonies, Earl Grey, eventually adopted the basic principles of Durham's report in 1846. He would oversee the institution of responsible government in the Canadas; a system whereby government ministers were answerable to the elected legislature rather than the governor.[4]

Seeing these concessions, colonists elsewhere began to call for the 'Canadian system' of representative government for themselves. In the Cape Colony, which had a nominated legislative council like that which had operated in New South Wales between 1823 and 1843, discontent with the council was so great by 1848 that Cape officials urged the Colonial Office to make constitutional reforms. When the British government announced in 1848 that it would do so, there were extensive debates over the form the new constitution should take, though it would be another five years before a constitution was passed.[5] In New Zealand, too, the political situation was unsettled through the late 1840s, the British government first passing a Constitution Act in 1846 and then suspending it for five years, a key issue being responsibility for relations with the Māori.[6]

In response to pressures at home and abroad, British policy finally shifted from resisting colonial demands for a more representative form of government, to seeking to extend it wherever possible. British statesmen accepted that if British people were to migrate to the colonies, they would expect to enjoy political rights at least to the extent they had in Britain.[7] In addition, Britain wanted to shift the costs of government to the colonists themselves. It was important to keep taxes low at home in order to avoid agitation of the scale of the 1848 revolutions on the European continent.[8] Furthermore, the growth in free-trade policies meant that British policy makers now expected

---

4 John M. Ward, *Colonial Self-Government: The British Experience, 1759–1856* (London: Macmillan, 1976), ch. 8.
5 Stanley Trapido, 'The Origins of the Cape Franchise Qualifications of 1853', *Journal of African History*, 5, 1 (1964): 40.
6 Tony Ballantyne, 'The State, Politics and Power, 1769–1893', in Giselle Byrnes (ed.), *The New Oxford History of New Zealand* (Oxford University Press, 2009), pp. 110–11.
7 Ward, *Colonial Self-Government*, pp. 209–11.
8 Miles Taylor, 'The 1848 Revolutions and the British Empire', *Past and Present*, 166 (2000): 146–80.

that trade rather than tight governmental controls would connect the settler colonies and the mother country.

Political and fiscal devolution to the colonies was only to occur on certain conditions. A commonality of belief and interest, and a civilised political sphere, were considered essential. Colonies with significant convict populations, or divided by religion or race, ought to remain under more direct British control. The political disputes within and between Britain and some of her Australian colonies in the late 1840s and early 1850s were fundamentally over the colonies' purpose. Where transportation of convicts had ended (or, in the case of South Australia, had never been), the question was whether the colonies had developed their settler populations and civil institutions sufficiently to be trusted to govern themselves well.

British birthright

From the 1820s colonists campaigning for more representative forms of government argued that Britons everywhere had the same political and legal rights, an idea Paul Pickering has termed 'popular constitutionalism'.[9] Australian colonists appealed to the history of English government abroad, going back at least to the seventeenth century, when the British crown granted the North American colonies local elective assemblies. They also voiced ideas about innate 'Anglo-Saxon' freedoms, asserted since the Glorious Revolution and revived by the popular Chartist movement, claiming that Anglo-Saxon people, whatever their political disagreements, shared an ancient and instinctive urge towards liberty and good government. This argument had many uses; it could give independent colonists a sense of continuity as well as rupture, and help to absorb other groups such as German migrants into a common civic community.[10] Many thought that just as the elected House of Commons gradually acquired power from the crown and the unelected House of Lords, so the colonies would acquire power from the imperial government.[11] Popular constitutionalism was not republicanism; rather, it was characterised by declarations of loyalty towards home,

9 Paul Pickering, 'Loyalty and Rebellion in Colonial Politics: The Campaign against Convict Transportation in Australia', in Phillip Buckner and R. Douglas Francis (eds), *Rediscovering the British World* (University of Calgary Press, 2005), pp. 98–103.

10 Reginald Horsman, *Race and Manifest Destiny: The Origins of American Racial Anglo-Saxonism* (Cambridge, MA: Harvard University Press, 1981), pp. 9–18, 23, 63; Colin Kidd, 'Race, Empire, and the Limits of Nineteenth-Century Scottish Nationhood', *Historical Journal*, 46, 4 (2003): 873–92.

11 Mark McKenna, *The Captive Republic: A History of Republicanism in Australia 1788–1996* (Cambridge University Press, 1996), p. 31.

and especially towards the unifying figure of Queen Victoria.[12] There was a strand of republicanism in the noisy debates leading up to self-government, notably in the oratory of the fiery Presbyterian minister J.D. Lang and the radical Irish nationalist Daniel Deniehy in New South Wales, but it, too, often appealed to the rights of Britons.[13]

British political rights did not, however, mean democracy as we might now understand it. Opinions varied widely on who should be included in the political sphere, and able to vote for representatives in a legislature. Many thought only men of property could be included, but through the 1840s and 1850s opposition to this class restriction grew. There was also some incorporation of non-British groups, notably the Germans, whose European, Protestant backgrounds were cited as proof that they could be responsible, active subjects. The Irish, despite fears of Roman Catholicism and sometimes Irish republicanism, were also to be included.

Yet even liberals and radicals understood British political rights to be restricted. While feminist movements were beginning in Britain and the United States, in the Australian colonies political life continued to be seen as a peculiarly masculine domain.[14] Furthermore, non-European groups such as the Chinese were to be excluded from the new polity. Colonists assumed that both the indentured Chinese who arrived in New South Wales from 1848 and the gold-rush Chinese immigrants who came to Victoria and New South Wales from 1852 were unable to assimilate and thus to share in the political rights and responsibilities of European colonists. This did not bother conservatives, who were content to include them as cheap and powerless labourers within the lower orders of society, but it worried liberals and radicals, whose view of a more equitable community required racial uniformity. As for Indigenous people, they may have been subject to British law in its punitive or charitable forms, but they were generally seen as outside civilised society, undeserving of rights or recognition – the objects of government,

---

12 Pickering, 'Loyalty and Rebellion in Colonial Politics', pp. 101–3.

13 McKenna, *The Captive Republic*, chs 3–5; Peter Cochrane, *Colonial Ambition: Foundations of Australian Democracy* (Melbourne University Press, 2006), p. 235; Mark McKenna, 'Transplanted to Savage Shores: Indigenous Australians and British Birthright in the Mid Nineteenth Century Australian Colonies', *Journal of Colonialism and Colonial History*, 13, 1 (2012): online.

14 Marilyn Lake, 'The Politics of Respectability: Identifying the Masculinist Context', in Susan Magarey, Sue Rowley and Susan Sheridan (eds), *Debutante Nation: Feminism Contests the 1890s* (Sydney: Allen & Unwin, 1993), pp. 1–15; Angela Woollacott, 'Political Manhood, Non-white Labour and White-settler Colonialism on the 1830s–1840s Australian Frontier', in Alison Holland and Barbara Brookes (eds), *Rethinking the Racial Moment: Essays on the Colonial Encounter* (Newcastle: Cambridge Scholars Publishing, 2011), pp. 75–96.

not its makers. Throughout the 1840s, calls for self-government regularly deployed the language of colonial conquest and racial superiority, as the Catholic *Sydney Chronicle* did in 1848 when it suggested the British government would surely support greater independence for the colonies if they could only see how far New South Wales had developed away from a 'howling wilderness', 'trodden only by the foot of the naked savage'.[15] The 'extinction' believed to be the inevitable and imminent fate of Indigenous people was sometimes given as an argument in favour of settler self-government; soon these colonies would be uniformly white, it was argued, and untroubled by racial divisions.

Towards self-government

The drive towards more representative government gathered pace in the eastern and southern colonies throughout the 1840s. Key sources of discontent were colonists' distance from the seat of government, imperial control over land policy and revenues, and convict transportation. One crisis occurred when the British authorities sought in 1844 to increase revenue from the sale and lease of land. The squatters, accustomed to seizing land from Aboriginal occupants and then occupying it for a low rent, were outraged, and noted that their loyalty to Britain was being sorely tested. Such talk evaporated, however, when their demands for security of land tenure at low rent were largely met in 1846.[16] Henceforth it was more likely to be the growing middle and working classes, some of them influenced by British Chartism, who would lead the demands for greater political freedoms. Giving expression to these radical aspirations was the Constitutional Association, formed in Sydney in December 1848 by democrats following a Chartist program, and the radical newspaper, the *People's Advocate*. Their demands included manhood suffrage, vote by ballot, more frequent elections and 'one man one vote'.[17]

One of the first problems they faced was the question of convict transportation. The system had long been controversial, especially since the 1837 Molesworth inquiry in Britain, which described transportation as degenerate and harmful, infecting free society with its vices. Throughout the British world, the anti-slavery arguments of the 1820s and early 1830s had been adapted to apply to other forms of unfree labour, including convict and indentured Indian and Chinese labour. Although some pastoralists wanted

15 *Sydney Chronicle*, 27 January 1848.
16 McKenna, *The Captive Republic*, pp. 36–9.
17 Ibid., p. 42.

continued access to convict labour, they struggled against the growing number of local activists who said penal labour kept free workers away, cost exorbitant amounts for police and gaols, and was a source of moral pestilence and sexual depravity.[18] The Whig government in Britain decided to abolish transportation to New South Wales in 1840 but to maintain it to Van Diemen's Land, where it would be reorganised and transformed. Despite substantial transportation to the latter colony in the 1840s, Britain still had a large and growing convict population, exacerbated by rising social turmoil in the wake of the Irish famine. In 1847 the Secretary of State for the Colonies, Earl Grey, decided to resume transportation to New South Wales (and introduce it to the Cape Colony), though this time the convicts would have already served part of their sentences in Britain and were to be called 'exiles'.

By 1849 the colonies were in uproar over the issue. Free immigration to both New South Wales and Van Diemen's Land had grown during the 1840s, bringing with it a more balanced sex ratio, increased marriage rate and a growing desire for respectability and political representation. Under the leadership of John West and his *Launceston Examiner*, an Anti-Transportation League was formed in Van Diemen's Land in January 1849. The League held huge public meetings in Hobart and Launceston, and sent petitions that in opposing transportation included a plea for a more representative system of government.[19] The League spread to the mainland after ships bringing 'exiles' arrived in Melbourne and Sydney.[20] One, the *Hashemy*, was greeted with a massive protest meeting on 11 June 1849 when it arrived in Sydney; although most of its convicts landed in Sydney and the rest in Moreton Bay, this was to be the last ship to bring convicts to New South Wales. Even employers who had appreciated cheap convict labour began to oppose transportation as deleterious to the development of a free and virtuous society.

Although less controversial than convict transportation, Aboriginal policy issues also helped create colonial dissatisfaction with the existing system of government. This became plainest in the late 1830s and 1840s, when local colonists' determination to consolidate their power over this newly seized land clashed with humanitarian concerns in Britain about the violent treatment of colonised people. These concerns were briefly influential in the British

18 Kirsten McKenzie, *Scandal in the Colonies: Sydney and Cape Town, 1820–1850* (Melbourne University Press, 2004), pp. 122–6, 142–52.

19 Ibid., pp. 172–3; L.L. Robson, *A History of Tasmania, Volume 1. Van Diemen's Land from the Earliest Times to 1855* (Oxford University Press, 1983), pp. 484–6, 491–502.

20 A.G.L. Shaw, *A History of the Port Phillip District: Victoria before Separation* (Melbourne University Press, 2003), pp. 153, 177–8.

government, especially after the House of Commons accepted many of the recommendations of the Report of the Select Committee on Aborigines (British Settlements) in 1836–7, which called for greater protection of native people from dispossession and destruction. Tensions between colonists and the British government became plain in 1838, when Governor Gipps tried to assert the rule of law over the frontier, pushing for the trial of twelve white men accused of the massacre at Myall Creek. The conviction and hanging of seven of the killers, greeted with outrage, was seen as proof of imperial interference in settlers' lives. This resentment, in turn, influenced the public response to another imperial initiative arising from the 1837 Report, the arrival of Aboriginal protectors to the Port Phillip District in 1839. The new protectors were opposed by local colonists, not only because their task was to help protect and represent the interests of Aboriginal people but also because they were unelected officials, representatives of a distant government. Discontented with being governed by a superintendent, Charles La Trobe, who was answerable only to the governor, and the Legislative Council, both far away in Sydney, the settlers of the Port Phillip District, who prided themselves on their free, liberal enterprise which had built up the district from a state of 'original savagery', were campaigning for separation from New South Wales. They cited the unwelcome presence of the protectorate as subverting 'the principles of the British constitution'.[21] The protectorate met with so much opposition that it ended in the late 1840s and settlement continued with little protection of Aboriginal people. By this time it had become popular colonial wisdom that Aboriginal people could not adopt British ways and would soon disappear. Aboriginal issues had thus largely been resolved in favour of the pastoralists by the time responsible government became a serious possibility.

The *Australian Colonies Government Act* (1850) and the colonial constitutions

As British policy towards the Australian colonies began to favour responsible government, colonials jostled for position. The conservatives wanted to ensure they remained in charge, while democrats feared the new system might entrench an oligarchy.[22] When news of the *Australian Colonies Government Act* finally arrived in Sydney in October 1850, the reaction was

---

21 *Port Phillip Herald*, 8 December 1840, 21 May 1841.
22 Cochrane, *Colonial Ambition*, p. 231.

mixed. Political reformers in New South Wales were disappointed – the Act did not authorise the hoped-for introduction of responsible government. It did, however, lay some foundational provisions that colonists in the future could use to seek to change their constitutions, in particular to create both an upper and a lower house on the British model. The Act also separated the Port Phillip District into a new colony called Victoria, and brought the political institutions in Van Diemen's Land, South Australia, and Victoria into line with those operating in New South Wales since 1843. That is, the legislative councils in all four colonies would now be two-thirds elected (on a limited property-based franchise) and one-third nominated by the governor. The new councils also gained the power that New South Wales had acquired seven years earlier to legislate on certain matters, such as the electoral system, local government, customs duties and the judiciary.[23]

Importantly, the Act widened the electorate for the legislative councils, extending the vote to all squatters, and significantly reducing the property requirements for eligibility to vote. Now those who owned freehold worth £100 or, significantly, who occupied dwellings worth £10 a year in rent, could vote. The House of Lords had passed this remarkably democratic measure because it had been convinced by Robert Lowe, a leading political figure in the colony recently returned to Britain, that a wider franchise would increase the immigrant influence in colonial politics and thus offset the influence of former convicts, the emancipists. On this count at least, the conservatives were dismayed and the liberals and democrats pleased.[24]

Lacking any reference to Aboriginal policy, the Act intimated that, with self-government, Britain would cease to be involved in it. The exclusion was not an oversight; when the government had been considering the Bill's provisions, the Aborigines Protection Society in London, concerned that there was no provision 'for imparting to the Natives the privileges enjoyed by British subjects', had visited the Secretary of State. The new constitutions, it urged him, should provide for Aboriginal possession of 'an adequate portion of the land of which they once had the undisputed possession', and be framed so that distinctions of race and colour should 'no longer operate against them'.[25] The government's reply was that as Aboriginal people were British subjects,

---

23 Irving, '1850–70', p. 127.
24 See J.B. Hirst, *The Strange Birth of Colonial Democracy: New South Wales, 1848–1884* (Sydney: Allen & Unwin, 1988), p. 26; Cochrane, *Colonial Ambition*, pp. 256–7.
25 Quoted in Julie Evans, Patricia Grimshaw, David Phillips, Shurlee Swain, *Equal Subjects, Unequal Rights: Indigenous Peoples in British Settler Colonies, 1830–1910* (Manchester University Press, 2003), pp. 67–8.

they would automatically gain the vote on the same basis as others. Nothing else was needed.

In New South Wales, the colony that had benefited least from the 1850 Act, there was lively debate over the colony's future. The campaign against transportation continued, as colonists sought confirmation that New South Wales would not again become a convict colony. So intense was the atmosphere of protest – mass meetings attracted up to 10,000 people – that conservatives began to fear rebellion.[26] Women, perhaps particularly concerned with morality and the protection of family life, were at times involved in this movement, producing in the early months of 1851 a Ladies Petition, and attending public meetings of the Anti-Transportation League.[27]

The two issues – opposition to transportation and the granting of responsible government – converged in an atmosphere of unrest. By December 1851, after elections that introduced more liberal-minded members, the New South Wales Legislative Council finally joined in the agitation and addressed a petition (in 'Declaration, Protest and Remonstrance') to the British government seeking approval to draw up a constitution along Canadian lines.[28] The mood was even more intense in Van Diemen's Land, which was still receiving large numbers of convicts. At the first elections for the new blended Legislative Council in 1851, anti-transportationists were successful. Even settlers who benefited from convict labour began to realise that a penal colony could not expect to receive more representative forms of government.[29]

The year 1852 would prove a watershed in the campaign to end transportation and introduce self-government. The gold rushes in Victoria and New South Wales were escalating, large anti-transportation meetings were held in Hobart, Melbourne and Sydney, and a select committee of the New South Wales Legislative Council began debating the shape of a new constitution. In Britain, the government changed from Whig to Tory in May, and then in December to a coalition of Whigs and Peelites, a breakaway group from the Tories. In the last days of the short-lived Tory government, on 15 December 1852, the Secretary of State, Sir John Pakington, announced to Governor FitzRoy a major change in British policy on both issues. Convict transportation to Van Diemen's Land would end, the dispatch noting the 'strong repugnance' of colonists towards the system. In addition, the British government

26 McKenna, *The Captive Republic*, pp. 56, 57.
27 Cochrane, *Colonial Ambition*, pp. 249, 309.
28 Ward, *Colonial Self-Government*, pp. 298–9.
29 W.A. Townsley, *Tasmania: From Colony to Statehood* (Hobart: St David's Park 1991), pp. 62, 91.

would allow the four eastern Australian colonies to devise constitutions similar to that of the United Canadas, including, most importantly, the control and disposal of crown lands.[30] Among other things, Pakington's dispatch cited 'those extraordinary discoveries of Gold which have lately taken place in some of the Australian Colonies' as a reason for the British government's change in thinking: these discoveries had 'imparted new and unforeseen features to their political and social condition' such that self-government was now entirely feasible.[31] In the following year, the Duke of Newcastle, having replaced Pakington as Secretary of State for the Colonies, wrote a further dispatch, withdrawing the earlier requirement that the new constitutions must provide for a nominated upper house; the colonies could now decide for themselves how their upper house would be formed.[32]

When the news of these two decisions arrived in the colonies in May 1853, colonists were overjoyed. Attention now turned to the shape of the new constitutions. With the British government open to substantial change in the way its Australian colonies were governed, and with immigration and economic diversification strengthening the number and hand of the democrats, the conservatives in the colonies were suddenly under pressure. W.C. Wentworth, who in his long parliamentary career had moved from being a leading radical to an outspoken conservative, suggested the creation of an upper house with a hereditary membership on the model of the House of Lords, to act as a buffer against excessive democracy.[33] His proposal was memorably laughed out of court, and ridiculed at a mass meeting in Sydney by the young colonial-born republican, Daniel Deniehy, as creating a 'bunyip aristocracy'. The Council eventually settled on a compromise: an upper house to be nominated by the governor on the advice of the Executive Council, and a lower house with broad but not universal franchise and a distribution of seats skewed to favour pastoralist interests. The malapportionment of electorates, whereby rural seats had considerably fewer voters than urban ones, was deeply embedded in British precedent, and was to continue as a State practice long after Federation.

Victoria reached a somewhat different solution. Here, the colonists were used to asserting their status as successful, free entrepreneurs, proud of their

---

30 Ward, *Colonial Self-Government*, p. 296.
31 Despatch from Pakington to FitzRoy, 15 December 1852, in The National Archives [TNA], CO 201/450.
32 Douglas Pike, *Paradise of Dissent: South Australia 1829–1857*, 2nd edn (Melbourne University Press, 1967), p. 468.
33 See Andrew Tink, *William Charles Wentworth: Australia's Greatest Native Son* (Sydney: Allen & Unwin, 2009), pp. 229–43.

achievements and confident of their capacity to govern themselves. After the discovery of gold in 1851, Victoria quickly developed an educated middle class and an environment that fostered literacy, education and political liberalism and radicalism. While a select committee appointed by the Legislative Council in September 1852 was deliberating on Victoria's new constitution, there was a surge in democratic politics, especially after the miners' protests that culminated in the Eureka rebellion of December 1854. The result was a proposed constitution that attempted to balance conservative and democratic interests. The Assembly was to be elected on a wide franchise and the Council elected by those with property worth £1,000; both were to have an electoral distribution favouring conservative rural seats and a property qualification for membership – £2,000 for the Assembly and £5,000 for the Council.[34] Like the other colonies, Victoria had created a system of 'strong bicameralism', whereby the two parliamentary houses had roughly equal powers, though money bills had to originate in the Assembly, and Council could reject, but not alter, them.

When South Australians campaigned for political rights, they spoke, like their countrymen everywhere, of themselves as Britons, heirs to a unique tradition of liberty and independence. They also articulated a sense that their colony was special – liberal, intelligently planned and free of the 'stain' of convict labour. Britain had promised them representative (though not responsible) government as soon as the white population was large enough; the figure nominated in 1834 and confirmed in the *South Australia Government Act* of 1842 was 50,000. Political progress was thus closely linked to population growth, and beyond that to economic development, both of which entailed the continued process of dispossession, displacement of Indigenous people and their replacement by settlers for purposes of pastoralism, agriculture, mining and commerce.[35] In the 1840s there had been some attempt to implement the new British policy of Aboriginal protection, with the appointment of a protector and the establishment of some schools, some provision of rations as compensation for dispossession, and some land grants for farming, but these protection policies were largely abandoned by the 1850s.[36]

---

34 Geoffrey Serle, *The Golden Age: A History of the Colony of Victoria, 1851–1861* (Melbourne University Press, 1963), p. 148.
35 John M. Ward, 'The Responsible Government Question in Victoria, South Australia and Tasmania, 1851–1856', *Journal of the Royal Australian Historical Society*, 63, 4 (1978): 231.
36 Charles Rowley, *The Destruction of Aboriginal Society* (Melbourne: Penguin, 1970), pp. 82–5.

During the extensive public debate over the form their new constitution should take, a select committee on constitutional reform was unable to reach agreement.[37] Under pressure and promises from Governor Young (who among other things withheld knowledge that the Council now had a free choice as to the nature of the upper house), the Legislative Council in 1853 passed a conservative constitution, with an upper house nominated for life. After news of widespread popular protests and Young's deceptions reached Britain, the Secretary of State for the Colonies returned the proposed constitution to the colony and insisted that a new Legislative Council be elected. The elections that followed in 1855 were highly successful for the reformers. The Constitution Act proclaimed in South Australia in 1856 was thus more democratic than the others, providing for universal male suffrage in the lower house and a franchise open to those with either £50 per annum property or paying rent over £20 per annum for the upper house. In addition, the constitution placed a ban on the practice of multiple voting, which in every other colony allowed wealthy men to vote in several districts.[38] Thus a relatively liberal system emerged with little popular division.

The confident liberalism that seemed so successful in South Australia and Victoria encountered much greater resistance in Van Diemen's Land. The population stagnated as many left for the Victorian goldfields, and the colony entered a period of economic depression.[39] As late as 1851, three-quarters of adult men were, or had been, prisoners, co-existing uneasily with a free upper class that enjoyed a privileged status.[40] The Aboriginal population was declining so rapidly that talk of its inevitable disappearance became commonplace. The Flinders Island settlement had closed in 1847, and its replacement at Oyster Cove saw further depopulation in the 1850s, as the authorities neglected it and the residents became ill and died, and failed to reproduce. Meanwhile, the conservative lieutenant-governor, William Denison, was opposed to responsible government and managed to minimise the influence of the Council's elected members.[41] The constitution proposed by the

37 Irving '1850–70', p. 32.
38 P.A. Howell, 'Constitutional and Political Development, 1857–1890', in Jaensch (ed.), *The Flinders History of South Australia*, pp. 116–17; Anna Munyard, 'Making a Polity: 1837–1857', in Dean Jaensch (ed.) *The Flinders History of South Australia: Political History* (Adelaide: Wakefield Press, 1986), pp. 67–72.
39 Wray Vamplew (ed.), *Australians: Historical Statistics* (Sydney: Fairfax, Syme & Weldon Associates, 1987), p. 28; see also Henry Reynolds, *A History of Tasmania* (Cambridge University Press, 2012), p. 170.
40 James Boyce, *Van Diemen's Land* (Melbourne: Black Inc., 2008), pp. 158–74, 183, 217, 224–5, 236–40.
41 Robson, *A History of Tasmania*, vol. 1, p. 520; Townsley, *Tasmania: From Colony to Statehood*, pp. 45–6.

Legislative Council in 1854 was the least liberal of the four the British government received at this time. The franchise for the Assembly was to be property-based, aimed at educated and successful men, and even more so for the Council, which furthermore had extensive powers and was to be chosen not through a general election but in a series of elections at which only one-third of the seats were up for election.[42] Nevertheless, when the arrival of responsible government was celebrated in 1856, there was a sense of a new beginning, augmented by British agreement to change the colony's name to Tasmania. The change had been advocated by the anti-transportationists, who were anxious to put the convict and Aboriginal past behind them.[43]

When the four proposed constitutions were discussed in the British parliament in mid-1855, they were passed with relatively minor amendments. The main change was that Britain retained its power of veto over internal colonial matters. In discussions within the Colonial Office and in the government, one of the reasons given for retaining the veto was the colonies' possible treatment of Aboriginal people and non-European immigrants.[44] However, that veto would be used sparingly in subsequent decades, and Aboriginal affairs were in effect left entirely to the colonial governments.

Queensland gained self-government, and indeed its existence as a separate colony, by a different route. Here, the democratic spirit so evident in South Australia, Victoria and New South Wales was far less apparent. Frontier violence still raged, and in 1852 convicts and ticket-of-leave men still comprised about a third of the white male population.[45] The question of transportation provoked some angry public debate, with pastoralists facing a shortage of free immigrant workers and turning first to convict and later to Indian and Chinese indentured labour, while middle and working-class townspeople complained that squatters were tying up the land and hindering free migration. Racial violence was common, particularly against the Chinese.[46] Like their southern counterparts, the northern squatters were unnerved by the rise of democratic politics in Sydney, especially its demands for land reform; they wanted, as Maurice French has put it, 'good government (by themselves), not self-government (by the masses)'.[47] At an inquiry held in 1858 in the New South Wales legislature

42 Reynolds, *A History of Tasmania*, pp. 65–675.
43 *Hobart Mercury*, 25 February 1856; Robson, *History of Tasmania*, vol. 1, p. 521.
44 Serle, *The Golden Age*, pp. 197–8.
45 Raymond Evans, *A History of Queensland* (Cambridge University Press, 2007), p. 61.
46 Ibid., pp. 65–6, 75
47 Maurice French, 'Squatters and Separation: A Synoptic Overview', *Queensland History Journal*, 20, 13 (2010): 806, 809.

into the workings of the Native Mounted Police in the north, rural colonists voiced their determination to proceed with the seizure of land and their impatient rejection of any authorities in Sydney who might fail to support them.[48]

It was not only the settlers who thought separation would serve them best; the Colonial Office had been considering it since 1840 as a means of exerting greater control over this large territory. Even though the non-Indigenous population was little over half the 50,000 that had been stipulated for South Australia's entitlement to self-government, and frontier violence was increasing rather than decreasing, the British government agreed in 1857 to accept the northern settlers' demands for separation. Since separation and responsible government would be introduced together, there was no representative body to draft the new constitution. Instead, Britain drafted an Order in Council to establish the new colony with the same constitution as that of New South Wales.[49] After prolonged debate over where the border should be drawn, northern colonists received word in July 1859 that their separation had been approved by the home government, and in December it became official with the arrival of Governor Bowen. The new name, Queensland, was chosen by Queen Victoria herself.[50]

Extending democracy

The new constitutions varied, but they all allowed for an Assembly elected on a generous but not universal franchise. They also enabled the parliaments to make further democratic reforms as they wished. Governments in Victoria, New South Wales and South Australia did so rapidly, while those in Tasmania and Queensland, with their smaller and less democratically inclined populations, were far more resistant to electoral reform. One reform, however, that all the colonies shared was the introduction of the secret ballot, a Chartist demand intended to make elections fairer and more orderly that was supported by radicals and liberals alike. This method of voting was adopted for the first elections under responsible government in Tasmania, Victoria and South Australia in 1856, and then by New South Wales in 1858, Queensland

48 'Report from the Select Committee on Murders by the Aborigines on the Dawson River together with the proceedings of the committee, minutes of evidence and appendix, 1858', *Votes and Proceedings of the New South Wales Legislative Council*, 1858.

49 George Shaw, '"Filched from us...": The Loss of Universal Manhood Suffrage in Queensland 1859–1863', *Australian Journal of Politics and History*, 26, 3 (1980): 372–3.

50 Evans, *A History of Queensland*, p. 77.

with separation in 1859, and Western Australia (still without responsible government) in 1877.[51]

The colonies differed, however, on who was allowed to vote for the Assembly. South Australia already had manhood suffrage, and it was introduced in Victoria in 1857 and New South Wales in 1858. In Queensland the Order in Council, having in error granted separation on the basis of the New South Wales arrangements as they were in 1856, the first elections in May 1860 were held on a more restrictive franchise than those of the previous year, which had been based on the much more democratic 1858 arrangements.[52] While the new Queensland legislature now had the power to restore universal male franchise, its conservative composition meant that it chose not to do so. To the same end, successive ministries increased the imbalance in the size of rural and urban electorates, until by 1872 some 30 of the 42 electorates were dominated by pastoral interests.[53] In such a situation, universal manhood suffrage posed little threat to those interests, and it was restored in 1872.[54] Voting rights were removed from Aboriginal people in 1885, however, and Queensland was the only colony at this time to make this exclusion explicit by legislation.

In Tasmania democratic reform took longer still. Responsible government in its first years of operation was shaky; there were six ministries between 1856 and 1861, as well as personal factionalism and tension between the Legislative Assembly and the Council.[55] Population growth remained slow, the government suffered from a chronic revenue shortage, and by the 1860s the colony entered an economic recession.[56] The strong centralised bureaucracy that had developed during the penal era withered away after 1856, as the colony's elite preferred to devolve responsibility to local bodies, charities and private businesses.[57] With only weak forces seeking political reform, it was not until 1900, with the advent of Federation, that Tasmania introduced universal manhood suffrage.[58]

51 Peter Brent, 'The Australian Ballot: Not the Secret Ballot', *Australian Journal of Political Science*, 41, 1 (2006): 41–2.
52 Shaw, '"Filched from Us"', p. 373.
53 Ibid., p. 384.
54 John Hirst, *Australia's Democracy: A Short History* (Sydney: Allen & Unwin, 2002), p. 58.
55 Townsley, *Tasmania from Colony to Statehood*, pp. 97–105, 112–13.
56 Bruce Felmingham, 'Economy', in Alison Alexander (ed.), *The Companion to Tasmanian History* (Hobart: Centre for Tasmanian Historical Studies, 2005), p. 421.
57 Stefan Petrow, 'The State', in Alexander (ed.), *The Companion to Tasmanian History*, pp. 484–5.
58 Reynolds, *A History of Tasmania*, p. 225.

Western Australia

The debates over self-government occurred 30 years later in Western Australia, in a quite different imperial context. Yet this was by no means an afterthought in the story of colonial self-government. In its specificity, it highlights many issues that the histories of the other colonies tend to take for granted: why colonists wanted self-government, and the place of Aboriginal people and policy in the new constitutions. In Western Australia the connections between self-government and Aboriginal–settler relations were explicit, different and illuminating.

Two years after convict transportation finally ended in 1868, Western Australia gained a part-nominated, part-elected Legislative Council of the kind the other colonies had had until the mid-1850s. For the time being, this system suited the most powerful and wealthy settlers. They feared that if the doors of parliament were opened to people without property – a likely consequence of a fully elected and responsible government – it might hinder the economic growth they wanted.[59] In short, it was better to negotiate with a governor than a working class. In any case, responsible government would mean additional costs. In this frame of mind, the Legislative Council in 1878 rejected a resolution for responsible government moved by the recently elected member for Perth, Stephen Henry Parker.[60] For its part, the Colonial Office in Britain was wary of surrendering control of so much territory to so few people; there were only 8,000 non-Aboriginal adults in Western Australia in 1874, of whom two-thirds had convict antecedents, and some of whom had been themselves convicts.[61]

The Council's attitude began to change in the mid-1880s as a result of major changes in the composition and economic character of the colony. As exports of wool, pearl products and timber grew, the pastoralists, pearlers and other employers demanded an extension of infrastructure such as railways, telegraph and shipping facilities.[62] Such projects necessitated large-scale government borrowing, and by the mid-1880s the colony's public debt had

---

59 Brian de Garis, 'Constitutional and Political Development, 1870–1890', in David Black (ed.), *The House on the Hill: A History of the Parliament of Western Australia 1832–1990* (Perth: Parliament of Western Australia, 1991), p. 52.

60 Ibid, p. 53.

61 A.C.V. Melbourne, 'The Establishment of Responsible Government', in J. Holland Rose, A.P. Newton and E.A. Benians, with Ernest Scott (eds), *The Cambridge History of the British Empire*, vol. VII, part 1: *Australia* (Cambridge University Press, 1933), p. 293.

62 Geoffrey Bolton, *Land of Vision and Mirage: Western Australia since 1826* (Perth: UWA Press, 2008), pp. 45–9.

doubled.[63] Gold discoveries in 1885 and an increase in free immigration enhanced economic development and led to a more diverse population, which wanted an extension of democracy.[64] Yet there were still very few immigrant or white workers in the pastoral industry, leading to the forced labour of Aboriginal people, often under brutal conditions. These conditions became contentious, especially after John Gribble, a missionary in the north, caused a storm in 1885 by publicising what he had witnessed: prisoners in chains and a system of labour contract that bordered on slavery.[65] Enraged settlers circulated a petition for his removal; the Church of England withdrew his missionary licence and closed his Gascoyne mission, and the Legislative Council hysterically denounced him.[66] Concerned by Gribble's and other similar claims, and under pressure from the Colonial Office, Governor Broome brought forward an *Aborigines Protection Act* in 1886.[67] Under its provisions, an Aborigines Protection Board was created.

At around the same time, the call for responsible government was becoming a bipartisan movement as the colonial elite began to think it might suit their purposes. The existing system of government, with its unstable relationship between the executive, the legislature and the judiciary, was in disrepute, especially after an extended bitter personal dispute between the Governor and the Chief Justice, Alexander Onslow.[68] Colonial pastoralists and businessmen wanted the government to raise loans for infrastructure development that were much larger than the British government would approve; they also wanted more control than Britain would allow over the sale and lease of crown land.[69] With popular democratic sentiment growing in the towns, and the colonial elite changing its views, the time at last seemed ripe for change. The Legislative Council passed a resolution favouring responsible government on 6 July 1887, and soon afterwards a Constitution Act with rather conservative provisions: a franchise based on strict property and residency requirements, plural voting and unequal electorates for the

---

63 Ibid., p. 46.
64 de Garis, 'Constitutional and Political Development', p. 55.
65 Neville Green, 'From Princes to Paupers: The Struggle for Control of Aborigines in Western Australia 1887–1898', *Early Days*, 11, 4 (1998): 448; Henry Reynolds, *This Whispering in our Hearts* (Sydney: Allen & Unwin, 1998), p. 163.
66 Su-Jane Hunt, 'The Gribble Affair: A Study in Colonial Politics', appendix to J.B. Gribble, *Dark Deeds in a Sunny Land* (Perth: UWA Press, 1987), pp. 65–7; Neville Green, 'Aborigines and White Settlers in the Nineteenth Century', in C.T. Stannage (ed.), *A New History of Western Australia* (Perth: UWA Press, 1981), pp. 101–3.
67 Reynolds, *This Whispering in Our Hearts*, p. 171
68 de Garis, 'Constitutional and Political Development', p. 54.
69 N.E. Smith and M. Rafferty, *Parliamentary Control of the Public Purse: Development of the Westminster System and its Application in Western Australia* (Perth: The Treasury, 1984), p. 39.

Assembly, and a Council that was to be appointed and then elected when the population reached a certain size.

Broome now emerged as a negotiator between the colonists and the Colonial Office, which by this time had a more cautious approach to responsible government than it had had in the 1850s. The interim period had seen some spectacular failures in colonial government as well as successes. Britain wanted to avoid mistakes such as those in New Zealand, Jamaica and Natal, where local settlers had provoked indigenous people to wars and uprisings costly to Britain. The Colonial Office also worried that responsible government in Western Australia would mean handing over to very small settler population huge tracts of land that perhaps ought to be kept for wider imperial purposes. It wanted to divide the colony into two, so that Britain could directly control land north of the 26th parallel. In order to allay British fears of settler treatment of Aboriginal people, and using his previous experience as colonial secretary in Natal, Broome suggested that if the constitution made special provision for Aboriginal people, responsible government could be granted without qualm. The Aborigines Protection Board could continue to be responsible directly to the governor and be funded by a reserved annual sum of £5,000 set aside from public revenues, to convert to one per cent of the annual revenue of the colony when it exceeded £500,000.[70] Though most speakers in the Legislative Council opposed these clauses, they passed the Bill as the price for responsible government. In 1890 the new governor, William Robinson, arrived to proclaim the new constitution.[71]

No sooner had the new constitution been put in place than pressure mounted for universal male suffrage for the Assembly, intensified by the gold rushes in Coolgardie and Kalgoorlie in 1893, which attracted over 100,000 people to the colony. The *Constitution Act Amendment Act* of 1893 removed the property qualification for white male voters, but, in the context of the intensely racial thinking of the time, retained it for 'aboriginal natives' of Australia, Asia, and Africa, and people of mixed descent.[72]

Responsible government did not bring with it the erasure of Aboriginal people the colonists confidently expected. The control of Aboriginal people and destruction of Aboriginal identity and society were to become an enduring and troubling concern. For their part, Aboriginal people did not share the colonists' idea that they belonged only to the past. As violent conflict

---

70 de Garis, 'Constitutional and Political Development', p. 57.
71 P.J. Boyce, 'The Governors of Western Australia under Representative Government 1870–1890', in *University Studies in History* (Perth: UWA Press, 1961–2), pp. 101–43.
72 Evans et al., *Equal Subjects, Unequal Rights*, p. 139.

came to an end, Aboriginal groups continued to assert their presence, and developed non-violent modes of making claims, through storytelling, performance, addresses, letters, petitions and protests. They never lost their desire to re-establish a system of self-government of their own, though now it would be in new circumstances.

7

The gold rushes of the 1850s

DAVID GOODMAN

The 1850s gold rushes in eastern Australia occurred in a post-invasion landscape. Aboriginal people had so recently been in possession of the lands on which gold was discovered that contemporaries quite naturally compared the new invaders' mode of living to that of the Indigenous inhabitants. A reporter sent to Australia's first significant gold rush at Ophir in New South Wales in 1851 noted that 'the whole settlement has the appearance of a vast aboriginal camp'.[1] An observer of the Ballarat diggings in Victoria in 1856 wrote that 'a solitary tree here and there, and prostrate trunks lying about, proclaimed the recent nature of the invasion of the haunts of the wildman by the gold-seekers'.[2] The gold rushes were, among other things, an extraordinarily effective invasion: it is difficult to think of anything else that would have populated the newly taken land so rapidly, with such numbers, so heedless of what lay in their way.

Discoveries and rushes

It was Edward Hargraves, returning in January 1851 from the California gold rush to New South Wales, who most single-mindedly tried to provoke a gold rush in Australia. With a small group of men he found gold in a creek near Bathurst in February 1851. Leaving the others to dig, Hargraves returned to Sydney; by April his party had four ounces of gold. He notified the New South Wales government of his find, and gave the *Sydney Morning Herald* the story. Soon newspapers were reporting the effects of the news: a *Herald* correspondent found the 'gold mania' in Bathurst 'still more violent than in Sydney' and speculated that there must be gold in 'unlimited

---

1 *Maitland Mercury and Hunter River General Advertiser*, 31 May 1851.
2 'The Past and Present of Ballaarat', (Sydney) *Empire*, 21 October 1856.

quantities, if such gold fields are scattered over such an extent of country as is reported'.[3]

Hargraves was feted and rewarded as first discoverer of gold, but his real achievement was in publicity. The London *Times* noted that, in addressing himself 'to the public instead of the Government', he had brought the discovery to the attention of the world.[4] Hargraves freely admitted that his public relations skills were greater than his geological acumen or mining expertise, and that his 'only intention' was 'to make the discovery and rely upon the Government and the country for my reward'.[5] In fact, Australian gold had been both discovered and predicted many times before 1851: the New South Wales government surveyor James McBrien reported a discovery in 1823; the zoologist John Lhotsky located gold in the Monaro region in 1834; Count Paul Strzelecki reported his 1839 find to New South Wales governor Sir George Gipps; the Rev. W.B. Clarke, a geologist, also reported a discovery in 1844 and from 1847 attempted to draw public attention to the existence of gold.[6] In London, the geologist, Sir Roderick Murchison, studied these reports and Strzelecki's specimens. In 1846 he not only predicted, on the basis of geological similarities with the Urals in Russia, that there would be gold in the Australian Great Dividing Range, but also urged the emigration of unemployed Cornish miners to look for it.[7] Years of acrimony between Murchison and Clarke followed, a classic contest between an imperial expert (who had never been to Australia) and a colonial informant with his own claims to expertise. Murchison's career prospered from the success of his prediction. He became the acknowledged imperial authority on gold; his followers, however, also absorbed his erroneous prediction that Australian gold lay mainly near the surface and diminished at depth.[8] Clarke had studied geology at Cambridge, but lacked access to academic outlets and published much of his work in Sydney newspapers. Considering these competing claims to priority, the nineteenth-century historian George Rusden concluded diplomatically

3 Edward Hammond Hargraves, *Australia and Its Goldfields* (London: H. Ingram and Co., 1855), ch. 4; *Sydney Morning Herald*, 28 May 1851.
4 Geoffrey Blainey, 'The Gold Rushes: The Year of Decision', *Historical Studies Australia and New Zealand*, 10, 38 (1962): 129–32; *The Times*, 16 January 1854.
5 Simpson Davison, *The Gold Deposits in Australia* (London: Longman, Green, Longman and Roberts, 1861), p. 294.
6 'William Branwhite Clarke', *Australian Dictionary of Biography*, vol. 3, pp. 420–2.
7 Davison, *The Gold Deposits in Australia*, pp. 271–2.
8 Robert A. Stafford, 'The Long Arm of London: Sir Roderick Murchison and Imperial Science in Australia', in R.W. Home (ed.), *Australian Science in the Making* (Cambridge University Press, 1988), pp. 74–6.

that stumblers upon gold were as entitled to credit as speculators about its likely existence.[9]

The first gold rushes in New South Wales were north and west of Bathurst, over the Blue Mountains from Sydney. Soon, a committee was offering a reward for finding gold in Victoria. Successive discoveries were announced in 1851, at Anderson's Creek near Melbourne, then in central Victoria – at Clunes, and then more significantly at Buninyong and Ballarat, which became the first major Victorian goldfield, and at Bendigo. Governor La Trobe wrote to a friend in early 1852 that 'the whole of my colony more or less seems to be larded with gold'.[10] Victoria did indeed contain great riches: between 1851 and 1860 it would produce 20 million fine ounces of gold to New South Wales' 2 million.[11]

A gold discovery was a necessary but not sufficient condition for a gold rush. The gold rushes of the 1850s were international in scale, made possible by modern communication, such as the telegraphs and newspapers that spread the word of new discoveries and the faster, safer and cheaper sailing ships of that decade; and manufactured goods, such as the transported wooden and tin houses that provided quickly assembled accommodation in the instant cities of Victoria.[12] More fundamentally, the mid-century gold rushes were made possible by a modern ethos that regarded uprooting oneself from home and undertaking a long and hazardous journey in pursuit of uncertain wealth as not only possible but desirable. We know this ethos was controversial because many contemporary commentators registered doubts about it, warning that nothing good could come from abandoning settled lives and responsibilities to search for randomly distributed gold. 'Gold hunting is not, *per se*, a desirable occupation', Melbourne lawyer Thomas à Beckett explained: 'its success is not dependent upon moral worth, and it has a tendency to destroy rather than promote the observance of those rules of conduct which, while they contribute to worldly welfare, elevate the individual who practises them, and promote social happiness'.[13]

---

9 G.W. Rusden, *History of Australia* (Melbourne: George Robertson, 1883), vol. 2, p. 602.
10 To John Murray, 16 January 1852, in C.J. La Trobe, 'Letters from the Colony', *La Trobe Journal*, 71 (2003): 135.
11 Rodney Maddock and Ian McLean, 'Supply-Side Shocks: The Case of Australian Gold', *Journal of Economic History*, 44, 4 (1984): 1050–1.
12 James Belich, *Replenishing the Earth: The Settler Revolution and the Rise of the Anglo-World, 1783–1939* (Oxford University Press, 2009), p. 310 argues the opposite case – that the gold rushes depended mainly on pre-industrial technology and animal power. On prefabricated houses, see Miles Lewis, 'The Diagnosis of Prefabricated Buildings', *Australian Journal of Historical Archaeology*, 3 (1985): 56–69.
13 'The Gold Mania', *Illustrated Australian Magazine*, 2 (1851): 377.

The Times in London editorialised that the moral and intellectual effects of the gold discoveries were likely to be 'repulsive and disheartening' because brute strength would now be honoured and rewarded more than 'trained skill or practiced intellect'.[14] In Victoria, Governor La Trobe reported in December 1851 that the presence of gold, 'requiring but little or no labour to collect', had acted 'completely to disorganize the whole structure of society'.[15]

Historical writing has often normalised the 1850s gold rushes as events, as though it were obviously thought reasonable and understandable at the time that so many men would abandon their life on one side of the world for a speculative and arduous pursuit on the other. It was, however, not a natural acquisitive instinct that led so many to rush after gold, but a particular way of thinking about the balance between individual wealth and community. Many contemporaries were indeed alarmed at the rushing after wealth at the expense of all that made it meaningful – family, community, social order – and at the congregation of so many men with fewer women on the goldfields.[16]

Governing

As with other nineteenth-century settlement booms (such as land booms), gold rushes were defined and made possible by government regulation – in the case of the Australian gold rushes of the 1850s, by the specific licensing provisions that opened up the goldfields to masses of individual miners. Historians have sometimes written as if the gold seekers were an almost unstoppable force, inevitably overwhelming attempts to regulate and control them. In 1850 however, an historically minded observer would have known of several historical precedents that appeared to demonstrate that government intervention could halt or limit gold digging, as well as determine its mode and manner. The 1690s Brazilian gold rush had drawn thousands in search of alluvial gold but the mines were subject over time to several taxing and regulatory measures, including a requirement for the payment of a fifth of the proceeds of gold mining to the Portuguese crown, limits on the number of slaves that could be imported to work the mines, and a poll tax on

---

14 *The Times*, 1 May 1852.
15 La Trobe to Grey, 3 December 1851, *Correspondence Relative to the Recent Discovery of Gold in Australia* (London: HMSO, 1852), p. 51.
16 See David Goodman, *Gold Seeking: Victoria and California in the 1850s* (Sydney: Allen & Unwin, 1994).

slave labour in the mines.[17] In Russia, the gold discoveries in the Urals in the 1740s did not at first lead to a gold rush because the state asserted a monopoly on gold production; it was only after 1812, when Russians gained the right to search for gold and silver in return for a royalty to the state bank, that private gold production overtook the state's.[18] In 1795 in County Wicklow, Ireland, miners who had already extracted £10,000 of gold were dispersed by militia, so the state could take over the mining.[19]

This historical record, familiar to at least some of the educated classes in the colonies, suggested that government intervention and regulation of gold rushes was the historical norm. Governor La Trobe learned of the 1828 Georgia gold rush (in which the state had initially claimed a monopoly of gold production) during his American travels in the early 1830s. He skirted around the gold district, commenting disdainfully that 'five thousand people were already collected, grasping and quarrelling, and it is probable that more gold will be sown than reaped'.[20] In Victoria, La Trobe held the same sceptical views about unregulated rushes; he responded to an incipient gold rush at Amherst in central Victoria in 1848 by sending the native police to disperse the gold seekers.

There has been continuing debate about whether governors in New South Wales attempted to suppress news of gold discoveries because they feared the consequences of gold in a penal society. Clarke famously reported that the governor of New South Wales, Gipps, had told him to 'Put it away, Mr Clarke, or we shall all have our throats cut'. Geoffrey Blainey has questioned whether Gipps actually uttered those words, and whether convicts and gold were really thought to be incompatible, arguing that there was 'no practical reason why convicts could not have worked the first gold mines in this continent'.[21] Much earlier gold mining had indeed been carried out by unfree labourers – Russian serfs, Brazilian, Colombian and American slaves – for the enrichment of others. It is only from a post-Californian perspective that Weston Bate's contention that gold was a 'democratic mineral' seems

---

17 C.R. Boxer, *The Golden Age of Brazil, 1695–1750: Growing Pains of a Colonial Society* (Berkeley: University of California Press, 1962), pp. 44–6; W.P. Morrell, *The Gold Rushes* (London: A. & C. Black, 1940), p. 27.

18 'Gold Mines in Russia', *Bankers Magazine*, 1 (1847): 206–7.

19 Timothy Alborn, 'An Irish El Dorado: Recovering Gold in County Wicklow', *Journal of British Studies*, 50, 2 (2011): 359–80.

20 C.J. Latrobe, *The Rambler in North America: 1832–1833* (London: R.B. Seeley and W. Burnside, 1835), vol. 2, p. 72.

21 Geoffrey Blainey, 'Gold and Governors', *Historical Studies Australia and New Zealand*, 9, 36 (1961): 341–2.

plausible.[22] W.B. Clarke was still claiming in 1849 that it was 'only in countries where labour is as cheap as it is with slaves and serfs, that...gold washing pays'; the democratic, international gold rush was being invented just as he uttered that warning, and was not the historical norm before 1848.[23]

To most newspaper-reading Australians, there was only one non-Australian gold rush worth talking about after December 1848 and that was the Californian. The transnational scale of the Californian and Australian gold rushes set them apart from previous events – both drew around 100,000 people annually in their peak years.[24] Californian experience informed Australian practice in many ways, and was carried in print and by immigrants; as many as 11,000 people may have travelled from Australia to the California gold rushes and perhaps 3,000 Americans came to the Australian goldfields.[25] The American journalist Walter Lummis claimed in 1900 that 'California not only invented the gold rush, but made it contagious'.[26] California, however, also served as a point of contrast for the Australian gold rushes, as exaggerated stories of disorder in California fostered a strong desire among colonial elites that any Australian gold rush should be more 'British' and orderly.

In California, for a mixture of strategic and legal reasons (including the incomplete transition of the recently conquered province from Mexican to US property law), the decision was made not to license gold mining but to 'permit all to work freely'.[27] Mining law in California encoded rather than dictated local practice; the late-nineteenth century American historian, Charles Shinn, romantically described the resultant communities as 'mining-camp commonwealths'.[28] Australian colonial governments, in contrast, at first attempted highly regulated gold rushes. Under British law, gold and silver belonged to the crown. New South Wales and then Victoria asserted crown ownership of the gold. Both colonies created a licence to 'dig, search for, and remove' gold, purchasable for 30 shillings a month by persons who could

22 Weston Bate, *Victorian Gold Rushes* (Melbourne: McPhee-Gribble/Penguin, 1988), p. 40.

23 *Sydney Morning Herald*, 16 February 1849.

24 Belich, *Replenishing the Earth*, p. 307.

25 Sherman L. Ricards and George M. Blackburn, 'The Sydney Ducks: A Demographic Analysis', *Pacific Historical Review*, 42, 1 (1973): 20; Geoffrey Serle, *The Golden Age: A History of the Colony of Victoria, 1851–1861* (Melbourne University Press, 1963), p. 76.

26 Charles F. Lummis, 'The Right Hand of the Continent', *Harper's New Monthly Magazine*, 100, 596 (1900): 174.

27 Peter Karsten, *Between Law and Custom: 'High' and 'Low' Legal Cultures in the Lands of the British Diaspora – The United States, Canada, Australia, and New Zealand, 1600–1900* (Cambridge University Press, 2002), p. 38.

28 Charles Howard Shinn, *Mining Camps: A Study in American Frontier Government* (New York: C. Scribner's Sons, 1885), p. 1.

show they were not 'improperly absent from hired service'. The revenue thus raised was to pay for administration of the goldfields – including operating the licensing system, escorting the gold to the treasury, paying the goldfields commissioners, who were responsible for resolving disputes between licensed miners, and generally assisting the maintenance of order, including by provision of magistrates courts, coroners, police (recruited from pensioned-off soldiers originally sent out as convict guards) and by subsidies for the deployment of clergymen and the building of (Church of England, Catholic, Presbyterian and Methodist) churches on the goldfields. Government thus involved itself with both order and morality on the goldfields. Victoria passed laws in late 1851 to criminalise gambling and the use of obscene language on the goldfields. Australian gold regulations from the beginning incorporated aspects of Californian practice – such as the priority given to first-comers, and the need to work a claim to retain it – but the ambition to achieve centralised regulation and moral order was far from Californian.[29]

The licensing of individual mining opened up the goldfields to all comers, regardless of nationality.[30] Blainey observed that this decision was 'unexpected and surprising'. The New South Wales governor, FitzRoy, and the colonial secretary, Thomson, were not democrats, harboured no belief that gold belonged to all, and yet became the architects of a system that had those effects.[31] The small size of the claims allowed – 20 feet (6.1 metres) square on flat land – initially made company mining difficult and helped create a highly mobile population, which moved rapidly from one claim to the next in what the New South Wales geological surveyor, Samuel Stutchbury, was already in 1851 describing as a 'perfect erratic life'.[32]

Politics

Licensing allowed for the mining of a public resource for private gain in return for payment of a fee, and this seemed to many a fair public policy. The New South Wales conservative politician, William Charles Wentworth, observed that 'the public at large had a right to expect great benefit from this gold

---

29 Jeremy Mouat, 'After California: Later Gold Rushes of the Pacific Basin', in Kenneth N. Owens (ed.), *Riches for All: The California Gold Rush and the World* (Lincoln: University of Nebraska Press, 2002), p. 270.

30 See below, however, on discriminatory financial imposts on Chinese immigrants and miners.

31 Blainey, 'The Gold Rushes: The Year of Decision', pp. 129–39.

32 Stutchbury to Colonial Secretary, 27 October 1851, in *Further Papers Relative to the Recent Discovery of Gold in Australia* (London: HMSO, 1853), p. 3.

discovery, as well as the private individuals who embarked in gold-seeking enterprise'.[33] A Victorian parliamentary select committee affirmed in 1853 that the licensing system was 'the best practical means of...maintaining the fundamental principle on which the rights of property, whether public or private, are founded'.[34] The miners themselves, however, soon began to resent the monthly fee because it fell equally on successful and unsuccessful diggers; they argued that it was a tax on labour not on production. As mining slowly shifted from the more easily won surface alluvial gold to deeper underground leads, the monthly licence fee imposed greater hardships; in deep-lead mining, months might pass without significant income. Resentment was increased by the sometimes high-handed and autocratic demeanour of the goldfields officials who, dressed in military-style uniforms, could ask to see licences at any time. Many of the officials were young men with connections in Britain but little colonial experience – 'unfledged aristocrats...useless at home', as Ballarat miners' leader John Basson Humffray described them – and this made the diggers' perception that they were being 'treated like felons and hunted out as kangaroos' all the more galling.[35] Non-compliance and protest grew in Victoria. Discontent was fuelled by the circumstance that the miners were taxed but could not, as itinerants, vote for the legislature that taxed them. The memory of the American Revolution and its mobilisation upon the principle of 'no taxation without representation' was still alive. Like the American revolutionaries, the dissident gold miners praised the British constitution and argued that they only sought their rights as Britons. Protests spread on the Bendigo fields, but came to a head in the Eureka rebellion at Ballarat in 1854.

James Scobie, a Scottish digger seeking a late drink at Bentley's Hotel in October 1854, was killed by a blow to the head with a spade. The hotelkeeper, Bentley, was widely suspected of the crime, but was exonerated by corrupt local magistrates. After a subsequent protest meeting, some of the crowd rushed the hotel; it burned down in the confusion. Three men selected from the crowd were charged with the arson, and the diggers' anger grew. Governor Hotham intervened, ordered Bentley's arrest (he was subsequently found guilty of manslaughter), and set up an inquiry that confirmed that corruption existed in the goldfields administration at Ballarat. Meanwhile the

---

33 Wentworth speech in New South Wales Legislative Council 2 December 1851, in *Correspondence Relative to the Recent Discovery of Gold in Australia* (1852), p. 32.
34 Victoria, *Report of the Select Committee of the Legislative Council on the Gold Fields*, 1 November 1853, p. vi.
35 (Melbourne) *Argus*, 16 November 1854.

Chartist-influenced Ballarat Reform League, formed to defend the arrested men, began calling not just for a reform of the autocratic goldfields' administration, but also for manhood suffrage, abolition of the licence fee, and – in their minds, crucially – the opening up of the colony's land to small farming settlement. On 11 November 1854 a public meeting of 10,000 at Ballarat resolved that 'it is the inalienable right of every citizen to have a voice in making the laws he is called upon to obey – that taxation without representation is tyranny'. The League's charter stated that it would 'endeavour to supersede…Royal prerogative by asserting that of the people, which is the most royal of all prerogatives, as the people are the only legitimate source of all political power'. In a British colony, that was self-consciously revolutionary language. In this tense environment, the symbolism of power and authority was crucial. A diggers' delegation to Hotham on 27 November 'demanded' the release of the three prisoners. Hotham objected to the word, but the delegation stood firm: 'the people…have, in their collective capacity, used that word'.

At a meeting held on 29 November, the rebel Southern Cross flag ('the Australian flag of independence', as Governor Hotham described it in a dispatch) was unfurled and gold licences burned.[36] One resolution, acknowledging that 'it would be wholly inconsistent, after refusing to pay a license, to call in a Commissioner for the adjustments of…disputes', set up alternative dispute resolution procedures – a small display of self-governing capacity.[37] The next day, Peter Lalor led the rebels to the Eureka field, where they built their stockade. Ballarat was now said to be 'in a state of open and undisguised rebellion'. At 4 a.m. on Sunday, 3 December, when most of those inside the stockade were asleep, troops attacked; about 20 diggers were killed, the military lost five dead and twelve seriously wounded. In early 1855, the Eureka rebels were put on trial in Melbourne, but juries refused to convict, despite Judge Redmond Barry's warning in one case after some thunder claps that 'the eye of heaven' was upon their deliberations.[38]

A post-Eureka Royal Commission recommended major changes to the regulation of gold mining. The licence fee was replaced with a 'miner's right', costing £1 a year, and an export tax on gold. Most importantly, the miner's right conveyed an entitlement to vote; it also allowed its holder to occupy land for a dwelling, assisting the settling of the gold regions and the

---

36 Hotham to Grey, 20 December 1854, in *Further Papers Relative to the Discovery of Gold in Australia* (London: HMSO, 1853), p. 63.

37 *Launceston Examiner*, 5 December 1854.

38 (Melbourne) *Argus*, 24 March 1855.

normalising of the population, as miners married and established families. Elected local courts were created on the goldfields to settle disputes and establish local mining rules. A system of leases was introduced to facilitate investment in company mining. From 1858, the local courts were restructured and augmented with mining boards, which until 1914 were responsible for making local regulations. These reforms made a significant step towards local autonomy in mining regulation. They produced a more institutionalised version of Californian practice and represented, Blainey suggested, 'the high tide of Australian democracy'.[39]

Eureka was an important turning point, but isolating the moment of rebellion from its context in a broader history of popular political discussion and agitation can distort its significance. What is striking in the record of Eureka is how deeply ingrained and sincere was the attachment to the forms of public meeting and discussion, the delegation, the petition, the remonstrance, the monster meeting and the demand for parliamentary representation, and how reluctantly and briefly they were abandoned.[40] The goldfields, despite the absorption of most energies in mining, were politically active regions, with their concentrations of people with united interests. They became important seedbeds of liberal and radical politics in colonial Australia; the kind of political mobilisation that facilitated a ready claiming of the voice of 'the people' speaking back to power – most importantly, in the movement to open up the lands for small farming settlement.

The political effects of gold rushes have been keenly debated by historians. C.M.H. Clark characterised the gold rush as a 'levelling flood' that created a '"pure democracy" – a society which acknowledged no distinction between man and man'; he portrayed those who worried about gold-rush society, on the other hand, as conservatives 'who believed society should be like a regiment in the army'.[41] For Clark, as for many historians since, there were only two kinds of people in gold-rush Australia – egalitarians who embraced the new conditions, and conservatives who lamented the loss of stable hierarchy. It is true that from the early rushes in New South Wales, radicals and democrats enthused about the levelling tendencies of the gold rush, seeing in it the possibility of independence from Britain and greater equality of

39 Ralph W. Birrell, *Staking a Claim: Gold and the Development of Victorian Mining Law* (Melbourne University Press, 1998), chs 3–4; Geoffrey Blainey, *The Rush that Never Ended: A History of Australian Mining*, 5th edn (Melbourne University Press, 2003), p. 57.
40 David Goodman, 'Eureka and Democracy', in Alan Mayne (ed.), *Eureka: Reappraising an Australian Legend* (Perth: Network Books, 2006), p. 110.
41 C.M.H. Clark, *A History of Australia. Volume 4, The Earth Abideth for Ever, 1851–1888* (Melbourne University Press, 1978), pp. 4–7.

opportunity.[42] But it was not only conservatives who worried about the social effects of gold. Many Victorian radicals in the 1850s saw gold mining as only a means to the end of land acquisition – it was the rights-bearing, voting, land-owning small farmer whose life they celebrated, not the transient alluvial miner.[43] Gold also hastened the transition to self-government. The British Colonial Secretary, Sir John Pakington, acknowledged in 1852 that the 'extraordinary discoveries of gold' had brought 'new and unforeseen' political and social conditions to the colonies, warranting the granting of a more complete self-government, including control of the process of sale of crown lands.[44]

Effects

The gold rushes brought economic disruption in the short term. The competition from gold seeking increased the price of labour and everything else. Some miners made more money than they would have at their ordinary occupations, but many did not; all had their earnings rapidly eroded by the high prices. Some persisted with digging for months and years, but many did not. Rewards for first-comers were high. Tony Dingle estimates the average annual income for Victorian gold miners at £390 in 1852, but dropping to £240 the following year and £148 the year after.[45] The rewards for arriving early meant that this was an information economy. Rumours might convey valuable information; newspapers were lively, plentiful and often highly regarded sources of information; scientific knowledge was scarcer but also circulated in various forms.

The gold rushes provoked short-term concern about the food supply and temporarily disrupted the pastoral industry. Gold replaced wool as Australia's leading export in the 1850s, and it was not until 1871 that wool again caught up. The population increase and elevated prices for food gave pastoralists an incentive to shift for a time to meat rather than wool production. In the longer term, however, as the Sydney *Empire* reflected in 1858, pastoralists

---

42 Paul A. Pickering, '"The Finger of God": Gold's Impact on New South Wales', in Iain McCalman, Alexander Cook and Andrew Reeves (eds), *Gold: Forgotten Histories and Lost Objects of Australia* (Cambridge University Press, 2001), pp. 38–9.

43 See Goodman, *Gold Seeking*, pp. 38–42.

44 Pakington to FitzRoy, 15 December 1852, in *Further Papers Relative to the Alterations in the Constitutions of the Australian Colonies* (London: HMSO, 1853), p. 44.

45 Tony Dingle, *The Victorians: Settling* (Sydney: Fairfax, Syme & Weldon Associates, 1984), p. 49.

realised that their industry 'instead of being injured or destroyed by the gold discovery, has, above all others, been benefited and enriched by it', as the value of land and livestock again increased, the price of labour fell, and the increased population settled down.[46]

After the initial disorganisation, gold stimulated economic growth, preparing the way for the long economic boom of 1860–90. Largely because of gold, the settler population of Australia increased from 437,000 in 1851 to 1,152,000 in 1861; the population of Victoria grew almost 100,000 between 1851 and 1852, and Melbourne became the largest city in the Australian colonies. The 1850s was the only decade of the nineteenth century in which as many Britons emigrated to Australasia as to the United States.[47] Economic historians conclude that it was the population increase, even more than the gold itself, which was the gold rushes' greatest contribution to Australian economic growth over the following decades. The extra people needed food, housing, manufactured goods, as well as infrastructure and services, so the gold immigration had 'multiplier effects' on other sectors of the economy.[48] Government as a supplier of administrative services was affected in the short term by inflation and high wages – the police force in particular found it difficult to retain recruits in the early 1850s – but soon there was a surplus of qualified applicants again as disappointed men seeking a regular income returned from the diggings. Unlike much twentieth-century mining, profits were to a large extent invested locally, assisting the unusual (for Australia) rise in non-metropolitan urban infrastructure in Victorian goldfields cities such as Bendigo and Ballarat.[49] The gold boom in New South Wales and Victoria temporarily debilitated the neighbouring colonies – in 1852 the male population of South Australia fell 3 per cent and that of Tasmania 17 per cent – but in the longer run provided them, too, with new markets.[50] As gold seekers married and formed families, there was a gradual normalising of the demographic imbalance in the gold regions. By the end of the 1850s, gold mining was becoming regularised and proletarianised, as more miners worked for a wage for local companies engaged in deep-lead mining.

46 (Sydney) *Empire*, 8 July 1858.
47 Gary B. Magee and Andrew S. Thompson, *Empire and Globalization: Networks of People, Goods and Capital in the British World, c. 1850–1914* (Cambridge University Press, 2010), p. 69.
48 W.A. Sinclair, *The Process of Economic Development in Australia* (Melbourne: Longman Cheshire, 1976), pp. 89–92.
49 Geoffrey Blainey, 'The Momentous Gold Rushes', *Australian Economic History Review*, 50, 2 (2010): 211.
50 Maddock and McLean, 'Supply-Side Shocks', pp. 1051–2.

The skills of the gold immigrants of the 1850s also assisted economic growth; indeed, the 'quality' of the gold migration has been a favourite theme of historians since the early twentieth century. T.A. Coghlan in 1918 thought a large majority of the gold immigrants had been 'brave, adventurous and resourceful', in contrast to the convict era when 'the inflow of population consisted mainly of degenerates'.[51] In 1932 G.V. Portus reported that the gold immigrants had been citizens of a 'new kind', 'eager for self-government'.[52] Geoffrey Serle's authoritative 1963 study of *The Golden Age* also emphasised the 'high quality' of the gold immigrants, observing that they were 'magnificent economic material with educational qualifications and professional and industrial skills superior to any other group of migrants to Australia, at least in the nineteenth century'.[53] Recent social history research has to some extent borne out these claims. Robert Tyler found, for example, that 40 per cent of English and Scottish immigrants to Ballarat had a father who was a skilled tradesman; in Bendigo in 1861, 17.3 per cent of miners were from Cornwall, and were quite likely to have brought personal or familial mining skills with them.[54] The gold immigrants were mainly British. The 1861 Victorian census showed that despite the apparent cosmopolitanism of gold-rush society, only about 7 per cent of the colony's population had been born outside Australia or Britain. The rushes did mix people from all parts of the British Isles together, reducing over time the significance, as well as the visibility and audibility, of regional and social differences.[55] But the celebrated egalitarianism of the diggings created a community with clearly defined boundaries.

Chinese miners came in considerable numbers from Guangdong and Fujian provinces in southern China. By the end of 1855 there were about 20,000 Chinese on the Victorian diggings, a fifth of the miners there; by 1861 there were almost 13,000 Chinese on the New South Wales goldfields, a quarter of the population there. Some of the Chinese had come under an 1848

---

51 T.A. Coghlan, *Labour and Industry in Australia: From the First Settlement in 1788 to the Establishment of the Commonwealth in 1901* (Oxford University Press, 1918), vol. 2, p. 875.

52 G.V. Portus, *Australia Since 1606: A History for Young Australians* (Oxford University Press, 1932), p. 135.

53 Serle, *The Golden Age*, p. 47.

54 R.L. Tyler, 'A Handful of Interesting and Exemplary People from a Country Called Wales, Identity and Culture Maintenance: The Welsh in Ballarat and Sebastopol in the Second Half of the Nineteenth Century', PhD thesis, University of Melbourne, 2000, p. 42, cited in Charles Fahey, 'Peopling The Victorian Goldfields: From Boom To Bust, 1851–1901', *Australian Economic History Review*, 50, 2 (2010): 154.

55 Eric Richards, *Britannia's Children: Emigration from England, Scotland, Wales and Ireland since 1600* (London: Hambledon and London, 2004), p. 127.

scheme as indentured labourers for pastoralists; a few had paid their own way from China; many more came on 'credit ticket' schemes sponsored by merchants in China or the Australian colonies who advanced their fare, which they then repaid with interest as they worked on the goldfields in groups under a supervising headman; most came directly from China but some had also sought gold in California.[56]

The capacity of the Chinese to work in large cooperative or directed groups gave them an advantage in alluvial mining over other miners.[57] The 1855 Victorian Gold Fields Inquiry Commission concluded, however, that the presence of so many Chinese would tend to 'demoralise colonial society by the low scale of domestic comfort, by an incurable habit of gaming, and other vicious tendencies and by the examples of degrading and absurd superstition'.[58] Victoria imposed a £10 entry tax on Chinese immigrants in 1855 (repealed in 1865) and a limitation on the number each ship could bring to the colony. As a result, many Chinese men walked overland to Victoria from the closest South Australian port at Robe (until that colony also imposed a landing tax in 1857, repealed in 1861) or from New South Wales (which introduced a tax in 1861, repealed in 1867).[59] The 1855 Victorian Act also sought to confine Chinese diggers to segregated camps under official Protectors, and to charge them a £1 annual protection fee for the privilege (repealed 1859).[60] These discriminatory taxes and often repressive 'protection' measures were significant governmental actions, but overt hostility to the Chinese came more significantly from European miners themselves. Because they defined the Chinese as racial outsiders to the colonial population, European diggers resented the gold the Chinese were taking, the water they were using, and

56 Ann Curthoys, '"Men of all Nations, except Chinamen": Europeans and Chinese on the Goldfields of New South Wales', in McCalman et al. (eds.) *Gold*, pp. 104–7; John Fitzgerald, *Big White Lie: Chinese Australians in White Australia* (Sydney: UNSW Press, 2007), pp. 61–9.

57 Barry McGowan, 'The Economics and Organisation of Chinese Mining in Colonial Australia', *Australian Economic History Review*, 45, 2 (2005): 124; Anna Kyi, '"The most determined, sustained diggers' resistance campaign": Chinese Protests against the Victorian Government's Anti-Chinese Legislation, 1855–1862', *Provenance*, 8 (2009): 35–49.

58 In William Westgarth, *The Colony of Victoria: Its History, Commerce and Gold Mining; Its Social and Political Institutions down to the end of 1863* (London: Sampson Low, Son and Marston, 1864), p. 220.

59 Arthur Reginald Butterworth, 'The Immigration of Coloured Races into British Colonies', *Journal of the Society of Comparative Legislation*, 2 (1897): 337–8. Each of these colonies reinstated Chinese immigration restriction measures in 1881.

60 Kathryn Cronin, *Colonial Casualties: Chinese in Early Victoria* (Melbourne University Press, 1982), ch. 5.

their hard-working and organised approach to gold seeking.[61] Anti-Chinese uprisings occurred at the Buckland field in Victoria, where 750 tents were destroyed and the gold of Chinese miners was stolen on 4 July 1856, and at Lambing Flat in New South Wales, where Chinese miners were expelled twice in 1860 by organised European miners, despite a military presence and government insistence that all diggers were entitled to British justice and the protection of the law.

On all sides, the Chinese issue was understood to have international as well as colonial dimensions. The British-imposed 'unequal treaties' after 1842 opened Chinese ports to trade and allowed foreigners to live and work in parts of China. At least some colonists saw a need for reciprocity: the American merchant George Francis Train argued that limiting Chinese immigration to Victoria would be 'contrary to the spirit of the age, opposed to the interests of this colony and opposed to the treaty with China'.[62] Recent work has emphasised the political sophistication of the Chinese diggers, their appeals as settlers to British justice, Christian values and democratic equality in campaigns against discriminatory taxes, their use of tax evasion as a means of resisting what they perceived as unjust discrimination, and the cosmopolitanism of the colonial Chinese leaders.[63] When the Victorian government proposed an additional £12 annual residence tax on Chinese miners in 1857, public protest meetings were held. In Castlemaine, Chinese spokesman Pon-Sa contested the idea that the proposed Victorian imposts on Chinese immigration paralleled earlier trade restrictions on the British in China; those restrictions he argued had been enacted only 'because they took in opium which was a bad thing for Chinamen'.[64]

Contemporary pessimists about the effects of the gold rush often cited its destructive and once-only character, always understood in invidious contrast to agriculture. The environmental effects of the gold rushes were significant and enduring.[65] Although the size of each claim was small, the number

---

61 Curthoys, '"Men of all Nations, except Chinamen"', pp. 108–10; Goodman, *Gold Seeking*, pp. 21–3.

62 (Melbourne) *Argus*, 24 April 1855.

63 Kyi, '"The most determined, sustained diggers' resistance campaign"'; Marilyn Lake and Henry Reynolds, *Drawing the Global Colour Line: White Men's Countries and the Question of Racial Equality* (Melbourne University Press, 2008), ch. 1; Mae M. Ngai, 'Chinese Miners, Headmen, and Protectors on the Victorian Goldfields, 1853–1863', *Australian Historical Studies*, 42, 1 (2011): 24.

64 (Melbourne) *Argus*, 7 August 1857; Ngai, 'Chinese Miners, Headmen, and Protectors', pp. 21–2.

65 Don Garden, 'Catalyst or Cataclysm? Gold Mining and the Environment', *Victorian Historical Journal*, 72, 1–2 (2001): 28–44.

of diggers who arrived, worked and left in a hurry meant that considerable environmental transformation was effected in a short time. In the first phase of alluvial mining, rivers were diverted from their courses, ground dug up and then abandoned, trees cut down to provide timber for fires, shelter and lining shafts, and animals hunted for food. The diggers, the literary traveller William Howitt noted, had 'two special propensities, those of firing guns and felling trees'.[66] Horse-drawn puddling machines accelerated the production of sludge, muddying waterways and increasing the likelihood of flooding. In the next phase of deep-lead mining from the later 1850s, there were different environmental effects – larger heaps of discarded dirt, the need for greater amounts of timber and water, the creation of miles of water races and channels, and the residue of chemicals. Mercury was widely used in the process of extracting gold from quartz and the contamination remained in waterways 150 years later; one study estimated that 900 tonnes of mercury had been released on the Bendigo goldfields.[67] The technique of hydraulic mining – the use of large, pressurised water hoses to wash away the topsoil – was introduced in the 1880s from California and the Urals, angering farmers who saw rivers silted and degraded and potentially good agricultural land destroyed.[68]

This environmental damage, and the human tide of alluvial gold seekers, produced a settler invasion that was even more rapid and intense than the earlier pastoral invasion. The pastoral industry was not labour-intensive; it destroyed the food supplies of Aboriginal people, but did not lead to a frenetic and unplanned peopling of the hills and valleys. Contemporary observers clearly perceived the detrimental effects of the gold rushes on the Aboriginal population; they dwelt in particular on the detrimental effects of the introduction of alcohol. Gold also brought some new economic opportunities for Aboriginal people, who in the short term replaced European workers (in particular, shepherds) who had fled to the gold fields. The Protector of Aborigines in South Australia reported in 1852 that there were now 'upwards of 200,000 sheep in the charge of native shepherds'.[69] Digging for desirable

---

66 William Howitt, *Land, Labour, and Gold: Or, Two Years in Victoria* (London: Longman, Brown, Green and Longmans, 1855), p. 176.

67 R.C. Churchill, C.E. Meathrel and P.J. Suter, 'A Retrospective Assessment of Gold Mining in the Reedy Creek Sub-catchment, Northeast Victoria, Australia: Residual Mercury Contamination 100 Years Later', *Environmental Pollution*, 132, 2 (2004): 355–63; B.M. Bycroft et al., 'Mercury Contamination of the Lerderderg River', *Environmental Pollution*, 28 (1982): 136.

68 Barry McGowan, 'Mullock Heaps and Tailing Mounds: Environmental Effects of Alluvial Goldmining', in McCalman et al. (eds.), *Gold*, pp. 88–9.

69 *South Australian Register*, 26 June 1852.

minerals – including greenstone, kaolin, ochres, basalt – was a traditional activity in Aboriginal society, and there is some evidence that Aboriginal people knew of and valued gold. In the gold-rush years, they alerted Europeans to gold, guided them towards it for pay, and sometimes dug it themselves.[70] There was a market for Aboriginal guides, even to established goldfields, which were not always easy to find in the absence of marked roads.[71] Aboriginal people understandably objected, sometimes eloquently, to paying for a license fee to dig on land that had so recently been all theirs.[72]

Nation

When William Charles Wentworth predicted in 1851 that gold 'must in a very few years precipitate us from a colony into a nation', he sounded a theme that has remained a favourite with historians ever since.[73] Nineteenth and earlier twentieth-century Australian historians liked the idea of the gold rushes as a rebirth of the nation, diluting or supplanting the earlier convict origins. Their interest in the quality of the gold migration also referred to the willingness to self-organise and take risks to improve life prospects. Gold seeking, they hypothesised, selected out a group with the self-governing, self-motivating qualities needed for nation building, and 'men with a far wider and more advanced liberalism', as Australia's second prime minister, Alfred Deakin, put it in 1912.[74] This gold rush as rebirth of the nation theme invoked a kind of Victorian exceptionalism, which dwelt on the gold-rush era rise to dominance of that colony over New South Wales, and clearly demarcated Victoria's free-settler, gold-era population and institutions from the convict origins of New South Wales, Queensland and Tasmania. Serle, career historian of Victoria, argued that the gold rush represented a 'fundamental change' from the direction set during the earlier decades of pastoral industry domination, because of Victoria's 'peopling by migrants with a more modern and progressive outlook'.[75] In reaction, other historians

70 David [Fred] Cahir, 'Finders not Keepers: Aboriginal People on the Goldfields of Victoria', in Mayne (ed.), *Eureka*, p. 145.
71 Fred Cahir, '"Are You off to the Diggings?" Aboriginal Guiding to and on the Goldfields', *La Trobe Journal*, 85 (2010): 22–36.
72 David [Fred] Cahir and Ian Clark, '"Why should they pay money to the Queen?" Aboriginal Miners and Land Claims', *Journal of Australian Colonial History*, 10, 1 (2008): 115–28.
73 See the discussion of the use of the quotation in Pickering, '"The Finger of God"', p. 38.
74 Deakin to Lionel Curtis, 13 March 1912, quoted in Stuart Macintyre, *A Colonial Liberalism: The Lost World of Three Victorian Visionaries* (Oxford University Press, 1991), p. 17.
75 Serle, *The Golden Age*, p. 380.

emphasised instead the continuities between the gold era and the pastoral and convict past. I.D. McNaughtan argued influentially in 1955 that the gold era did not divert the course of Australian development from 'the broad lines laid down before 1851'.[76] Russel Ward's nationalist account of *The Australian Legend* (1958) also argued that gold merely reinforced the egalitarian values and practices that had already developed among itinerant white male workers on the pastoral frontier.[77] The convict/free settler contrast can, however, be overstated. Not only did the Port Phillip District in the 1840s receive 1,700 holders of 'conditional pardons' from the Pentonville model prison in London, it also by the 1850s housed many former and escaped convicts from other colonies. The contemporary historian, William Westgarth, observed in 1855 that during the first years of the gold rush, 'the convict population of Tasmania literally swarmed into the colony'. Recent research confirms this intercolonial population movement. James Boyce observes that former Tasmanian convicts 'made up the overwhelming majority of the founding fathers of Melbourne'.[78] The conflict between the normalisers who emphasised the continuity of gold-rush society with existing colonial settlement, and those who viewed gold as a new beginning for Australian society, was a key twentieth-century historiographical debate; dogmatic insistence on one perspective at the expense of the other will clearly distort the history.

As Victoria settled into the more stable but less spectacular era of company mining, the centre of gold-rushing activity moved on, as Blainey noted, in an anti-clockwise direction around the continent.[79] There were further New South Wales rushes in the early 1860s. Queensland's first gold rush was in 1867 and significant finds followed at Charters Towers (which became for a time Australia's most productive field) and then in the 1870s further north at the Palmer River fields behind Cooktown, and in the Northern Territory. There were rushes in Western Australia in the Kimberley and Pilbara regions in the 1880s, and in the Murchison region and then at Coolgardie and Kalgoorlie – the richest field of all – in the 1890s. Gold was discovered at Mount Lyell in Tasmania in the 1880s. Australian gold production continued

---

76 I.D. McNaughtan, 'Colonial Liberalism, 1851–1892', in Gordon Greenwood (ed.), *Australia: A Social and Political History* (Sydney: Angus & Robertson, 1955), p. 99.

77 Russel Ward, *The Australian Legend* (Oxford University Press, 1958), ch. 5.

78 Ernest Scott and Herbert Burton, *A Short History of Australia* (Oxford University Press, 1947), pp. 196–8; Westgarth, *The Colony of Victoria*, p. 199; James Bradley et al., 'Research Note: The Founders and Survivors Project', *History of the Family*, 15, 4 (2010): 475; James Boyce, *1835: The Founding of Melbourne and the Conquest of Australia* (Melbourne: Black Inc., 2011), pp. 210–11.

79 Blainey, *The Rush that Never Ended*, p. 96.

at high levels through the century: in the 1860s averaging 2 million fine ounces a year, in the 1870s almost 1.5 million, and in the 1880s above 1 million, until Western Australia and Queensland lifted production to over 3 million ounces a year by the end of the century.[80] Outside Australia but in the region, gold was discovered in New Zealand in the 1850s and 60s, in New Guinea in the 1920s and Fiji in the 1930s. In each of these later rushes, the experience and memory of the 1850s Australian rushes was evident – in the administrative and legal models invented in New South Wales and Victoria, in transmitted mining expertise and lore, in understanding of the cycle of gold-rush history. 'All the world knows', observed Anthony Trollope in 1875, 'that Australia has been made what she is very much by her gold mines' – indeed, perhaps only Brazil had its national history so shaped by a mineral rush event.[81]

The individualist, democratic, international gold rushes of the 1850s were events specific to their time. Later gold discoveries were more quickly exploited by capital-intensive, often internationally financed companies; that was part of the reason that nostalgia for the freedom and independence of individual gold seeking had emerged so strongly in Australia by the 1890s. The consequences of the 1850s rushes for Indigenous people were seldom well remembered. That late-nineteenth century invention – the questing, heroic, romantic male gold seeker, who was an egalitarian yet nation-building individual – was to become an increasingly important figure in later Australian memory.

80 Maddock and Ian McLean, 'Supply-Side Shocks', p. 1051.
81 Anthony Trollope, *The Tireless Traveler: Twenty Letters to the Liverpool Mercury* (Berkeley: University of California Press, 1941), p. 99. The California rush was a major regional event, but rapidly dwarfed in the national history by slavery and the Civil War.

8

Colonial states and civil society, 1860–90

STUART MACINTYRE AND SEAN SCALMER

The first of the gold rushes was the most dramatic. In the decade following the original discoveries, 600,000 immigrants settled in the Australian colonies, taking the non-Aboriginal population to 1,152,000 by 1861; estimates of the Aboriginal population in that year range up to 180,000. While Victoria grew fastest, from 77,000 to 539,000, all the mainland colonies doubled in size.[1] The challenge Victoria faced as its richest alluvial fields were worked out was to stem the outflow of prospectors and consolidate local industries that had sprung up to serve their needs. The other colonies competed for labour and capital to fulfil their own aspirations.

They made rapid strides. Stimulated by a high rate of fertility and further migration, which brought nearly 750,000 additional settlers, the country's population reached 3,174,000 by 1891. Half lived in towns and cities, among which Melbourne (473,000), Sydney (400,000) and Adelaide (117,000) accounted for more than one third of their colonial populations.[2] The consolidation of settlement in the south-east corner of the continent was accompanied by a push into the north: separated from New South Wales in 1859, Queensland's population grew over the three decades from 30,000 to 394,000.[3] Economic progress outstripped the increase in population and gross domestic product increased more than threefold; the annual rate of economic growth averaged 4.8 per cent.[4]

---

1 Wray Vamplew (ed.), *Australians: Historical Statistics* (Sydney: Fairfax, Syme & Weldon Associates, 1987), pp. 4, 26.
2 J.W. McCarty, 'Australian Capital Cities in the Nineteenth Century', in C.B. Schedvin and J.W. McCarty (eds), *Urbanization in Australia: The Nineteenth Century* (Sydney University Press, 1974), pp. 21, 23.
3 Vamplew (ed.), *Australians: Historical Statistics*, p. 26.
4 Ian W. McLean, 'Australian Economic Growth in Historical Perspective', *Economic Record*, 80, 250 (2004): 332; N.G. Butlin, *Australian Domestic Product, Investment and Foreign Borrowing 1861–1938/39* (Cambridge University Press, 1962), pp. 460–1.

The growth was sustained across the 30 years, making this an epoch of rising prosperity matched only by the quarter-century following World War 2 and the two decades that spanned the end of the twentieth century. As with those subsequent long booms, this one was marked by successful innovation that lifted productivity and augmented living standards so that before 1890 Australians probably enjoyed the highest per-capita income in the world.[5] The improvement of physical conditions, the spread of education and opportunities for personal improvement built confidence in the future. As the children of the first gold rush came of age and formed their own households in the 1880s, the advance seemed to have achieved an irresistible momentum. By then, however, the pursuit of wealth was tilting over into reckless extravagance and the severe depression of the 1890s closed three decades of remarkable progress.

The economic historian, Noel Butlin, who laid down the contours of the country's wealth creation, emphasised the momentous transformation effected during this period. In 1860, he contended, the Australian colonies made up a loosely connected group of economies with no stable society, no sustained utilisation of resources, no definite composition of economic activity or foreign trade and no substantial capital equipment. Thirty years later he discerned the establishment of an enduring western society that was coherent, efficient and wealthy. It had achieved rapid and stable growth through a high rate of capital formation, which made for productive rural industries and at the same time allowed for rapid urbanisation. This dual pattern of development was made possible by a distinctively Australian pattern of activity – Butlin called it 'colonial socialism' – whereby governments borrowed overseas to finance the provision of the transport and communications infrastructure that linked the country and the city to the world economy.[6]

Butlin identified economy, society and government as components of this transformation, though he did not elaborate on the last two elements. While the colonial state was clearly an important economic actor, that was only one of its activities. Colonial society was undoubtedly acquisitive and enterprising, but it was more diverse in its composition and concerns than a narrative of material growth and progress allows. In the second half of the nineteenth century the Australian colonists worked by trial and error to tame a harsh

---

5 Angus Maddison, *The World Economy: A Millennial Perspective* (Paris: OECD, 2001), p. 186.

6 N.G. Butlin, *Investment in Australian Economic Development, 1861–1900* (Canberra: Department of Economic History, Research School of Social Sciences, ANU, 1972), pp. 3–15.

and obdurate environment, build family and community life, deal with differences of race, gender, class and faith, and explore the implications of their colonial condition. Civil society comprised the relationships and voluntary organisations that made up the fabric of society, along with the values and principles that animated public and private life.

Patterns of growth

To understand the form taken by the colonial state and the character of civil society it is necessary to look more closely at the patterns of growth. The nineteenth century saw a surge of European migration, trade and investment in which Britain, with the most advanced economy and largest territorial empire, played the leading role. Greatest success was achieved in regions in which Indigenous inhabitants could be pushed aside to allow for large-scale settlement, unhindered exploitation of resources and reproduction of British practices. This process developed new momentum in the second half of the nineteenth century as the transfer of people, money, technology, products and ideas became a mass transfer that transformed incremental colonisation into explosive colonisation.[7]

Between 1860 and 1889 woolgrowers pushed out beyond the established pastoral districts to occupy all the remaining grasslands on the vast inland corridor that stretched 3,500 kilometres from northern Queensland south to Victoria and then west into South Australia. The pastoralists invested heavily to construct fences, excavate dams, sink wells, install tanks and windmills and sow pasture, thereby increasing carrying capacity. Sheep numbers grew from 20 to 80 million. Fenced paddocks allowed more careful breeding, yielding higher volumes of finer wool. The railway and the steamship reduced the industry's transport costs. Local sales, which grew to more than half the clip by the end of the period, enabled growers to avoid the extra expense of transhipment to London auction houses; the telegraph provided faster and more accurate information about the market, and improvements in banking and finance reduced transaction costs.[8]

---

7 James Belich, *Replenishing the Earth: The Settler Revolution and the Rise of the Anglo-World, 1783–1939* (Oxford University Press, 2009); Gary B. Magee and Andrew S. Thompson, *Empire and Globalization: Networks of People, Goods and Capital in the British World, c. 1850–1914* (Cambridge University Press, 2010).

8 Graeme Davison, J.W. McCarty and Ailsa McLeary (eds), *Australians 1888* (Sydney: Fairfax, Syme & Weldon Associates, 1987), chs 6, 8; Simon Ville, 'The Relocation of the International Market for Australian Wool', *Australian Economic History Review*, 45, 1 (2005): 73–95.

Advances in mining were hardly less impressive. The gold discoveries in Victoria were followed by further rushes in New South Wales, New Zealand, then Queensland, the Northern Territory and by the mid-1880s the northern part of Western Australia; the following decade would bring the richest discoveries of all in Kalgoorlie. As surface deposits were worked out, mining companies employed advanced technologies to exploit deep ore bodies, using steam power to bring water to the surface and pump ventilation down to the leads, to drive pneumatic drills, haul cages up lifts and operate the batteries that released the gold. Similar techniques were applied to other minerals: copper, tin and the silver-lead lode discovered at Broken Hill in 1883.[9]

Gold was the principal export until 1871, when it was overtaken by wool. By the end of the 1880s wool earned £17.4 million, gold and other minerals £4.9 million, out of total exports of £29.6 million.[10] Both these sectors were characterised by ready access to natural resources, and substantial investment that created high ratios of capital to labour and correspondingly impressive levels of productivity. The initial expenditure on improvements to sheep runs provided much employment during the construction phase but then allowed the pastoralist to operate with a much smaller workforce, supplemented by casual labour during the shearing season. The mines employed larger workforces on wages and other forms of payment, but their productivity has been calculated at more than twice that of the British mining industry.[11]

The shift to other, more labour-intensive industries might therefore seem to reduce productivity and slow economic growth. Between 1861 and 1891 the number of farmers doubled. The family farm was a beguiling prospect of independence and self-sufficiency that lured many into ruin. Lacking the same access to long-term finance as pastoralists, the newcomer had to find the purchase cost of the land, clear it, erect a dwelling, buy livestock and equipment, plant a crop and bring it to harvest, and finally get the produce to market, meanwhile taking casual and seasonal jobs to supplement the farm's income and help ride out bad seasons. Many found this a Sisyphean labour, and the contrast between wealthy pastoralists and struggling selectors was pronounced, yet there were several reasons the growth of farming did not impede Australia's economic performance. First, the size of its agricultural labour force was smaller than in the United States and

9 Geoffrey Blainey, *The Rush That Never Ended: A History of Australian Mining* (Melbourne University Press, 1963).

10 Vamplew (ed.), *Australians: Historical Statistics*, p. 188.

11 Douglas A. Irwin, 'Australian Exceptionalism Revisited', *Australian Economic History Review*, 47, 3 (2007): 230.

other settler economies. Second, Australian farmers were quicker to adopt labour-saving machinery and improved methods. In South Australia and Victoria, where wheat growing was concentrated, they made use of new ploughs, strippers and reaper-binders. Among dairy farmers the introduction of the cream separator and refrigeration during the 1880s expanded the market. Third, farmers demonstrated a capacity to combine and advance their interests, whether through cooperative marketing schemes or by calling on government for assistance.

Transport was the principal form of government support, and vital since the cost of carting grain more than 30 or 40 kilometres was usually prohibitive. A rapid extension of the railway – just 390 kilometres of track were laid in 1861, but this extended to 1,657 kilometres by 1871, 6,456 kilometres by 1881 and 15,290 kilometres by 1891 – made farming profitable.[12] A study of probate records in northern Victoria found that whereas only 7 per cent of farmers left an estate of more than £1,000 at the end of the 1870s, with the spread of branch lines 38 per cent did so a decade later. The same figure was found for estates in the closing decades of the century in the farm district around Armidale, in the New England district of New South Wales, where the railway came in 1882.[13] One reason for improved fortunes was the consolidation of smaller farms into larger ones: whereas most landholdings in South Australia were under 100 hectares in 1861, by 1891 most exceeded 250 hectares.[14]

The rural sector made up 28 per cent of the workforce in 1871 but only 24 per cent in 1891. The great majority of Australians already worked in the manufacturing, construction and services sectors, which were concentrated in cities whose rapid growth was a distinctive feature of the settler societies. Here again, the unit of production was small and the ratio of capital to labour low. Secondary industries did not have the same natural resource advantage enjoyed by primary industries: there was some processing of wool, wheat and minerals but Australian commodities were more often exported in their raw form, so manufacturers had to rely on the domestic market. Construction and services in banking, transport and communications did benefit from linkages to commodity production and attracted substantial investment, but

12 Vamplew (ed.), *Australians: Historical Statistics*, p. 168.
13 Charles Fahey, 'The Wealth of Farmers: A Victorian Regional Study 1879–1901', *Historical Studies*, 21, 82 (1984): 29–51; John Ferry, *Colonial Armidale* (Brisbane: UQP, 1999), p. 212.
14 Eleanore Williams and Michael Williams, 'Rural South Australia in the Nineteenth Century', in Eric Richards (ed.), *The Flinders History of South Australia: Social History* (Adelaide: Wakefield Press, 1986), p. 523.

if we seek an explanation for Australia's high productivity we need to pay attention to other characteristics of the colonial economy.

One of these was immigration, which stimulated demand and made for a youthful population with a high rate of workforce participation. A preponderance of men (there were 140 males for every 100 females in 1860, 116 by 1890) had the same effect. High rates of literacy were consolidated by the provision of public education in the 1870s, while a flourishing metropolitan and rural press fostered the spread of ideas. Finally, the Australian colonies demonstrated a capacity for institutional innovation: they pioneered a simpler system of land title, extended water rights, introduced new banking practices so that land was accepted as collateral for mortgages, created more specialised financial institutions such as stock and station agencies, building societies and voluntary associations to provide protection against illness and accident.[15]

The movement of people into the colonies was facilitated by improvements in speed, safety and cost that followed the introduction of steamships. Subsidies made the cost of a passage to Australia little different from that of a voyage across the Atlantic, and also enabled the colonial authorities to choose those with appropriate skills.[16] Migrants were prepared to make the long journey from England, Scotland, Wales and Ireland in the expectation that they would improve their circumstances. One consequence of the improvement in transport and communications was that the six colonies were linked by passenger services, by sea and post from the 1850s, by telegraph in the 1870s and, apart from Western Australia, by rail at the end of the 1880s.[17] These services spread information, and one sign of economic integration was that living standards became more uniform. Victoria and New South Wales pulled ahead in per-capita gross domestic product during the 1850s and 1860s, but in the 1870s and 1880s the other colonies closed the gap.[18]

The average income was high in Australia but how widely were the benefits shared? There was a marked difference between the wages paid to men, who made up the majority of the paid workforce, and those of women and children. There was also a clear hierarchy: in descending order, it began with the skilled tradesmen and artisans, who constituted about a quarter of male

15 W.A. Sinclair, *The Process of Economic Development in Australia* (Melbourne: F.W. Cheshire, 1976), pp. 98–100.
16 Robin F. Haines, *Nineteenth Century Government Assisted Immigrants from the United Kingdom to Australia* (Adelaide: Flinders University, 1995).
17 Davison et al. (eds), *Australians 1888*, ch. 5.
18 Paul Cashin, 'Economic Growth and Convergence Across the Seven Colonies of Australasia: 1861–1991', *Economic Record*, 71, 213 (1995): 132–44.

wage-earners, then took in the ranks of semi-skilled workers such as miners and finally the unskilled labourers. Wage differences were narrower than in Britain: a blacksmith might earn as much as 80 shillings a week, a carpenter 60 shillings and a pick-and-shovel man 40 shillings.[19] But these rates fluctuated with the state of the labour market, and much Australian business – in transport, processing and construction – was highly seasonal.[20] The irregularity of employment made regular government work, on the railways, for example, attractive. Since most occupations relied on muscle power, and earnings diminished with old age or ill health, a clerical occupation with a regular salary was attractive; very few colonial Australians had the luxury of working while seated.

At the other end of the social scale, the largest fortunes were made in pastoralism, finance and commerce. Between 5 and 10 per cent of Australian income-earners were engaged in business and the professions, and many rose to prosperity on the crest of the long boom, especially if they took advantage of opportunities in the regions of new growth. Yet by international standards the richest Australians were hardly opulent.[21] The wealthiest in this period was probably William ('Big') Clarke, a pastoralist, who died in 1874 leaving an estate of £2.5 million and over 100,000 hectares of freehold.[22] Along with the financier and government minister Henry ('Money') Miller, who left £1.7 million in 1884, he was accused of corrupting officials and bribing members of parliament to enrich himself at the public expense.

The radicals who had agitated during the 1850s for democratic self-government expected the new colonial state to serve as an instrument of the popular will so that all could share in the fruits of economic growth. Those who had resisted the popular franchise warned of the threat to property rights and business confidence that radical measures would bring. In the three decades after 1860 the colonial state embarked on a number of such measures that restricted or supplemented the operation of the market. There is little reason to believe that these measures impeded economic growth, nor is there persuasive evidence that they had any powerfully redistributive effect. A recurrent feature of politics in this period is the attempt by diverse participants to reconcile their ambitions with the public good.

19 Charles Fahey, 'The Aristocracy of Labour in Victoria, 1881–1911', *Australian Historical Studies*, 26, 102 (1994): 77–96.
20 Charles Fahey and Jenny Lee, 'A Boom for Whom? Some Developments in the Australian Labour Market, 1870–1991', *Labour History*, 50 (1986): 1–27.
21 W.D. Rubinstein, 'Men of Wealth', in S.L. Goldberg and F.B. Smith (eds), *Australian Cultural History* (Cambridge University Press, 1988), pp. 109–22.
22 Michael Clarke, *'Big' Clarke* (Melbourne: Queensberry Hill Press, 1980).

Democracy and its discontents

A form of political democracy had been won in the decade after the gold rush. Colonists attained the power of self-rule; those who commanded a majority on the floor of the lower house of the parliament henceforth possessed the capacity to pass laws and to make governments. These lower houses were elected on something approaching full male suffrage, and elections protected by the secrecy of the ballot. Property ownership was removed as a qualification for office. The new arrangements encompassed the major points of the constitutional program of English radicalism; only the republics of the United States and France had advanced further towards complete self-government.[23]

Yet this was still far from full democracy. The privilege of the vote was not extended to women, except inadvertently when Victorian legislation to enfranchise all ratepayers in 1863 overlooked the fact that a tenth of them were women; after they took advantage of the opportunity in the following election, they were struck off the rolls.[24] While Indigenous men were not formally excluded, there is limited evidence of their participation. Parliamentary membership was at first unpaid – payment began in Victoria in 1870 and spread to other colonies in the 1880s – so working-class candidates were rare. The distribution of electorates favoured the wealthy and, except in South Australia, ownership of property in more than one electorate brought a corresponding right to plural voting. The upper houses of the colonial parliaments were relatively undemocratic: appointed in New South Wales and Queensland, elected in South Australia, Tasmania and Victoria on a property franchise, they were specifically designed to check the levelling impulse of the popular will.

Political life reflected the tensions of this arrangement. The newly enfranchised aimed to use parliament to shape their world. Anxious to win economic independence, they sought access to land; intent on moving their products to market, they campaigned for the extension of rail to new towns and hamlets. Workers in the cities were sometimes fearful of unemployment, and they combined with local manufacturers to argue for the protection of infant industries. Opposed to convict labour, and to workers from China or the Pacific Islands, they agitated to keep them out. They also expected

23 Robin Gollan, *Radical and Working Class Politics: A Study of Eastern Australia 1850–1910* (Melbourne University Press, 1960), p. 1.
24 Raymond Wright, *A People's Counsel: A History of the Parliament of Victoria 1856–1990* (Oxford University Press, 1992), p. 39

government to maintain the labour market when necessary by spending money on public works to alleviate unemployment.[25]

Agitation for such measures fluctuated in intensity, but even when the popular demand peaked, the structures of political life made their implementation difficult. Most members of parliament were wealthy men. At least initially, they resisted giving specific promises to their electors, and emphasised the virtues of independent judgement. Soon, however, they were subjected to the demands of their constituents for practical benefits: roads, bridge, railways and services. If the constituents wanted something done, they went in a deputation to the minister along with their local member. A representative who was unable to assist them was unlikely to retain his seat at the next election. The average length of service of a parliamentarian was just five years in New South Wales, six years in South Australia.[26]

Partly for this reason, parliamentarians rarely cohered into stable parties. Instead, there were loose and shifting factional alignments based on particular interests and personal loyalties. As these factions manoeuvred for influence and the spoils of office, so governments rose and fell at a dizzying rate: eleven months was the average duration of a ministry in South Australia, seventeen months in New South Wales and eighteen months in Victoria.[27] Stable arrangements were typically brokered by strong men with a personal following, adept in the art of patronage, with a capacity for intrigue and an indifference to principle that boded ill for any comprehensive program to meet popular aspirations.[28] The need for such attributes tended to deter the genteel and fastidious, allowing professional politicians to exercise leadership; none was more pertinacious and durable than Henry Parkes, who sat in the New South Wales Legislative Assembly from 1856 to 1895, representing nine different constituencies, surviving two bankruptcies and leading five ministries.[29]

25 Stuart Macintyre, *Winners and Losers: The Pursuit of Social Justice in Australian History* (Sydney: Allen & Unwin, 1985), chs 2, 4.

26 G.N. Hawker, *The Parliament of New South Wales 1856–1965* (Sydney: Government Printer, 1971), pp. 22–3.

27 Beverley Kingston, *The Oxford History of Australia. Volume 3, 1860–1900: Glad Confident Morning* (Oxford University Press, 1988), pp. 252–3.

28 P. Loveday and A.W. Martin, *Parliament, Factions and Parties: The First Thirty Years of Responsible Government in New South Wales, 1856–1889* (Melbourne University Press, 1966).

29 Geoffrey Bolton, 'Henry Parkes', in Graeme Davison, John Hirst and Stuart Macintyre (eds), *The Oxford Companion to Australian History* (Oxford University Press, 1998), pp. 493–4; A.W. Martin, *Henry Parkes: A Biography* (Melbourne University Press, 1980).

Popular dissatisfaction fostered mobilisation: the formation of pressure groups, organisation of public meetings, publication of newspapers and pamphlets. Thwarted in their aims, the advanced democrats came to the conclusion that something more was needed. If parliaments were to be properly representative, then working men needed to join the wealthy inside the chamber; if representatives were to be bound to serve their constituents, then something approaching a formal party was required; if the upper house continued to block the people's will, then it needed to be curbed and reformed. In this way, the quest to implement particular policies sometimes became a battle to reshape politics itself. The second half of the nineteenth century was marked by a series of major political conflicts.

Land was the chief cause. Many Europeans brought to Australia the dream of tilling their own patch of earth. The land had been seized from Aboriginal people and formally claimed by the crown. In the older colonies it was bestowed by governors upon soldiers, settlers and emancipated convicts, and occupied without consent by the most grasping and determined of pioneers. By the middle of the century, the south-eastern corner of Australia was mostly taken up by substantial sheep runs or subdivided by capitalists and let to tenant farmers. Frustrated by these barriers to a sharing of the wealth, the gold-rush generation initiated a campaign to 'Unlock the Land'.[30] Specifically, most sought the right to select a holding sufficient to support a family and to acquire it on terms that would allow those without capital to achieve independence.

The cause of land reform drew great support from existing tenants and disappointed gold seekers. Those colonies that had grown fastest would only retain their populations if the opportunity for land ownership was extended; further immigration only seemed possible if there was some prospect of newcomers gaining a farm of their own.[31] In consequence, the manufacturers of goods for the local market and many of the merchants who relied upon expanding trade also had reason to support reform. They might not have shared the same enthusiasm for a levelling democracy as the radicals who led the popular campaign, but they did want to make land rights subject to the operation of the market and replace squatterdom with the liberal

---

30 Alan Atkinson, *The Europeans in Australia: A History. Volume Two, Democracy* (Oxford University Press, 2004), p. 304.
31 Michael Hogan, 'The Land Question', in Michael Hogan, Lesley Muir, and Hilary Golder (eds), *The People's Choice: Electoral Politics in New South Wales* (Sydney: Federation Press, 2007), p. 21.

ideal of equality of opportunity.[32] The first land laws were enacted in Victoria in 1860 and New South Wales in 1861; South Australia followed in 1869 and Queensland, which had bestowed pastoral leases freely in the early years of self-government, in 1868.[33] In every colony new laws were needed to make good the defects of the original ones, and everywhere the first-comers clung to their patrimony.

The pastoralists could call on the support of those in the finance and service sector whose fortunes were tied to the wool industry. But large landowners in settled districts who had ruled over employees, tenants and local tradesmen found those loyalties crumbling under the pressures of rampant democracy. Land reform was thus the first demonstration of how the colonial state, with its distributive power, could serve as a counterweight to the dominant economic class – but it was also a reminder of the imperfections of this system of government.[34] A popular demand was blocked by a small, privileged elite, which mobilised its wealth to lobby – and in some notorious incidents, suborn – members of parliament. It used its entrenched position in the upper houses to block or sabotage the laws designed to throw open the land to the people.

As the opportunities for alluvial mining declined in Victoria a Land Convention assembled and constituted itself as an alternative, more popular assembly, its delegates elected from across the colony. When the obstructive Legislative Council refused to accept its demands, a large crowd marched in a torchlight procession on the new Parliament House in 1858, singing the 'Marseillaise' and 'Yankee Doodle', cheering liberty, equality and fraternity. Eleven conventionists, including the president, Moses Wilson Gray, entered the Legislative Assembly as members of parliament following the subsequent election.[35] In New South Wales the premier, Charles Cowper, faced a similarly obstructive upper house, though this was constituted by nominees rather than elected representatives. Cowper was able to pass land legislation in 1861 only by threatening to swamp the Legislative Council with new appointments. But

---

32 D.W.A. Baker, 'The Origins of Robertson's Land Acts', *Historical Studies Australia and New Zealand*, 8, 30 (1958): 166–82; J.B. Hirst, *The Strange Birth of a Colonial Democracy: New South Wales 1848–1884* (Sydney: Allen & Unwin, 1988), ch. 5.

33 J.B. Hirst, *Adelaide and the Country 1870–1917: Their Social and Political Relationship* (Melbourne University Press, 1971) pp. 78–95.

34 Gary Cross, 'Labour in Settler-State Democracies: Comparative Perspectives on Australia and the US, 1860–1920', *Labour History*, 70 (1996): 1–24.

35 Geoffrey Serle, *The Golden Age: A History of the Colony of Victoria, 1851–1861* (Melbourne University Press, 1963), pp. 266–82.

this was an action that itself prompted the mass resignation of many current Council members in protest, and hence a brief constitutional crisis.[36]

No mainland colony was able to formulate a land policy that resolved the conflict between the possessor and the aspirant. The battle over land was not a singular episode, but a recurring problem. Poorly designed schemes of land reform were at first manipulated by squatters to turn leasehold into freehold. Much of the territory set aside for selection by the landless was inhospitable and the rules that regulated its occupation were burdensome. For those seeking a place of their own, justice seemed perpetually deferred. One *Bulletin* cartoon of the late-nineteenth century showed an aged, bespectacled man, standing to hunched attention, right hand resting on a pile of earlier land Acts that rose to his waist, left hand holding a new land Bill: 'Now which will you have?' he asked, 'There is no difference'.[37]

The frustration of hopes stirred further activity. From the early 1870s, the Queensland liberal politician Charles Lilley sought to redistribute electorates as part of his campaign against the power of the squatters.[38] In South Australia, the campaign for land reform encouraged country residents to stand for office, prompted fresh debate about payment of members and inspired a new political institution, the Farmers' Mutual Association.[39] Likewise in New South Wales, dissatisfaction with the colony's land laws was one inspiration for the formation of local selectors' associations in the 1870s. These were the basis of the Amalgamated Farmers' Union and, much later, the Country Party.[40]

From the mid-1870s, new proposals were developed for a land tax: reformers hoped that this might strip wealth from the largest pastoralists and perhaps compel the break up of their estates. A major campaign in Victoria secured the election of a government dedicated to the cause, and again the Council blocked the measure, triggering a major constitutional crisis that would remain unresolved, even after a modified version of the tax was passed.[41] The land question persisted; like the fate of colonial democracy itself, it remained the subject of continuing anxiety, division and deadlock.

36 Hilary Golder, '1864–65', in Hogan et al. (eds), *The People's Choice*, p. 97.
37 *Bulletin*, 21 October 1882, reproduced in Lesley Muir, '1882', in Hogan et al. (eds), *The People's Choice*, p. 235.
38 H.J. Gibbney, 'Charles Lilley: An Uncertain Democrat', in Denis Murphy, Roger Joyce and Margaret Cribb (eds), *The Premiers of Queensland* (Brisbane: UQP, 1990), p. 81.
39 Hirst, *Adelaide and the Country*, p. 113.
40 G.L. Buxton, '1870–90', in F.K. Crowley (ed.), *A New History of Australia* (Melbourne: Heinemann, 1974), pp. 175–6.
41 Stuart Macintyre, *A Colonial Liberalism: The Lost World of Three Victorian Visionaries* (Oxford University Press, 1991), p. 159.

The protection of local industry was a second divisive issue, and sometimes overlapped with the conflict over land. Protective policies levied duties or 'tariffs' on imported goods. They attracted local producers struggling to compete with overseas manufacturers; the workless, hopeful that a thriving colonial industry might offer further employment; and ministries seeking some financial device to extract necessary revenue. Free trade, on the other hand, was enshrined in liberal political economy and by this time was the official policy in Britain, which bought most of Australia's exports and sold most of its imports. Export producers, seeking to keep their costs down, opposed tariffs, as did commercial enterprises reliant upon international trade and the workers that were employed in these sectors. Few consumers welcomed a tariff that increased their cost of living.

Victoria, with its greater reliance on manufacturing, smaller hinterland and more limited revenue from land sales, took the lead in protection of local industries. A Tariff Reform League was formed in 1859, and the Legislative Council's rejection of a tariff schedule precipitated the colony's first constitutional crisis in 1865.[42] The leading reformer in the 1870s, Graham Berry, rose to prominence as an advocate of the tariff. Berry used his newspaper, the *Collingwood Observer*, to argue for the policy, rebuilt his career from initial setback in the protectionist heartland of Geelong and implemented the first substantially protective tariff as Treasurer in 1871. With the powerful support of the *Age* newspaper, whose proprietor, David Syme, was wedded to protection, Berry mobilised the National Reform and Protection League that returned him to office in 1877. With more than 100 branches, it was the most developed political institution in the years before the formation of the Labor Party.

The Reform and Protection League was unusual in its combination of rural and urban interests. Assisted by the spread of the railway, Syme was building the circulation of his paper among the selectors as well as urban producers with a program of state support. Elsewhere, the policy of protection was less accepted. In New South Wales protection first emerged as an 'electoral bogey' in 1866, when Treasurer Eagar introduced a tariff principally as a means of raising revenue.[43] Likewise, in South Australia the success of wheat farmers encouraged support for free trade; here, the protectionist movement did not gain country allies.[44]

42 Ibid., pp. 102–5.
43 Hilary Golder, '1864–65', pp. 102–5.
44 Hirst, *Adelaide and the Country*, pp. 75–8.

A further feature of the constitutional crises was the role of the governor. The reformers resorted to desperate measures in their struggle against obstructive upper houses. Hence Charles Cowper's demand as premier in 1861 that the governor of New South Wales, Sir John Young, appoint new members to the Council to ensure the passage of his land legislation, and the decision in 1865 of the Victorian attorney-general, George Higinbotham, to 'tack' his government's tariff measures to an appropriation bill. The Colonial Office expected the governor to maintain neutrality between the warring Assembly and Council, whereas the reformers insisted that under a system of responsible government the governor was obliged to follow the advice of his ministers. An even more serious crisis occurred in 1877, when Graham Berry was thwarted by the Legislative Council over his proposed legislation to continue the payment of members. Berry resorted to the earlier tactic of attaching the measure to the annual appropriation bill, and when this too was rejected he took revenge by dismissing senior public servants thought to be conservative sympathisers. Seeking to curb the powers of the Council, the premier even undertook an 'embassy' to London in the forlorn hope that the British government might intervene on the government's behalf. As with earlier disputes, the immunity of the Council from the democratic will forced a compromise, and Berry eventually accepted coalition with more conservative parties.[45]

Whatever the political divisions over protection and land, there were growing reasons for some kind of accommodation. As the colonial state increased its activity, duties on imported goods – as well as duties on local products, notably alcohol – raised much-needed revenue. Equally, the sale of crown land generated substantial sums for the purposes of government. Land was the principal source of revenue in those colonies that were plentifully endowed with it, notably New South Wales, Queensland and South Australia. Customs duties were more important in Tasmania, Victoria and Western Australia (which had the land but not the buyers). Increasingly, however, all the colonies became dependent upon funds drawn from both sources. Where ideology divided, the imperatives of the state united.[46]

45 W.G. McMinn, *A Constitutional History of Australia* (Oxford University Press, 1979), pp. 65–72.

46 G.D. Patterson, *The Tariff in the Australian Colonies 1856–1900* (Melbourne University Press, 1968).

The work of the state

In a period of sustained growth the colonial state had to provide facilities and services – roads and bridges, police and courts, health and welfare – to more people across an enlarged area. There was also the need to increase the scale of water supplies, sewerage and waste disposal to deal with the effects of larger concentrations of people, and to invest heavily in the new technologies of transport and communication that were beyond the scope of private enterprise. The demographic consequences of the gold rush and continued immigration caused a major expansion of public education. For the most part governments funded their recurrent expenditure from revenue and borrowed, including very substantial loans raised in London, to finance public investment.

By far the largest item of public investment was railway construction, which rose steeply from £12 million in the 1860s to £22 million in the 1870s and £55 million in the 1880s.[47] The building of the railways involved large camps of surveyors, blacksmiths, carpenters, gangers and navvies that brought a sudden demand for materials, clothing, food, drink and amusements to a locality with effects comparable to a gold rush. At the peak of activity on the New South Wales northern line in 1885, there were 10,000 construction workers, and by 1889 just 500.[48] The location of railway workshops conferred more permanent benefits to inland towns such as Ballarat and Ipswich, and the operation of the service made all the difference to the fortunes of those along the route. Consequently, politicians took a keen interest in the location and operation of railway lines, which in turn raised the question of public administration.

At the advent of responsible government, a small number of ministers assumed control of an untidy machinery of departments, boards and other agencies, which continued to multiply as the colonial state took on new activities.[49] Since the rapid turnover of ministers made effective oversight of their operation difficult, much depended on the quality of the senior public servants who directed them. Yet the constant pressure on ministries to retain parliamentary support vitiated efficient administration. Financial controls were lax. Appointments were in the hands of the ministers and despite periodic

---

47 Butlin, *Investment in Australian Economic Development*, p. 322.
48 Denis Rowe, 'The Robust Navvy: The Railway Construction Worker in Northern New South Wales, 1854–1894', *Labour History*, 39 (1980): 42.
49 Paul Finn, *Law and Government in Colonial Australia* (Oxford University Press, 1987).

retrenchments, the size of the public sector rose inexorably: there were 3,600 in government employment in New South Wales in 1858 and 30,000 by the end of the period.[50] The solution adopted in that colony and Victoria during the 1880s was to create a public service board to replace patronage with appointment on merit, and to regularise classifications and salaries, though such reforms were contested.[51] The railways were placed under independent commissions, though these, too, were subject to repeated interference.

The railways were joined as the largest government employer by education departments. In 1860 schooling was provided to a minority of children by a mixture of small private schools run on commercial lines, church schools and public schools. Both church and public schools received government assistance, and the latter were hampered by a reliance on local initiative and obstruction by the principal denominations. From 1872 all six colonies created systems of public instruction under ministerial control and entirely supported by government funds. All children, moreover, were required to attend school until their early teens. The construction and staffing of these elementary schools was a major undertaking and the result was a highly centralised structure with a uniform curriculum.

The celebrated principles of free, secular and compulsory education were not fully realised. Most of the new elementary schools charged fees. While they provided no religious instruction and state aid was withdrawn from denominational schools, a Christian ethos pervaded the curriculum. The far-from-onerous attendance requirements were enforced loosely and not met by a significant minority of those on the rolls.[52] Public provision for further education remained far more restricted, with secondary education left largely to church schools and their fee-paying students dominating the meagre enrolments of universities in Sydney, Melbourne and Adelaide. However, we should not underestimate the significance of this assertion of state control over the training of children. It confirmed high rates of literacy, instilled habits of time discipline and regularity, and indeed provided a ladder of opportunity for able boys and girls.

The police forces followed a similar pattern of centralised, hierarchical control. Except in Tasmania, where local government controlled the magistracy

50 Hilary Golder, *Politics, Patronage and Public Works: The Administration of New South Wales. Volume 1, 1842–1900* (Sydney: UNSW Press, 2005), pp. 197, 232.
51 Graeme Davison, *The Rise and Fall of Marvellous Melbourne*, 2nd edn (Melbourne University Press, 2004), ch. 5.
52 Pavla Miller, *Long Division: State Schooling in South Australian Society* (Adelaide: Wakefield Press, 1986), ch. 4; Ann Larson, *Growing Up in Melbourne: Family Life in the Late Nineteenth Century* (Canberra: Demography Program, ANU, 1994), ch. 3.

and the constabulary, the colonial parliaments separated the enforcement of the law from prosecution of offences.[53] Each colony formed a single police force under the control of an inspector-general in New South Wales, a commissioner elsewhere, who was responsible to a government minister but in practice exercised substantial independence. These and the senior officers were likely to be British gentlemen with military backgrounds. The constabulary appealed particularly to Irish immigrants, many of whom had prior experience with the Irish Constabulary, which was organised on similar lines.[54] Such forces were ill suited to deal with the flurry of bushrangers that operated in rural New South Wales and Victoria, from the gold rushes to the celebrated exploits of the Kelly gang in the late 1870s. Police numbers in Western Australia and Queensland were disproportionately large, with violence and killing of Aboriginal people a marked feature of the pastoral frontier. In settled districts, town and cities, however, there was a decline in serious crime; of 166,000 arrests in the six colonies in 1888, 163,000 were dealt with in the lower courts and there were 120,000 convictions – less than 5 per cent of the population. The most common offences were drunkenness, disorderly conduct and vagrancy.[55]

A further feature was the weakness of local government. While provision was made in the early years of self-government for rural communities to form boards and councils that could build roads and provide essential services, the growing administrative reach of the colonial state left these bodies with attenuated responsibilities. Besides, residents had little incentive to incorporate when they would have to pay rates for services they expected the government to provide. Municipal government was similarly circumscribed. Activities such as education and public health were vested in central agencies that preferred uniformity to local initiative, and consolidated a paternal and managerial style of government.[56]

Care for the aged, the infirm and the destitute, on the other hand, was typically provided by voluntary organisations, albeit with government financial assistance. This preference for charity accorded with the reluctance to

---

53 Shane Breen, 'Local Authority in Colonial Tasmania', *Journal of Australian Colonial History*, 2, 1 (2000): 29–49.
54 Mark Finnane, *Police and Government: Histories of Policing in Australia* (Oxford University Press, 1994), ch. 1.
55 Davison et al. (eds), *Australians 1888*, p. 365; Mark Finnane and Stephen Garton, 'The Work of Policing: Social Relations and the Criminal Justice System in Queensland 1880–1914 (Part 1)', *Labour History*, 62 (1992): 52–70.
56 F.A. Larcombe, *A History of Local Government in New South Wales. Volume 2: The Stabilization of Local Government* (Sydney University Press, 1976); Hirst, *Adelaide and the Country*, ch. 3.

acknowledge that poverty coexisted with progress. 'Pauperism' was the British term, laden with the moral judgement used to distinguish the deserving from the undeserving poor, and since it epitomised the negative aspects of the social order the colonists had left behind, they were reluctant to see it take root.[57] Even so, there was a growing recognition of particular categories in need of treatment and support. Hence large public hospitals were built from the 1870s, along with government asylums for the aged and insane, and orphanages and industrial schools for children.[58]

Social patterns

As their aversion to a poor law indicated, the colonists aspired to a new social order free of the imperfections of the old. They would reproduce those voluntary associations that promoted autonomy and mutuality, but avoid divisive inequalities of wealth, power and status. A New Zealand study of the pursuit of this ideal society, with its abundance of natural resources promoting contentment and harmony, emphasises the difficulties of securing social cohesion. Footloose colonists met as strangers in scattered settlements, having few ties of kinship and little leisure for organised recreation.[59] There is a substantial Australian literature on community formation and the growth of the various institutions that made up civil society, but no similar consideration of atomisation.

A legacy of convict transportation to Australia and then the mass influx during the 1850s was the problem of origins. How was the ex-convict to be received in society, if indeed his or her penal background was known? How was the black sheep, exiled by his British family to the colonies, to be distinguished from an immigrant of good character? Character references and letters of introduction were one device, but these, too, were not always genuine. It was for this reason that manners assumed

---

57 Anne O'Brien, 'Pauperism Revisited', *Australian Historical Studies*, 42, 2 (2011): 212–29.

58 Stephen Garton, *Out of Luck: Poor Australians and Social Welfare 1788–1988* (Sydney: Allen & Unwin, 1990); Joan Brown, *'Poverty Is Not a Crime': The Development of Social Services in Tasmania* (Hobart: Tasmanian Historical Research Association, 1972); Brian Dickey, *Rations, Residence, Resources: A History of Social Welfare in South Australia since 1836* (Adelaide: Wakefield Press, 1986); Penelope Hetherington, *Paupers, Poor Relief and Poor Houses in Western Australia, 1829 to 1910* (Perth: UWA Press, 2009); Anne O'Brien, *Poverty's Prison: The Poor in New South Wales 1880–1918* (Melbourne University Press, 1988).

59 Miles Fairburn, *The Ideal Society and Its Enemies: The Foundations of Modern New Zealand Society 1850–1900* (Auckland University Press, 1989).

particular significance in colonial society. Dress, deportment, modes of speech, etiquette and even table manners marked out the boundaries of respectability.[60]

These devices served the landowning, mercantile and professional elite, but did little to promote the more inclusive bonds of the ideal colonial society. Ethnicity was a useful device for assimilation. New arrivals were likely to seek out the company of compatriots, so that Scots found work with Scottish entrepreneurs, the Cornish headed to mining towns where their skills were in high demand, the Irish gravitated to areas of Irish settlement and German settlers concentrated in agricultural districts. These networks provided advice, assistance and employment, leading in turn to ethnic organisations and practices: Caledonian and Hibernian societies, Burns suppers and eisteddfods. Such declarations of ancestral identity were a natural response to the novelty of a multi-ethnic society but carried few irredentist implications: rather, the newcomers advertised their particular national attributes in the expectation of equal standing and opportunity. The children of immigrants were by no means bound to marry within their national group, and by the end of the 1880s the Australian Natives Association – the title signifying that it was restricted to those born in Australia – outnumbered many of the ethnic associations.

Irish immigrants made up the largest non-English nationality. Australia's Irish were not the exiles of the great famine who huddled in the cramped neighbourhoods of inner New York or Boston, for most arrived in the years afterward and they settled more evenly across the new country. Women were nearly as common as men. Fenianism was less evident than support for home rule. Though less literate than the general population and more likely to become agricultural labourers and domestic servants, the Irish were also over-represented in the fields of law, politics and journalism, and prominent in many other meritocratic fields.[61] Intermarriage was common.

60 Penny Russell, 'A Wish of Distinction': Colonial Gentility and Femininity (Melbourne University Press, 1994); Penny Russell, Savage or Civilised? Manners in Colonial Australia (Sydney: UNSW Press, 2010); Dirk van Dissel, 'The Adelaide Gentry, 1850–1920', in Richards (ed.), The Flinders History of South Australia: Social History, pp. 337–70; Paul de Serville, Pounds and Pedigrees: The Upper Class in Victoria 1850–80 (Oxford University Press, 1991).

61 Oliver MacDonagh, 'The Irish in Australia: A General View', in Oliver MacDonagh and W.F. Mandle (eds), Ireland and Irish-Australia: Studies in Cultural and Political History (Sydney: Croom Helm, 1986), pp. 159–66; Malcolm Campbell, Ireland's New Worlds: Immigrants, Politics and Society in the United States and Australia, 1815–1922 (Madison: University of Wisconsin Press, 2008), p. 139.

Overall, Australia's Irish were less segregated than the children of Eire who migrated to other settler societies.[62]

Most Irish settlers were Catholics, and the overlapping of religious and national identities was a common pattern. Immigrants who came from Scotland and Ulster were mostly Presbyterian, and the 50,000 Germans in South Australia, Queensland and western Victoria were overwhelmingly Lutheran. The Church of England predominated among the English, but with a significant minority of Nonconformists – Baptists, Congregationalists and especially Methodists – drawn largely from the northern industrial counties, Wales and Cornwall. All these denominations already operated in Australia on a basis of equality, so much so that by 1860 the Nonconformists called their places of worship churches and not chapels. The challenge facing all was to build these churches and minister to the faithful, and over the next three decades the proportion of the population over the age of fifteen attending religious services increased from about a third to a half. The Presbyterians and Nonconformists, with a quarter of adherents, had the highest rates of participation; the Anglicans, who made up the largest denomination, found greater difficulty in adapting to the new circumstances, and the Catholics, who also made up a quarter of the population, fell between the two Protestant groups in their rate of worship.[63]

While the religious freedom of the colonies presented Catholics with opportunities, the religious plurality troubled them. An Irish Catholic who boarded an immigrant ship might find himself in conversation with a British Protestant for the very first time. Arrival brought no abatement of the danger, for whereas the British Protestant left a Protestant society for colonies that had the same character, the Catholic left a predominantly Catholic environment for one in which alien influences had the upper hand. Writing to Rome in the early 1870s, Mother Mary MacKillop explained that the Catholic spirit was often diminished because Catholics were afraid to lose the favour of their Protestant employers, while others dropped away in the absence of the sacraments.[64] Determined to guard against this danger, the Catholic

---

62 David Fitzpatrick, 'Irish Emigration to Nineteenth-Century Australia', in Colm Kiernan (ed.), *Australia and Ireland 1788–1988: Bicentenary Essays* (Dublin: Gill and Macmillan, 1986), pp. 138–44; Patrick O'Farrell, *The Irish in Australia* (Sydney: UNSW Press, 1986); Chris McConville, *Croppies, Celts and Catholics: The Irish in Australia* (Melbourne: Edward Arnold, 1987).

63 Walter Phillips, 'Religious Profession and Practice in NSW, 1851–1901: The Statistical Evidence', *Historical Studies*, 15, 59 (1972): 378–400; Vamplew (ed.), *Australians: Historical Statistics*, ch. 25.

64 H.R. Jackson, *Churches and People in Australia and New Zealand 1860–1930* (Sydney: Allen & Unwin, 1987), pp. 33, 35.

hierarchy brought out priests from Ireland, founded religious orders and lay sodalities, erected a separate system of education and raised barriers to mixed marriages. This strengthening of Catholic identity increased anti-Catholic prejudice, and sectarian divisions became more noticeable from the mid-1860s.

Historians have disputed the underlying causes. Recent scholarship has identified the importance of the context of economic change, marked by the growth of manufacturing and the failure of small farming; these might have heightened insecurity and hence encouraged communal conflict.[65] The sparks are more obvious. In 1868 Dublin-born Henry James O'Farrell shot a touring royal, Prince Albert, the Duke of Edinburgh, at a harbourside picnic in Sydney. O'Farrell falsely claimed to be an agent of Fenian conspiracy, and leading politicians such as Parkes exploited the incident for electoral gain. Suspicion of Roman Catholicism and the Irish increased greatly: the Loyal Orange Order expanded; a Protestant Political Association was formed in 1872. The arrival and then escape of Fenian convicts from Western Australia and the depredations of the Kelly gang in Victoria seemed to many further evidence of Hibernian treachery.[66] But Irish communities also organised themselves politically, often to great success, and Irish Catholic politicians were able to appeal to class as well as national or religious interests.[67]

Divisions over religious doctrine concealed a deeper agreement over the organisation of society. Like Roman Catholics, the Protestant churches laboured to safeguard the sanctity of the family. This was the primary social unit, a voluntary and yet binding partnership association considered crucial in ensuring members' life chances. With the pronounced sex imbalance, almost all women married but a significant minority of men remained single: 25 per cent in New South Wales and Queensland.[68] Women married young, typically in their early twenties, and were likely to bear children until menopause; seven, eight or more were common. But these norms conceal substantial differences between the country and city, as well as the demographic effects of sustained prosperity. In the country, where women were scarce, they married younger, had more children and shared more of the tasks; single men, on the other hand, were poorer, transient and vulnerable to misfortune. In cities there were more women, more spinsters, smaller

65 Campbell, *Ireland's New Worlds*, pp. 11, 126–9.
66 Robert Travers, *The Phantom Fenians of New South Wales* (Sydney: Kangaroo Press, 1986); Campbell, *Ireland's New Worlds*, pp. 114, 125.
67 McConville, *Croppies, Celts and Catholics*, p. 60.
68 Davison et al. (eds), *Australians 1888*, p. 309.

families and a higher incidence of dependence on absent fathers working in itinerant occupations. The difficulty of obtaining a divorce provided little protection against desertion and abuse.[69] Between 1860 and 1890 the birth rate was falling, life expectancy increasing and concern for the rising generation joined by a recognition of the problem of ageing; these strengthened the importance of family as a means of support.[70]

The town silhouette in colonial Australia was composed of the roofs of buildings of several storeys broken by the spires and towers of churches and other public buildings.[71] Much of the housing stock was new. In 1861 about a quarter of the residences in Ballarat were primitive structures – often just a single room of crudely sawn timber with a bark or shingle roof – and in that year a third of all housing in Australia was temporary in nature, a shack or lean-to made of timber or canvas. By the end of the 1880s, the typical house in Ballarat had grown to five or six rooms, laid out in an orderly pattern along properly formed streets, with parks, gardens and handsome state schools. The city centre boasted an imposing post office, a new mining exchange, an art gallery and academy of music, and grand hotels along with clubs and institutes; further out there was the hospital, the benevolent asylum and orphanage.[72]

Ballarat was Australia's largest inland city but hundreds of small country towns were springing up during the period. They began with a store and a smithy, then added a post office, bank, school, police station, hotel, flour mill and saleyards. A church was built as soon as a sufficient number of worshippers joined together, and the church hall was used for concerts and dances as well as civic meetings. Race meetings, cricket and football teams, an institute or school of arts, library, a brass band and progress committee followed. Soon those in business would build a residence away from the main street, more spacious and private, with a central hall dividing the house into separate spaces instead of the older arrangement whereby one room opened onto another. The town centre became a public space

---

69 Patricia Grimshaw, Ellen McEwen and Chris McConville (eds), *Families in Colonial Australia* (Sydney: Allen & Unwin 1985); Christina Twomey, *Deserted and Destitute: Motherhood, Wife Desertion and Colonial Welfare* (Melbourne: Australian Scholarly Publishing, 2002).

70 Davison et al. (eds), *Australians 1888*, ch. 17; Graeme Davison, '"Our Youth is Spent and our Backs are Bent": The Origins of Australian Ageism', *Australian Cultural History*, 14 (1995): 40–62.

71 David Denholm, *The Colonial Australians* (Melbourne: Allen Lane, 1979), p. 84.

72 Weston Bate, *Lucky City: The First Generation at Ballarat 1851–1901* (Melbourne University Press, 1978), pp. 207–9; R.V. Jackson, *Australian Economic Development in the Nineteenth Century* (Canberra: ANU Press, 1977), pp. 121–4.

of a new kind, more orderly and regulated, a site for promenading and displaying one's status.[73]

The principal cities grew fastest, for they were the seats of government and administration, centres of trade and finance. The railway and telegraph augmented the reach of their manufacturing and service sectors, while construction made a substantial contribution to the urban economy. It was in this period that some distinctive features of the Australian city became apparent. Single-family houses with increased floor space made for fresh air and improved health: even before installation of sewerage, the privy could be set well away from the house. These improvements increased the cost of housing, as well requiring a larger investment in the provision of water, roads and public transport over extended distances. With wages relatively high and the cost of food relatively cheap, residents were prepared to spend a higher proportion of their income to occupy their own home, even if that meant renting rather than purchasing. The rate of home ownership in Melbourne and Sydney slipped to around 40 per cent by the end of 1880s, forming a further fault-line in the ideal society.[74]

The city sustained a much greater variety of pastimes and pleasures, taking advantage of increased leisure time. Not all enjoyed such opportunities: the vaunted 8-hour day, first won by building workers in the 1850s, was always subject to the state of the labour market and beyond the reach of ordinary labourers, as well as shop assistants who often worked for twelve hours a day, and domestic servants whose numbers rose from 51,000 in 1861 to 104,000 by 1891.[75] Even so, the advance of the retail sector and growth of commercial entertainment and sport demonstrated that many colonists had disposable income and free time.

Plebeian culture, often associated with the neighbourhood pub, coexisted with high culture. An increasing regulation of public space was accompanied by an emphasis on rational recreation, served by public libraries, galleries and museums, and government support of institutes and learned societies. Chairs of science in the three universities supplemented the activity in colonial establishments of botanists, zoologists, geologists, mineralogists and technologists; Australian science was characterised by a readiness to adapt and improvise that in turn spawned inventiveness: there were 6,000 applications for patents in the 1880s.[76]

---

73 Buxton, '1870–1890', p. 184; Ferry, *Colonial Armidale*, pp. 176–80.
74 Lionel Frost, *The New Urban Frontier: Urbanisation and City-Building in Australasia and the American West* (Sydney: UNSW Press, 1991).
75 B.W. Higman, *Domestic Service in Australia* (Melbourne University Press, 2002), p. 282.
76 Ian Inkster and Jan Todd, 'Support for the Scientific Enterprise, 1850–1900', in R.W. Home (ed.), *Australian Science in the Making* (Cambridge University Press, 1988),

Australians were avid readers. Between 1870 and 1884 the import of books grew fourfold, making the colonies the principal overseas market for British publishers.[77] The local book industry was more restricted but there were hundreds of local periodicals that spanned business and the professions, fashion and religion, sport and politics. Newspapers proliferated: there were some 600 by 1890, 173 in New South Wales, 159 in Victoria. It cost only a few hundred pounds to start a country paper, and with advertising revenue a few hundred subscribers made it profitable. These papers carried reports on local, colonial and international affairs; financial information; court reports and public notices; announcements of birth, deaths and marriages, correspondence and editorials. Most of them were partisan, and in larger towns one paper spoke for the selectors, another for the landowners, while later there were rival free-trade and protectionist newspapers.[78]

By the 1890s the metropolitan dailies had overtaken the country press in circulation and influence; these newspapers had greater access to cables and agency news, free or reduced rates of postage, and they benefitted from the spread of the railway. Melbourne's *Age* cut its price to a penny in 1868 and achieved daily sales of 20,000. Its gaunt and remote proprietor, David Syme, an advanced liberal, then installed a rotary press and built circulation to 38,000 by 1879 and 81,000 in 1889, double that of his conservative competitor, the *Argus*, or indeed of any other Australian daily. Syme had trained for the ministry in Scotland and it was striking that many of the proprietors came from Nonconformist backgrounds: hence the Fairfax family, strong Congregationalists, employed Congregational ministers and laymen as editors of their cautious *Sydney Morning Herald*, while its more advanced rival, the *Daily Telegraph*, flourished in the 1880s under the direction of a former Wesleyan minister. Adelaide's leading paper, the *Advertiser*, was begun by Congregationalists and acquired by a Methodist.[79]

pp. 102–32; Ann Moyal, 'Invention and Innovation in Australia: The Historian's Lens', *Prometheus*, 1 (1987): 92–110.

77 Graeme Johanson, *A Study of Colonial Editions in Australia, 1843–1972* (Wellington: Elibank Press, 2000), p. 247.

78 Elizabeth Morrison, *Engines of Influence: Newspapers of Country Victoria, 1840–1890* (Melbourne University Press, 2005); Denis Cryle, *The Press in Colonial Queensland: A Social and Political History* (Brisbane: UQP, 1989); Rod Kirkpatrick, *Country Conscience: A History of the New South Wales Provincial Press 1841–1955* (Canberra: Infinite Harvest Publishing, 2000).

79 C.E. Sayers, *David Syme: A Life* (Melbourne: F.W. Cheshire, 1965); Gavin Souter, *Company of Heralds* (Melbourne University Press, 1981); E.J. Prest, *Sir John Langdon Bonython: Newspaper Proprietor, Politician and Philanthropist* (Melbourne: Australian Scholarly Publishing, 2011), ch. 2.

The newspaper was the dominant medium of civil society, recording, interpreting and disseminating public opinion. As the religious comparison suggests, its dominant tone was one of earnest moral uplift; but there was an alternative press that served the more popular tastes of the counter-public sphere. It sometimes took the form of the weekly illustrated magazine, using lampoons and cartoons to parody and mock respectable orthodoxies; by the 1880s there were also weeklies promoting the radical politics of organised labour, socialism and republicanism. These two forms came together in 1880 with the appearance of the *Bulletin*, the most successful of all the popular periodicals and a scourge of the establishment as the era of liberal progress came to an end.

The far north

The editor of the *Bulletin*, J.F. Archibald, commenced his career as a journalist with a country Victorian newspaper, and moved to Queensland in 1878 as clerk to an engineering firm. Working in isolated mining camps, he encountered a rough, polyglot community of white Australians, Chinese and Aboriginal people. In one of his recollections a young Aboriginal boy in a shanty was asked 'Where bin father belongah you?' and answered 'They bin shoot him'. The boy was adopted, sent to school and achieved sporting success, 'but among civilised surroundings Pompey was a failure. You could not make a white man out of him.'[80]

Many other colonists made the same journey north of the Tropic of Capricorn after 1860, bringing with them ideas of whiteness formed from earlier racial interactions. As settlement consolidated in the south-east and advanced further inland, it placed increasing pressure on Indigenous people. They could adapt to the intrusion, so that Aboriginal people worked on the goldfields and in some cases fossicked on their own behalf.[81] They found employment on pastoral runs, the men as shepherds, stockmen and shed-hands, the women as domestic servants; and during the initial phase of agriculture they helped clear and fence the land, clear it of vermin and get in the harvest. Closer settlement made it increasingly difficult for Aboriginal people to maintain their own forms of food production, while the consolidation of the family farm depleted their opportunities for employment.

---

80 Quoted in Sylvia Lawson, *The Archibald Paradox: A Strange Case of Authorship* (Melbourne: Allen Lane, 1983), pp. 35–6.
81 David Cahir and Ian D. Clark, '"Why should they pay money to the Queen?" Aboriginal Miners and Land Claims', *Journal of Australian Colonial History*, 10, 1 (2008): 115–28.

From 1860 governments in Victoria, South Australia and New South Wales responded to requests from Aboriginal people by setting aside a few small parcels of land for farming and subsistence. The most successful of these new reserves – at Coranderrk, near Healesville – became a symbol of Aboriginal self-reliance and possibility. But the independence and energy of Aboriginal residents here and elsewhere was mostly unrewarded: ownership remained with the state; profits were seized, land grants revoked, central control reasserted. The presence of Aboriginal people with European parentage provoked alarm and increased regulation of the reserves. Outside, opportunities were even more restricted. In Victoria at least an equal number of Aboriginal people eked out an existence as rural labourers and fringe dwellers. It has been estimated that four-fifths of Indigenous people in New South Wales were self-sufficient, but they also faced increasing segregation over time, with the introduction of curfews, exclusion from schools and the creation of protection boards imposing a tighter control.[82]

The other formative interaction was between British and Chinese colonists. More than 40,000 Chinese immigrants entered Victoria during the 1850s, and as many more were attracted by discoveries of gold elsewhere in the following decades. Most were young men, in keeping with the pattern whereby Chinese networks tested opportunities around the Pacific, and they found them in horticulture, service industries and commerce. These unfamiliar, enterprising settlers attracted resentment, and restrictions were imposed on their entry from as early as 1855 in Victoria. There were well-publicised cases of racial conflict on the goldfields, but recent scholarship has emphasised the Chinese contribution to the economy and the Chinese as themselves enterprising settlers.[83]

With these prior experiences of racial difference, the European colonists pushed north. In 1860 Burke and Wills led an ill-fated inland expedition from Victoria to the Gulf of Carpentaria. Following John McDouall Stuart's successful expedition from Adelaide in the following year, the Northern Territory was annexed to South Australia, and his stock route served as the foundation for the subsequent overland telegraph from Darwin, which was chosen as the northern harbour. Meanwhile in Western Australia, where the

82 Richard Broome, *Aboriginal Australians: Black Response to White Dominance 1788–1980* (Sydney: George Allen & Unwin, 1982), pp. 70–81; Heather Goodall, 'New South Wales', in Ann McGrath (ed.), *Contested Ground: Australian Aborigines Under the British Crown* (Sydney: Allen & Unwin, 1995), p. 74.

83 John Fitzgerald, *Big White Lie: Chinese Australians in White Australia* (Sydney: UNSW Press, 2007), chs 1–3; 'Dragon Tails: New Perspectives in Chinese Australian History', special issue of *Australian Historical Studies*, 42, 1 (2011).

population was just 10,000 in 1861 and confined to the south-west corner of the continent, pastoralists began moving up to the Pilbara and then to the Kimberley district.

The principal line of advance was in Queensland. Following the advent of self-government in 1859 there was a rapid settlement of the south-east of the colony, which then continued north. Pastoralists drove sheep and cattle across the lush mountain ranges of the coast, along the river gorges and onto the grasslands. They moved into the Gulf Country of the Northern Territory in the 1870s and some went on to take up runs in the Kimberley. These pioneers struggled initially with distance from markets. The transport system relied heavily on coastal shipping, with a string of ports that gained their own railway networks during the 1870s and 1880s, so that Brisbane did not attain the same dominance as the capital cities of the other colonies. Gold discoveries in the hinterlands of Townsville, Cairns and Cooktown brought an influx of miners in the 1870s, and the same decade saw a rapid growth of sugar plantations around Mackay. The European population of north Queensland grew from 16,000 in 1876 to 57,000 by 1891.[84]

The northern intrusion onto Aboriginal lands brought fierce resistance on an extended scale. This elongated frontier was at a vast distance from the seat of government. The exercise of authority was erratic and arbitrary, unchecked by the operation of civil society, and the newcomers brought far more advanced firearms than those available in their earlier conquest. Spearing of livestock, massacres and reprisals exacted a heavy toll.[85] The gold rush attracted large numbers of new Chinese miners – there were 17,000 on the Palmer River goldfield in 1876 – and in 1877 the Queensland government imposed a special tax to deter them.[86] A further feature was the use of Melanesian labour in the sugar industry. Around 60,000 Islanders were introduced to Australia between 1863 and the end of the century. They were recruited, and sometimes abducted, from the islands off the east coast of Papua New Guinea, on three-year contracts to work long hours at low wages and with a high mortality rate. A growing proportion of those who completed the initial engagement chose to remain, men far outnumbering women, and some became small farmers or self-employed in

84 G.C. Bolton, *A Thousand Miles Away: A History of North Queensland to 1920* (Canberra: ANU Press, 1971), p. 159.

85 Tony Roberts, *Frontier Justice: A History of the Gulf Country to 1900* (Brisbane: UQP, 2005).

86 Bolton, *A Thousand Miles Away*, pp. 56–8.

other occupations. The Queensland government introduced regulations to restrict their activity.[87]

Across the northern third of Australia the European population was approaching 70,000 by 1890, with perhaps 20,000 from Asia and the Pacific, and an Aboriginal population that can only be estimated but was probably at least 70,000. The Europeans were concentrated in four large centres: the gold town of Charters Towers (13,000) and the coastal regions of Townsville (11,000), Mackay (10,000) and Cairns, so that the 10,000 in western Queensland, the Northern Territory and the north-west of Western Australia were heavily outnumbered.[88] The cattle and sheep industries relied on Aboriginal labour.[89] In all of the ports there was a Chinese business community of merchants, fishermen, market gardeners, green grocers, tailors and shoemakers, keepers of boarding houses, restaurants, gambling houses and brothels. Some of the most exotic settings were the centres of sea-based industries. Thursday Island, just off the tip of Cape York, had a workforce of Japanese, Filipinos, Pacific Islanders and Malays engaged in pearling and harvesting *bêche de mer*. Broome, the base of Western Australia's pearling industry, was equally diverse.[90] The seeming inability of the white race to flourish in the tropics provoked fears of degeneration; the prominence of other races seemed to threaten the emerging nation's territorial integrity.

As the gold-rush generation saw their children come of age and take up their patrimony, they could look back on a remarkable transformation. Stimulated by celebration of the centenary of British settlement in Sydney and the ostentatious display of achievement in the International Exhibition in Melbourne, it became common to draw comparisons between the primitive circumstances they had encountered and the civilisation they created. Walk about in the city streets, wrote a later arrival, Francis Adams, and you could sense them expressing 'movement, progress, conscious power'.[91] The prodigious growth of the Australian colonies, their prosperity, advanced democracy and restless energy, attracted international visitors who duly

87 Clive Moore, *Kanaka: A History of Melanesian Mackay* (Port Moresby: Institute of Papua New Guinea Studies, 1985).

88 Henry Reynolds, *North of Capricorn: The Untold Story of Australia's North* (Sydney: Allen & Unwin, 2003), pp. xi–xvi.

89 Dawn May, *From Bush to Station: Aboriginal Labour in the North Queensland Pastoral Industry, 1861–1897* (Townsville: James Cook University, 1983).

90 Reynolds, *North of Capricorn*; Regina Ganter with Julia Martínez and Gary Lee, *Mixed Relations: Asian–Aboriginal Contact in North Australia* (Perth: UWA Press, 2006).

91 Francis W.L. Adams, *Australian Essays* (Melbourne: William Inglis, 1886), p. 5.

expressed admiration. The ebullient English novelist, Anthony Trollope, did so often during his tour and had only one piece of advice: 'Don't blow' (boast).[92]

But by the time of the centenary in 1888 there were signs the long boom was coming to an end. The prices of Australia's chief commodity exports were falling, the proportion of export income needed to service the external debt mounting. Banks and building societies had channelled investment into the housing market, so that two-thirds of private capital formation in Melbourne was directed to residential construction during the 1880s, whereas in Britain the figure was one-fifth.[93] The era of active colonial liberalism seemed spent, unable to contain the hardening of industrial relations as employers sought to deal with the pressures on their labour costs. The frontier of opportunity was closing, a growing restlessness becoming apparent.

In 1881 Patrick McMahon Glynn, an Irish lawyer recently arrived in Adelaide, wrote to his sister of the prosperity he found

> The working classes are well off, their houses cozey, with verandahs inter-laced with vines, flowery gardens, their daughters pianists, their children disobedient, their food cheap (mutton 1 ½ & 2d. per lb.) their working hours eight, their holidays many…Too many shops are being opened, too many towns built.[94]

As with many letters home, this was an exaggerated account of colonial circumstances. A decade later, when immigration stopped, shops closed and many workers had no holidays to enjoy because they had no work, it would seem a remote dream.

92 Anthony Trollope, *Australia and New Zealand* (London: Chapman and Hall, 1873), vol. 2, p. 387.
93 Jackson, *Australian Economic Development in the Nineteenth Century*, pp. 14–17; Frost, *The New Urban Frontier*, p. 158.
94 *Patrick McMahon Glynn: Letters to his Family 1874–1927*, ed. Gerald Glynn O'Collins (Melbourne: Polding Press, 1974), p. 23, quoted in Kingston, *The Oxford History of Australia*, vol. 3, p. 277.

9

Rethinking the 1890s

MELISSA BELLANTA

In 1895 a theatrical company associated with London's Gaiety Theatre brought musical comedy to Australia. Hailed as the latest thing in popular entertainment, musical comedy had a reputation for its emphasis on flirtation, fashion and the glamour of its female stars. Australian audiences, drawn by the publicity, gathered eagerly for the company's first production, *A Gaiety Girl*. Demand was so clamorous in Sydney that an auction was held for opening-night tickets, fetching the breathtaking sum of 24 shillings for the best seats. The theatre critic for the *Bulletin*, the Sydney-based weekly, was rapturous in his reviews. He urged all men of discernment to buy a ticket, regardless of the gloomy economic times.[1]

The romping frivolity of theatricals such as *A Gaiety Girl* was one reason the 1890s were later described as 'gay' or 'naughty' in Britain, parts of Europe and the United States. Outside intellectual circles, the decade was mythologised as an era of breezy hedonism: big nights out on London's West End, the rampant growth of New York's Tin Pan Alley, and *rouge*-tinted evenings at Montmartre dance halls. In Australia, terms such as 'Gay Nineties' or 'Naughty Nineties' – like their French equivalent, *Belle Epoque* – never came into currency.[2] The decade certainly attracted an extraordinary degree of myth making, some of which concerned the wine-fuelled hi-jinks of male bohemians in Sydney and Melbourne. Overwhelmingly, however, the nineties have been remembered for their intensity rather than gaiety, as a period of political and cultural experimentation rather than of racy gossip and glamorous nights on the town.

There are good reasons for the portrayal of Australia's 1890s as a period of such intensity. The decade began with bruising strikes, followed by the harrowing Depression in every colony but Western Australia. The Depression

---

1 *Bulletin*, 13 April 1895; 15 June 1895.
2 Melissa Bellanta, 'Naughty and Gay? Revisiting the Nineties in the Australian Colonies', *History Australia*, 9, 1 (2012): 137, n. 2.

punctured the confidence that had developed during the long boom in the eastern colonies between 1860 and 1890. Goaded by industrial conflict, unionists and their sympathisers formed the colonies' first labour parties in 1890–91, with an array of socialist leagues, single-tax societies, anarchist groups and utopian initiatives proliferating on their radical fringe. For the labour historians who once dominated accounts of the 1890s in Australian scholarship, these events were the only ones worth focusing upon.[3] As most of the radical groups disintegrated after a few years, the meaning of the 1890s for left-wing politics has also been debated at length – were they the cradle or graveyard of hopes for radical social change?[4]

The prodigious cultural output is another reason why Australia's 1890s have radiated heat over the years. The production of fiction, in particular, picked up during the decade; or more accurately, over the 'long nineties' between 1885 and 1905.[5] Utopian narratives, 'invasion-scare' serials, adventure fiction and domestic romances all appeared. So did writing by women, of the journalistic as well as literary kind. Although feminist and literary scholars have reminded us of this literature, the works of male artists associated with the so-called 'Heidelberg school' and bohemian writers associated with the *Bulletin* are still the best-remembered cultural products of the decade. Some of this work limned the sun-lit bush as a site of a self-conscious Australianness: a place airier, more down-to-earth and inviting of masculine fellowship than the old world. The cultural nationalism implicit in this work ensures that the 1890s continue to be romanticised as the era in which Australian national identity was born.[6] This is especially the case since a movement for the federation of the colonies gained momentum, coming to a triumphant conclusion at the end of the decade.

3 See, for example, Brian Fitzpatrick, *A Short History of the Australian Labor Movement* (Melbourne: Rawson's Bookshop, 1940), chs 6–8; Robin Gollan, *Radical and Working-Class Politics: A Study of Eastern Australia, 1850–1910* (Melbourne University Press, 1960), chs 7–8.

4 I paraphrase John Docker in *The Nervous Nineties: Australian Cultural Life in the 1890s* (Oxford University Press, 1991), p. xx. The key works debating the meaning of the 'nineties for left politics are Fitzpatrick, *A Short History of the Australian Labor Movement*; Humphrey McQueen, *A New Britannia: An Argument Concerning the Social Origins of Australian Radicalism and Nationalism*, 4th edn (Brisbane: UQP, 2004); Marilyn Lake 'The Politics of Respectability: Identifying the Masculinist Context', in Susan Magarey, Sue Rowley and Susan Sheridan (eds), *Debutante Nation: Feminism Contests the 1890s* (Sydney: Allen & Unwin, 1993), pp. 1–15; and Bruce Scates, *A New Australia: Citizenship, Radicalism and the New Republic* (Cambridge University Press, 1997).

5 Ken Stewart, 'Introduction', in Ken Stewart (ed.), *The 1890s: Australian Literature and Literary Culture* (Brisbane: UQP, 1996), pp. 6–10.

6 Vance Palmer, *The Legend of the Nineties* (Melbourne University Press, 1954); Richard White, *Inventing Australia: Images and Identity 1688–1980* (Sydney: Allen & Unwin, 1981), ch. 6.

That writers and artists enamoured of the bush linked Australianness to masculine qualities points to another reason for the emphasis on intensity in accounts of the 1890s. It was in this decade that Australian feminism first acquired critical mass. Following their New Zealand sisters in 1893, South Australian women were among the first in the world to win the vote in 1894, and the first to have the right to stand for parliament. Western Australian women were enfranchised in 1899, and those in the rest of the country won the same victory over the following decade.[7] Women's suffrage was not the only concern of Australian feminists. Like their counterparts overseas, they sought to change the conditions of marriage and work as well as citizenship, arguing passionately for women's right to be considered as something more than 'sex creatures'. Since these efforts were contentious, the 1890s were marked by defensive or aggressive reactions to feminism among men in Australian public and cultural life.[8]

In spite of the ardour and the rancour, the Depression and industrial conflict, there were still aspects of Australia in the 1890s that might be called 'gay'. Western Australia was caught up in a gold rush between 1892 and 1896. In western Tasmania, Queenstown was the centre of a copper-mining boom in the late 1890s.[9] There was certainly gaiety in the pubs and theatres that appeared seemingly overnight in these mining centres. The profound transformations in popular culture that caused the decade to become known as the 'Gay Nineties' elsewhere were also taking place in other Australian cities and towns. Cinema arrived in the colonies as in other parts of the globe in 1896; cricket and football developed as pay-for-view spectator sports. Big entertainment firms emerged with Harry Rickards' Tivoli vaudeville circuit and J.C. Williamson & Co.'s theatrical empire. The managers of these entertainment empires used gaiety – a celebration of fun and flirtation – as a key promotional strategy. If the auction for tickets to *A Gaiety Girl* in 1895 is anything to go by, this strategy proved successful even when the Depression was at its worst. Any account of Australia's 1890s must thus come to terms with the gay as well as the fervent and grim, noting developments in popular leisure alongside other transformative aspects of this remarkable decade.

7 Women gained the vote in New South Wales in 1902; Tasmania in 1903; Queensland in 1905; and Victoria in 1909. White women also won the right to vote in Commonwealth elections in 1902.
8 Lake, 'The Politics of Respectability'; see also the chapters by Susan Magarey, Patricia Grimshaw and Robert Dixon in Magarey et al. (eds), *Debutante Nation*; and Susan Magarey, *Passions of the First Wave Feminists* (Sydney: UNSW Press, 2001), p. 3.
9 Geoffrey Blainey, *The Rush That Never Ended: A History of Australian Mining*, 5th edn (Melbourne University Press, 2003), chs 16–19.

The Depression

No-one reading the financial news at the start of 1890 would have dreamed of calling the new decade 'gay'. The bleakest days would not come until the middle of the decade, but even in the summer of 1890 there was sufficient warning of the coming austerity. In eastern Australia, and especially Victoria, the 1880s had seen a heated boom in land and mining shares. The most feverish investment had been in Broken Hill silver-mining shares. Shares in the Broken Hill Proprietary Company (BHP) raced from £174 to over £400 between December 1887 and February 1888.[10] By the end of the year colonial banks had decided to raise interest rates and tighten their lending rules in an attempt to cool investors' temperatures.[11] The strategy worked all too well. After a brief lull, the cost of land and shares edged downward in 1889, and by 1891 entered free-fall. Formed to fund the great expansion of the city that had taken place during the previous decades – an expansion powered by population growth and the idealisation of suburban living – a succession of building societies and land and finance companies plunged into insolvency in 1891–92. Worse was to come in 1893, when numerous banks crashed spectacularly. Of eighteen banks with headquarters on the eastern Australian mainland, thirteen collapsed between January and May.[12]

The failure of institutions such as the Commercial Bank of Australia and City of Melbourne Bank had been almost unthinkable. Like the failure of the building societies, the collapse of these banks was influenced by international pressures as well as domestic ones. In this age of emergent economic globalisation, the November 1890 bailout of the Baring investment house by the Bank of London as a result of bad debts in Argentina caused British financiers to halt their flow of credit to the Australian colonies. A steep decline in world prices for commodities such as wool, silver and sugar contributed to this contraction of British investment in 1891.[13] Since the Australian colonies were so dependent on the export of commodities and import of capital, they experienced a much more severe downturn than North America and the old world.

10 Geoffrey Serle, *The Rush To Be Rich: A History of the Colony of Victoria, 1883–1889* (Melbourne University Press, 1971), p. 254.
11 E.A. Boehm, *Prosperity and Depression in Australia, 1887–1897* (Oxford: Clarendon Press, 1971), pp. 254–5.
12 Ibid., p. 271.
13 Luke Trainor, *British Imperialism and Australian Nationalism: Manipulation, Conflict and Compromise in the Late Nineteenth Century* (Cambridge University Press, 1994), ch. 10.

Though a lack of official statistics makes the effects of the Depression difficult to quantify, estimates place the unemployment rate in Melbourne (the worst affected city) somewhere between 26.5 and 28.3 per cent in 1893.[14] Many more worked less than a full week on reduced wages. Foreclosures on mortgagees meant that up to 6,000 Melbourne families lost their homes, bringing an abrupt end to dreams of independence and contentment in suburbia.[15] Harsher still was the fate of tenants evicted because they were behind on rent. Though Melbourne suffered most, followed by Sydney, other towns and cities also fared badly. Driven down by the falling price of sugar, land values in northern Queensland towns such as Cairns and Townsville fell earlier than in the south.[16] The sugar industry's reliance on indentured 'Kanaka' or Pacific Island labourers was already controversial. Back in the 1880s the Queensland government's attempts to stop recruitment to the cane fields had heightened sugar-planters' desires to create a separate northern colony. As the economic climate deteriorated in 1892, the sugar lobby convinced the government to allow Pacific Island labour schemes to continue for a further ten years.[17]

Aboriginal policy and racial anxieties

Like Pacific Islanders on the cane fields, Aboriginal workers were crucial to the survival of pastoralists and pearlers in northern Australia. This was particularly the case during the Depression and the so-called 'Federation Drought' that followed from 1895 until 1903. Concern about abuse and exploitation of Aboriginal labourers in these industries was part of the impetus for the establishment of new mission stations in the north during the 1890s: among them, the German Lutherans at Cape Bedford and Bloomfield, and the Jesuits on the Daly River. It also lent a sense of urgency to the work of anthropologists such as A.C. Haddon and his Cambridge colleagues, who conducted fieldwork in the Torres Strait in 1898. Like the ethnographic expeditions in central Australia, led by Walter Baldwin Spencer

---

14 G.L. Wood, cited in Ronald Lawson, *Brisbane in the 1890s: A Study of an Australian Urban Society* (Brisbane: UQP, 1973), p. 43; P.G. McCarthy, cited in Graeme Davison, *The Rise and Fall of Marvellous Melbourne*, 2nd edn (Melbourne University Press, 2004), p. 258.
15 Davison, *The Rise and Fall of Marvellous Melbourne*, p. 227.
16 Lennie Wallace, *Nomads of the Nineteenth-Century Queensland Goldfields* (Rockhampton: Central Queensland University Press, 2000), p. 125.
17 Raymond Evans, *A History of Queensland* (Cambridge University Press, 2007), pp. 132–5.

and F.J. Gillen in 1896–7, 1901–2 and 1903, this fieldwork was underpinned by a fear that Indigenous customs would soon disappear as a result of contact with white society.[18]

A more direct outcome of concern about the exploitation of Aboriginal labourers in the north was the Queensland government's *Aboriginal Protection and Restriction of the Sale of Opium Act*, passed in 1897. Ushering in an era of more formal and determined restrictions on Aboriginal freedoms, this Act placed every Aboriginal and 'half-caste' person under its regime. With its white racism and heavy-handed paternalism, the Queensland Act provided the model for similar legislation passed in South Australia, the Northern Territory and Western Australia over the following fifteen years.[19] It is partly for this reason that Penelope Hetherington refers to the late-nineteenth century as a 'rehearsal of the future'. In particular, the removal of 'half-caste' children from their families first began to be widely advocated in the 1890s, a policy that would wreak havoc on the lives of many Aboriginal people in the 1900s.[20] Southern Australians saw the north as a confronting place. This was partly due to the publicity given to the presence of 'Kanakas'; partly, too, because frontier conflict continued there between Aboriginal people and settlers after it had ceased in the south-east. In the Kimberley, for example, which was only settled in the 1880s, active Aboriginal resistance to colonisation continued through the 1890s and into the 1900s.[21]

If the humid north sometimes disturbed the public's dreams, then so did the inner suburbs of the colonial capitals. This was particularly the case in Melbourne, Sydney and Brisbane, the cities that had grown most rapidly in the preceding decades. The population density of inner-industrial districts such as Melbourne's Collingwood, Sydney's Redfern and Brisbane's Fortitude Valley had increased markedly during the long boom. 'Sweated' trades such as bootmaking and tailoring were also concentrated in these localities – especially in Collingwood – ensuring that their residents had shared little in the boom-time prosperity. It is perhaps unsurprising, then, that many inner

---

18 Henry Reynolds, *North of Capricorn: The Untold Story of the People of Australia's North* (Sydney: Allen & Unwin, 2003), chs 1–2; D.J. Mulvaney, *'So Much That is New': Baldwin Spencer, 1860–1929* (Melbourne University Press, 1985).

19 Richard Broome, *Aboriginal Australians: A History Since 1788*, 4th edn (Sydney: Allen & Unwin, 2012), pp. 118–20.

20 Penelope Hetherington, *Settlers, Servants and Slaves: Aboriginal and European Children in Nineteenth-Century Western Australia* (Perth: UWA Press, 2002), ch. 9.

21 Reynolds, *North of Capricorn*, ch. 8; Broome, *Aboriginal Australians*, pp. 112–14.

districts became infamous for delinquent gangs of youth known as 'larrikin pushes' even before the Depression began.[22]

Called 'savages' or 'white blackfellows' in the press, members of larrikin 'pushes' were involved in attacks on Chinese immigrants during the 1880s. The worst of these was in Brisbane's 'Frog's Hollow' in 1888. Male larrikins were also the perpetrators of a number of gang rapes of women in the same decade. As the economy headed into the Depression, Sydney pushes sparked a fear of descent into urban disorder. Some of their members rioted against police at a harbourside picnic on Eight Hours Day 1890; others kicked men to death in two separate incidents at the Rocks in 1892 and 1893. By the time these deaths took place, the inner-city neighbourhoods were becoming stigmatised as sites of crime and poverty. This was the case even for localities such as Richmond in Melbourne and Surry Hills in Sydney, which had once prided themselves on their professional and property-owning elites. Intensified by the outbreak of bubonic plague and 'slum' clearances in the following decade, this stigmatisation of the cities' inner-suburban rim would give impetus to the next great era of suburbanisation in the 1920s.[23]

Larrikin violence took place in a context in which many white male labourers perceived that women and Chinese immigrants were threatening their employment. Like white workers opposing black labour in the north, they were convinced that these groups were colluding with unscrupulous employers to undercut wages and take their jobs. While women were moving into paid employment in certain trades, this hardly meant that they were winning a contest between the sexes. On the contrary, they were among the poorest of those trying to eke out a living in inner-industrial districts. This was partly because the thousands of male workers who departed the eastern and southern colonies for Western Australia after gold was discovered at Coolgardie in 1891 left deserted wives and children to fend for themselves. Women swelled the queues at places such as the Night Refuge and Soup Kitchen for Women and Children, opened by Catholic nuns in Sydney's William Street in 1894.[24]

22 Melissa Bellanta, *Larrikins: A History* (Brisbane: UQP, 2012), ch. 1; Davison, *The Rise and Fall of Marvellous Melbourne*, pp. 69–71.

23 Bellanta, *Larrikins*, chs 3, 4.

24 Anne O'Brien, *Poverty's Prison: The Poor in New South Wales 1880–1918* (Melbourne University Press, 1988), p. 204.

Radicalism, protest and cooperative experiments

Charitable efforts to aid women were necessary because the limited aid provided by the state during the Depression was directed at men. In the worst
affected colonies, governments opened labour bureaus, began relief works
and doled out rations and shelter to unemployed men, offering only minimal assistance to women and fatherless families. In limited instances, they
offered leases and small loans to cooperatives of unemployed labourers in the
hope that they would form viable 'village settlements' on public land. These
schemes, which led to the creation of cooperative settlements on the Murray
River in South Australia, Queensland's Gayndah region and elsewhere, were
promoted by a rhetoric that suggested that men could escape the emasculat-
ing conditions of urban unemployment through small farming. Even though
they offered only paltry acreages and loans, such schemes were not offered as
a matter of course. Like other forms of state aid, colonial governments made
them available only after protest marches and rallies by aggrieved crowds.[25]

Along with demands for village settlements and relief works, members
of the unemployed kept a rowdy presence in urban spaces in the early 1890s.
Anger over the glaring inequality and the inertia of government in the face of
want fuelled motley gatherings in public places such as Melbourne's Queen's
Wharf, around the Queen's statue at the top of King Street in Sydney and
on the banks of the Torrens River near South Australia's Parliament House.
Radical groups also bloomed amid the ruins of bank savings and building
societies. Among them were the Australian Socialist League, Sydney's Active
Service Brigade, Melbourne's Anarchist Club, Adelaide's *Allgemeiner Deutscher
Verein* (an offshoot of Germany's Social Democratic Foundation), and numer-
ous Single Tax Leagues.[26]

The most *outré* of the radical movements that sprang up in the 1890s was
the campaign to create a New Australia in South America, based on cooperative socialist principles. Led by the former editor of the Queensland *Worker*,
William Lane, this movement took just under 240 men, women and children
to the fertile inlands of Paraguay. These participants felt the powerful mix
of utopian longing and back-to-the-land fervour found in diverse parts of
Western society at the time. The composition of the New Australia cooperative reflected the eclectic yearnings that had called it into being. It included

25 Scates, *A New Australia*, chs 4–5; O'Brien, *Poverty's Prison*, pp. 71–2, 74, 76.
26 Scates, *A New Australia*.

Lane himself, a club-footed teetotal who had pored over Edward Bellamy's utopian work, *Looking Backward* (1887), before writing his own radical novel, *The Workingman's Paradise* (1892). Since he had also written a racist 'Asian invasion' novel set in northern Queensland, it is not surprising that he hoped to maintain an all-white status for the New Australia, ruling out contact with its non-white neighbours. Others involved in this short-lived enterprise were the feisty Queensland shearers' unionist, Gilbert Carey; the puritanical socialist and writer, Mary Cameron (later Gilmore); and a contingent of 'single taxers' from Adelaide.[27]

The single-tax movement was an important part of the political landscape in the early 1890s. Following the American political economist, Henry George, its devotees called for all taxes to be removed except for one on land values. For those who had witnessed the excesses of the land boom, George's idea of abolishing the investment property market by means of a 'single tax' held a special allure. Thousands flocked to hear George speak when he visited Australasia on a lecture tour in 1890. Many of these Georgists were devout Nonconformists, chiefly Congregationalists and Primitive Methodists. Like those in the United States preaching the 'social gospel' or the Christian socialists in Europe, they were engaged in a process of adapting their evangelical beliefs to social justice concerns.[28] Others attempting this were the educated mavericks attending Rev. Charles Strong's Australian Church and Archibald Turnbull's Labour Church, both in Melbourne.[29]

The great strikes

The political ferment of the early 1890s was exacerbated by a series of industrial showdowns, later referred to as the 'Great Strikes'. These were the maritime strike of 1890; the shearers' strikes of 1891 and 1894; and the Broken Hill miners' strike of 1892. The biggest was the maritime strike. It began on 16 August 1890, when marine officers belonging to the Mercantile Marine Officer's Association walked off the job in the port of Melbourne. The officers were protesting their bosses' refusal to allow the Association to join Melbourne's Trades Hall Council. Because this amounted to a denial of their right to unionise, other maritime unions joined them in solidarity. By the time

---

27 Gavin Souter, *A Peculiar People: William Lane's Australian Utopians in Paraguay*, new edn (Brisbane: UQP, 1991).

28 Scates, *A New Australia*, pp. 14–15, 17, 29, 100.

29 C.R. Badger, *The Reverend Charles Strong and the Australian Church* (Melbourne: Abacada Press, 1971); 'Archibald Turnbull', *Australian Dictionary of Biography*, vol. 12, pp. 286–7.

it ended on 6 November 1890, the strike had spread across colonial boundaries and industries, involving some 50,000 seamen, wharf-workers, shearers, coal and silver-lead miners, gas-stokers and cart-drivers and at least 8,000 more in New Zealand.[30] A grab-bag of industrial issues had become involved during the action. The most intractable was a pre-existing dispute between shearers' unions and pastoralists over the employment of non-union labour.

In the years leading up to the maritime strike, shearers' unions had struggled for a place at the negotiating table with the owners of large sheep-stations. The shearers were campaigning for the 'closed shop', meaning the sole employment of union workers in the big shearing sheds. Unsurprisingly, most pastoralists resisted this. They called for 'freedom of contract', by which they meant the freedom to enter directly into agreements with workers, cutting out union negotiators and uniform wages and conditions. To preserve a role for organised labour, shearers' unions began courting the support of unionists in related industries. Chief among these were the carrier unions whose members transported export-bound wool; the maritime unions, whose members loaded the wool onto ships; and the coal-mining unions, whose members produced the ships' fuel.[31]

Attempts to foster collaboration between unions and across industries in the late-nineteenth century were sometimes called 'new unionism'. The new unionism was contrasted with the trade unionism of previous decades, whose representatives had been more narrowly focused on the interests of skilled workers in their own particular trade. An opportunity to put the new collaborative approach to the test came in Queensland in May 1890, when the managers of the massive Jondaryan sheep-station in Queensland's Darling Downs banned union labour. In response, the Queensland Shearers' Union solicited the aid of maritime unionists from Brisbane and London in a boycott on the movement of wool. Once this was granted, the Jondaryan managers found they had no way to export their product, and reluctantly agreed to a closed shop.[32]

Coming shortly after the successful London dockworkers' strike in 1889, the Jondaryan affair was celebrated in labour circles. It turned out to be a Pyrrhic victory, however, because it galvanised employers to begin organising

---

30 Stuart Svensen, *The Sinews of War: Hard Cash and the 1890 Maritime Strike* (Sydney: UNSW Press, 1995), p. xi.

31 John Merritt, *The Making of the AWU* (Oxford University Press, 1986).

32 R.J. and R.A. Sullivan, 'The London Dock Strike, the Jondaryan Strike and the Brisbane Bootmakers' Strike, 1889–1890', in D.J. Murphy (ed.), *The Big Strikes: Queensland 1889–1965* (Brisbane: UQP, 1983), pp. 50, 54–7; Trainor, *British Imperialism and Australian Nationalism*, p. 134.

among themselves. In the months after the dispute ended in May 1890, the owners of pastoral stations, shipping companies, coal mines and commercial firms formed a battery of federations. This activity accelerated after the union representing pastoral workers in New South Wales and Victoria issued pastoralists with an ultimatum. Agree to a closed shop for the upcoming season or face industrial action, the Amalgamated Shearers' Union proclaimed. Determined to defy this ultimatum, the pastoral lobby worked overtime to build a strike fund and shore up the support of capitalists in other industries. 'The common saying now is the fight must come, and most employers add the sooner the better', the president of the Sydney Chamber of Commerce declared. It was in this increasingly adversarial atmosphere, charged with the belief that what was at issue was the 'total framework of employer-labour relations', that the maritime strike broke out.[33]

Buoyed by the Jondaryan win, the union leaders who headed into the maritime strike were taken aback by the strength of employers' resistance. They were shocked both by their opponents' refusal to negotiate and the speed with which they arranged an alternative labour force. Unionists described workers who collaborated with employers to break the strike as 'scabs' or 'blacklegs'. Over the following weeks, nasty confrontations took place between 'scabs' and unionists, particularly in Melbourne, Port Adelaide, Sydney's Circular Quay and the coalfields in the Hunter Valley of New South Wales. Though unionists and their supporters set up pickets at mine entrances and on wharves, these proved ineffective after colonial governments sent police and troops to escort non-union workers through the picket lines. With police and military muscle behind them, employers were able to hold out until the unions' funds were depleted and the starvation of those on strike forced them to surrender.[34]

Almost as soon as the maritime strike was over, pastoralists drew up new rules for the next shearing season, due to begin in Queensland. The new rules were calculated to provoke a fight with Queensland unions. They reduced wages, omitted a ban on 'coloured' labour and provocatively repudiated the 8-hour day and any prior 'closed shop' arrangements. The outcome was the bitter shearers' strike involving approximately 10,000 unionists between 5 January and 18 June 1891. Fought in central and western Queensland, it led to ugly incidents in which desperate strikers burned paddocks and woolsheds,

---

33 John Rickard, *Class and Politics: New South Wales, Victoria and the Early Commonwealth, 1890–1910* (Canberra: ANU Press, 1976), pp. 13, 21.

34 Bruce Scates, 'Gender, Household and Community Politics: The 1890 Maritime Strike in Australia and New Zealand', *Labour History*, 61 (1991): 70–87.

and others armed themselves with rifles and rioted at stations where non-union workers arrived by train. The Queensland government responded by sending armed soldiers to Queensland's central highlands. At one stand-off at Peak Downs, the pastoralist Charles Fairburn (whose family owned 40 per cent of the Queensland wool clip) allegedly urged troops to open fire. Strikers were charged with a multitude of offences, and in many cases rural magistrates aligned with the pastoralists presided over their trials. Some 225 unionists served gaol terms as a result of the shearers' strike.[35]

A few months after the shearers' strike, another industrial conflict erupted among mining unionists at Broken Hill. They were protesting the fact that the Barrier Ranges Mining Companies' Association had decided to abolish the uniform day-wage, departing from an agreement long held with the Amalgamated Miners' Union. For the following eight weeks, unionists were surrounded by a massive police presence sent from Sydney via South Australia before being forced to back down. Further actions were staged and lost by unionists over the following few years: another shearers' strike in Queensland in 1894 and smaller ones by Newcastle coal miners in 1893 and 1896.[36] A letter written by a member of the Amalgamated Shearers' Union during the maritime strike in 1890 helps us to imagine the trauma suffered by participants during these angry, hungry and ultimately futile disputes. 'Our wives and children are starving, and we see misery everywhere', the letter-writer wrote to the union's president, William Guthrie Spence. 'You and your mates have ruined us all for the b__ Cause'.[37]

Civilising capitalism

The combined effects of the Depression and failed strikes led to a dramatic drop in union membership. While roughly one in five male wage earners had belonged to a union in 1890, that figure was closer to one in twenty in 1896.[38] Well before numbers had sunk that low, union leaders realised that they would need to adopt new strategies if they were to remain relevant. The

35 Stuart Svensen, *The Shearers' War: The Story of the 1891 Shearers' Strike* (Brisbane: UQP 1989), p. 107; Evans, *A History of Queensland*, pp. 122–3.
36 Brian Fitzpatrick, *The British Empire in Australia 1834–1939*, new edn (Melbourne: Macmillan, 1969), pp. 226–8; Trainor, *British Imperialism and Australian Nationalism*, pp. 138–9.
37 W.G. Spence, *Australia's Awakening: Thirty Years in the Life of an Australian Agitator* (Sydney: Worker Trustees, 1909), p. 84.
38 Stuart Macintyre, *A Concise History of Australia*, 3rd edn (Cambridge University Press, 2009), p. 125.

most innovative was their decision to participate in the formation of political parties. The idea of creating a political labour movement had germinated in the previous decade, when stray activists promoted themselves as Labour candidates come election time. This idea effloresced after the maritime and shearers' strikes, prompting the establishment of labour parties in the southern and eastern mainland colonies between November 1890 and May 1891. Western Australia and Tasmania had acquired their own labour parties by 1902, by which time the Australian Labor Party (as it became known) had also been born.[39]

The first labour candidates fared remarkably well for raw recruits to a new political movement. In New South Wales, they won 36 out of 141 seats in the lower house to hold the balance of power after the election of 1891. Their South Australian counterparts won ten lower house seats in the 1893 election, while those in Queensland won fifteen seats the same year. Big employers were alarmed by these electoral gains. They formed lobby groups known as National Associations – 'National Asses' to their adversaries – with the intention of opposing legislation introduced by labour members of parliament. In 1892 a member of the New South Wales 'National Ass' claimed that he and his fellows were 'the chief representatives of what may be termed Conservatism, or opposition to mob rule'.[40] In truth, the colonial labour parties were far from any kind of rule. The world's first labour government was admittedly formed in Queensland in 1899 – but it lacked a parliamentary majority and lasted only a week. Plenty of people wanted Labor to have a voice, but few considered it capable of running a government.

The overwhelming longing among Australian voters in the 1890s was for political stability. In each colony, the governments elected during the Depression remained in power until the end of the decade. In the dog days of 1894, for example, the jowl-faced liberal, George Reid, a free trader, became premier of New South Wales. He stayed in power until 1899, when he was replaced by another liberal, the pro-tariff William Lyne. After turbulence in 1892–93, the cautious liberal, George Turner, became premier between 1894 and 1899. In South Australia, the more advanced liberal, Charles Kingston, took over the reins with Labor backing in 1893 and kept hold of them for the following six years. Tasmania was governed by Edward Braddon between 1894 and 1899, while the so-called Continuous Ministry stayed at the helm from 1890 to 1899 in Queensland. Conditions were different in Western

39 Ross McMullin, *The Light on the Hill: The Australian Labor Party, 1891–1991* (Oxford University Press, 1991), ch. 1.
40 Quoted in Rickard, *Class and Politics*, p. 59.

Australia, which had only achieved self-government in 1890 and immediately embarked on a period of boom rather than bust. 'Big John' Forrest provided a similar period of political stability there, however, working adroitly to reconcile diverse political interests while serving as premier between 1890 and 1899.[41]

Mindful of the industrial savagery of the Great Strikes, both liberal and labour members of parliament in the late 1890s were keen to 'civilise capitalism'.[42] Most of the policies that would make Australia famous as a social laboratory in the new century were introduced by colonial governments in the second half of the 1890s. Chief among these were attempts to fix a minimum wage, provide welfare payments for those most in need, create courts for the arbitration of industrial disputes, ramp up protective tariffs and restrict the entry of 'coloured' immigrants. In 1900, for example, the New South Wales ministry led by Lyne introduced an old-age pension and a compulsory arbitration scheme for industrial disputes. Four years earlier, in 1896, Reid's ministry had passed a slew of significant laws with the support of Labour members of parliament. These included the *Coloured Races Restriction and Regulation Act*, presaging the federal government's white Australia policy in the following decade; the *State Children Relief Act*, providing that destitute single mothers receive a 'boarding-out' allowance for their children; a *Public Health Act*, extending government control over community health; and two laws intervening in labour relations, the *Coal Mining Regulation Act* and the *Shops and Factories Act*.[43]

Fuelled by what some would call 'new liberal' beliefs, shops and factories Acts were passed in South Australia and Victoria as well as New South Wales in the mid-1890s. Replacing the colony's earlier factory laws, Victoria's was the most adventurous. It set up wages boards to establish minimum wages and standards in the most notoriously sweated trades such as baking and boot and shirt making. By making it less profitable for employers to outsource work, these wages boards helped to begin a transition from 'an

41 Ibid., chs 3–4; Margaret Glass, *Charles Cameron Kingston: Federation Father* (Melbourne University Press, 1997); Henry Reynolds, *A History of Tasmania* (Cambridge University Press, 2012), pp. 205–6; Geoffrey Bolton, 'Robert Philps: Capitalist as Politician', in Denis Murphy et al. (eds), *The Premiers of Queensland* (Brisbane: UQP, 2003), pp. 1–29; Geoffrey Bolton, *Land of Vision and Mirage: Western Australia Since 1826* (Perth: UWA Press, 2008), pp. 59–86.

42 Bede Nairn, *Civilising Capitalism: The Beginnings of the Australian Labor Party* (Melbourne University Press, 1989).

43 John Murphy, *A Decent Provision: Australian Welfare Policy, 1870 to 1949* (Farnham: Ashgate, 2011), p. 55; Desley Deacon, *Managing Gender: The State, the New Middle Class and Women Workers 1830–1930* (Oxford University Press, 1989), pp. 101–2, 125.

essentially pre-industrial manufacturing structure reliant on sweating and small units to a modern factory-based industrial system' in Victoria, albeit one that would take some decades to complete.[44] This same transition began to take place in other parts of Australia after a similar wage-board system was adopted in some other States, though a separate system of wage arbitration by a tribunal was introduced at the federal level in the early 1900s.[45]

Gender and the first-wave feminists

The legislative experimentation that took place in the late 1890s went beyond seeking a stable compromise between labour and capital. It was also directed at re-establishing separate spheres between the sexes. For the male politicians and public servants involved, a crucial part of the process of reorganising society involved reinforcing men's role as breadwinners. The most strenuous attempts were in Victoria. Its wages boards instituted a host of new segregations between the sexes, banning girls from apprenticeships in many trades and making it impossible for women to be employed in the best-paid, highest-status work. Married women were excluded from employment in the public service, a policy that remained in effect until the 1970s. In 1893–94, for example, the education departments in New South Wales and Victoria stopped recruiting married women. In 1896, the New South Wales Post Office and Telegraph Department sacked all its married women workers. By 1903 attempts were being made to prevent even single women from employment in an array of government offices throughout New South Wales.[46]

Attempts to restrict women's movement into the workforce were the most overt instances of a backlash against campaigns to enlarge female opportunity. Australia's 'woman movement' had begun in the 1880s, the decade in which women were first permitted to graduate from universities. The first women's suffrage societies were founded in the 1880s: first in Victoria in 1884, then South Australia in 1888. When the South Australia's Women's Suffrage League was formed, its leading lights had already acquired experience as

44 Janet McCalman, *Struggletown: Public and Private Life in Richmond 1900–1965* (Melbourne: Hyland House, 1998), p. 28.
45 Stuart Macintyre and Richard Mitchell (eds), *Foundations of Arbitration: The Origins and Effects of State Compulsory Arbitration 1890–1914* (Oxford University Press, 1989), ch. 9; Raelene Frances, *The Politics of Work: Gender and Labour in Victoria 1880–1939* (Cambridge University Press, 1993), Part 1.
46 Magarey, *Passions of the First Wave Feminists*, pp. 132–5; Deacon, *Managing Gender*, chs 5, 6.

activists for the colony's Social Purity Society, which fought successfully to raise the age of female sexual consent from thirteen to sixteen in 1885. They were actively supported by the South Australian branch of the Woman's Christian Temperance Union (WCTU) after it was galvanised by a visit from the US temperance reformer, Jessie Ackermann, in 1889. Though it would not acquire a suffrage society until 1891, New South Wales was the site of Australia's first feminist newspaper and club in 1888. Known respectively as the *Dawn* and the Dawn Club, these were founded by the journalist and writer, Louisa Lawson. Another Sydney woman, Maybanke Wolstoneholme (later Anderson), began the colonies' second feminist newspaper, the *Woman's Voice,* in 1896, by which time South Australian women already had the vote and suffragists in the other colonies were hopeful of achieving the same.[47] In such a context, it is little wonder that an anti-feminist reaction was underway by the mid-1890s.

Australia's first-wave feminists were a diverse group. Politically, they ranged from the liberal Lady Mary Windeyer, wife of a Supreme Court judge in Sydney, to the Brisbane shirtmaker Emma Miller, a keen unionist and supporter of Queensland's political labour movement. On sexual issues, they varied from the agnostic shopkeeper-suffragist, Brettana Smyth, who sold 'French preventatives' at her North Melbourne drapery store, to the high-minded Bessie Lee, organiser for the influential Victorian branch of the WCTU, who urged married women to practise chastity. For some, like New South Wales' Rose Scott and Victoria's Vida Goldstein, raising the age of female sexual consent was a burning issue, but not for others. The same applied to the temperance movement, which had acquired momentum in the 1880s. The WCTU was a key player in the colonies' push for women's suffrage, but not all feminists supported restrictions on the sale and consumption of alcohol.[48] What most Australian feminists had in common was an excitement about the growth of the 'woman movement' in the colonies. This excitement detracted from their ability to see the retraction of opportunities for women in the paid workforce taking place at the time.

The rhetoric of first-wave feminism was filled with optimistic talk of a new day dawning in 1890s Australia. The fact that many feminists supported the campaign for federation heightened this emphasis on fresh beginnings.

---

47 Magarey, *Passions of the First Wave Feminists*, ch. 3; Brian Matthews, *Louisa* (Melbourne: McPhee Gribble, 1988); Jan Roberts, *Maybanke Anderson: Sex, Suffrage & Social Reform* (Sydney: Hale & Iremonger, 1993).

48 Magarey, *Passions of the First Wave Feminists*, chs 3–5; Pam Young, *Proud to be a Rebel: The Life and Times of Emma Miller* (Brisbane: UQP, 1991), pp. 47–9.

As they saw it, the imminent birth of the Australian nation, often symbolised by a radiant virginal girl, held the promise of full citizenship for white women. A rash of popular novels portraying a new type, the 'Australian girl', was the perfect accompaniment to this view. These coltishly spirited, golden-haired figures appeared in works such as Ethel Turner's *Seven Little Australians* (1894) and David Hennessey's *An Australian Bush Track* (1896), testament to the expanding market for fiction with Australian settings.[49] Though neither Australian-girl characters nor their creators were necessarily advocates for the 'woman movement', they complemented feminists' confidence that a new breed of sure-minded and able-bodied Australian women was on its way.

With their emphasis on youthful promise, a number of Australia's leading feminists were attracted to the 'child rescue' campaigns that intensified throughout western society at the turn of the century. Aimed at transforming poor urban children into productive future citizens, these campaigns included efforts to abolish child labour, establish crèches and parks, and place needy children in what we now call foster care. (By the end of the Edwardian era, they would also incorporate the removal of 'half-caste' Aboriginal children to industrial schools or 'homes'.[50]) After years of advocacy for 'boarding out' schemes for impoverished children, for example, the woman's suffragist and novelist, Catherine Helen Spence, was appointed to South Australia's Destitute Board by the Kingston government in 1897. She would later document the same government's creation of a dedicated children's court in 1896, a landmark event marking the beginnings of a juvenile justice system in Australia. In Sydney, Maybanke Wolstenholme was prominent in the Kindergarten and Playground Unions of New South Wales.[51]

Bohemianism and Australian national identity

While activists were working to create green spaces for 'slum' children, male artists and writers from the cities were embarking on their own discoveries of the outdoors. Some Australian artists had started roughing it in bush camps back in the 1870s, at the same time as Claude Monet and his

---

49 Magarey, *Passions of the First Wave Feminists*, pp. 44–8; Robert Dixon, *Writing the Colonial Adventure: Race, Gender and Nation in Anglo-Australian Popular Fiction, 1875–1914* (Cambridge University Press, 1995), pp. 91–4; Richard White and Hsu-Ming Teo, 'Popular Culture', in Deryk M. Schreuder and Stuart Ward (eds), *Australia's Empire* (Oxford University Press, 2008), pp. 345–50.

50 Shurlee Swain and Margot Hillel, *Child, Nation, Race and Empire: Child Rescue Discourse, England, Canada and Australia, 1850–1915* (Manchester University Press, 2010), pp. 146–8.

51 Roberts, *Maybanke Anderson*; Susan Magarey, *Unbridling the Tongues of Women: A Biography of Catherine Helen Spence* (University of Adelaide Press, 2010), p. 88.

fellow French impressionists were venturing into the countryside around Fontainebleu. When young male artists began camping out in the country around Heidelberg, on the outskirts of Melbourne, in the late 1880s, they considered themselves at the vanguard of a radical new *en plein air* school on Australian shores. Youthful men of Anglo heritage were not alone in attempting to capture momentary sensations of light and mood in paintings of the Australian countryside. Others included the Melbourne artist, Jane Sutherland, and an Italian aristocrat, Girolamo Nerli.[52] Australian impressionism was nonetheless dominated by strapping young fellows. The most notable were Tom Roberts and Arthur Streeton, who left Melbourne to spend portions of the early 1890s camping with other male artists they called 'the boys' at Little Sirius Cove on Sydney Harbour.

When George du Maurier's novel, *Trilby,* appeared in book form from 1895, drawing on memories of the author's Parisian youth, Streeton read it avidly by the light of an 'aesthetic' Japanese lantern in his artists' camp. He and his friends fancied themselves to be wilder, fresher variants of Parisian bohemians, painting by the water by day and holding bush soirees with daring young women by night. They still liked to frequent urban venues, however – particularly Sydney's Café Francais, once described as 'so Frenchy that it might have been on the "Boule Miche"'.[53] Some of the *en plein air* painters attended gatherings of a group calling itself the Supper Club at the Café Francais. Others joined writers and journalists in alternative, all-male bohemian clubs such as Sydney's Dawn and Dusk Club, or Melbourne's Ishmael Club. There, they discussed symbolism and *art pour l'art* aestheticism between rowdy pranks and rounds of cheap beer or wine.[54]

When the Australian journalist, Arthur Jose, published a reminiscent work called *The Romantic Nineties* in the 1930s, he claimed that the bohemians he had known had been too preoccupied with national possibilities to concern themselves with the risqué pleasures enjoyed by decadents in London.[55] The mythology surrounding the decade by the mid-1900s insisted similarly that 1890s bohemians cultivated their mix of bush fervour and Francophilia in order to resist effete British influences on Australian culture. These men

52 'Jane Sutherland', *Australian Dictionary of Biography*, vol. 12, pp. 140–1; Barry Pearce and Linda Slutzkin (eds), *Bohemians in the Bush: The Artists' Camps of Mosman* (Sydney: Art Gallery of New South Wales, 1991), p. 18.

53 Pearce and Slutzkin, *Bohemians in the Bush*, pp. 27–30.

54 Tony Moore, *Dancing with Empty Pockets: Australia's Bohemians* (Sydney: Pier 9, 2012), ch. 2.

55 Arthur Jose, *The Romantic Nineties* (Sydney: Angus & Robertson, 1933).

did participate in the growing interest in national identity that was widely apparent in the period – whether in consumer objects decorated with native blooms or sentimental pro-Federation poetry in the press.[56] Yet they still maintained a profound interest in British cultural production. For all their Gallic pretensions, they felt a keen kinship with the members of London bohemia, that network of clubs, taverns and theatres in which men spoke the 'egalitarian language of "the boys" on the spree'.[57] Whether this interest included a curiosity in the homosexual subculture that overlapped with London's bohemian scene is a matter of speculation. It is notable, however, that an article called 'The Oscar Wilde's [sic] of Sydney', published in the scandal-sheet *Scorpion* in 1895, claimed that flamboyantly dressed, effeminate men paraded in certain Sydney pubs and billiard halls – seamy venues possibly known to the city's bohemians.[58]

An example of Australian bohemians' interest in British cultural production can be found in the similarities between images of cockneys and those of larrikins produced in the 1890s. Caricatures of jolly cockney bruisers and their 'donahs' (girlfriends) were rife in English popular culture in this period, whether in music-hall acts or cartoons appearing in the likes of *Punch* or *Ally Slope's Half Holiday*. There were striking parallels between these caricaturised cockneys and the larrikin hedonists sketched for the *Bulletin* by the Melbourne bohemian artists Tom Durkin, Ambrose Dyson and Norman Lindsay.[59] Portraying larrikin woman-beaters who delighted in the levelling effects of the spree, these caricatures were part of a defence of rowdy masculine pleasure at a time when it was under attack from temperance and feminist reformers. Durkin, in particular, had revealed a hostility to feminism when he depicted Australian suffragists as plain-faced killjoys in an 1895 cartoon. It had been criticised by Melbourne socialist Henry Hyde Champion for its 'hysterical prejudice' against the suffrage cause.[60]

Among the general public, an interest in Australian national identity coexisted with a passionate commitment to British culture and imperial might. This was apparent in the push for Federation, which had a substantial

---

56 White and Teo, 'Popular Culture', p. 342; John Hirst, *The Sentimental Nation: The Making of the Australian Commonwealth* (Oxford University Press, 2000), p. 24.
57 Peter Bailey, *Popular Culture and Performance in the Victorian City* (Cambridge University Press, 1998), pp. 53, 124.
58 Robert French, *Camping by a Billabong: Gay and Lesbian Stories from Australian History* (Sydney: Blackwattle Press, 1993), pp. 43–6.
59 Bellanta, *Larrikins*, ch. 2.
60 Marguerite Mahood, *The Loaded Line: Australian Political Caricature 1788–1901* (Melbourne University Press, 1973), p. 239.

popular following.[61] It was also evident during the South African War between 1899 and 1902. An outpouring of public support attended Australian troops who volunteered to aid Britain in South Africa during these hostilities. Before the Anzac 'digger' was mythologised as a national type, these troops were lionised for their possession of supposedly Australian traits (bush practicality, laconic humour, anti-authoritarianism) and for their adoption of native marsupials and a sheep dog, 'Bushie', as mascots.[62] At the same time, theatrical managers pandered to the public's pro-British patriotism by staging songs such as 'When the Empire Calls'. One such manager was Kate Howarde, head of a travelling theatre company that toured the Western Australian goldfields and northern Queensland towns among other locations in the late 1890s. Tellingly, Howarde's repertory was a mix of popular British melodramas and local bushranger plays.[63]

Popular culture

The 1890s have long been characterised in trans-Atlantic histories as a crucial period for the development of mass cultural production and consumption. This claim needs to be qualified in Australia's case. Circuses, small vaudeville troupes and travelling theatre companies such as Howarde's continued to tour into the new century. Concentrating on suburban and provincial locations, they worked hard to develop relationships with local communities, with entertainments that were far from mass-produced. Even so, there was evidence of a move towards mass culture in 1890s Australia. It was apparent in the growing interest in Tin Pan Alley songs and dance crazes such as the cakewalk; in the presence of phonograph operators in public spaces; and in the exhibition of film reels in rented halls and vaudeville shows from 1896. Perhaps more significantly, the corporate foundations for large-scale commercial entertainment in Australia were laid in the decade. In urban districts, at least, the small players who had once offered a multitude of live performances were ousted by well-capitalised companies holding the rights to perform the latest international acts. These firms soon controlled circuits extending throughout Australia and New Zealand,

---

61 Helen Irving, *To Constitute A Nation: A Cultural History of Australia's Constitution* (Cambridge University Press, 1997).

62 White and Teo, 'Popular Culture', p. 343; Craig Wilcox, *Australia's Boer War: The War in South Africa 1899–1902* (Oxford University Press, 2002).

63 Barbara Garlick, 'Australian Travelling Theatre: A Study in Popular Entertainment and National Ideology', PhD thesis, University of Queensland, 1994, ch. 2.

which was effectively regarded as a single territory for the entertainment industry.[64]

The best example of the emergence of a big player in popular entertainment can be found in the former English music-hall star, Harry Rickards. After opening with his Tivoli Minstrels and Speciality Company in Sydney's Garrick Theatre in 1892, he built up what became known as the Tivoli vaudeville circuit across Australasia. By the early 1900s, Rickards was staging shows in Sydney, Melbourne, Adelaide, Brisbane, Perth and many New Zealand cities. The Australian public was first introduced to cinema in a Tivoli show: in an act by the magician, Carl Hertz in 1896.[65] In the same period, the company formed by J.C. Williamson and his partners came to dominate the elegant end of the urban theatrical market. Though firms such as Bland Holt's offered big-budget sporting melodramas at the turn of the century, Williamson & Co. promoted itself as the last word in sophistication. It staged comic opera, lavish costume drama and fashionable musical comedy to a middling to middle-class clientele.[66]

First performed in Australia in the mid-1890s, musical comedies such as A Gaiety Girl were signal examples of the shift from the high-Victorian emphasis on rational recreation to what the historian Peter Bailey has called the 'gospel of fun' preached by turn-of-the-century entertainment entrepreneurs.[67] They invited audiences to conclude that gaiety could be enjoyed for its own sake. With scenes in up-to-date spaces such as gleaming department stores and gymnasiums, they also complemented the hedonistic consumerism on which developers of urban pleasure resorts relied. Significantly, too, musical comedy presented flirtation between the sexes as a bit of harmless fun.[68] It was probably for this reason that A Gaiety Girl appealed so markedly to the Bulletin's bohemian theatre reviewer in 1895. Filled with ideas of 'innocent libertinism' among urbane couples, musical comedies could be read as an endorsement of male sexual prerogatives in the face of challenges by feminist 'killjoys'. It is thus important to acknowledge the presence of a 'Gay Nineties' in Australia – if only to note that the politics of gaiety was part of the broader gender struggles taking place at the time.

---

64 Veronica Kelly, The Empire Actors: Stars of Australasian Costume Drama 1890s–1920s (Sydney: Currency Press, 2009), p. 2.
65 Richard Waterhouse, From Minstrel Show to Vaudeville: The Australian Popular Stage, 1788–1914 (Sydney: UNSW Press, 1990), ch. 8.
66 Kelly, The Empire Actors, pp. 2–4.
67 Peter Bailey, 'The Politics and Poetics of Modern British Leisure', Rethinking History, 3, 2 (1999): 157.
68 Bailey, Popular Culture and Performance in the Victorian City, ch. 8.

That theatrical productions such as *A Gaiety Girl* could attract audiences in Australia even in the midst of the Depression makes it clear that by no means everyone was rendered penniless by the economic upheaval of the day. Department stores such as Anthony Horderns and David Jones were in fact filled with customers throughout the Depression, taking advantage of the drop in prices.[69] An innovative business begun by the feminist Alice Henry in 1896 also underlines the fact that some rural folk continued to have disposable income. After quitting her job as a Melbourne journalist, Henry set herself up as a city-based buyer for country women.[70] One can imagine her buying the enormous hats a-quiver with trimmings that became popular during the decade – or perhaps enquiring about the bicycles that enjoyed a craze in 1895. Enough consumers had bought bicycles by 1896 for Australian football fans to be observed riding to Saturday-afternoon matches in Melbourne on two-wheeled vehicles emblazoned with the colours of their team.[71] Such observations remind us that there were other aspects of 1890s street life apart from protests and soup-kitchen lines.

The expansion of spectator sports was another aspect of 1890s Australia that requires us to look beyond the misery caused by the Depression and Great Strikes. This was most notably the case for boxing, cricket, Australian rules football and rugby union.[72] On the other hand, Australia showed little interest in the first modern Olympics, held in Athens in 1896, although one Australian athlete competed there.[73] Pictures of boxing matches held in turn-of-the-century Sydney reveal tight-packed, boisterous male crowds – including one at the aptly named Gaiety Hall.[74] Cricket and football attracted women as well as men, with those at football matches wearing coloured ribbons or waving flags at carnival-like Saturday games. The New South Wales Rugby Union grew so fat on ticket sales that rumblings of discontent had already

---

69 Gail Reekie, 'The Sexual Politics of Selling and Shopping', in Magarey et al. (eds), *Debutante Nation*, p. 62.

70 Diane Kirkby, *Alice Henry, The Power of Pen and Voice: The Life of an Australian-American Labor Reformer* (Cambridge University Press, 2000), p. 56.

71 Rob Hess, 'A Mania for Bicycles: The Impact of Cycling on Australian Rules Football', *Sporting Traditions*, 14, 2 (1998): 9–11.

72 June Senyard 'Marvellous Melbourne, Consumerism and the Rise of Sports Spectating', in Matthew Nicholson (ed.), *Fanfare: Spectator Culture and Australian Rules Football* (Melbourne: Australian Society for Sports History, 2005), pp. 25–40; Richard Cashman *'Ave a Go, Yer Mug! Australian Cricket Crowds From Larrikin to Ocker* (Sydney: Collins 1984), pp. 38–40; Martin Sharp '"A Degenerate Race": Rugby and Cricket Crowds in Sydney 1890–1912', *Sporting Traditions*, 4, 2 (1988): 134–49.

73 Douglas Booth and Colin Tatz, *One-Eyed: A View of Australian Sport* (Sydney: Allen & Unwin, 2000), p. 114.

74 For example, photograph of Jack McGowan versus Bob Turner, Gaiety Hall, Sydney, 24 November 1902, National Library of Australia, PIC / 8395 / 977 LOC Drawer PIC / 8395.

begun among working-class players about its refusal to compensate them for loss of earnings or injury. A push to professionalise the game would not come to fruition until 1907, when breakaway players decided to form the New South Wales Rugby League, adopting the rules of England's Northern Union – followed by the formation of a similar league in Queensland the following year. In Melbourne, too, rising ticket sales and debates about professionalisation of the sport were part of the context in which the strongest teams in Victoria's Football Association broke away to form the Victorian Football League in 1896.[75] In a range of sports, debates about professionalisation went hand in hand with the commercialisation of leisure, developing apace at the time.

*

The term *fin de siècle* has often been used to characterise the maelstrom of artistic experimentation appearing in Europe at the end of the nineteenth century, whether among impressionists, symbolists, decadents, aesthetes or practitioners of Art Nouveau. With its connotations of exhaustion and decay, it has also been used to describe the proliferation of fears about the possible degeneration of the white race expressed by a range of intellectuals, public figures and cultural producers. Along with the obvious significance of Australian impressionism, symbolist influences were evident on work published in the *Bulletin* after A.G. Stephens began to edit its literary 'Red Page' in 1896.[76] There was also concern about the potential degeneration of the white race in 1890s Australia, expressed in 'Asian invasion' novels, or fears of barbarous larrikin pushes, or anxiety that the Depression signalled an end to progress.

Ultimately, however, the term *fin de siècle* is misleading because it distracts attention from the extent to which 1890s Australia was preoccupied with the birth of the new century rather than the end of the old. Whether among feminists, bohemians or politicians intent on 'civilising capitalism', there was too much excitement expressed about what the twentieth century would bring to describe the period in terms of anxiety and decline. For the same reason, the phrase *fin de siècle* belies how many consumers and producers of

75 Chris Cunneen, 'The Rugby War: The Early History of Rugby League in NSW', in David Headon (ed.), *The Best Ever Australian Sports Writing: A 200 Year Collection* (Melbourne: Black Inc., 2001), pp. 313–25; Rob Hess, 'The Victorian Football League Takes Over, 1897–1914', in Rob Hess and Bob Stewart (eds), *More Than a Game: An Unauthorised History of Australian Rules Football* (Melbourne University Press, 1998), pp. 86–113.

76 Peter Kirkpatrick, '"New Words Come Tripping Slowly": Poetry, Popular Culture and Modernity, 1890–1930', in Peter Pierce (ed.), *The Cambridge History of Australian Literature* (Cambridge University Press, 2009), p. 204.

1890s popular culture placed a premium on gaiety. This was important not only to the male bohemians who resented feminist efforts to restrict their libertine pleasures, not only to the retailers and entertainment entrepreneurs who expanded during the decade, but also the crowds flocking to musical comedies, sporting matches and vaudeville shows as an antidote to the anxieties of the day.

The term 'turn of the century' is more apt than *fin de siècle*. With its evocation of movement and transformation, it points to the multiple ways in which the future of twentieth-century Australia was rehearsed during the decade. This was evident in its racial and gender struggles, in the emphasis on youth, the attempts to 'civilise capitalism' and the commercialisation of leisure taking place in theatres and at football matches. Debate might still rage about the extent to which this turn-of-the-century era was characterised by nationalist feeling, or whether or not the demise of its utopian idealism represents the graveyard of dreams for radical social change. Regardless of one's views on these issues, the 1890s occupy a compelling place in Australian history: economically grim, politically intense, creatively prolific and at times insistently, even aggressively, gay.

10

Making the federal Commonwealth, 1890–1901

HELEN IRVING

On 8 January 1901 an anonymous Australian 'special correspondent' for the London *Morning Post* recorded the momentous events that had taken place in Sydney one week earlier. As midnight struck, hymns, choruses and a 'tumultuous uproar' sounded in the streets; whistles, bells, gongs and the clanging of kitchen utensils joined the hooting and shrieking of people, boats and steam pipes.[1] Later that morning, a great procession moved through the city streets, passing under a sequence of ornamental arches and making its way to the vast Centennial Park south-east of the city, created in 1888 for the centenary of Britain's colonisation of New South Wales. There, the Federation of Australia's six colonies was completed, and the Commonwealth of Australia inaugurated. Under a white pavilion, the Lord's Prayer was recited and Queen Victoria's Proclamation of the Commonwealth read out. The first Australian governor-general, John Adrian Louis Hope, Seventh Earl of Hopetoun and representative of Victoria, Queen of the United Kingdom and Ireland, was sworn in by the Chief Justice of New South Wales. The first prime minister, Edmund Barton, and his handful of executive ministers were then sworn in by Hopetoun. As the ceremony concluded, a massed choir broke into the Hallelujah Chorus and children sang Australian and British patriotic songs, while a vast crowd of spectators, seated on the grassy slopes around the pavilion, applauded.

Among the men who took the oath of office was none other than the *Morning Post* correspondent, Alfred Deakin, the new attorney-general, spiritualist, writer, barrister, former colonial politician and undisputed leader of Victoria's federalist movement, who would secretly comment on Australia's progress for the following thirteen years, even while he occupied (three times) the office of prime minister. On the day of the inauguration, he wrote,

---

1 Alfred Deakin, *Federated Australia: Selections from Letters to the Morning Post 1900–1910*, ed. J.A. La Nauze (Melbourne University Press, 1968), p. 19.

'a very self-conscious nation...[had] just made its appearance in the centre of the Southern Seas'.[2]

Federation had created a new polity, but what was it? Was it a nation? The Federationists had called it a 'commonwealth', but this term – controversial at first, because of associations with republican history – did not signify any particular type of government, and the framers who defended its adoption were at pains to suggest nothing more than a general sense of benevolence, an etymological reference to the common good, or 'weal'.

The Commonwealth of Australia was established under a Constitution, written by elected delegates from the Australian colonies at a convention held in 1897–98. It was approved by the electors of the colonies in the referendums held between 1899 and 1900 (after an unsuccessful round of referendums in 1898), adopted by the colonial parliaments, and then passed as an enactment of the British imperial parliament, receiving Queen Victoria's formal assent on 9 July 1900. The Constitution turned the six self-governing Australian colonies into States under a new federal government; its preamble describes this arrangement as an 'indissoluble Federal Commonwealth'. But the Constitution was also a statute, a British Act. This dual identity was to make classification difficult.

The new Constitution designated and established the institutions of federal government, with the now-familiar three arms – the parliament (with two houses, one representing the people of the nation; the other, the States), the executive and the 'judicature'. It conferred important national powers upon the federal arms; it described the fiscal and trading relations between the States and the Commonwealth; it gave the Australian people the power of constitutional amendment, through popular referendum. But it also included provisions that kept Australia tied to Britain. The British monarch was to remain the Australian monarch; the governor-general had the power to reserve assent on bills passed by the Commonwealth parliament, and the Queen (in reality, the British government) retained the power to disallow Australian Acts. These provisions, which mirrored the old arrangements between Britain and its self-governing colonies embedded in the *Colonial Laws Validity Act* of 1865, were potentially large, but in practice restrained. As under the 1865 Act, Britain's oversight was confined to laws that conflicted with British Acts that expressly or necessarily applied to Australia. No Commonwealth Acts were ever disallowed. Still, Australia remained closely linked to Britain in matters of defence, trade, international relations,

2 Ibid.

diplomacy and citizenship, until the second half of the twentieth century. The British *Statute of Westminster* (1931) freed the Dominions from British legislative interference, but British common law was followed in Australia for another 40 years. In constitutional matters, however, Australia was almost fully sovereign from the start.

If statehood is to be measured by unimpaired sovereignty and international recognition, the newly inaugurated Commonwealth was not yet a state. But many thought, as Deakin did, that it was a nation. Henry Lawson, the celebrated Australian nationalist writer, also heralded the event. In a poem written in 1901, he had a character say

> 'I hear that our Country's a nation at last!
> I hear they have launched the new ship of the State
> And with men at the wheel who are steering it straight...
> That all things are coming we fought for so long'.[3]

A 'ship of state' *and* a nation. This was a significant endorsement.

Australia's federationists had followed the progress of Europe's nationalist movements and many were inspired by the romantic image of their leaders. The death in 1882 of 'the model patriot', Giuseppe Garibaldi, who had led Italy's unification 20 years earlier, was mourned in Sydney by a crowd of 10,000. Giuseppe Mazzini, the intellectual of the *Risorgimento*, was a particular hero of Alfred Deakin and the Tasmanian federalist leader, Andrew Inglis Clark.[4] The evolution of the United States from a handful of separate colonies to a powerful modern state under the world's first federal constitution was a particular inspiration. The knowledge of what others had achieved nurtured the vision of a federated Australia. Yet the methods of its achievement were always to be different. A revolt against Britain was neither desired by, nor logical for, the Australian colonies. How far, then, was the urge to create a *nation* the driver behind, even a factor in, Federation?

A federal union or federal authority for the Australian colonies had, in one form or another, been promoted in Australia or Britain in every decade from the 1840s to the 1890s. Historians seeking to explain why it finally occurred when it did – why, in Manning Clark's words, 'the nibble at federation' became the 'bite' that developed into the Commonwealth of Australia – have disagreed.[5] In particular, the claim that nationalism prompted Federation has

3 Henry Lawson, 'Jack Cornstalk', in *When I was King* (Sydney: Angus & Robertson, 1906).
4 John Hirst, *The Sentimental Nation: The Making of the Australian Commonwealth* (Oxford University Press, 2000), pp. 9–11.
5 C.M.H. Clark, *Select Documents in Australian History, 1851–1900* (Sydney: Angus & Robertson, 1955), p. 444.

been disputed. The observation that Australia, voluntarily and even eagerly, followed British policies after 1901, strengthened the view that nationalism could not have been a factor. For some decades after the federationists them-selves had passed away and the accounts they left of their work had been discounted or forgotten,[6] historical interpretation favoured the view that the motivation was little more than 'utilitarian'.[7] For certain historians, the deal went beyond mere utility or pragmatism; it was designed to promote the interests of capital and to suppress the emerging labour movement.[8] The federationists, such historians noted, included a provision in the Constitution mandating 'absolutely free' trade and commerce among the States, and this, it seemed, prohibited national economic regulation and ruled out the social-isation of industry.[9] This provision was treated as a constitutional synecdoche standing for the whole idea behind Federation.

It is undisputed that economic values played a part in the federation movement, but the 'economic explanation' itself is not consistent. For some historians, enhanced access to the international money market was the key motivator, and the trading and investment interests of British businesses were uppermost.[10] For others, the economic interests were regional, and could be traced in patterns of voting in the federal referendums of the late 1890s.[11] One historian has emphasised recovery from the 'economic catastrophes' of the Depression of the 1890s as the 'driving force' behind Federation.[12] Such variations point to complexity in contemporary motivations.

Other historians, highlighting the complexity, note the 'sentimental' or 'romantic' character of the federation movement, the idealism of the

6 Alfred Deakin, *The Federal Story* (Melbourne: Robertson & Mullens, 1944); Robert Garran, *Prosper the Commonwealth* (Sydney: Angus & Robertson, 1958); George Reid, *My Reminiscences* (Melbourne: Cassell, 1917); Bernhard Wise, *The Making of the Australian Commonwealth* (London: Longmans, Green and Co., 1913).

7 Hugh Collins, 'Political Ideology in Australia: The Distinctiveness of a Benthamite Society', in Stephen Graubard (ed.), *Australia: The Daedalus Symposium* (Sydney: Angus & Robertson, 1985), pp. 147–69.

8 C.M.H. Clark, *A History of Australia. Volume 1, From the Earliest Times to The Age of Macquarie* (Melbourne University Press, 1962); Peter Botsman, *The Great Constitutional Swindle: A Citizen's View of the Australian Constitution* (Sydney: Pluto Press, 2000).

9 For many years, the High Court of Australia interpreted the relevant constitutional provision (section 92) in this light.

10 R. Norris, *The Emergent Commonwealth: Australian Federation, Expectations and Fulfilment 1889–1910* (Melbourne University Press, 1975).

11 R.S. Parker, 'Australian Federation: The Influence of Economic Interests and Political Pressures', *Historical Studies Australia and New Zealand*, 4, 13 (1949): 1–24. Parker's anal-ysis is disputed by Geoffrey Blainey, 'The Role of Economic Interests in Australian Federation', *Historical Studies Australia and New Zealand*, 4, 15 (1950): 224–37.

12 David Meredith, 'Meat and Potatoes beneath the Southern Cross: The Economic Interpretation of Australian Federation Revisited', *Australian Studies*, 17, 1 (2002): 101.

federation goal, and the fact that economic interests could have been served without the huge and uncertain task of federating.[13] They note that labour itself was not socialist at the time, nor was it uniformly opposed to the goal of Federation or the specifics of the Constitution (in Western Australia and Queensland, it was largely favourable); furthermore, labour opposition (as in New South Wales) was not principally directed at the Constitution's economic arrangements. Against the view that Federation was antithetical to nationalism, they point to a distinctively Australian style of art, literature and music that was emerging contemporaneously and featured prominently in federationist iconography and campaigns. The celebration of Australian sporting victories against the 'mother country' and the determination of Australians to frame their own Constitution without British interference are further (if rarely associated) illustrations.

The resolution of these seemingly conflicting impulses lies in what Alfred Deakin (describing himself) called the 'independent Australian Briton'. There was no stark conflict between imperialism and nationalism. Those who imagined an Australian Commonwealth and led the movement for its creation thought of themselves as both visionary and practical, socially progressive and economically interested, Australian *and* British. The conjunction did not indicate subservience. There were moments, in particular, in the 1880s – the decade in which Federation took its first serious steps – when Australia's fondness for Britain was severely tested and thoughts of 'cutting the painter' were stirred. Most strikingly, Britain failed to understand Australian alarm over increasing European incursions in the South Pacific. This was starkly illustrated in 1883, when the Queensland government attempted to pre-empt German occupation of eastern New Guinea by claiming the territory in Britain's name, only to have its actions repudiated by the British government. This, and other indicators of British neglect or condescension, caused deep resentment in the colonies. By the end of the decade, however, fences were being mended.

At the same time, specifically Australian sentiments were taking shape. The sons and daughters of the many immigrants who had swollen the colonies' populations in the gold rushes of the 1850s had reached maturity. They were part of a young, literate and self-improving generation, with an abundance of Australian literature and numerous local newspapers to nourish their interests. The Australian Natives Association, a mutual society

13 Hirst, *The Sentimental Nation*; Helen Irving, *To Constitute a Nation: A Cultural History of Australia's Constitution* (Cambridge University Press, 1997).

formed in Melbourne in 1871, which offered membership to men born in the colonies, became one of the earliest advocates of Federation. With some few exceptions (small, colonial republican parties),[14] Australian nationalism was neither revolutionary nor anti-British. It was compatible with both independence and a sense of Britishness, with national identity and membership of the wider imperial 'family'.

Modernising influences played an important part. The idea of government was changing. Governments were assuming greater regulatory powers and involving themselves in previously 'private' matters: social welfare, marriage, the regulation of business, labour relations. Communications technologies were expanding; railways were linking city and country; ocean and overland telegraph cables were being laid over long distances, and international treaties were concluded to govern such initiatives.[15] Women were beginning to makes claims upon democracy, forming suffrage and temperance organisations, and giving expression to an expanded understanding of equality and articulating their experiences as political, even constitutional matters.

These expressions of modern life were especially attractive in the New World, and aligned with the idea that a nation could shape itself through progressive legislation. The new forces found their way into the Constitution. The Commonwealth parliament was given powers to make laws regarding (among other subjects) corporations, industrial arbitration, old age and invalid pensions, and marriage and divorce. The Constitution protected the right to vote of women enfranchised in their colony before Federation (South Australia, Western Australia, and – had it chosen to join the Commonwealth – New Zealand), and thereby reflected an understanding that the 'adult vote' would be adopted under the first Commonwealth Franchise Act.

The promise of a new century and a 'new age', the ideals of self-improvement, spiritualism and free-thinking contributed to a deeply aspirational and optimistic movement. A self-conscious sense of destiny pervades the writings of the federationists. Their goal, however, was not fanciful. Indeed, for some in the colonies it was not enough; in 1893, the radical Queensland union leader, William Lane, left with several hundred followers to establish a utopian 'New Australia' in Paraguay. Their experiment was ultimately unsuccessful, but their departure at that time may have eased the way for the more pragmatic federationists.

14 Mark McKenna, *The Captive Republic: A History of Republicanism in Australia, 1788–1996* (Cambridge University Press, 1996).
15 K.T. Livingston, 'Anticipating Federation: The Federalising of Telecommunications in Australia', *Australian Historical Studies*, 26, 102 (1994): 97–117.

There were negative visions, too. The colonies' commitment to a 'white Australia' – meaning, an Australia in which the Asian population (the Chinese, in particular) would be dramatically reduced, even to the point of non-existence – had been taking shape well before the federation movement. As in other parts of the New World, Acts designed to limit Chinese immigration had been passed in several colonies.[16] In 1870 Britain had conceded power to colonial parliaments over their own naturalisation laws, and colonial Acts soon denied naturalisation to Asians. Restrictions were also imposed on Chinese employment in key industries. In 1888 an Australian Intercolonial Conference on the Chinese Question concluded with a commitment to a common restrictive immigration policy. This goal of 'whiteness' was a powerful unifying factor. It brought together erstwhile antagonists, and the promise of keeping cheap Chinese labour out of Australia helped 'convert' the colonial labour parties to Federation.

In the weight given to colour as a criterion for exclusion, we see a further indicator of nationalism. 'Whiteness' was also a claim about ethnicity. Australians, it was said, were part of the British 'race'. In the words of the so-called Father of Federation, Henry Parkes (five times premier of New South Wales),'the crimson thread of kinship' ran through all colonial Australians.[17] By comparison with many countries, it was a relatively mild form of nationalism, but it was significant. It found its indirect way into the Constitution, in a provision empowering the Commonwealth parliament to pass 'special laws' for the people of any race.[18] Constitutional powers over immigration also permitted the passage of racially restrictive immigration laws at the national level.

This idea of 'whiteness' had little to do with the Indigenous population. Aboriginal Australians were viewed by most as little more than outsiders, irrelevant to the nation-building project of the federationists. This did not necessarily mean antipathy. A surprising number were sympathetic. Edward Dowling, secretary of the New South Wales Central Federation League, expressed regret that Aboriginal people had 'not received adequate compensation for the grand island continent which was taken from them by the

---

16 For example, the *Chinese Immigration Act 1855* (Vic.); the *Chinese Immigration Restriction and Regulation Act 1861* (NSW).

17 'Crimson Thread', in Helen Irving (ed.), *The Centenary Companion to Australian Federation* (Cambridge University Press, 1999), p. 355.

18 The 'races power' – section 51 (xxvi) of the Constitution – was not, in the event, employed; the immigration power – section 51 (xxvii) – was sufficient. The latter supported the Commonwealth's *Immigration Restriction Act* of 1901.

British Crown'.[19] But the taking was treated as a *fait accompli*. The new nation was to be built upon it. Constitutionally, Aboriginal people were identified as a local problem, a matter for the States alone.[20]

Federation was more than visionary, of course. There were many practical attractions, as well as challenges. Since Britain had abandoned its insistence on a single imperial tariff policy in 1873, the issue of the colonial tariff had emerged as the greatest challenge. Dubbed the 'lion in the way' (afterwards known as 'the lion in the path') by a former Victorian premier, James Service, colonial differences in trade policy created continuing conflict, in particular between protectionist Victoria (with artificially high tariffs on imports, protecting local industry) and free-trade New South Wales (with minimal tariffs, for revenue-raising alone). Tariffs also caused inconvenience, even embarrassment, in the lives of ordinary people, who were subjected to customs inspections as they crossed colonial borders. Attempts had long been made to create an intercolonial customs union, but had consistently failed. The 'lion', Service warned, had to be killed or it would kill Federation.[21]

There was an alternative. Early in the 1890s, the New South Wales Free Trade leader, Henry Parkes, and Protectionist leader, Edmund Barton, took the momentous step of agreeing that the lion's fate could simply be left for later. They resolved to work together on the goal of Federation, setting aside the attempt to reconcile their tariff policies. A similar arrangement was effectively struck between New South Wales and Victoria, and although fiscal powers between the Commonwealth and the States were a major battleground in the framing of the Constitution, tariff policy was left for the post-Federation parliament.

Such agreements signalled the strength of aspirations that transcended colonial lines, but there were lines of fragmentation too. Each colony was wary of the disadvantages that might follow its transformation into a State; the protectionist colonies feared loss of industry; the wealthier colonies feared subsidising the poorer ones; the smaller colonies feared domination by the larger. Official inquiries were held in each colony into the financial prospects

---

19 Dowling in *Commonweal* (Journal of the New South Wales Federation League), no. 1, October 1894, quoted in Irving (ed.), *The Centenary Companion to Australian Federation*, p. 51.
20 Until the provisions were deleted in 1967, they were expressly excluded from the scope of the Commonwealth's 'races power', section 51 (xxvi), and from being included in 'reckoning the numbers' of the people of the Commonwealth (for the purposes of calculating numbers of State seats in the House of Representatives) under section 127.
21 J.A. La Nauze, *The Making of the Australian Constitution* (Melbourne University Press, 1972), p. 11.

under federation; each concluded that it would find itself worse off. But still they proceeded. Individual benefits were also anticipated. The long-running tariff war between Victoria and New South Wales would be resolved. South Australia would be rid of the burden of the Northern Territory. Queensland would find new markets for its produce, and its ambivalence about its sugar industry's reliance on indentured Pacific Islander labour would be settled.[22] The geographical and fiscal isolation of Western Australia would be eased. Tasmania's weak economy would be strengthened, and the 'historic project of restitution' from its convict past might be completed.[23] Together, the future States could also picture themselves as members of a team, a great new nation in the southern seas, better equipped for defence, forming a bulwark against undesirable immigration, and an unbroken tariff wall to protect Australian industry.

Steps towards Federation

The goal of Federation was thus built on visions and practical challenges, carrots and sticks. None of these, however, could have effect without organisation. While the Federation story is much larger than the practical steps, those steps were critical. Many attempts had been made in the past, and all had failed. Numerous intercolonial meetings on subjects of common interest (postal services were the most frequent) had taken place in the second half of the nineteenth century, but intercolonial rivalries had proven equally persistent. In 1867 Parkes, the then-New South Wales colonial secretary, had spoken of his vision of 'the footprints of Six Young Giants in the morning dew', but in reality the 'giants' were reluctant to walk side by side. Things began to change in the 1880s. Most significantly, the Federal Council was created. It had been suggested by Parkes in 1880 and then planned at an Intercolonial Convention in 1883, in the immediate aftermath of Queensland's failure to annexe New Guinea. This Convention had concluded with a resolution to form a federal authority that, it was hoped, would generate 'national' laws.

The Federal Council of Australasia (formalised in 1885 by an Act of the imperial parliament) was described by Deakin as unique, like a platypus, 'a perfectly original development compounded from familiar but entirely

---

22 Kay Saunders, 'The Workers' Paradox: Indentured Labour in the Queensland Sugar Industry to 1920', in Saunders (ed.), *Indentured Labour in the British Empire 1834–1920* (London: Croom Helm, 1984), pp. 213–59.

23 James Warden, 'Tasmania', in Irving (ed.), *The Centenary Companion to Australian Federation*, p. 215.

unassociated types'.[24] The Act empowered the Council to make laws on a limited range of subjects at the request of two or more member colonies. However, like the American Congress of the Confederation, formed under the Articles of Confederation in 1781 (an analogy later made by Parkes), it had no executive authority or power to raise revenue. It could not compel membership. Victoria, Queensland, Tasmania and Western Australia joined, but South Australia held off for several years. Fiji (an unlikely co-federationist, but at that time still part of the Australasian colonial 'club') joined, but New Zealand did not. Most damagingly, New South Wales stayed out. Parkes had been touring the United States during the Council's creation, and he had witnessed the fruits of full Federation. He returned enamoured with what he had seen and convinced, in his own words, that the adage 'half a loaf is better than no bread' was 'of ill sound' when it came to nation building.[25] Still, the Federal Council was a start. It served as a practice forum for those who belonged to it, as well as a model of what to avoid, for those who did not.

For a short time, another federal idea was also in circulation. The Imperial Federation League, founded in London in 1884, promoted the political union of all the self-governing colonies of the Empire. Its goal was a remodelled imperial parliament in London, wielding powers over defence, foreign policy and other 'imperial' matters, while the colonies, retaining control of their own domestic matters, elected its members. The League attracted some prominent Empire leaders, and a branch was established in Victoria, but the scheme gained little support in Australia. Its failure provides another counterweight to the claim that Australia's federationists were subordinate to Britain in their thinking. Their willingness to retain the crown did not extend to envisaging Australia as no more than a 'state' of the Empire.

Unification of the colonies was another possible model. It offered a centralised means of resolving common problems as well as coordinating the economy, and at least one prominent New South Wales politician, sometime premier, George Dibbs, promoted it. The colonies, however, were too well practised in their own self-government, too jealous of their own spheres of power and too conscious of their differences, to accede. Anti-unification did not rule out coordinated policies or common efforts, but federalism alone fitted their vision of the new nation. The colonies saw themselves as future

24 Alfred Deakin, 'The Federal Council of Australasia', *Review of Reviews*, 20 February 1895, p. 154.
25 Henry Parkes, *Fifty Years in the Making of Australian History*, vol. 1 (London: Longman, Green and Co., 1892), p. 336.

States and, when the time came, they made sure that this commitment was embedded in the Constitution.

Federalism did not preclude the centralised control of matters that required a national solution. Defence was the outstanding example, one upon which all were agreed. In 1887, at the first Colonial Conference in London (held to coincide with Queen Victoria's Golden Jubilee) the Australian representatives finally persuaded the British government of their colonies' strategic vulnerability and secured its cooperation. Britain, it was agreed, would furnish an enlarged naval fleet (it would be docked in Sydney and maintained jointly by Britain and the colonies) and an expert would be sent to assess the colonies' defence capabilities. Major-General James Bevan Edwards was appointed to this task. He toured Australia in early 1889, and in October that year reported in no uncertain terms. The colonies were incapable of defending themselves. The immediate Federation of the existing defence forces under a single command was essential, as was the standardisation of colonial railway gauges.

The Edwards report was alarming; it also served as a prompt for Federation. Returning from Brisbane, where he had been promoting the idea of a Federation conference, Henry Parkes stopped in the small northern New South Wales town of Tenterfield and, at the local School of Arts, delivered what was to become a legendary 'oration'. It drew heavily on the findings of the Edwards report, and urged Australians to accomplish, in peace, what Americans had done through war. It concluded with an urgent call for a convention.

A conference and a convention

Queensland was quickly persuaded, but the others, understandably, objected that a federal body – the Federal Council – already existed; New South Wales, they declared, should simply join and work through it. On the conclusion of these conflicting alternatives, the prospects for Federation effectively hung. A timely compromise resulted in a federal conference of what were referred to simply as 'representative men'. Thirteen delegates from the parliaments of seven colonies assembled in Melbourne in February 1890. (Fiji had planned to take part, but did not; New Zealand was still in the ring.) They began with a resolution to open their deliberations to the public. It was an important departure from other countries' constitution making and one that, creating a precedent for the later conventions, arguably assisted in popularising the Federation goal. Six days of lengthy speeches followed. Visions of national greatness, alternative constitutional models and intercolonial jealousies were tossed around, and agreements were finally struck. They would seek Federation 'under the Crown', with federal arrangements modelled on the United States. Despite affinities as a 'sister colony' in the imperial family (and notwithstanding the fact that many provisions of the Australian Constitution were ultimately copied from the 1867 Canadian Constitution), the example of the confederated Dominion of Canada was rejected, unequivocally, as too centralist and insufficiently federal.[26] The strange and untried marriage of Westminster parliamentary government and American federalism was to be the alternative. The Conference also concluded – a vital admission – that, despite its 'valuable services', the Federal Council could not accomplish this goal. Instead, it was agreed, the colonial legislatures would appoint delegates to a National Australasian Convention, 'empowered to consider and report upon an adequate scheme for a Federal Constitution'.[27]

Their resolution was put into effect. The planned convention assembled in the New South Wales Legislative Assembly chamber, in Sydney, on 2 March 1891. Among the 42 representatives from seven colonies (all chosen by their colonial parliaments, including New Zealand's) were men who would spend the following decade on the Federation project, several of whom would become leaders in the new Commonwealth. These included Edmund Barton (New South Wales), first Prime Minister and later Justice of the first High Court of Australia; Samuel Griffith (Queensland), first Chief Justice of the High Court of Australia; Charles Kingston (South Australia), first Minister for Trade and Customs; Alfred Deakin (Victoria), first Attorney-General and subsequently three-times Prime Minister; and John Forrest (Western Australia), (effectively) first Defence Minister.[28] Two other men were indispensable to the convention and their influence would be enduring, although they would play no role in the Commonwealth they had helped to create: Andrew Inglis Clark (Tasmania), later Justice of the Supreme Court of Tasmania, who (for reasons never fully understood) kept his distance from the federation movement after 1891, and Henry Parkes himself, president of the convention, robbed by death in 1896 of the chance to complete his mission.

---

26 Helen Irving, 'Sister Colonies with Separate Constitutions: Why Australian Federationists Rejected the Canadian Constitution', in Linda Cardinal and David Headon (eds), *Shaping Nations: Constitutionalism and Society in Australia and Canada* (University of Ottawa Press, 2002), pp. 27–37.

27 *Official Record of the Proceedings and Debates of the Australasian Federation Conference* (Melbourne: Government Printer, 1890), p. 261.

28 The first appointed defence minister, James Dickson, died on 10 January 1901, nine days after he was sworn in.

Both Clark and Charles Kingston (perhaps mindful of James Madison at the Philadelphia Convention in 1787) had already circulated draft constitutions for the convention's consideration. Clark, the great 'Americanist', had successfully promoted the United States constitutional model at the 1890 conference, and his own constitution included much that was drawn from that country. A great many of his ideas were adopted in 1891, including an 'equal protection of the laws' provision copied from the United States Fourteenth Amendment. Ultimately, however, the provision was omitted. By contrast, a proposed federal industrial arbitration power that had featured in Kingston's draft was defeated in 1891, but re-appeared in the final Constitution. It was to prove vital in the iconic 'Australian settlement' of the twentieth century,[29] in which the national arbitration of industrial disputes and the establishment of a minimum wage and progressive labour laws were central.

At the convention, the press and the public were again admitted. Committees worked on constitutional detail, and a drafting subcommittee convened during the Easter recess on board the Queensland government steamship, the *Lucinda*, in a now-celebrated three day cruise on Sydney's waters.[30] A fully drafted Constitution, elegant and spare in its wording, was adopted. The convention wound up on 9 April, with modest words about its own achievements and with three cheers for the Queen and for Henry Parkes.

The Constitution Bill, it had been decided, would now be taken to the individual colonial parliaments for adoption, followed by a process (unspecified) of popular approval and a swift, even painless, enactment in London. It was not to be. Of the many reasons, the most dramatic was the economic Depression that hit in the early 1890s. Bank collapses, high unemployment, capital and investment losses, combined with drought and labour unrest, distracted from grander visions of nation building. Colonial governments concentrated on immediate economic strategies for recovery.

In New South Wales, the political success of the newly formed Labor Electoral League provided another distraction. Having suffered a devastating defeat in the great shearers' and maritime workers' strikes in the previous year, the labour movement had turned to politics, immediately winning the balance of power in the 1891 colonial election. It was a portent of things to come: the realignment of the political priorities and allegiances that had

29 Paul Kelly, *The End of Certainty: The Story of the 1980s* (Sydney: Allen & Unwin, 1992), pp. 7–10.
30 La Nauze, *The Making of the Australian Constitution*, pp. 64–8.

marked the late-Victorian era. It was also a signal about the democratising project of the nineteenth century. Members of parliament had recently been awarded salaries. Government would no longer be closed to 'ordinary' men. These shifts would soon benefit the federation movement. From the perspective of the working men of New South Wales, however, a distant, uncertain goal offered no advantages.[31]

In Victoria the effects of the Depression were especially severe. Victoria had surged ahead after the gold-rush years to become the most populous and prosperous colony; it now suffered a dramatic reversal. Tasmania and South Australia, also hard-hit, made some attempts towards adopting the Constitution Bill, but could go no further without the larger colonies. Western Australia was just then enjoying its newly conferred self-government; the discovery of gold in that colony would soon shelter it from the worst effects of the Depression, and would also stir long-running doubts about the value of joining the others. Queensland, too, was less affected but had its own distractions.

There were some unanticipated positives in the decade. An extraordinarily long period of stability in colonial leadership played an under-recognised but critical part in federation's ultimate success. In an era when ministries typically lasted a matter of months, all the men who were premiers by 1894 remained in office for the following five or six years, guaranteeing continuity in policy, allowing intercolonial familiarity and even friendships to grow, and underpinning the viability of Federation planning. The longer-term effects of the Depression would also provide a paradoxical silver lining; among other things, the uneven effect around the country would 'bring the six colonies closer in size and status...[making] it easier to present the case for Federation as a coming together of equals'.[32] Whatever the reality, the case was crucial. Still, the open-ended nature of the 1891 convention's commitments had allowed the distractions to prevail. The Constitution Bill was set aside.

The popular turn

During the six years that passed before a new convention picked up the work abandoned in 1891, much changed in the politics and cultures of the colonies. The final Constitution was, in important respects, more democratic than the first. It was also closer to Britain's orbit. This was not necessarily a paradox.

---

31 L.F. Crisp, *Australian National Government* (Melbourne: Longmans, 1965).
32 John McCarty, 'Depression', in Irving (ed.), *The Centenary Companion to Australian Federation*, p. 356.

Britain itself was democratising, albeit more slowly than in the Australasian 'social laboratories'. It was also self-consciously adopting a more tolerant approach towards parts of the Empire, partly for democratic reasons and partly out of prudence. Britain's resources, also heavily hit by the Depression, were under strain. Maximum autonomy for the self-governing colonies (soon to be known as dominions) would serve Britain's interests, relieving it of some of its responsibilities, and at the same time helping to keep the Empire together. The new British Secretary of State for the Colonies, Joseph Chamberlain (appointed in 1895), was an ardent imperialist. He wanted the Empire to rest on ties of affection and loyalty, and he championed colonial self-government alongside central imperial institutions such as the Judicial Committee of the Privy Council acting as infrequent, but unifying, 'paternal' authorities.

Social and demographic changes also played their part. The children born to the gold-rush immigrants had tilted the population; the native-born were now numerically dominant. The colonies were becoming increasingly urbanised. A lower rate of marriage and a falling birth rate coincided with the emergence of the 'new woman', and incremental steps were taken towards the achievement of women's political rights. While these steps appear small to later eyes, they were momentous in their context. When the women of New Zealand, and then South Australia, were enfranchised in the early 1890s, they gained not merely a technical right to vote but also a validation of their identity as citizens, and with that, a recognition of all women's potential as active members of the future Commonwealth. Had Federation been accomplished in 1891, this would not have been part of its story.

There were other reasons for the persistence of popular interest in Federation. It promised relief for some of the daily disadvantages of colonial separation: not only the inconvenience of customs inspections on border crossings but, among other things, the high price of food and household goods in the protectionist or more distant colonies, and difficulties caused by the sharing of common river water in the trade and irrigation projects of riparian colonies. These domestic concerns kept enthusiasm alive when the politicians' attention was elsewhere.

It comes as no surprise, then, that a renewed federation effort started in a district in which the greatest inconvenience of colonial separation was felt. Riverina in southern New South Wales, immediately north of Victoria's Murray River border and just north-east of South Australia, was distant from the decision-makers in Sydney, and caught between the conflicting tariff regimes and the schemes governing rail freight and river water use in the surrounding colonies. The first of the so-called citizens' Federation Leagues was established there in early 1893, and its leaders quickly urged a Central League into life in Sydney. By the end of the decade there were more than 100 leagues in New South Wales, and leagues were also found in most other colonies, including Fiji (although it was never a realistic prospect as a State of the Commonwealth) and New Zealand (still making up its mind). Women's leagues were also formed: in the Riverina, in Sydney and in the eastern gold-fields of Western Australia, another isolated and disadvantaged region.

League members campaigned at public meetings. They lobbied politicians; they wrote letters to the press and published their own journals; they held conferences. One particular conference was to prove the turning point in Federation's fortunes. Delegates from the Murray River border leagues, representatives of other pro-Federation organisations, and politicians met in the Riverina town of Corowa in late July 1893. There, the Victorian parliamentarian, John Quick, representing the Bendigo branch of the Australian Natives Association, met the young New South Wales federationist, Robert Garran.[33] Together, they successfully proposed a new means of achieving Federation. It would require a new convention, directly elected this time, where a new federal Constitution Bill would be written; the Bill would then be put to the electors for approval in colonial referendums. The conference resoundingly adopted the plan, and (adding the imperial parliament's passage of the Constitution Bill at the end of the process) Quick immediately drafted an Enabling Bill to show how it could be done. The Central Federal League adopted it too, and members of government, including New South Wales Premier George Reid (a former Federation sceptic, now converted), were convinced. Reid had skilfully managed his colony's recovery from the Depression, overseeing its restoration to the pre-eminence it considered its birthright. Making use of this strategic advantage, he now called a meeting of all the premiers, opportunistically to coincide with a Federal Council meeting in Hobart in January 1895. There, Reid argued successfully for the plan. Four colonies adopted it, adding a step that would allow the colonial parliaments to debate the Bill in between sessions of the convention. While Western Australia and Queensland had reservations about details, they joined the majority in committing to the core. The 'Corowa Plan' was doubly ingenious: popular participation would be mandated and all commitments would

33 They were to go on to form a legendary partnership as authors of the enduring 'Quick and Garran': John Quick and Robert Randolph Garran, *The Annotated Constitution of the Australian Commonwealth* (Sydney: Angus & Robertson, 1901).

be locked in from the start; if followed, they would lead, step by step, to Federation. Nothing, this time, would be left to chance.

In the event, however, it took two years before the planned convention became a reality. During the interim, a further 'people's' event urged the politicians forward. A so-called People's Federal Convention was organised by the Federation League of Bathurst, in New South Wales, in November 1896. It quickly became almost an official event, bringing together not only representatives of pro-Federation organisations, but also many colonial politicians and other leading men, and attracting wide press coverage. The attendance and the energy signalled Federation's growing momentum.

The convention heard speeches from prominent federationists. 'Federal' poetry was read and a 'Federation hymn', composed for the occasion, was sung. The 1891 Constitution Bill was debated, section by section, and proposals for amendments were adopted, a number of which (concerning finance, railways and the election of senators) would ultimately make their way into the final Constitution. The marriage of US-style federalism and parliamentary government was endorsed. A proposal for the governor-general to be elected by the Australian people was soundly defeated; it would reappear, unresolved, in the republican debates of the 1990s. A 'manifesto' issued to the press by Thomas Machattie, president of the convention, confidently asserted that the convention had 'given an impulse to the cause of Australian Federation and stirred numbers, previously indifferent'.[34] The convention's motto, *Foedere Fato Aequamur* ('By our union we are made equal to our destiny') reflected the now self-conscious assumption that something great, even transcendent, was being created: a 'real Australian nation, not a mere makeshift Government'.[35]

Enabling Bills, copied from Quick's draft, had already been adopted by the colonial parliaments and were now activated. The first step was the election of ten representatives per colony to the new convention. Western Australia's parliament elected its representatives; Queensland could not agree on the method of choice and ended up unrepresented; New Zealand, this time, made no move to participate. In early 1897 a total of 138 candidates, including all the premiers and many other politicians (as well as Australia's first female political candidate, Catherine Helen Spence, in South Australia) submitted themselves to the voters' judgement. It was a remarkable and counter-instinctive undertaking for the politicians in particular. The election

34 *Proceedings of the Bathurst People's Federal Convention* (Sydney: Gordon and Gotch, 1896), p. 196.
35 Ibid., p. 195.

might have resulted in a convention of political amateurs, men who were inexperienced, even inept, and unsuited to the negotiations, let alone the technicalities that would be necessary for constitution-making. It might, equally, have delivered men opposed to Federation, or dedicated to republicanism or other forms of government at variance with the commitments made in 1890. In the event, the democratic gamble paid off. Thirteen of the 40 elected (plus four of the appointed Western Australians) had been at the 1891 convention. All the premiers and all the federalist leaders were chosen. Only one candidate who was not a sitting or former politician (James Walker, a banker from New South Wales) was elected. The politicians' experience, better resources, familiarity with the voters and, no doubt, personal worth, had given them the lead.

The limited franchise, combined with the low turnout of voters in some colonies for both the convention elections and the subsequent Constitution Bill referendums, have been treated by some historians as evidence that the process was neither truly popular nor genuinely democratic.[36] This conclusion rests on an ideal. In comparison with other countries and taking into account the public nature of the process,[37] Australia's nation building was far from undemocratic. In one participating colony, all women were enfranchised alongside all men, and all white women and men in a second. In 1902 the first Commonwealth Franchise Act would exclude Aboriginal Australians from enrolling to vote, but in the late 1890s all Aboriginal men were enfranchised in four colonies and all Aboriginal women in one. The fact that in some of the colonies the voter turnout was poor, while it was robust in others, was not in itself undemocratic.

The 1897–98 convention

Fifty men, from five colonies, assembled at the second federal convention in Adelaide on 22 March 1897. The large majority were Protestants; there were two Jews and two Catholics. Almost a third were lawyers by training or profession. One alone, William Trenwith from Victoria, represented the labour movement. For some historians, this result also demonstrates that Federation was the work of a virtually homogeneous group of conservative, middle-class

---

36 Botsman, *The Great Constitutional Swindle*; Meredith, 'Meat and Potatoes Beneath the Southern Cross', p. 86; Alastair Davidson, *The Invisible State: The Formation of the Australian State, 1788–1901* (Cambridge University Press, 1997), p. 237.

37 Helen Irving, 'Democratic Experiments with Constitution-Making', in Marian Sawer (ed.), *Elections, Full, Free and Fair* (Sydney: Federation Press, 2001), pp. 115–28.

men. Heterogeneity is a matter of degree; certainly, the men who wrote the Constitution were neither unionists nor radical socialists, but many were liberal progressives, and the conservatives were almost all moderate. Secularists mingled with advocates of religious recognition; proponents and opponents of women's suffrage debated each other; defenders of States' rights faced advocates of centralised powers, as did protectionists and free traders. Certainly, all believed in a 'free' economy, in the sense of its being principally a matter for private initiative, and all agreed on internal 'free trade', in the sense that discriminatory and protectionist tariffs should not be levied by any State against the others. But national powers that permitted, even required, governmental intervention in the economy and that encouraged progressive legislation were also adopted at the convention. Rising above the detail, all were committed to the creation of democratic national institutions and to a federal distribution of powers. Most wanted to maximise Australia's powers over its own policies and laws. Almost all shared the racism that was virtually universal in 'white' communities at the time. All agreed that Australia should remain 'under the Crown', although some anticipated that this would not be permanent. In these commitments were reflected the values of the majority of Australians, including most working men and women.

The convention opened with a series of resolutions, designed, in the words of convention leader, Edmund Barton, 'to enlarge the powers of self-government of the people of Australia'.[38] As in 1891, proposals were debated in plenary sessions, and subcommittees worked and reworked provisions of the evolving new Constitution Bill, frequently turning to the 1891 draft to guide deliberations or suggest departures. The principle of free trade and commerce among the States was accepted, as it had been in 1891. Time-honoured 'national' subjects of defence, postal services, quarantine, immigration, lighthouses and currency found their way, without challenge, into the list of Commonwealth powers. The design of the executive and judiciary was largely unchanged. But there were also alterations, both to content and layout. New legislative powers reflected new thinking about the sphere of government. New communications technologies had been anticipated, and the Commonwealth's power over postal, telegraphic and telephonic services was extended to take in 'other like services'. There were democratising shifts. Senators would be directly elected, rather than chosen by the State parliaments. The means of amending the Constitution would

---

38 *Official Record of the Debates of the Australasian Federal Convention*, new edn (Sydney: Legal Books, 1986), Adelaide session, vol. 2, p. 17.

be by popular referendum, rather than elected State conventions. But certain issues, unresolved in 1891, still failed to attract consensus. A protracted debate over railways and rivers concluded with constitutional provisions that, to this day, remain opaque. Conflict over federal fiscal relations and the respective financial powers of the Commonwealth houses of parliament almost broke the convention. The constitutional compromises satisfied neither side.

Still, the Bill was thought satisfactory, and it was submitted to the colonial parliaments at the end of the session for their consideration. During the break between convention sessions, the colonial premiers travelled to London for the Queen's Diamond Jubilee, joining other Empire leaders in the celebrations and another Colonial Conference. There, too, Premier Reid was approached by Colonial Secretary Chamberlain, conveying British concerns over the new Constitution Bill, in particular its design for a largely independent High Court. Chamberlain, in confidence, gave Reid three memoranda with recommendations for amendments and a request to promote these as if they were Reid's own. The decision to act in secret is revealing. Notwithstanding their routine assertions of imperial loyalty at each Federation event, Australians, it was well understood, were obstinate and likely to resent any outside interference in their constitution making.

Chamberlain felt free, however, to raise one matter openly. He reminded the Australians that Britain was opposed to race-based immigration laws, and that many subjects of the Empire were not white. Britain had resisted the colonies' immigration restriction laws in the past and, Chamberlain hinted, it would take the same line on future national laws. His audience was unmoved. A 'white' Australia was, after all, the very thing that most wanted. To be an Australian, they agreed, was to be a member of the British race. But membership, in the Australians' eyes, did not extend to all 'subjects of the Queen'.

Meanwhile, the colonial parliaments debated the Constitution Bill, and produced more than 300 proposals for amendment. The majority came from New South Wales, where, among others, the principle of equal Senate representation for all States was opposed, and a restriction on the Senate's powers over money bills was recommended. The New South Wales Legislative Council also recommended that the Constitution should guarantee Sydney's claim to be the federal capital. It was to be the issue that most captured the popular eye.

In September 1897 it was Sydney's turn to host the next session, where the proposed amendments were scheduled for discussion. Three weeks only were available before the Victorian delegates had to leave for their colony's general election, and in the event, little progress was made. Time ran out, and a third, unanticipated session had to be called. So, on 20 January 1898 the delegates returned to Melbourne, where the serious business of Federation had begun eight years earlier. For the better part of two months, in heat that was 'phenomenal, both in intensity and duration',[39] the Convention worked on completing the draft Constitution. It settled the distribution of powers between the Commonwealth and the States, wrestled over fiscal issues, debated matters provoked by persistent petitioners – notably, the recognition of God in the Constitution's preamble, which was finally conceded – and concluded, contrary to the wishes of New South Wales, that the choice of federal capital should be left to the future Commonwealth parliament.

Unlike in 1891, the convention wound up in a spirit of self-congratulation and hyperbole. 'A charter of liberty is enshrined in this Constitution, which is also a charter of peace', declared Alfred Deakin.[40] The new Commonwealth, declaimed future federal attorney-general, Josiah Symon, 'will be a union with strong foundations set deep in justice, a union which will endure from age to age, a bulwark against aggression and a perpetual security for the peace, freedom, and progress of the people of Australia'.[41] The delegates concluded with three cheers for the Queen, and this time, 'for Australia'.

Within three months, referendums on the Constitution Bill were held in Victoria, South Australia, Tasmania and New South Wales. The 'No' campaign was especially intense in the last, where the Constitution's financial arrangements, composition of the Senate, and above all, the federal capital issue, all worked against a positive vote. Two members of the New South Wales delegation joined with the colony's Labor Party and the dedicated Anti-Convention Bill League in the 'No' campaign. At a town hall meeting, premier Reid declared himself duty-bound to support the Bill, but made his doubts about the Constitution so clear that he might as well have said the opposite; the speech earned him the nickname 'Yes-No Reid'. A threshold number of 80,000 affirmative votes had been set for the referendum's success. Notwithstanding an equally intense affirmative campaign, including on the part of the newly formed Women's Federal League (its members not yet enfranchised), the result was failure.

Robust successes had been recorded in the three other colonies, and all the Enabling Acts had allowed for Federation to proceed with the agreement of three colonies alone, but this was never realistic in the absence of New South

---

39 Reid, *My Reminiscences*, p. 162.
40 *Official Record of the Debates of the Australasian Federal Convention*, vol. 5, p. 2507.
41 Ibid., p. 2509.

Wales. Concessions, albeit reluctant, could not be avoided. In January 1899 a 'secret' conference of all the premiers (closed to the public, this time) concluded with agreements that subtly, if significantly, strengthened the House of Representatives over the Senate, empowered the Commonwealth to make conditional grants to the States, and, most importantly, if popular approval were to be secured in New South Wales, offered the federal capital to that colony, although ruling out Sydney and allowing Melbourne to enjoy the 'seat of government' until the site in New South Wales was ready.

A new round of referendums was held that year and, having waited to see which way the wind blew, Queensland joined in at last. The campaigns in New South Wales intensified. New Federal Leagues, including Women's Leagues, sprang up to promote the 'Yes' case, and many of the previous year's opponents, including some of the Labor leaders, were won over. The 'working-man's bible', the *Bulletin*, came out in support. The opponents, too, were strengthened, and prominent women suffragists also joined the opposition. Although the turnout and voting patterns varied considerably around the continent, the result this time was positive in each colony, particularly convincing in Victoria and Tasmania, and exceptionally so in the Northern Territory of South Australia. Western Australia alone held back. Its premier, John Forrest, under pressure from the pro-Federation goldfields, now threatening secession under the slogan 'Separation for Federation', still hesitated. The other colonies would not wait. They had given up hoping for New Zealand to join; now, with or without Western Australia, they were ready to federate. Addresses to the Queen requesting the passage of the Constitution Bill were adopted in their parliaments. The next step was through the imperial parliament.

The battle in London

A delegation of leading federationists was assembled: Edmund Barton (New South Wales), Alfred Deakin (Victoria), Charles Kingston (South Australia), Phillip Fysh (Tasmania) and James Dickson (Queensland). Their role – so they thought – was to take the Bill to London and 'secure [its] passage without amendment'.[42] Britain, however, saw things differently. As in 1897, Joseph Chamberlain had ideas about amending the Constitution, and he knew that Reid's efforts on his behalf had been mostly unsuccessful. As before, his particular concern was the section of the Constitution that would

---

42 Deakin, *The Federal Story*, p. 104.

severely limit appeals from the Australian courts to the Judicial Committee of the Privy Council.

A battle of wills ensued. Still unaware of Chamberlain's secret strategy in 1897, the Australians were understandably puzzled about the British government's failure to have made its views known earlier. They appealed for support in Australia and they appealed to the British public. They gave addresses to every organisation that invited them. The campaign lasted twelve weeks, and was followed closely in the press. Eventually, some small concessions were made by the Australians, and Chamberlain accepted a compromise on the status of Australia's courts: the Privy Council would be available for criminal and civil appeals from the High Court of Australia (as well as the State Supreme Courts) and it could hear appeals in a limited class of constitutional matters, but the High Court would be conclusive on most constitutional questions. The Commonwealth parliament, furthermore, would have the power to bring all Privy Council appeals to an end when it chose. This compromise, Deakin wrote, was 'the golden bridge over which we passed to union'; at its conclusion the Australians took each other's hands and did a little victory dance.[43]

On 5 July 1900 the imperial parliament passed the Constitution Bill, and on 9 July it received the Royal Assent. Three weeks later, Western Australia held its referendum. With a high turnout and a resounding 'Yes' vote (registered by women as well as men), the colony's inclusion in the Commonwealth was assured. New Zealand, having watched from afar since 1891, now held a Royal Commission on the question of joining; six months later, it concluded in the negative. That colony, in its own view, was not merely too distant and geographically different, but also too advanced in race, labour and social relations to risk its own national aspirations, including its own foreign policy, by merging with Australia.[44]

The shape of the new Commonwealth was now clear. One last official task fell to Britain: the newly commissioned first governor-general would choose the first Commonwealth prime minister, pending elections. The task (at least in Australian eyes) was mishandled. In what would become known

43 Ibid., p. 155.
44 Nicholas Aroney, 'New Zealand, Australasia and Federation', *Canterbury Law Review*, 16 (2010): 31–46; Philippa Mein Smith, 'New Zealand', in Irving (ed.), *The Centenary Companion to Australian Federation*, pp. 400–5. Textual evidence of the hopes that New Zealand would join can still be found in the Constitution, and it remains an interesting counterfactual to imagine what difference this would have made. The New Zealanders' more generous approach to their indigenous population may, for example, have influenced the other States; alternatively, perhaps, it may have been compromised.

as the 'Hopetoun blunder', New South Wales premier, William Lyne (who had defeated George Reid in September 1899) was nominated.[45] Hopetoun's idea was simply to appoint the incumbent premier of the senior colony. Lyne, however, was known as an anti-federationist. Furthermore, he was disliked by the Federation leaders and was generally unpopular. It was Edmund Barton, the tireless federationist who seemed incapable of making enemies, who had long been the favourite. A transcolonial campaign against Lyne, led by Deakin, was now waged by the men who expected a place in the new ministry. At last Lyne stepped aside and Barton was rightfully recognised. It was Barton who entered the white pavilion on 1 January 1901, to take the oath, as the first prime minister.

The inauguration of the Commonwealth, which began with Deakin's 'tumult', captured a distinctively Australian national identity shaped in a British imperial context. Long-held certainties of racial and masculine superiority mingled with new and emerging values and forces. Although religious leaders quarrelled over precedence in the inauguration procession, and some declined to take part, trade unions were well-represented in the celebrations, as were non-British communities: German, Scandinavian, Italian, French, American and even, in Melbourne, the Chinese. Aboriginal men were on display, performing a 'corroboree' in Centennial Park and a re-enactment of James Cook's landing in New South Wales in 1770. This pantomime of inclusiveness was not insincere. It was the expression of aspirations: a generous, celebratory moment, before the reality – captured in the political machinations that Deakin's *Morning Post* columns would soon record – inevitably took over.

The colonies, now transformed into States, would see many, but not all, of the dilemmas that had prompted them into Federation resolved by Commonwealth legislation. But a shared dismay at the rapid centralising of power would blunt much of their enjoyment. Pre-Federation rivalries would endure. Western Australia would soon regret its last-minute decision to join, and in the 1930s would unsuccessfully seek to leave the Commonwealth altogether. The vision of Australia as another United States, growing mightily in size, wealth and international importance, while bearing British values in the southern seas, would have genuinely mixed results.

With the old Queen's death, three weeks to the day after the inauguration, the certainties of the nineteenth century gave way to a more turbulent age.

---

45 J.A. La Nauze, 'The Hopetoun Blunder', in J.A. La Nauze, *No Ordinary Act: Essays on Federation and the Constitution*, eds Helen Irving and Stuart Macintyre (Melbourne University Press, 2001), pp. 36–81.

Less than a decade and a half later, the world was convulsed by war, and the new nation, under a fracturing Labor government, had its national powers tested to the extreme. It emerged and, in a process that was slow and sometimes halting, took its place on the international stage as – in the formula adopted at the 1926 Imperial Conference in London – an 'autonomous' community 'equal in status, [and] in no way subordinate' to the other members of the Empire, including Britain itself.[46]

In the event, it would take many decades before full autonomy was achieved (or even desired). But the federationists' vision and the political arrangements they put in place to support it must be considered a success. Unquestionably, significant parts of the Constitution would have been written differently, had the process taken place 100 years later. But it is doubtful that the core commitments – to federalism, responsible and representative government, a democratic electoral system and popular control of constitutional alteration – would change.

46 'Balfour Declaration', Report of the Inter-Imperial Relations Committee, Chaired by the former British prime minister, Arthur Balfour, adopted at the Imperial Conference, London, 1926.

PART II

★

11

Environmental transformations

ANDREA GAYNOR

Australia is an old continent, home to the Earth's most ancient rocks. By 542 million years ago most of the present Australian landmass had been formed, though it was joined to the future Indian and Antarctic landmasses and lay far to the south of its present location. The Tasman Sea began to open between 80 and 60 million years ago, and the final separation from Antarctica commenced. So began the long period of isolation in which Australia's distinctive flora and fauna would evolve. At this time, much of Australia was covered with well-watered, species-rich rainforests. The wet conditions produced deep weathering and leaching of the land surface, contributing to the characteristically infertile soils found over much of the continent today.[1] Nowhere but Tasmania and the Snowy Mountains in the south-east would soils be renewed by glacial activity, and only along parts of the eastern seaboard and a few other small areas would volcanic activity produce young, fertile soils comparable to those in other continents.[2]

Australia drifted north and by 11 million years ago it was over 2,000 kilometres from Antarctica.[3] As the circumpolar ocean current began to flow, Australian climates became cooler, drier and more seasonal. Rainforests gave way to woodlands, shrublands and grasslands. Fires increased. Eucalypts and acacias, both present since at least 45 million years ago, became prominent. Western Australian plants, previously separated from eastern species by an inland sea, became isolated by the arid Nullarbor Plain, producing highly distinctive flora.[4]

---

1 David Johnson, *The Geology of Australia*, 2nd edn (Cambridge University Press, 2009), pp. 90–2, 146–54.
2 Mary E. White, *After the Greening: The Browning of Australia* (Sydney: Kangaroo Press, 1994), pp. 55, 131, 151.
3 Johnson, *The Geology of Australia*, pp. 146–7. Today Australia lies almost 3,000 kilometres from Antarctica, and is still moving in a northerly direction by almost 7 centimetres per year.
4 White, *After the Greening*, p. 127.

Then, from approximately 2.4 million years ago, the Earth entered a period of rapid climatic change, alternating between cold and arid glacial phases, and warmer and wetter interglacial periods, with long intervals of cool and dry conditions. Sea levels fell and rose as water was frozen in or released from polar icecaps. Seasonal aridity in the inland was well established by 700,000 years ago with salt lakes and shifting dunes found in some parts, while others supported a flora dominated by sheoaks, saltbushes and grasses. As the climate shifted between glacial and interglacial periods, many ecosystems were extinguished, and populations of less adaptable plants and animals were fragmented into smaller areas in which conditions were more suitable. There, they evolved separately, extending their range again when more favourable conditions returned.[5] This process fostered the high biodiversity evident in some areas of the continent today.

Overall, the wetter interglacial periods were insufficient to halt the evolutionary trend toward a flora adapted to fire and dry conditions. This trend was amplified when, around 140,000 years ago, there was a great increase in fire. The reasons for this are unknown; some have suggested early human activity.[6]

By 2 million years ago, many of Australia's most familiar animals were present, including kangaroos, emus, bandicoots, bats and crocodiles. At this time they existed alongside megafauna, such as flightless birds standing 3 metres high, a plant-eating marsupial – diprotodon – that was the size of a hippopotamus and kangaroos growing to a massive 230 kilograms. Then, around 46,000 years ago, 23 of the 24 kinds of large land mammals became extinct.[7] The reasons are hotly debated. Scientists believe that ancestral Aboriginal people probably arrived in the north of Australia around 50,000 years BP. Was the extinction a consequence of Aboriginal hunting and use of fire, or a result of climate change? The evidence remains inconclusive.[8]

Aboriginal people were and often remain skilful users of fire, and records of European exploration and settlement provide abundant evidence of its historical ubiquity. Willem de Vlamingh, sailing near present-day Perth in January 1697, observed 'great numbers of fires burning the whole length of

5 Ibid., pp. 145–7.
6 Stephen J. Pyne, *Burning Bush: A Fire History of Australia* (Sydney: Allen & Unwin, 1992), p. 76.
7 Johnson, *The Geology of Australia*, p. 159.
8 Tim Flannery, *The Future Eaters: An Ecological History of the Australasian Lands and People* (Sydney: New Holland Publishers, 1997), pp. 180–216.

the coast'.[9] Subsequent observers reported on the multiple and complex roles played by fire within Indigenous cultures. Domestic fires were the centre of family life and gave Aboriginal people 'the nighttime for story, ceremony, and companionship'.[10] Signal fires were used for long-distance communication; fires set for hunting drove or flushed out game. In 1846 John Lort Stokes noted that in Aboriginal hands, fire 'seems almost to change its nature, acquiring, as it were, complete docility'.[11]

How did Aboriginal people change the land? Some scholars propose that they 'made' the Australian landscape through 'constant and purposeful' management, especially the carefully planned burning of country in small patches or 'mosaics'. Over time this made grasslands and open woodlands with a grassy understorey the dominant vegetation types. With the expansion of colonial frontiers and the ensuing death and dispossession of Indigenous people, burning gradually declined and vegetation became more dense: 'new' forests grew.[12] Other scholars acknowledge that Aboriginal people engaged in burning but propose that vegetation was first shaped by climate and soil, then by the ecological cataclysm of large-scale clearing and cultivation that followed colonisation.[13] Still others seek to emphasise the diversity of Indigenous practices, while combining historical observations with current scientific understandings.[14]

British responses

Over thousands of years of occupation, Indigenous people developed an intimate understanding of climate that relied on adept reading of ecological indicators of seasonal change, rather than a fixed calendar. By contrast, European newcomers understood that they could expect seasons to be inverted, but struggled to come to terms with the highly variable climate.

9 Quoted in Sylvia J. Hallam, *Fire and Hearth: A Study of Aboriginal Usage and European Usurpation in South-Western Australia* (Canberra: Australian Institute of Aboriginal Studies, 1975), p. 16.
10 Quoted in Pyne, *Burning Bush*, p. 91.
11 Ian Abbott, 'Aboriginal Fire Regimes in South-West Western Australia: Evidence from Historical Documents', in Ian Abbott and Neil Burrows (eds), *Fire in Ecosystems of South-West Western Australia: Impacts and Management* (Leiden: Backhuys, 2003), p. 135.
12 See, for example, Eric Rolls, *A Million Wild Acres: 200 Years of Man and an Australian Forest* (Melbourne: Thomas Nelson, 1981); Bill Gammage, *The Biggest Estate on Earth: How Aborigines Made Australia* (Sydney: Allen & Unwin, 2011).
13 See, for example, Karl W. Butzer and David M. Helgren, 'Livestock, Land Cover, and Environmental History: The Tablelands of New South Wales, Australia, 1820–1920', *Annals of the Association of American Geographers*, 95, 1 (2005): 97–9.
14 See, for example, Abbott, 'Aboriginal Fire Regimes'.

When the *Endeavour* put in to Botany Bay in August 1770, Lieutenant James Cook noted that 'The Country in general is not badly water'd'. But the First Fleet arriving in the same location eighteen years later did so at the beginning of a severe and persistent El Niño event that generated drought conditions from India to the Caribbean. As crops failed and water sources dried up at Port Jackson in 1791, Governor Phillip wrote 'I do not think it probable that so dry a season often occurs' – an optimism perhaps grounded in Aboriginal knowledge.[15] Marine officer Watkin Tench, at Port Jackson from 1788 to 1791, observed that 'Of rain, we found in general not a sufficiency, but torrents of water sometimes fall'[16] – an impression amplified in the 'droughts and flooding rains' of Dorothea Mackellar's famous poem, 'My Country', published after some 120 years of bitter European experience of the effects of the El Niño Southern Oscillation in eastern Australia.

The experience of environmental degradation in colonies such as St Helena and Mauritius in the eighteenth century gave rise to a new awareness of the need for resource conservation.[17] By 1788 colonial officials well understood the requirement for environmental management, and regulations intended to protect food, water and timber supplies were passed in New South Wales within a few years. For example, by 1793 the 'Tank Stream', which provided Sydney with water for the first 40 years, was fenced and regulations prohibiting the felling of nearby trees were enacted. Not all residents shared the officials' concerns, and governors struggled to protect the stream from erosion and pollution.[18]

Early European perceptions of the environment of New South Wales have commonly been described as negative: the newcomers despised the strange and harsh landscape in which they found themselves. In fact responses varied, and delight and wonder were expressed alongside fear and alienation. Observers could not help but see and describe the unfamiliar land using the ideas and language of their homelands, but perceptions varied according to

15 Quoted in Richard Grove, 'Revolutionary Weather: The Climatic and Economic Crisis of 1788–1795 and the Discovery of El Niño', in Tim Sherratt, Tom Griffiths and Libby Robin (eds), *A Change in the Weather: Climate and Culture in Australia* (Canberra: National Museum of Australia Press, 2005), pp. 128–9.

16 Watkin Tench, *1788: Comprising A Narrative of the Expedition to Botany Bay and A Complete Account of the Settlement at Port Jackson* (Melbourne: Text, 1996), p. 235.

17 Richard Grove, *Green Imperialism: Colonial Expansion, Tropical Island Edens, and the Origins of Environmentalism, 1600–1860* (Cambridge University Press, 1996).

18 Tim Bonyhady, *The Colonial Earth* (Melbourne: Miegunyah Press, 2000), p. 5; J.M. Powell, *Environmental Management in Australia, 1788–1914* (Oxford University Press, 1976), p. 18.

personal backgrounds and motives, as well as the environments encountered.[19] A few themes stand out.

Enlightenment sensibilities valuing reason, order and the idea of progress framed the scientific gaze, which sought to collect and classify the abundant 'new' nature. The same Enlightenment principles informed notions of antipodean nature as raw material for improvement: a brute wilderness waiting to be transformed into congenial, 'civilised' surrounds.[20] Judge advocate David Collins observed with pride 'a country gradually opening, and improving everywhere…with a spirit universally prevalent of cultivating it'.[21] Although the hardships associated with arriving in a strange place that lacked familiar conveniences shaped many early views, the success of early cultivation efforts gave rise to perceptions of the young settlement as a luxuriant garden.

The stamp of Enlightenment was also evident in town planning, and soon after arrival Arthur Phillip laid out the settlement's first grand avenue. He envisaged a spacious settlement, proposing that streets must 'afford free circulation of air', and that no more than one house would be built on any of the town allotments.[22] Phillip also sought public controls on private development. However, land was such an important element in networks of colonial patronage that Phillip flouted his own plan, and it attracted little respect from his successors. When William Bligh arrived as governor in 1806, he was confronted by the disorder of building on short and informal leases in Sydney. However, his efforts to assert public control over private property in the interests of more equitable and orderly development won him the enmity of many, including those who would ultimately depose him.[23] By the 1820s Sydney and Hobart were both open settlements dominated by detached housing on large lots. The dust and noise of the growing towns, and the desire to achieve greater distance from the lower classes, soon saw colonial elites join their counterparts in London and New York in a flight to new suburban villa estates.[24]

19 Grace Karskens, *The Colony: A History of Early Sydney* (Sydney: Allen & Unwin, 2010), chs 8–9; R.L. Heathcote, 'Early European Perceptions of the Australian Landscape: The First Hundred Years', in George Seddon and Mari Davis (eds), *Man and Landscape in Australia* (Canberra: AGPS, 1976), p. 31.
20 John Gascoigne with the assistance of Patricia Curthoys, *The Enlightenment and the Origins of European Australia* (Cambridge University Press, 2002), pp. 70–1, 86–96; Bernard Smith, *European Vision and the South Pacific*, 2nd edn (Sydney: Harper & Row, 1985), p. 177.
21 Quoted in Karskens, *The Colony*, p. 238.
22 Quoted in Graeme Davison, 'Australia: The First Suburban Nation?' *Journal of Urban History*, 22, 40 (1995): 43.
23 Bonyhady, *The Colonial Earth*, pp. 41–66.
24 Davison, 'The First Suburban Nation', pp. 49–51.

English migrants – forced or free – were understandably nostalgic for home, and with imported technologies, seeds and animals they set about re-making England in the antipodes. By 1827 one visitor to Sydney found himself 'scarcely to be sensible that I was out of England'.[25] Gardens were an important symbol of transformation, marking possession as well as providing food and evoking memories of home.[26] But in the gardens of Sydney's Government House, visitors encountered native banksias, tea-trees and eucalypts alongside cherry, pear and apricot trees. Although the growing towns, in particular, were filled with sights and sounds familiar to the English visitor, the landscape would inevitably be a hybrid: 'a foreign place made English, and England turned exotic'.[27]

Where colonial officials, visitors and, later, free settlers delighted in the transformation of the bush, the convict majority in New South Wales saw it as a site of opportunity: a means of temporary or permanent escape. In Van Diemen's Land, convicts and emancipists hailing from non-industrial parts of Britain saw the bush as a place of redemption and hope, a bountiful landscape that opened up the possibility of a frugal independence.[28] As the bush became associated with convict rebellion, bushranging and 'vagabonds', the elite was even more keen to transform it.[29]

Other early views were informed by the romantic predilection for the 'noble savage' and wild landscapes as symbols of the primeval nature that was home to a human estate uncorrupted by civilisation. Such ideas informed James Cook's well-known reflection on the Aboriginal people of Australia as 'far more happier than we Europeans'. Romantic notions of an antipodean Eden were bolstered when the colony's five cows and a bull that had strayed into the bush five months after the first fleet's arrival were found seven years later, 32 kilometres inland, having expanded to a herd of over 60 animals.

Romantic attitudes were most keenly reflected in aesthetic responses, with many observers finding sublime or picturesque qualities in the landscape around Port Jackson. Aesthetic and utilitarian appreciation came together in the views of the open woodlands of the Cumberland Plain, where Eora

---

25 Quoted in Alan Frost, 'Going Away, Coming Home', in John Hardy and Alan Frost (eds), *Studies from Terra Australis to Australia* (Canberra: Australian Academy of the Humanities, 1989), p. 231.
26 Katie Holmes, Susan K. Martin and Kylie Mirmohamadi, *Reading the Garden: The Settlement of Australia* (Melbourne University Press, 2008), pp. 8, 26.
27 Ibid., p. 231.
28 James Boyce, 'Return to Eden: Van Diemen's Land and the Early British Settlement of Australia', *Environment and History*, 14, 2 (2008): 289–307.
29 Karskens, *The Colony*, ch. 9.

'firestick farming' had created extensive areas of widely spaced trees with luxuriant grass between. The newcomers likened these to a 'nobleman's park', after the landscapes created by Lancelot 'Capability' Brown and his followers for the English gentry.[30] In each region in which Aboriginal burning had produced these grassy woodland landscapes, Europeans described them in similar terms. Although some observers acknowledged the role of Aboriginal burning in their creation, the dominant view was that nature had provided this landscape, ready for pastoralists' use. Near Parramatta, however, as the destruction of Aboriginal society and prohibitions on burning put an end to their firing, the forest began to reclaim the parkland. As explorer Thomas Mitchell noted, by 1848:

> The omission of the annual periodical burning by natives, of the grass and young saplings, has already produced in the open forest lands nearest to Sydney, thick forests of young trees, where, formerly, a man might gallop without impediment, and see whole miles before him. Kangaroos are no longer to be seen there; the grass is choked by underwood; neither are there natives to burn the grass.[31]

Exploiting sea and land

Well before that time, early colonial entrepreneurs, who often possessed maritime skills but little capital, were looking to the sea. There they saw wealth in the guise of whales. The industrial revolution in Britain had given rise to an insatiable demand for whale oil: the spinning frames of northern England were lubricated with it, and lamps burning it illuminated factories long into the night. Illumination was also increasingly demanded by urban populations as a basic modern amenity, and by 1809 the streets of London were lit by 35,000 whale oil lamps.[32] Whalebone (or baleen) revolutionised corsetry, and whale products were used in soap, candles, cosmetics and the processing of wool and leather. By the end of the eighteenth century, northern whale fisheries were depleting, and whaling fleets were moving to southern waters.

There, the two main species pursued for oil were the southern right whale and sperm whale. The southern right whale migrates north from Antarctic

---

30 Smith, *European Vision and the South Pacific*, pp. 179–80.
31 T.L. Mitchell, *Journal of an Expedition into the Interior of Tropical Australia* (London: Longman, Brown, Green and Longmans, 1848), p. 413.
32 Roger Fouquet, *Heat, Power and Light: Revolutions in Energy Services* (Cheltenham: Edward Elgar, 2008), p. 198.

waters to breed, passing alongside Tasmanian and southern Australian shores. Sperm whales were less likely to be found inshore.[33] Both were hunted in a similar fashion, being harpooned from open boats until dead, when they were towed to the ship or land station and the blubber was cut off or 'flensed'. Pregnant females and those with young calves were especially vulnerable to shore-based whaling, as they often sought sheltered waters in bays and estuaries to birth and suckle their young.

Both species were abundant in Australian waters in the late eighteenth century. Captain Melville of the *Britannia*, one of five whaling ships serving as transports for the Third Fleet, declared after a voyage from Port Jackson that he had seen more sperm whales in a fortnight than 'in all his former life'.[34] Another master of a Third Fleet whaling vessel noted, ominously for the whales, that they were 'the least shy of any he had ever seen'.[35] Similar observations were made as British settlement extended to other areas. Major Edmund Lockyer reported that the coast at King George Sound (now Albany, in Western Australia) 'abounds with the sperm whale'. Lockyer also observed, with some prescience, that the local stocks of both whales and seals would be 'irreparably injured if not destroyed altogether' unless hunting was regulated.[36]

Colonial officers were keen to establish a whaling industry, not only for revenue but also the increased opportunities for communication arising from additional shipping. As a result, barriers to development such as the imperial injunction against ship-building and the East India Company's monopoly over shipping were overlooked, creatively bypassed and progressively dismantled. Since offshore hunting for sperm whales required large boats and considerable capital, colonial entrepreneurs favoured shore-based or bay whaling, which commenced in the estuary of the Derwent River around 1805. When shore whaling peaked in the 1830s, there were at least 60 whaling stations around Van Diemen's Land, each year exporting oil worth £100,000.[37] As one of the few occupations open only to free men, whaling was a source of pride as well as profit; the morality of the industry was not questioned.

---

33 Susan Lawrence and Peter Davies, *An Archaeology of Australia Since 1788* (New York: Springer Verlag, 2011), pp. 101–2.
34 Tench, *1788*, p. 271.
35 Quoted in J.C.H. Gill, 'Genesis of the Australian Whaling Industry: Its Development up to 1850', *Journal of the Royal Historical Society of Queensland*, 8, 1 (1966): 117.
36 Quoted in Martin Gibbs, 'Conflict and Commerce: American Whalers and the Western Australian Colonies, 1826–1888', *The Great Circle*, 22, 2 (2000): 3.
37 Susan Lawrence, 'A Maritime Empire: Archaeological Evidence for Van Diemen's Land Whaling in the Southern Oceans', *Tasmanian Historical Studies*, 13 (2008): 15.

In 1839 alone, Van Diemen's Land whalers took more than 1,000 southern right whales. The bonanza could not last. The 1841 season opened with 1,000 men employed on 35 stations, but whale populations were declining and the survivors had learned to avoid Tasmanian estuaries and bays: fewer than 300 were killed. Between 1828 and 1850 whalers registered in New South Wales and Van Diemen's Land alone took more than 11,700 southern right whales. Thereafter, reduced populations, along with economic factors, all but finished shore whaling in eastern Australian waters.[38] In Western Australia whaling was dominated by American vessels. Their numbers peaked in the 1840s, but by the end of the decade catches comprised fewer right whales and more of the less-desirable humpbacks. The last locally recorded right whale caught was in 1866.[39] A recent study suggests that southern right whale populations have still not re-established their distribution prior to the advent of commercial southern whaling in the late eighteenth century.[40]

Sealing followed much the same pattern as whaling, and indeed there was a good deal of overlap between the two industries. Seal oil was used in similar ways to whale oil and in the 1790s Thomas Chapman invented a method for ridding seal fur of its coarse hairs, making it a valued commodity in England. The potential for sealing in the region was first demonstrated in 1792, when William Raven left a gang of sealers at Dusky Bay in New Zealand. They slaughtered and skinned 4,500 seals.[41] Five years later, when Matthew Flinders was sent to recover salvaged supplies from a shipwreck on the Furneaux Islands at the east end of Bass Strait, he declared that 'the number of seals exceeded anything we had, any of us, before witnessed'.[42] The first to test these claims was a visitor to New South Wales, Captain Charles Bishop, who returned to Sydney with 5,200 sealskins and 350 gallons of seal oil.[43] Sealing soon became popular with local entrepreneurs as the

---

38 W.H. Dawbin, 'Right Whales Caught in Waters Around South-Eastern Australia and New Zealand During the Nineteenth and Early Twentieth Centuries', *Report of the International Whaling Commission*, 10 (1986): 262; Gill, 'Genesis of the Australian Whaling Industry', p. 129.

39 Gibbs, 'Conflict and Commerce', p. 18; John Bannister, *Western Australian Humpback and Right Whales: An Increasing Success Story* (Perth: Western Australian Museum, 1994), p. 37.

40 Rhys Richards, 'Past and Present Distributions of Southern Right Whales (*Eubalaena australis*)', *New Zealand Journal of Zoology*, 36, 4 (2009): 447–59.

41 D.R. Hainsworth, 'Exploiting the Pacific Frontier: The New South Wales Sealing Industry 1800–1821', *Journal of Pacific History*, 2, 1 (1967): 60, 68.

42 Quoted in John K. Ling, 'Exploitation of Fur Seals and Sea Lions from Australian, New Zealand and Adjacent Subantarctic Islands during the Eighteenth, Nineteenth and Twentieth Centuries', *Australian Zoologist*, 31, 2 (1999): 324.

43 Hainsworth, 'Exploiting the Pacific Frontier', p. 61.

equipment required was modest, and they could use their vessels to deposit crews on sealing grounds and while the slaughter was going on, return to port or engage in other regional trade before returning to collect sealers, skins and oil. From 1801 large numbers of seals were being taken on King Island in Bass Strait; soon after, the slaughter began on other rookeries along the south coast. The main target was the fur seal, though two species of sea lion were also hunted, and on King Island the elephant seal was hunted to local extinction.

By 1840, over 240,000 sealskins had been taken from Bass Strait by colonial and English crews alone. Almost half of the total harvest was taken in the peak years of 1803–06; thereafter decline was rapid, and never would the harvest again approach even half of the early nineteenth-century peaks. Across the entirety of southern Australia, at least 317,000 fur seals were taken before 1825. Not all of the decline in production was due to reduced populations: the imposition of duties on skins and oil disadvantaged colonial producers, and sealskin markets collapsed in China and England in response to a vast over-supply of skins from the South Atlantic.[44] However, the dwindling populations did not go unnoticed: as early as December 1802 it was obvious that there were fewer seals on King Island, and in May 1803 Governor King was talking of the need for restrictions. Concern was not only utilitarian: the wholesale slaughter of sea elephants was denounced by the naturalist and explorer François Péron not only as economically myopic, but also because it inflicted cruelty on 'gentle and peaceful' animals.[45] By the early 1810s Bass Strait seal populations were 'totally annihilated', though sealing was not regulated in Tasmania until 1889. Recovery was slow: in 1985 it was estimated that there were only 20 to 50 percent as many Australian fur seals in Australasia as there were prior to sealing.[46] Sealers also contributed to the extinction of the diminutive King Island emu and local extinction of a wombat subspecies. Neither had learned to fear humans.[47]

Sealing and whaling provided a start for many colonial entrepreneurs, and in stimulating ship-building these industries opened up further possibilities for commerce. Directly and indirectly, thousands were employed, at a time

---

44 Ling, 'Exploitation of Fur Seals', pp. 329, 337–40.
45 Quoted in Bonyhady, *The Colonial Earth*, p. 6.
46 Hainsworth 'Exploiting the Pacific Frontier', p. 66; Ling, 'Exploitation of Fur Seals', pp. 329, 339.
47 Flannery, *The Future Eaters*, p. 191.

when there were no other staple export industries. However, these rewards came at a high ecological cost.

Even before the unsustainable exploitation of these maritime resources was nearing its end, covetous eyes were turning inland. The searing heat and drought of the summer of 1813 provided an incentive for landholders in New South Wales to find a passage through the Blue Mountains to the interior, which was rumoured to contain a vast, open plain ideal for grazing. Expansion into the interior was rapid. Attempts to regulate it were made in vain, and by 1835 squatters and their quadrupeds were illegally occupying land over 500 kilometres from Sydney. This pattern of pastoral expansion would later be repeated in South Australia.

In Van Diemen's Land, pastoral expansion played out a little differently. The first whites to move out into the open grasslands were poor emancipists and their descendants, who were little touched by the Enlightenment and industrial revolution. Hunting dogs stolen from the officer class enabled them to live independently in the bush on the abundant kangaroos that had never known such predators.[48] They lived simple lives shaped by the available resources, sharing the land – for the most part peacefully – with Aboriginal people. Sheep integrated into the kangaroo economy multiplied on the rich native pastures, to about 172,000 by 1819 – more than twice the number found in New South Wales.[49] However, in the wake of the Bigge report, free settlers arrived in the 1820s to take up land, which was granted them in proportion to their capital. This new class of immigrant sought to increase its own wealth and status and, as one of them put it, 'to exhibit on a small scale something like the beauties which rise at every step in the land to which we have bade adieu'.[50] These motives gave rise to a much more energetic transformation of the land, as well as social relations.

Visions and ambitions, then, were clearly an important determinant of landscape change. However, as the environmental historian, Alfred Crosby, has pointed out, the Europeans were not entirely in control of their destiny. Rather, their 'portmanteau biota' of germs, plants and domestic animals helps to explain why populations of colonial Europeans increased so dramatically, while those of native peoples crashed.[51] In Australia, pathogens that

48 James Boyce, 'Canine Revolution: The Social and Environmental Impact of the Introduction of the Dog to Tasmania', *Environmental History*, 11, 1 (2006): 107, 111.
49 Boyce, 'Return to Eden', p. 295.
50 Quoted in ibid., p. 301.
51 Alfred W. Crosby, *Ecological Imperialism: The Biological Expansion of Europe, 900–1900* (Cambridge University Press, 1986).

Aboriginal populations had never before encountered gave rise to deadly epidemics and weakened many survivors. Old World plants spread to become fodder for stock. Domesticated animals, once established, were 'walking sources of food, leather, fibre, power, and wealth', and enabled the transfer of British culture and technology with relatively little adaptation.[52] Both plants and animals disrupted native ecologies.

Sheep were 'the shocktroops of land seizure', enabling the imposition of an imperial economy on a 'wild' land, with tragic consequences for its Aboriginal custodians.[53] They eroded the banks of creeks and waterholes, and fouled the water with dung. They ate out the sweet native grasses that protected the soil, leaving it open to invasion by annual weeds in winter, and erosion by summer winds. In the Port Phillip District, the *murnong* or yam daisy – a stable Aboriginal food – declined.[54] The immediacy of effects varied between regions, according to the soil, vegetation, weather, stocking rates and grazing practices. Before 1852 pastoral leasehold was practically non-existent, and grazing rights were obtained through payment of an annual licence fee. Under such conditions there was little incentive to look after the land, though the lack of formal boundaries meant that sheep could readily be moved around, offering some protection against over-grazing. As pastoral claims were recognised and boundaries fenced, the exponentially increasing sheep population was much less mobile, and so placed more pressure on the land, especially in dry seasons.[55] As early as 1853, the pastoralist John Robertson realised that 'for pastoral purposes the lands here are getting of less value every day…and will carry less sheep and far less cattle'.[56] By the 1880s the environmental problems arising from overstocking were widely acknowledged, though indebtedness saw it widely practised. The considerable wealth that sheep generated for individuals and colonies was obtained at the expense of many of the ecologies that had sustained Indigenous people, physically and spiritually, for countless generations.

52 Alfred W. Crosby, *Germs, Seeds and Animals: Studies in Ecological History* (Armonk, NY: M.E. Sharpe, 1994), p. 34.
53 Stuart Macintyre, *A Concise History of Australia* (Cambridge University Press, 1999), pp. 59–70.
54 Richard Broome, 'Changing Aboriginal Landscapes of Pastoral Victoria, 1830–1850', *Studies in the History of Gardens & Designed Landscapes*, 31, 2 (2011): 93–4.
55 Quoted in Butzer and Helgren, 'Livestock, Land Cover, and Environmental History', p. 104.
56 Tony Dingle, *The Victorians: Settling* (Sydney: Fairfax, Syme & Weldon Associates, 1984), p. 38.

From mining gold to mining soil

The invasion of European biota and the consequent destabilisation of local ecologies might have played a role in the most catastrophic bushfires then known to Europeans in Australia. In February 1851, perhaps a quarter of Victoria's desiccated country erupted into roaring flame.[57] Settlers were shocked at the scale and ferocity of the 'Black Thursday' fires, though their contemplation was soon overtaken by the discovery of gold in New South Wales, then Victoria. A vast influx of diggers swept into the colonies, all with hopes for a better life and material needs to be met. Increased exploitation of natural resources followed the immigrants' demands for food, fuel, housing and other goods. As the discovery and mining of gold generated unprecedented material wealth, levels of consumption rose in both goldfield towns and colonial capitals.

By 1861 Victoria was producing around one-third of the world's gold, and 46 per cent of the non-Indigenous population of Australia lived there. Melbourne had grown rapidly to a town of some 125,000 people. It struggled with such growth and the Yarra River was fast becoming a fetid drain, carrying sewage and industrial effluent slowly to the sea. A law passed in 1855 'to prevent further pollution' of the Yarra was not enforced after objections from business leaders who, characteristically favouring economic development over environmental amenity, found it a convenient sewer for industries operating in the surrounding working-class suburbs.[58]

The lack of affordable and efficient public transport meant that working-class people had little choice but to accept accommodation close to employment opportunities, however crowded or substandard. Under gold-rush conditions of rampant speculation, jerry-building on tiny blocks in inner areas was rife. Ownership rates were high and residents valued this independence, though William Howitt, visiting Melbourne in 1852, deplored its 'wilderness of wooden huts of Lilliputian dimensions…delightfully interspersed with pigs, geese, hens, goats, and dogs innumerable'.[59] Sanitation was poor and gastroenteric diseases extracted a deadly toll among the booming urban population. Wealthier residents continued to retreat to outlying suburbs, and by the 1860s commuting by carriage to suburban villas was well established.

57 Pyne, *Burning Bush*, pp. 221–4.
58 John Lack, '"Worst Smelbourne": Melbourne's Noxious Trades', in Graeme Davison, David Dunstan and Chris McConville (eds), *The Outcasts of Melbourne: Essays in Social History* (Sydney: Allen & Unwin, 1985), pp. 172–80.
59 Quoted in Powell, *Environmental Management in Australia*, p. 36.

Gold mining also had local effects. The first phase of mining was alluvial, often symbolised by the romantic image of the lone miner panning for gold in a stream. The reality was rather different. As William Howitt exclaimed, 'every feature of Nature is annihilated'.[60] To get at the alluvial gold miners first had to clear the vegetation, sealing the fate of its bird and animal residents. The earth was then dug, washed for gold and left in barren mullock heaps. Streams were diverted and muddied; their 'thick and foul' waters sustained little aquatic life.[61] Any remaining low plants were grazed into oblivion; native animals shot for food or sport; trees felled for shelter, firewood and shaft construction. In the Western Australian rushes of the 1890s, the woodlands for many miles around Kalgoorlie were stripped bare to meet the demands of mining machinery and infrastructure and to feed the voracious appetites of condensers producing fresh water from saline bore water. The deforestation, as local residents attested, played a major role in the frequent dust storms that plagued the settlements.[62] Processes used to extract gold from ore mined in deep leads contaminated surrounding environments with toxic substances, including mercury and arsenic. Although the danger of arsenic compounds was recognised at the time and the means to recover the arsenic were known, polluters were rarely prosecuted despite numerous complaints.[63]

As the surface gold began to run out, there was a surge in demand for land reform: landless former miners and their town and trades allies sought to 'unlock the land' held by the squatters. They envisioned instead a society of yeoman farmers, in which stability and contentment would be found in dignified work, moral virtue and manly independence. Victorian land reform Acts in the 1860s were generally ineffective in achieving closer settlement, though some small farms were established, particularly in the goldfields. Small acreages forced over-cropping of land, however, and by the 1870s many of these farms were exhausted, overrun with weeds and abandoned. Oblivious to this outcome, the colonial government pressed on with reform, introducing the *Land Act* of 1869, which enabled prospective settlers to select up to 320 acres (130 hectares) for £1 per acre over 10 years, conditional upon

60 Quoted in ibid., p. 37.
61 Don Garden, 'Catalyst or Cataclysm? Gold Mining and the Environment', *Victorian Historical Journal*, 72, 1–2 (2001): 33; see also Dingle, *Settling*, pp. 50–2.
62 Andrea Gaynor and Jane Davis, 'People, Place and the Pipeline: Visions and Impacts of the Goldfields Water Supply Scheme, 1896–1906', in Marnie Leybourne and Andrea Gaynor (eds), *Water: Histories, Cultures, Ecologies* (Perth: UWA Press, 2006), p. 25.
63 Ian D. Rae, 'Gold and Arsenic In Victoria's Mining History', *Victorian Historical Journal*, 72, 1–2 (2001): 165–6.

certain 'improvements' within the first three years.[64] The required improvements, reflected in similar legislation in other colonies, would dramatically transform landscapes across Australia, precipitating a frenzy of clearing, ring-barking and fencing as selectors strove to carve out viable farms.

Demand for land was immense, and hopes for Australia's agrarian future high. Together, dreams and political ambition produced some reckless policy decisions. One of these episodes occurred in South Australia. There, the surveyor-general, George Goyder, had carefully observed the land and the Aboriginal people, and had come to understand the critical importance of rainfall variability. In 1865 he mapped the boundary of the agricultural land with reliable rainfall, and seven years later 'Goyder's line' was declared the northern limit of the area in which agricultural land could be purchased on credit. Soon afterwards, however, under intense political pressure from inexperienced and over-confident settlers and those who believed that 'rain follows the plough', the government released land beyond the line. At the end of the decade, Goyder's judgement was painfully vindicated when dry seasons returned to the northern lands and farmers beyond the line had little choice but to abandon their desiccated and degraded farms.[65]

In less marginal areas, first yields were often high, but the soils – mostly old and weathered – were rapidly exhausted. As yields began to decline many farmers sold their land and moved further out. This strategy of 'mining the soil', though decried by contemporaries, was encouraged by the ready availability of 'virgin' land on cheap terms. As land became scarce, farmers increasingly sought means of sustaining their enterprise. By the end of the nineteenth century, superphosphate, new methods of fallowing and new wheat varieties had made farming more economically sustainable. Many had also turned to mechanisation, and extended their holdings by purchasing or having family members select adjacent blocks.[66] The strategy of increasing farm size would become a commonplace one as the yeoman ideal retreated before the capital-intensive and export-oriented reality of Australian farming. For farmers, since at least the 1870s

Land was potential wealth and wheat was the proven means of reaping the potential. His wheat was not for his family and the village grist mill, it

---

64 Charles Fahey, 'The Free Selector's Landscape: Moulding the Victorian Farming Districts, 1870–1915', *Studies in the History of Gardens & Designed Landscapes*, 31, 2 (2011): 99.

65 D.W. Meinig, *On the Margins of the Good Earth: The South Australian Wheat Frontier 1869–1884* (Adelaide: Rigby, 1970).

66 Dingle, *Settling*, pp. 113–14; Fahey, 'The Free Selector's Landscape', pp. 102–3.

was wheat for the millions of the new industrial world. He farmed not as a member of an intimate, stable, localized society, but as a member of a world-wide, dynamic, competitive society.[67]

Yet the yeoman dream died hard: in 1893 the Western Australian government offered free 160-acre 'homestead farms' to the head of a family or any adult male who did not already own more than 100 acres. Such small farms, on ancient, infertile soils and remote from markets, could never be sustainable.

Small farmers across Australia had to contend not only with drought, bushfire and remote markets, but also increasingly unstable ecologies. In the high-rainfall Great Forest of South Gippsland, the selectors laboriously hacked out the understorey, chopped down small trees, ringbarked large trees and burned the lot, but then expected a relatively smooth transition to British-style farming. Instead they were confronted with a barrage of native pests. Hardy pioneer plant species – many poisonous or prickly – sprung up in dense thickets after a burn. Arduous and expensive secondary clearing became a key factor in neglect and abandonment of land: by the 1920s over 180,000 hectares of South Gippsland had been cleared and no fewer than 125,450 of them were abandoned or overgrown.[68] As farming commenced, many forest animals found the new fare much to their liking. Grasshoppers and caterpillars laid pasture bare. Bandicoots dug out and ate seed; wallabies devoured growing crops and pasture; cockatoos feasted on ripening maize; dingoes ate lambs. Similar challenges were experienced in the well-watered forests of New South Wales, Queensland and Tasmania.

The changes to the landscape wrought by ringbarking and clearing did not go unremarked. In the 1840s and 50s the author and artist, Louisa Meredith, voiced objections to the transformation of Australian nature, deploring the 'most bare, raw, and ugly appearance' of clearing, and the 'indescribably dreary and desolate appearance' of ringbarked forests.[69] Such aesthetic appreciation of the environment was a significant factor motivating nineteenth-century advocates of landscape and species preservation, though such was the power of the cultural and economic forces promoting rapid development that they struggled to translate their ideals into practice.[70] Furthermore, their opposition to colonial capitalist expansion was highly

---

67 Meinig, *On the Margins of the Good Earth*, p. 121.
68 Warwick Frost, 'European Farming, Australian Pests: Agricultural Settlement and Environmental Disruption in Australia, 1800–1920', *Environment and History*, 4, 2 (1998): 136.
69 Quoted in Holmes et al., *Reading the Garden*, p. 11; Bonyhady, *The Colonial Earth*, p. 149.
70 Bonyhady, *The Colonial Earth*.

selective and did not extend, for example, to the destruction of Aboriginal societies.[71]

Arguments for conservation were also articulated in ethical terms. The leading colonial botanist and naturalist, Ferdinand von Mueller, proposed in a public lecture of 1871 that

> individual life, whatever it may be, which we so often so thoughtlessly and so ruthlessly destroy, but which we never can restore, should be respected. Is it not as if the sinking tree was speaking imploringly to us, and when falling wished to convey to us its sadness and its grief?[72]

Ethical considerations also drove Louisa Meredith's mid-century opposition to animal cruelty and hunting for sport.[73]

More prominent were utilitarian arguments for the conservation of natural resources. In the 1860s and 70s these were particularly influenced by the 1864 publication of *Man and Nature*, by the American naturalist George Perkins Marsh. In this pivotal book, Marsh promoted the idea that humanity had the power to transform and destroy nature. This understanding is today commonplace, but in the early nineteenth century it was still widely believed that nature was so immense and enduring as to be virtually immune to exhaustion at human hands.

The book stimulated discussion of environmental degradation, especially in South Australia and Victoria. Prominent concerns included the relationships between forest, climate and water supplies, as well as the supply of timber. In Victoria these were investigated by a committee of scientists and public servants, which called in 1865 for the creation and extension of forest reserves, as well as afforestation projects. South Australia possessed relatively few timber resources and Adelaide suffered from acute water shortages, leading to considerable anxiety over the possibility that rainfall might decline with deforestation. There, following the example of New Zealand, a Forest Board was created in 1875, which established reserves and took the lead in development and management of tree plantations.[74] In spite of such developments, woodcutters, pastoralists and selectors continued to plunder forests and woodlands. Licensing systems failed to discourage wasteful and

---

71 Caroline Jordan, 'Progress Versus the Picturesque: White Women and the Aesthetics of Environmentalism in Colonial Australia 1820–1860', *Art History*, 25, 3 (2002): 352–6.
72 Quoted in Powell, *Environmental Management in Australia*, p. 70.
73 Bonyhady, *The Colonial Earth*, pp. 132–5.
74 Powell, *Environmental Management in Australia*, pp. 63–7, 89–92; James Beattie, *Empire and Environmental Anxiety: Health, Science, Art and Conservation in South Asia and Australasia, 1800–1920* (Basingstoke: Palgrave Macmillan, 2011), pp. 166–7.

excessive exploitation, and administration was underfinanced and largely impotent. Although the concept of sustained-yield management was quite well understood in colonial scientific circles, it was not implemented effectively because there was insufficient public support for it, particularly among influential people.[75]

Animals, water, cities

Though some colonists were sympathetic to native nature, all believed that it required 'improvement' to realise its productive and aesthetic potential. Members of the acclimatisation movement, which emerged from the 1850s and flourished in the British and other European empires, sought to achieve this through the transfer and establishment in the wild of the most 'useful' and 'beautiful' species from around the world. In Australia, acclimatisation societies imported and exported various species and transferred them within and between colonies, aiming to create a garden landscape that was abundant, profitable and morally uplifting.[76] Although their efforts were sometimes too successful, not all new introductions thrived. For example, only seven of the sixteen bird species introduced into South Australia between 1863 and 1885 became established in the wild.[77]

The work of acclimatisation societies was supported by the promulgation of game laws, which were passed in most of the colonies during the 1860s in spite of working-class opposition to perceived similarities with 'the evil of the game laws in the mother country'.[78] The colonial laws generally aimed to protect imported fauna, though some also provided for the protection of native animals, and more especially birds.[79] Acclimatisation societies were also behind the first fisheries protection Acts, which were intended to protect imported species as well as iconic native species such as Murray Cod. Though the game laws were impossible to enforce effectively, they did

75 Ibid., p. 77.

76 Ian Tyrrell, *True Gardens of the Gods: Californian-Australian Environmental Reform, 1860–1930* (Berkeley: University of California Press, 1999), p. 27.

77 Ian Abbott, 'Historical Perspectives of the Ecology of Some Conspicuous Vertebrate Species in South-West Western Australia', *Conservation Science Western Australia*, 6, 3 (2008): 156.

78 Geoffrey Bolton, *Spoils and Spoilers: Australians Make Their Environment 1788–1980* (Sydney: George Allen & Unwin, 1981), p. 98.

79 Brett J. Stubbs, 'From "Useless Brutes" to National Treasures: A Century of Evolving Attitudes Towards Native Fauna in New South Wales, 1860s to 1960s', *Environment and History*, 7, 1 (2001): 27.

signal a growing awareness of the desire to conserve 'wild' species, native and exotic, if only for their utility to humanity.

The acclimatisers' understanding of the land was derived largely from natural history, a form of scientific inquiry concerned with classifying and naming the natural world.[80] This approach dealt with nature's pieces rather than systems, leaving colonists poorly equipped to understand interactions between species and what would later be understood as ecosystems. Few counselled caution. In the 1840s and 50s, many attempts were made to establish rabbits in the wild on the mainland, as game. One man who advertised his success widely was Thomas Austin of Barwon Park, near Geelong. Seeking suitable animals to hunt, in 1859 Austin imported 24 wild rabbits, along with partridges and hares, from England. They bred quickly and soon Austin was holding grand shooting parties.[81] With plentiful food and shelter, relatively few predators and climates similar to its Iberian homeland, the rabbit spread faster than any other introduced mammal anywhere in the world. As the furry scourge ate whole fields of ripening crops and stripped paddocks of grass, sheep starved and farmers walked off the land. Rabbits killed trees and shrubs – native and exotic – by stripping them of bark. By 1930 the historian W.K. Hancock was certain that the rabbit had 'made new deserts'.[82]

Colonial governments responded with legislation establishing regimes of inspection and punishment for failure to control rabbits, to little effect. Government employees and besieged landholders fought the rabbits with shovels and explosives, poison baits and gases, and the release of mongooses and cats. The optimistic belief that vast regions could be protected like paddocks saw the erection of barrier fences across thousands of kilometres. Often built too late, their effectiveness was further reduced by fires, floods, open gates and human helpers. In the wake of the rabbit, enthusiasm for acclimatisation waned. Yet many profited from the pest. From 1883 to 1885 nearly £1 million was paid in bounties and wages for rabbit control in New South Wales alone, and some rabbiters became wealthy men.[83] They had a clear incentive to sustain their source of revenue, assuring the futility of bounty schemes. Though introduced for gentlemen's pleasure and deplored by farmers, rabbits sustained many among the poor and landless.

---

80 Thomas R. Dunlap, *Nature and the English Diaspora: Environment and History in the United States, Canada, Australia and New Zealand* (Cambridge University Press, 1999), p. 55.
81 Eric C. Rolls, *They All Ran Wild: The Animals and Plants that Plague Australia*, new edn (London: Angus & Robertson, 1984), pp. 19, 23.
82 W.K. Hancock, *Australia* (London: Ernest Benn, 1930), p. 32.
83 Brian Coman, *Tooth & Nail: The Story of the Rabbit in Australia* (Melbourne: Text, 1999), p. 99.

As generations grew up with the rabbit, it also became intricately enmeshed in Australian life and culture, from the iconic rabbit-fur felt slouch hats worn by Australian troops, to the bunny hunting that enlivened quiet evenings on the farm.

Cats were another introduction, arriving as domestic pets and mouse-catchers. Around south-eastern Australia and Perth, cats had taken up independent life in the bush by 1840, with wild-born generations growing larger than their domesticated forebears. In several areas they were deliberately released to help control rabbits, and by 1890 they could be found over 90 per cent of the mainland.[84] Although they preyed upon small mammals and reptiles, it is unclear whether they were responsible for as much ecological damage as the red fox. Like rabbits, foxes were released to satisfy a desire for a fashionable sport, and it also took some time for them to become established. Indeed, it is likely that only the exponential increase in wild rabbits from the mid-1860s enabled the initial proliferation of foxes. The first foxes to breed and disperse across south-eastern Australia were probably released in the mid-1870s by the wealthy Chirnside family at Werribee Park, outside Melbourne. The foxes proceeded to prey on domestic and native animals alike, and in 1889 joined a growing list of animals declared vermin.[85]

Foxes played a role in the decline of some native fauna, though clearing, grazing, rabbit damage and changes in fire regimes were more to blame. Hunting was also implicated. Numerous birds and marsupials, including lyrebirds, platypus and koala, were trapped or shot for their fur or plumage. Trapping and poisoning of native 'pest' species was common, and in Queensland and New South Wales landholders were required to destroy 'noxious animals' found on their property, including wallabies, kangaroos and dingoes. In 1892 bounties were paid on the scalps of 27,736 pademelons (a kind of small wallaby) in the Lismore district alone.[86] Animal diseases also took a toll: it is likely that one introduced near Shark Bay around 1875 resulted in the decline and even extinction of several species of native animal in Western Australia.[87] Yet the effects of colonisation on native animals were

84 Ian Abbott, 'The Spread of the Cat, Felis catus, in Australia: Re-examination of the Current Conceptual Model with Additional Information', Conservation Science Western Australia, 7, 1 (2008): 1, 5.

85 Ian Abbott, 'The Importation, Release, Establishment, Spread, and Early Impact on Prey Animals of the Red Fox Vulpes vulpes in Victoria and Adjoining Parts of South-Eastern Australia', Australian Zoologist, 35, 3 (2011): 526.

86 Stubbs, 'From "Useless Brutes" to National Treasures', p. 31.

87 Ian Abbott, 'Mammalian Faunal Collapse in Western Australia, 1875–1925: The Hypothesised Role of Epizootic Disease and a Conceptual Model of Its Origin, Introduction, Transmission, and Spread', Australian Zoologist, 33, 4 (2006): 530–61.

diverse: while some were pushed to extinction, others proliferated. In some areas, kangaroos were threatened by hunting and ecological change; elsewhere, populations boomed as they took advantage of new water sources, crops and pastures intended for sheep and cattle.

As well as seeking to control animal populations, colonial governments made some attempts to control water resources. Although landowners had been carrying out small-scale irrigation in Victoria since the 1850s, efforts to promote larger schemes were stymied by short memories and a run of good seasons, as well as a lingering association of irrigation with Chinese rice paddies.[88] Not until the El Niño droughts of 1877 and 1880–81, which caused widespread misery on the Victorian northern plains, was there sufficient interest to support the emergence of an irrigation movement, based in Melbourne. Proponents saw irrigation not merely as insurance against drought and investment in production, but also a means by which to realise the ideal of an independent white rural yeomanry. The irrigationists' landscape vision was Edenic, and their rhetoric laden with biblical imagery, even though their project was inescapably modern and technological.[89]

In 1884 a Royal Commission on Water Supply was established in Victoria, with Alfred Deakin, later Australia's second prime minister, as chair. His 1886 *Irrigation Act* was inspired by the Californian example, though control of rivers was vested in the crown while irrigation was managed through local trusts. An agreement with the Canadian Chaffey brothers enabled their private development of irrigation colonies at Mildura on the Murray and Renmark rivers in South Australia. However, Victorian farmers generally regarded irrigation as supplementary, and failed to adopt the more intensive cropping that would enable recovery of costs. The Chaffey brothers' ventures ended in bankruptcy, and even before the century's end salt was an emerging problem.[90] The dream of irrigation did not die, but its practice was thereafter centralised and tightly controlled with a view to economic efficiency.

Water was also central to the expansion of pastoralism inland. As the southern colonies sought to replace pastoralists with selectors, Queensland aimed to attract pastoral interests by reducing rents and increasing the size of leases. Groundwater had been harvested on a large scale in England since the

---

88 Dingle, *Settling*, p. 119.
89 Tyrrell, *True Gardens of the Gods*, pp. 121–40; Melissa Bellanta, 'Irrigation Millennium: Science, Religion and the New Garden of Eden', *Eras*, 3 (2002) <http://arts.monash.edu.au/publications/eras/edition-3/bellanta.php> accessed 15 August 2012.
90 Hilary Susan Howes, 'The Spectre at the Feast: The Emergence of Salt in Victoria's Irrigated Districts', *Environment and History*, 14, 2 (2008): 229.

1820s, and understanding of the hydrology of artesian basins had increased greatly in subsequent decades. Efforts to tap artesian sources in Australia were sporadic before the 1880s, when drought hit the inland pastoral industry. In 1886 the Queensland squatter Simon Fraser hired a Canadian well-borer whose massive drill reached water – and lots of it – at the unheard-of depth of 512 metres. More deep bores were drilled over subsequent years, with the artesian water enabling grazing to expand into Aboriginal country previously considered too arid for stock. Pastoralism in Queensland boomed, and a few graziers became very wealthy indeed, while Aboriginal resistance was repressed and fragile ecologies were crippled.[91]

Australians were increasingly located not in the outback but in the rapidly growing cities and towns: the ports and administrative centres for prosperous rural hinterlands. The largest city was sprawling Melbourne. In 1888, when there were 122 Parisians and 53 Londoners per acre, there were only three Melbournians.[92] They lived mainly in detached or semi-detached, owner-occupied, single-storey houses, and as public transport networks grew they were increasingly located in the suburbs. Similar patterns of development would prevail in Perth and Adelaide; Sydney, Brisbane and Hobart remained more compact.[93]

Three main factors combined to make extensive suburbanisation possible in colonial cities: the commercial rather than industrial nature of the cities (which freed up capital to invest in city-building); the relative affluence of Australian workers; and their preference for the domestic independence conferred by suburban home-ownership. In the suburbs of all Australian cities, land around the house was put to a range of uses. Front gardens were an important means of creating privacy and displaying taste. White-collar workers could achieve a semblance of the yeoman's manly independence by growing fruit and vegetables in the backyard, making use of the manure produced by abundant urban horses. Working-class households favoured animals for food production, and as late as 1903, up to 8 per cent of Perth households kept a house cow.[94]

As more people were separated from the bush in cities, the sentimental attachment to it began to grow. This, along with the growth of railway

91 Michael Cathcart, *The Water Dreamers: The Remarkable History of Our Dry Continent* (Melbourne: Text, 2009), pp. 167–74.
92 Graeme Davison, *The Rise and Fall of Marvellous Melbourne* (Melbourne University Press, 1978), p. 12.
93 Lionel Frost, *Australian Cities in Comparative View* (Melbourne: McPhee Gribble, 1990)
94 Andrea Gaynor, *Harvest of the Suburbs: An Environmental History of Growing Food in Australian Cities* (Perth: UWA Press, 2006), p. 20.

networks and a rising popular interest in outdoor recreation, led to modest pressure for the preservation of native landscapes in reserves. Many early arguments revolved around their value for middle-class tourism. Caves, waterfalls, fern gullies, mountains and lakes were prominent among the early reservations, satisfying nineteenth-century romantic predilections for the sublime, the beautiful and the picturesque. The Fish River (Jenolan) Caves in the Blue Mountains region are an early example, reserved in 1866 to protect 'a source of delight and instruction to succeeding generations and excite the admiration of tourists from all parts of the world'.[95]

The rise of popular nature study also saw amateur naturalists join the few professional scientists to lobby for reserves to protect flora and fauna, not least so they could study it. Belair National Park near Adelaide was declared in 1891 after pressure from the Field Naturalists' section of the Royal Society of South Australia, although most visitors sought 'brass bands, flower picking and a bit of sylvan peace', and the development of tennis courts, kiosks and other infrastructure limited its conservation value.[96] Furthermore, reservation did not guarantee protection: over time many reserves were revoked, reduced or subjected to illegal resource extraction.[97]

Agitation for other reserves was informed by the belief that people's health, morality and productivity were affected by their surrounds: whereas dark, crowded housing on dirty streets begat criminality and disease, sun, air, exercise and contact with nature were morally, physically and intellectually uplifting. Royal National Park, accessible from Sydney by rail, was declared in 1879 'to ensure a healthy and consequently vigorous and intelligent community' through mass recreation.[98] Similar sentiments also informed campaigns for urban parkland, and against cruelty to animals.[99]

Not all of the hazards associated with urban environments were imaginary. By the late nineteenth century colonial cities were struggling to cope with the waste produced by their human and animal populations. Wells were frequently contaminated by nearby cesspits. Where nightsoil was collected in pans, disposal became a problem: although some was used to fertilise parks and market gardens, it was often dumped illegally in local waterways or

95 Powell, *Environmental Management in Australia*, p. 114.
96 Derek Whitelock, *Conquest to Conservation: A History of Human Impact on the South Australian Environment* (Adelaide: Wakefield Press, 1985), p. 124.
97 Julia Horne, *The Pursuit of Wonder: How Australia's Landscape Was Explored, Nature Discovered and Tourism Unleashed* (Melbourne: Miegunyah Press, 2005), pp. 149–50.
98 Michael Colin Hall, *Wasteland to World Heritage* (Melbourne University Press, 1992), p. 92.
99 Drew Hutton and Libby Connors, *A History of the Australian Environment Movement* (Cambridge University Press, 1999), pp. 81–2.

vacant land. Decades after the sanitary reform movement emerged in Britain, colonial inquiries in the 1880s revealed a range of sanitary abominations. In Perth, for example, two earth closets without bucket or cesspit served 26 residents of one inner-city terrace. In Melbourne, the Yarra remained a stinking receptacle for all manner of solid and liquid waste – from water closets, urinals, stables, kitchens, abattoirs, knackers, tanneries and more.[100] Flies flourished; typhoid was rife. Efforts to redress woefully inadequate sanitation were hampered by fragmented administrative structures and the lack of a 'metropolitan consciousness' that would enable sacrifices to be made for the greater long-term good.[101] Yet urban reform movements sometimes reflected cultural anxieties and capitalist imperatives more than actual environmental hazards. The 'city improvement' movement of 1880s Sydney saw over 1,500 buildings demolished. Presented primarily as a public health measure, it was largely driven by popular representations of 'the slum', as well as parochial self-interest. Little consideration was given to the working-class need for adequate housing.[102]

The 1890s brought social upheaval and economic depression to the eastern colonies. Then three El Niño periods between 1895 and 1903 cumulatively produced the most severe drought known to Europeans in Australia. They were particularly vulnerable to this drought because of the psychological and economic conditions created by the prior Depression; the expansion of pastoralism and small farming; and the environmental degradation caused by over-exploitation. Scorching winds blew the exposed red soil of the outback all the way to New Zealand. Human suffering was widespread, though animals bore the brunt of the disaster. Only half of the sheep in affected areas survived, and 40 per cent of cattle perished.[103] From 1892, and increasingly as the drought set in, many men – though fewer women and children – left the eastern colonies to chase the dream of finding gold on the Western Australian fields. They formed part of a mass migration that spared Western Australia from the worst effects of Depression and gave rise to processes of

---

100 Su-Jane Hunt and Geoffrey Bolton, 'Cleansing the Dunghill: Water Supply and Sanitation in Perth 1878–1912', *Studies in Western Australian History*, 2 (1978): 4–5; Lack '"Worst Smelbourne"', pp. 172–200; David Dunstan, 'Dirt and Disease', in Davison, Dunstan and McConville (eds), *Outcasts of Melbourne*, pp. 144–6.

101 Dunstan, 'Dirt and Disease', p. 171; Hutton and Connors, *A History of the Australian Environment Movement*, p. 80.

102 Alan Mayne, *The Imagined Slum: Newspaper Representation in Three Cities, 1870–1914* (Leicester University Press, 1993), pp. 98–124, 165–87.

103 Don Garden, *Droughts, Floods & Cyclones: El Niños that Shaped Our Colonial Past* (Melbourne: Australian Scholarly Publishing, 2009), pp. 238, 242.

growth and environmental exploitation similar to those witnessed earlier in the east.

*

The extensive environmental change wrought during the nineteenth century rested, perhaps most obviously, on the dominant colonial understanding that the Indigenous people did not possess the land, which was therefore available for Europeans to occupy and use. It also arose from animal actors – in particular sheep, cattle, rabbits and foxes, but also kangaroos and dingoes. The variable climate was indifferent to the colonists' dreams, and old soils repaid ignorant zeal with dust.

The hubris and greed that drove the seizure of New World lands and prevented significant learning from Indigenous people caused much nineteenth-century environmental devastation. However, aesthetic, utilitarian and ethical arguments for conservation were articulated at every stage. That they were rarely acted upon with efficacy was due to beliefs about the sanctity of private property, the popularity of colonial development in its many forms, and the fact that most non-Indigenous Australians – urban and rural – stood to benefit materially in some way from the exploitation of resources and the many transformations that entailed.

12

Population and health

JANET McCALMAN AND REBECCA KIPPEN

The Aboriginal population

The history of colonial Australia's population is one of stark contrasts: a largely opaque record of the decline of the Aboriginal people, and a conscientiously documented populating of the continent by the forced and voluntary immigration of external settlers. Estimates of the pre-colonial population have risen as archaeologists and anthropologists progressively have revealed the antiquity of Aboriginal societies, re-writing Europeans' understanding of Aboriginal land management and food gathering.[1] There is now an appreciation of the role of women in dispersed horticulture, seed harvesting and fishing, and of the significance of eel farming and men's pasture management by fire for hunting. Working from this new understanding of the capacity of the land to support denser populations, it has been calculated that before 1788 this alleged *terra nullius* supported 1.6 billion people to survive until their first birthday.[2]

The population is estimated to have been around 1 million in 1788, but in April 1789 smallpox erupted at Port Jackson, killing entire communities of Aboriginal people within the sight of the Europeans. The economist Noel Butlin was the first to hold the British responsible for the introduction of this notorious agent of ecological imperialism, but more complex cases have since been made for the prior penetration of Aboriginal Australia by the smallpox variole from the Indonesian archipelago, through Macassan

1 Harry Lourandos, *Continent of Hunter-Gatherers: New Perspectives in Australian Prehistory* (Cambridge University Press, 1997); Grace Karskens, *The Colony: A History of Early Sydney* (Sydney: Allen & Unwin, 2009).
2 Len Smith, 'How Many People had Lived in Australia Before it was Annexed by the English in 1788?', in Gordon Briscoe and Len Smith (eds), *The Aboriginal Population Revisited* (Canberra: Aboriginal History Incorporated, 2002), pp. 9–15.

trepang fishermen.[3] Those who doubt that a contagious disease could make its way along rivers through sparsely populated inland Australia, or around the coast, perhaps underestimate the complexity of Aboriginal trade and communication lines. Smallpox travelled inland twice again: in the late 1820s and in the early 1860s, each time 'clearing' the country for the advance of pastoralist pioneers, first into south-east Australia across the Murray River, and second into inland Queensland.

Other biological agents that came directly with the Europeans were 'slow-burning' infections that enabled carriers to be asymptomatic or at worst chronically ill, but still upright and breathing. Tuberculosis, sexually transmitted infections and typhoid (first known as 'colonial fever') began to kill Aboriginal people of all ages, or to prevent women from reproducing. Tuberculosis remained a disproportionate killer of Aboriginal Australians until the last quarter of the twentieth century.[4] Sexually transmitted infections added to the misery of women who were captured or enticed by frontier men from land or sea.

The visible invaders were the vast herds of grazing animals that crowded people and native animals out of sources of water and open land. By 1850 there were almost 17 million sheep and cattle grazing the best land. And in 1851 the discovery of gold unleashed a tidal wave of European and Chinese incomers – half a million in a decade to Victoria alone – who drove the most rapid colonisation yet seen of a landscape by modern technology in roads, towns, railways, industries and small-scale farming. Armed imperialism took fewer lives than ecological imperialism, but its psychic and cultural effects were no less severe than the destruction of Aboriginal Australians by invisible destroyers.

If, in 1788, when the First Fleet of some 1,300 people landed at Botany Bay, the number of Aboriginal people was around 1 million, by the end of the nineteenth century the colonising population had grown to 3.5 million while the Aboriginal population had fallen precipitously. We still know very little about the timing and extent of that fall, but it is now estimated in Victoria to have been from 60,000 in 1788 to around 650 in 1901, with

---

3 N.G. Butlin, *Our Original Aggression: Aboriginal Populations of Southeastern Australia, 1788– 1850* (Sydney: George Allen & Unwin, 1983); Judy Campbell, *Invisible Invaders: Smallpox and other Diseases in Aboriginal Australia 1780–1880* (Melbourne University Press, 2002).

4 Janet McCalman et al., 'Colonialism and the Health Transition: Aboriginal Australians and Poor Whites Compared, Victoria 1850–1985', *History of the Family*, 14, 3 (2009): 253–65.

smallpox having already cut the population in half twice before European permanent settlement in 1834.[5]

Settler population growth and distribution

From the beginning of colonisation, the administrative obsession with documenting the European population in Australia contrasted with the dearth of statistics on Aboriginal people. Australia is the only New World settler society that possesses data on the height, eye colour, precise birthplace, skills, temperament, literacy and religion of a large segment of its founder population through the records of convicts transported between 1788 and 1868. But while the 165,000 convicts and the penal system that managed them had significant effects on early Australian society and economy, their demographic impact was rather less. As with the French in Quebec, Canada,[6] the founding population among the transported and their minders that created the lineages that survive to the present day might well have been quite small. Certainly in Van Diemen's Land, where the sex ratios were even more unbalanced than in New South Wales, most male convicts who finished their servitude failed to find a wife in the colonies and left no discoverable descendants. Convict women did better, simply through their shortage, but their fertility was often compromised by the consequences of penal servitude and sexually transmitted infection. Australia's history of convict founders has been written by the 'winners'; the descendants of those who arrived early when land grants were more readily available, and married young when marriage during servitude was officially encouraged to settle the community, and who avoided the worst of convict punishment and hard labour. The historian Lloyd Robson estimated that just 16 per cent of those who were transported before 1821 became something more than labourers, whereas of those who had been 'on strength' in 1810 fully 50 per cent become landowners of some description.[7] Although research is continuing, convicts who arrived later, especially during the hungry 1830s

5 Len Smith et al., 'Fractional Identities: The Political Arithmetic of Aboriginal Victorians', in Per Axelsson and Peter Sköld (eds), *Indigenous Peoples and Demography: The Complex Relation between Identity and Statistics* (New York: Berghahn Books, 2011), pp. 15–31.
6 Marc Tremblay et al., 'Distant Kinship and Founder Effects in the Quebec Population', in Tommy Bengtsson and Geraldine P. Mineau (eds), *Kinship and Demographic Behavior in the Past* (Dordrecht: Springer, 2008), pp. 259–77.
7 L.L. Robson, *The Convict Settlers of Australia: An Enquiry into the Origins and Character of the Convicts Transported to New South Wales and Van Diemen's Land 1788–1852* (Melbourne University Press, 1965).

and 1840s, were even less likely to marry, establish viable families and die owning property.

The free settler population grew slowly in the first four decades of settlement, with the convict stigma and distance deterring most. By 1838 colonised Australia could still be mapped as an 'archipelago' of Europeans 'pullulating timidly on the edge of alien shores' (as the poet A.D. Hope would later write), as gentleman investors and emigration schemes to bring useful, respectable settlers provided a slow stream of newcomers to New South Wales and Van Diemen's Land. From 1830 free immigrants and the native-born overtook the bond population in New South Wales, and the same process took place in Tasmania two decades later.[8] From the 1830s, in the wake of the second terrible smallpox epidemic that swept down the Murray-Darling basin, pastoral land was seized on the mainland; new colonies were established in South Australia and Victoria, and convict transportation, especially to Van Diemen's Land, increased. Planned colonisation in South Australia along the lines advocated by E.G. Wakefield created an English Protestant enclave,[9] leavened by German and Wendish religious refugees in the 1840s. The discovery of gold in the 1850s accelerated settlement by free immigration, extinguishing the convict stigma that had hampered recruitment, and the post-gold slump stimulated assisted immigration. In the gold decade, 1851–61, the population of Australia nearly trebled, from 405,000 to 1,145,000, and Victoria overtook New South Wales – an ascendancy it would maintain until the 1890s.[10]

The great European peopling of Australia thus occurred between 1850 and 1890. It was distinctive among the Anglophone settler societies of the nineteenth century for the high level of government-assisted immigration, paid for by the sale of land seized by the crown. The settling was characterised by an unusual degree of planning and calculation: importing settlers who were needed to fulfil specific needs. These were young couples and established families who could become self-sufficient pioneers and independent workers, and single women who could redress the gender imbalance bequeathed by convict transportation. These assisted immigrants, with the exception of the almost 5,000 Scottish highland and island-famine refugees and the 4,000 Irish female orphans, were more likely to have some means, because even assisted

8 W.D. Borrie, *The European Peopling of Australasia: A Demographic History, 1788–1988* (Canberra: Demography Program, ANU, 1994).

9 Edward Gibbon Wakefield, *A View of the Art of Colonization, with Present Reference to the British Empire* (London: John W. Parker, 1849).

10 James Jupp, *Immigration* (Oxford University Press, 1991).

immigration to Australia was more expensive than the 'coffin ships' that took the Irish to Canada or the United States.

But there was a singular exception: the power of gold to lure relatively well-off settlers who paid their own way and who were more educated and skilled than the government-assisted immigrants recruited from depressed agricultural counties of England and famine-stricken districts of Ireland and Scotland. In particular, Victoria's self-funded founding population in the 1850s brought a wave of modernity to an otherwise traditional, pre-industrial out-post of the British Empire.[11]

While the convict population was exhaustively documented in Van Diemen's Land, the civilian population also came to be extensively regis-tered. Van Diemen's Land was the first colony to introduce governmental registration of births, deaths and marriages in 1838 – one year after its intro-duction in England and Wales[12] – but it was Victoria that arguably had the best records of births, deaths and marriages in the world from the 1850s. Among the wave of immigrants to Victoria was the statistician William Henry Archer, a self-described disciple of the father of English vital statistics and the census, Dr William Farr.[13] In the social laboratory of small-scale colonial Victoria, Archer was able to institute Farr's original vision of vital registrations and social statistics. His successor, H.H. Hayter, and the New South Wales statistician, Timothy Coghlan, completed the triumvirate who set the Australian colonies and the subsequent Commonwealth on a firm statistical foundation. The wealth of population data collected in Victoria, and to a lesser extent New South Wales, means that we must rely on these colonies for a demographic picture of colonial Australia at the expense in particular of Queensland, South Australia and Western Australia. Those colonies are sorely in need of demographic historical research. In the absence of official statistics, family and community reconstitution in partnership with family and local historians may be productive.

Victoria also kept the most accurate statistics of Aboriginal populations in the second half of the nineteenth century, in large part due to the *Aboriginal Protection Act* of 1869, which became the model for the rest of the country. The Protection Board recorded the statistics of Victorian Aboriginal people

---

11 Geoffrey Serle, *The Golden Age: A History of the Colony of Victoria, 1851–1861* (Melbourne University Press, 1963).

12 Rebecca Kippen, 'An Indispensable Duty of Government: Civil Registration in Nineteenth-Century Tasmania', *Tasmanian Historical Studies*, 8, 1 (2002): 42–58.

13 John L. Hopper, 'The Contribution of W.H. Archer to Vital Statistics in the Colony of Victoria', *Australian Journal of Statistics*, 28, 1 (1986): 124–37.

who lived within the official reserves and those known to the police who were living 'free'. Registrations of their vital events appeared in the official record, although after the 1870s individuals were rarely identified as 'Aboriginal' except by family name and lineage.

In the nineteenth century Victoria was also the colony most shaped by self-funded immigration, building a solid middle class to challenge the pastoral elite for political and cultural leadership. Each colony developed subtle differences in religious and ethnic characteristics that remained influential in education, social institutions and politics until after World War 2. New South Wales and Victoria had both absorbed larger numbers of Irish-Catholic incomers, between them creating the largest proportional Irish diaspora, apart from Boston and New York. On the other hand, South Australia remained noticeably Protestant into the 1980s, and Tasmania the most 'Anglican'.[14]

Crowley's analysis of British assisted and unassisted immigration between 1861 and 1900 illuminates the different historical trajectories of the colonies. In those four decades, 1.2 million people emigrated from Britain to the Australian colonies, a third of them to Queensland alone, almost half of whom were government-assisted. Assisted immigration peaked in Queensland in the 1880s, reaching 107,000, while in the same decade Victoria received just two assisted immigrants and around 150,000 who paid their own way. By 1900 Queensland had absorbed four times the number of assisted immigrants as Victoria, providing a pioneering population far less endowed with both educational and financial capital. Free immigration exceeded assisted immigration in all the other colonies, most noticeably in Tasmania, where, like Victoria, it was four times the assisted rate. Immigration to New South Wales and South Australia declined markedly from the second half of the 1880s. Western Australia remained lightly settled, with communities clustering around ports, until the discovery of gold in the late 1880s. The surge of immigrants came from the other Australian colonies, notably Victoria and South Australia, fuelling its growth through secondary migration.[15]

These immigrants, self-funded and assisted, continued to be movers. 584,000 people arrived in Victoria between 1851 and 1860, 85 per cent of them paying their own way, but just under half that number was to move on, looking for a new 'El Dorado'. This mobility persisted, and was one of the notable characteristics of the historian James Belich's template for the explosive

14 J.C.R. Camm and John McQuilton (eds), *Australians: A Historical Atlas* (Sydney: Fairfax, Syme & Weldon Associates, 1987).
15 Borrie, *The European Peopling of Australasia*, p. 127.

Anglo settler cultures of the nineteenth century, driven by the mass transfer of people, capital and technologies, both non-industrial and industrial.
The result was a cycle of booms and busts, underpinned by demographic
booms created by migration of cohorts of young settlers. Australia shared
this demographic history with Canada, the United States, New Zealand,
Argentina, Siberia and Mongolia.[16] Internally, these fertility booms affected
economic and institutional development: beginning with communities of
young couples and children bereft of grandparents, and maturing into societies dominated by the founding generation grown old.[17] Generational vested
interests therefore dominated politics and institution building: a politico-
demographic dynamic that was to be repeated by the baby boom after World
War 2, and that generation's skewed investment in property as the key source
of private security.

The common response of individuals to booms and busts was to move on:
to the Māori wars and New Zealand goldfields in the 1860s, Queensland in
the 1870s, Western Australia and even South Africa in the 1890s. Distinctive
maritime economies transported these second-stage migrants: east–west
along the southern coast of the continent from Fremantle, including
Tasmania to New Zealand, and north–south between Sydney and Brisbane.
Within colonies, new settlers moved from town to town, starting businesses,
finding partners, fleeing creditors. The 'nomad tribes' of unmarried and
unskilled males moved with seasonal labour, drought and new gold rushes,
while farmers moved on and off selections that failed. The high masculinity
of the frontiers, the uncertainty of the economy and the flow-on effects of
high birth cohorts resulted in employment crises, rural poverty traps and
outbreaks of criminal activity.[18]

New South Wales was by far the most populous colony in 1851, with almost
180,000 people. Victoria, South Australia and Tasmania each held 60–80,000,
while Queensland and Western Australia had populations of around 10,000
each. The total population was just over 400,000. Fifty years later, New South
Wales and Victoria each housed more than 1 million people, with populations
in the other four states ranging from half a million to less than 200,000, and
the total population of Australia heading towards 4 million (see Table 12.1).

16 James Belich, *Replenishing the Earth: The Settler Revolution and the Rise of the Anglo-World,
1783–1939* (Oxford University Press, 2009).
17 Jennifer A. Jones, 'Old Age in a Young Colony: Image and Experience in South Australia
in the Nineteenth Century', PhD thesis, University of Adelaide, 2010.
18 John McQuilton, *The Kelly Outbreak 1878–1880: The Geographical Dimensions of Social
Banditry* (Melbourne University Press, 1979).

Table 12.1 Total population by colony, 1851; percentage distribution of birthplace by State, 1901; total population by State, 1901

Colony/State	NSW	Vic.	Qld	SA	WA	Tas.	Total Australia
Total population 1851	178,688	77,345	8,575	63,700	11,743	70,130	437,665
Birthplace 1901	%	%	%	%	%	%	%
Same State	72.2	73.3	57.1	75.0	28.7	79.4	69.0
Other Australia	7.5	5.4	7.8	4.9	40.4	6.6	8.2
New Zealand	0.8	0.8	0.3	0.2	1.5	0.7	0.7
England	9.4	9.6	13.9*	10.5	13.9	7.6*	10.5*
Wales	0.3	0.3	N/A	0.2	0.5	N/A	N/A
Scotland	2.3	3.0	4.0	1.9	3.0	1.8	2.7
Ireland	4.5	5.2	7.6	3.1	5.4	2.3	4.9
Other Europe	1.5	1.4	4.3	2.5	3.3	0.8	2.0
Asia	1.1	0.7	2.8	1.3	2.6	0.5	1.3
Other	0.5	0.4	2.2	0.3	0.8	0.3	0.7
Total	100.0	100.0	100.0	100.0	100.0	100.0	100.0
Total population 1901	1,354,846	1,201,070	498,129	358,346	184,124	172,475	3,773,801

* England and Wales counted together

Sources: J.C. Caldwell 'Population', in Wray Vamplew (ed.), *Australians: Historical Statistics* (Sydney: Fairfax, Syme & Weldon Associates, 1988), pp. 23–41; C.A. Price, 'Birthplaces of the Australian Population 1861–1981', *Working Papers in Demography*, no. 13 (Canberra: ANU, 1984), reproduced in W.D. Borrie, *The European Peopling of Australasia: A Demographic History, 1788–1988* (Canberra: Demography Program, ANU, 1994); 'Historical Census and Colonial Data Archive', *1901 State Census Reports*, Australian Data Archive <hccda.ada.edu. au>, accessed April 2012.

In 1901 Australian-born people made up around 80 per cent of the population in New South Wales, Victoria and South Australia. A smaller percentage of native-born were seen in Queensland (65 per cent) and Western Australia (69 per cent), reflecting relatively high immigration in the late nineteenth century, while low immigration to Tasmania meant that 86 per cent of the population in 1901 had been born in Australia. In all States a relatively high proportion of the population had been born in the British Isles; 10 per cent in England and Wales, 3 per cent in Scotland and 5 per cent in Ireland. For Australia as a whole, 96 per cent of the population in 1901 had been born in Australia, New Zealand or the British Isles.

Most of Australia's population lived in coastal areas. In 1901 one-quarter of the population was concentrated in the two coastal capital cities of Melbourne and Sydney. The most highly urbanised state was South Australia, with 45 per cent of its population living in the metropolis, and the least urbanised, Western Australia and Tasmania, each with 20 per cent.

Family formation and fertility decline

Traditional Aboriginal fertility and family formation were acutely disrupted by colonisation: by premature death, by illness that compromised fertility and by the effects on sex ratios of the predations of European men on young Aboriginal women. Aboriginal people who remained outside the reach of the frontier and governments in the colonial period continued to control family size by prolonged lactation, as had all human communities that remained mobile food procurers. But when Aboriginal people were brought under the 'protection' of the colonial state, as happened first in Victoria in the 1860s, they were forced to live a largely settled existence, which increased exposures to respiratory and diarrhoeal diseases. Aboriginal babies born on the reserves typically died of respiratory diseases before late weaning, and after weaning from diarrhoeal and infectious diseases caught from the sick adults around them. This was in contrast to European babies who perished more often from gastro-enteric diseases and failure to thrive before their first birthday, leaving their mothers more likely to conceive again quickly.[19] Aboriginal birth spacing remained longer and completed families smaller until the twentieth century, by which time Europeans were in the midst of the fertility transition to smaller families. From the 1890s, after the passage of the amended *Aborigines Protection Act* of 1886, known as the 'Half-Caste Act', Victorian Aboriginal families adopted natural fertility with shorter birth intervals, caused in part by rising infant mortality.

The peculiar circumstances of convict colonisation – with most prisoners being male – led to a severe imbalance in the sex ratio of the colonising population. In Van Diemen's Land, for example, there were six men for every woman in the early 1820s, and still more than twice as many men than women by the early 1850s.[20] Although the imperial government and various local authorities attempted to redress this imbalance through assisted immigration, by the end of the nineteenth century there were still 15 per cent

---

19 Janet McCalman et al., 'Colonial Health Transitions: Aboriginal and "Poor White" Infant Mortality Compared, Victoria 1850–1910', *History of the Family*, 16, 1 (2011): 62–77.

20 Rebecca Kippen and Peter Gunn, 'Convict Bastards, Common-Law Unions and Shotgun Weddings: Premarital Conceptions and Ex-nuptial Births in Nineteenth-Century Tasmania', *Journal of Family History*, 36, 4 (2011): 387–403.

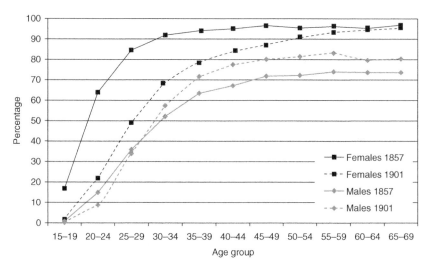

Figure 12.1 Percentage of the population ever married by age and sex, Victoria, 1857 and 1901
Source: Censuses of Victoria, 1857 and 1901, Historical Census and Colonial Data Archive, Australian Data Archive, Canberra <http://hccda.ada.edu.au>, accessed December 2011.

more men than women, and the cohort effects of settlement distributed this sex imbalance unevenly. The imbalance led to singular marriage patterns. Marriage rates for women – as a rare commodity – were high, while many men were cut out of the marriage market. In Victoria in the late 1850s, for example, almost two-thirds of women aged 20–24 years were ever married, compared with 36 per cent of men aged 25–29 years – their traditional marriage partners. Proportions of women ever married rose to well over 90 per cent from age 30–34, while just half of men at the same age were or had been married. By 1901 proportions married for both sexes followed much more similar trajectories, although female proportions were still higher at each age (see Figure 12.1).

Convict Van Diemen's Land was an exception to the high rates and proportions of female marriage seen in the other colonies.[21] Those still under sentence who wished to marry had to apply to the authorities for permission to do so. They were often refused. Marriage rates in Tasmania peaked in the mid-1850s at the time the convict system was being dismantled and a large proportion of the population no longer had to request permission

21 Borrie, *The European Peopling of Australasia*.

to marry.[22] Along with low levels of female marriage in Tasmania went high levels of births outside marriage. This became such a concern to the convict authorities that they introduced the 'offence of an illegitimate child', punishable by six months' imprisonment after weaning. Ex-nuptial birth rates fell precipitously in the mid-1850s, concurrently with the collapse of the convict system.[23]

The near-universal marriage rates for women in most parts of Australia, and high birth rates within marriage, contributed to high overall birth rates. Founding-generation couples practised natural fertility, with completed families of more than ten and twelve children being common. In suburbs or rural districts, these families intermarried, rapidly producing dense kinship networks. Continued habits of geographical endogamy produced within two generations communities that had begun as mutual strangers and were now tightly bonded by intermarriage. In Tasmania, social class and fear of the 'convict stain' impelled the 'quality' in the Midlands to intermarry to such an extent that there is still a distinctive genetic heterogeneity.[24]

In the mid-nineteenth century, Australian women had an average of six children each over their lifetimes. Birth rates fell steadily over the remainder of the century, so that by 1901 the average number of children per woman was between 3.0 and 4.5 across the former colonies (see Figure 12.2). Most of the reduction in fertility between 1861 and 1881 was due to declining proportions married (since most births occurred within marriage) rather than lower numbers of births for married women.[25] However, from 1881 to the end of the century, declining fertility resulted from falls in both proportions of women married and marital fertility.

The high geographical mobility of European Australians and the accompanying domestic insecurities affected the home life and training of the first-born generations. Settler families began in communities poorly provided for in terms of schools, the trade societies, family affiliations and, in particular, an equivalent social organiser to the parish that had traditionally apprenticed out those without families to find them occupations and placements.[26]

22 Kippen and Gunn, 'Convict Bastards, Common-law Unions and Shotgun Weddings', pp. 387–403.
23 Ibid.
24 R. John Mitchell, Mark Kosten and J. Williams, 'Historical Demography and Genetic Structure of Tasmania', in Hilary King (ed.), *Epidemiology in Tasmania* (Canberra: Brolga Press, 1987), pp. 1–22.
25 Elise F. Jones, 'Fertility Decline in Australia and New Zealand 1861–1936', *Population Index*, 37, 4 (1971): 301–38.
26 Jane Beer et al., *Colonial Frontiers and Family Fortunes: Two Studies of Rural and Urban Victoria* (Melbourne: History Department, University of Melbourne, 1989).

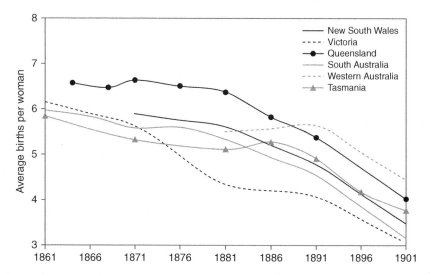

Figure 12.2 Average number of births per woman, Australian colonies, 1861–1901

Source: Elise F. Jones, 'Fertility Decline in Australia and New Zealand, 1861–1936', *Population Index*, 37, 4 (1971): 301–38.

Children moved home frequently, even within cities, and work training was often impossible, resulting in a second generation less skilled than its immigrant predecessor. The plentiful work available for cheap juvenile labour in the boom-era urban and rural economies of the 1870s and 1880s tempted people to enter the workforce as early as possible, thereby setting them up for a lifetime of increasing unemployability as their physical strength and dexterity waned.[27] Intergenerational downward social mobility was therefore a paradoxical phenomenon in a dynamic settler society. The informal economy was over-supplied with unskilled casual male and female workers, which created a pool of intractable urban and rural poverty that would not begin to be resolved until World War 2. Colonial families thus divided into those whose breadwinners produced a regular, secure income, a permanent place to live and an imaginable future, and those whose families were trapped into day-to-day survival, 'midnight flits', or leaving with unpaid rent, with absent or failing fathers who were 'up the bush' or in the pub. The casual economy

27 Ann Larson, *Growing Up in Melbourne: Family Life in the Late Nineteenth Century* (Canberra: Demography Program, ANU, 1994).

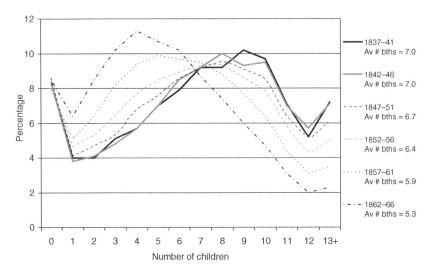

Figure 12.3 Percentage distribution of number of births, Australian married women born 1837–41 to 1862–66
Source: Patricia Quiggin, *No Rising Generation: Women & Fertility in Late Nineteenth-Century Australia* (Canberra: Department of Demography, ANU, 1988).

made it impossible to imagine a future, sapped energies and blighted children's development. Those who could imagine a future could also plan for it, and from the 1880s Australians began, along with many others around the world, to plan smaller families. Figure 12.3 shows birth distributions for Australian married women born from the 1830s to the 1860s. Married women born 1837–46 – who would have experienced peak fertility in the 1860s and 70s – had an average of seven births each. Numbers of children within marriage began to fall for cohorts born from the late 1840s, with married women born 1862–66 having an average of 5.3 children each. Although the proportion of married women with no births remained relatively constant across the cohorts at 8 per cent, the proportion with eight or more births declined sharply from half to a quarter.

The methods that Australian families began to employ to control their family sizes were rarely technologies for prevention of conception. The pattern of family formation continued to be a string of births spaced by weaning or infant death: if babies died, the gaps were shorter; if a new conception started after weaning, the gap was usually two to three years. However, from the 1870s women stopped their childbearing after the third or fourth, suggesting a decision to limit the family. Abstinence and withdrawal were the most common methods, and Simon Szreter has suggested that partial abstinence (infrequent intercourse) in older couples was often sufficient to make conception rare.[28] With the demands of competing children, heavy work and children sharing parental bedrooms, sexual relationships suffered. (It was widely believed that children's attendance at Sunday school was inflated by the need of parents to snatch some privacy.)

Contraceptive devices such as condoms and pessaries were expensive and difficult to purchase, generally being sold only in urban unorthodox venues: radical bookshops and brothels. The technology that women had under their direct control, however dangerous and unreliable, was termination of pregnancy. By the 1890s newspapers teemed with advertisements for the correction of 'irregularity' and sale of herbal abortifacients, while ancient remedies abounded. New surgical tools became available from the 1880s with the invention of the curette and, particularly in cities, the Higginson syringe became ubiquitous in household lavatories and washrooms, employed for enemas, douching after intercourse and inducing abortion. Someone always knew 'someone' who would know how to 'bring it on' and, from the 1890s, post-abortal sepsis cases began appearing in increasing numbers in hospitals. As women became more determined to limit their families, so self-administered and procured abortion became more common and deaths from post-abortal sepsis began to inflate the maternal death rate, while death from puerperal sepsis fell after the gradual adoption of antiseptic midwifery in larger hospitals from the late 1880s.[29]

By the end of the nineteenth century, as a result of later and less-universal marriage, the widespread use of effective birth-control methods and the 1890s Depression, average births per woman had fallen dramatically (Figure 12.2). The decline in fertility, and its effect on population growth, was of such concern that in 1903 the New South Wales government set up a Royal Commission of Inquiry on the decline of the birth rate. A parade of doctors, police officers, pharmacists and clergy reported to the commission, which in turn laid blame for the decline in fertility on the selfishness of couples. This selfishness led to the 'deliberate prevention of conception

28 Kate Fisher and Simon Szreter, '"They Prefer Withdrawal": The Choice of Birth Control in Britain, 1918–1950', *Journal of Interdisciplinary History*, 34, 2 (2003): 263–91; Simon Szreter, Robert A. Nye and Frans van Poppel, 'Fertility and Contraception During the Demographic Transition: Qualitative and Quantitative Approaches', *Journal of Interdisciplinary History*, 34, 2 (2003): 141–54.

29 Janet McCalman, *Sex and Suffering: Women's Health and a Women's Hospital, 1856–1996* (Baltimore: Johns Hopkins University Press, 1999), pp. 128–33.

and destruction of embryonic life', enabled by a decrease in religiosity and an increase in knowledge of, and access to, birth-control methods.[30]

Health, sickness and death

The end of life also had distinctive characteristics. If a frontier society proved deadly for Aboriginal people, it was also very dangerous for immigrants, and deaths from violence, accidents and drowning were high, especially for men and children. The summer heat and hot winds took a toll before new settlers learned to adjust, particularly with the care of babies at risk of dehydration. Infant mortality on the frontier peaked in El Niño years, according to the figures extracted by the early twentieth-century director-general of health and medical historian J.H.L. Cumpston. But it was the inevitability of poor sanitation, abetted by the ubiquitous fly, that inflicted the greatest toll of death on both young and old. 'Colonial fever', later recognised to be typhoid, would have arrived with asymptomatic carriers and soon took out adults and children wherever soil and water were contaminated. It remained a problem in urban areas, rising to a peak in Melbourne by the late 1880s and the principal reason for sewering the metropolitan area despite the financial stringencies of the 1890s.[31]

Infant mortality (deaths under the age of one year) was also aggravated by the singularity of the age structure of a frontier society that lacked grandmothers and older women who could provide advice, support and nursing for childbed and the lying-in. Mothers learned by hard experience, often losing their first child due to difficulties with feeding or gut infections after weaning. The greatest risk to infant life came when new mothers had no supporting husbands, extended families or tolerant employers. The frontier society was one of unstable marriages and de facto relationships, and the loss of young men through accidents left many young mothers alone in a world of strangers. As everywhere, the hand-fed child of the unmarried mother who had to become a wet nurse or go out to work had little future: the mortality of illegitimate infants born at Melbourne's Lying-In Hospital reached 80 per cent in the 1880s. The introduction of antiseptic midwifery from 1887 and the effects of the *Infant Life Protection Act* of 1893 that policed feeding practices in the 'baby farming' private nursing industry reduced the death rate dramatically: 'failure to thrive' resulted from sick mothers,

---

30 Quoted in Neville D. Hicks, *'This Sin and Scandal': Australia's Population Debate 1891–1911* (Canberra: ANU Press, 1978).

31 J.H.L. Cumpston, *Health and Disease in Australia: A History* (Canberra: AGPS, 1989).

neglect, careless artificial feeding and repeated gut infections.[32] The real fall in the infant death rate, which mirrored that of the United Kingdom, did not begin until the turn of the century. As the first generation of more healthy children became mothers themselves, families became smaller: knowledge about the importance of hand-washing and the boiling of water spread from school education, health inspectors and public discourse, and manufactured infant foods improved in nutritional value.[33]

Despite difficult conditions in the colonies, infant mortality was relatively low. Tasmania and South Australia had the lowest mortality of the Australian colonies in the late nineteenth century, with just over 10 per cent of babies dying before their first birthday. Higher rates in Queensland and Western Australia, of 13 per cent in the early 1880s, reflected the particular dangers to infant life on the frontiers of settlement. However, these rates were still much lower than those seen in many countries of Europe, which were typically 15 per cent and above. Visitors and European settlers brought most sicknesses with them, introducing a fatal suite of infectious diseases that had never appeared before on a continent that had no herd animals that could be domesticated. Even mosquito-borne diseases were rare because of the low density of both human and animal hosts. But if the biological encounter was fatal for Aboriginal people, the new land was healthful for the Europeans, provided they did not live too close to one another. The length of the sea voyage to Australia delayed the introduction of rapid infections, but when measles, whooping cough, scarlet fever and new strains of influenza eventually survived the voyage, their effects on the colonial-born, and therefore immunologically naive, was severe. In Tasmania in the early 1850s, successive waves of scarlet fever, influenza and measles killed one in fifteen children, with some families losing four or five children within days. Death rates at some ages rose 400 per cent.[34]

The worst epidemics in Sydney and Melbourne were in the 1870s, with high mortalities among children, and linked spikes in maternal mortality and later tuberculosis infection.[35] These mortality crises – the distinctive mark

32 Philippa Mein Smith, *Mothers and King Baby: Infant Survival and Welfare in an Imperial World: Australia 1880–1950* (London: Macmillan, 1997); McCalman et al., 'Colonial Health Transitions', pp. 62–77.

33 Mein Smith, *Mothers and King Baby*.

34 Rebecca Kippen, '"A Pestilence Stalks Abroad": Familial Clustering of Deaths during the Tasmanian Scarlet Fever, Measles and Influenza Epidemics of 1852–54', *Genus*, 67, 2 (2011): 57–75.

35 Cumpston, *Health and Disease in Australia*; Peter H. Curson, *Times of Crisis: Epidemics in Sydney, 1788–1900* (Sydney University Press, 1985).

of the regime of disease and death before the epidemiological transition – constituted the greatest threat to children apart from gut infections, contaminated food and milk (transmitting bovine tuberculosis). As population densities and travel between centres of population grew, epidemics became less severe and mortality crises diminished. The exception was the influenza pandemics, which afflicted all age groups in the 1890s and then returned dramatically in 1919. Diphtheria emerged as a major threat to children, but it was the insidious Group A streptococcus that continued to wreak most damage on life-course health with skin infections, scarlet fever, rheumatic fever and outbreaks of contagious puerperal fever spread by the ubiquitous 'strep throat'. Young victims would suffer the consequences later in life with aortic valvular heart disease and renal failure: a chain of poverty and infection that in the European community would not be halted until the slum clearances of the 1950s. Streptococcal infections remain the scourge of remote Aboriginal communities struggling with poor housing and lack of water and bathing facilities.

In his landmark discussion of the epidemiological transition in Australia, the historian F.B. Smith identified the decline in tuberculosis and infant mortality as the distinctive changes in mortality in the late colonial and early Federation era.[36] Improvements in survival, as in England and Wales, began first in childhood with the reduction in death rates from infectious diseases. McKeown's case for improved nutrition above medical intervention or sanitary reform has received considerable qualification by British historians such as Szreter and Hardy, who have demonstrated the gradual effectiveness of the local medical officers of health, municipal clean-ups and home visiting nurses and advisors.[37] Australia's major cities, especially Melbourne, were keen adaptors of the latest from Britain, with the first *Public Health Act* passed in 1854.[38]

As with all complex social changes, multiple factors combined to enable children to survive to their fifteenth birthday: the mellowing of the frontier society, the effects of compulsory schooling from the 1870s, the better

---

36 F.B. Smith, 'The First Health Transition in Australia, 1880–1910', in Gavin W. Jones et al. (eds), *The Continuing Demographic Transition* (Oxford: Clarendon Press, 1997), pp. 29–50.

37 Simon Szreter, 'The Importance of Social Intervention in Britain's Mortality Decline c.1850–1914: A Re-interpretation of the Role of Public Health', *Social History of Medicine*, 1, 1 (1988): 1–37; Anne Hardy, 'Rickets and the Rest: Child-care, Diet and the Infectious Children's Diseases, 1850–1914', *Social History of Medicine*, 5, 3 (1992): 389–412; Anne Hardy, *The Epidemic Streets: Infectious Disease and the Rise of Preventive Medicine, 1850–1900* (Oxford University Press, 1993).

38 Milton J. Lewis, *The People's Health. Volume 1, Public Health in Australia, 1788–1950*, (Westport: Praeger, 2003).

distribution of food to urban centres with the growth of railways and spread of Chinese market gardens in cities and large towns, and especially the gradual improvement in the reticulation of drinking water in urban areas. Infant mortality in metropolitan Brisbane fell four decades before the city was sewered. The provision of clean drinking water in cities in the United States has now been demonstrated to be the single most important factor in the health transition in comparable New World urban aggregates.[39]

The medical profession was newly armed with 'germ theory' by the 1880s, and by the 1890s antiseptic practices in surgery, midwifery and nursing the sick improved recovery from infection. Indeed the survival of children from infectious diseases depended most of all on the quality of home nursing: keeping children in bed, feeding them and maintaining fluid intake. Anne Hardy has demonstrated the significance of childcare in the improvement of child health and therefore survival among the poor in the second half of the nineteenth century.[40] Children had more time and care to recover as they came to be less depended upon as juvenile breadwinners, and as there were more grandmothers to nurse sick children than there had been for the pioneers.

By the 1880s the various colonies and major towns were served by public hospitals, either descendants of the convict and military institutions or voluntary hospitals on the English model, partially supported by government funds. Most babies were born at home, and many surgical procedures were undertaken in private homes or doctors' private hospitals. But the poor increasingly had access to modern hospitals that were the sites of nursing and medical training, led by honorary consultants. These hospital communities were in turn linked to European and US medical practice by the scientific literature. Melbourne, in particular, was fortunate in a profession whose leaders were reading German and French publications as well as the British medical literature. This intellectual culture spread to regional hospitals such as Victoria's remarkable institutional network built by the gold miners. Half a century before antibiotics, doctors and nurses and public hospitals had become skilful at keeping the very ill alive long enough for their natural recuperative powers to save their lives. There was no cure for tuberculosis and it is likely that a majority of Australians were infected by the time they reached 30 years of age. However, over time fewer of them developed tuberculosis disease, and the mathematics of

39 David M. Cutler and Grant Miller, 'The Role of Public Health Improvements in Health Advances: The Twentieth-Century United States', *Demography*, 42, 1 (2005): 1–22.
40 Hardy, 'Rickets and the Rest', pp. 389–412.

transmission – ten infective cases to produce one active infectious case – saw the retreat of the 'white plague'. Better nutrition for some would have assisted, and lower densities and larger rooms in dwellings reduced the load of bacillus that the uninfected aspirated. However, tuberculosis continued to afflict Aboriginal people, while it declined in the most vulnerable of the urban poor, charity babies born at the Melbourne Lying-In Hospital in the period 1857–1900.[41]

The decline in tuberculosis and later diarrhoeal disease in infancy brought death in adulthood from heart disease, stroke and cancer into greater prominence. They had always been there, but now, as certain infectious diseases declined, more people survived long enough to die of non-communicable disease. Many of the adult causes of death had their origin in earlier infectious diseases that damaged hearts and kidneys. Nonetheless, colonial Australia was a more healthful place to live than Britain, for settlers not Aboriginal Australians. Australians enjoyed a slight survival advantage over their British cousins, until the 1940s.[42] Life expectancy in late nineteenth-century Australia was around five years higher than in England and Wales. The proportion of people surviving from birth to age 20 years increased slightly from 76 per cent in New South Wales in 1856–66 to just over 80 per cent for Australia in 1891–1900. By the 1890s more than half the population could expect to survive to their 60th birthday (see Table 12.2). For each cohort, a higher percentage of females than males survived to each age. Life expectancy at birth increased significantly over the second half of the nineteenth century from 45 years to over 50 years. Those who survived to age 60 could expect to live for another 15 years (see Table 12.3).

Life in the country, where even the very poor had some access to fresh food, was certainly healthier than life in the city. The results were seen in the heights of recruits to the Australian Imperial Force in World War 1, with men from the inner cities displaying a distinct urban penalty.[43] Indeed the anthropometrics suggest a decline in living standards in 1890s that reflect the economic Depression and long droughts.

---

41 McCalman et al., 'Colonialism and the Health Transition', pp. 253–65; McCalman et al., 'Colonial Health Transitions', 62–77.

42 Richard Taylor, Milton Lewis and John Powles, 'The Australian Mortality Decline: All-Cause Mortality 1788–1990', *Australian and New Zealand Journal of Public Health*, 22, 1 (1998): 27–36.

43 Greg Whitwell, Christine de Souza and Stephen Nicholas, 'Height, Health and Economic Growth in Australia, 1860–1940', in Richard H. Steckel and Roderick Floud (eds), *Health and Welfare During Industrialization* (University of Chicago Press, 1997), pp. 379–422.

Table 12.2 Percentage of population surviving from birth to selected ages

Age (years)	1856–66 NSW Males and females %	1870–81 Vic., NSW, Qld Males %	Females %	1881–90 Australia Males %	Females %	1891–1900 Australia Males %	Females %
0	100	100	100	100	100	100	100
1	89	87	89				
10	79	78	80	80	82	83	85
20	76	75	77	77	79	80	82
40	63	64	66	64	67	70	72
60	39	43	48	44	50	50	57
80	6	10	14	10	16	13	19

Table 12.3 Average age at death (years) for population surviving to selected ages

Age (years)	1856–66 NSW Males and females	1870–81 Vic., NSW, Qld Males	Females	1881–90 Australia Males	Females	1891–1900 Australia Males	Females
0	45.6	46.5	49.6	47.2	50.8	51.1	54.8
1	50.9	53.1	55.6				
10	57.1	59.2	61.7	58.9	62.0	61.4	64.5
20	58.6	60.8	63.3	60.6	63.4	62.8	65.7
40	64.1	66.2	69.0	66.5	69.1	67.7	70.5
60	72.0	73.8	75.5	73.8	75.4	74.0	75.9
80	83.6	85.4	85.7	85.1	85.3	85.0	85.5

Source: Gigi Santow, W.D. Borrie and Lado T. Ruzicka (eds), *Landmarks in Australian Population History* (Canberra: Australian Population Association, 1988).

By 1901 the demographic transition to lower fertility and lower mortality rates was well advanced and the settler population had come to depend on natural increase rather than migration for growth in a stagnant economy after the financial failures of the 1890s. The Aboriginal population in large stretches of the country remained insulated by distance from the advancing frontier, but in the relatively well-watered, fertile regions where Aboriginal Australia had traditionally flourished, the population was either coming under the control of 'total institutions' in reserves and missions or had suffered catastrophic declines. In Tasmania, 'official Aborigines' were supposedly extinct and in Victoria reduced to 1 per cent of their original strength. Yet in both colonies 'unofficial Aborigines' – the descendants of relationships between Aboriginal people and incomers – were beginning to rebuild their communities.

By 1901 this settler colony had become one of the most urbanised societies in the world. Its Europeans still clung to the shore, concentrated in two cities of world size in Sydney and Melbourne. Regional Australia was in decline, leeching young immigrants to the city in search of work, better spouses and excitement. The new Australian States were now populated with 3.8 million people, including 2.9 million native-born, 760,000 Europeans, 47,000 Asian-born and fewer than 100,000 Aboriginal people. As a collection of colonies became a federated nation, the values and behaviours that affected reproduction, health and survival were in transition. Collectively, along with other similar societies around the world, the 1890s, while a decade of acute crisis, had witnessed a modernising turn as increasingly people imagined a future and had some control over the destiny of their families. They decided, obviously as couples because the methods of family limitation depended on the agency of men as well as women, that they would plan their families. They were learning to boil milk and water to protect against disease. As the old frontier population of unattached men and unsupported women spent their last days in benevolent asylums, the riotous drinking and fighting that had blighted many private lives was quietening down. Regulation of alcoholic beverages and fresh and packaged food reduced illness and premature death and the state was maturing as the critical agent in the protection of public health.

13

The economy

LIONEL FROST

Henry Parkes made his 1889 speech calling for federation at the School of Arts at Tenterfield in New South Wales. Located close to the Queensland border, Tenterfield was much nearer to Brisbane than Sydney and was disadvantaged by customs duties on intercolonial trade. The 1893 federal conference was held at Corowa, another New South Wales town that was closer commercially to another colony's capital city, Melbourne. Tenterfield and Corowa exemplified towns of no more than around 1,000 inhabitants that were 'emporium and depot' for the pastoral, agricultural and mining regions in which most Australians lived at that time.[1] For much of the second half of the nineteenth century, such towns hummed with economic and civic activity. A wide range of stores, commercial and professional services were available; local manufacturers prospered and sporting, social and cultural institutions were diverse and vigorous. In 1901, two out of every three Australians lived in rural areas and provincial towns, and the remainder lived in capital cities.[2]

The capitals were the gateways at which the produce of their hinterlands was shifted between various forms of land transportation and ocean-going ships, and then distributed to external markets. Between 1861 and 1901 the population of Australia's three largest cities – Melbourne, Sydney and Adelaide – quadrupled. Sydney became more crowded as its housing stock trailed population growth, but in inner suburbs such as Paddington skilled workers rented well-built terrace houses that were finished to a high standard and provided 'comfort quite undreamt of by an English tradesman'.[3]

---

1 Brian Burton, *Flow Gently Past: The Story of the Corowa District* (Corowa: Corowa Shire Council, 1973), p. 85.
2 Bernard Salt, *The Big Shift: Welcome to the Third Australian Culture* (Melbourne: Hardie Grant, 2001), p. 2.
3 Lionel Frost, *The New Urban Frontier: Urbanisation and City-Building in Australasia and the American West* (Sydney: UNSW Press, 1991), p. 106; R.E.N. Twopeny, *Town Life in Australia* (Harmondsworth: Penguin, 1883), p. 46; Max Kelly, *Paddock Full of Houses: Paddington 1840–1890* (Sydney: Doak Press, 1978).

In Melbourne and Adelaide families revealed a preference for new, detached suburban houses, even though there were cheaper but smaller dwellings available closer to the city centre. Although wealth was distributed unevenly, the average housing stock was of high quality.[4]

This wellbeing was made possible by high rates of economic growth. Within two generations of the first European settlement, Australians were better off materially than their counterparts in Britain: in 1854 Australian real wages were 138 per cent higher than those of Britain.[5] Between 1870 and 1890 Australian labour productivity grew by an average of 8 per cent per annum and per capita incomes were on average 51 per cent higher than those of the United States.[6] The Depression of the 1890s signalled the end of a 30-year boom, but the development of refrigerated shipping for meat and dairy products and the rise of the Western Australian goldfields fuelled an 'export rescue' that allowed growth to continue, albeit at a slower pace.[7] Australia remained one of the world's fastest growing nations at the end of the colonial era.[8]

When Keith Hancock was appointed director of the Research School of Social Sciences at the ANU in 1957, his first project was to develop a series of multidisciplinary seminars on the subject of wool.[9] The pastoral industry was an Australian icon and in his book *Australia* (1930) Hancock had described it as the 'corner-stone of Australia's economic and social edifice', having played the key role in the exploration and conquest of the continent.[10] The largely descriptive, pioneering economic history texts of Edward Shann and Brian Fitzpatrick, which appeared between the wars, also associated economic change with expansion of the wool industry and export-led

4 Martin P. Shanahan, 'Personal Wealth in South Australia', *Journal of Interdisciplinary History*, 32, 1 (2001): 55–80.
5 Jeffrey G. Williamson, 'The Evolution of Global Labour Markets Since 1830: Background, Evidence and Hypotheses', *Explorations in Economic History*, 32 (1995): 164–5.
6 Rajabrata Banerjee, 'Population Growth and Endogenous Technological Change: Australian Economic Growth in the Long Run', *Economic Record*, 88, 281 (2012): 1–2; Ian W. McLean, 'Why Was Australia so Rich?' *Explorations in Economic History*, 44, 4 (2007): 635–6.
7 James Belich, *Replenishing the Earth: The Settler Revolution and the Rise of the Anglo-World, 1783–1939* (Oxford University Press, 2009), pp. 85–9.
8 David Greasley and Les Oxley, 'A Tale of Two Dominions: Comparing the Macroeconomic Records of Australia and Canada since 1870', *Economic History Review*, 51, 2 (1998): 294–318.
9 Geoffrey Bolton, 'Rediscovering Australia: Hancock and the Wool Seminar', in D.A. Low (ed.), *Keith Hancock: The Legacies of an Historian* (Melbourne University Press, 2001), pp. 180–200.
10 W.K. Hancock, *Australia* (London: Ernest Benn, 1930), p. 1.

growth.[11] Subsequent monographs examined primary industries and related sectors such as banking.[12] At an early Wool Seminar, Noel Butlin, who had been a research fellow at the ANU since returning to Australia from Harvard in 1951, used a blackboard to sketch a revolutionary approach to Australian economic history.[13] For Butlin, the source of economic growth lay in capital formation – the creation of assets that could be used for production. The gold rush fuelled population growth and internal migration that exacerbated housing shortages and drew labour from the rural sector, but also generated wealth and bigger markets that expanded opportunities in commerce, trade and financial activities. Shann and Fitzpatrick had argued that when the security of land rights was confirmed in 1847, pastoralists could invest in wire fencing to reduce labour costs, and that allowed the wool industry to resume its dominant role in economic activity once the peak of gold production had passed.[14] Butlin's estimates of national production, investment and trade, derived from colonial statistics and verified by qualitative data from institutional records, showed that after 1860 growth depended on investment in four related areas: pastoral production, transport (mainly railways), residential construction and service occupations (mainly in urban areas).[15] Wool remained Australia's most valuable export, but Butlin's data revealed the economic importance of the urban sector and its associated construction, industrial and service activities. In a period of growth that was sustained until the onset of the Depression in 1889, Australia built an expanding industrial sector on the foundations of a highly productive rural economy.

As the rate of capital formation increased from the 1870s, capital imports became increasingly important and rates of net immigration accelerated. As Table 13.1 shows, the increase in capital imports during the 1880s helped to finance a sharp rise in domestic capital formation, but also increased Australia's current account deficit (the excess of the value of imported goods and services over exported goods and services). The transfer of labour and

11 Edward Shann, *An Economic History of Australia* [1930] (Melbourne: Georgian House, 1948); Brian Fitzpatrick, *The British Empire in Australia: An Economic History 1834–1939* (Melbourne University Press, 1941).

12 See, for example, S.J. Butlin, *Foundations of the Australian Monetary System 1788–1851* (Sydney University Press, 1953).

13 For the text of Butlin's paper, 'substantially as delivered', see N.G. Butlin, 'The Shape of the Australian Economy, 1861–1900', *Economic Record*, 34, 67 (1958): 10–29.

14 Shann, *An Economic History of Australia*, pp. 123–5; Fitzpatrick, *The British Empire in Australia*, pp. 123–4.

15 N.G. Butlin, *Australian Domestic Product, Investment and Foreign Borrowing 1861–1938/39* (Cambridge University Press, 1962); N.G. Butlin, *Investment in Australian Economic Development 1861–1900* (Cambridge University Press, 1964).

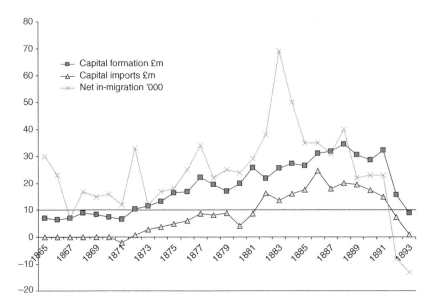

Figure 13.1 Australian capital formation, capital imports and net in-migration, 1865–93
Source: N.G. Butlin, 'The Shape of the Australian Economy, 1861–1900', *Economic Record*, 34, 67 (1958): 14.

Table 13.1 Australian national accounts, 1861–1900 (£ million)

Period	GDP Haig	GDP Butlin	Domestic capital formation	Net capital imports	Current account balance
1861–70	676	636	85	41	−41
1871–80	945	1,116	181	25	−24
1881–90	1,482	1,761	344	174	−72
1891–1900	1,903	1,667	218	48	−28

Sources: Bryan Haig, 'New Estimates of Australian GDP: 1861–1948/49', *Australian Economic History Review*, 41, 1 (2001): 28–9; N.G. Butlin, *Australian Domestic Product, Investment and Foreign Borrowing 1861–1938/39* (Cambridge University Press, 1962), pp. 6, 10–11, 411, 413–14.

capital from Britain, where rents were high and wages and interest rates low, combined with an expanding local workforce, allowed Australians to accumulate capital and develop the productive assets needed to enter world trade and meet local demands. Butlin's estimates of real gross domestic product (GDP) per capita show an average rate of growth of almost 1.5 per cent per annum from 1861 to 1889. Real GDP grew by 4.8 per cent per annum. In a recent reassessment, Bryan Haig argued that Butlin's estimates overstated levels of pastoral and construction investment, and understated the level of employment in manufacturing. Haig's estimates showed an economy that grew at only around 0.5 per cent per capita annually during the boom, with real incomes per capita falling by 10 per cent during the 1890s.[16]

During what J.M. Keynes called 'the magnificent episode of the nineteenth century', the world economy was transformed as reduced trade barriers and transport costs allowed consumers and producers around the world to reap the maximum benefits from commercial exchange.[17] Long-distance trade had hitherto been a risky, expensive business, confined to low-bulk, high-value products such as precious metals, silk, porcelain and tea. The costs of migration were prohibitive and the international movement of people was largely confined to slaves, indentured servants and convicts.[18] The value of world trade grew during the nineteenth century by 3.9 per cent per annum; in the preceding century the growth rate was 1.3 per cent per annum.[19] After the Napoleonic wars, Britain enjoyed a long period of military mastery and the freedom to seek new markets and sources of raw materials. The industrial revolution increased demand for imports of inputs to manufacturing, such as cotton, wool, tin and rubber. Economic growth increased demand for luxury foodstuffs such as sugar, tea, coffee and meat. Bulkier commodities, such as flour and raw materials for cheap textiles, which were key items of working-class consumption, became important items of trade. International freight rates were slashed – by around 1.5 per cent per annum between 1840 and 1913 – with the introduction of steamships and subsequent technological changes that cut coal consumption.[20] The richest and fastest growing European economies championed free trade and used their growing military power to establish colonies in Asia and Africa. Force was used – explicitly in

---

16 Ian W. McLean, *Why Australia Prospered: The Shifting Sources of Economic Growth* (Princeton University Press, 2013); Bryan Haig, 'New Estimates of Australian GDP: 1861–1948/49', *Australian Economic History Review*, 41, 1 (2001): 1–34.

17 Elizabeth Johnson (ed.), *The Collected Writings of John Maynard Keynes. Volume 17, Activities 1920–1922, Treaty Revision and Reconstruction* (Cambridge University Press, 1978), p. 442.

18 Timothy J. Hatton and Jeffrey G. Williamson, *The Age of Mass Migration: Causes and Economic Impact* (Oxford University Press, 1998), p. 7.

19 Kevin H. O'Rourke and Jeffrey G. Williamson, 'Once More: When Did Globalisation Begin?' *European Review of Economic History*, 8 (2004): 112.

20 Kevin H. O'Rourke and Jeffrey G. Williamson, *Globalization and History: The Evolution of a Nineteenth-Century Atlantic Economy* (Cambridge, MA: MIT Press, 1999), pp. 35–6.

China's case and implicitly in Japan's – to enter large markets from which European traders had hitherto been restricted.[21] The telegraph reduced uncertainty about prices. Faster ships and cheaper fares stimulated mass migration and the settlement of new primary producing regions. As world wheat production shifted from Europe, exchanges of information across international boundaries reduced the cost of developing seed varieties and cultivation methods suited to drier and less fertile regions.[22] The resulting 'grain invasion' cut food prices and increased disposable incomes in Europe. Because most countries adopted gold as their monetary standard, the Californian (1848) and Australian (1851) rushes increased the amount of money in circulation and allowed overseas countries to pay for British products. British investors then pumped funds back into the world economy through investment in railway building. While the nineteenth-century increases in the world's production potential encouraged rapid population growth – from 180 to 390 million in Europe and 26 to 152 million in the Americas and Oceania – output and per-capita incomes accelerated at greater rates through technological change.[23]

Butlin's interpretation repositioned colonial Australia as more than a mere appendage of this international economy. Shann and Fitzpatrick had seen the nineteenth century from different philosophical vantage points – the former championed free trade as the key to prosperity and the latter developed a Marxist theme of exploitation of people and resources by British capital – but they shared a Eurocentric view of the Australian colonies as technologically inferior satellites. For Butlin, the changing world economy and the availability of British capital and migrants were exogenous factors that presented Australians with opportunities that they were empowered to resist or embrace. The high degree of Australian urbanisation added an 'internal dynamic' to economic development, with the critical decisions about the orientation of the economy being made 'in Australia, by Australians and in the light of Australian criteria'.[24] This directed investment into three broad

---

21 Daniel R. Headrick, *Power Over Peoples: Technology, Environments, and Western Imperialism, 1400 to the Present* (Princeton University Press, 2010).
22 Alan L. Olmstead and Paul W. Rhode, 'Biological Globalization: The Other Grain Invasion', in Timothy J. Hatton, Kevin H. O'Rourke and Alan M. Taylor (eds), *The New Comparative Economic History: Essays in Honor of Jeffrey G. Williamson* (Cambridge, MA: MIT Press, 2007), pp. 115–40.
23 Jakob B. Madsen, James B. Ang and Rajabrata Banerjee, 'Four Centuries of British Economic Growth: The Roles of Technology and Population', *Journal of Economic Growth* 15, 4 (2010): 263–90; Colin McEvedy and Richard Jones, *Atlas of World Population History* (Harmondsworth: Penguin, 1978), pp. 18, 270, 320.
24 Butlin, *Investment in Australian Economic Development, 1861–1900*, p. 5.

categories: the building and servicing of cities, the building of links between cities and their hinterlands, and the development of those hinterlands. Government capital outlays, mainly for railway construction, accounted for up to half of all capital outlays. In later work, Butlin found that the concentration of a high proportion of the Australian population in towns, where activities-based specialisation and exchange took place, originated from the establishment of convict colonies.[25]

Colonial Australia's success in a booming, rapidly changing world economy illustrates a paradox of economic growth. The Australian economy provided incomes and housing standards that were on average very high by international comparison, through the extraction of non-renewable resources and conversion of native vegetation into pastoral and agricultural land use. This involved a hostile takeover of ancient Indigenous societies and destruction of their way of life. Settlers who turned the land over to European plants and animals in search of profits were usually uninterested in conserving resources. A purely triumphal view of this history is thus inappropriate, and recent scholarship has explored the violence, racism, poverty, social exclusion and environmental damage that is the dark side of Australian economic development. But destructive ecological change often went hand-in-hand with the development of creative solutions to the challenges of settling an unfamiliar and sometimes hostile land. As Geoff Raby observes, growth and change are inseparable issues and 'we cannot make our history *à la carte*'.[26] A broad survey of the colonial economy that accommodates these perspectives must use a coarsely grained analysis.

Competing for resources

'Competition', wrote Samuel Johnson, is 'the act of endeavouring to gain what another endeavours to gain at the same time'.[27] Economic competition takes place in markets, where sellers of goods and services adjust production to meet the expectations and changing wants of consumers at the lowest possible cost. Buyers reveal their preferences by accepting or rejecting the price nominated by sellers. Prices, the measure of the combined preferences

---

25 N.G. Butlin, *Forming a Colonial Economy: Australia 1810–1850* (Cambridge University Press, 1994), p. 105.

26 Geoff Raby, *Making Rural Australia: An Economic History of Technical and Institutional Creativity, 1788–1860* (Oxford University Press, 1996), p. 1.

27 Quoted in Friedrich A. Hayek, *Individualism and Economic Order* (University of Chicago Press, 1948), p. 96.

of consumers and the relative scarcity of products, provide the information that people need to make decisions. These interactions take place voluntarily and, when the market works smoothly, the wellbeing of participants and society in general is maximised.

When a resource becomes scarce, an efficient market will send signals to consumers and producers in the form of rising prices. These are likely to encourage conservation of the resource, the search for new reserves and the development of substitutes. Owners of land and capital are likely to take action to prevent excessive resource depletion to prevent their assets from declining in value. When property rights are not well defined, competition will exhaust resources because users have no incentives to conserve them. This type of market failure – the 'tragedy of the commons' – was a characteristic of the early white exploitation of the Pacific. After James Cook completed the exploration of the Ocean – landing at Botany Bay in the process – British and American traders had maps that enabled them to roam free in search of whales, seals and sea otters. The Pacific was 'an internationalised free trade waterscape' that was outside any national boundary.[28] If seal traders curbed their killing to conserve animal populations and prolong the trade, they would have simply left seals for their rivals.[29] Traders also created negative externalities – costs that spilled over onto the Indigenous population that was not involved in producing or consuming these products. Fishermen from Macassar, where smallpox was endemic, likely carried the virus to the shores of the Gulf of Carpentaria.[30] American sealers operating in Bass Strait and on to Kangaroo Island depleted Aboriginal people's food sources and spread pulmonary and sexually transmitted infections through violence and enslavement of Aboriginal women.[31]

The British government planned its New South Wales colony as a command economy, in which a self-sufficient convict population would live under authoritarian rule. No local treasury was established, and Spanish dollars, barter (notably rum) and informal currency such as promissory notes were used in market exchanges.[32] To meet expectations that the colony would become self-supporting, colonial governors established principles of private property

28 David Igler, 'Diseased Goods: Global Exchanges in the Eastern Pacific Basin, 1770–1850', *American Historical Review*, 109, 3 (2004): 693–719.
29 Geoffrey Blainey, *The Tyranny of Distance: How Distance Shaped Australia's History* (Melbourne: Sun Books, 1966), pp. 106–7.
30 N.G. Butlin, *Economics and the Dreamtime: A Hypothetical History* (Cambridge University Press, 1993), pp. 104–20.
31 Ibid., pp. 197–8.
32 Butlin, *Foundations of the Australian Monetary System*, pp. 12–50.

and free labour markets that allowed the application of British market principles to Australia. The convicts were not habitual criminals and were more skilled and literate than historians once supposed.[33] Their crimes were often work-related and involved participation in black markets for stolen goods. Many convicts brought goods and cash with them, and an important early function of colonial banks was to receive deposits from convicts.[34] Most convicts were urban working people who embraced the new consumer culture of the industrial revolution, which made cheaper clothes, food and possessions available.[35] They were generally not confined to cells or barracks and their assignment to government work gangs or to free or emancipist farmers and entrepreneurs created an efficient supply of labour. Convicts and free settlers brought 'intellectual baggage' that included knowledge and appreciation of market mechanisms and British practices and legal arrangements.[36] Sealers and whalers who called at Sydney and Hobart for repairs and provisions hired convicts and ex-convicts, and provided information that encouraged local business people to enter those industries. Women – mostly married and widowed – were actively involved in business activities and accounted for one-third of the first shareholders of the Bank of New South Wales.[37] The muster record of 1805–06, an incomplete census, shows that only 42 per cent of Sydney's adult male population were convicts. The variety of non-agricultural occupations and industries, and the thriving private market for land are evidence 'for a highly – one might say, extraordinarily – successful establishment of a colonial bridgehead economy'.[38]

The rate of transportation accelerated in the 1810s, which expanded the domestic market and made more labour available for the construction of roads and bridges. The settlement of the Cumberland Plain began with land grants to free settlers and former convicts. Governor Macquarie's enlightened policy of emancipation and his orders to cut a road through the Blue Mountains, which led to the founding of Bathurst in 1815, confirmed that the colony would expand inland. In 1819 Macquarie sent a shipment of merino sheep to Van Diemen's Land to speed up the development of the fine-wool

---

33 Stephen Nicholas (ed.), *Convict Workers: Reinterpreting Australia's Past* (Cambridge University Press, 1988).
34 Butlin, *Forming a Colonial Economy*, pp. 107–9.
35 Grace Karskens, *The Colony: A History of Early Sydney* (Sydney: Allen & Unwin, 2009), p. 65.
36 Butlin, *Forming a Colonial Economy*, pp. 107–36.
37 Leanne Johns, 'The First Female Shareholders of the Bank of New South Wales: Examination of Shareholdings in Australia's First Bank, 1817–1824', *Accounting, Business & Financial History*, 16, 2 (2006): 293–314.
38 Butlin, *Economics and the Dreamtime*, p. 146.

industry.[39] By that time the Napoleonic wars were over and the British government was cutting back on direct participation in the establishment of colonies. Britain now preferred to allow private companies to expand the Empire, which resulted in the foundation of the Swan River colony in 1829 and the South Australian Company in 1835.[40]

The origins of Australasia's first economic boom can be traced to Van Diemen's Land in 1828, when increasing numbers of ships carrying free settlers arrived in Hobart.[41] The colony had separated from New South Wales three years earlier and its boosters promoted Hobart and its hinterland as an Arcadian land of opportunity. The British government invested heavily in roads, bridges and other infrastructure. Capital from Britain began flooding in and new banks were created that directed investment into pastoral expansion.[42] The scramble to occupy land that was suited to pastoral activity swept aside all previous attempts at consolidated settlement, despite uncertainty about the consequences of trespassing on crown land. Tasmania's grazing land was occupied so quickly that in 1833 Lieutenant-Governor George Arthur attempted to persuade the British government to extend the colony to the Port Phillip District, on the southern coast of the mainland.[43] When squatters from Van Diemen's Land established a camp on the banks of the Yarra River, where Melbourne would be sited, the event signified that 'the continent was fully opened to conquest'.[44] During the pastoral boom, which ended in 1841, Australasia's population increased fourfold and squatters occupied nearly 20 million hectares of the most productive and best-watered Aboriginal homelands beyond the Great Dividing Range and then north across the Liverpool plains to the New England plateau in New South Wales and the grasslands of what are now Victoria, South Australia and southern Queensland.[45]

The wool industry allowed European owners or providers of factors of production – land, labour and capital – to interact with each other in the expectation of profit. Squatters took up sheep runs to increase the size of their flocks and the woolclip, financed by borrowings from local banks and

39 Raby, *Making Rural Australia*, p. 29.
40 Ian Berryman, 'Swan River Mania', in Jenny Gregory and Jan Gothard (eds), *Historical Encyclopedia of Western Australia* (Perth: UWA Press, 2009), pp. 854–5; Michael Williams, *The Making of the South Australian Landscape: A Study in the Historical Geography of Australia* (London: Academic Press, 1974), pp. 23–5.
41 Belich, *Replenishing the Earth*, pp. 267–72.
42 Butlin, *Foundations of the Australian Monetary System*, pp. 228–43.
43 James Boyce, *1835: The Founding of Melbourne & the Conquest of Australia* (Melbourne: Black Inc., 2011), pp. 16–25.
44 Ibid., p. xi.
45 Belich, *Replenishing the Earth*, p. 261; Boyce, *1835*, p. xi.

merchants and British investors. Annual pastoral licence fees provided revenue for colonial governments. Licence fees were low and the land required little investment, other than the purchase of sheep to make it productive. Shearers, shepherds and urban workers offered the services needed for profitable wool production in return for wages. English millers appreciated Australian wool because it was cheaper than European wool and could be used to produce the superfine cloths that were demanded by fashion-conscious buyers, as well as the plain cloths that appealed to a mass market.[46] The high value of raw wool, and the lack of barriers to enter the industry, allowed the holders of pastoral licences to establish profitable enterprises despite high costs of labour, capital and land transport. This form of production and the value it placed on private property clashed with the nomadic, customary nature of Aboriginal society that was based on communal property, intergroup order and obligations and laws.[47] As Richard Broome observes, squatters were risking their capital on land they did not own. 'For Aboriginal people, their very ownership of land, which was not only their livelihood but the source of their culture, identity and spiritual essence, was at stake'.[48] The whites monopolised and fenced local water supplies, destroyed the habitats of native animals, pursued black women and attacked hunting and gathering bands. The blacks hunted sheep and cattle and attacked shepherds. There was some cooperation – Aboriginal guides often accompanied squatters who were searching for land and ate European food. Aboriginal people shared valuable information about the Australian environment and worked on pastoral stations. But the differences between the British and Aboriginal economies were wider than either side appreciated. The 'cost of information required to span the gulf...made errors of understanding virtually certain and, in the last resort, was a price that neither side was willing to pay'.[49]

Investment in boom times was usually a rational decision based on observations of the profitability of past investment. What was irrational was the assumption that resources were unlimited and that wealth creation would go on indefinitely.[50] By 1842 it was apparent that the most productive pastoral land had been taken up. British investors became less confident in the future profitability of wool growing in drier interior lands. Capital inflow,

46 Alan Barnard, *The Australian Wool Market, 1840–1900* (Melbourne University Press, 1958), pp. 22–3.
47 Butlin, *Economics and the Dreamtime*, pp. 199–201.
48 Richard Broome, *Aboriginal Victorians: A History Since 1800* (Sydney: Allen & Unwin, 2005), pp. 54–5.
49 Butlin, *Economics and the Dreamtime*, p. 199.
50 Belich, *Replenishing the Earth*, pp. 275–8.

which peaked at £1.6 million in 1840, fell to £400,000 in 1842 and there was net outflow of capital in 1844.[51] In-migration ceased. Recovery from this depression was based on increasing exports of wool through a reconstruction of the industry. The more efficient pastoralists bought out bankrupt neighbours. Improved methods of wool packing, buying and shipping were developed. South Australian wheat and copper provided other important export industries.

A resource blessing

The colonies that were established by European powers after 1500 can be distinguished by the institutions that evolved in response to differing mortality rates among setters.[52] Where disease environments were unfavourable to Europeans, a small range of commodities was extracted from large production units using a forced non-European labour force. These colonies were set up to allow Europeans to derive rents quickly and transfer them to their home countries. Institutions that might have offered property rights, the administration of justice and checks on the ability of imperial governments and elites to take a large enough share of the proceeds of resource extraction to crowd out productive investment, were weak. Where environments were more benign, 'neo-Europes' were created by settlers who wanted to build permanent homes and expected the same legal rights as existed in their home countries. These institutional frameworks evolved in a path-dependent way, exerting lasting influences on economic activity that sustained high incomes in low-mortality colonies and persistent poverty in the other colonies.

It may be that Australian squatters, in their ruthless pursuit of 'possessive individualism', were as motivated by the desire for wealth as the seventeenth-century plantation and slave owners of the American south and the Caribbean.[53] Pastoral expansion devastated the Indigenous population, but for the colonial economy, government provision of infrastructure and stable property rights meant that no landed elite or political authority could capture all of the proceeds of resource development. The rule of law and democracy

---

51 W.A. Sinclair, *The Process of Economic Development in Australia* (Melbourne: Cheshire, 1976), p. 66.
52 Daron Acemoglu, Simon Johnson and James A. Robinson, 'The Colonial Origins of Comparative Development: An Empirical Investigation', *American Economic Review*, 91, 5 (2001): 1369–401.
53 Richard Waterhouse, 'Settling the Land', in Deryck M. Schreuder and Stuart Ward (eds), *Australia's Empire* (Oxford University Press, 2008), pp. 54–6.

allowed institutions to develop that directed resources to the formation of human capital – education and health – rather than public spending on physical capital that would benefit the interests of a small number of powerful rent-seekers.[54] Australian colonial governments were involved in the development of primary industries through the disposal of crown lands for settlement and the building of railways and other infrastructure. Under the rules of the gold standard, gold was exported and imported freely. After the discoveries of the 1850s gold increased the amount of money in circulation, and Australian colonial governments could borrow more cheaply on the London capital market than private investors could. In Australia, as in California – where there was a common experience of transport problems linked to distance and isolation and bursts of growth due to mining and agricultural booms – the rents from capitalist resource extraction 'were ploughed back into productive enterprise, not frittered away'.[55] Compared to those of the United States, Australia's natural resources were developed at a low cost, without high levels of capital. Labour-market participation rates, and therefore labour input per capita, were high and the labour force itself grew slowly due to the costs of migration. Despite the tyranny of distance, Australians grew rich due to the abundance of resources.[56]

Most immigrants to Australia came from British cities, but they retained folk memories of a pre-industrial age and their act of emigration reflected a desire for a better quality of life.[57] Owning a farm of one's own was equated with independence and membership of a stable, morally virtuous community. Colonial governments sought to create a class of hardworking yeoman farmers who would conserve the fertility of smallholdings in areas of concentrated settlement.[58] Popular demands to 'unlock the land' were heightened by the expanded population of the gold rush, and new legislation aimed to settle the land more intensively and prevent individuals from accumulating large holdings. The New South Wales, Victorian, Queensland and South Australian land legislation of the 1860s limited the size of holdings and by the mid-1870s one square mile (640 acres or 259 hectares) was

54 David de la Croix and Clara Delavallade, 'Growth, Public Investment and Corruption With Failing Institutions', *Economics of Governance*, 10, 3 (2009): 187–219.
55 Richard A. Walker, 'California's Golden Road to Riches: Natural Resources and Regional Capitalism, 1848–1940', *Annals of the Association of American Geographers*, 91, 1 (2001): 167–99.
56 McLean, *Why Australia Prospered*.
57 Graeme Davison, 'Colonial Origins of the Australian Home', in Patrick Troy (ed.), *A History of European Housing in Australia* (Cambridge University Press, 2000), p. 9.
58 Williams, *The Making of the South Australian Landscape*, p. 24.

commonly regarded as the ideal holding size. Land could be purchased on credit and selectors were required to live on the land and improve it through cultivation.[59]

The ideal of a closely settled rural society was at odds with the reality of Australian conditions: the climate was generally drier and the soil less fertile than that of Britain. Labour and capital were scarcer. To farm profitably, settlers needed to develop land-extensive systems that circumvented government restrictions.[60] Rural expansion depended on larger farm units being made available at affordable terms, which made it imperative for farmers to maximise profits to pay their debts and, in time, help their children to buy farms of their own. As one farmer put it in 1901, for those who failed to make farming pay, 'our only alternative would be to enter the ranks of the labourers'.[61] Creative responses to these challenges generated new information about production possibilities that could not be monopolised by any one farmer. New information gained through experimentation and learning by doing was circulated through newspapers and agricultural societies. There was thus a connection between the spread of settlement and the rate of discovery of new technology that allowed resources to be exploited more efficiently.[62] By the time settlers began seeking new property beyond the initial core of agricultural land, Williams argued, 'the ideal of a self-supporting yeomanry was gone and in its place there had emerged the reality of a footloose population engaged in a business-like approach to agriculture, specializing in wheat-growing for a world-wide competitive market'.[63]

An examination of the case of South Australia will illustrate how governments supported the increasing commercialisation of agriculture and provided incentives for productivity growth. The South Australian Company eschewed speculators and convict labour, adopting the Wakefield system of land sales to raise the capital needed to establish a new colony and assist free immigrants. Once it had been surveyed, land was offered for sale at auction in lots of up to 80 acres, at a minimum price of £1 per acre. Purchasers had to pay a 10 per cent deposit and the balance in cash within

59 Michael Williams, 'More and Smaller is Better: Australian Rural Settlement 1788–1914', in J.M. Powell and M. Williams (eds), *Australian Space, Australian Time: Geographical Perspectives* (Oxford University Press, 1975), pp. 70–80.
60 Charles Fahey, '"A Splendid Place for a Home": A Long History of the Australian Family Farm 1830–2000', in Alan Mayne and Stephen Atkinson (eds), *Outside Country: Histories of Inland Australia* (Adelaide: Wakefield Press, 2011), pp. 231–66.
61 *Quorn Mercury*, 13 December 1901.
62 Paul M. Romer, 'The Origins of Endogenous Growth', *Journal of Economic Perspectives*, 8, 1 (1994): 11–3.
63 Williams, *The Making of the South Australian Landscape*, p. 37.

a month. Farm labour would be provided by new arrivals who were saving to buy their own land.

The proximity of grasslands to ports that offered cheap sea transport made South Australia the epicentre of the Australian wheat-growing industry. The discovery and mining of copper at Kapunda (1843) and Burra (1844) increased the size of the market for primary producers. The Victorian gold rushes had a similar effect – Melbourne food prices remained high throughout the 1850s and grain was imported from California and Chile.[64] Resource booms have the potential to create 'supply shocks' by diverting resources from farming and manufacturing, and increasing their costs.[65] Labour was in such short supply in 1846 that some employers rowed out to meet ships as they arrived at Port Adelaide to gain first choice amongst the new arrivals. Wages for various trades increased by 50 per cent in 1846 and almost doubled in 1852.[66] Despite rising costs, the South Australian economy was able to respond to these stimuli through supply-side changes. Wool production increased almost fourfold during the 1850s as cashed-up squatters invested in land purchase, fencing and water supply. The number of farmers increased from 2,500 to 7,000 after new land was surveyed around Kapunda and Burra, and during the 1850s the amount of land under cultivation in the colony rose from 65,000 to 362,000 acres (26,000 to 129,000 hectares). South Australia now had more wheat acreage than all the other Australian colonies combined – a situation that remained until the 1891–92 season.[67] When the Kapunda mines began working in 1843 the colony's population was 17,000; by the time the Yorke Peninsula copper mines at Wallaroo and Moonta were operating in 1861 the figure had increased to 127,000.[68]

The success of South Australian farmers in the 1850s and early 1860s was based on the development of simple techniques of 'extensive' cultivation. Most 'scratched' the soil to economise on labour and capital and cropped their land continuously with wheat to generate quick cash flows. Once the soil was exhausted, farmers needed to expand their holdings or find new

64 James Gerber, 'Gold Rushes and the Trans-Pacific Wheat Trade: California and Australia, 1848–57', in Dennis O. Flynn, Lionel Frost and A.J.H. Latham (eds), *Pacific Centuries: Pacific and Pacific Rim History since the Sixteenth Century* (London: Routledge, 1999), pp. 133–6.
65 Rodney Maddock and Ian McLean, 'Supply-Side Shocks: The Case of Australian Gold', *Journal of Economic History*, 44, 4 (1984): 1047–67.
66 T.A. Coghlan, *Labour and Industry in Australia: From the First Settlement in 1788 to the Establishment of the Commonwealth in 1901* (Oxford University Press, 1918), pp. 455, 745–7.
67 J.B. Hirst, *Adelaide and the Country 1870–1917: Their Social and Political Relationship* (Melbourne University Press, 1973), p. 11; Wray Vamplew (ed.), *Australians: Historical Statistics* (Sydney: Fairfax, Syme & Weldon Associates, 1987), pp. 76, 82.
68 Vamplew, *Australians: Historical Statistics*, p. 127.

areas of cheap land. Beyond the Adelaide plains and central hill country the land was either covered with mallee scrub – thick, tough vegetation that was difficult to clear – or was in the hands of pastoralists. New land legislation in 1869 was a reaction to the increasing number of South Australians who were moving to Victoria, where land was available on credit before it had been surveyed. South Australian land, once surveyed, was offered for sale in lots of up to 640 acres. Clearing mallee scrub in a cost-effective way became easier after 1868, when Charles Mullen, a farmer from near Gawler, invented a technique of dragging a heavy log over the surface of roots and stumps after the trees had been felled by axe and the timber sold as fuel. Stubble was burnt after harvest to subdue mallee shoots. Farmers who practised 'mullenising' used another South Australian invention, the stump-jump plough, to prepare seed beds despite the obstructions of stumps and roots.

The official limit of 'safe' wheat cultivation in South Australia was based on surveyor-general George Goyder's observations of drought-stricken pastoral country in 1865. Goyder's 'Line of Rainfall' became the government's accepted boundary between the lands that were suitable for agricultural use and those that were not. After a run of favourable seasons – popularly explained by the idea that broken soil absorbed more moisture and thus 'rain followed the plough' – public pressure grew to make land available on the Yorke Peninsula and beyond the northern margins of settlement. The Line, and even Goyder himself, who maintained his faith in the concept, was treated with contempt by farmers and the press. In 1874 the government opened the whole of South Australia for selection, withdrawing from judging the land and leaving its appraisal to individual settlers. A million acres was surveyed in 1876 as settlers clamoured for land.[69] Thereafter the trend was for average wheat yields to fall as acreage increased (Figure 13.2).

Goyder was vindicated when the northern areas were hit hard by droughts in the early 1880s. Some settlers abandoned the land – 600,000 acres were forfeited in 1883 and 1884 – but many stayed to try and recoup the capital they had outlaid.[70] Those who could afford to buy more land were able to rest paddocks from cultivation and plough it more deeply after it had been softened by winter rainfall. By the late 1890s farmers had developed new methods of cultivation, fallowing, sowing, fertilising and harvesting that were cost effective in dry conditions and on poor-quality soils. A new type of farming system, based on improved seed varieties, keeping sheep on fallow paddocks

69 D.W. Meinig, *On the Margins of the Good Earth: The South Australian Wheat Frontier, 1869–1884* [1962] (Adelaide: Rigby, 1970), pp. 56, 61.
70 Ibid., p. 91.

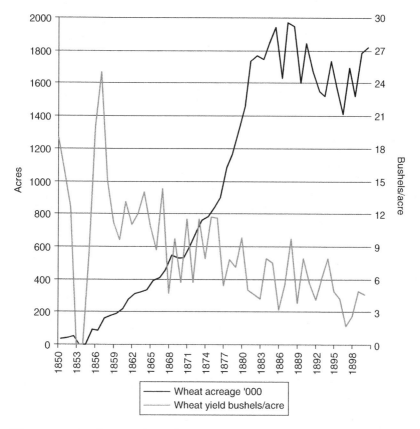

Figure 13.2 South Australian wheat acreage and yields (bushels per acre), 1870–1900
Source: Wray Vamplew (ed.), *Australians: Historical Statistics* (Sydney: Fairfax, Syme & Weldon Associates, 1987), p. 76.

and the use of superphosphate, was developed in South Australia and diffused through the other colonies in time for farmers to profit from excellent growing and market conditions in the period before World War 1.[71]

Colonial governments also provided infrastructure to help producers stay on the land. Most public investment was in rural areas and directed mainly to railway building, which was expected to increase the profitability of farming by reducing production costs. Empirical studies show that new railways increased the level and volatility of real incomes in the regions they served by reducing the

71 Lionel Frost, 'The Correll Family and Technological Change in Australian Agriculture', *Agricultural History*, 75, 2 (2001): 239–41.

cost to farmers of participating in inter-regional and world trade.[72] The process of allocating resources to railway building was subject to political pressure, but parliamentary checks and balances reduced the scope for corruption and unproductive investment.[73] The South Australian parliament was dominated by members who represented or lived in Adelaide and was less swayed by parochial pressures than a parliament of local members would have been.[74] It was official policy to place railway facilities within 15 miles of every major farming district. A government commission, chaired by Goyder, was established in 1875 to rank the order in which proposed routes would be investigated, based on the value of the surrounding farmland.[75] Further select committees would consider issues of construction costs, proposed routes and the extent of settlement in the area to be served. Finally, the matter would be debated and voted on in parliament and this scrutiny resulted in several proposals being shelved. In Victoria, large-scale irrigation works, which were beyond the means of local communities, were constructed to distribute water in a cost-effective way to the greatest possible number of farmers. Colonial governments also promoted rural development through agricultural education and research, building long rabbit-proof fences and tapping artesian water supplies in pastoral areas, providing incentives for communities to establish cooperative butter factories and building refrigerated railway cars and cool stores.

Town and country

In a 1902 ballad, 'The Road to Gundagai', A.B. 'Banjo' Paterson used the crossroads 'where the roads divide' between Sydney and Gundagai as a metaphor for the choice people had to make about whether they would live in rural or urban Australia.[76] For Paterson, the turnoff to the city symbolised a great divide in Australian society, where the country changed direction materially and morally. Country work and living was widely held to be noble and pure, whereas the cities were places of vice, selfishness, trickery, dirt and overcrowding. Like Tenterfield and Corowa, Gundagai was a concentration

---

72 Dave Donaldson, *Railroads of the Raj: Estimating the Impact of Transportation Infrastructure* (Asia Research Centre Working Paper 41, London School of Economics and Political Science, 2010).

73 Lionel Frost, 'Government and the Colonial Economies: An Alternative View', *Australian Economic History Review*, 40, 1 (2000): 71–85.

74 Hirst, *Adelaide and the Country*, p. 105.

75 Meinig, *On the Margins of the Good Earth*, pp. 135–40.

76 Andrew Barton Paterson, 'The Road to Gundagai', in *Rio Grande's Last Race and Other Verses* (Sydney: Angus & Robertson, 1902), p. 77.

Table 13.2 Capital city populations ('000s) and populations as a percentage of colonial populations (in italics)

Year	Sydney	Melbourne	Adelaide	Brisbane	Perth	Hobart
1851	54 (28)	29 (38)	18 (28)	3 (34)	N/A	N/A
1861	96 (27)	125 (23)	35 (28)	6 (20)	5 (33)	25 (28)
1871	138 (27)	191 (26)	51 (27)	15 (13)	N/A	26 (25)
1881	225 (30)	268 (31)	92 (30)	31 (14)	9 (30)	27 (23)
1891	400 (35)	473 (41)	117 (35)	94 (24)	16 (32)	33 (22)
1901	496 (37)	478 (40)	141 (37)	119 (24)	61 (33)	35 (20)

N/A = not available
Source: J.W. McCarty, 'Australian Capital Cities in the Nineteenth Century', *Australian Economic History Review*, 10, 2 (1970): 119, 125.

of people who were engaged in a wide variety of non-agricultural occupations. It had all of the trappings of an urban place: commercial and civic buildings, specialist stores, hotels, medical surgeries, churches and schools.[77] Yet, as Russel Ward observed, 'country towns, even the largest of them, have always been centres of "bush" values where the country-dweller's hostility to the wicked city finds expression'.[78] In economic terms, the countryside was thought to be the source of all wealth, while towns were seen as parasites that inflated primary production costs by devouring scarce capital and labour. Even in the capital cities themselves there was a perception that an unhealthy imbalance existed between the colonies' urban and rural populations (see Table 13.2). Capital city growth was seen not 'as a sign of economic progress, but as a threat to it'.[79]

Economists tend to associate city growth with productivity-raising activities. The generation of agglomeration economies, derived from bringing together workers with valuable and diverse skills, allows information to be created and spread through face-to-face contact. This creates external effects as people learn from random formal and informal contacts with others who are more highly skilled.[80] Diverse urban environments, as Edward Glaeser has put it, 'can foster the unexpected combination of seemingly unrelated ideas that may provide the most important forward leaps of knowledge',

77 Cliff Butcher, *Gundagai: A Track Winding Back* (Gundagai: A.C. Butcher, 2002), pp. 189–206.
78 Russel Ward, 'The Australian Legend Re-Visited', *Historical Studies*, 71 (1978): 173.
79 Hirst, *Adelaide and the Country*, p. 61.
80 Alfred Marshall and Mary Paley Marshall, *The Economics of Industry*, 2nd edn (London: Macmillan, 1881), p. 53.

embodied in new or modified products.[81] A Scot, James Harrison, established the world's first ice-making plant at Geelong in 1851. Harrison moved his plant to Melbourne, and then Sydney, but the domestic market for ice was limited. Thomas Mort and his associates developed refrigerated shipping in 1873, which was used to land Australian meat and butter in Europe.[82] The convergence of railway systems near capital-city ports encouraged efficient production of farm inputs and processing of rural output. H.V. McKay, a Ballarat agricultural implement manufacturer, built a new factory west of Melbourne in 1904 to take advantage of efficient shipping and rail facilities and the proximity of specialist producers of rivets, metals, oils and paints.[83] Urbanisation increased the size of the domestic market and encouraged innovative entrepreneurs to develop new processes and products.[84] Economies of scale reduced the costs of introducing new technology for the owners of city breweries, brick makers and butter factories.

The benefits of city growth may be diluted if markets for labour, housing and infrastructure provision fail to work effectively. New arrivals, acting on imperfect information about urban job opportunities, can flood the labour market and force wages down, which reduces effective demand for housing and causes overcrowding of the housing stock. Underinvestment in urban infrastructure creates unhealthy environments that reduce labour productivity and quality of life. The concept of market failure is implicit in several case studies of Australian urban poverty, slum housing and pollution.[85] All of the capital cities had areas of old, overcrowded and poorly serviced housing, but this does not mean that the urban labour market in general was characterised by excess labour. The income levels enjoyed by Australian urban workers were higher than those of their counterparts in Britain; this suggests that Australian cities were generally short of labour.[86] Their population growth

---

81 Edward L. Glaeser, 'Cities, Information, and Economic Growth', *Cityscape*, 1, 1 (1994): 9.
82 K.T.H. Farrer, *A Settlement Amply Supplied: Food Technology in Nineteenth Century Australia* (Melbourne University Press, 1980), pp. 183–200.
83 John Lack, *A History of Footscray* (Melbourne: Hargreen, 1991), pp. 167–8.
84 Gary B. Magee, 'Patenting and the Supply of Inventive Ideas in Colonial Australia: Evidence from Victorian Patent Data', *Australian Economic History Review*, 36, 2 (1996): 30–58.
85 See, for example, Dan Coward, *Out of Sight: Sydney's Environmental History 1851–1981* (Canberra: Department of Economic History, ANU, 1988); Shirley Fitzgerald, *Rising Damp: Sydney 1870–90* (Oxford University Press, 1987); Max Kelly, 'Picturesque and Pestilential: The Sydney Slum Observed 1860–1900', in Max Kelly (ed.), *Nineteenth-Century Sydney: Essays in Urban History* (Sydney University Press, 1978), pp. 66–80.
86 Lionel Frost, 'The Contribution of the Urban Sector to Australian Economic Development Before 1914', *Australian Economic History Review*, 38, 1 (1998): 56–61.

was mainly due to the in-migration of adults of working age who brought skills and incomes with them and added to the level of aggregate demand. Much of the cities' core business – such as the loading and unloading of ships, railway wagons and drays, and the delivery of building materials, food and drink and firewood – involved heavy manual work. Roads, railways and drains were formed by men with picks and shovels. Builders' labourers carried bricks on hods and timber was sawn and nailed by hand. Women worked as laundresses, charwomen or domestic servants. These non-tradeable services could only be provided on the spot, which meant that as the city grew, so did its demand for labour. Although contemporaries saw migration from rural to urban areas as draining the economy's life-blood, wages for unskilled work remained higher in the cities than in the countryside, even if allowance is made for higher urban living costs.[87] High wages helped to compensate for urban disamenities and allowed workers to buy good-quality housing.

The growth of the capital cities promoted agricultural change in their hinterlands.[88] City demand for meat, fruit, vegetables, dairy products, hay and firewood created incentives for farmers in nearby areas to diversify and work with greater efficiency. The average farm became increasingly capable of serving a larger urban population. Melbourne's population grew by 278 per cent from 1861 to 1891, while the number of farmers in Victoria grew by 188 per cent. The number of Melbourne residents served by every 100 Victorian farms increased from 357 to 446 – an increase in productivity of 25 per cent , or 0.8 per cent per annum. As farm production grew faster than rural population, food prices fell, increasing disposable incomes and effective demand for housing. This understates the overall rise in productivity, as some produce was sold to smaller towns and to markets outside Victoria.[89]

'All country people have some business in Adelaide', a government official noted in 1875.[90] This observation indicated awareness that every farmer, pastoralist or small town resident in the colony was connected in a commercial sense to the capital city. Within each of the Australian colonies was a range of settlements of different size and function between the metropolis and the farm gate. A large number of small towns developed as a practical means of serving frequently occurring needs; a smaller number of larger towns provided a more complex range of goods and services, the demand for which

---

87 Ibid., pp. 58–9.
88 Lionel Frost, '"Metallic Nerves": San Francisco and its Hinterland During and After the Gold Rush', *Australian Economic History Review*, 50, 2 (2010): 129–47.
89 Frost, 'The Contribution of the Urban Sector', pp. 55–6.
90 Quoted in Hirst, *Adelaide and the Country*, p. 1.

arose intermittently, while a single metropolis was the major centre of government, industry and commerce. Smaller towns were in frequent contact with primary producers, who could conveniently travel only short distances over rough roads by horse and cart or bicycle, and encouraged increased production that generated work for the larger towns. In turn, the larger towns provided products that were distributed by agents and salesmen who lived in or visited smaller towns. Rural expansion and improvements in farm productivity created urban jobs. Capital cities became 'urban' as people built the first houses, workshops, docks and warehouses, at the same time that the territory around them became 'rural' as settlers transformed native vegetation into paddocks and pastures. As in North America, 'city and country shared a common past, and had fundamentally reshaped each other' in a relationship of mutual dependence.[91]

In observing the high degree of Australian urbanisation, Butlin noted that 29 per cent of the population in 1891 lived in non-metropolitan towns of at least 500 inhabitants.[92] This understates the size of the urban sector, as towns with less than 500 inhabitants provided urban services, and towns with as few as 100 inhabitants provided a sufficient range of basic services, such as hotels, stores, schools, churches and post offices to be classed as urban. If towns of at least 100 inhabitants are classed as urban, 69 per cent of the population of Victoria, New South Wales and South Australia was urban in 1891, with 44 per cent of the urban population living outside the capital cities.[93] Many towns were established at river crossing points before much of the surrounding land was sold and occupied. Soon after their foundation, pastoral towns such as Hamilton in western Victoria and Wagga Wagga in the Riverina district of New South Wales were providing government, professional and personal services to areas well beyond their boundaries.[94] At Shepparton and Wangaratta in northern Victoria, storekeepers worked actively to promote agricultural settlement and offered credit to selectors. These towns were established when transport and manufacturing technologies were simple, and the marketing and financial services provided by merchants and stock and station agents were consumed on the spot.[95] Mechanics

91 William Cronon, *Nature's Metropolis: Chicago and the Great West* (New York: W.W. Norton, 1991), pp. 7–8.
92 Butlin, *Investment in Australian Economic Development 1861–1900*, p. 184.
93 Meinig, *On the Margins of the Good Earth*, pp. 189–93; Frost, 'The Contribution of the Urban Sector', pp. 50–1.
94 J.M. Richmond, 'Country Town Growth in South-Eastern Australia: Three Regional Studies, 1861–1891', PhD thesis, ANU, 1969, pp. 146–56.
95 Simon Ville, *The Rural Entrepreneurs: A History of the Stock and Station Agent Industry in Australia and New Zealand* (Cambridge University Press, 2000).

institutes and schools of arts provided technical education for crafts and trades and meeting places for agricultural societies and other community groups. More than 1,000 Mechanics institutes were founded throughout Victoria during the nineteenth century.[96] Australia's largest inland cities were mining towns that created local markets for manufacturing and to stimulate the growth of non-metropolitan ports, such as Geelong, Rockhampton and Port Pirie. Railways from Melbourne to Sandhurst (Bendigo) and from Geelong to Ballarat opened in 1862, and were showcases of engineering that reflected the optimism and affluence of the times. These trunk lines were the foundation for branch lines to Victoria's wheat-growing regions and a railway to the paddle-steamer port of Echuca on the Murray River, which encouraged the opening up of new pastoral areas in New South Wales.[97]

Depression and recovery

In the 1880s Melbourne was Australia's investment 'hot spot'. The city increased its population from 268,000 to 473,000 during that decade and its boosters revelled in calling it the 'metropolis of Australia'.[98] Melbourne's financial institutions directed British capital to the expansion of pastoral runs in the Riverina district in southern New South Wales, cattle runs in Queensland's Darling Downs region, silver and lead mining at Broken Hill, sugar plantations in Queensland and Fiji, and the New Zealand timber industry. The city's tertiary sectors – transport, finance, communications and public administration – were reorganised technologically and spatially in response to the growing volume of economic activity. The increasing number of workers employed in construction, the growing variety of specialist building trades and the growth of building materials, metals and vehicle construction industries reflected the city's growing size. Melbourne exuded brashness and bustle, and Richard Twopeny contrasted its 'Yankee' feel to the 'languor' and 'old-fashionedness' of Sydney.[99] While almost of all Sydney's population lived in a compact core of terrace housing close to Sydney Cove, Melbourne grew by adding suburbs in which working and

---

96 Richard Myers, *Berwick Mechanics Institute and Free Library: A History* (Berwick Mechanics Institute and Free Library, 1999), p. 8.

97 Weston Bate, *Lucky City: The First Generation at Ballarat 1851–1901* (Melbourne University Press, 1978); Susan Priestley, *Echuca: A Centenary History* (Brisbane: Jacaranda Press, 1965), pp. 63–74.

98 McCarty, 'Australian Capital Cities', p. 119; Graeme Davison, *The Rise and Fall of Marvellous Melbourne*, 2nd edn (Melbourne University Press, 2004), p. 7.

99 Twopeny, *Town Life in Australia*, pp. 21, 26.

middle-class people could live in detached, single-family houses set on relatively large lots. Melbourne's population was 20 per cent greater than Sydney's in 1891, but its built-up area was seven times larger.[100] Melbourne's decentralisation was made possible by siting the town away from its port, and the grid layout that provided space for railway termini was suited to trams. Railways were built and operated by colonial governments and in the 1880s Melbourne's suburban rail system was extended lavishly to assist suburban developers. At the height of the land boom, six of the eight-member Cabinet were directors of building societies or mortgage companies.[101]

Melbourne profited during the 1880s from economic stagnation elsewhere in Australia.[102] South Australia remained depressed and Western Australia and Tasmania were growing slowly, if at all. Victoria's wheat yields were low and farmers were struggling to make a living. The dairy export trade and irrigated agriculture were in their infancy. Economic conditions in New South Wales and Queensland were stronger, but the opening of new mines and pastoral and farming land depended on the transfer of capital and labour from Victoria. Capital and labour was highly mobile and investors and workers voted with their feet: during the 1880s Melbourne's share of Australia's population increased from 12 per cent to 15 per cent, with 70 per cent of this growth due to migration. Melbourne's share of Australian private capital formation grew from 7 per cent in 1880 to 19 per cent in 1888.[103]

These conditions fuelled a boom in land purchase and house building. Commuter suburbs along new railways to the Melbourne suburbs of Caulfield and Camberwell tripled in population during the 1880s.[104] Further extensions to the system encouraged investors to buy house lots to sell on to builders or farmland that could be subdivided into new estates. This was a high-risk strategy, usually financed on credit based on expectations of future demand, but for a time the rewards offered ample compensation. At the peak of the land boom in 1887, the average annual net rate of return was 78 per cent and the average mortgage for land purchase was paid off in less than 20 months. In the following year the total amount of land purchased increased from 458 to

---

100 Frost, *The New Urban Frontier*, pp. 26–7.
101 Graeme Davison, 'The Capital Cities', in Graeme Davison, J.W. McCarty and Ailsa McLeary (eds), *Australians 1888* (Sydney: Fairfax, Syme & Weldon Associates, 1987), p. 223.
102 E.A. Boehm, *Prosperity and Depression in Australia, 1887–1897* (Oxford: Clarendon Press, 1971).
103 Butlin, 'The Shape of the Australian Economy, 1861–1900', p. 22; Butlin, *Investment in Australian Economic Development 1861–1900*, pp. 28, 47; Frost, 'The Contribution', p. 54.
104 Davison, *Marvellous Melbourne*, pp. 191–2.

1,170 acres.[105] With as little as £10 in starting capital, new builders could secure finance from a building society and build houses ahead of demand, in anticipation that they would sell quickly.[106] Confidence that rising land prices and economic expansion were irreversible underpinned this speculative process. As more land buyers entered this competitive market returns began to decline and after 1888 the turnover in land and house sales fell sharply. A collapse of land values reduced the equity of borrowers and many defaulted when it became clear that they could only sell their land at a loss.

The collapse of the Melbourne land boom unmasked several inherent weaknesses in the Australian economy. Victoria's banks competed with non-bank financial institutions that had grown in number during the boom and were willing to lend for speculative purposes. The banks lowered their credit standards and began lending to land-finance companies. The total value of lending grew faster than the growth of productive assets: the share of credit in GDP increased from 34 per cent in 1880 to 73 per cent 1893.[107] An increasing reliance on short-term foreign loans left the banking system vulnerable to a decline in the property sector, a loss of confidence by British and domestic investors and a general economic downturn. By the end of the 1880s the immediate prospects for growth in the export sectors of the economy were limited. High wage costs and the limited size of the domestic market choked off profits and discouraged investment in manufacturing. Rural industries were growing more slowly as farming was pushed into areas of lower rainfall and fertility, and pastoral enterprises were set up in dry areas that were distant from natural waterways. The inland expansion of rural industries led to overcropping and overstocking, leaving the land vulnerable to erosion and drought.[108] Low wheat yields meant that new railways did not generate enough revenue to service the overseas loans that been taken out to finance their construction.[109]

After the Baring crisis (1890) that followed the near collapse of the London merchant bank, Baring Brothers, as a result of losses in Argentina, British investors lost confidence in emerging markets, including Australia.[110] As the

---

105 R. Silberberg, 'Rates of Return on Melbourne Land Investment, 1880–92', *Economic Record*, 51, 2 (1975): 203–17.

106 Davison, *Marvellous Melbourne*, pp. 92–3.

107 Christopher Kent, 'Two Depressions, One Banking Collapse: Lessons from Australia', *Journal of Financial Stability*, 7, 3 (2011): 128.

108 Butlin, *Investment in Australian Economic Development 1861–1900*, pp. 166–80.

109 Lionel Frost, 'A Reinterpretation of Victoria's Railway Construction Boom of the 1880s', *Australian Economic History Review*, 26, 1 (1986): 40–55.

110 Kris James Mitchener and Marc D. Weidenmier, 'The Baring Crisis and the Great Latin American Meltdown of the 1890s', *Journal of Economic History*, 68, 2 (2008):

cost of raising credit in London increased, Australian banks began rationing credit, which dampened expectations about asset values. During the second half of the 1880s the assets of deposit-taking building societies and pastoral finance companies grew by 80 per cent; these assets fell by 45 per cent over the 1890s. Between 1891 and 1893, 54 non-bank financial institutions closed their doors; 60 per cent permanently.[111] Thirteen of Australia's 22 note-issuing (trading) banks failed in the early months of 1893 and tens of thousands of depositors were unable to obtain their money for years.[112] Falling wages and cutbacks in consumer and government spending hit Melbourne's economy hard. No other Australian capital city was as badly affected by the Depression of the 1890s, and during that decade its population increased by only 5,000. An estimated 28 per cent of Victoria's trade unionists were out of work by the end of 1893 and much of the burden of dealing with distress fell on institutional and informal charities.[113] The 1890s Depression was more prolonged than that of the 1930s, and the index of real GDP fell further from its peak.[114]

The economy began to show signs of recovery after 1895. People from Victoria and South Australia flocked to the mines in Kalgoorlie, which would yield more gold than Bendigo and Ballarat did in the 1850s.[115] World demand for primary products increased and the development of new technology improved productivity in wheat growing. A revival in wool production and exports of meat and butter improved the balance of payments position. During the boom industrialists faced high labour and capital costs due to the profitability of the residential and commercial sectors. A reduction in spending on imports during the Depression provided new opportunities for local manufacturers of consumer goods such as woollen products and boots and shoes.[116]

These changes suggested new possibilities for future growth that would involve more than the application of capital and labour to resource extraction.

462–500; Ian W. McLean, 'Recovery from Depression: Australia in an Argentine Mirror 1895–1913', *Australian Economic History Review*, 46, 3 (2006): 215–41.

111 David Pope, *Bank Deregulation Yesterday and Today: Lessons of History* (Canberra: Department of Economic History, ANU, 1991), p. 156.

112 D.T. Merrett, 'Australian Banking Practice and the Crisis of 1893', *Australian Economic History Review*, 29, 1 (1989): 61.

113 P.G. McCarthy, 'Labor and the Living Wage, 1890–1910', *Australian Journal of Politics & History*, 13, 1 (1967): 83; John Murphy, *A Decent Provision: Australian Welfare Policy, 1870 to 1949* (Farnham: Ashgate, 2011), pp. 29–53.

114 Kent, 'Two Depressions', p. 129.

115 Geoffrey Blainey, *The Golden Mile* (Sydney: Allen & Unwin, 1993), p. 35.

116 W.A. Sinclair, *Economic Recovery in Victoria 1894–1899* (Canberra: ANU Social Science Monograph no. 8, 1956), pp. 84–103.

In the colonial era the transfer of British law, institutions and skills helped Australians to adapt to a new environment and develop a high-productivity export trade in primary products. Australia's relatively high incomes were derived from resources that could be exploited cheaply and were abundant in relation to the supply of labour. In urban areas, the supply of labour grew more slowly than the demand for labour and the inflow of capital, which created high effective demand for housing. Diminishing returns to pastoral land use and investment in city building reduced the competition for other forms of rural and urban production. Australia's growth rates were checked by drought from 1895 to 1903 and remained lower than those of Canada and Argentina.[117] The income advantage that Australia enjoyed over Britain and the United States had all but vanished by World War I.[118]

---

117 McLean, 'Recovery from Depression'.
118 Jeffrey G. Williamson, 'The Evolution of Global Labor Markets Since 1830: Background Evidence and Hypotheses', *Explorations in Economic History*, 32, 2 (1995): 141–96; Ian W. McLean and Jonathan J. Pincus, 'Did Australian Living Standards Stagnate Between 1890 and 1940?' *Journal of Economic History*, 43, 1 (1983): 193–202.

14

Indigenous and settler relations

TRACEY BANIVANUA MAR AND PENELOPE EDMONDS

At the close of the eighteenth century, contact between Aboriginal people and Europeans was localised along coastal regions of the continent. Penal settlements at Port Jackson and in Van Diemen's Land sat at the edge of vast Aboriginal worlds. The crown's Instructions to Governor Phillip were to 'endeavour by every possible means to open an Intercourse with the Natives and to conciliate their affections', 'to live in amity and kindness with them', and to 'punish' those who would 'wantonly destroy them'.[1] But small British military garrisons and coastal settlements were unstable contact zones in which rituals of diplomacy could mix easily with aggression.[2] Contact, conciliation and conflict would always be closely intertwined.

Newcomers often depended on Indigenous knowledge for their survival. Acts of curiosity, accord and handshakes could be performed by British and Aboriginal people and then followed swiftly by ritualised acts of judicial violence: a highly choreographed British hanging, for example, or a closely sequenced Aboriginal spearing. In the early years, when debates over the reach of British sovereignty were in flux, the British responded to conflict with Aboriginal people in localised and disparate ways, and it was nearly half a century before the authority claimed by the British crown was settled legal doctrine.

Aboriginal people experienced the arrival of British colonists as an invasion. First contact was accompanied by the transmission of new diseases, which travelled ahead of the physical frontier along Indigenous trading and cultural networks. In 1789 smallpox devastated Aboriginal populations in the Port Jackson, Botany Bay and Broken Bay regions. Some scholars estimate that up to 80 per cent of the population died in the Sydney region, causing

---

1 Governor Phillip's Instructions, 25 April 1778, *Historical Records of Australia [HRA]*, series 1, vol. 1, pp. 13, 14.
2 Tiffany Shellam, *Shaking Hands on the Fringe: Negotiating the Aboriginal World at King George's Sound* (Perth: UWA Press, 2009), p. 71.

massive social and cultural disruption. Smallpox spread inland and later moved along river systems, decimating networks of people on the Murray and Darling rivers.[3] Likewise, tuberculosis, measles and influenza-like diseases were fatal in these early years when Aboriginal people had little or no immunity. Moreover, as the Port Jackson settlement became established, vegetation and native animals were depleted, depriving Aboriginal people of food, leading to intense, often violent, competition for resources. Increased reports of starving Aboriginal people would be repeated around the coastal fringes of the continent, and later the interior as frontiers of settlement and occupation moved from the south-east of the continent to Western Australia and Queensland, and then later to the northern reaches of Australia.[4]

Until the mid-1790s the presence of Aboriginal people in Sydney's streets was commonplace, creating an urban frontier. On the outer pastoral frontier a brutal war raged between settlers and Aborigines. The Eora lands of the Sydney region were bounded by those of the Kuringai people to the north, the Darug to the west, and the Dharawal and Gandangara to the south. Settlers rapidly pushed into these areas, known to them as the Cumberland Plain, in pursuit of fertile farmlands along the Parramatta and Hawkesbury rivers. The latter was rich Darug land and became the site of a war of occupation that lasted until the early 1800s. Convict settlers on new farms prevented Darug people from harvesting native yams that were crucial to the Indigenous economy. Some also kidnapped Darug children to work as forced labourers.[5] Aboriginal resistance was widespread, farms were raided and sheep and cattle were killed. The impact of Darug attacks was so intense that in May 1795 officials feared settlement of the Hawkesbury would be abandoned. A military detachment was deployed, with orders

---

3 For various perspectives on the origins of smallpox, see Judy Campbell, *Invisible Invaders: Smallpox and Other Diseases in Aboriginal Australia 1780–1880* (Melbourne University Press, 2002); N.G Butlin, *Our Original Aggression: Aboriginal Populations of Southeastern Australia, 1788–1850* (Sydney: George Allen & Unwin, 1983). See also Craig Mear, 'The Origin of the Smallpox Outbreak in Sydney in 1789', *Journal of the Royal Australian Historical Society*, 94, 1 (2008): 1–22; Christopher Warren, 'Could First Fleet Smallpox Infect Aborigines? A Note', *Aboriginal History*, 31 (2007): 152–64.

4 Heather Goodall, *Invasion to Embassy: Land in Aboriginal Politics in New South Wales, 1770–1992* (University of Sydney Press, 2008). Debates over the magnitude and nature of frontier violence became a key area of contention in Australia's 'history wars'. See Robert Manne (ed.), *Whitewash: On Keith Windschuttle's Fabrication of Aboriginal History* (Melbourne: Black Inc., 2003); Stuart Macintyre and Anna Clark, *The History Wars* (Melbourne University Press, 2003); Bain Attwood and S.G. Foster (eds), *Frontier Conflict: The Australian Experience* (Canberra: National Museum of Australia, 2003).

5 Goodall, *Invasion to Embassy*, p. 30.

from Lieutenant-Governor William Paterson to shoot any Darug people on sight and hang the bodies from gibbets as a warning to others. European expansion in this early period remained precarious but colonists' determination and further Aboriginal resistance led by the warrior Pemulwuy caused officials to place a military garrison on the Hawkesbury River, second in size only to Sydney.[6]

The major achievements of Governor Macquarie's period of administration (1809–22) are usually seen to be civic and infrastructure development. He also pioneered strategic manoeuvres to 'pacify' and govern Aboriginal peoples. In 1814 he established the experimental 'Native Institution' at Parramatta to 'effect the civilization of the Aborigines' and train children as farmers and labourers, a village at Elizabeth Bay for the 'Sydney tribe', and an Aboriginal farm at George's Head, Sydney.[7] Although Macquarie sought good relations, a series of fatal conflicts between Aboriginal people and settlers in the Appin area south of Sydney strained his commitment. Macquarie counselled conciliation and forbearance to settlers, stating he would punish further aggression against Aboriginal people.[8] Yet conciliation and violence went hand-in-hand in linked acts of aggression and retribution. Macquarie announced in April 1816 that 'unwillingly' he had come to the 'painful resolution of chastening these hostile tribes...to inflict terrible and exemplary punishment upon them'.[9] He ordered three military detachments into Dharawal lands, with instructions to hang 'guilty' Aboriginal people in the trees 'to strike the great terror into the survivors'. At least sixteen Dharawal people were subsequently killed by the military.[10]

In 1816 Macquarie issued a Proclamation that sought to reclaim Aboriginal people 'from their barbarous practices and to conciliate them to the British government', proscribed Aboriginal entry to towns and initiated a pass system.[11] No more than six Aboriginal people could gather near farms of the interior, and settlers were permitted to drive them away by force. Conversely, Aboriginal people who desired the protection of the British crown were issued 'passports or certificates signed by the governor' and would be protected from 'injury or molestation' if they conducted themselves peaceably

6 John Connor, *The Australian Frontier Wars, 1788–1838* (Sydney: UNSW Press, 2002), pp. 38, 39.
7 Governor Macquarie to Earl Bathurst, Despatch no. 15, 1814, *HRA*, series I, vol. 8, pp. 367–73.
8 M.H. Ellis, *Lachlan Macquarie: His Life, Adventures and Times* [1965] 4th edn (Sydney: Angus & Robertson, 2010), p. 355.
9 Quoted in ibid., p. 353.
10 Quoted in Goodall, *Invasion to Embassy*, pp. 31, 32.
11 Quoted in Ellis, *Lachlan Macquarie*, p. 356.

and were unarmed.[12] This Proclamation was among the first formal attempts to impose a spatial segregation between Aboriginal people and settlers.

Macquarie sought to forge political alliances with preferred Aboriginal groups, a strategy used by the British and French in North America. On 28 December 1816, six months after the military's retaliatory violence in the Appin area, he held a 'Native Feast' in Parramatta for people from the wider region. At this strategic gathering the governor bestowed 'badges of distinction' on a select group of men to designate them as 'chiefs', partly to pacify them in the wake of the Appin massacre, and partly to create an Indigenous hierarchy to facilitate governance and improve relations.[13]

By 1820 such conciliatory efforts were in decline. The Native Institution had failed, Aboriginal people had abandoned their farms, and conflict had resumed as settlement expanded into inland New South Wales.[14] Settlers crossed the Blue Mountains onto the Bathurst Plains and faced resistance from Wiradjuri warriors, who killed or wounded both stock and their keepers. Governor Thomas Brisbane (1822–25) proclaimed martial law on the Bathurst Plains on 14 August 1824, following the killing of seven stockmen by Aboriginal people in the ranges north of Bathurst, and the murder of Aboriginal women and children by settler-vigilantes, in what the *Sydney Gazette* on 14 October 1824 called 'an exterminating war'.[15] Brisbane also established a mounted police force whose first frontier deployment to 'pacify' Aboriginal people was in the upper Hunter Valley in 1826.[16] Despite extenuating claims that the frontier was a place of lawlessness, Julie Evans has argued that the declaration of martial law served to formalise the frontier as a legal space of violence and was thereby crucial to advance the settler project.[17]

Some scholars have argued that Brisbane's policy towards Aboriginal people was ambivalent, on the one hand imposing martial law and on the other seeking to compensate them for lost land. Exemplary was a grant to the London Missionary Society of 10,000 acres (4,047 hectares) for an Aboriginal reserve at Lake Macquarie in 1825.[18] Rather, this policy reflected the growing

---

12 Ibid., p. 356.
13 R.H.W. Reece, 'Feasts and Blankets: The History of Some Early Attempts to Establish Relations with the Aborigines of New South Wales, 1814–1846', *Archaeology & Physical Anthropology in Oceania*, 22, 3 (1967): 190–206.
14 'Lachlan Macquarie', *Australian Dictionary of Biography*, vol. 2, pp. 185–7.
15 See Henry Reynolds, *Frontier: Aborigines, Settlers and Land* [1987] (Sydney: Allen & Unwin, 1996), pp. 4, 5.
16 Connor, *The Australian Frontier Wars*, pp. 63, 64.
17 Julie Evans, 'Where Lawlessness is Law: The Settler-Colonial Frontier as a Legal Space of Violence', *Australian Feminist Law Journal*, 30 (2009): 3, 22.
18 'Sir Thomas Makdougall Brisbane', *Australian Dictionary of Biography*, vol. 1, pp. 151–5.

tensions of colonisation as retaliatory and offensive violence sat alongside an emergent humanitarianism that sought to compensate and protect Aboriginal people.

Violence and conciliation in Van Diemen's Land

In the earliest years of the penal settlement of Van Diemen's Land an uneasy coexistence endured between Aboriginal people and convicts, alongside sporadic moments of violence. Convict hunters seeking supplies such as kangaroo meat for an at-times starving settler population gained access to Aboriginal hunting grounds and for almost two decades engaged in a relatively peaceful shared land use.[19] By the late 1820s, however, with the encroachment of an aggressive new pastoral economy, free settlers began an extensive land-grab that escalated tensions with Aboriginal people dramatically. As competition for food increased, and with the abuse and kidnapping of Aboriginal women and children, people resisted settler incursion with widespread guerrilla raids on shepherds' huts and farms. Settlers retaliated violently, often with night attacks on Aboriginal camps.[20]

On 15 April 1828 Lieutenant-Governor George Arthur issued a Proclamation dividing the island into settled and unsettled districts, and forbade Aboriginal entry into settled areas without a pass granted by the governor. Like his counterparts on the mainland, Arthur used partition to protect settlers and 'bring about a temporary separation of the coloured from the British population' to avert conflict.[21] On 1 November 1828, amidst growing frontier violence, Arthur declared martial law against the 'Black or Aboriginal natives' within the settled districts of the Island, established military 'roving parties' to search out Aboriginal people in the settled districts, and encouraged civilian parties to capture them. This extended conflict between 1824 and 1834 was known as the Black War.[22]

19 Marie Fels, 'Culture Contact in the County of Buckinghamshire, Van Diemen's Land, 1803–11', *Tasmanian Historical Research Association Papers and Proceedings*, 29, 2 (1982): 47–69; James Boyce, *Van Diemen's Land* (Melbourne: Black Inc., 2008), pp. 66–8.

20 Lyndall Ryan, *Tasmanian Aborigines: A History Since 1803* (Sydney: Allen & Unwin, 2012), pp. 87–105; Henry Reynolds, *Fate Of A Free People*, new edn (Melbourne: Penguin, 2004).

21 'Proclamation, 15th April 1828, By His Excellency Colonial George Arthur, Lieutenant Governor of the Island of Van Diemen's Land and Its Dependencies', *House of Commons Papers*, 1831, vol. 19, pp. 22–4; Ryan, *Tasmanian Aborigines*, p. 101.

22 'Governor's Proclamation, 1 Nov. 1828', *British Parliamentary Papers, Colonies, Australia* (Shannon: Irish University Press, 1970), pp. 4, 184, 192.

On initial contact in 1803 there were 6–8,000 Aboriginal people living in Van Diemen's Land, but by 1838 only around 60 survived and they were sequestered on the northerly Flinders Island in Bass Strait.[23] Governor Arthur, a Calvinist Evangelical, had attempted a range of conciliation strategies but did not stop short of kidnapping to effect communication. When Umarrah, the leader of the North Midlands nation, was captured, the event was celebrated in the settler press. 'White people had been murdered', Umarrah told his captors, because they had driven his people from their kangaroo hunting grounds. His 'determined purpose' was to destroy as many white people as he could, which he 'considers his patriotic duty'.[24] Arthur detained the Aboriginal leader for more than a year and later attempted to persuade him to convince his people of the government's good intentions. Refusing, Umarrah escaped at the first opportunity.[25] In a further effort, Arthur arranged in 1829 for a series of illustrative boards depicting apparently equal justice under the British crown for Aboriginal people and Europeans. With the central image of a handshake between a British governor and an Indigenous chief, the boards were intended to serve as instruments of diplomacy. Yet the humanitarian precepts expressed on the boards, such as the brotherhood of man, and Indigenous transformation to civilisation, were integral to the aggressive expansion of Britain's settler empire. Throughout the Australian colonies calls for conciliation came most often at times of severe violence. Indeed, the so-called 'conciliation' boards were made between two declarations of martial law. In 1830 Arthur appointed George Augustus Robinson to the post of 'Protector of Aborigines' in a further attempt to communicate and convey his conciliatory intentions.[26] A religious man who believed that conciliation was possible, Robinson carried the boards with him on his 'friendly mission' in six extensive journeys across Van Diemen's Land to contact groups in the interior.

On 11 February 1830, Arthur offered a reward of £5 for every adult Aboriginal person and £2 for every child captured and delivered alive to police. This strategy revealed his strained position whereby Aboriginal people

23 Ryan, *Tasmanian Aborigines*, p. 14; N.J.B. Plomley, *The Aboriginal/Settler Clash in Van Diemen's Land, 1803–1831* (Hobart: Queen Victoria Museum and Art Gallery, 1992), p. 10.
24 Quoted in Ryan, *Tasmanian Aborigines*, p. 107.
25 'Eumarrah', *Australian Dictionary of Biography*, Supplementary Volume, pp. 117–18.
26 N.J.B. Plomley (ed.), *Friendly Mission: The Tasmanian Journals and Papers of George Augustus Robinson, 1829–1834* (Hobart: Tasmanian Historical Research Association, 1966); Penelope Edmonds, '"Failing in every endeavour to conciliate": Governor Arthur's Proclamation Boards to the Aborigines: Australian Conciliation Narratives and their Transnational Connections', *Journal of Australian Studies*, 35, 2 (2011): 214.

were apparently to be protected, but temporarily were placed outside any protection offered by the King's Peace under martial law. By October 1830 Arthur had lost faith in the possibility of conciliation and extended martial law to the whole island to enable an 'active and extended system of military operations against the natives'.[27] Such was the tension that Arthur called for civilian volunteers to join a combined civil and military force; the aim was to remove all Aboriginal people from settled districts. This military-style operation, the 'Black Line', was conducted from 7 October to 24 November 1830, and sought to capture or force Aboriginal people into the Forestier and Tasman Peninsulas. The settler community responded enthusiastically and a force of around 2,200 men, including armed convicts, was assembled; only 550 were troops. Arthur later reported that 'all classes of the Community had manifested the greatest alacrity and zeal in seconding the measures of the Government'.[28]

The 'Black Line' captured only a few Aboriginal people. While many historians regard the operation as a failure, it drove numerous Aboriginal groups into the north-east, and settlers celebrated its success. Subsequent efforts at conciliation were left to Robinson and his 'friendly mission'. The so-called conciliation of the 'Big River tribe' has been described as an Aboriginal 'surrender' into government protection; it was the final chapter in Robinson's mission and the end of the Black War, at least in the minds of settlers. Mannalargenna, Aboriginal leader of the Oyster Bay people, negotiated a verbal covenant with Arthur that the government would ensure their future welfare, including the possibility that they could stay in their own country. Although these agreements were later dishonoured, the historian Henry Reynolds rightly credits these Aboriginal leaders with a key role in negotiating the end of the Black War.[29] After the peak of violence in Van Diemen's Land, Arthur lamented that it 'was a fatal error...that a treaty was not entered into' and the results of such devastation and loss of Aboriginal life 'must ever remain a stain upon the colonisation of Van Diemen's Land'.[30]

Over the course of his 'friendly mission' Robinson travelled with an Aboriginal group, which, seeking to save their people, aided him in

---

27 John Connor, 'British Frontier Warfare Logistics and the "Black Line", Van Diemen's Land (Tasmania), 1830', *War in History*, 9, 2 (2002): 142–57, 153.
28 George Arthur despatch to Murray, 20 November 1830, *HRA*, Series III, vol 9, p. 590.
29 Reynolds, *Fate of A Free People*, p. xxii.
30 George Arthur to Secretary Hay, September 1832, Tasmanian Archive and Heritage Office, CO280/35.

persuading many small groups to relocate to the Flinders Island mission of Wybalenna in the Bass Strait. The intention was that they would be converted to Christianity and taught to be farmers. Truganini, a Nuenonne woman from Bruny Island, accompanied Robinson on all his missions between 1830 and 1834. She was an astute negotiator whose political acuity enabled Robinson's safe movement through various Aboriginal territories, and at one point saved his life. By 1834 there were 134 Aboriginal people at Wybalenna, but by late 1847 many of this virtually captive group had died. A mere 47 people were moved in that year to the Aboriginal settlement at Oyster Cove. Truganini, one of the last so-called 'full blood' people at Oyster Cove, later moved to Hobart to live with a guardian family. Towards the end of her life she greatly feared she would be 'cut up' after her death in the name of racial science, as had the Aboriginal man William Lanney. Telling the Rev. H.D. Atkinson, 'I know that when I die the Museum wants my body', she pleaded that she be buried in the 'deepest part of the D'Entrecasteaux channel'.[31] After she died in 1876 she was buried, but her body was exhumed two years later by the Royal Society of Tasmania.[32] Truganini's body was prized in a climate of aggressive collection of Indigenous human remains the world over, and as part of the particular scramble for Tasmanian Aboriginal remains. She endured as a putative symbol of an 'extinct race', with her skeletal remains exhibited in the Tasmanian Museum in Hobart from 1904 to 1947. By the late twentieth century descendants of Tasmanian Aboriginal women such as Fanny Cochrane Smith and Bass 'Straits people' descended from Dolly Dalrymple, scattered across northern Tasmania, were living proof that such powerful extinction narratives were entirely mistaken.[33]

New frontiers

The 1830s marked a period of intense land rushes in eastern Australia. Mounted police and military detachments were engaged increasingly across New South Wales in the 'pacification' of Aboriginal people as they resisted settler incursion and competed with settlers for territory and food.

---

31 Quoted in Ryan, *Tasmanian Aborigines*, p. 269; 'Trugernanner (Truganini) (1812–1876)', *Australian Dictionary of Biography*, vol. 6, p. 305.
32 Ryan, *Tasmanian Aborigines*, p. 270.
33 Ibid., p. xviii.

In northern New South Wales the conflict radiated from the penal colony at Moreton Bay, the site of modern-day Brisbane. In the Swan River colony, established in 1829, a similar pattern of conflict emerged. Noongar people pushed from their lands were starving and began taking stock and raiding farms. After several years of conflict, the Western Australian governor, James Stirling, established a mounted police force, and in October 1834 led a detachment of 25, including two surveyors, on an expedition south of Fremantle to open up further land at the Murray River. This resulted in conflict with a group of Pinjarup people south-east of Perth, known as the Battle of Pinjarra or the Pinjarra Massacre. One white man and between 20 and 25 Aboriginal people were killed, including three women and a child.[34]

The land hunger that drew settlers and Indigenous people into such conflict continued in New South Wales, leading to two particularly violent inland incidents in 1838. A five-week pursuit and then massacre of the Kamilaroi people at Waterloo Creek, led by Major James Nunn, resulted in what most historians agree was 40 to 50 Aboriginal deaths.[35] At Myall Creek, stockmen and convict-shepherds, goaded by sheep and cattle spearings, killed and burned the bodies of at least 22 Aboriginal men, women, and children. Governor Gipps, an Evangelical humanitarian, ordered an investigation and tried eleven of the offenders for murder. They were speedily acquitted and Gipps ordered a retrial, which found seven defendants guilty. Despite public outcry, the seven were hanged in December 1838 in one of the rare instances when white men were tried, convicted and executed for the mass killing of Aboriginal people.[36] The hangings enraged many settlers: such frontier violence, with and without government sanction, had been so common it was barely regarded a crime.

The 1838 trials highlighted the opposing forces that would govern race relations in the Australian colonies for the remainder of the nineteenth century. While humanitarians emphasised the moral imperatives of a humane colonisation, pastoralists and agriculturalists insisted on having access to cheap labour and land. By the 1830s humanitarian precepts had gained influence throughout the British colonies. After ending the slave trade in 1833, abolitionists turned their attention to the welfare of indigenous peoples, particularly in the Cape Colony, the Australian colonies and

---

34 See Pamela Statham, 'James Stirling and Pinjarra: A Battle in More Ways than One', *Studies in Western Australian History*, 23 (2003): 167–94.

35 Lyndall Ryan, 'Waterloo Creek, Northern New South Wales, 1838', in Attwood and Foster (eds), *Frontier Conflict*, pp. 33–43.

36 'Sir George Gipps', *Australian Dictionary of Biography*, vol. 1, pp. 446–53.

the Pacific, and established the Aborigines Protection Society in 1837. In both metropolitan and colonial governing circles, humanitarians did not generally oppose colonisation, but increasingly promoted a benevolent or 'Christian colonisation', a civilising mission of moral enlightenment.[37] This was challenged in the Australian colonies by an emerging assertion of settler' rights and entitlements. A strong doctrine of supercessionism – that settlers should rightly replace Indigenous people – was promoted, based on claims of British moral and racial superiority, and Lockean principles of civilisation, property and the imperative to cultivate land. As the settler John Cotton wrote from Sydney in the 1840s, 'the worthless idle Aborigine has then been driven back from the land that he knew not how to make use of, and valued not, to make room for a more noble race of beings who are capable of estimating the value of this fine country. Is it not right that it should be so?'[38]

In 1837 a Select Committee of the British Parliament investigated the condition of the indigenous populations of British colonies.[39] Directed by the abolitionist Thomas Fowell Buxton, the inquiry and its report reflected the views of his Evangelical abolitionist circle. Seeking to draw attention to the grim realities of Britain's expansion, their report painted the far reaches of Britain's Empire as 'dark places of the earth, full of the habitations of cruelty'. The extreme settler violence caused many reformers to seek a Christian transformation of settlers and Indigenous people alike.[40] Recommendations included the reservation of lands to allow Aboriginal people to continue to hunt until persuaded to till the soil; education of their children; increased funds for missionaries and protectors; and, if necessary, the prosecution of violent settlers. The Report's recommendations did not end the abuses that its broad investigation revealed, and over the following century many recommendations were largely ignored. The Select Committee did, however, influence the establishment of experimental protectorates in the Australian colonies.

37 Elizabeth Elbourne, 'The Sin of the Settler: The 1835–36 Select Committee on Aborigines and Debates Over Virtue and Conquest in the Early Nineteenth-Century British White Settler Empire', *Journal of Colonialism and Colonial History*, 4, 3, (2003): 1–46; Hilary M. Carey, *God's Empire: Religion and Colonialism in the British World, c. 1801–1908* (Cambridge University Press, 2011), p. 321.

38 John Cotton, in George Mackaness (ed.), *The Correspondence of John Cotton, Victorian Pioneer, 1842–1849*, part 3 (Dubbo: Review Publications, 1978), p. 9.

39 *Report of the Parliamentary Select Committee on the Aboriginal Tribes (British Settlements), Reprinted with Comments by the Aborigines Protection Society* (London: William Ball, 1837).

40 Ibid., preface; Elbourne, 'The Sin of the Settler', p. 4.

The rise of 'protection' policy and racial governance

The rise of British humanitarianism in the 1830s coincided with the rapid expansion of settlement in the Australian colonies. The Port Phillip Protectorate, established in 1839 following the colonial settlement of that district, experimented with the 1837 Select Committee's recommendations. The 'conciliator', George Augustus Robinson, was appointed Chief Protector of Aborigines, and with four assistants was to promote Aboriginal people's wellbeing and represent their interests to the colonial executive and British government. They were also to civilise, convert and instruct Aborigines in European agriculture and house construction.[41] As would be the case elsewhere, these protection strategies were eventually harnessed to colonial efforts that disenfranchised and dispossessed Indigenous people.

In South Australia settlement had proceeded through the private South Australian Colonisation Association, an organisation modelled on Edward Gibbon Wakefield's doctrine of 'systematic colonisation' to promote productive enterprise while converting British paupers and indigenous people into compliant colonial labourers and farmers.[42] It had a range of enthusiastic supporters, including the liberal John Stuart Mill, a proponent of empire who argued that unlike previous colonial projects, South Australia 'will be a civilised country from the very commencement'.[43] From 1836 the Association used humanitarian claims to promote its endeavour, asserting that 'far from being an invasion of the rights of Aborigines', South Australia would be settled by 'industrious and virtuous settlers' who would protect Aboriginal people from 'pirates, squatters and runaway convicts'.[44] The governor's Proclamation to inaugurate the new colony also stated that the same protections enjoyed by settlers would be given to Aboriginal people.

From the 1830s a system of conciliatory 'native feasts' and distribution of rations, modelled on Macquarie's efforts in New South Wales, was established as part of the South Australian humanitarian experiment. The provision of food was seen as an important 'protective' measure, and one

41 M.F. Christie, *Aborigines in Colonial Victoria, 1835–86* (Sydney University Press, 1979), pp. 87, 89.

42 Jan Kociumbus, *The Oxford History of Australia. Volume 2, 1770–1860: Possessions* (Oxford University Press, 1986), p. 180.

43 Quoted in Katherine Smits, 'John Stuart Mill on the Antipodes: Settler Violence Against Indigenous Peoples and the Legitimacy of Colonial Rule', *Australian Journal of Politics and History*, 54, 1 (2008): 1.

44 Robert Foster, Rick Hosking and Amanda Nettelbeck, *Fatal Collisions: The South Australian Frontier and the Violence of Memory* (Adelaide: Wakefield Press, 2001), pp. 2, 3.

destined to instil dependence amongst Aboriginal people. By the 1840s these distributions were replaced with policed ration depots on the frontier as competition for land and resources peaked and Indigenous people prevented overlanders from New South Wales from bringing stock along the Murray into the colony. Resistance elsewhere drove a third of the settlers in Port Lincoln away, leaving what the Government Resident described as a 'melancholy and convincing proof of [Aboriginal] hostility and success'.[45] In response, government ration depots came to be staffed by a protector and magistrate, with armed police. Under these arrangements, conciliation frequently gave way to violence as the ration system became critical to managing frontier conflict, bringing Aboriginal people into regular contact with police, and imposing discipline on resistant groups. By the 1850s the rations system had been transformed. No longer a means of offering conciliation, protection or compensation, it had become a frontier weapon capable of instilling dependence and imposing discipline on Aboriginal recipients. Self government later in the decade ensured that settler interests continued to prevail.[46] The office of the Protector, established in 1836, was abolished in 1856 and by 1860 the majority of reserves set aside for Indigenous people's use were leased to settlers.

The appropriation of protection strategies to serve the interests of settlers in South Australia was indicative of the wider changes that accompanied the advent of responsible government. In New South Wales and Moreton Bay, the few privately run missions were either closed or eclipsed by widespread violence. Australian humanitarian sentiment had become laced with the pessimistic conviction that Aboriginal people were a race doomed to extinction.[47]

In the Port Phillip District the experimental protectorate had lasted only to 1849. Aboriginal groups disrupted stock routes and speared stock, making surprise attacks on shepherds' huts and squatters' homes, and targeting those known to have abused Aboriginal women.[48] In turn, as assistant protector William Thomas recounted, settlers 'openly avowed their willingness to

---

45 Government Resident in Port Lincoln, quoted in Robert Foster, 'Feasts of the Full-Moon: The Distribution of Rations to Aborigines in South Australia: 1836–1861', *Aboriginal History*, 13 (1989): 68.

46 Peggy Brock, 'South Australia', in Ann McGrath (ed.), *Contested Ground: Australian Aborigines under the British Crown* (Sydney: Allen & Unwin, 1995), pp. 208–22.

47 Jessie Mitchell, *In Good Faith? Governing Indigenous Australia through God, Charity and Empire* (Canberra: ANU E Press, 2011), p. 14.

48 Lyndall Ryan, 'Settler Massacres on the Port Phillip Frontier, 1836–1851', *Journal of Australian Studies*, 34, 3 (2010): 257–73.

destroy [the Aborigines]'.[49] European reprisals were often swift and vicious, yet after the Myall Creek judgment, they became more covert, and protectors remained powerless to effect substantial change beyond the distribution of rations. By the end of the protectorate experiment, humanitarian motives were largely subordinated to settler interests. In Melbourne, for example, the distribution of rations to displaced and destitute Indigenous people merged with efforts to 'prevent them coming into Melbourne and interfering with the white population'.[50]

From 1835 the Indigenous population in the Port Phillip District plummeted by around 80 per cent within a generation. While millions of sheep had already destroyed food sources and fouled water supplies, the advent of gold seekers in the 1850s further transformed Victoria, pushing more Indigenous people off their lands.[51] As trespassers in their own country, Indigenous Victorians survived on station work, seasonal harvesting and occasional rations. They developed effective strategies of accommodation by incorporating new languages, methods of gathering food and resources, and developing new forms of protest. In 1840 the Wauthawurrung people from near Geelong asked the missionary Francis Tuckfield for land of their own, and from 1843 the Woiwurrung clan near Melbourne repeatedly called on assistant protector William Thomas for 'land in our own country'.[52] By 1847 they also sought new alliances with the previously hostile Kurnai of Gippsland.[53] These early political networks and demands for land as both refuge and compensation would develop into cultures of protest and a 'powerful narrative of entitlement'; it would also bring Indigenous people and their supporters into political engagement with colonial governments.[54]

In 1858 the newly self-governing colony of Victoria established a parliamentary committee to inquire into Aboriginal living conditions. Capitulating to Aboriginal requests, it recommended the reservation of pockets of land

49 William Thomas Journal, Aboriginal Protector, 26 April 1839, Mitchell Library MSS214/1, frames 44–46, *The Thomas Papers in the Mitchell Library A Comprehensive Index* (Melbourne: Monash University Centre for Indigenous Studies, 2004), 14.

50 *Victorian Parliamentary Debates*, vol. 3, p. 110 (6 October 1858).

51 George Augustus Robinson (1845), quoted in Richard Broome, 'Changing Aboriginal Landscapes of Pastoral Victoria, 1830–1850', *Studies in the History of Gardens & Designed Landscapes*, 31, 2 (2011): 91.

52 Ann Curthoys and Jessie Mitchell, '"Bring this Paper to the Good Governor": Aboriginal Petitioning in Britain's Australian Colonies', in Saliha Belmessous (ed.), *Native Claims: Indigenous Law Against Empire, 1500–1920* (Oxford University Press, 2012), p. 188.

53 R.E. Barwick and Diane E. Barwick, 'A Memorial for Thomas Bungaleen, 1847–1865', *Aboriginal History*, 8, 1 (1984): 9.

54 Curthoys and Mitchell, 'Bring this Paper to the Good Governor', p. 190.

where government-funded supply depots would distribute rations.[55] The government received the recommendations favourably, spurred on by a Woiwurrung deputation led by Simon Wonga requesting 'a block of land in their own country'.[56] After attempting to settle at several small stations, the Woiwurrung subsequently squatted at a traditional site (near Healesville, north-east of Melbourne) they named 'Coranderrk'. This was gazetted as a reserve and by 1863 five reserves, also known as stations and missions, and 23 camping places and ration depots had also been established around Victoria.[57] While these reserves eventually became sites of confinement, many Indigenous people saw and treated them as compensatory land and a critical means of continuity and survival.

Not all Victorian reserves were the product of Indigenous people's insistence, and by 1869 only one in four Aboriginal people lived on them permanently.[58] Seeking legal authority to compel individuals to stay on reserves, the Victorian government passed the *Act to Provide for the Protection and Management of the Aboriginal Natives of Victoria* of 1869. This created the Board for the Protection of Aborigines (BPA) with executive power to determine the identity of Aboriginal people, their place of residence, the terms on which they could be employed, the distribution and protection of earnings, and the loosely defined 'care, custody and education' of Aboriginal children. Under section 5, all rations, including blankets, bedding and clothing, were 'on loan only and...the property of Her Majesty', and Aboriginal recipients were not free to sell or dispose of them. Like the ration system, protection legislation produced dependency.

Control over residence was a key means of limiting the Aboriginal political activity that intensified in Victoria after 1869. The BPA's attempt to manage Louisa Briggs is exemplary. From 1836 Briggs spent her childhood in the Bass Strait with her mother, a Woiwurrung woman taken by sealers. When she was seventeen Louisa joined the gold rush and worked on stations in western Victoria until work ran out. Unemployed and destitute in 1871, Louisa and her husband, John Briggs, went to Coranderrk station but her family was later expelled because John refused to get BPA permission before undertaking paid work. They were allowed to return in 1876 when Louisa, by then a nurse and matron, became an outspoken advocate for Coranderrk residents as they

---

55 'Report of the Select Committee of the Legislative Council on the Aborigines, 1858–9', *Victorian Parliamentary Papers*, 1858–9, vol. 1, no. 8.
56 Diane E. Barwick, *Rebellion at Coranderrk* (Canberra: Aboriginal History Inc., 1998), p. 40.
57 Broome, *Aboriginal Victorians*, p. 126.
58 Ibid., p. 86.

fought the BPA's replacement of a popular station manager and attempts to sell the station. The protests have become known as the Coranderrk rebellion, and the outspoken Louisa gave crucial evidence at the resulting inquiry. Widowed in 1878, she was ordered off Coranderrk by the BPA in the same year following her further political agitation, but returned in 1882 to rejoin her political and cultural community.[59]

Aboriginal residents' dissatisfaction with the management of reserves and stations was widespread, and mobile individuals such as Briggs were important political agitators who connected stations all over Victoria.[60] In 1886 the Victorian government amended the *Protection Act* to strengthen the powers to remove younger activists from stations.[61] Dubbed the 'Half-Caste Act', it introduced the additional legal category of 'half-caste' for Aboriginal people who, thus identified, were to be prevented from visiting or living on missions and stations. Determined nominally by blood quanta, the new category reflected an intensification of racial biopolitics in Australia and internationally. While the 1886 legislation adopted the terminology of scientific racism, the process of defining who was a 'half-caste' was profoundly unscientific. The category could include all people with 'any mixture of aboriginal blood', and under the age of 34. If so identified, sections of the Act rendered 'half-castes' trespassers on the stations and missions. Compelled to live in settler society unaided and without the benefits that came with being non-Aboriginal, they remained subject to the BPA's care, oversight and management until 1893.

Insistent letters written to the BPA by Aboriginal men and women as parents, children and siblings of expelled people, testify to the lasting impact of the 1886 legislation.[62] In Louisa Briggs' case, she and her children were ordered off Coranderrk in 1886 as 'half castes'. Unable to gain admission to any Victorian reserve, they sought refuge on Maloga mission on the New South Wales side of the Murray River. Briggs repeatedly pleaded with the BPA to allow her access to her community at Coranderrk, but was refused. When 'half-castes' were excluded from Cummeragunga, the new mission

---

59 'Louisa Briggs', *Australian Dictionary of Biography*, Supplementary Volume, pp. 45–6; Diane Barwick, 'This Most Resolute Lady: A Biographical Puzzle', in Diane Barwick et al. (eds), *Metaphors of Interpretation: Essays in Honour of W.E.H. Stanner* (Canberra: ANU Press, 1985), p. 5.

60 Penny van Toorn, 'Hegemony or Hidden Transcripts? Aboriginal Writings from Lake Condah, 1876–1907', *Journal of Australian Studies*, 86 (2006): 15–27.

61 Bain Attwood, *Rights for Aborigines* (Sydney: Allen & Unwin, 2003), p. 28.

62 Patricia Grimshaw et al. (eds), *Letters from Aboriginal Women of Victoria, 1867–1926* (Melbourne: History Department, University of Melbourne, 2002).

near Maloga, in 1895, she and her family camped, destitute, at Barmah on the Victorian side of the river. At the age of 67, Louisa applied again to the BPA for rations, and was refused.

Despite the BPA's erosion of the autonomy of Victorian Aboriginal people, the movement between missions of those it termed 'dangerous wanderers' ensured that Indigenous political, social and cultural networks spread.[63] At the height of the Coranderrk rebellion in 1881, for example, the YortaYorta residents of Maloga mission petitioned the New South Wales government for land. The Coranderrk leader, William Barak, had visited Maloga when the petition was being formulated and one of the signatories, David Berrick, was Barrak's son.[64] Such ventures formed part of what has been described as a nineteenth-century land rights campaign, spanning Victoria and New South Wales from the 1840s. Aboriginal people directly requested grants of land, recruited white supporters to convey their desire for land or reoccupied and squatted on land in their country.[65] The movement appears to have been informed by the traditions established in Victoria, and reached into South Australia and as far north as Queensland, where three Aboriginal men, James Diper, William Watiman Nilepi and Charles Diper Ghepara, petitioned for land that their ancestors had owned from time immemorial.[66]

Unlike the Victorian government's establishment of managed reserves, the New South Wales government briefly pursued an alternative model of granting land requests. Between the 1860s and 1884, 31 Aboriginal reserves were gazetted, and by 1894 a further 85 were granted by the New South Wales Aborigines Protection Board, established in 1883.[67] Many were granted at the request of Aboriginal people or validated Aboriginal re-occupations, and nearly all were unsupervised, leaving Indigenous people to live independently. This supported the high level of autonomy in New South Wales at the time, where over 80 per cent of Aboriginal people lived self-sufficiently from wages, ration labour or traditional subsistence.[68]

63 Van Toorn, 'Hegemony or Hidden Transcripts?', p. 22.
64 Maloga Petition, 5 July 1881, in Bain Attwood and Andrew Markus (eds), *The Struggle for Aboriginal Rights: A Documentary History* (Sydney: Allen & Unwin, 1999), pp. 51–2; Barwick, *Rebellion at Coranderrk*, p. 302.
65 Heather Goodall, '"Land in Our Own Country": The Aboriginal Land Rights Movement in South-Eastern Australia, 1860–1914', *Aboriginal History*, 14, 1 (1990): 1.
66 'The Reverend Duncan McNab and the Aborigines', *Queensland Votes and Proceedings*, 1876, vol. 3, pp. 165, 172; Tracey Banivanua Mar, *Violence and Colonial Dialogue: The Australian-Pacific Indentured Labor Trade* (Honolulu: University of Hawai'i Press, 2007), pp. 82–3; Graham Jenkin, *Conquest of the Ngarrindjeri* (Adelaide: Rigby, 1979), pp. 126–31.
67 Goodall, 'Land in Our Own Country', pp. 8, 12.
68 Ibid., pp. 8–9.

Rather than segregate Aboriginal people on reserves, the approach of the New South Wales government briefly favoured the support of Aboriginal autonomy. By the mid-1880s, however, other Australian colonies had moved, like Victoria, to manage and segregate Aboriginal people. In 1881 South Australia re-appointed a Protector of Aborigines and in Western Australia the *Aborigines Protection Act* of 1886 provided for the distribution of rations, and the removal or imprisonment of Aboriginal people in towns. Governments around Australia organised and separated settler and 'native' spaces in broadly similar ways. But Victoria's 'Half Caste Act' had introduced a new level and kind of racial governance. The introduction of a racial caste that legally diluted Aboriginal identity for administrative purposes reflected a wider settler colonial 'blood logic' whereby Indigenous people's identities were racialised and blood quanta acted as a convenient, though not exclusive, mechanism for control.[69] Over the following century 'Aboriginality' would be defined and managed in 67 different ways in over 700 separate pieces of legislation, diluting or strengthening identity according to the needs and burdens of the state.[70]

The pastoral occupation of the interior, north and west

While Aboriginal people were increasingly concentrated on segregated sites in the southern, more densely occupied regions of Australia, a distinct set of race relations emerged in the sparsely settled grazing country spanning western Queensland and New South Wales, northern South Australia and the north-east and north of Western Australia. Overlanders from Queensland and South Australia only began to occupy central and northern Australia with cattle by the 1880s, and regions such as the Kimberley in Western Australia experienced until at least the 1920s the kind of frontier violence that had occurred earlier in the south.[71] Under such conditions the management of settler and Indigenous relations remained starkly uneven. In New

---

69 J. Kēhalani Kauanui, *Hawaiian Blood: Colonialism and the Politics of Sovereignty and Indigeneity* (Durham: Duke University Press, 2008), p. 4.
70 John McCorquodale, 'The Legal Classification of Race in Australia', *Aboriginal History*, 10, 1 (1986): 7–24.
71 Two of the highest profile twentieth-century massacres are the Forrest River massacre of 1926, and the Coniston Station massacre of 1928. Both were subject to numerous inquiries and publicity. Mary Anne Jebb, *Blood, Sweat and Welfare: A History of White Bosses and Aboriginal Pastoral Workers* (Perth: UWA Press, 2002); Pamela Smith, 'Into the Kimberley: The Invasion of the Sturt Creek Basin (Kimberley Region, Western Australia) and Evidence of Aboriginal Resistance', *Aboriginal History*, 24 (2000): 62–74.

South Wales, for example, while the government granted reserves of land in settled areas to Aboriginal petitioners in the 1880s, the north-west of the colony was still engaged in violent conflict. In these regions, as Aboriginal people integrated pastoral industries into Indigenous economies, and as pastoralists sought to run stations cheaply and efficiently, a delicately balanced interdependence emerged.

Pastoral occupation devastated Indigenous people's food stocks and limited their access to sites of social, legal and cultural importance.[72] This was compounded by impoverishment caused by the confiscation of weapons, tools and other goods following frontier raids. As a rural newspaper in Western Australia reported in 1888, a single punitive raid netted thousands 'of spears, axes, tomahawks…two small boys…a large number of glass and stone spears, beautifully carved spear heads, string made of bark, women's hair and dog's hair; coolamans…and some splendid pearl shells'. About 'two tons' of material was later burned.[73]

Faced with finding new means of survival, Indigenous people incorporated the rations that accompanied occupation into their economies, and attractive and addictive commodities such as tobacco, or *nigi-nigi*, ensured that many Aboriginal people moved closer to, or camped on, stations.[74] These camps became labour pools that incorporated men, women and children into the pastoral economy as shepherds and stockmen, and in the labour-intensive work of clearing, fencing and carting, and domestic maintenance.[75] Throughout the pastoral industries of Queensland, South Australia (which included the Northern Territory after 1862) and Western Australia, Aboriginal people provided essential and skilled 'colonised labour' that was typically unpaid beyond subsistence rations.[76] In South Australia, where ration depots shifted from being government-run police stations in the south to adjuncts of pastoral stations in the north and west by the 1890s, the reliance of the industry on Indigenous people was widely acknowledged.[77] A select committee heard in

---

72 Pamela Smith, 'Station Camps: Legislation, Labour Relations and Rations on Pastoral Leases in the Kimberley Region, Western Australia', *Aboriginal History*, 24 (2000): 82–4.

73 Quoted in Christine Choo and Chris Owen, 'Deafening Silences: Understanding Frontier Relations and the Discourse of Police Files through the Kimberley Police Records', *Studies in Western Australian History*, 23 (2003): 149–50.

74 Smith, 'Station Camps', p. 81.

75 Peggy Brock, 'Pastoral Stations and Reserves in South and Central Australia, 1850s–1950s', *Labour History*, 69 (1995): 105; Smith, 'Station Camps', pp. 82–3.

76 Bill Thorpe, 'Aboriginal Employment and Unemployment: Colonized Labour', in Claire Williams and Bill Thorpe, *Beyond Industrial Sociology: The Work of Men and Women* (Sydney: Allen & Unwin, 1992), pp. 94–7.

77 Robert Foster, 'Rations, Coexistence and the Colonisations of Aboriginal Labour in the South Australian Pastoral Industry, 1860–1911', *Aboriginal History*, 24 (2000): 10.

1899 that Aboriginal labour was so essential in the pastoral districts that stations would be abandoned without it.[78]

Given the effects of occupation on Indigenous people's lives and economies, there were ameliorations inherent in accommodating pastoralists. While camped and working on pastoral stations, Indigenous groups could more easily maintain connection to country and a semblance of autonomy, albeit radically altered.[79] Unlike the confined reserve system developing in Victoria or the culturally invasive expectations of Christian missions, employment in the pastoral industry had fewer effects on religious, economic and cultural practices. During the first 80 years of engagement with settlers, for example, the Adnyamathanha of the Flinders Ranges in South Australia practised marriage, kinship and religious rituals with limited intervention. Stock and domestic work supplemented their economic activities after the 1860s, and although more vulnerable to unemployment than white workers, the Adnyamathanha and many other Aboriginal pastoral workers developed skills inaccessible through the missions.[80] Pastoralists' dependence on Aboriginal people's labour was entwined with a tacit reliance on them exercising their rights of possession to country; an arrangement with continuing ramifications in native title law after 1996.

Policing and administering miscegenation in Australia's north

In the north of Western Australia, the Northern Territory, Queensland and the Torres Strait, particularities of geography, climate and industry produced a virulent strain of racial prejudice that extended the blood logic manifest in Victoria in 1886. But these new frontiers also produced alternative models of interaction between Indigenous people and newcomers. By the mid-1880s a colonial pearl and shell industry had followed cattle up the West Australian coast to Broome, and developed into a diverse, multi-racial and multilingual trade that built on longstanding Indigenous pearling and *trepang* industries.[81] By the end of the nineteenth century the vast majority of pearlers, indentured

---

78 Ibid., p. 2.

79 R.M. Berndt and C.H. Berndt, *End of an Era: Aboriginal Labour in the Northern Territory* (Canberra: Australian Institute of Aboriginal Studies, 1987), p. 279.

80 Harry Green, 'Harry Green Remembers', unpublished manuscript cited in Brock, 'Pastoral Stations and Reserves', pp. 109–10.

81 Campbell Macknight, 'The View from Marege': Australian Knowledge of Makassar and the Impact of the Trepang Industry across Two Centuries', *Aboriginal History*, 35 (2011): 121–43.

and free, were from Japan, Malaysia, Singapore, the Philippines and west Timor, and the trade encompassed the entire north coast, including the port town of Darwin and the Torres Strait islands, annexed to Queensland in 1879. Aboriginal and Torres Strait Islanders were mostly excluded from the trade by the 1880s, but Indigenous communities along the coast continued to trade extensively with pearling luggers.[82]

The tropical communities that emerged throughout Australia's north were different from those in the southern colonies. Broome, known at the turn of the century as 'Japanese Town', had a pearling population in 1901 of 1,358 people, of whom only 132 were white settlers. The town's stratification was typical of many tropical communities. A middle class of Asian workers, pearl dealers and business owners bridged the gap between white settlers and an Aboriginal underclass of temporary service workers.[83] In Queensland, with the exception of Thursday Island, the tropical communities that emerged along the coast between Bundaberg and Cairns to service a booming sugar industry after 1860 were different again. Significant populations of Pacific Islanders – more than 60,000 in total between 1868 and 1906 – brought to Queensland as indentured workers, generally joined Aboriginal people as itinerant, casual and seasonal workers when their indentures expired.

Throughout the north, Aboriginal people and non-Europeans mostly resided on the fringes and margins of colonial towns, in temporary camp settlements or in segregated commercial quarters that serviced the margins. Labelled 'Chinatowns' ('Kanaka towns' in Queensland), these commercial areas were sites of both segregation and refuge, their separateness from the white quarters policed from outside and from within. On the one hand, town by-laws and curfews often regulated the movement of Aboriginal people and non-Europeans.[84] On the other, within these cordoned spaces communities of Indigenous, Southeast Asian, African American, European, Papuan and Pacific Islander peoples developed their own dynamics. The ideas of race that regulated their contact with the increasingly self-conscious 'white' community were not necessarily the dominant cause for division. In Pacific Islander communities, islands of origin, kinship or gender were principal organisers of social relations; and on Thursday Island 'race' was merely one

---

82 Christine Choo, 'Asian Men on the West Kimberley Coast, 1900–1940', *Studies in Western Australian History*, 16 (1995): 105–6.

83 Ibid., p. 96; Sarah Yu, 'Broome Creole: Aboriginal and Asian Partnerships along the Kimberley Coast', *Queensland Review*, 6, 2 (1999): 58–73.

84 Tracey Banivanua Mar, 'Belonging to Country: Racialising Space and Resistance on Queensland's Transnational Margins, 1880–1900', *Australian Historical Studies*, 43, 2 (2012): 174–90.

of a range of linguistic, gendered, cultural and economic causes for division or cohesion.[85] So, too, the ethnic composition of the Torres Strait Islands, where the Indigenous Islander population was halved in 1875 during a measles epidemic, was transformed through sexual and cultural unions between (mostly) Islander women and men from Europe, the Pacific, Sri Lanka, the West Indies and the Philippines. Many newcomers were integrated into Indigenous kinship networks, sometimes being granted parcels of land or usage rights to land and sea.[86] It was not until the late nineteenth century that racial ideologies and practices labelled and policed these communities as 'interracial'.

The emergence of diverse polyglot communities in Australia's north was less the result of racial tolerance and more a reflection of the prominence of ideologies of racial difference that distinguished geography and labour on racial lines. While government policy was to maintain the Australian colonies as places of British migration, the need for cheap labour presented a problem, especially after the 1840s, when convict labour was gradually abolished. As pastoralists experimented with importing free or indentured Indian, Afghan, Chinese, Māori and Pacific Islander labourers, the Colonial Office, governors and a growing number of colonists opposed the practice, fearing the 'admixture of races'.[87] But while the southern colonies adopted restrictive immigration policies from the 1850s, the tropical north was treated as an exception. Many argued that indentured so-called coloured labour was critical, supported by the conviction that the climate debased white men and produced racial degeneration. This belief persisted into the twentieth century and ensured the dependence of tropical industries on cheap, non-white labour.[88]

The communities that developed in the north were kept under intense scrutiny. Both the Queensland and Western Australian governments repeatedly interrogated the numbers of 'coloured aliens' and collected statistics showing patterns of crime, marriage and employment.[89] Their collection reflected wider popular anxieties regarding the imagined imminent 'invasion of the

85 Noel Fatnowna, *Fragments of a Lost Heritage, 1929–59* (Sydney: Angus & Robertson, 1989); Banivanua Mar, *Violence and Colonial Dialogue*, pp. 101–20.

86 Anna Shnukal, 'A Double Exile: Filipino Settlers in the Outer Torres Strait Islands, 1870s–1940s', *Aboriginal History*, 35 (2011): 161–78.

87 Janet Doust, 'Setting Up Boundaries in Colonial Australia: Race and Empire', *Australian Historical Studies*, 35, 123 (2004): 160.

88 Ibid., pp. 160–6; Warwick Anderson, *The Cultivation of Whiteness: Science, Health and Racial Destiny in Australia* (Melbourne University Press, 2002).

89 Banivanua Mar, *Violence and Colonial Dialogue*, pp. 70–100.

black and yellow races' from the north, as well as fears of miscegenation, or 'a hybrid race springing up'.[90] Marriage or other unions between Aboriginal women and men of colour were the subject of widespread disapproval.[91] Relationships between Indigenous women and Asians or Pacific Islanders were labelled as 'interracial' and described in terms of contamination, disease and immorality.[92] A range of methods of controlling contact between Asian and Pacific Islander men and Aboriginal women was introduced, including the imposition of white-only restrictions on the employment of Aboriginal people, and the creation of prohibited areas and 'anti-native reserves'.[93]

Through popular anxiety over miscegenation, attempts to produce a racially exclusive white Australia merged legislatively by the end of the nine-teenth century with the administration of Indigenous people. Industrial and immigration restrictions in both Queensland and Western Australia, which forced many people of colour from tropical industries, were the corollary of a new era of Aboriginal and settler relations.[94] In 1897 Queensland was the first to introduce legislation comparable to Victoria's Protection Acts with the *Aboriginals Protection and Restriction of the Sale of Opium Act* of 1897. Described as systematically making Aboriginal people's 'disappearance...as light to them as possible', it made provision for a network of missions and reserves.[95] The Act responded to interactions between Aboriginal women and Asian men by restricting and punishing the sale of opium, seen largely as an Asian vice. Extensive controls over Aboriginal people rendered them wards of the state, while 'harbouring' clauses required Aboriginal women to seek permission to marry or cohabit with non-Indigenous men. Punitive rather than protective, the Act explicitly sought 'discipline and good order' on missions with a range of sections suspending the legal rights of Indigenous residents, and empowering reserve managers to impose summary punishment and imprisonment. Queensland's version of the protection legislation

90 *Brisbane Courier*, 14 March 1899; *Queensland Parliamentary Debates*, vol. 31, p. 139 (26 October 1880), p. 161 (28 October 1880).

91 Katherine Ellinghaus, 'Absorbing the "Aboriginal problem": Controlling Interracial Marriage in Australia in the Late 19th and Early 20th Centuries', *Aboriginal History*, 27 (2003): 182–207.

92 Shnukal, 'A Double Exile', p. 167.

93 Choo, 'Asian Men', p. 110; Victoria Haskins, '"The Privilege of Employing Natives": The Quan Sing Affair and Chinese-Aboriginal Employment in Western Australia, 1889–1934', *Aboriginal History*, 35 (2011): 145–60.

94 Ronald Moore, 'The Management of the Western Australian Pearling Industry, 1860 to the 1930s', *Great Circle*, 16, 2 (1994): pp. 127–9; Choo, 'Asian Men'; Banivanua Mar, *Violence and Colonial Dialogue*, pp. 82–100.

95 The Home Secretary, Justin Foxton, in *Queensland Parliamentary Debates*, vol. 82, p. 117 (26 September 1899).

was overtly designed to isolate Aboriginal people – physically, spatially and reproductively – by giving robust powers of removal to local protectors. Few Aboriginal people on the Queensland mainland would remain unaffected by the Act's removal powers as they were used readily to erase fringe camps, discipline individuals and separate families of mixed descent.[96]

The shift in Queensland in 1897 to more invasive management mirrored a hardening of relations between Indigenous people and settler states elsewhere. In Victoria, the 1886 Half Caste Act was exacerbated by a concentration policy that closed five of six Aboriginal stations and reserves between 1890 and 1924. Framlingham in the Western District was the only one defended by the local white community in solidarity with Aboriginal residents.[97] In New South Wales from the mid-1890s, 45 new reserves were created to encapsulate existing Aboriginal camps at the request of white town residents. Abandoning the earlier support for autonomous Aboriginal settlements, the New South Wales government turned to what Heather Goodall has described as 'segregation reserves'.[98] They would in turn supply 'apprenticed' Aboriginal girls to white families to be 'absorbed' into the white working class from the mid-1890s – an early version of twentieth-century assimilation policies.[99]

After Federation all the Australian States, having retained the power to govern Aboriginal affairs, introduced legislation that echoed elements of Queensland's and Victoria's Acts, creating a national legislative web that governed Indigenous people's residence, employment, marriage and cohabitation. Western Australia was first, replacing its much weaker *Aborigines Protection Act* of 1886 with new Queensland-style legislation in 1905; New South Wales followed in 1909. The Commonwealth did the same in the Northern Territory in 1910, South Australia in 1911 and Tasmania in 1912.[100] These Acts ushered in an era of administered violence against Aboriginal people. As the historian Thom Blake put it, if 'the sight of a trooper or policeman with a rifle evoked terror in the nineteenth century, in the twentieth century it was a policeman with a removal order'.[101]

---

96 Thom Blake, '"Deported...at the sweet will of the government": The Removal of Aborigines to Reserves in Queensland 1897–1939', *Aboriginal History*, 22 (1998): 51–61.
97 Jan Critchett, *Our Land Till We Die: A History of the Framlingham Aborigines* (Warrnambool: Warrnambool Institute Press, 1980).
98 Goodall, 'Land in our own Country', pp. 13–14.
99 Victoria Haskins, '"& so we *are* 'Slave Owners'!" Employers and the NSW Aborigines Protection Board Trust Funds', *Labour History*, 88 (2005): 147–64.
100 *Bringing Them Home: Report of the National Inquiry into the Separation of Aboriginal and Torres Strait Islander Children from their Families* (Canberra: Human Rights and Equal Opportunity Commission, 1997).
101 Blake, 'Deported...at the sweet will of the government', p. 61.

By the end of the nineteenth century, as concerns over miscegenation, an increasingly articulated desire for racial purity and an embryonic eugenics movement sharpened racial discourse in Australia, governments increasingly defined and implemented internal racial frontiers. Excluded peoples were first defined racially and then managed through a range of policies and laws governing immigration, forced deportation, the franchise, access to state benefits, the ability to rent or buy land, marry, join unions, own a dog, open bank accounts, buy alcohol, or get a job and receive wages.[102] For Indigenous people, legislation had constructed the segregated categories of 'Aboriginal' or 'Half-Caste' as legal anomalies within the administration of the state. Coupled with the spatial strategies of establishing reserves and missions, this oversaw the production of racialised zones of exception throughout Australia that enabled extraordinary intervention and control.[103]

*

In the first half of the nineteenth century race relations in the Australian colonies were shaped through the politics of territory and the taking of land, using physical violence and the rhetoric of conciliation. Governors sought to secure peace and to manage relations, protecting both Aboriginal people and settlers through the creation and patrolling of legal and physical partitions. Yet governors were also charged with the task of promoting settlement, and if Aboriginal people did not cede their land and dominion peaceably, punitive measures were taken. Multiple instances of martial law allowed for the violent but sanctioned removal of Aboriginal people in the course of taking their land. In this early period, humanitarian ideas of protection emerged that would later become central to the management of Aboriginal peoples and non-white others in post-frontier societies.

Aboriginal people maintained degrees of autonomy in the aftermath of occupation. Although colonial strategies of segregation emerged as the dominant model of governing race relations, it was not the only one. In the southern colonies Indigenous movements to acquire land as inalienable freehold, to be managed independently by Aboriginal landowners, was another post-frontier response that operated briefly. So, too, the delicately

---

102 Julie Evans, Patricia Grimshaw, David Phillips and Shurlee Swain, *Equal Subjects, Unequal Rights: Indigenous Peoples in British Settler Colonies, 1830–1910* (Manchester University Press, 2003), pp. 63–87, 134–56.

103 Gerald Neuman, 'Anomalous Zones', *Stanford Law Review*, 48, 5 (1996): 1197–234; Lauren Benton, *A Search for Sovereignty: Law and Geography in European Empires, 1400–1900* (Cambridge University Press, 2009), pp. 6–10.

balanced model of mutual dependence that developed in pastoral country, although underpinned by the potential for violence, nevertheless created a middle ground through which Aboriginal people remained on their country in exchange for providing much-needed labour. In the deep north Aboriginal and non-Aboriginal peoples, of whom often only a minority were white, developed communities that mutually and autonomously found economic, emotional and genealogical common ground. As international ideas of race merged with the intensification of settlement and the rise of a virulently 'white' settler-nationalism towards the end of the century, this era of self-sufficient autonomy came under threat. In this historical pattern, genuine ideals of liberal humanitarianism articulated too easily with the more brutal realities of establishing a white settler nation. This would intensify before it improved.

15

Education

JULIA HORNE AND GEOFFREY SHERINGTON

Individuals and societies acquire and construct knowledge in various ways. In the nineteenth century the transmission of knowledge became closely associated with specific educational institutions that promised both moral enlightenment and material improvement and benefits. Most of all, ideas of the universal school and notions of widening social access for all were born and adopted, particularly in societies of settlement such as Australia. Education seemed to promise much, especially to those of perceived merit and talent. It partly overcame boundaries of gender and class, though not the division between Indigenous populations and new settlers.

Cultures, faiths and ventures

Indigenous people had long engaged in educational practices, including the acquisition of hunting and gathering skills, initiation through ceremony and knowledge of country. Place and environment shaped these experiences. Around Sydney Harbour and Botany Bay the various language groups lived close together in 1788, catching fish by bark canoe or spear, while initiation ceremonies took place on the foreshores.[1] Across the continent, at what is now Albany on the shores of King George Sound, the Nyungar people avoided the sea; their country was close to the edge of the great jarrah forests, although they ranged for food across a much wider domain and their young accompanied them on long journeys, learning by imitation and initiated by ceremony and tasks into understanding the surrounding environment.[2] Such practices were part of the cultural web of education when the new settlers arrived in 1788.

1 David Collins, *An Account of the English Colony in New South Wales* [1798], ed. Brian H. Fletcher (Sydney: Reed, 1975), pp. 451–514.
2 W.C. Ferguson, 'Morake's Domain', in D.J. Mulvaney and J. Peter White (eds), *Australians to 1788* (Sydney: Fairfax, Syme & Weldon Associates, 1987), pp. 120–45.

The British had their own forms of apprenticeship and training, practices that were augmented in the new colony by the pressing need for skilled craftsmen. The governors brought with them Christianity as the foundation to education. The 'word' of God had become a guide for men and women of faith and, with the invention of the printing press, followed by the Reformation, education had become closely associated with words and numbers and the culture of the book, particularly the Bible.

Words were the foundation of knowledge in the new society of settlement. Just as there were various Aboriginal languages in the Sydney basin, so the spoken word continued to divide the colonial settler population through accent and dialect according to regional origin, class and caste, and even occupation.[3] In contrast to speech, the written word was a means of communicating knowledge, ideas and faiths. From the end of the eighteenth century in Britain, evangelical Christian reformers saw the prospect of universal literacy as a way to convert the heathen and the unfaithful to God. The Rev. Richard Johnson, first chaplain to the new settlement at Sydney Cove, brought with him numerous religious tracts. In England the Society for the Propagation of the Gospel sought to assist Johnson by 'holding out an encouragement to school masters and school mistresses, as the most likely means of effecting a reformation must be by paying all the attention that can be to the instruction and morals of the rising generation'.[4] The idea of the school for all would soon be seen as a form of pastoral care and a way to guide the souls of the young into good citizenship.[5]

The history of early colonial schools also gave rise to private ventures. In Britain the tradition of 'dame schools' had already emerged, whereby mainly working-class women supervised other people's children and provided basic instruction in reading and writing, for a fee. In the new colony, some convict women soon found teaching a form of enterprise that brought both respect and a livelihood. The first known teacher in New South Wales was the convict Isabella Rosson, who began her own school in 1789. Married to a schoolmaster, William Richardson, her venture could be seen as also the

---

3   Alan Atkinson, *The Europeans in Australia: A History. Volume One, The Beginning* (Oxford University Press, 1997), pp. 1–98.
4   Proceedings of the Society for the Propagation of the Gospel, 1794–95, in D.C. Griffiths (ed.), *Documents on the Establishment of Education in New South Wales, 1789–1880* (Melbourne: Australian Council for Educational Research, 1957), p. 7.
5   Ian Hunter, *Rethinking the School: Subjectivity, Bureaucracy, Criticism* (Sydney: Allen & Unwin, 1994).

first family enterprise in education in Australia. Richard Johnson became the school's benefactor, providing grants to maintain it.[6]

The initial state involvement in education came through the efforts of wives of the early governors. Elizabeth Paterson and Anna King strove to establish a government Female Orphan School for convicts' children; for 'if we ever hope for worth or honesty in this settlement, we must look to them for it, not the present degenerate mortals'.[7] Their successor, Elizabeth Macquarie, continued this hope by establishing a boarding residence for 'orphans' on the banks of the Parramatta River, modelled on her ancestral home in Scotland and outside the influences of the township of Sydney.[8] Governor Macquarie had his own priorities in education. He supported the efforts of the missionaries William and Elizabeth Shelley to establish a Native Institution, first at Parramatta and later at Black Town. But removed from their families and kin, Aboriginal children soon left the institution. Increasingly Christian missions sought to separate and protect Aboriginal people from white settlement, while seeking to convert them, instruct them in the English language and offer some vocational or domestic skills.[9]

The first attempt to start a system of schools in Australia was the Church and Schools Corporation, established in New South Wales in 1826. The Church of England received land grants that would provide for the support of Anglican clergy and churches as well as school teachers and schools. The Corporation proposed to oversee infant and parochial schools, grammar schools, colleges, male and female orphan schools, native schools and evening schools, with special provision for mechanics' institutes and the new school at Black Town for 'children of the Blacks', who would be received from under the age of five only.[10] This was a comprehensive attempt to cater for the nature of colonial society in the 1820s, and anticipated the educational institutions that would emerge as part of the patterns of settlement. The corporation received grants but the scheme foundered, in part on its ambitions but principally on the differences and jealousies between the emerging colonial churches. As the first bishop of Australia, William Broughton maintained that the Church of England remained the one true established faith and that

---

6 John F. Cleverley, *The First Generation: School and Society in Early Australia* (Sydney University Press, 1971), pp. 23–6.

7 Quoted in Grace Karskens, *The Colony: A History of Early Sydney* (Sydney: Allen & Unwin, 2009), p. 342.

8 Ibid.

9 J.J. Fletcher, *Clean, Clad and Courteous: A History of Aboriginal Education in New South Wales* (Sydney: Fletcher, 1989), pp. 13–38.

10 Griffiths (ed.), *Documents on the Establishment of Education*, pp. 38–9.

only Anglican schools could receive government funds.[11] The argument failed on the strength of other denominations in the settler population.

By the late 1830s it had become accepted that where the state distributed funds to Church of England schools it could only do so on the basis of equitable provision for all denominations that sought aid. This helped to foster an expectation of church entitlement to state funds that would persist for much of the following half century as new colonies were established.[12] In South Australia the colonial administration initially granted aid to church schools, only to withdraw such provision within a decade because of the views of the Nonconformist Protestant churches, such as the Congregationalists and Methodists. There were also Lutherans, who established their own system of German-speaking schools, initially free from any state oversight and control.[13] Elsewhere in Australia, the major churches – particularly the Anglicans and Catholics and, for a period, the Presbyterians – expected the colonial state to provide for a growing system of schools. In Western Australia the Catholic church was often the pace setter, setting up the first schools and forcing the state to compete.[14]

Centralisation rather than local administration became a feature of state-supported education. Central boards or agencies were established throughout all the colonies to administer funds, although each church tended to continue its separate educational endeavours without much supervision. These church-run elementary schools were established principally in the colonial capitals and major towns. They were generally associated with the local church and parish of each religious denomination. Different church schools could be found on neighbouring street corners of the cities, although those attending were not confined to the denomination adherents.

Church-affiliated schools remained the majority of schools across Australia in the mid-nineteenth century. At the 1861 census 'denominational' schools probably enrolled more than half the students attending school in Victoria and New South Wales, although small 'private' schools, run for a profit and

---

11 G.P. Shaw, *Patriarch and Patriot: William Grant Broughton 1788–1853, Colonial Statesman and Ecclesiastic* (Melbourne University Press, 1978).

12 A.G. Austin, *Australian Education, 1788–1900: Church, State and Public Education in Colonial Australia* (Melbourne: Pitman, 1961). For a more recent overview see Craig Campbell, 'Schooling in Australia', in Craig Campbell and Geoffrey Sherington (eds), *Going to School in Oceania* (Westport: Greenwood, 2007), pp. 9–77.

13 Pavla Miller, *Long Division: State Schooling in South Australian Society* (Adelaide: Wakefield Press, 1986), pp. 1–17.

14 Ladaan Fletcher, 'Education of the People', in C.T. Stannage (ed.), *A New History of Western Australia* (Perth: UWA Press, 1981), pp. 551–74.

often with only one teacher, continued to proliferate in urban areas.[15] By the mid to late-nineteenth century, most church schools faced increased competition from the government secular schools discussed below.

The last quarter of the nineteenth century was a turning point in Australian education. Facing pressures, Protestants, including the Anglicans, agreed to give up their elementary schools; but the Catholic church refused to do so, even when the colonial governments withdrew funding. The Catholic position was determined by both international and local circumstances. From the mid-nineteenth century the Papacy had resisted many modern developments including liberalism and the power of democratic states. It was closely associated with the growth of the Irish church, from where many of the Australian Catholic bishops now originated. Support for Catholic education and schools thus became one of the clearest expressions of Irish-Australian Catholicism.[16] The Catholic schools also depended on the local efforts of parishes and communities. In contrast to the growing centralisation of the state, localism would become one of the ways in which Catholic communities and their schools survived. Finally, the Catholic system of schools was able to depend upon congregations of religious orders from overseas as well as Australian nuns and brothers who became teachers.[17] Under these influences Catholic schools soon became the clearest Australian expressions of faith-based schools with their own inherited traditions: authoritarian in approach; religious in tone, practice and symbols; overwhelmingly single-sex; and 'Irish' in submission to law and devotion to the faith.[18] They also ensured that schools were available to the very poor and particularly Catholic immigrants from Ireland, who made up a large section of the working class.

Other patterns of education emerged. Family and local ventures remained important in various forms of education for middle-class Australia. Wealthy families in cities and large landholders in the country sometimes employed governesses and tutors for their own children. Elsewhere, many clergy in the Church of England and in the Presbyterian church were university graduates,

---

15 Wray Vamplew (ed.), *Australians: Historical Statistics* (Sydney: Fairfax, Syme & Weldon Associates, 1987), pp. 330–2.
16 Patrick O'Farrell, *The Catholic Church and Community* (Sydney: UNSW Press, 1985). See also Gregory Haines, *Lay Catholics and the Education Question in New South Wales* (Sydney: Catholic Theological Faculty, 1976).
17 Ronald Fogarty, *Catholic Education in Australia, 1806–1950*, 2 vols (Melbourne University Press, 1959). See also Geoffrey Sherington, 'Religious School Systems', in James Jupp (ed.), *The Encyclopedia of Religion in Australia* (Cambridge University Press, 2009), pp. 668–76.
18 Tom O'Donoghue, *Upholding the Faith; The Process of Education in Catholic Schools in Australia, 1922–65* (New York: Peter Lang, 2001).

and often provided local educational leadership. Some clergy became educational entrepreneurs, setting up their own private-venture schools, mainly for the colonial middle class. Around Sydney, between 1830 and 1850, there were numerous academies offering curricula that provided a 'commercial', mathematical or English education for boys, with some limited provision for classical studies in Latin and Greek. Clergymen and other tutors often taught in their own homes, while governesses and other educated women offered to girls studies in the 'polite accomplishments' of music, dance and other refinements of an 'English' education.[19]

Education was a major area of female enterprise. Two unmarried women who arrived in Van Diemen's Land in 1823 established a school. Later named Ellinthorp Hall, after a family home in Yorkshire, this educational enterprise became a main source of family income.[20] Some schools survived only a few years, others for a decade or more. A personal and intimate atmosphere marked teacher–pupil relationships in residences that were domestic rather than institutional in form. In Victoria the gold rushes helped to create individual and family ventures in both the regions and Melbourne. Cosmopolitanism was marked in such enterprises as Vieusseux Ladies' College, the 'high point of the private girls' school in nineteenth-century Australia'.[21] Owned by Julie and Lewis Vieusseux, respectively from Holland and Belgium, the college had a reputation for high academic standards as well as instruction in creative arts and accomplishments from different European cultures. Beginning in modest premises, the school moved on a number of occasions to a larger mansion, which was later overhauled. The Vieusseux were said to have accumulated a 'goodly fortune'.[22]

Private ventures remained a part of the landscape of Australian education throughout the nineteenth century. Some even survived the 1890s Depression because of their low fees and costs as well as promises to produce results in the public examinations that led on to university and paid employment. But the corporate came increasingly to prevail over individual enterprise. In contrast to private ventures that relied on individual efforts, or a partnership or family ownership, the corporate school was governed by a board, was often associated with a church and reflected corporate as well as religious values and

19 Christopher Mooney, 'Securing a Private Classical Education In and Around Sydney: 1830–1850', *History of Education Review*, 25, 1 (1996): 38–53.
20 Marjorie Theobald, *Knowing Women: Origins of Women's Education in Nineteenth-Century Australia* (Cambridge University Press, 1996), p. 35.
21 Ibid., p. 44.
22 Ibid.

identities. Corporate colleges or schools were sometimes business enterprises. As early as 1825, the Sydney College was founded on joint stock principles, allowing each shareholder to nominate pupils.

The corporate model took different forms across Australia, although mostly with reference to British examples. By the early nineteenth century the idea of 'public schools' in England implied a school with a national reputation for educating the governing elite. Such schools were sometimes proprietary in nature but were also associated with a governing council and professed attachment to the Church of England. The earliest and most continuous example of the English public school tradition in Australia was the Collegiate School of St Peter Adelaide, founded in 1847. In part created for the training of clergy, St Peter's soon had a chapel and extensive grounds as well as boarding houses for pupils from outside Adelaide.[23] In 1867 the Methodist church established Prince Alfred College in Adelaide to honour the visit of the son of Queen Victoria and challenge the primacy of the Anglican Church.

Just as the gold rushes reinforced private ventures in Melbourne, so the idea of corporate models was soon transposed from Britain. At first these were for males. All the major churches established boys' schools and colleges in Melbourne and surrounding districts from the 1850s to the 1870s: Scotch College (1851), Geelong Grammar (1855), Melbourne Grammar (1858), Geelong College (1861), Wesley College (1866) and Xavier College (1878). These soon became known as the six 'public' schools of Victoria, drawing upon what was seen as the English public school tradition, even though in Australia this was merged with the different religious patterns of Anglican, Presbyterian, Methodist and Catholic. So Scotch College began as the Melbourne Academy, reflecting Scottish academic traditions as a variant of the English public school. In New South Wales and Queensland, the term Great Public School (GPS) would soon be applied to the schools that participated in sporting competitions, thus bestowing a status of association and common values.

By 1900 the major cities and most Australian regional centres had similar schools, many well endowed with dedicated buildings and grounds well beyond the resources of the earlier private schools. While the private schools were often transitory, the corporate schools were mostly permanent, governed by councils and with headmasters who usually came from Britain to

23 John Tregenza, *Collegiate School of St Peter Adelaide: The Founding Years 1847–1878* (Adelaide: Collegiate School of St Peter, 1996).

find a post in the Empire. Just when most of the churches were abandoning elementary education they were assuming a more prominent place in defining corporate secondary schools: catering to the middle classes, academic in orientation, but also devoted to organised games and with codes of practice designed to produce the future leaders of Australia.[24] This was all part of a common British imperial culture that crossed ethnic and religious lines, uniting Protestants and Catholics.[25]

The corporate model was extended further across the lines of gender. Increasingly, during the last quarter of the nineteenth century, in the wake of the universities admitting women, the churches founded new girls' schools that mirrored many of the educational patterns of the boys' institutions. Even the new private girls' schools of this period often assumed a corporate form and identity, prior to many being later taken over or brought into association with the churches.[26]

The Catholic church stood apart from such trends, continuing to found its own colleges and convents under religious orders. From the mid-century convents sought to cater for both Catholics and Protestants, with a curriculum that stressed motherhood and family. In Perth, the Sisters of Mercy founded the convent school Mercedes in 1849, attracting the daughters of Protestants as much as Catholics, and setting a precedent that was adopted in parts of the eastern colonies.[27] In 1857 the Mercy Mary Immaculate Academy opened in Melbourne and by 1863 there was the Sisters of Mercy All Hallows convent in Brisbane. In contrast to the private-venture schools, the nuns were not paid. A number of Catholic boys' schools were founded from the 1860s in both rural areas and the cities, although some of the more significant foundations came later, including the Jesuit St Aloysius (1879), Riverview (1880) and the Marist St Joseph's (1881) in Sydney, the Christian Brothers Wakefield in Adelaide (1878), St Joseph's in Brisbane (1875) and Nudgee (1891) and Aquinas in Perth (1874).

Being part of religious congregations, both girls' and boys' Catholic schools had practices of devotion and faith. But the Catholic and Protestant

---

24 Geoffrey Sherington, R.C. Petersen and Ian Brice, *Learning to Lead: A History of Girls' and Boys' Corporate Secondary Schools in Australia* (Sydney: Allen & Unwin, 1987).

25 Geoffrey Sherington and Mark Connellan, 'Socialisation, Imperialism and War: Ideology and Ethnicity in Australian Corporate Schools 1880 to 1918', in J.A. Mangan (ed.), *Benefits Bestowed: Education and British Imperialism* (Manchester University Press, 1987), pp. 132–49.

26 Ibid., pp. 184–5.

27 Noeline Kyle, *Her Natural Destiny: The Education of Women in New South Wales* (Sydney: UNSW Press, 1986), pp. 69–130.

boys' schools shared more on questions of masculinity and manhood than the convents and other Catholic girls colleges had in common with the private and Protestant girls' schools. In this way the Catholic view of the corporate sought to maintain the sacred and the religious, even though all secondary schools now tended to follow a common academic curriculum. Increasingly matters of faith were merged into affairs of the world.

Secular and public

The idea of a secular civil society emerged during the eighteenth century with the increasing separation between the state and church, as well as the rise of a political ideology of 'secularism' that reflected a growing religious and social pluralism. This context fostered a 'secularisation' of western society and belief, based particularly on reason and science.[28] Secular and public institutions in the Australian colonies were designed not so much to displace religion as to provide modes of engagement between the world of the sacred and the world of secular affairs. In this way secular educational institutions became part of a 'public' culture. Three examples were the learned societies and mechanics institutes of the early nineteenth century, the universities and the public, or state, schools. Each had different institutional forms.

As elsewhere in the British Empire and North America, mechanics' institutes and schools of arts were established in the colonies from the 1820s. They were community enterprises established locally both in urban and rural areas for the conveyance of knowledge especially through libraries, reading rooms, lectures and classes. Their funding – precarious at times – came from a combination of subscriptions, donations and, in some colonies, generous grants from colonial governments.[29] Their intended audiences were the working classes, in particular 'mechanics' who might benefit from instruction in practical subjects, though their appeal was far broader than mechanics, and it is not entirely clear whether mechanics made much use of them.[30]

Most institutes aimed to provide classes in basic literacy and numeracy, general education and technical and scientific education, but the latter was

28 Marion Maddox, 'Religion, State and Politics in Australia', in Jupp (ed.), *Encyclopedia of Religion in Australia*, pp. 608–9.

29 Jill Eastwood, 'The Melbourne Mechanics' Institute: Its First Thirty Years', and M. Whiting, 'The Education of Adults in Schools of Arts in Colonial New South Wales', in P.C. Candy and J. Laurent (eds), *Pioneering Culture: Mechanics' Institutes and Schools of Art in Australia* (Adelaide: Auslib Press, 1994), pp. 71–3, 160–2.

30 P. Candy, '"The Light of Heaven Itself": The Contribution of the Institutes to Australia's Cultural History', in Candy and Laurent (eds), *Pioneering Culture*, pp. 1–10.

often neglected. The Victorian government surveyed technical education in Victoria in 1869 and found that out of 51 mechanics' institutes, only two offered instruction useful to trade skills. In the government's view, mechanics' institutes had failed in their duty to the working classes.[31] Imbued with nineteenth-century, middle-class views of knowledge as self-improvement, topics for lectures and courses were wide-ranging, though with a preponderance for liberal education – history, languages, the natural sciences and philosophy were commonly the subject of lectures, which were often amply supported by libraries of books, journals and newspapers. It is therefore likely that their chief appeal was to the growing middle classes. Women attended institute lectures and classes. In 1860 John Woolley, professor of Classics at the University of Sydney and enthusiast for mechanics' institutes as a means to spread liberal education to the broader population, argued for the social value of opening institute reading rooms to women as a way to diffuse civilising thought throughout broader society.[32] Institutes around Australia began to take on women as 'junior' members and created ladies' reading rooms, which helped to stem declining revenues.

By the mid-nineteenth century institutes and schools of art were joined by other institutions that reflected the 'people's learning', a consequence of the colonies becoming self-governing liberal democracies.[33] The need for knowledge to build successful colonies justified state subsidies to such organisations, which also reached usefully into both urban and rural areas. It was also a period when colonial governments began to establish city-based public institutions such as museums, libraries and art galleries to consolidate this knowledge base. Perhaps the most ambitious of these newly created institutions were the colonial universities.

By 1900 Australia had four universities. The first two of these, the University of Sydney (1850) and the University of Melbourne (1853), were both founded as meritocratic institutions with students admitted on academic ability. The University of Sydney was based originally on the University of London (1836) and the Queen's Colleges in Ireland (1845). When professors were appointed to the University of Sydney, a new vision of reformed Oxford in the antipodes emerged: a strong, central teaching university with entry by examination. The University was to be secular in

---

31 Ibid., p. 11.
32 John Woolley in Whiting, 'The Education of Adults', p. 176.
33 Kathleen Fennessy, *A People Learning: Colonial Victorians and their Public Museums 1860–1880* (Melbourne: Australian Scholarly Publishing, 2007), pp. 1–5.

instruction and form, not anti-religious as the churches feared, but open to all faiths and with preference for none.[34]

Sydney University was established by an optimistic government, spurred on by gold-generated economic growth. Victoria's gold created even greater optimism and the University of Melbourne, largely based on the Sydney model, was established to cater for the interests of the gold-rush generation and new colonial professional classes. The foundation of both universities established an Australian model with features not previously seen in the British Empire. The education historian R.J.W. Selleck has described this new model as 'a state university: urban, secular, professional, non-residential and non-collegiate, centralised in government, controlled by a laity and possessing power to teach and examine. Other universities had some of these characteristics but none had this particular combination.'[35]

Imperial connections remained important. Both universities had imperial charters that provided recognition for their degrees in the Empire and allowed for their graduates to seek attachment to the University of London. Imperial expertise was also sought for appointments of professors. The governing bodies of both universities used London-based selection committees – a practice retained throughout the antipodes until well into the twentieth century. F.B. Smith has argued that while Sydney recruited from and was 'shackled' to Oxbridge colleges, Melbourne was more 'adventuresome', having established an early Irish connection with professors from Trinity College, Dublin.[36] But recent research presents different patterns which, in addition to Oxbridge, also drew from other educational and social backgrounds, particularly Scottish.[37] Nonetheless, the Oxbridge connection explains Sydney's long attachment to a liberal classical curriculum, and Melbourne's connection with Trinity College, Dublin explains the early

---

34 C. Turney et al., *Australia's First: A History of the University of Sydney. Volume 1, 1850–1939* (Sydney: Hale & Iremonger, 1991), pp. 82–8; Julia Horne and Geoffrey Sherington, *Sydney, The Making of a Public University* (Melbourne: Miegunyah Press, 2012), pp. 6–7.

35 R.J.W. Selleck, *The Shop: The University of Melbourne 1850–1939* (Melbourne University Press, 2003), p. 27.

36 F.B. Smith, 'Academics In and Out of the Australian Dictionary of Biography', in F.B. Smith and P. Crichton (eds), *Ideas for Histories of Universities in Australia* (Canberra: Division of Historical Studies, Research School of Social Sciences, ANU, 1990), pp. 1–14; F.B. Smith, 'Stalwarts of the Garrison: Some Irish Academics in Australia', in John O'Brien and Pauric Travers (eds), *The Irish Emigrant Experience in Australia*, (Dublin: Poolberg, 1991), pp. 74–93.

37 Tamson Pietsch, 'A Commonwealth of Learning? Academic Networks and the British World, 1890–1914', DPhil. thesis, University of Oxford, 2008.

rejection of the Oxbridge classical tradition as well as the introduction of professional schools in law and medicine.[38]

The forerunner to the University of Tasmania (1890) was the Tasmanian Council of Education (1858), created out of debates in the 1840s and 1850s about university models best suited to Tasmanian conditions. The Council was an examining authority and offered an opportunity for students to apply for the newly established Associate of Arts based on recent reforms at Oxford; it also offered scholarships to study in Britain. Unlike the universities of Melbourne and Sydney, which for decades grappled with problems of access to university for rural populations, the Tasmanian system reached out more effectively into its rural heartland by conducting examinations in many places outside Hobart.[39]

The University of Adelaide emerged as a 'civic university' in 1874, with its origins and purpose more clearly related to its city than in the case of Sydney and Melbourne.[40] Its civic origins lay in the strength of Congregationalism and its educational ideals, the local philanthropic support of Thomas Elder's benefaction of £20,000, and the formation of a civic movement that argued for a secular university with 'a fair representation of all classes in the province'.[41] The government was prepared to provide entrance scholarships and an initial grant of £10,000 for buildings on five acres on North Terrace, significantly smaller than either Sydney or Melbourne universities in a precinct that soon developed as a hub for education and culture. But the annual endowment was small and its development relied heavily on support from philanthropists.[42] This was very much a university of the interested public rather than a generous state.

The idea of Australian universities as public also lay in the role of philanthropy as a form of public duty. In Melbourne, private endowment such as that which the Scottish-born Francis Ormond provided, helped to establish and strengthen the residential colleges in ways similar to Oxford. In Sydney, philanthropy supported the endeavours of the central university. Of highest significance was the grand general bequest of £276,000 from the merchant

38 Selleck, *The Shop*, pp. 192–201.

39 Maurice French, 'The Prehistory of the University of Tasmania', *Australian University*, 11, 3 (1973): 185–94; Richard Davis, *Open to Talent: The Centenary History of the University of Tasmania 1890–1990* (Hobart: University of Tasmania, 1990), pp. 5–12.

40 W.J. Gardner, *Colonial Cap and Gown: Studies in the Mid-Victorian Universities of Australasia* (Christchurch: University of Canterbury, 1979), p. 35.

41 Minutes of the University Association, 17 September 1872, quoted in Geoffrey Sherington and Julia Horne, 'Empire, State and Public Purpose in the Founding of Universities and Colleges in the Antipodes', *History of Education Review*, 39, 2 (2010): 47.

42 W.G.K. Duncan, *The University of Adelaide, 1874–1974* (Rigby: Adelaide, 1974), pp. 4–6.

John Henry Challis. By 1900 private foundations provided about one-third of the University of Sydney's income, compared to 37 per cent from state grants and 29 per cent from fees.[43]

The idea of non-denominational universal instruction grew up alongside the public universities. In the early colonial context some were initially prepared to claim the term of 'public school' as part of attachment to the established Church of England, which received financial aid from government. As Samuel Marsden boasted in 1810, 'Roman Catholics, Jews, and persons of all persuasions, send their children to the public schools where they are all instructed in the principles of our established religion'.[44] By the 1830s others were seeing a more inclusive role for 'public' – or what had become known as 'national' – schools. The latter term arose when the Anglo-Irish governor, Richard Bourke, proposed that New South Wales adopt the Irish 'national' state-funded systems whereby Catholic and Protestant children attended a common school with provision for access by clergy and priests. The proposal met opposition from the local Anglican and Catholic bishops as well as many others in the community.[45] Instead, Bourke and others were forced to concede that aid would have to be extended to all religious schools rather than to schools for all pupils.

By mid-century, the idea of 'national' schools for all was beginning to gain acceptance. In 1850 the liberal Catholic, William Augustine Duncan, delivered a *Lecture on National Education* in the new settlement of Moreton Bay near Brisbane. Drawing on the general idea of public education in the past, Duncan argued that education had now fallen into a 'miserable state' with the churches competing so that there were '*four* kinds of public schools, in which the different doctrines are taught at public expense'. The answer lay in adopting 'national education', as was occurring in Europe. As a liberal, Duncan even included the Indigenous population as part of his universal scheme. As a Catholic, he rejected the view that national education would undermine religion, for 'no education can be perfect which is not based upon Christianity'.[46]

By then there were already moves to establish a system of state-funded and state-provided education, based in part on secular principles that would

---

43 Turney et al., *Australia's First*, p. 207; Horne and Sherington, *Sydney*, pp. 207, 312.
44 Quoted in Cleverley, *The First Generation*, p. 41.
45 John Cleverley, 'Governor Bourke and the Introduction of the Irish National System', in C. Turney (ed.) *Pioneers in Australian Education: A Study of the Development of Education in New South Wales in the Nineteenth Century* (Sydney University Press, 1969), pp. 27–58.
46 W.A. Duncan, *Lecture on National Education* (Brisbane: James Swan, 1850).

still embrace common elements of Christianity. A National Board of Education was established in New South Wales in 1848. One of its main missions soon became to found schools in the new areas of settlement. In 1849 the Board appointed George William Rusden to travel the remote districts of New South Wales, which then included Moreton Bay and Port Phillip. Son of an Anglican clergyman who had migrated in the 1830s, on the voyage out Rusden had met the wealthy Charles Nicholson, one of the founders of the University of Sydney. Nicholson became Rusden's patron, securing for him the post of agent for national schools. Over eighteen months, Rusden travelled 10,000 miles and visited remote hamlets.[47] After transferring to the new colony of Victoria, Rusden later drew on his experiences to write his own pamphlet on national education. Acquainted with overseas developments, including the emerging public school system of the United States, he claimed that the denominational schools in Australia had failed to extend education to all the population. The principles of 'national education' were to 'contend for Christianity as zealously as any one' while achieving 'what the Denominationalists cannot' – 'the formation of a sound Christian National School in any part of the colony'.[48]

The national school idea prevailed throughout Australia as much the result of an efficient system as the assertion of values. The mounting of a campaign for public education was most clearly seen in New South Wales. Here, William Wilkins, appointed headmaster of Fort Street Model (Training) School in 1850 and then inspector and superintendent of schools under the Board of National Education in 1854, was the most significant campaigner. The apprenticeship system of pupil teachers working under a master ensured a supply of future teachers recruited directly from the national schools. School inspectors oversaw the standards of the curriculum and school buildings.[49] By the late 1850s Wilkins could claim that in Sydney alone children in national schools came from many social backgrounds:

> They are of all denominations, and among them their parents may be found representatives of all classes of society – *ministers of religion*, merchants, professional gentlemen, tradespeople, mechanics and labourers.[50]

---

47 A.G. Austin, *George William Rusden and National Education in Australia 1849–1862* (Melbourne University Press, 1958).

48 W.G. Rusden, *National Education* (Melbourne: The Argus, 1853), p. 231.

49 Cliff Turney, *William Wilkins: His Life and Work* (Sydney: Hale & Iremonger, 1992).

50 Geoffrey Sherington and Craig Campbell, 'Middle Class Formations and the Emergence of National Schooling', in Kim Tolley (ed.), *Transformations in Schooling: Historical and Comparative Perspectives* (Basingstoke: Palgrave Macmillan, 2007), p. 28.

The national schools were popular because they were efficient in instruction. By 1866 a *Public Schools Act* in New South Wales created a council to oversee public and denominational schools. Now new public schools could be established in any locality in which 25 pupils could attend regularly, while enrolment provisions imposed on denominational schools became more restrictive. Denominational schools found it harder to meet the new standards of council inspectors. Even Catholic parents began to drift away from Catholic schools towards the public schools. The state began to take over denominational schools as well as former private schools.[51]

Beginning with Victoria in 1872 and ending with Western Australia in 1895, the parliaments of all the Australian colonies enacted the 'free, compulsory and secular' Acts that provided the foundation for state-provided schools under a centralised bureaucracy accountable to the oversight of a minister of the crown. Such schools were generally neither free nor compulsory until the early twentieth century. The major issue of controversy and division was the nature of proposed 'secular' education. The Victorian Act of 1872 effectively endorsed 'non-sectarian' instruction, excluding denominational education.[52] In the later Acts of the other colonies there was some provision for the churches to have some 'right of entry' to public schools, or to allow Bible instruction.

Even before this legislation was enacted, the emerging concept of 'secular' created a sectarian divide. Protestants supported secular education and secular schools as a form of common Christianity that would unite all sects. Premier Henry Parkes told the New South Wales parliament that the bill that would become the *Public Instruction Act* of 1880 would establish:

> a splendid system of instruction for the young…making no distinction in faith, asking no question where the child has been born, what may be his condition of life, or what the position of his parents, but inviting all to sit side by side in receiving that primary instruction which must be the foundation of all further education…What is aimed at is that he should be considered as belonging to a family forming part of the population of this free and fair country.[53]

In contrast, the Catholic church, many of whose Australian bishops had experienced the national schools in Ireland, had come to believe that secular

---

51 Ibid., pp. 28–30.
52 Denis Grundy, *'Secular, Compulsory and Free': The Education Act of 1872* (Melbourne University Press, 1972).
53 J.J. Fletcher (ed.), *Documents in the History of Aboriginal Education in New South Wales*, (Sydney: Fletcher, 1989), pp. 73–4. As Fletcher points out, literally applied, the 1880 Act embraced both settler and Indigenous populations.

education was at best a Protestant effort to convert Catholics from their faith, and at worst a form of schooling that would undermine religion and morality. Catholics would be taxed to support secular schools, to which the bishops held strong objections:

> We condemn them, first, because they contravene the first principles of the Christian religion; and secondly, because they are seed plots of future immorality, infidelity, and lawlessness, being calculated to debase the standard of human excellence, and to corrupt the political, social, and individual life of future citizens.[54]

In Britain and Canada, educational settlements in the late nineteenth century allowed churches to receive aid for schools. In Australia, the secular Acts became a major divide with consequences that lasted for almost a century. Schooling now split generations of Australian children along sectarian lines. Rather than creating a common Christianity, the new public schools arising out of the secular Acts were primarily Anglo-Protestant in outlook. Through legislation or practice, Protestant clergy gained access to them, often appearing at ceremonies to celebrate the Empire. Under the central direction of state departments, schools sprang up in small hamlets as well as in the cities and suburbs. A new workforce of mainly female teachers was recruited, trained and appointed, sometimes to rural one-teacher schools.[55]

Children growing up by 1900 were part of a generation educated either in the schools of the state or the schools of the Catholic church, which sought to match the standards of state secular education. At the turn of the twentieth century, most of the non-Indigenous population was schooled to at least the age of twelve. And state education was now firmly in control of a generation of the Australian-born, such as Frank Tate, a child of the goldfields who became a student teacher, university graduate and progressive inspector in the Mallee district of Victoria – and on the eve of the new century, aged just in his mid-30s, about to become Victorian Director of Education in 1902.[56]

Beyond the elementary stages of education, there were intermittent government efforts to create institutions that would compete with the corporate

---

54 Pastoral Letter of the Archbishops and Bishops Exercising Jurisdiction in New South Wales, June 1879, in C.M.H. Clark (ed.), *Select Documents in Australian History 1851–1900*, new edn (Sydney: Angus & Robertson, 1977), p. 722.

55 Kay Whitehead, *The New Women Teachers Come Along: Transforming Teaching in the Nineteenth Century* (Sydney: Australia and New Zealand History of Education Society, 2003).

56 R.J.W. Selleck, *Frank Tate: A Biography* (Melbourne University Press, 1982).

schools and thus prepare some students for university and the professions. Sydney Grammar School had been founded with state endowment in 1857 to act as a 'feeder' school to the university. In Queensland, just after the establishment of responsible government, legislation had been enacted for local grammar schools endowed with central funds and scholarships but controlled by local boards. This would open up opportunities for both boys and girls in Brisbane and rural areas, some of whom attended local state schools before going on to the grammar schools, often with scholarship support. Over the following three decades endowed grammar schools were established in Ipswich (1863), Brisbane (1868), Toowoomba (1875), Brisbane Girls (1876), Rockhampton (1881), Townsville (1888), Ipswich Girls (1892) and Rockhampton Girls (1892).[57]

The 1880 Act in New South Wales created 'superior' public schools with a curriculum allowing students to matriculate to university or go on to teachers' training college. There were also the fee-paying Sydney Boys High School and Sydney Girls High School, opened in the wake of the 1880 Act, although efforts to carry the principle of single-sex high schools into rural regions failed. In South Australia, just after the foundation of the University of Adelaide, the state Adelaide Advanced School for Girls was established in 1876 to provide an academic curriculum. But in Victoria the strength of the corporate schools ensured that state education would not go beyond elementary schools. Instead, scholarships enabled a small number of state school students to proceed to these increasingly prestigious schools. It was similar in Tasmania, where the existing corporate schools remained tied to a traditional classical curriculum enshrined through examinations for the Associate of Arts, which actually prepared scholarship holders to receive state scholarships to proceed to Oxford and Cambridge.[58]

Beyond the schools, secular knowledge was applied to the material world. Opened during the 1870s, in the wake of the gold rushes, the Ballarat School of Mines developed an international reputation for education in the technology of mining. Economic imperatives helped to bring into being agricultural and technical colleges. In part this was a recognition that reason and applied science could assist rural and industrial development, and contribute to the

---

57 Rupert Goodman, *Secondary Education in Queensland 1860–1960* (Canberra: ANU Press, 1960).

58 Craig Campbell, Carol Hooper and Mary Fearnley-Sander, *Toward the State High School in Australia: Social Histories of State Secondary Schooling in Victoria, Tasmania and South Australia 1850–1925* (Sydney: Australia and New Zealand History of Education Society, 1999).

economic challenges to the British Empire from Germany. By the 1870s there was a number of initiatives throughout Australia, with South Australia the most progressive and forward-looking. Roseworthy Agricultural College was founded in 1883 to spread scientific knowledge among farmers. The large and impressive South Australian School of Mines and Industries was opened in 1889. Offering diplomas and certificates in such traditionally male areas as engineering, mechanics and bookkeeping, and also skills for females such as dressmaking, these colleges crossed some of the boundaries between schools and universities.[59]

Aspirations

Education was not restricted in the nineteenth century to religious faiths and secular knowledge. It engaged the aspirations of individuals, families, communities and other social groups. The creation of different educational institutions and systems helped to sustain such aspirations for large parts of the population.[60]

The landed elites were educated in Australia and abroad. As the eldest son of John Macarthur, James Macarthur was first taught at home by a governess and then a tutor, who was a French émigré. John then took James and his brother William to Europe. On board ship and again in England, he instructed his sons in classical literature and history. They were enrolled in a small boarding academy rather than one of the English public schools, which still had a reputation for vice and violence. On finishing his schooling James went to work in a 'counting house' to learn business principles. The five-year trip concluded with a grand tour of France, Switzerland and northern Italy.[61] Australians from wealthy families continued to aspire to an education at 'home' in Britain or on the continent.

Educational aspirations were more clearly seen in the 'middling ranks' of society. From almost the beginning Australia had literacy rates higher than much of Britain.[62] The waves of migration from the 1830s reinforced the

---

59 Annely Aeuckens, *The People's University: The South Australian School of Mines and Industries and the South Australian Institute of Technology 1889–1989* (Adelaide: South Australian Institute of Technology, 1989).

60 For an overview of colonial education systems in the nineteenth century, see Alan Barcan, *A History of Australian Education* (Oxford University Press, 1980).

61 John Manning Ward, *James Macarthur: Colonial Conservative, 1798–1867* (Sydney University Press, 1981), pp. 15–20.

62 Eric Richards, 'Migrations', in Deryck M. Schreuder and Stuart Wards (eds), *Australia's Empire* (Oxford University Press, 2008), p. 166.

ranks of the literate and skilled free settlers seeking fulfilment for themselves and their children. As so many immigrants were young couples, and with the high birth rates of the mid-century, Australia was a 'youthful' society that saw children as the future, but in ways that maintained continuity with past traditions.[63]

The German-speaking Lutherans of South Australia were one early example of a pattern of ethnic settlement with traditional aspirations for their young. Church and school were entwined; the pastors the leaders of the community. Lutherans of a traditional faith did not aspire initially to engage with the wider community, nor to seek educational qualifications for places in the wider world of professions, commerce and trade. Rather, their ambitions were linked to their faith and the land, much in the way of their German forefathers. But over the century Lutheran children increasingly patronised state education, so that by 1900 only half the number of Lutheran children in South Australia were in German-speaking, faith-based schools.[64]

Many other families and communities embraced secular education as a means to a better future. In the 1840s Scots-Irish settlers from Ulster arrived at Kiama, south of Sydney. At first these settlers kept faithful to their different denominational schools, mainly Anglican and Presbyterian. Within a generation they had come to support the Kiama Public School, built in stone and opened in 1871, just after the University of Sydney's public examinations had been extended to students in rural areas. By the 1890s it was claimed that 25 former pupils from Kiama Public School had become lawyers, judges and politicians.[65]

There was an equal passion for education among the Catholic Irish. Denied state aid, the Catholic church focused on the regions and the bush as much as the cities. Nuns and brothers replaced the laity in teaching children, first in outback areas in South Australia and Queensland, and then in the urban areas.[66] Drawing from their experiences in Ireland, Irish-born Catholic bishops based in rural regions sought to counter indifference among their

63 Patricia Grimshaw, Chris McConville and Ellen McEwen (eds), *Families in Colonial Australia* (Sydney: Allen & Unwin, 1985); Marjorie Theobald and R.J.W. Selleck (eds), *Family, School and State in Australian History* (Sydney: Allen & Unwin, 1990).

64 Ian Harmstorf, 'German Settlement in South Australia until 1914', in James Jupp (ed.), *The Australian People: An Encyclopaedia of the Nation, Its People and Their Origins* (Cambridge University Press, 2001), pp. 360–5.

65 Winfred Mitchell and Geoffrey Sherington, 'Children and Families in Nineteenth Century Illawarra', in Grimshaw et al. (eds), *Colonial Families*, p. 109. See also Michael Hogan (ed.), *A Lifetime in Conservative Politics: Political Memoirs of Sir Joseph Carruthers* (Sydney: UNSW Press, 2005), pp. 30–43.

66 Whitehead, *The New Women Teachers Come Along*, pp. 38–42.

congregations by creating in large country towns 'schools of high class to save our Catholic boys from Protestant establishments'.[67] The intention was to create regional boarding colleges to draw in boys from rural properties, who might then go on to the university and its residential colleges. It was a strategy that soon drew in Catholics from the eastern colonies, predating even some of the Catholic boys' colleges in the cities, which also maintained boarding houses. Then there was Queensland, with its endowed local grammar schools and Catholic boarding schools near and outside Brisbane. Without a local university, students in these Queensland schools sat for the public and matriculation examinations of Sydney and Melbourne and then went south to enrol in the universities.[68]

The universities were thus not restricted to elites or even the urban middle class. From the start, they aimed to admit students who passed the matriculation examination, regardless of their class, region of origin or religion, though women were not admitted until the 1870s and 1880s. Sydney's academic meritocracy had some success in extending 'educational franchise' to the broader population. There were aristocratic features at Sydney, particularly in the male colleges with their growing fascination with Oxbridge and sport.[69] But the student population was drawn from a much wider social spectrum. During the first decade, one-third of undergraduates held scholarships but only 40 per cent of these came from professional backgrounds normally associated with university education, and the same number – possibly more – from mainly lower middle-class occupations (including older occupations such as artisans and shopkeepers as well as newer ones such as white-collar workers), but also from the unskilled trades.[70] About 40 per cent of all matriculants in the first decade were Anglican. Just over one-quarter were Protestant dissenters and Presbyterians, and just under one-fifth were Catholic. Together they outnumbered the Anglican matriculants, at a time when both groups were still excluded from Oxford and Cambridge.

67 David Bollen, *Up On the Hill: A History of St Patrick's College Goulburn* (Sydney: UNSW Press, 2008), p. 27.
68 Goodman, *Secondary Education in Queensland*, pp. 242–54.
69 Geoffrey Sherington and Julia Horne, 'Modes of Engagement: Universities and Schools in Australia, 1850–1914', in P. Cunningham (ed.), *Beyond the Hall: Universities and Community Engagement from the Middle Ages to the Present Day* (Cambridge: Faculty of Education and Institute of Continuing Education, University of Cambridge, 2009), pp. 133–49.
70 Julia Horne and Geoffrey Sherington, 'Extending the Educational Franchise: The Social Contract of Australia's Public Universities, 1850–1890', *Paedagogica Historica*, 46, 1–2 (2010): 212–14.

Across Australia the social composition of students varied.[71] The University of Melbourne remained largely captive to the Anglican and Presbyterian professional middle classes, despite the early introduction of university scholarships. Opposition to state secondary schools in Victoria strengthened the corporate schools, not least in the way they came to dominate the university matriculation exams and the award of state scholarships.[72] In contrast, in New South Wales, the corporate schools were weak until at least the 1880s, and it was the University of Sydney that used scholarships and the exam system to establish a state-endowed grammar school and then support a public school system.

Academic meritocracy also helped to break down the gender divide in Australian universities. Girls from the newly founded corporate and state schools of the 1870s and 1880s, which taught an academic curriculum, began to sit for university examinations. The first university in Australia to admit women was Adelaide from 1876, even though the British Colonial Office originally refused Adelaide's request to offer degrees to women.[73] Women sat for Melbourne's and Sydney's examinations from 1871, though the universities refused to matriculate women. In 1880, after long debate, the University of Melbourne agreed to admit women, though there were special arrangements made for those who wished to study medicine.[74] Sydney admitted its first women students on the same basis as men in 1882, with the Chancellor reasoning that 'the sexes have an equal right to participate... seeing that this University has been founded for the general benefit of the Public, and is maintained at the general public cost'.[75]

In these ways Australian higher education was different. Historians of the university in Europe and North America have argued that the transformation of higher education from the mid-nineteenth century involved expansion, diversity, wider social access, and increasing professionalisation. This was all associated with the emergence of the urban 'middle class university', whereby merit and competition became pre-eminent, allowing

71 Whitehead, *The New Women Teachers Come Along*.
72 Carole Hooper, 'Opposition Triumphant', in Campbell et al. (eds), *Toward the State High School in Australia*, pp. 29–54; Geoffrey Blainey, *A Centenary History of The University of Melbourne* (Melbourne University Press, 1957), pp. 17–18; Selleck, *The Shop*, pp. 53–5.
73 Theobald, *Knowing Women*, pp. 55–64; Horne and Sherington, 'Empire, State and Public Purpose', pp. 47–8; Helen Jones, *Nothing Seemed Impossible: Women's Education and Social Change in South Australia 1875–1915* (Brisbane: UQP, 1985), pp. 86–95.
74 Selleck, *The Shop*, pp. 119–24, 162–5.
75 Quoted in Turney et al., *Australia's First*, pp. 183–8; Horne and Sherington, *Sydney*, pp. 65–71.

access to those once denied higher education.[76] Higher education in the Australian colonies was part of a process that engaged secular foundations, merit and gender. Being secular from the outset was crucial for Australian universities. Once the idea of religious tests had been abandoned, the question became who could be admitted on merit, for in the end all these colleges and universities needed to grow in order to survive. As in Britain, the Australian universities and colleges only reached a small proportion of the population, but scholarships, bursaries and part-time enrolments seem to have slowly extended educational opportunities and increased student numbers.

The higher education of women was also associated closely with the new girls' schools and the creation of teaching as the main profession for women. A system of informal teacher training had begun in the private girls' schools by the mid-nineteenth century. From the 1880s the first generation of women educated in the universities, in both Britain and Australia, began to assume prominence as heads and principals, sometimes of their own private schools, and sometimes of corporate or state girls' high schools. There was often a tension between the expectations of parents for their daughters and the ambitions of the headmistresses for their students. But a foundation was laid by the end of the nineteenth century for the emergence of the 'new women' teachers committed to career rather than motherhood and children.[77]

The aspirations of the mass of the population were restrained. School was generally accepted, sometimes welcomed. In the cities and the suburbs state schools became part of the civic landscape. Often built in a neo-gothic form, they seemed to be modest cathedrals of learning. In the bush there were appeals from communities for the spread of new schools. In Victoria alone in 1880 there were 350 applications for new schools, of which only 25 were refused.[78] But disillusion arose with the practice of instructing large mass classes, particularly in the urban areas. Earlier views about child-centred education gave way to technologies of control, with students placed in tiers or rows for supervision.

---

76 Konrad H. Jarausch, 'Higher Education and Social Change: Some Comparative Perspectives', in Konrad Jarausch (ed.), *The Transformation of Higher Learning, 1860–1930: Expansion, Diversification, Social Opening, and Professionalization in England, Germany, Russia, and the United States* (University of Chicago Press, 1983), pp. 9–36.

77 Theobald, *Knowing Women*; Whitehead, *The New Women Teachers Come Along*.

78 Theobald, *Knowing Women*, p. 205.

Among sections of the population there was continuing resistance to the regular patterns of education that schools of the state provided. Instead there was support for the older and more informal forms of private dame schools, which suited the nature of working-class life in which the labour of children was sometimes needed to support the household.[79] The kindergarten or nursery school also emerged in the late nineteenth century, not through the state but from the initiatives of middle-class women conscious of the needs of the working-class mother as well as the interests of the child.[80] In rural and mining areas there was sometimes little incentive for boys or girls to remain at school beyond the minimum age. Those who did attend school did so irregularly. Disaster at work could lead to the death of the father as the breadwinner. Strikes brought further pressure on the family budget and ability to keep children in school. For those who left school, the prospect for boys was paid but often irregular work and for girls unpaid assistance in the family household.[81]

School held out few prospects for the original inhabitants of Australia. At the end of the nineteenth century, Aboriginal people of the interior were still coming into contact for the first time with missionaries, who hoped to convert and educate them. In the south and south-east of the continent long-standing Aboriginal communities were now living close to white settlements. Following the secular Acts some Aboriginal families were able to enrol their children in local public schools, but many were denied access because of pressure from white parents.[82]

*

On the eve of the new century, with mounting tensions between settlers and Indigenous communities, white parents sought outright exclusion of Aboriginal children from all public schools. In New South Wales this arose as a direct consequence of an incident at Gulgong, in the central tablelands, where Jimmy Governor, an Aboriginal man, murdered nine white settlers, including his employer's family and local teacher, many of whom had humiliated and taunted him as 'black rubbish'. In the wake of these murders, the

---

79 Ian Davey, 'Growing Up in a Working-Class Community: School and Work in Hindmarsh', in Grimshaw et al. (eds), *Families in Colonial Australia*, pp. 163–72.
80 Ruth Harrison, *Sydney Kindergarten Teachers' College, 1897–1981* (Sydney: KTC Graduate Association, 1985).
81 Mitchell and Sherington, 'Families and Children in the Illawarra', pp. 111–17.
82 Fletcher, *Clean, Clad and Courteous*, pp. 61–91.

minister of education in New South Wales resolved that any Aboriginal child could be excluded from a public school on the demand of just one white parent. As a teacher told a local inspector, parents objected to Aboriginal children on the following grounds '1. Because they are black. 2. Education makes rogues of them. 3. They are dirty.'[83] Denying access to schools would widen the divide between white settlers and Indigenous people.

83 Fletcher (ed.), *Documents in the History of Aboriginal Education*, p. 87.

16

Law and regulation

MARK FINNANE

Legal institutions were scarcely visible at the founding of New South Wales. It was nearly half a century before the scope of the legal authority claimed by the British settlers over the country's Indigenous inhabitants was determined.[1] Law meant different things to the settlers and the Indigenous people. For the latter, as settlers were only slowly to discover, life and law intersected, overlapped and were inseparable. Law was comprehensive and normative in ways that settlers could not imagine and failed to appreciate. For settlers, law was mutable, its claims over lives and ways of living expanding and contracting as modernity was in process. It was also a weapon that individuals could wield against each other, a shield that might repel the harms directed by others, even by those in authority, against those who had few of the world's resources. Law also meant different things to those in power and those without. In the first century of Australian settlement law was the twin of government; sometimes its critic, at others its instrument. The nineteenth century proved a creative era for law in the scope of regulation, in the reform and refinement of its penalties and in the design of its institutions. But that was only possible after the taking of the country from its first peoples.

Martial law

Dispossession proceeded with the aid of military force, and occasionally under the warrant of that emergency act of executive government, martial law. While even in a penal colony the military remained accountable to law for its actions, martial law rendered immune from prosecution the actions of agents of government. Its deployment against both Indigenous resistance and rebellious settlers signalled the fragility of authority at critical stages of

---

1 Lisa Ford, *Settler Sovereignty: Jurisdiction and Indigenous People in America and Australia, 1788–1836* (Cambridge, MA: Harvard University Press, 2010).

the colonial period. In March 1804 a rebellion at Castle Hill, west of Sydney, by mainly Irish convicts was put down by soldiers despatched by Governor King under a declaration of martial law. The extraordinary conditions created by a marauding gang of bushrangers in Van Diemen's Land in 1814 prompted Lieutenant-Governor Davey to a declaration of martial law, to the pleasure of suffering settlers and the dismay of Governor Macquarie. The declaration was illegal since only Macquarie had such power, and the episode helped bring Davey's posting to an end. When bushranging next became a major problem for the colonial government in New South Wales in the 1830s, the government responded not with martial law, but with criminal statutes to be enforced through newly created mounted police. At Ballarat late in 1854 Lieutenant-Governor Hotham proved very reluctant to declare an emergency, putting his faith initially in conciliation and then in the use of combined police and military forces to collect licence fees from protesting miners. When more forceful action seemed inevitable to combat what he saw as an increasingly revolutionary challenge to his authority, he declared martial law. The position had been reached, so Hotham later told the Secretary of State for the Colonies, when 'a Riot was rapidly growing into a Revolution, and the professional agitator giving place to the man of physical force'.[2] Hotham repealed the martial-law declaration after three days.

Later crises and conflicts involving a challenge to government were met more confidently without resort to martial law – in part because self-government enabled coercive legislation, and the creation of large colonial police forces facilitated early repression of rebels and agitators. There was an element of bluff in the politics of emergency in colonial Australia. While Queensland premier Sir Samuel Griffith called out the defence forces and issued a proclamation outlawing assembly under arms during the 1891 shearers' strike, he also admitted that the proclamation 'has of course no legal effect but it is not, I think, unusual for the head of state in case of emergency to exercise his influence in such a manner'.[3]

There was no bluff when martial law was deployed against Indigenous resistance in the first half of the nineteenth century. Typically a martial law declaration was preceded by an attempted conciliation; in some cases it was accompanied by measures that presumed a restoration of amicable relations, but on white terms and in an expectation of gradual acculturation. In 1826 Governor Darling opposed his attorney-general, Saxe Bannister, who

2 Hotham to Grey, 20 December 1854, 'Eureka Documents', *Historical Studies Australia and New Zealand* (Special Eureka Supplement, 1954): 4.
3 Roger B. Joyce, *Samuel Walker Griffith* (Brisbane: UQP, 1984), p. 161.

had suggested the necessity of martial law to repress Aboriginal resistance. Darling thought 'Martial Law could not be necessary to put down a few naked Savages', but his reluctance was also informed by his sense that 'the Natives had not been altogether unprovoked'. And indeed he prosecuted Lieutenant Lowe, whose murderous behaviour in the Hunter Valley included the shooting of prisoners.[4] But two years earlier Saxe Bannister's advice to declare martial law in the Bathurst region had been received favourably by Governor Brisbane, a resort to emergency against sustained pressure by the Wiradjuri.[5]

Facing prolonged and damaging resistance on the Cumberland Plain, Macquarie did not declare martial law in 1816 but instead proclaimed that ten named Aboriginal men were outlaws and so subject to exceptional measures, to be arrested or killed through prolonged military action.[6] In South Australia, on the other hand, Governor Gawler confessed he was led by the 'principles of martial law' in directing reprisals against Indigenous people thought responsible for a massacre of the survivors of the *Maria* shipwreck in 1840. Even so, he was reluctant to tarnish the colony's reputation as a favoured destination of free emigrants by actually making the declaration.[7] Such a misgiving had not been a consideration for Governor George Arthur in Van Diemen's Land in 1828. Following an earlier drawing of boundaries for 'settled districts', Arthur proclaimed martial law in November 1828 to facilitate the suppression of Aboriginal resistance within those districts. In 1830 he extended this to the entire island, facilitating the military operation known as the Black Line for the removal of Aboriginal people into an enclave.[8]

Martial law was law's extreme, exposing the force that lay behind the more mundane exercise of the common law and its institutions. In regretting its necessity the colonial governors who deployed martial law spoke to the violence of colonial settlement and the possibility of that violence being displaced by a rule of law and legal institutions they brought with them.

4 *Historical Records of Australia*, series 1, vol. 12, p. 609; John Connor, *The Australian Frontier Wars, 1788–1838* (Sydney: UNSW Press, 2002), pp. 64–7.

5 David Roberts, 'Bells Falls Massacre and Bathurst's History of Violence: Local Tradition and Australian Historiography', *Australian Historical Studies*, 26, 105 (1995): 621–3.

6 Grace Karskens, *The Colony: A History of Early Sydney* (Sydney: Allen & Unwin, 2009), pp. 503–14.

7 S.D. Lendrum, 'The "Coorong Massacre": Martial Law and the Aborigines at First Settlement', *Adelaide Law Review*, 6, 1 (1977): 29.

8 James Boyce, *Van Diemen's Land* (Melbourne: Black Inc, 2008), pp. 272–7.

Legal institutions and authority

The imperial statutes framing the founding of the successive Australian colonies authorised the establishment of courts for the adjudication of civil disputes and the prosecution of criminal law. The *New South Wales Act* of 1823 established Supreme Courts in both Sydney and Hobart, with a chief justice in each colony. The Supreme Courts of the other colonies came later, in South Australia in 1837, just a year after its establishment as a free colony, in Victoria (1852) and Queensland (1861) following their constitution as self-governing colonies, and in Western Australia only in 1861, more than three decades after the founding of the Swan River colony. In comparison with England, the courts of the colonies were unified, with the Supreme Court jurisdiction encompassing civil and criminal matters as well as equity and chancery.[9]

The delay in establishing Supreme Courts did not mean an absence of legal remedies or the familiar forms of legal combat. In both New South Wales and Van Diemen's Land the governor from the outset established military courts sitting under a civilian judge advocate, with trial by juries of military officers. The later colonies were free of the aggravation of military justice, though not of the sense of justice subordinated to the authority of the governor: at Swan River one of Governor Stirling's first acts was the establishment of a court of civil jurisdiction and, not much later, a criminal court. In each, justice was administered by a legally qualified advocate. But in the years before the establishment of the respective Supreme Courts, appeals were only to the governor of each colony, assisted by his judge advocate. Appeals in civil cases in early New South Wales could, and did, proceed to the Privy Council in London, a line of authority that endured for almost two centuries until the Australia Act in 1986.

What kind of law and what kind of authority did such institutions exercise? Some have considered the judiciary an excessively powerful presence in the Australian political landscape, even an 'invisible state' constraining democratic possibilities.[10] In another view, Australia was a 'Benthamite society', utilitarian and legalist in its political culture, a place where there was less interest in the language of rights than in what governments might deliver to

---

9 Bruce Kercher and Brent Salter (eds), *The Kercher Reports: Decisions of the New South Wales Superior Courts, 1788 to 1827* (Sydney: Francis Forbes Society for Australian Legal History, 2009), pp. xiii-xviii.

10 Alastair Davidson, *The Invisible State: The Formation of the Australian State 1788–1901* (Cambridge University Press, 1991).

the people, through bureaucratic institutions.[11] Law was never monolithic, however, in institutions, norms or personnel; it was shaped by, as well as shaping, colonial social relations and increasingly by colonial political interests.[12] The common law of England (judge-made law, moulded by precedent over centuries of court-room practice) influenced the forms and procedures, the reasoning, remedies and punishments available in the colonial courts. That tradition weighed heavily on the colonial judiciary. As an historian of Australian administrative law has observed, 'the freedoms enjoyed by the colonists in erecting their governmental systems were not given to the judges in regulating it'.[13] But the first century of Australia's European settlement was also an era in which the common law was increasingly modified by the creation by parliament of statutes for the government of the people. The new regulatory state was adding and taking away rights and liberties, expanding the reach of government through new agents such as the police and public medical officers.[14] In colonial Australia those new agents were the product of statutes passed by colonial parliaments, only in some respects on models framed at Westminster. Even after Federation it remained unclear quite what the scope of the law might be – with the High Court of Australia being called to judge whether offences created by the British parliament did or did not hold in Australian jurisdictions. This was in spite of what appeared to be clear authority for defining what law prevailed in Australia when the *Australian Courts Act* of 1828 declared that the law was what the common and statute law provided at that date in England.[15]

The Colonial Office exercised a close watch over colonial lawmaking after 1828, disallowing statutes it considered infringed the equal status of Aboriginal people, for example.[16] Although the imperial hand loosened its grip after self-government, there were some areas of legislative innovation (divorce law a notable example) that still provoked Colonial Office objection.[17] Correlatively, an extraordinary display of judicial activism by Justice

---

11 Hugh Collins, 'Political Ideology in Australia: The Distinctiveness of a Benthamite Society', *Daedalus*, 114, 1 (1985): 147–69.

12 Bruce Kercher, *An Unruly Child: A History of Law in Australia* (Sydney: Allen & Unwin, 1995).

13 P.D. Finn, *Law and Government in Colonial Australia* (Oxford University Press, 1987), p. 165.

14 Alison Bashford, *Imperial Hygiene: A Critical History of Colonialism, Nationalism and Public Health* (Baskingstoke: Palgrave Macmillan, 2004).

15 Alex Castles, *An Australian Legal History* (Sydney: Law Book Co., 1982), pp. 426–36.

16 Damen Ward, *'Savage Customs and Civilised Laws': British Attitudes to Legal Pluralism in Australia, c. 1830–48* (London: Menzies Centre for Australian Studies, 2004).

17 Hilary Golder, *Divorce in 19th Century New South Wales* (Sydney: UNSW Press, 1985).

Boothby in South Australia provoked imperial action to *validate* colonial legislative powers. Boothby had insisted that a succession of statutes passed by the South Australian legislature was invalid, being repugnant to English law. His determined campaign against local lawmakers and eventually his fellow judges brought his own removal from the bench. The imperial *Colonial Laws Validity Act* of 1865 sharpened the definition of repugnancy, clarifying the scope of colonial self-government.[18]

The move from crown colony to self-government in Australia was mirrored by a transformation in the relation of the judiciary to the executive. While many early colonial judges asserted their autonomy, the constitutional structures before self-government did not respect such ideals. For one thing, the governor was the final court of appeal, and the authority of law in the early colonial period was therefore a gubernatorial authority. For another, judges were typically intimately involved in the exercise of government broadly considered, advising on or drafting new statutes, and in some colonies serving as members of the governor's executive council. By the end of the colonial era such overlapping of roles would be long past, and judicial autonomy more jealously guarded. That did not prevent some traffic between the different arms of government. Although their careers were exceptional in this respect, two of the most influential colonial politicians, George Higinbotham (Victoria) and Sir Samuel Griffith (Queensland), made the move from politics to the bench, becoming chief justices in their respective jurisdictions and Griffith later becoming the first chief justice of the High Court of Australia.

The administration of justice did not lie with judges alone. Within each jurisdiction the Supreme Court was the pinnacle of a court system that was dependent on the work of magistrates and justices of the peace. In the British homeland local justice had long been the preserve of unpaid justices of the peace. In the colonies, too, governors from an early date appointed justices with a variety of functions: attestation of oaths; conduct of inquests; and hearing of minor criminal cases. Colonial conditions constrained both the efficiency and fairness of such a system. In the frequently chaotic conditions of colonial expansion, the patrician hierarchies of local order in English counties were but a memory. In consequence, from the time of Governor Macquarie there developed a system of paid magistrates, variously known

---

18 Alex Castles and Michael C. Harris, *Lawmakers and Wayward Whigs: Government and Law in South Australia 1836–1986* (Adelaide: Wakefield Press, 1987), pp. 125–34; John McLaren, *Dewigged, Bothered, and Bewildered: British Colonial Judges on Trial, 1800–1900* (University of Toronto Press, 2011), 190–216.

as police or resident magistrates and eventually as stipendiary magistrates. What Golder describes as a 'dual system' of amateur and stipendiary magistrates developed as a characteristic feature of colonial justice systems.[19] The stipendiaries were officers of government as well as law – in particular, they were responsible for overseeing local constabularies of police from as early as 1810, when Governor Macquarie made D'Arcy Wentworth a salaried superintendent of a Sydney police force. Even after police administration was centralised from the 1850s (and gradually detached from the control of the magistrates), these officers continued to function as key agents of administration, the representatives at local level of the reach of government into the remote spaces of settlement. Their role did not displace the function of local justices of the peace, who continued to be appointed by colonial governments, but the stipendiary system spoke to the centralised character of colonial administration before and after self-government. Only in Tasmania did a system of local administration of policing survive to the end of the colonial period, before in turn it adopted the Australian model and displaced the guiding role of local magistrates.[20]

Authority in the administration of law and justice derived not simply from the possession of office, an appointment as judge or magistrate. It was a cultural construct, visible in the accoutrements of office, in the garb of the office-holder and the architecture of spaces in which an office-holder performed his duties – his, for appointment of a woman was never imagined in the nineteenth century. Judicial robes on the English model were widely adopted in the colonies, although wigs were dispensed with during trials in north Queensland in deference to the extremities of the climate.[21] The donning of a black cap accompanied the pronouncement of a death sentence, while at the opening of judicial terms and on circuit in the country districts the formalities of an English assizes were mimicked with the reading of the 'Queen's proclamation against vice and immorality'.[22] These archaic forms were vulnerable to mockery when even the staidest urban newspapers wondered about the language of such 'commands' as were contained in the

---

19 Hilary Golder, *High and Responsible Office: A History of the NSW Magistracy* (Sydney University Press, 1991).

20 Stefan Petrow, 'Economy, Efficiency and Impartiality: Police Centralisation in Nineteenth Century Tasmania', *Australian and New Zealand Journal of Criminology* 31, 3 (1998): 242–66.

21 B.H. McPherson, *The Supreme Court of Queensland, 1859–1960: History, Jurisdiction, Procedure* (Sydney: Butterworths, 1989), pp. 66–7.

22 J.M. Bennett, *Sir John Pedder: First Chief Justice of Tasmania, 1824–1854*, (Sydney: Federation Press, 2003), p. 12.

proclamation, whose 'new' form in 1860 exhorted 'all our loving subjects, of what degree or quality soever, from playing on the Lord's day, at dice, cards, or any other game whatsoever, either in public or private houses, or other place or places whatsoever'.[23]

Authority was also the product of architecture, colonial courthouses displaying the central role of law in the imagination and government of colonial society. More than 300 courthouses were built in New South Wales after European settlement, the great majority of them during the nineteenth century. Not without exaggeration, the Chief Justice of New South Wales congratulated the inhabitants of Goulburn in 1887 on 'the possession of so splendid a court...which takes rank amongst the best in any part of Her Majesty's dominions'.[24] The extravagance of some of these buildings reflected the prosperity of the sporadic boom-decades of the different colonies. In leaner times judges and magistrates had to make do with makeshift accommodation – an adapted gaol in Perth, complete with leaking roof, served for many years the Supreme Court that was established in Western Australia in 1861,[25] while public houses frequently provided the setting for justice and inquests administered in rural outposts. The determination to secure a standard of accommodation that respected the dignity of proceedings was a telling signal of the authority thought to lie in the performance of law.

Authority was above all the product of the rhetoric and discourse of legal proceedings. The reporting of trials and civil disputes contributed to the daily diet of those who consumed the myriad colonial newspapers. Sensational trials were reported and then reproduced in all newspapers from one colony to the next, while local police offences and civil disputes were routinely recorded in every town's local outlet. To a degree unknown today, the transcripts of evidence and examination in both criminal and civil trials were published; judicial observations, reasoning and judgment all were carefully noted. Law and litigation saturated colonial society, providing entertainment, instruction and moral tales that defined identities, boundaries and norms.[26] Was there a better illustration of this than the field of reference

23 *South Australian Register*, 20 August 1860.
24 Peter Bridges, *Historic Court Houses of New South Wales* (Sydney: Hale & Iremonger, 1986), p. 11.
25 G.C. Bolton and Geraldine Byrne, *May It Please Your Honour: A History of the Supreme Court of Western Australia 1861–2005* (Perth: Supreme Court of Western Australia, 2005).
26 Alan Atkinson, *The Europeans in Australia: A History. Volume Two, Democracy* (Oxford University Press, 2004), pp. 53–8; Kirsten McKenzie, *Scandal in the Colonies: Sydney and Cape Town, 1820–1850* (Melbourne University Press, 2004); Kirsten McKenzie, *A Swindler's Progress: Nobles and Convicts in the Age of Liberty* (Sydney: UNSW Press, 2009).

invoked by a Queensland Supreme Court judge in 1870 when he presided at the Toowoomba assizes over successive trials in which the first defendant had bitten off part of a man's ear and a second did the same to another man's nose? In such conditions the deterrent function of criminal proceedings was, said Justice Lutwyche, to 'prevent the colony becoming another Nebraska or another Kansas'.[27] Such ambition imagined a people moulded to a mode of civility that conditions in a new society might undo, without law's guiding or disciplinary hand.

Boundaries

The nineteenth century was a period of enormous expansion in law's capacity to shape populations, define the boundaries of acceptable behaviour and express preferences for a certain style of urban order. The Australian colonies shared in this revolution in ordering, sometimes prompted by the imperial government, at other times readily adapting the legal frameworks and institutions that constituted a new and intensive management of some populations. While self-government (of state and individual) was an abiding precept of colonial settler society, the paradigm of the liberal subject capable of managing his or her own life in a condition of steady work and respectable behaviour highlighted the deficiencies of those who could not match that high ideal. Laws, institutions and policing created and governed a variety of populations defined by boundaries of exclusion, rarely permanent, but always conditional. Lunatics, street urchins, larrikins, orphans, prostitutes, vagrants and criminals were named in legislation or constructed in colonial discourse as demanding the attention of police. In part, these boundaries operated as norms that helped define what urban order was, and what it must not be. But the jurisdictions that governed social life in the Australian colonies were geographically vast. The policing of these boundaries was one that extended far beyond the cities and main towns of the colonies, not least in respect of the Indigenous populations that were progressively caught in the web of administrative expansion that characterised the developing colonial state.

Law's commanding presence was found in the exercise of criminal jurisdiction. Prior to the foundation of Supreme Courts, there were courts of criminal jurisdiction before which offenders were brought, tried and punished when convicted. In the earliest decades charges in the criminal jurisdiction were laid by the victims of offences, acting as complainants.

27 *Brisbane Courier*, 10 February 1870.

As the elements of a bureaucratic justice system were put in place, complainants were typically displaced from this role in the courtroom by police constables and later public prosecutors. The expansion of a criminal justice bureaucracy did not, however, result in an increase in prosecutions.[28] The proportion of police to population numbers decreased over time.[29]

Improved economic and social conditions might have contributed to declining prosecutions over the century, but the official statistical picture was also shaped by a shift of some offences into summary jurisdiction as well as by changing demographies. Towards the end of the century creative law-makers also contributed to the apparent decline of serious criminality, if that was to be measured by use of imprisonment. The introduction of probation for first offenders and the increasing use of fines in place of imprisonment contributed to aggregate prison populations being lower at 1900 than they had been in the 1880s.[30]

As in Britain and Ireland, the criminal law was systematised by nineteenth-century statutory innovation. There were two significant developments: the enactment of policing laws expressed in the police offences Acts from the 1820s; and the codification of serious criminal offences from the 1850s. For the most part, the colonies followed and adapted Westminster legislation, sometimes at a distance. Late nineteenth-century media ventilation of the horrors of baby-farming, with its links to abhorred but widely practised infanticide, prompted colonial legislation to police private maternity hospitals and adoption, more than 20 years after the English model.[31] In other matters there was a determined rejection of the example of the British parliament; for example, in abolishing capital punishment for rape.[32] A powerful factor shaping domestic politics in Australia was an anxiety about the threat of black men, especially to white women. The exemplary use of hanging in interracial offences was a sign of that anxiety, though even here the

---

28 S.K. Mukherjee, E.N. Jacobsen and J.R. Walker, *Crime and Punishment in the Colonies: A Statistical Profile* (Sydney: History Project Inc., 1986), pp. 120–44.

29 Mark Finnane, *Police and Government: Histories of Policing in Australia* (Oxford University Press, 1994), p. 21.

30 Mark Finnane and Stephen Garton, 'The Work of Policing: Social Relations and the Criminal Justice System in Queensland 1880–1914 (Part 1)', *Labour History* 62 (1992): 52–70; Peter N. Grabosky, *Sydney in Ferment: Crime, Dissent and Official Reaction, 1788–1973* (Canberra: ANU Press, 1977); Michael Sturma, *Vice in a Vicious Society: Crime and Convicts in Mid-Nineteenth Century New South Wales* (Brisbane: UQP, 1983), pp. 64–82.

31 Shurlee Swain and Renate Howe, *Single Mothers and Their Children: Disposal, Punishment and Survival in Australia* (Cambridge University Press, 1995), pp. 100–12.

32 G.D. Woods, *A History of Criminal Law in New South Wales: The Colonial Period, 1788–1900* (Sydney: Federation Press, 2002), pp. 311–12, 346.

politics of mercy mitigated the heavy hand of white justice.[33] Clemency was also at issue in punishment of women convicted of capital offences, a large number of whom were convicted for infanticide and almost all for killing of intimates, including husbands and lovers. Few went to the gallows; those who did always inspiring a controversy that helped limit the future use of the death penalty.[34]

The shifting regimes of nineteenth-century penality were distinguished by their refinement of populations according to particular attributes of age, gender and race. The convict system itself was a vast exercise in penal experimentation, evident not only in the ticket-of-leave system and secondary punishment settlements, but also in the gender separation that led to the housing of women convicts in their own institutions.[35] Complementing the penal institutions were the lunatic asylums, whose design and function only gradually departed from their penal origins.[36] The colonial lunacy laws, beginning with that of New South Wales in 1843, were in effect a branch of penal legislation, empowering police to channel a sizable population of men and women from police cells and prisons into the new asylums. Unlike the prisons, asylums and their populations grew steadily.[37]

The regulatory apparatus of lunacy law and the large financial outlay on lunatic asylums were part of a growing investment in regimes of population management. The convict foundations of settlement, requiring a precise and comprehensive bureaucratic control system, may be seen as a precursor of

33 Simon Adams, *The Unforgiving Rope: Murder and Hanging on Australia's Western Frontier* (Perth: UWA Press, 2009); Tracey Banivanua Mar, *Violence and Colonial Dialogue: The Australian-Pacific Indentured Labor Trade* (Honolulu: University of Hawai'i Press, 2007); Mark Finnane and Jonathan Richards, 'Aboriginal Violence and State Response: Histories, Policies and Legacies in Queensland 1860–1940', *Australian and New Zealand Journal of Criminology*, 43, 2 (2010): 238–62; Carmel Harris, 'The "Terror of the Law" as Applied to Black Rapists in Colonial Queensland', *Hecate*, 8, 2 (1982): 22–48; John McGuire, 'Judicial Violence and the "Civilizing Process": Race and the Transition from Public to Private Executions in Colonial Australia', *Australian Historical Studies* 29, 111 (1998): 187.

34 Kathy Laster, 'Arbitrary Chivalry: Women and Capital Punishment in Victoria, Australia 1842–1967', *Women & Criminal Justice*, 6, 1 (1994): 67–95; Carolyn Strange, 'Discretionary Justice: Political Culture and the Death Penalty in New South Wales and Ontario, 1890–1920', in Carolyn Strange (ed.), *Qualities of Mercy: Justice, Punishment, and Discretion* (Vancouver: University of British Columbia Press, 1996), pp. 156–7.

35 Joy Damousi, *Depraved and Disorderly: Female Convicts, Sexuality and Gender in Colonial Australia* (Cambridge University Press, 1997).

36 James Semple Kerr, *Out of Sight, Out of Mind: Australia's Places of Confinement, 1788–1988* (Sydney: S.H. Ervin Gallery, 1988).

37 Catharine Coleborne, *Madness in the Family: Insanity and Institutions in the Australasian Colonial World, 1860–1914* (Basingstoke: Palgrave Macmillan, 2010); Stephen Garton, *Medicine and Madness: A Social History of Insanity in New South Wales 1880–1940* (Sydney: UNSW Press, 1988).

later systems for the surveillance of mobility. As islands in remote destinations, the Australasian colonies proved ideal sites for the refinement of immigration controls in the later nineteenth century. The racial discriminations of Chinese-restriction legislation were complemented by the refinement of quarantine controls to prevent the spread of infectious diseases, and draconian segregations targetting leprosy.[38] In expanding the reach of government in the management of populations, the Australian story shared much with that of other parts of the Empire and beyond. The story of child-rescue is a striking example, with the colonies sharing in the mid-Victorian British anxiety over the status of children in a rapidly changing urban environment. The response in Australia, however, was characteristically state-directed rather than voluntaristic; indeed, child welfare and protection had a history going back to the earliest convict days.[39] In the 1860s both the largest colonies, New South Wales and Victoria, enacted legislation for state institutional provision for neglected children and juvenile delinquents.[40] The development of juvenile reformatories, separating young offenders or those at risk of the criminal underworld from the dangers of contamination by adult prisoners, expressed nineteenth-century liberalism's faith in rehabilitation through the separation of vulnerable individuals from malign influences. In New South Wales this institutional solution owed much to the dominant voice of Henry Parkes. His chairing of the 1860 select committee on the condition of the working classes set out a program of social amelioration that presumed a major role for state provision of institutional remedies to poverty, distress and crime.[41] The resulting institutions, industrial schools and juvenile reformatories proved no panacea and in the longer term became the object of severe criticism and demands for reform. Child-saving and rescue was a persistent object of women's philanthropic activism, which did much to shape the later development of alternatives to state institutional provision in the form of the boarding-out or fostering system.[42] Hence the readiness with which colonial liberal politicians welcomed the globe-trotting reformers Florence and Rosamond Hill. Before a

---

38 Bashford, *Imperial Hygiene*.
39 Damousi, *Depraved and Disorderly*, pp. 128–53.
40 John Ramsland, *Children of the Back Lanes: Destitute and Neglected Children in Colonial New South Wales* (Sydney: UNSW Press, 1986); Christina Twomey, 'Gender, Welfare and the Colonial State: Victoria's 1864 Neglected and Criminal Children's Act', *Labour History*, 73 (1997): 169–86.
41 A.W. Martin, *Henry Parkes: A Biography* (Melbourne University Press, 1980), pp. 174–6.
42 Brian Dickey, *Rations, Residence, Resources: A History of Social Welfare in South Australia Since 1836* (Adelaide: Wakefield Press, 1986); Susan Magarey, *Unbridling the Tongues of Women: A Biography of Catherine Helen Spence* (Sydney: Hale & Iremonger, 1985); Swain and Howe, *Single Mothers and Their Children*.

New South Wales parliamentary committee in 1873 Rosamond Hill advocated at length the merits of the continental, family based provisions at Mettray in France and Rauhe Haus near Hamburg, Germany, as examples of progressive reform that were frequently appraised in the colonial press.[43] In this respect the regulatory apparatus of the nineteenth century was also an imperial legacy, with the debates and moral drivers constantly referring to British example, which in turn mediated European and North American innovation.[44] The effects in social policy were widespread, and enduring. Its legacy could be found in the institutional design and substantive interventions in Australian Indigenous life through the protection systems and the practices of child removal.[45]

A different kind of imperial context shaped the controversial regulation of prostitution. While the practice of prostitution was not itself criminalised, the category of prostitute was the object of vagrancy legislation that delivered broad discretionary powers into the hands of police. Reputation as a 'common prostitute' was sufficient in the contagious diseases acts of the second half of the nineteenth century to justify police certification for the purposes of medical examination. Originating in a governmental ordinance of 1857 in India aimed at protecting solders of the British Army, from 1864 a series of contagious-diseases statutes were enacted at Westminster, providing for the medical inspection in proclaimed towns of women who were identified by inspectors as engaged in prostitution. In the United Kingdom and many colonial legislatures, the legislation was articulated to the felt need to protect the imperial army and navy forces. In the Australian setting, however, from which imperial forces were withdrawn in 1870, the legislation was articulated for the protection of the white population.[46] In Queensland, where an *Act for the Prevention of Contagious Diseases* was passed in 1868, the regulations could apply in any town proclaimed by the governor. Under such legislation women within defined territorial boundaries might be detained for medical inspection, and confined in a lock hospital if found to have a venereal disease. Only Tasmania followed Queensland's example, with other colonies faltering in their attempts to follow the imperial parliament. In Victoria, a

---

43 John Ramsland, 'The Agricultural Colony at Mettray: A 19th Century Approach to the Institutionalization of Delinquent Boys', *Melbourne Studies in Education*, 29, 1 (1987): 64–80.

44 Stephen Garton, *Out of Luck: Poor Australians and Social Welfare 1788–1988* (Sydney: Allen & Unwin, 1990).

45 Anna Haebich, *Broken Circles: Fragmenting Indigenous Families 1800–2000* (Fremantle Arts Centre Press, 2000), pp. 148–50; Rosalind Kidd, *The Way We Civilise: Aboriginal Affairs – The Untold Story* (Brisbane: UQP, 1997), pp. 20, 47, 51.

46 Philippa Levine, *Prostitution, Race, and Politics: Policing Venereal Disease in the British Empire* (New York: Routledge, 2003).

spirited campaign for the enactment of legislation aimed specifically at syph-
ilis (but not venereal diseases generally, as in Queensland and Tasmania)
resulted in the *Conservation of Public Health Act* of 1878. Strong resistance to
the recognition of prostitution entailed in such legislation was evident in the
Victorian government's reluctance to make the Act effective by proclaiming
a lock hospital for the purpose of inspections and treatment. Consequently
the legislation was never enacted. Attempts in both New South Wales and
South Australia failed to result even in a statute, with social reformers in both
places opposing the idea of de facto regulation of prostitution.[47]

The uneven colonial response to the threat of 'contagious diseases' is
no model for the effects of other modes of population regulation through
law. By the late nineteenth century the Australasian colonies were places in
which ideals of health and purity, of individuals and of race, were marshalled
enthusiastically. The regulation of population along dimensions of productive and responsible versus vagrant and idle was imported with English
vagrancy law, replicated in the towns and police Acts of the early nineteenth
century. Egalitarian sentiment in the colonies was comforted by the absence
of a poor law, with its detested regimes of workhouse, work test and lesser
eligibility – even if colonial governments absorbed some of its principles in
their centralised systems of poor relief.[48] Yet in the hands of urban police the
vagrancy statutes were an instrument for surveillance of the criminal and
dangerous classes of the Victorian era, among whom prostitutes, 'incorri-
gible thieves' and other social enemies were the objects of attention. The
notorious flexibility of the vagrancy charge, with its reverse onus of proof
in a summary jurisdiction, rendered it an alternative to contagious diseases
legislation.[49] Indeed, another kind of public order concern shaped the policing of prostitution – the concern to limit its visibility evident in campaigns
against street prostitution.[50] Social purity campaigns were nevertheless limited
in their capacity to shape policing in colonial cities. After the 1850s (except
for Tasmania, where police administration was centralised only in 1898), the

---

47 Raelene Frances, *Selling Sex: A Hidden History of Prostitution* (Sydney: UNSW Press,
2007); Milton Lewis, *Thorns on the Rose: The History of Sexually Transmitted Diseases in
Australia in International Perspective* (Canberra: AGPS, 1998).

48 Robert Dare, 'Paupers' Rights: Governor Grey and the Poor Law in South Australia',
Australian Historical Studies, 25, 99 (1992): 220–43.

49 Susanne Davies, '"Ragged, Dirty, Infamous and Obscene": The Vagrant in
Late-Nineteenth-Century Melbourne', in David Phillips and Susanne Davies (eds), *A
Nation of Rogues? Crime, Law and Punishment in Colonial Australia* (Melbourne University
Press, 1994), p. 149.

50 Judith A. Allen, *Sex & Secrets: Crimes Involving Australian Women Since 1880* (Oxford
University Press, 1990); Frances, *Selling Sex*.

police force was not subject to local direction but answerable to central government; its cherished notions of independence and discretion allowed police officers to resist the demands to eradicate whatever nuisance of the streets happened to exercise various strands of public opinion from time to time. Yet public order and crime control remained important drivers in the use of vagrancy regulation. Criminals congregated around brothels and hotels, making them a constant focus of police surveillance and interference.[51] These powers and their manipulation in the policing of such populations also laid the ground for police corruption.

By the end of the nineteenth century no population within colonial jurisdictions was as vulnerable to regulation as the Indigenous. That vulnerability was also a function of particular local histories of contact and of preferred structures of administration, constructed and expressed through legislation. A later review of legal definitions of 'Aboriginal identity' found no less than 67 distinct definitions, reaching back into the 1830s.[52] Through vagrancy laws colonial authorities sought variously to limit the debasement of the country's original peoples by those imagined most capable of degrading them (white or Asian, especially Chinese), and to avoid the dangers of a miscegenation that would apparently dilute the vigour of a British population in the antipodes. Adapting English vagrancy law to the conditions of New South Wales in 1835, Governor Richard Bourke penalised idle associations between the settlers and 'black natives'; in turn that law was adapted in newly self-governing Victoria in 1852, the prohibition now applying to any person not an Aboriginal 'lodging or wandering with any of the Aboriginal Natives'. A residual recognition of the different position of Indigenous people lay at the heart of this segregating legislation. A petition to the New South Wales parliament from the New England district sought protection from the local Aboriginal people by bringing them within the reach of the *Vagrants Act* and confining them within their own localities, a proposal that gestured towards the domiciliary framework of English poor law and vagrant regimes. The *Sydney Morning Herald* thought the proposition absurd: 'although we have taken the black man's land – although, vagrant-like, we have unauthorisedly settled on his possessions, we have not yet ventured under color of law to seize upon his body or to restrict his personal freedom'.[53] This disingenuous

---

51 Dean Wilson, *The Beat: Policing a Victorian City* (Melbourne: Melbourne Publishing Group, 2006), p. 184.

52 J.C. McCorquodale, 'Aboriginal Identity: Legislative, Judicial and Administrative Definitions', *Australian Aboriginal Studies*, 2 (1997): 24–35.

53 *Sydney Morning Herald*, 30 August 1853.

characterisation of surviving Aboriginal freedom retains its interest as a sign of colonial uncertainty about the scope and rationale of regulation of the country's Indigenous people, a hesitation replaced by certitude in the necessity of total control by the end of the century.

Policing

The police played its role in the violent displacement of the country's original inhabitants. It might also have been the means of averting even worse bloodshed. Colonial policing in Australia was of a type with its contemporaries in other parts of the Empire, and a product of the twofold influence of British and Irish policing. Police officers complained of their multiple roles and duties but the development of the capacity of government to administer the vast spaces of Australia was unthinkable after 1850 without the agency of police.

In the early decades policing was a function of the magistracy. Constables were appointed by and overseen by magistrates. Their functions were narrowly defined; thief-taking and murderer-hunting, as well as acting at the magistrates' direction in urban peace-keeping. In the convict colonies their functions were also controversial, especially when governors such as Macquarie started to regulate more actively what they expected of local populations. In Sydney there was much resentment at the surveillance exercised by local constables over the free population, aggravated by the fact that some of the constables were convicts or emancipated convicts. Even so, it has been observed that constables paid close attention to the evidence required in bringing cases to court during these decades.[54]

The association between policing and government in the penal and crown colonies was consistent with the long-term evolution of police institutions. Governor Macquarie established the Sydney police in 1810, and Governor Stirling appointed police constables at Swan River in one of his earliest actions in 1830. In Van Diemen's Land Lieutenant-Governor Arthur established authoritarian and highly centralised policing, with two-thirds of police also being convicts, an arrangement continued by his successors.[55] Later, colonial policing was shaped profoundly by the two models developed at the heart of Empire in the 1820s and 1830s.[56] The London Metropolitan Police (1829)

54 Paula J. Byrne, *Criminal Law and Colonial Subject: New South Wales, 1810–1830* (Cambridge University Press, 1993).
55 Stefan Petrow, 'Policing in a Penal Colony: Governor Arthur's Police System in Van Diemen's Land, 1826–1836', *Law and History Review* 18, 2 (2000): 351–95.
56 Finnane, *Police and Government*; Robert K. Haldane, *The People's Force: A History of the Victoria Police* (Melbourne University Press, 1986).

was the reference point for urban policing in the colonies, while the Irish Constabulary (1836) shaped policing organisation and method in the rural areas. But there was no simple divide between urban and rural policing, for the weakness of local government in Australia meant that at an early point police were controlled from the colonial capitals. In the manner that Dublin Castle controlled the policing of Donegal or Cork, so a police commissioner residing in Perth would exercise remote control over the Kimberleys in the northern parts of Western Australia, or one in Adelaide over the vast expanses of central Australia and the entire Northern Territory (even down to its cession to the Commonwealth in 1911).[57]

Policing of Indigenous resistance was the second phase of government response, succeeding military action under the orders of the governor. The widespread adoption in Imperial policing of recruitment of selected Indigenous people to police their own was the subject of early experiment in Australia.[58] The earliest Native Police Corps was established in Port Phillip District (later Victoria) in 1837. The aims were more benign than the later history of such forces suggests. The administrator, Captain Lonsdale, thought that enlistment of local Aboriginal men in a 'Police Corps' would foster the 'desirable objectives of making them useful to society, of gradually weaning them from their native habits and prejudices, of habituating them to civilised customs'. Enlisting them as police would have the advantage that they would not be tied 'to any definite labor or irksome routine of employment', allowing them to continue some of their traditional pursuits, such as the 'recreation of hunting'. To the Aboriginal people, of course, hunting was not recreation but work, the necessary means of subsistence. Through the fog of cultural preconceptions there was in Lonsdale's conception a transformative, rather than simply destructive object.[59] Later colonials were less sanguine, and more brutal in their views of what the uses of a Native Police would be.

The archetype of brutality in the Native Police was found in Queensland. Dating from 1849 when the colony of New South Wales acted to control

57 Andrew Gill, 'Aborigines, Settlers and Police in the Kimberleys, 1887–1905', *Studies in Western Australian History*, 1 (1977): 1–28; Amanda Nettelbeck and Robert Foster, *In the Name of the Law: William Willshire and the Policing of the Australian Frontier* (Adelaide: Wakefield Press, 2007); Gordon Reid, *A Picnic with the Natives: Aboriginal–European Relations in the Northern Territory to 1910* (Melbourne University Press, 1990).

58 David M. Anderson and David Killingray, *Policing the Empire: Government, Authority, and Control, 1830–1940* (Manchester University Press, 1991).

59 Marie Hansen Fels, *Good Men and True: The Aboriginal Police of the Port Phillip District, 1837–1853* (Melbourne University Press, 1988), pp. 16–17.

conflict between settlers and Aboriginal people on its northern frontiers, the Queensland Native Police continued after separation to police the expanding borders of settlement to the end of the century. On a principle derived from the Irish Constabulary, a key feature of the Native Police was that the troopers were recruited from districts foreign to those they would be policing. Sometimes they were discharged convicts, having spent time in prisons for previous killings. But their activities proceeded under the authority of officers whose duties were above all to limit the threat of Aboriginal resistance to white settlement. Unlike the regular police of Queensland, replete with the paperwork of the modern constabulary, the Native Police proceeded under limited supervision: historians have often found it difficult to track their activities, and estimates of fatalities remain highly speculative.[60] The violence of frontier policing was not without its critics, in Queensland and in other colonies. Occasional public inquiries and even prosecutions of some police signalled by the 1890s the tension between two visions of policing, one paramilitary, the other administrative and ambiguously 'protective'. An important outcome, critical to the future development of policy affecting Indigenous Australians in the twentieth century, was the elaboration during the 1880s of a new policing focused on the 'protection' of the Indigenous populations in north Queensland.[61]

There was another policing of the Australian colonies that was almost as controversial as that controlling and regulating the lives of Indigenous people. Much of colonial policing was shaped by the direct transmission of law and regulation from the centre of the Empire. Well before the formation of the New South Wales Police Force in 1862, its antecedent Sydney constabulary was responsible for enforcing the new codes of urban order embodied in the *Towns Police Act* of 1833. This was no less than an amalgam of the powers police in London were then deploying under the *London Metropolitan Police Act* of 1829. The constables were expected to be the moral street cleaners of the growing cities and towns of the colonies, the domestic guardians of secure settler dominions.[62] In newly self-governing Tasmania after 1856 such a focus was the very principle of police organisation, following a rejection of

---

60 W. Ross Johnston, *The Long Blue Line: A History of the Queensland Police* (Brisbane: Boolarong, 1992), pp. 82–99; Noel Loos, *Invasion and Resistance: Aboriginal-European Relations on the North Queensland Frontier 1861–1897* (Canberra: ANU Press, 1982); Jonathan Richards, *The Secret War: A True History of Queensland's Native Police* (Brisbane: UQP, 2008), pp. 193–200.

61 Loos, *Invasion and Resistance*, pp. 170–82.

62 Wilson, *The Beat*.

Governor Arthur's centralised policing in favour of local police run by each municipal district, a system persisting to 1898.[63]

The mundane world of patrolling the beat and arresting drunks and vagrants formed a strong contrast to another and more dangerous pursuit. Beyond the town boundaries, in a sparsely occupied land behind the frontiers of white settlement, the small colonial villages and their linking roads were vulnerable to the rural bandits known as bushrangers. From the exploits of the most famous, Ned Kelly, were moulded the mythologies of an Australian vernacular that placed a high value on rebellion and opposition to authority. Kelly's capture and execution in 1880 was, however, the denouement of the bushrangers. Their lives and exploits were shaped by a variety of colonial circumstances, not the least of which was the challenge to police them.

It would be tempting to explain the phenomenon of bushranging in terms of the weakness of colonial government in a large, open land. Yet the exploits of the Kelly gang took place in the relatively small and more densely populated colony of Victoria. The police were by the 1870s well established, more on the Irish model than that of London – not only was more than 80 per cent of the Victorian constabulary of Irish birth, but nearly half of these had already served in the Irish constabulary.[64] In spite of this background of administrative and occupational experience, the Victorian police was seriously challenged by the Kelly gang's outlawry.

One reason was that the police force found itself combatting a foe whose strength derived in part from a wider community of support. In north-eastern Victoria many selectors struggling to make a living in the wake of the gold rushes, with their inevitable disappointments, found Kelly's defiance of authority appealing. Rural poverty was only part explanation: family and faction were as likely important here as in rural Ireland. There were other rural areas of Australia, too, where the police found itself battling not only the outlaws who robbed banks and stagecoaches but the sympathies of those who supported the bushrangers. Some bushrangers cultivated a style of chivalry, or a flashness of language and dress, that helped to build sympathy.[65] In New South Wales a decade and more before the Kellys, Ben Hall and Frank Gardiner had kept police at bay in a series of adventures that forced a restructuring of police, brought government to its knees and inspired the Chief

---

63 Petrow, 'Economy, Efficiency and Impartiality'.
64 Haldane, *The People's Force*, pp. 78–90.
65 Graham Seal, *The Outlaw Legend: A Cultural Tradition in Britain, America and Australia* (Cambridge University Press, 1996).

Justice to draft an 'outlawry' statute, later adopted as the *Felons Apprehension Act* of 1865.[66]

For the most part the bushrangers were white. But in 1864 the small coastal town of Mackay (Queensland) was the scene of a bank robbery by a black American named Henry Ford and his Aboriginal bushranging partner, William Chambers. They escaped with £746 and then led a settlers' posse on a fruitless chase, stopping to have a beer on their way to freedom. Nine months later they were arrested after another incident in northern New South Wales, hundreds of miles away.[67] Other Aboriginal people assumed outlaw status when they led local resistance to white settlement or else absconded from service on pastoral stations, taking to killing stock and the occasional robbery. The legendary Toby of central Queensland in the 1880s was one such outlaw. A series of stock killings, theft of liquor and abduction of a white woman led to his eventual capture and killing, not before he had killed a constable with a tomahawk he had allegedly held between his toes to conceal it while he was arrested.[68] Indigenous outlawry and its respondent policing strategies, paramilitary more than conciliatory, remained a feature of the frontier landscape to the end of the nineteenth century and, in northern Australia especially, into the twentieth.[69]

Aboriginal resistance was a formidable impediment to colonial settlement in some districts, its incidence following the contours of the frontier. Among its most spectacular examples was the late-nineteenth century story of Jandamarra ('Pigeon', as he was long remembered in Bunuba folklore) in the Kimberley district of north-western Australia. Like other such outlaws, Jandamarra's initiative and power derived partly from his life bridging two cultures; he had himself been a police tracker. This three-year resistance over 1894–97 delayed settlement in that region, brought only to an end by large-scale policing operations. The police killed Jandamarra after earlier

66 J.B. Hirst, *The Strange Birth of Colonial Democracy: New South Wales 1848–1884* (Sydney: Allen & Unwin, 1988); Susan West, *Bushranging and the Policing of Rural Banditry in New South Wales, 1860–1880* (Melbourne: Australian Scholarly Publishing, 2009); Woods, *A History of Criminal Law in New South Wales*, pp. 203–4.

67 Gordon Reid, *A Nest of Hornets: The Massacre of the Fraser Family at Hornet Bank Station, Central Queensland and Related Events* (Oxford University Press, 1982), pp. 145–6.

68 Ibid., p. 169.

69 Richard Broome, 'The Statistics of Frontier Conflict', in Bain Attwood and S.G. Foster (eds), *Frontier Conflict: The Australian Experience* (Canberra: National Museum of Australia, 2003), pp. 88–98; Chris Owen, '"The Police Appear to Be a Useless Lot up There": Law and Order in the East Kimberley 1884–1905', *Aboriginal History* 27 (2003): 105–30; Tony Roberts, *Frontier Justice: A History of the Gulf Country to 1900* (Brisbane: UQP, 2005).

police massacres of Indigenous people across the Kimberley.[70] Occurring at the same time as police in Queensland were mapping the demise of the Native Police in favour of a new model of 'protection', the Kimberley violence underscored the ineradicable foundation of colonial law in the use of force.

The later colonial allure of bushranging is at odds with the more hostile reception of earlier decades, but the sense of domestic emergency inspired by the bushrangers had a long history in the colonies. The term originated indeed in the early convict decades, with both Van Diemen's Land and New South Wales experiencing earlier crises in authority provoked by rural banditry, as runaway convicts turned to robbing travellers or isolated farms. Since bushranging originated in a convict society, subject to the autocratic rule of a governor, it was scarcely surprising that responses to it were draconian: as the historian Alan Atkinson has noted, 'in dealing with bushrangers the government [in Van Diemen's Land] was not just putting down outlaws. It was trying to prove that it was in fact the government.'[71] Large numbers were hanged in New South Wales and Tasmania in the penal colony years.[72] But then and later, more was needed than the governor's command: catching the bushrangers came to be aided by new powers to the police during the very periods of their formation. In New South Wales the 'Bushranging Act' (in fact the *Robbery and Firearms Act* of 1830) was a drastic statutory response that reversed the onus of proof in criminal proceedings and gave broad powers of detention to the authorities. As a symbol of all that was wrong with a colony subject to autocratic and irresponsible rule, the repeal of the Bushranging Act became a *cause célèbre* for the liberal press of the day. It endured until 1853.[73]

Enacting such laws and hanging an exemplary lot of bushrangers were methods of response that depended in the long term on the efficiency of the police. It was here that bushranging played an even more significant role. In the 1850s and early 1860s in New South Wales, and again in Victoria in the late 1870s, the police were found wanting. Their skills and organisation proved

---

70 Howard Pedersen and Banjo Woorunmurra, *Jandamarra and the Bunuba Resistance* (Perth: Magabala Books, 2000).

71 Atkinson, *The Europeans in Australia*, vol. 2, p. 69.

72 Tim Castle, 'Watching Them Hang: Capital Punishment and Public Support in Colonial New South Wales, 1826–1836', *History Australia*, 5, 2 (2008): 43.1–15; Richard Davis, *The Tasmanian Gallows: A Study of Capital Punishment* (Hobart: Cat & Fiddle Press, 1974).

73 David Neal, *The Rule of Law in a Penal Colony: Law and Power in Early New South Wales* (Cambridge University Press, 1991); Woods, *A History of Criminal Law in New South Wales*, pp. 77–8.

inadequate in combatting the serious challenge posed by bushranging to rural settlements. The consequence in New South Wales was the centralisation of police and an enhancement of their bush-patrolling skills. In Victoria the Kelly outbreak was put down only with an extreme display of police violence at Glenrowan, and led to one of the most extensive inquiries into colonial policing held in Australia. The Longmore Commission scrutinised not only the series of events resulting in the death of police and Kelly's open defiance of authority. The detective force was also shown to have been inept, and was reintegrated into the general police. Improved training and organisation, promotion by examination and a new police code were among other recommendations.[74] The resulting changes were predictably partial: a generation later there were further inquiries into corruption, and in 1923 maladministration provoked Australia's only police strike in Melbourne. By that time, however, bushrangers could not be blamed; although the representation of their exploits in silent cinema of the 1920s led to new police powers, this time in aid of censorship of film.[75]

The role of policing in regulating a particular kind of social order was accentuated by these great social conflicts of the colonial period. The dual face of policing – the potential use of ultimate force combined with an accountable and restrained use of it – was shaped by the controversies arising from the policing of Indigenous communities and the failures as well as successes of the battle against bushranging. The organisation of policing as a function of central government in the colonies, operating with an increasing armoury of statutory as well as common-law powers, spoke to the ambitions of a society that had a limited tolerance for disorder. But the egalitarian legacy of a society that had allowed convicts access to the law was also evident in the restraint with which police powers were used, which appeared often to be in inverse proportion to the volume of criticism engendered by their use. Colonel Tom Price was notoriously remembered as having ordered his volunteers facing 40,000 protesters at Flinders Park in Melbourne during the maritime strike of 1890 to 'fire low and lay them out'. But Price was a military officer; there was no firing from his volunteer military officers and it was police who kept command on the day, earning a parliamentary compliment that 'all the working men who assembled at the great meeting on Sunday regarded the police not as enemies but as brothers'.[76] This was a

74 Haldane, The People's Force, pp. 90–101.
75 Ina Bertrand, Film Censorship in Australia (Sydney: Australian Film and Television School, 1981).
76 Haldane, The People's Force, p. 118.

different view from that which informed the furious invective of Ned Kelly's Jerilderie letter, which slated the police as corrupt and servile, traitors to the people from whom they came, in the 1870s still largely Irish emigrants. 'I would manure the Elevenmile with their bloated carcasses and yet remember there is not one drop of murderous blood in my Veins', he castigated the police who had threatened his family. His expressed grievance was with a system that failed to live up to its ideals. '[I]t seems that the jury was well chosen by the Police as there was a discharged Sergeant amongst them which is contrary to law...they thought it impossible for a Policeman to swear a lie but I can assure them it is by that means and hiring cads they get promoted', he charged. Even in the midst of Kelly's anger it seemed possible to imagine a policeman who might serve fairly a law that dispensed a justice worth respecting.[77]

77 'Ned Kelly's Jerilderie Letter', <http://www2.slv.vic.gov.au/collections/treasures/jerilderieletter/jerilderie25.html> (accessed 27 March 2012).

17

Religion

ANNE O'BRIEN

A 'peculiar colony'

When the British arrived at Sydney Cove in 1788 – Warrane, the local people called it – the continent had been richly inscribed with the Dreaming stories of about 250 language groups and 500 clans of Indigenous people for around 50,000 years. Stories of the Ancestral Beings, whose travels had created land forms, people, animals, plants, sea and stars, provided both an explanation of origins and a law to govern behaviour.[1] The ancestral beings connected Indigenous people to specific sites, but Christianity was a mobile faith. Its all-powerful, all-knowing God was a personal companion who accompanied his people on trips of exploration and guided their acquisition of new lands. Unlike the early seventeenth-century settlement of 'pilgrims' in Massachusetts, however, religion was not foundational to the formation of New South Wales. This colony was a government outpost, a repository for criminals and a potential base for trade with Asia. Its first chaplains were part of the military apparatus, dependent on the goodwill of the governors. They were also evangelicals, products of the revival that swept England in the eighteenth century, with its radical critique of the established church; they preached a gospel that prohibited most of the pleasures available to the British lower orders.

It is unsurprising, then, that narratives of doom surrounded the first years of the Christian history of New South Wales. Certain stories are retold because of their symbolic power: Richard Johnson, the first chaplain of the colony, was given no support to build a church and when he built his own in 1796, the convicts burned it down; when the New South Wales Corps took charge of the colony in the early 1790s, its drum sergeant humiliated Johnson by summoning the convicts to parade halfway through his sermon.

---

1 Howard Morphy, Francoise Dussart and M.J. Charlesworth, *Aboriginal Religions in Australia: An Anthology of Recent Writings* (Burlington: Ashgate, 2005).

The governors disagreed with the chaplains about religion's role. Governor Phillip urged Johnson to confine his sermons to 'moral subjects' but Johnson wanted to preach a message of salvation through personal conversion. Most of the governing men were indifferent to evangelical strictures; they took convict mistresses, drank alcohol, allowed blood sports and showed so little respect for the Sabbath that they allowed the theatre to open on Easter Sunday.[2] The lack of interest in Christianity of the Eora people, who lived in the coastal areas occupied by the settlers, also contributed to the narrative of failure. After the first smallpox epidemic of 1789 a few settlers, including Rev. Johnson and his wife Mary, 'adopted' children from the Gadigal band, but the children either died or ran away.[3] Defining failure depends, of course, on one's perspective. Despite the enormous disruption that colonisation brought to their lives and the devastating effects of smallpox in 1789, the Eora people continued to practice traditional rituals in the heart of Sydney into the 1830s.[4]

The picture is also more complex regarding settler religion. Many of the governing men might have been suspicious of evangelical enthusiasm, but they also believed in a providential God and in the Church of England. If few saw the church as a 'spiritual entity' or 'the conscience of society' in the manner of traditional churchmen, most saw it as a source of stability, civilisation and public good.[5] The women of the elite also modified the received stories about the early colony's unrelieved irreligion. The grazier Elizabeth Macarthur was an Anglican of 'more than formal piety and much comforted by faith'. Anna King's faith guided her public and personal philanthropy, for she was instrumental in the foundation of the Female Orphan School in 1802 and she included her husband's illegitimate children within the circle of family affection.[6] Nor should we assume that all evangelicals saw themselves as failures. Johnson's younger assistant chaplain, the Rev. Samuel Marsden, adapted well to colonial conditions. When he found neither 'the higher ranks' nor the convicts wanting 'the Great Physician of Souls', he turned his energies to farming and became one of the wealthiest landowners in the

2 Alan Atkinson, *The Europeans in Australia: A History. Volume 1, The Beginning* (Oxford University Press, 1997), pp. 168–92.

3 Niel Gunson (ed.), *Australian Reminiscences & Papers of L.E. Threlkeld, Missionary to the Aborigines, 1824–1859* (Canberra: Australian Institute of Aboriginal Studies, 1974).

4 Grace Karskens, *The Colony: A History of Early Sydney* (Sydney: Allen & Unwin, 2009), pp. 424, 440–6.

5 Stephen Judd and Kenneth Cable, *Sydney Anglicans: A History of the Diocese* (Sydney: Anglican Information Office, 1987), p. 10.

6 'Elizabeth Macarthur', *Australian Dictionary of Biography*, vol. 2, pp. 144–7; 'Anna King', *Australian Dictionary of Biography*, vol. 2, pp. 52–4.

colony.[7] He saw no clash between public order and mission; indeed, order was the 'fixed point' in his life.[8] It underpinned his ruthless treatment of Irish convicts and his responses in the wars with Aboriginal people. A Calvinist, Marsden saw his worldly success as a sign of God's pleasure and blessed the God who had 'made him to differ' from the convicts. He and his wife, Eliza, 'adopted' two Gadigal boys, an experiment whose failure confirmed his conviction that Aboriginal people were incapable of conversion and 'civilisation', and discouraged British missionary societies from working in Australia for the first two decades of the nineteenth-century.[9] He was more confident that the Māori would accept Christianity and commerce, and sailed to New Zealand on behalf of the evangelical Church Missionary Society (CMS) in 1814, thus formalising Sydney's role as a base for missionary work in the Pacific. The first London Missionary Society (LMS) missionaries to Tahiti, forced to abandon their mission there in 1797, had established school chapels at various settlements around Sydney, and some moved between the colony and the Tahitian mission over the following decades.[10]

The early histories of religious belief are more complex still when we consider that in this 'peculiar colony', as Governor King described New South Wales in 1804, the vast majority of the settler population comprised convicted criminals from the lower orders. They shaped the nature of the early colonies as much as, if not more than, the officers and clergy. What do we know of their beliefs? There is abundant evidence of anti-clericalism, deriving not just from old resentments against the abuses of the church in England, but also from the fact that colonial chaplains were magistrates endowed with the power to punish and to grant tickets of leave. There are reports of convicts using religious tracts as scrap paper and of the women curling their hair with them; they feigned piety and mimicked the clergy behind their backs.[11] There is also evidence that convicts responded well to clergy they respected: Johnson provided for the sick out of his own provisions. In the first four years, when attendance at Sunday services was effectively voluntary, between a quarter and a half of the convicts attended his services, with congregations

---

7 Karskens, *The Colony*, p. 140.
8 Judd and Cable, *Sydney Anglicans*, p. 4.
9 See Karskens, *The Colony*, p. 479; A.T. Yarwood, *Samuel Marsden: The Great Survivor* (Melbourne University Press, 1977), pp. 79, 112–13.
10 Judd and Cable, *Sydney Anglicans*, pp. 5–6; 'James Cover', *Australian Dictionary of Biography*, vol. 1, pp. 251–3.
11 Allan M. Grocott, *Convicts, Clergymen and Churches: Attitudes of Convicts and Ex-Convicts towards the Churches and Clergy in New South Wales from 1788–1851* (Sydney University Press, 1980), pp. 56, 61, 201–4

of between 600 and 800. Convict women took their children to be baptised, and some sent their children to church on Sundays. A rereading of the convicts' burning of Johnson's church suggests it may have been as much a reaction against compulsory attendance as rebellion against religion.[12]

Nor was anti-clericalism necessarily irreligious. Some convicts had religious symbols tattooed on their bodies: crucifixes, anchors and talismanic verses seeking God's protection.[13] Folk beliefs and interest in astrology were common. Convicts were frightened if they could not bury their dead – unbaptised, stillborn babies or those lost at sea.[14] Almanacs, published in Sydney from 1806 until the 1850s, showed the positions of the heavenly bodies so readers could predict their horoscopes or be guided on when to pick healing herbs.[15] It is difficult to know how widespread folk beliefs were or what they meant to 'ordinary' people. Some professed contempt for any aspect of the supernatural: Charles Williams, one of the settlers who took possession of the Hawkesbury River area, prefaced his testimony in court in 1792 by saying 'he was not of any religion at all, but that of the Cock and Hens'.[16] There are reports of the Irish, however, 'sitting up with the corpse' all night at wakes and celebrating St Patrick's Day for two weeks at a time.[17] If traditional customs represented mayhem and ignorance to the clergy, they provided immigrants with links to the Old World, and perhaps some sense of control in the New.

The Irish-Catholic convicts complicate the politico-religious dynamic. They comprised about a quarter of all convicts transported and, since the Church of England was the only denomination to receive official recognition and support before 1820, they were forced to attend its services. Compulsion may have sharpened their desire for their own rites. During the first 30 years of settlement, small groups of Irish Catholics repeatedly petitioned the government to send them a priest, particularly for those facing execution; observers noted small communities of Irish Catholics coming together for prayer in the main centres around Sydney.[18] Catholic priests ministered in the

---

12 Atkinson, *The Europeans in Australia*, vol. 1, pp. 142–3, 177–80.

13 Hamish Maxwell-Stewart and Ian Duffield, 'Skin Deep Devotions: Religious Tattoos and Convict Transportation to Australia', in Jane Caplan (ed.), *Written on the Body: The Tattoo in European and American History* (London: Reaktion, 2000), p. 132.

14 Grace Karskens, 'Death was in his Face: Dying, Burial and Remembrance in Early Sydney', *Labour History*, 74 (1998): 21–39.

15 Maureen Perkins, '"An Era of Great Doubt to Some in Sydney": Almanacs and Astrological Belief in Colonial Australia', *Journal of Religious History*, 17, 4 (1993): 465–74.

16 Quoted in Atkinson, *The Europeans in Australia*, vol. 1, p. 170.

17 Patrick O'Farrell, *The Irish in Australia* (Sydney: UNSW Press, 1986), pp. 27–8, 42.

18 Edmund Campion, *Australian Catholics* (Melbourne: Viking, 1987), pp. 3–9.

colonies for two brief periods before 1820. Both ended abruptly and both fed the sense of persecution that characterises much of Catholic historiography in Australia.

The first Irish-Catholic priest was James Dixon, who was transported for his alleged role in the 1798 rebellion at Wexford. He was held to have contributed to the attempted uprising at Castle Hill by Irish convicts in 1804, and his public ministry was immediately terminated. The second swiftly aborted ministry was that of Jeremiah O'Flynn, who arrived in Sydney in 1817 without approval and was deported the following year. His escapade – its legendary status heightened because he was said to have left the Blessed Sacrament as a gift to Catholics before his departure – was a turning point in the attitudes of both Roman and British authorities, pressing home the need for an officially approved ministry.[19] In 1820 John Joseph Therry was appointed Catholic chaplain to New South Wales and Phillip Connolly to Van Diemen's Land. Irishness was pivotal in the persistent but fluctuating sectarian bigotry that was a distinctive feature of Australian religion. Marsden's observation in 1807 that Catholic convicts were from 'the lowest Class of the Irish Nation, who are the most wild, ignorant and savage Race that were ever favoured with the Light of Civilisation' captures at its most intense the disgust for Irish Catholics in the early nineteenth-century Protestant gaze.[20]

More than any other governor, Lachlan Macquarie believed in religion as a source of order and a means for reform. He tried to impose respect for the Sabbath; convicts on public works were to attend service, publicans were to close their doors and the *Sydney Gazette* was to change its publication date from Sunday to Saturday.[21] He commissioned the brilliant convict architect Francis Greenway to design churches for the centre of Sydney and at Liverpool and Windsor, where they would take civilisation to the edge of the 'wilderness'.[22] Institutions and societies were intrinsic to Macquarie's goal of moral reform, and a number were established under his governance by the trickle of evangelical laymen, Dissenting missionaries and chaplains who arrived in the 1810s. The evangelical and radical newspaper proprietor, Edward Smith Hall, was the driving force behind the foundation of the Benevolent Society in 1813. Thomas Hassall, the son of one of the most prominent

19 Patrick O'Farrell, *The Catholic Church and Community: An Australian History* (Sydney: UNSW Press, 1985), pp. 1–39.

20 Yarwood, *Samuel Marsden*, p. 98.

21 John Ritchie, *Lachlan Macquarie: A Biography* (Melbourne University Press, 1986), p. 131.

22 John Gascoigne with the assistance of Patricia Curthoys, *The Enlightenment and the Origins of European Australia* (Cambridge University Press, 2002), p. x.

LMS missionaries, Rowland Hassall, founded the New South Wales Sunday School Institution in 1815.[23] The first Methodist minister to New South Wales in 1815, Samuel Leigh, was prominent in the formation of the Bible Society.[24] The idea for the Native Institution came from the former LMS missionary, William Shelley, who had taken some Aboriginal children into his home at Parramatta and, unlike most other colonists, found them 'remarkably teachable'. He realised that 'adopting' them within European families would not work for they were 'rejected by the other Sex of Europeans' and needed to 'go into the Bush for a companion'. Macquarie supported the Institution in order to stem the new outbreak of violence on the Cumberland Plain in 1815 but it was Elizabeth Shelley, the missionary's wife, who taught the students the rudiments of literacy and numeracy after her husband's death. When one student, Maria Lock, won first prize in the anniversary school examination ahead of all non-Indigenous children, it looked like the school might succeed, but there was only ever a handful of children there and most of them escaped once they reached marriageable age. The Native Institution was closed in 1822 but some of the girls visited Elizabeth Shelley after they had left. They laughed when she asked them about their catechism.[25]

Church, state and the colonial mission

The 1820s and 1830s saw significant and rapid shifts in the church's relationships with government. These followed changes in British politics but also suggest the imperial government's uncertainty about how colonial religion might best serve the needs of Empire. In the 1820s, when Tory conservatism was on the ascendant, the wealth and power of Australian Anglicanism increased to the point of 'quasi-establishment'; ten years later the mounting pressures of liberal reform led to the removal of the formal precedence of the Anglican Church.

The immediate context of the first change was the report commissioned from J.T. Bigge by the British government on the state of the Australian colonies in 1819. Coming in the wake of the Napoleonic wars and the government's vigilance against unrest, it sought to create a gentrified society in which the Church of England would be a source of stability and order.

23 'Rowland Hassall', *Australian Dictionary of Biography*, vol. 1, pp. 521–2.
24 Don Wright and Eric G. Clancy, *The Methodists: A History of Methodism in New South Wales* (Sydney: Allen & Unwin, 1993), p. 5.
25 J. Brook and J.L. Kohen, *The Parramatta Native Institution and the Black Town* (Sydney: UNSW Press, 1991).

Accordingly, New South Wales was made an archdeaconry under the Bishop of Calcutta in 1824, and Thomas H. Scott was appointed archdeacon, a position that ranked second in authority to the governor and included a seat in the newly formed Legislative Council. Generous funding was provided to the Church and Schools Corporation: one-seventh of crown land was to be reserved for the church and the funds raised from the sale or cultivation of this land were to support Anglican clergy and schools. Though short-lived, the arrangements of the 1820s bequeathed greater wealth to the church in Sydney than any other diocese.

By the 1830s the political winds had changed. The new governor, Richard Bourke, was a liberal opponent of ecclesiastical privilege; he had supported the removal in England of the civil disabilities of Dissenters in 1828 and of Catholics in 1829. With responsibility for a colony in which less than half the population was adherent to the Church of England, Bourke wound back and then terminated the Church and Schools Corporation, and introduced the Church Acts in 1836 and 1837. These made financial aid available to the four largest denominations – Anglican, Catholic, Presbyterian and, a little later, Methodist – in proportion to the size of their congregations.[26]

The Church Acts were something of a political conundrum. Intended to reveal the state's neutrality on religious matters, they succeeded in privileging four denominations rather than one.[27] Australia was not the only colonial outpost with multiple establishments in the 1830s, but in a voluntarist age – after all, the separation of church and state was a sacred tenet of the American Revolution – state aid to religion seemed to run against the tide.[28] Indeed, many of the smaller Nonconformist denominations refused to apply for support, and in the new colony of South Australia the influence of these Dissenters was such that state support was introduced only in the depression of the 1840s, and then for only five years.[29] The significant fiscal commitment represented by the Acts suggests the importance to colonial authorities of 'civilising' the outposts of empire, and indicated fears of 'white' vulnerability to savagery.

26 Brian Fletcher, 'The Anglican Ascendancy', in Bruce Kaye (ed.), *Anglicanism in Australia* (Melbourne University Press, 2002), pp. 14–19; Judd and Cable, *Sydney Anglicans*, pp. 7–28.

27 Patricia Curthoys, 'State Support for Churches 1836–1860', in Kaye (ed.), *Anglicanism*, pp. 31–51.

28 Hilary M. Carey, *God's Empire: Religion and Colonialism in the British World, c. 1801–1908* (Cambridge University Press, 2011), p. 52; Michael Hogan, *The Sectarian Strand: Religion in Australian History* (Melbourne: Penguin, 1987), pp. 38–40.

29 David Hilliard and Arnold Hunt, 'Religion', in Eric Richards (ed.), *The Flinders History of South Australia: Social History* (Adelaide: Wakefield Press, 1986), pp. 200–2.

The Acts were never intended to be permanent and they were rescinded in New South Wales in 1862. Their effects, at a crucial stage in the development of the colonies, however, were profound. They reconfigured the status hierarchy of British religion, removing the privileges of the Church of England and putting old enemies on an equal fiscal footing. William Broughton, appointed Bishop of Australia in 1836, protested vehemently against the Anglican Church's loss of privileged status, though it gained more funding than any other denomination and, as the religion of the monarch, the governor and the colonial gentry, it retained considerable prestige. Since the major denominations were now competing for funds, the Acts exacerbated sectarian animosity between them all, but the Catholic Church's receipt of assistance heightened fears of 'priestcraft and popery', especially after Rome erected the Vicariate of New Holland in 1834. It was hoped the appointment of an educated, upper-class Englishman and Benedictine monk, John Bede Polding, as Catholic Bishop of Australia would assuage fears of Catholicism, but the influx of Irish convicts, immigrants and priests in the 1830s and 1840s, and the creation of an Australian Catholic hierarchy in 1842, made them worse. To John Dunmore Lang – the first Presbyterian minister in New South Wales and an evangelical with enormous capacity for moral outrage – the 'Question of Questions' was whether the colony was to be 'transformed into a Province of Popedom'.[30]

This early state aid influenced the character of Australian sectarianism. Funding made the Catholic Church a more formidable enemy than it was in the United States, where the Catholic Irish were poorer and more 'alien'.[31] The appointment of John Hubert Plunkett as attorney-general and Roger Therry as judge in the 1830s demonstrated the greater opportunities for a Catholic elite in public office than in either Britain or the United States, but also fuelled extreme Protestant suspicion.[32] The Church Acts also shaped sectarian culture through their effects on Protestantism. By rewarding the largest denominations, they encouraged orthodoxy, discouraged the 'multiplication of creeds' that nineteenth-century travellers saw as defining colonial North American religion, and encouraged a generalised Protestant identity that defined itself against Roman Catholicism.[33]

30 Quoted in O'Farrell, *The Catholic Church and Community*, p. 56
31 O'Farrell, *The Irish in Australia*, pp. 62–9.
32 David Hilliard, 'Australasia and the Pacific', in Adrian Hastings (ed.), *A World History of Christianity* (Michigan: William B. Eerdmans, 1999), p. 520; Hogan, *The Sectarian Strand*, p. 52.
33 K.J. Cable, 'Protestant Problems in New South Wales in the Mid-Nineteenth Century', *Journal of Religious History*, 3 (1964–5): 119–36.

The material effects of this funding cannot be overstated. By providing financial aid to the largest denominations in eastern Australia at a seminal moment in their development, it produced a steady growth in the numbers of churches and clergy, laying the foundation for the acceleration that occurred after the influx of gold-rush immigrants in the 1850s. The adherents of the four largest denominations that received government funding in these years – Anglican, Catholic, Methodist and Presbyterian – remained remarkably stable: 80 per cent of the population identified with these faiths until the 1960s.[34]

State assistance was introduced as increasing numbers of convicts poured into New South Wales and Van Diemen's Land, to face a system designed to be more severe than it was under Macquarie and of greater economic benefit to the empire. This was also a period of increasing frontier violence, for Bigge's blueprint required that Aboriginal lands be turned over to sheep. To the British colonial missionary societies, to Rome and to the Catholic Church in Ireland, this was a frontier in dire need of religious ministration and it offered opportunities to enterprising and improving missionaries. A small but steady stream flowed into the colonies, some encouraged by the passage of the *Colonial Clergy Act* of 1819, which enabled clergy to serve in the colonies without requiring them to have the training necessary for the home church. By 1836 the government paid for eighteen Anglican chaplains; by 1839 there were 35 of them and by 1847 there were 64.[35]

The primary concern of missionary Christianity was the convict population but ministry in the new penal settlements was not highly prized. William Schofield was recruited to Van Diemen's Land by the Wesleyan Missionary Society in 1824 and only agreed to go to Macquarie Harbour – known as 'Hell's Gates' – after being 'brow-beaten' by Lieutenant-Governor Arthur.[36] Most colonial missionaries were not confined to penal settlements. On the contrary, the thinly dispersed population made itinerancy the mark of a successful pastor. The Irishman John Joseph Therry, the only Catholic priest in Sydney from 1820 to 1826, was revered for traversing the countryside to take the sacraments to the sick and condemned; stories of his horsemanship became legendary.[37] Similarly, the Methodist missionary Joseph Orton, who successfully led the fractious Wesleyans in Sydney in the early

---

34 Hilliard, 'Australasia and the Pacific', p. 520.
35 Judd and Cable, *Sydney Anglicans*, pp. 26–7.
36 Hamish Maxwell-Stewart, *Closing Hell's Gates: The Life and Death of a Convict Station* (Sydney: Allen & Unwin, 2008), p. 251.
37 O'Farrell, *The Catholic Church and Community*, pp. 23–5.

1830s, was noted for his journeys over the Blue Mountains, visiting prisoners in chain gangs on the way.[38] The Sisters of Charity, who arrived in Australia from Ireland in 1838, visited convict women at the Female Factory – one of whom left them property in her will – and ran the Roman Catholic Orphan School at Parramatta.[39] Trans-imperial missionary travellers, the English Quakers James Backhouse and George Walker, were influential in Alexander Maconochie's reforms of Norfolk Island between 1840 and 1844.[40]

When Schofield first went to the 'moral desert' of Macquarie Harbour, he saw the local Aboriginal people as 'a noble race' of 'poor destitute creatures' more deserving of salvation than the convicts.[41] This view of the relative moral 'innocence' of Aboriginal people – deeming them 'savage' because they had not seen 'the Light of Civilisation' – was not unusual. It prompted a number of missions in the 1820s and 1830s, none of which endured. Governors saw missions as a way to stem frontier conflict. In 1828, when frontier violence in Van Diemen's Land had assumed the dimensions of a 'black war', Lieutenant-Governor Arthur commissioned the Wesleyan autodidact, George Augustus Robinson, to 'pacify' and convert Aboriginal people.[42] In 1825 Governor Brisbane granted Lancelot Threlkeld's mission 10,000 acres (4,047 hectares) at Port Macquarie. Threlkeld acted as an advocate for Aboriginal people in legal cases in the 1820s and, with the help of his Awakabal mentor, Biraban, compiled the first study of Aboriginal language. In addition to resisting the invaders through warfare, the Wiradjuri people made adaptations to their cosmology as a form of resistance. After the smallpox epidemic of 1829, the journal of the CMS mission at Wellington in New South Wales recorded the development of a travelling nativist cult in Wiradjuri country that expressed hostility to the Europeans and the diseases they brought.[43]

Religious visions of various sorts played their part in the development of the colonies. Jewish communities in Sydney, Hobart, Launceston, Melbourne and Adelaide built synagogues in the 1840s.[44] St John's Camden, built on the top of a hill so that its spire could be seen for miles around, embodied

38 'Joseph Orton', *Australian Dictionary of Biography*, vol. 2, p. 303.
39 Anne O'Brien, *God's Willing Workers: Women and Religion in Australia* (Sydney: UNSW Press, 2005), pp. 21–2.
40 'James Backhouse', *Australian Dictionary of Biography*, vol. 1, pp. 45–6.
41 Maxwell-Stewart, *Closing Hell's Gates*, p. 247.
42 J.D. Bollen, 'English Missionary Societies and the Australian Aborigine', *Journal of Religious History*, 9, 2 (1977): 263–90.
43 Hilary M. Carey and David Roberts, 'Smallpox and the Baiami Waganna of Wellington Valley, New South Wales, 1829–1840: The Earliest Nativist Movement in Aboriginal Australia', *Ethnohistory*, 49, 4 (2002): 822.
44 Suzanne Rutland, *The Jews in Australia* (Cambridge University Press, 2005), p. 21.

James Macarthur's paternalist hope of recreating an English village with the Church of England at its centre.[45] South Australia, founded by respectable Dissenters who sought to evade the pervasive power of the Church of England, remained a receptive environment throughout the century for unorthodox believers such as the New Church, 'radicals' and Unitarians.[46] The colony's wealthiest backer, the Baptist merchant George Fife Angas, acted as patron to a group of 200 German Lutherans who, led by their pastor, August Kavel, were escaping the King of Prussia's attempts to create a unified state church.[47] While there was no equivalent of the outpouring of religious enthusiasm in the United States, revival was not unknown. A range of millenarian sects – such as the Christian Israelites from south-east Lancashire and west Yorkshire – drew on the distress of immigrants assisted to the Australian colonies in the 1830s and 1840s; others, such as Plymouth Brethren and Christadelphians, were founded in Britain, but came to Australia by way of the United States.[48] There was at least one 'home grown' popular millenarian sect, in the 1860s, led by the farmer James Fisher, from Nunawading in Victoria.[49] Historians of evangelicalism estimate that there were about 70 localised and mostly Methodist revivals in the years between 1834 and 1894.[50] The demographic contours of the biggest of these, at Moonta in South Australia in 1875, had much in common with the 'Burned Over District' of New York State. As in New York, Moonta's population of Cornish miners was relatively homogenous, and a large number had migrated from areas with a strong tradition of religious revival.[51]

Churchmen, and sometimes women, were part of the turbulent world of colonial politics. They made various contributions to what one historian has described as 'moral enlightenment', the belief that the possibility of human betterment might be realised in Australia.[52] The evangelical Edward Smith

---

45 Alan Atkinson, *Camden* (Oxford University Press, 1988), pp. 44–6.
46 David Hilliard, 'Unorthodox Christianity in South Australia', *History Australia*, 2, 2 (2005): 38.2–38.3.
47 Douglas Pike, *Paradise of Dissent: South Australia 1829–1857* (Melbourne University Press, 1967).
48 Alan Atkinson, *The Europeans in Australia: A History. Volume 2: Democracy* (Oxford University Press, 2004), pp. 178–9.
49 Guy Featherstone, 'The Nunawading Messiah: James Fisher and Popular Millenarianism in Nineteenth-Century Melbourne', *Journal of Religious History*, 26, 1 (2002): 42–64.
50 Stuart Piggin, 'The History of Revival in Australia', in Mark Hutchinson and Edmund Campion (eds), *Revisioning Australian Colonial Christianity* (Sydney: Centre for the Study of Australian Christianity, 1994), pp. 176–7.
51 H.R. Jackson, *Churches and People in Australia and New Zealand 1860–1930* (Sydney: Allen & Unwin, 1987), pp. 55–6.
52 Michael Roe, *Quest for Authority in Eastern Australia 1835–1851* (Melbourne University Press, 1965)

Hall was inspired by Thomas Paine, Adam Smith and Jeremy Bentham, but read the Bible most assiduously and used his long-running newspaper, *The Monitor* (1826–40), to keep tabs on instances of injustice, particularly against convicts.[53] The struggle for democracy united many whom sectarianism might otherwise have divided, including the Scottish Catholic William Duncan and the Irish Protestant Henry Macdermott, who joined forces as 'friends of the people' in the 1840s.[54] Complex and contradictory religious ideas were central to the humanitarian movement that extended its concern to colonisation itself by the 1830s. While colonisation was justified on biblical grounds – 'go forth and multiply' – churchmen warned of divine retribution for the 'neglect and oppression' of Aboriginal people. The Catholic convert, Caroline Chisholm, the most significant mid-century woman philanthropist, thought a system of family colonisation that empowered women would end 'the gradual destruction and extermination of the aborigines'.[55] The discourse of evangelical humanitarians was inflected with the idea of justice, but more frequently it represented Aboriginal people as objects of charity.[56]

Faith in the age of gold

The gold rushes of the 1850s stimulated the growth of religion, particularly in Victoria. At first conservative clergy feared the disruptive effects of gold: the Anglican bishop, Charles Perry, thought it might lead to 'an age of barbarism' and he struggled to interpret the rushes in the light of God's providence.[57] In the longer term the influx of wealth and population strengthened religious practice. The American 'California Taylor' was credited with generating 'an outburst of religious exaltation' in the Victorian gold towns, and colonists proclaimed their faith through a spate of church building: 36 churches were built in Ballarat in the 20 years after 1851.[58] Social upheavals brought about by the gold rushes intensified the appeal of radical sects: the Christian Israelites

---

53 Erin Ihde, *Edward Smith Hall and the Sydney Monitor 1826–1840: A Manifesto for New South Wales* (Melbourne: Australian Scholarly Publishing, 2004).

54 T.H. Irving, *The Southern Tree of Liberty: The Democratic Movement in New South Wales before 1856* (Sydney: Federation Press, 2006), p. 59.

55 Quoted in Mary Hoban, *Fifty-One Pieces of Wedding Cake: A Biography of Caroline Chisholm* (Melbourne: Lowden Publishing, 1973), p. 290.

56 Anne O'Brien, 'Humanitarianism and Reparation in Colonial Australia', *Journal of Colonialism and Colonial History*, 12, 2 (2011): online.

57 Quoted in David Goodman, *Gold Seeking: Victoria and California in the 1850s* (Sydney: Allen & Unwin, 1994), pp. 58–9.

58 'William Taylor', *Australian Dictionary of Biography*, vol. 6, pp. 250–1. Anne Doggett, '"The Old Vexed Question": Divergent Attitudes and Practices in the Sacred Music of Early Ballarat', *Journal of Religious History*, 33, 4 (2009): 401–17.

grew in Victoria in the 1850s when their popularity had fallen off in England, and a splinter group of German Lutherans founded a utopian community, Herrnhut, in western Victoria.[59] The great cultural mix of the gold-rush population was reflected in the diversity of religions transferred. The Jewish community in Victoria increased tenfold in the 1850s, and by the 1860s it had built three synagogues in Melbourne.[60] Chinese gold miners built temples in South Melbourne, Bendigo, Ballarat and Castlemaine, often of canvas, timber and hand-made brick. By the late 1860s, when overt hostility toward the Chinese had receded, Chinese dragons were included in street processions, to honour the tour of the Duke of Edinburgh in 1868, for example, and to help raise money for the Bendigo Benevolent Asylum.[61] Victoria's wealth drove the development of the interior, and for this Muslim cameleers, who transported food and water, were essential. Though Muslims were generally temporary residents, there were two mosques and a community of 300 Muslims in Coolgardie, Western Australia, by the end of the century.[62]

In the longer term, the gold rushes accelerated the growth in denominational Christianity that had been developing since the passage of the Church Acts. In New South Wales in the 1860s the number of Anglicans and Presbyterians going to church more than doubled. The growth rate was greater among Catholics and among Methodists it was spectacular.[63] Half of Ballarat's 36 post-gold churches were built by branches of Methodism; ten were Wesleyan, four Primitive Methodist and four Bible Christian.[64] Described as a religion 'perfect for pioneers', Methodism's doctrines were simple and had direct emotional appeal, particularly through graphic images of Christ's suffering conveyed in Charles Wesley's hymns.[65] Evangelical religion offered a personal relationship with Jesus that brought consolation to lonely immigrants. 'I new no one, nor had I a friend to take my hand, but thank God I had Him who Never (?) has forsaking', Isabella Wyly, an 18-year-old

---

59 Featherstone, 'The Nunawading Messiah'; William J. Metcalf and Elizabeth Huf, *Herrnhut: Australia's First Utopian Commune* (Melbourne University Press, 2002), p. 62.
60 Rutland, *The Jews in Australia*, pp. 22–3.
61 Amanda Rasmussen, 'Networks and Negotiations: Bendigo's Chinese and the Easter Fair', *Journal of Australian Colonial History*, 6 (2004): 79–92.
62 Bilal Cleland, 'The History of Muslims in Australia', in Abdullah Saeed and Shahram Akbarzadeh (eds), *Muslim Communities in Australia* (Sydney: UNSW Press, 2001), p. 17.
63 Atkinson, *The Europeans in Australia*, vol. 2, p. 290.
64 Doggett, 'The Old Vexed Question'.
65 Janet McCalman, *Journeyings: The Biography of a Middle-Class Generation 1920–1990* (Melbourne University Press, 1995), p. 32; Joanna Cruickshank, '"Appear as Crucified for Me": Sight, Suffering, and Spiritual Transformation in the Hymns of Charles Wesley', *Journal of Religious History*, 30, 3 (2006): 311–30.

domestic servant, wrote home in 1851.[66] Methodist organisation – circuits, classes and semi-itinerant lay preachers – was designed for evangelising the countryside.[67] Between 1852 and 1867 those colonists affiliated with the Methodist church increased by 300 per cent, nearly twice the population increase.[68]

If the work of the church was to communicate the message of eternal salvation, church attendance also offered temporal advantages with more immediate effects. In a fluid colonial society in which respectability was social capital, it fortified the reputations of the anxious but improving, and provided useful connections for their 'betters'. It offered a range of relatively inexpensive and regular social activities – from literary societies and Sunday-school picnics to tennis and cricket clubs – and it provided aesthetic experience not readily found elsewhere.[69] Congregational hymn singing gave all worshippers the chance to participate and, in the large city churches, choirs and orchestras performed the music of Mozart, Beethoven, Rossini, Handel, Mendelssohn and Pergolesi. The church building itself was 'set apart'; its large, high and open internal space evoking the transcendent. The widespread use of Gothic revival style, particularly in New South Wales where in the 1840s and 1850s it was favoured by the architect Edmund Blacket and encouraged by Bishop Broughton, gave the reassuring appearance of tradition and authenticity to colonists unaware that the landscape itself was sacred to Indigenous people.[70] Music and architecture had liturgical meanings that stemmed from the battles of the Reformation. The Presbyterians initially prohibited the playing of instrumental music in church, considering it too close to Roman idolatry, just as some evangelicals' preference for neoclassical or Romanesque styles derived from neo-Gothic's Catholic associations.[71] Theology might have influenced design but economics determined its expression. For example, in north-eastern Victoria, where selectors were hard pressed to make a living

---

66 Quoted in David Fitzpatrick, '"This is the Place that Foolish Girls are Knowing": Reading the Letters of Emigrant Irish Women in Colonial Australia', in Trevor McClaughlin (ed.), *Irish Women in Colonial Australia* (Sydney: Allen & Unwin, 1998), p. 170.

67 Cable, 'Protestant Problems in New South Wales', pp. 124–7.

68 Barry Chant, 'The Nineteenth and Early Twentieth Century Origins of the Australian Pentecostal Movement', in Mark Hutchinson and Stuart Piggin (eds), *Reviving Australia: Essays on the History and Experience of Revival and Revivalism in Australian Christianity* (Sydney: Centre for the Study of Australian Christianity, 1994), pp. 97–122.

69 David Hilliard, *Godliness and Good Order: A History of the Anglican Church in South Australia* (Adelaide: Wakefield Press, 1986).

70 Colin Holden, 'Anglicanism, the Visual Arts and Architecture', in Kaye (ed.), *Anglicanism in Australia*, pp. 247–69.

71 Doggett, 'The Old Vexed Question'; Hilary M. Carey, 'Anglican Imperialism and the Gothic Style in Australia', *Australian Religion Studies Review*, 23, 1 (2010): 6–28.

from the land, Christ Church, Greta, located in the heart of 'Kelly' country, was a small timber church designed by the contractors of the Wangaratta Post Office.[72] It was typical of most country churches on the struggling frontiers of settlement.

Despite the growth of the churches, between about 30 and 40 per cent of the population were not regular attenders in 1871, a cause of concern to all denominations.[73] To some extent, this was a product of geographical challenge, and various missions were established to assist the evangelisation of 'the bush'. One of the earliest was the Bush Missionary Society which, when it was founded in Sydney in 1859, included Randwick and Waverley as fields of mission.[74] If missionaries' horsemanship (or its lack) entered into folklore, the bicycle came into its own at the end of the century: Edgar Caust of the Bible Christian Bush Mission, for example, rode several thousand kilometres from Peterborough in South Australia to Broken Hill in 1897.[75] The 'bush brotherhood' was a unique response to Australian conditions: an innovation of English Anglo-Catholics, it sent young graduates to western New South Wales and northern Queensland for fixed terms of ministry from 1897.[76] Not all non-attendance, however, was a result of distance, as city missionaries knew. From the early 1840s the Irish revivalist, Nathaniel Pidgeon, fought the devil in Sydney and between 1852 and 1867, interdenominational Protestant city missions were founded in Hobart, Melbourne, Sydney and Adelaide. Their greatest foes were alcohol and prostitution, but they counselled against all evil doing, including gambling, horse-racing, dog and cock-fighting, and against false creeds such as socialism, Roman Catholicism and Mormonism. For the people of the inner city, being visited by a missionary carried a degree of odium, implying 'fecklessness' at best, 'degradation' at worst, and as the missionaries' journals show, plenty of people despised them. Those who were desperate, however, particularly women with no-one else to help, trusted them and treated them with deference.[77] Though most city missions did not give 'relief' before the 1890s Depression, they acted as intermediaries, directing people to organisations that provided material aid.

72 Holden, 'Anglicanism, the Visual Arts and Architecture', p. 254.
73 Walter Phillips, 'Religious Profession and Practice in NSW, 1850–1901: The Statistical Evidence', *Historical Studies*, 15, 59 (1972): 378–400.
74 Bush Missionary Society, *Annual Reports*, 1857–64.
75 Arnold Hunt, *This Side of Heaven: A History of Methodism in South Australia* (Adelaide: Lutheran Publishing House, 1985), p. 114.
76 R.M. Frappell, 'The Australian Bush Brotherhoods and their English Origins', *Journal of Ecclesiastical History*, 47 (1996): 82–97.
77 Roslyn Otzen, 'Charity and Evangelisation: The Melbourne City Mission 1854–1914', PhD thesis, University of Melbourne, 1986.

A feminine church

In the nineteenth century Anglophone world ideas about femininity, morality and Christianity were closely associated and religion was seen as women's special province. Ireland's mid-nineteenth century 'devotional revolution' emphasised new patterns of female piety, reinforced by Rome's proclamation of the doctrine of the Immaculate Conception in 1854. The primary site of women's influence was the home. Despite their numerical dominance – observers reckoned that women outnumbered men in the pews by two or three to one – women were largely excluded from formal ministry, preaching and church governance. Most women worked for the church as Sunday-school teachers, musicians, fundraisers, arrangers of flowers, embroiderers of linen and visitors of the poor. The boundaries of exclusion, however, were shifting and uncertain. The transatlantic, evangelical revival of the 1860s gave rise to a new generation of female evangelists. The Bible Christian preacher Serena Thorne was an immediate success when she arrived in Adelaide in 1870, filling the town hall to capacity for three weeks; but she was seen as having an 'exceptional' call, not one that sanctioned women's preaching generally and, commended for her 'chaste eloquence', she was represented in the language of respectability.[78] Melbourne's Unitarian Church – dubbed a 'half-way house to infidelity' – was the only church to elect a woman as minister when Martha Turner took over in 1873.[79]

In rural settlements in which there was no church building, women exercised leadership when their homes were used for worship, as they had in the 'cottage religion' of the early English Methodist connexions and on isolated Aboriginal mission stations missionary wives sometimes crossed the line of ecclesiastical order and led services when their husbands were itinerating.[80] Religion was an agent of colonialism but some Indigenous women took on Christian practice. Fanny Cochrane Smith was at the centre of an extended-family Methodist community: her kitchen was used as a church at Oyster Cove, Tasmania, before a church was built on land she donated. As a child she had suffered 'conditions of appalling squalor, neglect and brutality' at the Aboriginal compound, Wybalenna, on Flinders Island and she was

78 Jennifer M. Lloyd, 'Women Preachers in the Bible Christian Connexion', *Albion*, 36, 3 (2004): 451–81.

79 'Martha Webster', *Australian Dictionary of Biography*, vol. 6, pp. 314–15.

80 Jessie Mitchell, '"The Nucleus of Civilisation": Gender, Race and Australian Missionary Families, 1825–1855', in Amanda Barry, Joanna Cruickshank, Andrew Brown-May and Patricia Grimshaw (eds), *Evangelists of Empire? Missionaries in Colonial History* (Melbourne: University of Melbourne eScholarship Research Centre, 2008).

one of the institution's few survivors. As well as following Methodist rituals, she sang and told her people's stories and continued to carry out traditional ceremonies.[81]

Catholic women were constrained by the hierarchy's insistence that they work in religious orders. Responding to the extreme distress of early nineteenth-century Ireland, Catherine McAuley founded the Sisters of Mercy, a congregation that proliferated in Australia, but she commented later: 'I never wanted to become a nun. I only wanted to serve the poor'.[82] There was ample opportunity for cloistered women to serve the poor in Australia. The Sisters of Charity opened St Vincent's Hospital in Sydney in 1857, and in 1867 Mary MacKillop, a young school teacher from Penola in South Australia, founded the Sisters of St Joseph to teach the children of isolated settlers. Many of the earliest women religious, including the first Sisters of Mercy who arrived in Perth in 1846, had volunteered for Australia on the mistaken assumption they would be working with Aboriginal people.[83] Like most religious sisters they were directed to teach the children of the settler population, work that reflected the class aspirations of the Catholic bishops as well as the distinctions of the wider society: different religious congregations taught children of different social classes.

The education of Protestant daughters by religious sisters was both symptom and cause of the softening of sectarianism that often marked rural communities, but the Protestant–Catholic divide deepened in the broader canvas of late nineteenth-century politics, particularly over the issue of education. If there was widespread agreement that it was necessary to improve elementary education following the extension of democracy in the 1850s, there was no agreement about how religious education should be managed. A 'war of words' ensued, inflamed by serendipitous incidents as well as deeper structural changes. In Sydney in 1868 a mentally ill Irishman claiming Fenian connections attempted to assassinate the Duke of Edinburgh, an abomination made worse by the fact that a group of Fenians had just been transported to Western Australia.[84] It did not help that the early 1860s were years of particularly high Irish immigration to Australia, 75 per cent of all those who arrived between 1863 and 1865. Internationally the Catholic Church felt itself under siege and responded with renewed authoritarianism manifest in

81 'Fanny Cochrane Smith', *Australian Dictionary of Biography*, vol. 11, p. 642.
82 Quoted in Catherine Kovesi Killerby, *Ursula Frayne: A Biography* (Fremantle Arts Centre Press, 1996), p. 19.
83 Kovesi Killerby, *Ursula Frayne*, pp. 92, 121.
84 Keith Amos, *The Fenians in Australia 1865–1880* (Sydney: UNSW Press, 1988), pp. 54–77.

the proclamation of the 'syllabus of errors' in 1864 and of papal infallibility in 1870, which in turn heightened fears of 'papal aggression'.[85] The appointment of six Irish bishops to rural dioceses in New South Wales and to Brisbane between 1859 and 1869 strengthened the Irish influence on the Catholic Church in Australia. All had studied in Rome and were protégés of the powerful Irish prelate, Cardinal Paul Cullen. They envisaged Australia as a new and better 'Irish spiritual empire' and to varying degrees were aggressively defensive of Irish Catholics.[86] This shifting context altered the discourse of the Australian Catholic hierarchy in its address to the faithful and to the world. Its pastoral message became more uncompromising and oppositional over time, with the emphasis on support for the church rather than the individual's relationship with God.[87] On the question of education, its political stance was immovable: religious education could not be separated from secular education. When government funding to church schools was removed in all colonies between 1872 and 1896, the Catholic bishops expanded and entrenched their alternative education system, staffed largely by orders of religious women.

Foreign missions on Indigenous lands

Foreign missions were not a high priority for the churches in the Australian colonies. George Stanton, the first bishop in northern Queensland, surveying the vastness of his diocese and having encountered an English girl who had never heard of God, encapsulated the fears of many when he commented in 1880 that 'white savages are far worse than blacks'.[88] The churches had, however, established missionary boards from mid-century: the Australian Board of Missions (1850), the Australasian Wesleyan Methodist Missionary Society (1855) and the Heathen Mission Committee of the Presbyterian Church (1865). They prioritised missions to the Pacific and to Asia. The arrival of large numbers of Chinese gold seekers in the 1850s was seen as 'a true mission field

---

85 Hogan, *The Sectarian Strand*, p. 91.

86 O'Farrell, *The Catholic Church and Community*, pp. 128–9.

87 Gavin Brown, '"The Evil State of Tepidity": Mass-Going and Absenteeism in Nineteenth-Century Australian Ecclesiastical Discourse', *Journal of Religious History*, 33, 1 (2009): 28–48.

88 Cited in Noel Loos, 'Concern and Contempt: Church and Missionary Attitudes Towards Aborigines in North Queensland in the Nineteenth Century', in Tony Swain and Deborah Bird Rose (eds), *Aboriginal Australians and Christian Missions* (Adelaide: Australian Association for the Study of Religions, 1988), p. 102.

opening before us' for they would be agents for the conversion of China, the highest missionary prize, on their return.[89]

Some missions for Aboriginal people were opened in the middle of the century. They were most numerous in Victoria, where pastoral incursion was swift and religious currents relatively strong. The Port Phillip Protectorate, an outcome of humanitarian advocacy in the late 1830s, was abandoned in 1849 but just over a decade later six mission stations were set aside. In Western Australia the Methodist John Smithies established a school for Aboriginal children in 1842 and Spanish Benedictine monks, under Dom Rosendo Salvado, established New Norcia as a monastic mission in 1846. In South Australia, the Anglican archdeacon of Adelaide, Mathew Hale, established Poonindie in 1850. In New South Wales, where the early missionary efforts had seemed so fruitless, no missions were established between the closing of the Wellington Valley Mission in 1844 and the establishment of the Maloga Mission on the Murray River, near Echuca, in 1874.[90]

Missionaries wanted to stop Indigenous people from 'wandering', encourage them to work, increase their desire for consumer goods and save their souls. They gathered people from varied linguistic and tribal backgrounds together in the same compounds and sought to change their understandings of time and space and encourage them to think as individuals rather than members of a kinship network. Most missionaries treated Aboriginal people as members of a 'child-race', attempting to impose a foreign discipline and to eradicate traditional custom. They recorded a few Aboriginal 'conversions', and Daniel Matthews recorded a revival at Maloga in 1883–84.[91] The claim to have wrought the 'first' Aboriginal conversion was made several times, suggesting not just that missionaries of different denominations worked in isolation, but that the idea of Aboriginal people's capacity for change was so fragile that it had to be continually rediscovered and reasserted.

The responses of Indigenous people to Christian teaching were shaped by their experiences of colonialism. The Kurnai, who had experienced violence and disruption for 20 years in southern Victoria, were attracted to the Moravian mission, Ramahyuck, because there was nowhere else they could live without disturbance. Early efforts to convert them produced conflict,

---

89 *The Australian Witness*, 6 March 1875.
90 John Harris, *One Blood: 200 Years of Aboriginal Encounter with Christianity* (Sydney: Albatross Books, 1990).
91 Peggy Brock, *Outback Ghettos: Aborigines, Institutionalisation and Survival* (Cambridge University Press, 1993), p. 34; Claire McLisky, 'The Location of Faith: Power, Gender and Spirituality in the 1883–84 Maloga Mission Revival', *History Australia*, 7, 1 (2010): 8.1–20.

sometimes violence, within their communities. Those who showed interest in Christianity probably did so as a survival strategy; later a core group, who were neither 'strangers' from different parts nor had been raised by missionaries from a young age, identified as converts.[92] Any conversion was a dynamic interaction to which Indigenous people brought their pre-existing beliefs. A recent exploration of the conversion of the Wotjobaluk man who took the name Nathanael Pepper at Ebenezer station, considers the importance of recounted dreams and of shared understandings of blood and animals. There were connections between the image of Jesus sweating blood at Gethsemane and the shedding of blood in Aboriginal ritual; between the evangelists' descriptions of Jesus as the Lamb of God and animals as of totemic significance.[93] The Maloga revival took place under conditions that foreground Indigenous agency; in the presence of a respected Sri Lankan missionary teacher, in the absence of a white missionary, on land of ancestral significance and following their acquisition of land with the missionary's help.[94] Despite these conversions there was far less use of Indigenous evangelists in Australian missions than in the Pacific Islands or in Africa in the same period.[95]

The approach taken by missionaries also influenced Indigenous people's reception to Christianity. As superintendent of Coranderrk mission, near Healesville in Victoria, the Scottish Presbyterian John Green was unusual in treating Aboriginal people as friends and 'equals', encouraging their self-governance and respecting their rights to land. While Green was at Coranderrk 1863–74, the Wurundjeri leader, Simon Wonga, was 'very glad' to know 'plenty of good words from the Bible' and that his people remembered their trek to Coranderrk in biblical terms.[96]

Realignments

There were discernible shifts in the place of the churches within the late nineteenth-century cultural landscape. Slow processes of secularisation, growing out of improved patterns of consumption and medical advances, encouraged the idea that the earthly realm would continue to improve. Science and higher criticism questioned the literal truth of the Bible but most

92 Bain Attwood, *The Making of the Aborigines* (Sydney: Allen & Unwin, 1989), pp. 6, 43.
93 Robert Kenny, *The Lamb Enters the Dreaming: Nathanael Pepper and the Ruptured World* (Melbourne: Scribe, 2007), p. 16.
94 McLisky, 'The Location of Faith'.
95 Hilliard, 'Australasia and the Pacific'.
96 Quoted in Jane Lydon, 'The Experimental 1860s: Charles Walter's Images of Coranderrk Aboriginal Station, Victoria', *Aboriginal History*, 26 (2002): 78, 89–90.

clergy were more concerned about vice. Observance of the Sabbath and divorce law reform were subjects of long, intense battles. In South Australia and Victoria there were considerably more Dissenters than in New South Wales. Proportionately, there were far fewer Catholics in South Australia than in New South Wales, and marginally fewer in Victoria. Sabbatarians gained ground: public transport was restricted to before and after church, hotels were closed and in Melbourne the public library was closed.[97] This is not to underestimate the effects of intellectual challenges to orthodoxy. In the 1880s the Australian Secular Association, under the former Methodist lay preacher Joseph Symes, was a small, localised but pugnaciously animated group. Its theological objections – to literal interpretations of the Bible, to conceptions of a vengeful God and the doctrine of eternal damnation – were met by the churches with varying degrees of hostility and accommodation. The Anglican bishop of Melbourne, James Moorhouse, reassured the faithful that contemporary thought was compatible with Christianity but Melbourne's Presbyterians forced one of their thoughtful questioners, Charles Strong, minister of Scots Church, to resign in 1883.[98] It was a context in which alternative religions, such as Theosophy, spiritualism and Christian Science, gained followers. At the 1901 census 2 per cent of the population of New South Wales answered 'other persuasion' or 'no religion'; in 1851 it had been 0.4 per cent.[99]

These challenges were met with a renewed missionary vigour that linked Australia more closely to the Anglophone Christian world. In the 1870s the visiting revivalist Alexander Somerville had coupled 'sermon with song' and in 1880 the Salvation Army brought military-style organisation to the techniques of popular culture and had a lasting effect on Australian religion and welfare. Populist in tone and working-class in personnel, these missions stimulated the large conservative churches to create forums for revival.[100] George Grubb's Keswick-inspired mission in the depressed 1890s inspired hordes of Melburnians to yield to the Lord. The arrival of religious orders of

97 Beverley Kingston, *The Oxford History of Australia, Volume 3, 1860–1900: Glad Confident Morning* (Oxford University Press, 1988), pp. 86–7; Richard Waterhouse, *Private Pleasures, Public Leisure: A History of Australian Popular Culture Since 1788*, (Sydney: Longman, 1995), p. 108.

98 Geoffrey Serle, *The Rush to be Rich: A History of the Colony of Victoria, 1883–1889* (Melbourne University Press, 1971), pp. 127–75; David Hilliard, 'Intellectual Life in the Diocese of Melbourne', in Brian Porter (ed.), *Melbourne Anglicans* (Melbourne: Mitre Books, 1997), pp. 27–48.

99 Phillips, 'Religious Profession and Practice', p. 381.

100 Jackson, *Churches and People*, pp. 57–65

priests in the 1880s – Redemptorists (1882), Vincentians (1885) and Passionists (1887) – signalled the advent of Catholic parish missions.[101]

With Catherine Booth as its co-founder, the Salvation Army's proclamation of women's spiritual equality pressured the churches to open up formalised roles to women. W.G. Taylor, Superintendent of Sydney's Central Methodist Mission, established the Sisters of the People in Sydney only after a young woman from Grafton, Laura Frances, threatened to join the Salvationists. Churchmen were ambivalent about employing women. Mervyn Archdall, who founded the Deaconess Institution in Sydney in 1890, asserted that women's leadership was needed in public life but not if they showed 'any unwomanly or unreasonable ambition'. In a context of growing militarism and athleticism, churchmen were also concerned that employing women would encourage the seepage of men from a church already feminised. On the other hand, churchmen needed women's labour, and they believed in the pervasive ideology of maternalism; that women's influence in public life would lead to social betterment, and that women were best suited to minister to women. Women's professionalisation, then, was accompanied by their marginalisation: deaconesses and sisters worked mainly with women and children and rarely preached to mixed audiences. Churchwomen's voluntary organisations in the 1890s were also maternalist though their emphases varied. The Protestant Woman's Christian Temperance Union was pivotal in raising support for women's franchise while the Anglican Mother's Union devoted its energies to re-affirming the 'sanctity' of marriage.[102]

The new ministries for women, paid at lesser rates than men, expanded during the 1890s Depression. The Depression revealed the inadequacies of religious charity – many charities closed in Melbourne in 1892 – but in the longer term stimulated its expansion. The Depression also saw shifts in understandings of deservedness. A few Protestant contributors to public debate became more sympathetic to social, as well as personal, reform.[103] The 1891 papal encyclical *Rerum Novarum*, a condemnation of both socialism and excessive capitalism, influenced Cardinal Patrick Moran's public support of the labour movement. In a cruel paradox, Indigenous people in the north of Australia came to be seen as 'deserving' of missionary control and protection as settlement moved north into Queensland and as they were formally

101 Judd and Cable, *Sydney Anglicans*, pp. 150–2; Brown, 'The Evil State of Tepidity', p. 45.
102 O'Brien, *God's Willing Workers*, p. 98.
103 J.D. Bollen, *Protestantism and Social Reform in New South Wales 1890–1910* (Melbourne University Press, 1972), p. 5.

excluded from the franchise and from the welfare measures introduced by the Commonwealth government. The establishment of the new missions – the most enduring of which were the Anglican mission at Yarrabah and the Moravian (later Presbyterian) mission at Mapoon – took place in a context of hardening racial determinism. Those who spoke out against frontier violence ran the risk of being mocked, derided and expelled from the community, as John Gribble found in Western Australia in 1887. Some missionaries rejected the Darwinian pessimism underpinning the theory of the dying race, but the essence of the missionary project had not substantially changed. Missions continued to be under-funded, to have no security of tenure on their lands and were on the periphery of the vision of the Australian churches, who preferred to support missions almost everywhere else.[104]

*

How, on the cusp of nationhood, did Australians understand the meanings of religion? In 1901 less than half of the population attended worship regularly, even though 96 per cent identified as Christian.[105] 'The parson' and the umbrella-wielding temperance feminist were easy targets of parody in popular magazines but the language of Christianity retained serious import; during the strikes of the early 1890s one procession of the unemployed carried through Sydney an effigy of a man on a cross, his side smeared with blood and affixed to it a sign saying 'murdered by the rich'.[106] How did the historians of the major denominations interpret their experience in Australia? As in other British colonies, traditions other than British establishment religion felt they had most to be proud of. To Patrick Moran in his *History of the Catholic Church in Australasia* (1894) the 'open persecution' of the convict era had well and truly gone, and he looked forward to the church 'spreading abroad the light of truth'.[107] To George Lane, introducing James Colwell's *The Illustrated History of Methodism* (1904), Australian Methodism had exerted a 'wonderful influence' on 'modern Christianity'.[108] But there was considerable ambiguity in understandings of religion in the Australian colonies, symbolised not only by the outcome of churchmen's struggles for public recognition of God in the federal constitution, but by the very project of Federation itself.

---

104 Henry Reynolds, *This Whispering in our Hearts* (Sydney: Allen & Unwin, 1998).
105 Phillips, 'Religious Profession and Practice'.
106 Manning Clark, *A Short History of Australia*, new edn (New York: Signet, 1969), p. 170.
107 Patrick Moran, *History of the Catholic Church in Australasia* (Sydney: Frank Coffey & Co., 1894), pp. 24–5.
108 James Colwell, *The Illustrated History of Methodism: Australia: 1812 to 1855, New South Wales and Polynesia, 1856 to 1902* (Sydney: William Brooks and Co., 1904), p. 12.

The Preamble of the Constitution declared that the people were 'humbly relying on the blessing of Almighty God' in forming the Commonwealth; and yet, to allay the fears of secularists and Seventh-day Adventists (whose celebration of the Saturday Sabbath required them to work on Sunday) Section 116 excluded any establishment of religion and insisted that the Commonwealth practise strict neutrality regarding religion.[109] At the time, there was no agreement about the extent to which Section 116 detracted from the Preamble, and historians have debated it since.[110] At a deeper level, the makers of Federation, including seekers such as Alfred Deakin and Andrew Inglis Clark, envisaged their project as having serious religious meaning, not only fulfilling the destiny of a young nation, but also showing the world what the future of humanity might be.[111] Perhaps the most profound ambiguities stem from the support provided by religion for the whitening that accompanied Federation. There was some resistance to the exclusionary nature of the new immigration policy from Christian churchmen but there was no buffer against the demonising in the Christian imagination of the oldest sacred traditions in the land.

109 Richard Ely, *Unto God and Caesar: Religious Issues in the Emerging Commonwealth 1891–1906* (Melbourne University Press, 1976).
110 Walter Phillips, *Defending a Christian Country: Churchmen and Society in New South Wales in the 1880s and After* (Brisbane: UQP, 1981), pp. 254–67.
111 John Hirst, *The Sentimental Nation: The Making of the Australian Commonwealth* (Oxford University Press, 2000), pp. 4–25.

18

Colonial science and technology

JOHN GASCOIGNE AND SARA MAROSKE

One of the great aims of the Enlightenment was to shine the light of science on those corners of the Earth that were little known to the European world. Australia and the Pacific provoked particular intellectual curiosity and excitement as parts of the globe yet to be drawn into the Enlightenment's maps of nature.[1] Eighteenth-century exploration of the Pacific had a strong scientific character because, with the growing sophistication of systems of classification and methodology, science was increasingly regarded as the dominant means by which to understand the world and thus control it. The familiar goals of imperial rule and economic advantage were major spurs to Pacific voyaging but the language used to justify such endeavours assumed an increasingly scientific cast. Developments in science and technology in the nineteenth century reinforced the dominance of scientific understandings of the world, especially with the acceleration of the industrial revolution and the rise of Darwinism. Nevertheless, the light generated by science also revealed a world that challenged some of the basic tenets of the Enlightenment. There was pattern and bounty, but nature also emerged as brutal, dangerous and, as the Australian experience attested, surprisingly fragile.

European attention to the Pacific reached new heights in the aftermath of the Seven Years' War (1756–63), which placed mastery of the New World of North America in British rather than French hands, thus diverting great power rivalry to other possible new worlds in the southern hemisphere. The French absolutist state devoted more lavish resources to scientific enquiry than the British, although both nations' voyages were intended to advance the frontiers of science as well as those of empire. Cook's *Endeavour* voyage of 1768–71 had as its most immediate goal participation in the worldwide observation of the Transit of Venus of 1769, with an astronomical base at

---

1 Bernard Smith, *European Vision and the South Pacific*, 2nd edn (Sydney: Harper & Row, 1985).

Tahiti providing a new vantage point. Once this was completed the secret instructions from the British Admiralty ordered Cook to turn his attention to the South Pacific, the better to chart such sketchily known regions as the islands of New Zealand and to shed light on the claim that the southern hemisphere might contain a great land mass that balanced the continents of the north. The quest took Cook along the east coast of the Australian continent, a region hitherto unknown to Europeans. Along with records of astronomical observations of the little-known southern skies, the *Endeavour* brought back copious specimens of the natural history of Australia and the south Pacific. On board was the gentleman-botanist, Joseph Banks, and the naturalist, Daniel Solander, who had studied under his fellow Swede, Carl Linnaeus – the figure who had done most to bring order and system to the bewildering variety of nature through his characteristically Enlightenment project of constructing a system of classification.

Included in the remit of eighteenth-century natural history was the observation and description of indigenous peoples, and Cook as well as Banks recorded details of encounters with Australian Aboriginal people. It was the French explorers, however, who first treated Aboriginal people as the subject of a discrete scientific study that they called 'anthropology'.[2] Influenced by the Enlightenment idea of the 'noble savage', the scientists on Bruny d'Entrecasteaux's expedition to Van Diemen's Land in 1793 looked for, and found, a people living in conditions 'the closest that may be found to the state of nature'. They managed to idealise the Aboriginal people while at the same time retaining their own sense of superiority. The Nicolas Baudin expedition to Shark Bay, Western Australia in 1801, and Van Diemen's Land in 1802, commissioned the zoologist, François Péron, to produce anthropology's first fieldwork report and it took as its subject the Aboriginal people of Maria Island, off the east coast of Van Diemen's Land. Péron's anthropological remarks were made in the context of an emerging, racially based interpretation of human diversity that typically placed these people in the lowest rank of classification systems. This set the tone for future French voyagers' accounts.[3]

2 Stephanie Anderson, 'French Anthropology in Australia, a Prelude: The Encounters between Aboriginal Tasmanians and the Expedition of Bruny d'Entrecasteaux, 1793', *Aboriginal History*, 24 (2000): 212–23; M.J. Hughes, 'Philosophical Travellers at the Ends of the Earth: Baudin, Péron and the Tasmanians', in R.W. Home (ed.), *Australian Science in the Making* (Cambridge University Press, 1988), pp. 23–44.

3 Stephanie Anderson, 'French Anthropology in Australia, the First Fieldwork Report: François Péron's "Maria Island – Anthropological Observations"', *Aboriginal History*, 25 (2001): 228–42.

The scientific impulses behind voyages of discovery continued to be woven into the foundational years of the Australian colonies. Australia provided a different perspective on both the Earth and the heavens that continued to be a source of fascination to the European scientific world. When the eminent clergyman-geologist, the Rev. W.B. Clarke, gave his inaugural address to the Royal Society of New South Wales in 1867, he pointed enthusiastically to the scientific possibilities its members enjoyed since, as he tellingly put it, 'We have, as it were, a new heaven for Astronomy and a new earth for Geology'.[4]

In the early decades of British settlement, science in Australia was largely watched over by Joseph Banks, who had recommended Botany Bay as a site for a penal settlement on the basis of his voyage with Cook. Up to his death in 1820, Banks was the infant colony's main advocate in London. Other British patrons succeeded him, and while none matched his overwhelming significance, they all testified to the remarkable importance of key British-based scientists in the development of the natural sciences in Australia, especially in the first half of the nineteenth century. William and Joseph Hooker at Kew prosecuted the case for imperial and colonial resources being spent on Australian botany;[5] Roderick Murchison, of the British Geological Survey, interested himself in Australian geology;[6] and Richard Owen, at the British Museum of Natural History, in Australian zoology and palaeontology.[7] The natural history specimens and observations collected in the colonies, the scientific papers published about them and the reputations thereby boosted were mostly to be found in Britain, making the history of Australian science and technology in this period often indistinguishable from the history of British science and technology.

Improvement and exploration

While best known for his interest in botany, Joseph Banks' preoccupation in the early decades of the Australian colony was with the task of agricultural

---

4 Quoted in Ann Moyal (ed.), *The Web of Science: The Scientific Correspondence of the Rev. W.B. Clarke, Australia's Pioneer Geologist*, 2 vols (Melbourne: Australian Scholarly Publishing, 2003), vol. 1, p. 50.
5 Richard Drayton, *Nature's Government: Science, Imperial Britain, and the 'Improvement' of the World* (New Haven: Yale University Press, 2000).
6 Robert A. Stafford, *Scientist of Empire: Sir Roderick Murchison, Scientific Exploration and Victorian Imperialism* (Cambridge University Press, 1989).
7 A.M. Moyal, 'Sir Richard Owen and His Influence on Australian Zoological and Palaeontological Science', *Records of the Australian Academy of Science*, 3, 2 (1975): 41–56.

improvement.[8] Drawing on the successes of the agrarian revolution in Britain, and the vastly increased production of food it made possible, Banks sought to apply such lessons to the new colony (as he had, very profitably, to his own Lincolnshire estate). Under his direction the First Fleet brought with it a wide range of crops and fruits to cultivate, with the aim of rendering the colony independent and ultimately a source of profit to the British Empire.[9] A keen sheep breeder, Banks helped to develop the merino strands that were eventually to make the colony profitable.[10] Indicative of Banks' view of the possibilities of agricultural improvement enabled by the rational techniques embodied in science, was his exhortation to Governor Hunter in 1797 (two years after he took up office) 'to press forward the improvements. The climate and soil are superior to most which have yet been settled by Europeans.'[11]

Even before the First Fleet set sail a London newspaper of 1787 sought to appeal to the ideal of improvement as a way to elevate the establishment of a penal colony: 'The Expedition to Botany Bay comprehends in it more than the mere Banishment of our Felons; it is an Undertaking of Humanity' for, it added, 'a capital Improvement will be made in the Southern part of the New World'.[12] One way in which this improving agricultural ethic eventually took root in Australia was in the adaption of farming practice to suit Australian conditions. The depressed trade in wool in the 1840s led to the development of boiling-down works and a trade in sheep tallow. In the same decade labour shortages in South Australia led to the invention in 1843, by the flour miller, John Miller, of a horse-drawn stripper, saving much labour in harvesting wheat.

The engagement of a significant proportion of the European population in agriculture led to exceptional technological innovation across the nineteenth century.[13] The iconic stump-jump plough was invented by Richard Bowyer

8 John Gascoigne, *Joseph Banks and the English Enlightenment: Useful Knowledge and Polite Culture* (Cambridge University Press, 1994). See also the companion volume, *Science in the Service of Empire: Joseph Banks, the British State and the Uses of Science in the Age of Revolution* (Cambridge University Press, 1998).

9 Alan Frost, *Botany Bay Mirages: Illusions of Australia's Convict Beginnings* (Melbourne University Press, 1994), pp. 127–9.

10 Quoted in H.B. Carter, *His Majesty's Spanish Flock* (Sydney: Angus & Robertson, 1964).

11 Banks to Hunter, 30 March 1797, *Historical Records of New South Wales* [HRNSW], vol. 3, p. 202.

12 Quoted in Alan Frost, '"As it Were Another America": English Ideas of the First Settlement in New South Wales at the End of the Eighteenth Century', *Eighteenth-Century Studies*, 7, 3 (1974): 271.

13 Lynette J. Peel and D.E. Tribe, 'Innovation, Science and the Farmer', in *Technology in Australia, 1788–1988* (Melbourne: Australian Academy of Technological Sciences and Engineering, 1988), pp. 1–68.

Smith in 1876 to deal with the difficulty of clearing mallee roots. William Farrer began breeding new strains of wheat suited to local conditions as early as the 1880s,[14] while other agriculturists experimented with non-standard European crops such as sugar cane,[15] cotton and tobacco (partly under the influence of the acclimatisation movement). The development of irrigation began in 1886, when the Chaffey brothers selected a derelict sheep station on the Murray River, known as Mildura, for an irrigation settlement, and the Goulburn Weir (the first major diversion structure for irrigation in Australia) was built between 1887 and 1891. Attempts were also made to deal with some of the problems caused by European settlement, such as the explosion in numbers of introduced pests, including livestock diseases, thistles and rabbits.[16] Motivated by self-interest, pioneer pastoralists and farmers learned to back their own judgement over the received wisdom of the British agricultural tradition. These agricultural 'practitioners' were generally suspicious of the 'experts' appointed to departments of agriculture and the agricultural colleges that existed in most Australian colonies by the end of the century.[17] This tension between knowledge gained by experience and that gained by education persisted into the twentieth century.

While British interest in Australian settlement was motivated primarily by economic and political objectives, these were linked with the desire to know the land in scientific terms. Such scientific enquiry gave British imperial claims greater legitimacy and also raised the possibility of more effective utilisation of the land through the techniques of scientifically based improvement. The inclusion on the *Endeavour* of an astronomer and a party of natural historians under Banks was emulated by the major exploration voyages dispatched under the auspices of the Imperial or colonial governments. The *Investigator* voyage under Matthew Flinders, which in 1801–03 circumnavigated the continent,

14 M. Cawte, 'William Farrer and the Australian Response to Mendelism', *Historical Records of Australian Science*, 6, 1 (1984): 45–58; C.W. Wrigley, 'W.J. Farrer and F.B. Guthrie: The Unique Breeder-Chemist Combination that Pioneered Quality Wheats for Australia', *Records of the Australian Academy of Science*, 4, 1 (1979): 7–25.

15 Peter Griggs, *Global Industry, Local Innovation: The History of Cane Sugar Production in Australia, 1820–1995* (Bern: Peter Lang, 2011).

16 Geoff Raby, 'Science in the "Pastoral Age": Veterinary Responses to the New South Wales Catarrh Epizootics of the 1830s', *Historical Records of Australian Science*, 6, 2 (1985): 189–94; Stephen Dando-Collins, *Pasteur's Gambit: Louis Pasteur, the Australasian Rabbit Plague and a Ten Million Dollar Prize* (Sydney: Random House, 2008).

17 Christopher Soeterboek, '"Who Are You to Tell Me How to Farm?" Farmers and Experts in the Goulburn Valley of Victoria', PhD thesis, University of Melbourne, 2011; David J. Collins and Ian D. Rae, 'R.W.E. MacIvor: Late-Nineteenth-Century Advocate for Scientific Agriculture in South-Eastern Australia', *Historical Records of Australian Science*, 19, 2 (2008): 125–59.

included an astronomer, a mineralogist, a botanist and a Kew gardener. The voyage was organised by Joseph Banks to consolidate the British hold over what – largely thanks to Flinders – became known as Australia at a time when the French were actively beginning to explore the region. As its chief metropolitan patron, Banks hoped that Australia, like North America before it, would add to the wealth of empire through its resources and a river system that could make them accessible. The continent's size, he thought, suggested the presence of 'vast rivers capable of being navigated into the heart of the interior' along with 'some native raw material of importance to such a manufacturing country as England is'.[18]

Banks's belief in the possibility of a river system was shared by some in the colonial government and did much to determine the goals of many of the early exploring expeditions.[19] The first two expeditions of John Oxley (appointed surveyor-general of New South Wales in 1812) were focused on the mapping of rivers: the first in 1817 followed the Lachlan and Macquarie rivers, and the second in 1818 involved further exploration of the Macquarie along with the Castlereagh and Hastings rivers. Accompanying Oxley on the first expedition were the Kew collector, Allan Cunningham, and the superintendent of the Sydney Botanical Gardens, Charles Frazer, together with a mineralogist. Frazer also formed part of Oxley's second expedition, while Cunningham sailed with Lieutenant Phillip Parker King on three of his maritime expeditions (in 1819, 1820 and 1821–22) to chart the Australian coastline.

The exploration of the inland river system was taken much further by Charles Sturt. His first expedition of 1828–29 travelled along the rivers of western New South Wales with exploration of the Macquarie River and its tributaries, leading him to the Darling River. It was, however, his second expedition of 1829–30 that did most to unravel the disappointingly meagre inland river system of eastern Australia. By travelling down the Murrumbidgee to its confluence with the Murray, which in turn linked with the Darling, he showed that all the rivers of the region formed one interconnected system, with the Murray-Darling at the centre. Such an achievement excited the jealousy of Thomas Mitchell, who succeeded Oxley as surveyor-general in 1828; hence his expedition of 1835 to prove that the Darling did not flow into the Murray River. This, ironically, had the effect of strengthening Sturt's claims that the Darling and the Murray formed the core waterways into which the other major inland rivers flowed. The following year Mitchell set out on the

18 Banks to Under-Secretary John King, 15 May 1798, HRNSW, vol. 3, p. 383.
19 Michael Cathcart, The Water Dreamers: The Remarkable History of Our Dry Continent (Melbourne: Text, 2009).

expedition for which he is best known; by exploring the lands along and south of the Murray he opened up 'Australia Felix', the relatively fertile western districts of Victoria, thus laying the foundation for the rapidly growing Port Phillip District. Such expeditions contributed to an Enlightenment-tinged quest to promote science and improvement, with Mitchell urging the need for further such explorations to 'spread the light of civilisation over a portion of the globe yet unknown...where science might accomplish new and unthought-of discoveries'.[20]

Charting new country or recording its flora and fauna meant on many occasions seeking the guidance of those who knew the land best, the Indigenous population.[21] On Mitchell's expedition to the Darling, for example, he followed Aboriginal guides at times; Leichhardt did likewise.[22] Flinders' *Investigator* expedition had included two Aboriginal men, Bungaree (or Bongaree) and Nanbaree. Scientific collectors were, on occasion, reliant on Indigenous expertise. The naturalist George Caley had remarked to Joseph Banks as early as 1801 that he employed Aboriginal assistants since 'they can trace anything so well in the woods, and can climb trees with such ease'.[23]

The emergence of a colonial scientific culture

The first signs of an Australian-based science were more evident in the field of astronomy than in natural history and followed the settlement of Sydney and the appointment of scientifically trained naval officers to administrative posts. Lieutenant William Dawes set up a small astronomical observatory in 1788 near the harbour, using instruments that had been supplied by the Board of Longitude. In 1791, however, he returned to England, taking this equipment with him.[24] A more promising start to an Australian study of the southern skies occurred with the arrival of the amateur astronomer Sir Thomas Brisbane, as governor of New South Wales. He erected a twin-domed observatory alongside Government House at Parramatta and equipped it, at his own

20 T.L. Mitchell, *Three Expeditions into the Interior of Eastern Australia*, 2 vols (London: T. & W. Boone, 1839), vol. 1, p. 5.

21 Philip A. Clarke, *Aboriginal Plant Collectors: Botanists and Australian Aboriginal People in the Nineteenth Century* (Sydney: Rosenberg Publishing, 2008).

22 Geoffrey Badger, *Explorers of Australia* (Sydney: Kangaroo Press, 1981), p. 142; Clarke, *Aboriginal Plant Collectors*, p. 94.

23 Quoted in Clarke, *Aboriginal Plant Collectors*, p. 63.

24 Ragbir Bhathal and Graeme White, *Under the Southern Cross: A Brief History of Astronomy in Australia* (Sydney: Kangaroo Press, 1991), pp. 13–16.

expense, with instruments that he brought with him.[25] Brisbane was recalled in 1825, in part because of complaints that he was more concerned with 'star-gazing' than government business. The major work of the observatory was not published until ten years later as the *Catalogue of 7385 Stars*; only the second account of the southern skies to appear, although it was already known to contain many inaccuracies.[26]

After Brisbane's departure the gubernatorial observatory became more formally a state institution, with Brisbane's instruments being purchased by the government. His assistant, Carl Rümker, became the government astronomer from 1827 until 1830, when he returned permanently to Europe, having incurred the ill will of the president of the Royal Astronomical Society. Brisbane's other assistant, James Dunlop, followed as government astronomer, a post he held until his resignation in 1847 in the face of an unfavourable report on the observatory, which led to its being closed. The instruments were put in storage and eventually passed on to the Sydney Observatory that was opened in 1855, when another scientifically minded governor, Sir William Denison, took up office. The following year the Rev. William Scott was appointed to the revived post of government astronomer. It was an indication of how important gubernatorial leadership was in science; as lieutenant-governor of Van Diemen's Land from 1847 to 1855 Denison had breathed new life into scientific activity in that colony and he was to do the same as governor of New South Wales from 1854 to 1861.

It was under Sir John Franklin, another scientifically disposed lieutenant-governor of Van Diemen's Land, that the Magnetical and Meteorological Observatory was established at Hobart in 1840 although this was a metropolitan initiative forming part of a larger imperial network. Fluctuations in terrestrial magnetism were a major concern to the British Admiralty because of reliance on the magnetic compass for navigation. Along with other such institutions around the world, the Hobart observatory provided scientifically accurate information to that most basic arm of British imperial power, the Royal Navy; hence its funding by the Admiralty.[27]

---

25 Simon Schaffer, 'Keeping the Books at Paramatta [sic]', in David Aubin, Charlotte Bigg and H. Otto Sibum (eds), *The Heavens on Earth: Observatories and Astronomy in Nineteenth-Century Science and Culture* (Durham: Duke University Press, 2010), pp. 118–47.

26 Shirley D. Saunders, 'Sir Thomas Brisbane's Legacy to Colonial Science: Colonial Astronomy at the Parramatta Observatory, 1822–1848', *Historical Records of Australian Science*, 15, 2 (2004): 177–209; Nick Lomb, 'The Instruments from Parramatta Observatory', *Historical Records of Australian Science*, 15, 2 (2004): 211–22.

27 Raymond Haynes et al., *Explorers of the Southern Sky: A History of Australian Astronomy* (Cambridge University Press, 1996), p. 70.

The Hobart Magnetical and Meteorological Observatory was an instance of how the Australian colonies could serve as a base for the study of the physical as well as the natural sciences. The greatest effect in the physical sciences internationally came from observations of the southern skies, where the work of the Parramatta Observatory led the way. Astronomical observatories were established in Sydney in 1858, Melbourne in 1862, Adelaide in 1874, Brisbane in 1879 and Perth in 1896. The scope and significance of their work gathered momentum as the sophistication of telescopes developed. The manufacture of scientific instruments was mostly undertaken in Britain or Europe, but Henry Chamberlain Russell, government astronomer of New South Wales from 1870, designed and built at least 23 scientific instruments. He was also a pioneer in astronomical photography and in 1874 the Royal Astronomical Society of London judged his photographs of the Transit of Venus 'the best and most complete they had seen'.[28] Henry Evans Baker, a retired sea captain and first superintendent of the Ballarat Observatory, built a workshop and foundry and constructed a number of telescopes, including the 26-inch 'Great Equatorial Telescope' in 1886.[29] The Great Melbourne Telescope was manufactured in Ireland in 1868, but was possible because of colonial backing. The second-largest reflecting telescope in the world, it was designed to observe changes in southern nebulae and, despite technical problems, produced some remarkable drawings of the Carina Nebula.[30]

Botany also established an early institutional presence in the Australian colonies, aided substantially by its practical applications, and importance to Joseph Banks. After 1821 Charles Frazer was formally known as the colonial botanist, a post he held until his death in 1831. For a time, too, there was a royal botanist employed not by the colonial government but by the Royal Gardens at Kew, the centre of an imperial network of which Australia increasingly became a part.[31] It was under the auspices of Kew that Allan Cunningham arrived in Sydney in 1816 as a botanical collector. After Cunningham's brief and unhappy time as royal botanist in 1837, the post lapsed, but the Botanic Garden in Sydney survived, and by the end of the century all the colonial

28 Bathal and White, *Under the Southern Cross*, pp. 23–7.
29 Wayne Orchiston, *A Brief Outline of the History of the Ballarat Observatory* (Melbourne: Astronomical Society of Victoria, Historical Section, 1982).
30 Richard Gillespie, *The Great Melbourne Telescope* (Melbourne: Museum Victoria, 2011), pp. 67–8, 104.
31 Lucile H. Brockway, *Science and Colonial Expansion: The Role of the British Royal Botanic Gardens* (New York: Academic Press, 1979).

capitals boasted such an institution.[32] In 1853, Ferdinand Mueller, the first government botanist of Victoria, claimed that the Melbourne Botanic Garden (initiated in 1846) was an institution 'for diffusion of knowledge, for the experimental introduction of foreign plants into our adopted country or for multiplying the treasures, which our own Flora offers and as a healthy locality for recreation'.[33] This view prevailed until the 1870s, when competition from museums and universities, and a rise in the influence of the horticultural industry, led to a shift in public support away from science in botanic gardens to recreation and display. Although botanists in Sydney and Adelaide were able to negotiate this transition successfully, Mueller was not, and was removed from the directorship of the Melbourne Botanic Garden in 1873, although not from the position of government botanist.[34]

In the first 50 years of European settlement a river of natural history specimens flowed from the Australian colonies to Europe, and a much smaller stream went the other way, bearing a handful of scientifically minded settlers. These settlers – the Macleay family, for example – were integral to the development of colonial science. Alexander Macleay was nearly 60 years old when he was appointed colonial secretary of New South Wales in 1825, and had already accrued 'the finest and most extensive collection' of entomological specimens 'of any private individual', a library to interpret it, and his own system of classification with which to arrange it.[35] Scientific visitors to Sydney such as Joseph Hooker were astonished to find a well-stocked library and museum in the Macleay villa, Elizabeth Bay House, resources that were utilised by male and female members of the family.[36] When visiting Sydney, the English naturalist, Thomas Huxley, declared it was one of the 'two or three houses where I can go and feel myself at home at all times'.[37] The collection

32 Lionel Gilbert, *The Royal Botanic Gardens, Sydney: A History 1816–1985* (Oxford University Press, 1986); R.T.M. Pescott, *The Royal Botanic Gardens, Melbourne: A History from 1845 to 1970* (Oxford University Press, 1982); Richard Aitken, *Seeds of Change: An Illustrated History of Adelaide Botanic Garden* (Melbourne: Bloomings Books, 2006).

33 Quoted in R.W. Home et al., (eds), *Regardfully Yours: Selected Correspondence of Ferdinand von Mueller Volume 1, 1840–1859* (Bern: Peter Lang, 1998), p. 164.

34 H.M. Cohn and Sara Maroske, 'Relief from Duties of Minor Importance: The Removal of Baron von Mueller from the Directorship of the Melbourne Botanic Gardens', *Victorian Historical Journal*, 67, 1 (1996): 103–27; Stephen Jeffries, 'Alexander von Humboldt and Ferdinand von Mueller's Argument for the Scientific Botanic Garden', *Historical Records of Australian Science*, 11, 3 (1997): 301–10.

35 Derelie Cherry, *Alexander Macleay: From Scotland to Sydney* (Sydney: Paradise Publishers, 2012).

36 Ibid., pp. 235–37.

37 Quoted in Julian Holland, 'Diminishing Circles: W.S. Macleay in Sydney, 1839–1865', *Historical Records of Australian Science*, 11, 2 (1996): 119–47.

eventually formed the basis of the Macleay Museum at Sydney University.
The Macleays were also prime movers in the formation of the oldest public
museum in Australia, the Australian Museum, established in Sydney in 1827.

Those interested in achieving scientific recognition in particular disciplines
might have needed to invoke imperial patrons, but for others the study of
local problems could loom larger. Joining with those who shared scientific
interests could also bring social or even political advantages. The study of
nature could combine fresh air, mixed companionship and recreation with
Victorian canons of the need for moral, intellectual and even religious
self-improvement.[38] The colonial scientific societies that rose and fell in the
first half of the nineteenth century reflected diverse personal and social goals.
They were generally not devoted to specific scientific disciplines but were
established more in the scientifically inclusive spirit of the British provincial
scientific societies.[39] The first in Australia, the Australasian Philosophical
Society, lasted only from 1821 until 1822 when, as Barron Field, the editor
of its major publication, put it, 'the infant society soon expired in the bane-
ful atmosphere of distracted politics'.[40] The arrival of Sir John Franklin as
lieutenant-governor of Van Diemen's Land from 1836 to 1843 (along with his
wife, Jane, Lady Franklin) led to that island colony taking the scientific lead
with the formation of the Tasmanian Society in 1838. The year 1844 saw the
formation of the first Royal Society outside the United Kingdom, the Royal
Society of Van Diemen's Land for Botany, Horticulture and the Advancement
of Science.[41] Scientific organisation in New South Wales was revived when
Governor Denison took up office in 1855 and encouraged the formation of
the Philosophical Society of New South Wales in 1856 (after 1866, the Royal
Society of New South Wales). In New South Wales and the other colonies
scientific life also received some sustenance from a range of agricultural societies, botanical gardens and a growing number of museums.

British, and to a lesser extent French, influences dominated early colonial
science. But it was also shaped significantly by a group of Germans arriving in the colonies from the 1840s, highly trained beneficiaries of a German

38 Sybil Jack, 'Cultural Transmission: Science and Society to 1850', in Home (ed.),
   Australian Science in the Making, pp. 45–68; G. Melleuish, 'Beneficial Providence and the
   Quest for Harmony: The Cultural Setting for Colonial Science in Sydney, 1850–1890',
   Journal and Proceedings of the Royal Society of New South Wales, 118, 3–4 (1986): 167–80.
39 Colin Finney, *Paradise Revealed: Natural History in Nineteenth-Century Australia*
   (Melbourne: Museum of Victoria, 1993), p. 17.
40 Barron Field, *Geographical Memoirs on New South Wales by Various Hands* (London: John
   Murray, 1825), p. v.
41 David Branagan, 'Words, Actions, People: 150 Years of Scientific Societies in Australia',
   Journal and Proceedings of the Royal Society of New South Wales, 104, 3–4 (1972): 129.

university-based scientific tradition. Fired with enthusiasm, they sought to emulate the travels and big-picture science of their famous compatriot, Alexander von Humboldt, who argued that a knowledge of all the natural sciences, and the connections between them, was necessary to discover the laws that governed nature.[42] Included in this group were Carl Rümker, Ferdinand Mueller, Ludwig Leichhardt, Wilhelm Blandowski, first director of the first public museum in Melbourne, Gerard Krefft, a director of the Australian Museum, Georg Neumayer, who in 1857 established the Flagstaff Observatory for Geophysics, Magnetism and Nautical Science,[43] and Richard Schomburgk, long-serving curator of the Adelaide Botanic Garden.[44] These scientists did not feel the weight of British imperial expectations to enrich the great institutions of London. They made connections with British-based scientists to facilitate their work in an English-speaking environment, but at the same time looked toward continental Europe for inspiration and validation. Neumayer and Blandowski eventually returned to Europe, but the others stayed, contributing significantly to local knowledge, institutions and research endeavours.

Perhaps the most under-appreciated of the German scientists (largely due to his premature death) is Ludwig Leichhardt, who led three privately funded exploring expeditions in northern Australia in the 1840s.[45] The first scientist in much of that territory, Leichhardt's natural history observations and collections remain fundamentally important in geology and botany, although still not completely analysed and published. With the interests of his Australian patrons in mind, Leichhardt identified the pastoral potential of northern Australia, and the aridity of the centre of the continent.[46] Leichhardt's fate remains mysterious as he and his party disappeared in 1848 while on an expedition from Moreton Bay to Perth. Many subsequent inland expeditions were motivated by the search for Leichhardt.

42 R.W. Home, *Science as a German Export to Nineteenth Century Australia* (London: Sir Robert Menzies Centre for Australian Studies, 1995); Sara Maroske, 'Germans at the Melbourne Botanic Garden and Herbarium, 1853–96', in Ellen I. Mitchell (ed.), *Baron von Mueller's German Melbourne* (Melbourne: Plenty Valley Papers, 2000), pp. 24–34.

43 R.W. Home and H. Kretzer 'The Flagstaff Observatory, Melbourne: New Documents Relating to its Foundation', *Historical Records of Australian Science*, 8, 4 (1989): 213–43.

44 Pauline Payne, *The Diplomatic Gardener: Richard Schomburgk, Explorer and Botanic Garden Director* (Adelaide: Jeffcott Press, 2007).

45 E.M. Webster, *Whirlwinds in the Plain: Ludwig Leichhardt – Friends, Foes and History* (Melbourne University Press, 1980).

46 Matthew Stephens, 'From Lost Property to Explorer's Relics: The Rediscovery of the Personal Library of Ludwig Leichhardt', *Historical Records of Australian Science*, 18, 2 (2007): 191–227.

The discovery of gold in the eastern colonies of Australia in the 1850s boosted small-scale exploration and prospecting, and led directly to rapid government-funded developments in the sciences of geology and mineralogy.[47] New South Wales established a geological survey in 1850, and two years later Victoria appointed British-trained Alfred R.C. Selwyn as a geological surveyor. Selwyn assumed the directorship of the Victorian geological survey in 1855, and this body had a long-term influence on that field throughout the colonies.[48] Victorian government surveyors quickly worked out the colony's broad geological structure, establishing the stratigraphic succession of rocks and producing a series of topographical and geological maps on the grid system used in Great Britain.

While the maps of colonial geological surveys represent an early high point of local scientific endeavour, they were not without controversy. The identification and interpretation of geological features involved testing and adapting systems of classification and theories generated by European-based geologists. Differences of opinion over the distribution of gold in quartz deposits, the age of coal fields, geological succession, and the existence of glaciation in Australia rent the nascent geological community.[49] They also revealed the strength of allegiances formed by geologists before they assumed colonial appointments. While these disputes contributed to international scientific discussions, they were of less interest to Australian users and funders of geological maps and, in a restructuring process similar to that experienced at the Melbourne Botanic Garden, the 'scientific' Geological Survey of Victoria was disbanded in 1868 in favour of a more 'practical' Department of Mining. This body was expected to find coal deposits that could support the development of colonial industry. The Geological Survey of Victoria was reinstituted in 1878, by which time many of its seasoned former staff were boosting the capacity of geological surveys in other Australian colonies or overseas.

47 D.A. McCann, 'Alfred Selwyn and Frederick McCoy to John Walter Gregory: 19th century British Experience Applied in S.E. Australia' in Roger Pierson (ed.), *The History of Geology in the Second Half of the Nineteenth Century: The Story in Australia, and in Victoria, from Selwyn and McCoy to Gregory 1853 to 1903* (Melbourne: Earth Sciences History Group, 2007), pp. 55–6.

48 E.W. Skeats quoted in T.A. Darragh, 'The Geological Survey of Victoria under Alfred Selwyn, 1852–1868', *Historical Records of Australian Science*, 7, 1 (1987): 1.

49 Darragh, 'The Geological Survey of Victoria', p. 3; T.G. Vallance, 'The Fuss about Coal: Troubled Relations between Palaeobotany and Geology', in D.J. and S.G.M. Carr (eds), *Plants and Man in Australia* (Sydney: Academic Press, 1981), pp. 136–76. David Branagan, *T.W. Edgeworth David: A Life* (Canberra: National Library of Australia Press, 2005).

The era of British dominance of natural science in colonial Australia culminated in the North Australian Exploring Expedition (NAEE) of 1855–56, which traversed the continent on a diagonal from the mouth of the Victoria River in the future Northern Territory to Brisbane. Liberally funded by the imperial government, the expedition's scientific personnel included a naturalist, geologist, botanist (Ferdinand Mueller) and artist, with Augustus Gregory, a surveyor, as leader. The expedition confirmed Leichhardt's predictions that central Australia offered poor prospects for settlement, but returned after nearly two years in the field with a full complement of staff and abundant natural history collections. Most of the specimens were sent to, and worked on, in Britain, but Ferdinand Mueller was able to retain a set of botanical specimens for the Melbourne Herbarium, and to publish most of the new species it contained. This was a significant coup, and helped to establish his reputation as an authority in descriptive and geographical botany.[50]

In the aftermath of the NAEE, Ferdinand Mueller was invited to join other colonial expeditions, to advise on routes and scientific personnel and to analyse botanical findings. He thus became one of the earliest and most powerful locally based patrons of the natural sciences in Australia, and expeditions led by John McDouall Stuart, Burke and Wills and their relief parties, the Forrest brothers in Western Australia, Ernest Giles and the Elder Scientific Exploring Expedition were all influenced by him to a greater or lesser extent. Mueller's largest ambition, to write a flora of Australia, was thwarted by the imperial botanists at Kew, but Mueller ensured that his work on unique and diverse Australian vegetation reached an international audience by issuing his own taxonomic journal in Latin, and by establishing a correspondence with hundreds of international scientists.[51]

Mueller took a leading role in the Geographical Society of Australasia, formed in 1883. An early instance of federation, the society was made up of largely self-governing bodies in New South Wales, Victoria, Queensland and South Australia.[52] Its aim was to promote the exploration not just of the Australian continent, but also the nearby islands, reflecting and fostering an emerging Australian imperialism. In 1885 the New South Wales branch of the society sponsored an expedition to the Fly River in the recently annexed

---

50 Helen M. Cohn, 'Botanical Researches in Intertropical Australia: Ferdinand Mueller and the North Australian Exploring Expedition', *Victorian Naturalist*, 113, 4 (1996): 163–8.

51 Home et al., *Regardfully Yours: Selected Correspondence of Ferdinand von Mueller Volume 2, 1860–1875* (Bern: Peter Lang, 1998), pp. 21–6.

52 Susan Lizabeth Blackwood, 'Jungle, Desert, Ice: The Royal Geographical Society of Australasia, Victorian Branch', PhD thesis, Deakin University, 2006.

south-east New Guinea, led by Captain H.C. Everill; and, in the context of the International Polar Year of 1882–83, members of the New South Wales and Victorian branches began pushing for Australian involvement in the exploration of Antarctica. An Antarctic Exploration Committee was set up in Melbourne in 1886 and was instrumental, nationally and internationally, in 'turning eyes southward' from the Arctic to the Antarctic, and in casting the exploration of Antarctica as 'a task for scientists'. The Committee disbanded in 1896, but its aims were more than realised in the remarkable developments in Antarctic research and exploration that occurred shortly afterwards.[53]

Until the establishment of universities in Australia in the 1850s, colonial scientists were necessarily educated overseas. The colony of New South Wales initiated the first Australian university in Sydney in 1850 with three foundation professors, including Morris Birckbeck Pell and John Smith in the chairs of mathematics, and chemistry and experimental physics respectively. Three years later Melbourne followed suit with four foundation professors, including William Wilson and Frederick McCoy in the chairs of mathematics and natural science. Applied sciences were also taught in the schools of mines established in capital cities and regional centres such as Ballarat in Victoria, Zeehan in Tasmania and Charters Towers in Queensland. Science subjects were at first restricted to male students, and at universities only as part of an arts degree. In 1883 the first female graduate at the University of Adelaide, Emily Dornwell, was also Australia's first Bachelor of Science. Graduates of Australian universities applied for chairs in the sciences as they were created in the 1880s, in response to expanded interest in science education. Three Melbourne alumni were appointed to chairs in chemistry, anatomy and natural philosophy at the University of Melbourne in 1882, due as much to an upsurge in Australian chauvinism as to the outstanding talent of the graduates.[54] More typically and uncontroversially, Australian universities filled their senior scientific positions with men from British universities well into the twentieth century.

While there were relatively few professional scientific positions in colonial Australia, the study of natural history was open to all, an enterprise that helped to compensate for a perceived lack of cultural history. Amateur

---

53 R.W. Home et al., 'Why Explore Antarctica? Australian Discussions in the 1880s', *Australian Journal of Politics and History*, 38, 3 (1992): 386–413.
54 R.J.W. Selleck, *The Shop: The University of Melbourne 1850–1939* (Melbourne University Press, 2003), pp. 192–9.

naturalists, men and women, played a significant part in making known new species to the larger scientific world;[55] particularly in the more remote regions. Thanks to the work of Georgiana Molloy, who sent rare specimens from the hitherto little-known Western Australia, John Lindley, the foundation professor of botany at the University of London, published in 1840 a description of the flora of Swan River.[56] While holding a variety of public and private managerial positions in Tasmania, Ronald Gunn sent back a large variety of botanical specimens to Joseph Hooker. Such data was later incorporated in Hooker's *Flora Tasmaniae* (1855–60), published after Hooker became assistant director of Kew Gardens. Gunn saw this task of recording the flora and fauna of Tasmania as being particularly important since, as he poignantly and accurately remarked to Hooker, 'Many of our animals and Birds will become extinct or nearly so'.[57]

The pursuit of natural history was given strong cultural reinforcement by its close connection with natural theology. Divine revelation, it had long been argued, could be studied through two books: that of the Scriptures and that of nature. Natural history was thought to be a strong support for the argument from design, since the more one demonstrated the complexity and intricate character of the natural world the more evident was the need for a purposeful Creator. This was, for example, the view advanced by the Anglican clergyman, W.B. Clarke, who became the most eminent of Australian colonial geologists.[58] Clergy were among the most active naturalists, with the first chaplain, the Rev. Richard Johnson, setting a precedent.[59] As well as being morally uplifting, natural history also had the potential to be useful and even profitable. As the Australian Floral and Horticultural Society report of 1841 put it, natural history was a study that could bring 'beneficial results to the whole community' through the 'fabrication and diffusion of Nature's productions' along with its role in leading from 'viewing nature, to a love of Nature's God'.[60]

---

55 Sara Maroske, '"The whole great continent as a present"': Nineteenth-century Australian Women Workers in Science', in Farley Kelly (ed.), *On the Edge of Discovery: Australian Women in Science* (Melbourne: Text, 1993), pp. 13–34.

56 Clarke, *Aboriginal Plant Collectors*, p. 86.

57 T.E. Burns and J.R. Skemp (eds), *Van Diemen's Land Correspondents: Letters from R.C. Gunn, R.W. Lawrence, Jorgen Jorgenson, Sir John Franklin and others to Sir William J. Hooker, 1827–1849* (Launceston: Queen Victoria Museum, 1961), p. 59.

58 W.B. Clarke, *The Signs of the Times* (London: J.G. & F. Rivington, 1838), p. 4.

59 L.A. Gilbert, 'Plants and Parsons in Nineteenth Century New South Wales', *Historical Records of Australian Science*, 5, 3 (1982): 17–32.

60 Australian Floral and Horticultural Society, *Third Report* (Sydney, 1841), p. 5.

Darwin, acclimatisation and the emergence of a national scientific tradition

The publication of Darwin's *On the Origin of Species* in 1859 challenged this view in Australia, as elsewhere. Darwin's version of nature emphasised change as inevitable, but not progress, and defined relations between individuals by the harsh 'struggle for existence' and 'survival of the fittest'. Australia can claim a contribution to the *Origin* because Darwin visited the area around Sydney for two months in 1836 toward the end of the *Beagle* voyage. Zoological curiosities such as the kangaroo and emu, and especially for him the mysterious platypus, were a source of great interest to a naturalist engaged in elucidating the origin of species. This is reflected in a famous passage in Darwin's journal, in which he raised the possibility that two Creators were involved in bringing into being the life forms of Australia and elsewhere.[61] Darwin subsequently obtained information about the natural history of Australia by correspondence with at least eight local naturalists, including William S. Macleay, Sir Thomas Mitchell and Ferdinand Mueller. Data from Mueller on northern European plants in the Australian Alps made its way into a chapter in the *Origin*, where Darwin considered the influence of geography and climate change on evolution.[62]

Darwin himself sent two presentation copies of the first edition of the *Origin* to the Australian colonies; one to Mueller and one to Charles Moore, Director of the Sydney Botanic Garden, but there were other copies of the first and second editions available in Australian bookshops by 1860.[63] Within a year of the *Origin's* publication, Australian scientists, presidents of scientific societies and church leaders were joining forces to warn the public about the moral dangers of what was known as the 'transmutation theory' or 'development hypothesis'. Nevertheless, by the end of the century, Darwinism was being taught in Australian universities and many theologians had comfortably accommodated natural selection and natural theology.[64] This generational

61 B.W. Butcher, '"Adding Stones to the Great Pile?" Charles Darwin's Use of Australian Resources, 1837–1882', *Historical Records of Australian Science*, 8, 1 (1989): 1–14; Iain McCalman, *Darwin's Armada: Four Voyages and the Battle for the Theory of Evolution* (New York: W.W. Norton, 2009).

62 Janet Garber, 'Darwin's Correspondents in the Pacific', in Roy MacLeod and Philip F. Rehbock (eds), *Darwin's Laboratory: Evolutionary Theory and Natural History in the Pacific* (Honolulu: University of Hawai'i Press, 1994), p. 178.

63 A.M. Lucas, 'Early Copies of the First Edition of *Origin of Species* in Australia', *Archives of Natural History*, 37, 2 (2010): 346–54.

64 Barry W. Butcher, 'Darwin Down Under: Science, Religion and Evolution in Australia', in Ronald L. Numbers and John Stenhouse (eds), *Disseminating Darwinism: The Role of Place, Race, Religion and Gender* (Cambridge University Press, 1999), pp. 39–60.

change is evident in the contrary reactions to evolution of Frederick McCoy on the one hand, foundation professor at the University of Melbourne and Director of the National Museum of Victoria, and Walter Baldwin Spencer on the other, who arrived in Australia in 1887 to take up the new chair of biology at the University of Melbourne and who replaced McCoy as director of the Museum in 1899.[65] McCoy echoed the opposition to evolution of his former teachers in Great Britain (Roderick Murchison and Adam Sedgwick) and held with the Biblical story of creation as it had come to be rendered in the light of modern geology.[66] The scientific education of Spencer, who was 43 years younger than McCoy, was shaped by the Darwinists Milnes Marshall and H.N. Moseley, and resulted in Spencer becoming an evolutionary biologist and abandoning conventional religion.[67] McCoy and Spencer were both teaching at the University of Melbourne in the 1890s, which gave students a unique opportunity to hear articulate advocates of both sides of the evolutionary debate.[68]

More than any other scientific theory in the nineteenth century, Darwinism influenced the wider community. This was exemplified in 1865 by the crowds that flocked to the Melbourne Museum when Frederick McCoy unveiled an exhibit of a 'family' of gorillas, the first great apes (albeit stuffed) to arrive in Australia.[69] McCoy asked the crowds to judge for themselves whether gorillas were 'infinitely remote' from humanity (his view) or a missing link between apes and humans. Thus the ground was prepared for speculations about human ancestry and relationships with non-human animals to enter the consciousness of the Australian public. Evolution became personal. The *Argus* journalist Frederick Sinnett described the gorilla group in the Museum as 'our poor relations'.[70] The French sculptor Emmanuel Frémiet expressed darker imaginings about interspecies intimacy in a sculpture of 'A gorilla carrying off a woman' in 1859. The public of Melbourne was able to draw its own conclusions about this exhibit, too, when a bronze version of the sculpture was installed in the National Gallery of Victoria in 1908; a gift of the artist.[71]

65 Ronald L. Numbers and John Stenhouse, 'Introduction', in Numbers and Stenhouse (eds), *Disseminating Darwinism*, p. 2.
66 Barry W. Butcher, 'Frederick McCoy's Anti-Evolutionism – the Cultural Context of Scientific Belief', *Victorian Naturalist*, 118 (2001): 226–30.
67 'Sir Walter Baldwin Spencer', *Australian Dictionary of Biography*, vol. 12, pp. 33–6.
68 Butcher, 'Frederick McCoy's Anti-Evolutionism', p. 229.
69 Barry W. Butcher, 'Gorilla Warfare in Melbourne: Halford, Huxley and "Man's Place in Nature"', in Home (ed.), *Australian Science in the Making*, pp. 153–69.
70 (Melbourne) *Argus*, 26 September 1865.
71 Ted Gott, 'An Iron Maiden for Melbourne – The History and Context of Emmanuel Frémiet's 1906 Cast of *Jeanne d'Arc*', *La Trobe Journal*, 81 (2008): 53–68.

McCoy and other Darwin sceptics articulated an alternative scientific theory of variation in the context of the acclimatisation movement. Although the first acclimatisation society was not established in Paris until 1854, its aims were based on the quintessentially Enlightenment idea of improvement. Acclimatisers regarded nature as a garden that could be planted and weeded according to people's needs, using organisms drawn from anywhere in the world. Melbourne set up the first Australian society in 1861 with McCoy and Mueller among its leading members.[72] Societies were established in all the other Australian colonies in the nineteenth century. Acclimatisation, as defined by French scientist Isidore Geoffroy Saint-Hilaire, was 'a rationally forced adaptation to new environments'. It connoted permanent physical change at a sub-specific level, a kind of 'conservative evolution', and it led French acclimatisation societies to attempt to introduce a variety of unlikely animals such as ostriches and yaks into France and its colonies.[73] In Australia the influence of Saint-Hilaire was most evident in the writings of Ferdinand Mueller, an honorary member of the Paris society since 1861, although both he and Frederick McCoy advised local societies to focus on introducing organisms into Australia that already lived in similar environments. They called this process 'acclimation' or 'naturalisation' and predicted, correctly, that they would not need to resort to forced adaptations to augment the Australian biota.[74]

In 1871 Darwin published *The Descent of Man*, which applied his theory of natural selection to the discipline of anthropology. As early as the second edition of the *Origin*, Darwin had already somewhat altered his original meaning of 'survival of the fittest' to suggest that individuals who were 'more fit' were generally also developmentally 'higher'.[75] This did not bode well for the Aboriginal people who were mentioned in *The Descent of Man*, and influentially so. Darwinian anthropologists such as Baldwin Spencer tended to regard Indigenous people in Australia as an example of 'what an early man must have been like before he learned to read and write', and to assume that

---

72 L. Gillbank, 'The Origins of the Acclimatisation Society of Victoria: Practical Science in the Wake of the Gold Rush', *Historical Records of Australian Science*, 6, 3 (1986): 359–74.

73 Quoted in Michael A. Osborne, 'Acclimatizing the World: A History of the Paradigmatic Colonial Science', *Osiris*, 15 (2000): 135–51.

74 Sara Maroske, 'Science by Correspondence: Ferdinand Mueller and Botany in Nineteenth Century Australia', PhD thesis, University of Melbourne, 2011, pp. 121–6; A.M. Lucas, 'Ferdinand von Mueller's Interactions with Charles Darwin and his Response to Darwinism', *Archives of Natural History*, 37, 1 (2010): 102–130.

75 Dov Ospovat, *The Development of Darwin's Theory: Natural History, Natural Theology, and Natural Selection 1838–1859* (Cambridge University Press, 1981), pp. 232–3.

Aboriginal people would not survive the 'inevitable' struggle with 'more fit' Europeans. Darwinism can be said to have 'scientised' Enlightenment notions of progress in relation to human history, while at the same time jettisoning its respect for 'primitive' peoples.[76] Spencer was humane towards Aboriginal people in his personal dealings, but modern anthropology is more grateful for the artefacts, observations and photographs collected by him and other anthropologists, such as Daisy Bates and Francis Gillen, than for their attempts at evolutionary anthropology, which have been comprehensively discredited.[77]

Colonial science and technology were largely defined by the efforts of individuals, but when viewed as whole they made an impressive display in the great exhibitions of the nineteenth century. Beginning with the London 1851 Royal Exhibition, these occasions provided another way to advertise to a larger world what the colonies had to offer. The 1850 report of the Australasian Botanic and Horticultural Society referred excitedly to the way in which the impending exhibition 'under the auspices of His Royal Highness Prince Albert' had prompted the society to assemble 'suitable subjects for representing the varied capacities of the colony'.[78] Distance and delay blighted Australia's first appearance on that world stage, although it had a more successful debut at the Paris exhibition of 1855.[79] This included display of a geological history of New South Wales prepared by William Clarke, which won him an International Exhibition Medal. A succession of international exhibitions followed in Paris, Moscow, Chicago, Philadelphia, and in the 1870s and 1880s in Melbourne and Sydney. Professional and amateur scientists and naturalists participated as organisers, exhibitors and commissioners, and instruments, machines, models, sketches, maps, specimens, samples and essays that were displayed formed the corpus of permanent exhibits at technological museums founded in Melbourne and Sydney.[80]

---

76 Butcher, 'Darwin Down Under', pp. 39–60.
77 'Sir Walter Baldwin Spencer', pp. 33–6.
78 *Second Annual Report of the Australasian Botanic and Horticultural Society* (Sydney, 1850), p. 6.
79 Peter Hoffenberg, *An Empire on Display: English, Indian, and Australian Exhibitions from the Crystal Palace to the Great War* (Berkeley: University of California Press, 2001), p. 129.
80 Kathleen M. Fennessy, '"Industrial Instruction" for the "Industrious Classes": Founding the Industrial and Technological Museum, Melbourne', *Historical Records of Australian Science*, 16, 1 (2005): 45–64; Carolyn Rasmussen et al., *A Museum for the People: A History of Museum Victoria and its Predecessors, 1854–2000* (Melbourne: Scribe, 2001); Lionel Gilbert, *The Little Giant: The Life & Work of Joseph Henry Maiden, 1859–1925* (Armidale: Kardoorair Press, 2001).

Involvement in international exhibitions was one of the ways in which Australian scientists helped to build momentum for Federation. The earliest example of intercolonial scientific cooperation dates back to the 1840s when the *Tasmanian Journal of Natural Science* became a de facto national periodical. In the 1860s all the colonies except Western Australia contributed funds towards the publication of George Bentham's *Flora Australiensis*. Its publication was also an example of international scientific cooperation because the British botanist, George Bentham, shared the title page with Ferdinand Mueller (albeit not with equal billing).[81] Examples of intercolonial scientific cooperation multiplied in the 1870s and 1880s in the disciplines of astronomy, geography and meteorology,[82] and culminated in 1888 with the foundation of the Australasian Association for the Advancement of Science (AAAS, later ANZAAS). The prime mover in establishing this body was Archibald Liversidge, Professor of Geology and Mineralogy at the University of Sydney, but all the leading Australian scientists eventually signed on. The AAAS was modelled on the British Association for the Advancement of Science and had a similarly wide range of specialist sections, which included economics and other social sciences. The governing council of the AAAS had the power to appoint committees to investigate special problems, and oversaw the staging of annual congresses.[83] These meetings quickly became the leading Australian forums for the announcement of new scientific discoveries and remained so until well into twentieth century, when their significance was undermined by a proliferation of specialist national scientific bodies.

The development of laboratory-based sciences in Australia lagged behind that of the field sciences, in large part because they required expensive equipment for lines of research that were not obviously useful to settlers. The appointment of British-trained Richard Threlfall to the University of Sydney in 1886 was decisive in establishing physics as a laboratory-based discipline in Australia.[84] His research on the propagation of explosions led to his being

81 A.M. Lucas, 'Assistance at a Distance: George Bentham, Ferdinand von Mueller and the Production of *Flora australiensis*', *Archives of Natural History*, 30, 2 (2003): 255–81.

82 'The Australian Eclipse Expedition', *Nature*, 29 February 1872, p. 351; M.E. Hoare, 'The Intercolonial Science Movement in Australasia 1870–1890', *Records of the Australian Academy of Science*, 3, 2 (1975): 9; R.W. Home and K.T. Livingston, 'Science and Technology in the Story of Australian Federation: The Case of Meteorology, 1876–1908', *Historical Records of Australian Science*, 10, 2 (1994): 109–27; J. Gentilli, ' A History of Meteorological and Climatological Studies in Australia', *University Studies in History*, 5, 1 (1967): 54–88.

83 Hoare, 'The Intercolonial Science Movement in Australasia 1870–1890', pp. 7–28.

84 R.W. Home, 'First Physicist of Australia: Richard Threlfall at the University of Sydney, 1886–1898', *Historical Records of Australian Science*, 6, 3 (1986): 333–57; R.W. Home with Paula J. Needham, *Physics in Australia to 1945: Bibliography and Biographical*

used as a consultant by the Australian military after Federation.[85] Laboratory work was undertaken in chemistry in the sugar and pharmaceutical industries from the 1860s,[86] but substantial academic research awaited the appointments of Liversidge in 1874, and David Orme Masson in 1886, at Sydney and Melbourne universities respectively.[87] Both of these chemists made use of the AAAS to develop their discipline across Australia, dominated research outputs at their universities, and attracted talented research students whose careers extended Liversidge's and Masson's influence well into the twentieth century.

The discipline of scientific medicine was another late developer in Australia. Unique environmental conditions and the presence of an Indigenous population did provide possibilities for the identification of new diseases and treatments, but the colonial apparatus of hospitals, universities and medical societies was largely concerned with the dissemination of European medical knowledge.[88] There were exceptions, especially in pharmacology, when Aboriginal practices were investigated. The Melbourne pharmacist, Joseph Bosisto, produced eucalyptus oil (a well-known traditional medicine in a number of Aboriginal tribes) in the 1850s, marketed as a product that could ameliorate the air and subdue contagion.[89] Later, when a microbial theory of disease emerged, eucalyptus oil was recommended for its antiseptic properties. Joseph Bancroft, surgeon at the Brisbane Hospital, presented a series of papers to the Queensland Philosophical Society in the 1870s on the therapeutic properties of 'pituri' (or *Duboisiahopwoodii*), a narcotic well known to the Aboriginal people of western Queensland. A drug derived from *Duboisia* was used to control pupil dilation in ophthalmic surgery in Australia, the United States and Europe.[90]

While European ideas about what constituted science dominated in colonial countries, the rapid, often destructive, changes in the landscape that accompanied settlement resulted in the development of a proto-ecological

Register (Melbourne: Department of History and Philosophy of Science, University of Melbourne, 1990).

85 'Sir Richard Threlfall', *Australian Dictionary of Biography*, vol. 12, pp. 220–1.

86 J.E. Kolm, 'The Chemical Industry: Australian Contributions to Chemical Technology', in *Technology in Australia, 1788–1988*, pp. 607, 618–21.

87 Roy MacLeod, *Archibald Liversidge, FRS: Imperial Science Under the Southern Cross* (Sydney University Press, 2009); Ian D. Rae, 'Chemical Organizations in Australia and New Zealand', *Ambix*, 42, 1 (1995): 28–49; 'Sir David Orme Masson', *Australian Dictionary of Biography*, vol. 10, pp. 432–5.

88 John Pearn (ed.), *Pioneer Medicine in Australia* (Brisbane: Amphion Press, 1988).

89 'Joseph Bosisto', *Australian Dictionary of Biography*, vol. 3, pp. 197–9.

90 Luke Keogh, 'Duboisia Pituri: A Natural History', *Historical Records of Australian Science*, 22, 2 (2011): 199–214; Clarke, *Aboriginal Plant Collectors*, pp. 138–9.

sensibility in which the importance and complexity of relationships between organisms and their environments was recognised. In Australia the 'scientisation' of this sensibility initially took place in the acclimatisation movement as key members such as McCoy and Mueller moved away from the imperial idea of improving nature towards a position better described as its 'renovation'. In three public lectures given in 1870 and 1871, Mueller established himself as a pioneer ecological and environmental thinker by articulating new ideas about the sustainable management of natural resources, especially forests.[91] German romanticism and Humboldtian science played a part in Mueller's ideas, but they mainly emerged from his personal experience of rapid change in the landscapes he knew well through extensive fieldwork. Deforestation and the decline and disappearance of native species were mainly caused by agriculture, mining and settlement, but the acclimatisation movement itself was not above reproach. The introduction of the sparrow as an agent of biological control, and the blackberry to stabilise river banks, are examples of experiments conducted under its auspices that had unforeseen and unwelcome consequences. The introduction of rabbits by Thomas Austin in the late 1850s preceded the foundation of the Acclimatisation Society of Victoria – though that society compounded the problem by importing pedigree strains of what became Australia's greatest introduced pest.[92]

*

Such a movement away from natural history, as understood in the eighteenth century, toward the discipline of ecology, sums up much of the scientific history of colonial Australia. Founded under the shadow of the Enlightenment, the early colony reflected its desire to catalogue the plants, animals, fossils, rocks, minerals, weather and stars of this corner of the globe as yet unexamined by European science. With the Enlightenment's confidence in the possibilities of progress it was hoped, too, that Australia could be reshaped in accordance with European conceptions of improvement; an impulse that underlay the acclimatisation movement. The nineteenth century also brought greater knowledge of the environmental distinctiveness of Australia and the need to confront the limitations as well as possibilities of European settlement. Exploration made plain that there was no great river system of the sort that had opened up North America. Farming the land made evident

---

91 Ian Tyrrell, *True Gardens of the Gods: Californian-Australian Environmental Reform, 1860–1930* (Berkeley: University of California Press, 1999), p. 17.
92 Don Garden, *Australia, New Zealand, and the Pacific: An Environmental History* (Santa Barbara: ABC-CLIO, 2005), p. 366.

that European techniques had severe constraints in a poorly watered land-mass, where the scale of cultivation had to compensate for poor quality soil. The gold rushes transformed forests into wastelands for the extraction of a finite resource.

Such experiences required an adjustment of thinking, not in order to end the exploitation of Australian resources but to find more information about them. Thus the rise of the technological and laboratory-based sciences toward the end of the nineteenth century is also part of the scientific history of colonial Australia. This process was assisted by the growth of institutions, positions and projects that investigated local as well as international scientific questions, thereby complicating the divide in power relations between a colonial periphery and a metropolitan scientific centre. The Europeans (mainly but not solely British) who dedicated themselves to science and technology in colonial Australia were always relatively few in number, but they were always part of a larger scientific imperial network. The colony's development was linked with greater scientific understanding of its possibilities, and thus from its beginnings science formed part of the emerging nation's wider culture and identity. Scientifically minded settlers participated in discovering, describing and knowing the land in physical terms and negotiated for themselves tensions between faith and science, and between progress and destruction. The scientific history of colonial Australia reveals that science has always been at the core of how European Australia defined itself when it took possession of that ancient continent.

19

Gender and colonial society

PENNY RUSSELL

'What's in a name?' demanded George Stevenson, controversial editor of the *South Australian Register* in a very young Adelaide in 1839.[1] Unlike Shakespeare's Juliet, he thought there was a good deal in it. South Australia had been established as a province in 1836 but in everyday conversation was more often spoken of as a 'colony', and this word, he thought, had an unfortunate effect on opinion and sentiment. It conveyed 'nothing of home or domestic life', and tended instead 'to foster a sense of strangerism which it would be well to avoid'. Women in particular were 'morbid on the subject of "the colony," and difficult to reconcile to what is unavoidably new in their circumstances'. Similarly, the use of the blanket term 'bush' to designate even the most beautiful of country districts tended to frighten women away from a 'delightful rural life' in which they might enjoy the 'dignity of usefulness'.[2] Stevenson's repudiation of the word 'colony' reflected a deeper concern that would trouble Australian colonists throughout the nineteenth century. When so many colonists were strangers to the environment and strangers to each other, how could they develop a sense of community, familiarity and belonging? Could this atomised agglomeration of emigrants and native-born become a society, with all that implied?[3] Could they overcome a 'sense of strangerism' and learn how to feel at home?

Stevenson's editorial also laid out what was already a familiar formula for achieving that feeling of domestication and belonging. 'Woman's presence and care is all the bush of Australia requires', he asserted.[4] Like so many of his generation, his vision for colonial society was one in which closer settlement would transform the undifferentiated 'bush' into communities of

---

1 'George Stevenson', *Australian Dictionary of Biography*, vol. 2, pp. 481–2.
2 *South Australian Register*, 31 August 1839.
3 Compare Miles Fairburn, *The Ideal Society and Its Enemies: The Foundations of Modern New Zealand Society, 1850–1900* (Auckland University Press, 1989).
4 *South Australian Register*, 31 August 1839.

independent farming families. Variations on this vision of a settled rural society comprising a sturdily independent 'yeomanry' held sway throughout the nineteenth century as the ideal form of cultivated society. At different times it could be upheld as offering hope for the rehabilitation of convicts, the civilisation of Aboriginal people, the independent prosperity of hopeful immigrants or the peaceful cohesion of colonial society. Rarely did social reality match these expectations. The competing interests of different classes, the desire to consolidate land holdings and exploit labour, the marked preference of many immigrants for the more familiar social landscape of the towns and the vagaries of terrain and climate combined to produce a society that was diverse, amorphous and contested. The yeoman ideal so regularly invoked served as reproach as often as promise.

Despite the manifest human presence, early colonisers of Australia insistently represented the land as an unmarked wilderness, a blank canvas on which the great panorama of civilisation was yet to be painted. It awaited the impress of history – and from the outset Europeans identified Aboriginal people with that timeless, uncultivated space.[5] The challenge for the colonisers, as they understood it, was to create a society where none had existed before, to transform 'a vast territory...hitherto appropriated to a handful of the rudest savages...into a scene of prosperous industry'.[6] Here was a test indeed for the power of civilisation as an idea, a habit and way of being. Stripped of familiar possessions, assumptions and contexts, individuals might find little to assure themselves of who they were. The risk seemed ever present that the baking heat and harsh environment might scorch the thin veneer of civilisation from optimistic settlers and draw them back into some more primitive form of existence.

Bond and free

In penal societies there was all the more reason to worry. Both convicts and their masters seemed at times to plumb the depths of human brutality, and even colonists who were convinced that cruelty must accompany punishment felt some qualms about its effect on the society that began to form alongside the gaol. Some of the military officers sent to guard the prisoners

---

5 Rod Macneil, 'Time after Time: Temporal Frontiers and Boundaries in Colonial Images of the Australian Landscape', in Lynette Russell (ed.), *Colonial Frontiers: Indigenous–European Encounters in Settler Societies* (Manchester University Press, 2001), pp. 47–67.
6 William Westgarth, quoted in Penny Russell, *Savage or Civilised? Manners in Colonial Australia* (Sydney: UNSW Press, 2010), p. 29.

had brought their wives; many soon acquired grants of land and found time to pursue domestic, agricultural and social interests amid their official duties. Some of the convicts had served the bulk of their seven-year sentences before they ever reached the colony, and were soon liberated from penal servitude: they, too, sought parcels of land and means of livelihood; they, too, forged relationships, produced children, worked, loved, fought and drank. The trickle of expirees became a flood; many convicts were pardoned or released on tickets-of-leave even before their sentences had expired. Moralists feared that society would be forever damned by the pervasive presence of criminals, drawn mainly from the underclasses of Britain. The released prisoners, unconcerned, called themselves 'emancipists' and claimed the rights of free men and women. Indeed they occasionally, with mordant humour, laid claim to more than that, arguing that the colony was theirs by special privilege. Had they not been personally selected for settlement by His Majesty's government and supplied with a free passage? Accordingly, they looked upon free settlers with contempt and suspicion, as 'bloody emigrants come to take the country from us'.[7]

The early free settlers seemed intent on 'taking the country' indeed, and wresting a rapid fortune from the rich pastoral lands. In New South Wales, it seemed for a while that policy and topography would combine to create a colonial aristocracy with a monopoly over land, labour and power. From the 1820s, generous land grants and the assignment of convict labour to rural districts saw land brought rapidly under settlement, much of it concentrated in the hands of a few 'gentry' families. Their vision of society was very different from that of the emancipists. With vast acres and free convict labour at their disposal, they envisaged a society almost feudal in character. Self-styled 'Major' James Mudie, for one, lorded it over his convict servants at his Hunter Valley estate, 'Castle Forbes', until his tyranny led them to revolt in 1833.[8] Mudie considered that colonial society should remain forever divided into two separate castes, the 'felonry' and the 'free'. The felonry – convicts, ex-convicts and their offspring – should be denied political liberties or property. It was a vision that came closer to realisation in Van Diemen's Land, where the rapid alienation of almost all the accessible grasslands to a small number of free settlers (almost 2 million acres were given away between 1823 and 1831) encouraged the creation of two societies, separate but

---

7 Comment reported by J.D. Lang, quoted in K.S. Inglis, *The Australian Colonists: An Exploration of Social History 1788–1870* (Melbourne University Press, 1974), p. 16.

8 Kirsten McKenzie, *A Swindler's Progress: Nobles and Convicts in the Age of Liberty* (Sydney: UNSW Press, 2009), pp. 172–3.

coexistent. The landholding settlers of a colony they liked to call 'Tasmania' held themselves aloof, avoiding all contact with the 'untouchable majority' of Van Diemen's Land, the convicts and emancipists.[9]

But the thinly spread pastoral populations seemed, as Edward Gibbon Wakefield warned, to invite 'a descent into barbarism'.[10] From 1831 government policy changed: crown lands were to be sold, not given away, and the proceeds used to assist emigrants to the colonies. In Van Diemen's Land the change came too late to have much effect and in New South Wales it did nothing to curb land hunger. Settlers swarmed out beyond the designated limits of settlement, including into the Port Phillip District where, since none of that land had been officially alienated for settlement, all alike were 'squatters', establishing a claim to tenure through presence and use. This rapid pastoral expansion unsettled the social structures of the colony. The squatters' easy access to free land and convict labour challenged the hegemony of an older landholding class that had tried to emulate on their estates the ordered communities of rural England.

While some squatters revelled in their pared-down social existence, their anonymity and freedom from the pressures of respectability, others found these things deeply discomforting. The lawlessness of the new pattern of settlement, the hand-to-mouth existence and primitive living conditions that gentlemen were prepared to tolerate in their race for fortune, and above all the escalating violence between settlers and Indigenous Australians, seemed to confirm the justice of Wakefield's warnings. The Presbyterian squatter Niel Black, for one, found many aspects of colonial society repugnant. The 'great aim of life' everywhere was money, he wrote in his journal soon after his arrival. Men seemed to have placed themselves 'under Servitude' by agreeing 'to forego all their former comforts and live in any way for a time', sinking 'every other feeling in the love of gain' in hopes that their reward for sacrifice would be an early return home. Black himself saw the art of colonisation differently, and was keen to bring 'the comforts and little elegances of life' as soon as possible to his new abode in the Western District.[11]

Other squatters urged that, despite appearances, they were not descending into barbarism but taking the first necessary steps towards civilisation. The squatter loved the wilderness not for its own sake, argued one advocate, John Henderson, but 'for the independence it confers'. As the 'pioneer of

9 James Boyce, *Van Diemen's Land* (Melbourne: Black Inc., 2008), p. 146, pp. 158–9.

10 Quoted in ibid., p. 150.

11 Maggie Mackellar, *Strangers in a Foreign Land: The Journal of Niel Black and Other Voices from the Western District* (Melbourne: Miegunyah Press, 2008), pp. 58–9, 131.

civilization', he opened the way 'for the smiling villages, the good old British institutions, and the happy population which follow'. In the process he inevitably lost touch with the social niceties, and the 'spirit that drove him on' might also drive him into acts of horrific violence against Aboriginal people, a 'cunning' and 'untiring' enemy. Yet surely, Henderson pleaded, the squatter 'deserved at least leniency at our hands'. Let none of those 'comfortable and luxuriant philanthropists' who never strayed beyond their native cities condemn the 'hardy and adventurous backwoodsman' whose right arm was his 'only defence', for if a man were unable or unwilling to defend himself, then 'the bush is indeed no place for him'.[12] While they laboured to extend the reach of civilised society for the benefit of those who would follow, squatters voluntarily made themselves into social outsiders. When they chose to return they must be allowed to do so, their conduct and character as social, civilised beings untouched by anything that had occurred in the wilderness.

Despite such vigorous defences, concern about the degrading effects of a violent, lawless and comfortless bush life would continue throughout the nineteenth century, with some fearing that the white man was deteriorating into a 'semi-civilised nomad who escaped his responsibilities by constantly moving further out'.[13] Commentators noted, with varying degrees of disapproval, that the pastoral frontiers were a curious social world, characterised by hard riding, hard swearing and hard drinking. The bush life encouraged at once a tough, hard-headed pragmatism, continual watchfulness and a delightful sense of irresponsibility about domestic demands and social niceties. It could also be, at times, almost intolerably lonely.

The image of bush life as lonely, comfortless and on the brink of barbarism was frequently linked with the relative absence of women and families. Caroline Chisholm, who arrived in Sydney in 1838 with her army officer husband, was one of those who actively sought to domesticate 'the Bush' – and in so doing hoped to solve the problem of the future for many young women. Her particular concern was with young emigrant women. Brought from poverty in the orphanages and workhouses of Britain and Ireland to swell the ranks of domestic servants in the colony, they were liable to find themselves instead unemployed, homeless and vulnerable in an unwelcoming city. When Chisholm's husband returned to his military duties

12 John Henderson, quoted in Russell, *Savage or Civilised?* pp. 46–7.
13 Jan Kociumbas, 'Lost in the Bush: Searching for the Australian Child', *History of Education Review*, 30, 2 (2001): 43; Richard Waterhouse, *The Vision Splendid: A Social and Cultural History of Rural Australia* (Fremantle: Curtin University Books, 2005), pp. 113–24.

in Madras, she remained in Sydney, determined to make a difference. She converted the disused Immigration Barracks into a refuge for vulnerable women, and moved in herself to supervise the homeless girls who flocked there. She enquired into the possibilities of work for the women in the country, identified households in which a woman was present to provide protection and then accompanied wave after wave of nervous young women into the interior. Married couples also drew her enthusiastic support. Men with young children generally had to seek waged employment in Sydney, for they were unlikely to be welcomed by rural employers. Chisholm found the situation most irritating. She considered that the 'Bachelor System' had nearly ruined the colony, and gloried in her project to 'introduce matrimony into the bush'.[14] Linking the politics of home life with the democratic language of independence and self-sufficiency, she argued for the closer settlement of families on the land, where they would be accountable only to themselves.[15] In 1846 she took her campaign to London, where she argued vigorously for migration assistance for single women, wives and children and, with the support of her husband, established the Family Colonization Loan Society.[16]

From the 1830s onwards, growing numbers of free migrants flocked to the colonies, outstripping the number of transported felons and further complicating the social landscape. Although Sydney long remained the most popular destination, new settlements at Swan River, Port Phillip and South Australia offered prospects for independence and opportunity without the stigma of the convict presence. Some of these new immigrants hoped to forge an independent living through agriculture; others had no thought but to acquire sheep and rush 'up country' to join the pastoral boom – but for many the growing towns proved an altogether stronger drawcard. Their diverse skills and entrepreneurial interests expanded urban society and altered its character. Doctors, lawyers, clergymen, newspaper editors, midwives, stationers, printers, pharmacists, toy-makers, grocers, drapers, publicans, craftsmen and artisans sought a livelihood in the emerging cities. They came in a spirit of resignation, despair or high adventure: some in search of health or opportunity, others to escape dishonour or hunger. Some came to appointments in the church or civil service arranged before they left Britain;

14 Patricia Grimshaw, 'The Moral Reformer and the Imperial Major: Caroline and Archibald Chisholm', in Penny Russell (ed.), For Richer, For Poorer: Early Colonial Marriages (Melbourne University Press, 1994), pp. 102–8.
15 Alan Atkinson, The Europeans in Australia: A History. Volume 2, Democracy (Oxford University Press 2004), pp. 262–4.
16 Grimshaw, 'The Moral Reformer and the Imperial Major', pp. 109–10.

some brought capital to support new ventures; many brought nothing but their own strength and skills. By the 1830s Sydney rejoiced in many flourishing retail businesses. But the economic depression of the 1840s hit hard. Tradesmen who had left Britain in expectation of high wages and cheap land found instead land monopolies and high unemployment. They voiced their discontent at this unequal state of affairs in a radical press and, increasingly, through political disorder.[17]

Now squatters and landowners, their differences merging, shared a common cause. They fought to secure their monopoly over land and (with growing urgency during the 1840s, as depression deepened) to maintain the supply of cheap convict labour from England. Squatters, too, now dreamed of a future as landed gentry, perhaps with hereditary powers. Within the decade such dreams would be laughed to scorn by the new political interests arising in the towns as the delusions of a 'bunyip aristocracy'. A sturdy alliance of radicals and liberals, arguing that the social and economic development of the colony depended on commercial interests and free immigration, demanded the abolition of transportation. When in 1840 transportation to New South Wales ceased, it became clear the future of the colony lay elsewhere.[18]

With the 1850s the forces of change became even more apparent. The announcement of the discovery of gold in New South Wales and Victoria stimulated a rush of immigrants, lured by the prospect of freedom, adventure, excitement and an easy fortune. Again both domesticity and social order seemed to be lost as men of vastly different backgrounds dressed alike, shared backbreaking manual labour and endured damp, fleas, monotonous diets and domestic misery in tents or hastily constructed huts, barely distinguishable from each other in appearance and a burning desire to make their fortune. Diggers rushed from field to field, their attachments to home, family, community and propriety all apparently loosened. Gold broke the ties of 'modesty, duty and respect'. It promised the transformation of individuals and society: rough diggers boasted, 'It is our turn to be masters now'.[19]

---

17 See Terry Irving, *The Southern Tree of Liberty: The Democratic Movement in New South Wales before 1856* (Sydney: Federation Press, 2006).

18 See J.B. Hirst, *The Strange Birth of Colonial Democracy: New South Wales 1848–1884* (Sydney: Allen & Unwin, 1988); Ged Martin, *Bunyip Aristocracy: The New South Wales Constitution Debate of 1853 and Hereditary Institutions in the British Colonies* (Sydney: Croom Helm, 1986).

19 Stuart Macintyre, *A Colonial Liberalism: The Lost World of Three Victorian Visionaries* (Oxford University Press, 1991), pp. 18–19; David Goodman, *Gold Seeking: Victoria and California in the 1850s* (Sydney: Allen & Unwin, 1994), pp. 56–63; Geoffrey Serle, *The Golden Age: A History of the Colony of Victoria 1851–1861* (Melbourne University Press, 1971), pp. 66–94.

The goldfields were at once a space outside colonial society – a new frontier wilderness threatening social values everywhere – and a symbol of the transformative power that lay at its heart, in the opportunities for wealth and rapid upward mobility that threw accustomed social relations into chaos. The discoveries were a temporary setback to Caroline Chisholm's hopes, prompting a new rush of single men to the colonies who were doomed as so many convicts had been to 'the demoralizing state of bachelorism'. In 1854 Chisholm returned to Australia and toured some of the goldfield towns of Victoria, making speeches about the joys of home life and urging greater amenity on the diggings so more wives and families would feel able to live there, too.[20] Yet her words struck a chord precisely because of the paradox that lay at the heart of gold fever. It inspired both an extreme version of the transient, masculine, mannerless colonial world and a new yearning towards a respectable, domestic independence.

For the more prosperous, 'roughing it' on the diggings held a certain theatricality. Early squatters in their makeshift bark huts had lived that way partly because they had no audience: in the indifferent bush there was little social benefit to be gained by playing the part of a gentleman. On the goldfields, however, men embraced the costume and style of the digger because they were everywhere under observation. To stand out as a 'new chum' or a 'gentleman' was to invite undesired attention – anything from ridicule to theft, claim-jumping and violence. Men strove to assume the appearance of a seasoned digger with minimal delay, and many wrote home to their families of their success in doing so, perhaps enjoying the imagined horror of their readers. Where clothing and living conditions marked no distinction of status, and where all alike shared – or seemed to share – in a compulsory egalitarian conviviality and the grind of the working day, the distinctions of class did not disappear but rather went underground.

These frenzied bursts of egalitarian fortune-seeking were short-lived and often illusory. Capital backing was generally an advantage; so too was education; friends in high places could be helpful; as could habits of thrift and prudence engrained since birth. When the alluvial gold gave out, company mines took over. A successful digger like John Boyd Watson of Bendigo, son of an emigrant Scottish Presbyterian cabinet-maker, might progress from mining to quartz reefing, eventually becoming the owner of a mine that yielded over 12 tonnes of gold and a shareholder in mining companies, banks, real estate,

20 Atkinson, *The Europeans in Australia*, vol. 2, pp. 262–4.

hotels, railways, tramways and wharves. Watson died a millionaire in 1889;[21] but in the meantime many miners had returned from the diggings no richer, and perhaps poorer, than they had set out, resuming old trades in their quest for a livelihood. Opportunities to acquire wealth – and with it social position – certainly existed, and there were plenty of rags-to-riches stories to cement the idea of social mobility deep in colonial culture. 'I little thought, when I put up that there centre piece in the ceiling, that I should ever be a dining under it with His Excellency', a guest at a Government House dinner was said to have remarked to his bemused neighbour at the table.[22] But the prevalence of such anecdotes probably exaggerated the extent of such experiences in reality.

The modern industrialising city was built in Australia by thousands of immigrants, many initially lured by gold, who brought with them their trade skills, political ideals, religious beliefs, domestic ideology and above all their social aspirations, hoping to 'better themselves' in this new world. The Australian colonies were from the outset some of the most urbanised societies of the nineteenth century: immigrants were never as enthusiastic about rushing up-country in search of work and settled homes as migration agents hoped they would be. Each colony had its metropolis, a port city where the traffic of goods, people and news formed an emotional and economic hub for the whole region. The growth of cities gathered pace with each new injection of capital and immigration, the gradual transfer of political responsibility from imperial to colonial governments, and the consolidation and expansion of centralised infrastructure. Urban growth, steadily fuelled by immigration, created its own logic of expansion, as builders and labourers, shopkeepers and accountants, lawyers and politicians found in cities the most reliable markets for their services. Industries flourished around the wharves and rail centres.

Inevitably, the hopes and expectations of many were disappointed. Opportunity, after all, was not the same thing as a classless society – and many unskilled labourers who rushed hopefully to the 'workingman's paradise' found that secure employment was still hard to come by, while the high cost of food and housing put considerable pressure on daily life. Poverty, disease, slums and malnutrition were features of the colonial cities from the beginning.

---

21 'Death of a Sandhurst Millionaire', (Melbourne) *Argus,* 5 June 1889; 'John Boyd Watson', *Australian Dictionary of Biography,* vol. 6, pp. 363–4.
22 Samuel Curtis Candler, quoted in Russell, *Savage or Civilised?* p. 195.

Class mattered in colonial society, although class relations were fluid, complex and unpredictable. Inequalities – of success, if not of 'opportunity' – abounded, and social groupings as well as political loyalties clustered around the separate material interests of colonists: the pastoralists who thought their large 'stake' in the country gave them a natural right to run it; the merchants and bankers whose fortunes (like those of the pastoralists) were tied to the imperial economy; retailers and skilled tradesmen whose prosperity depended on thriving local markets and growing cities; professional men – lawyers, doctors and clergy – whose interests were similarly tied to local markets but whose education and kinship bound their hearts nevertheless to the ruling elites; aspiring diggers and farmers who found their own hopes for a stake in the country thwarted again and again by land monopolists; and of course the working man, who had nothing on which to build a fortune but the strength of his own labouring body, and who seemed caught between dreams of independence and recurring nightmares of renewed enslavement to the forces of land and capital.

Neither the dream nor the nightmare was entirely without foundation. Class consciousness remained closely associated with the hopes and disappointments of colonisation itself. Working-class radicalism was a factor in society from the 1840s, and by the 1890s was a force to be reckoned with, edged with the bitterness of aspirations to security, land ownership and independence thwarted.

Social distinctions

Nevertheless, the growing diversity of the economy and immigrants ensured that the Australian colonies always contained an element of social fluidity. Those who dreamed of exclusiveness, caste and inherited social position were forced to give way before the material and social realities of a brash, democratic, colonial world. This did not mean that social status was rendered insignificant in colonial life. On the contrary, anxieties about status were, if anything, exacerbated in this uncertain society.

The tension between order and opportunity was apparent even in convict times. While the old 'gentry' class advocated a complete separation between felonry and free, moralists opposed such a permanent segregation of classes. Such fixed inequality, they feared, would not only enforce the slavish dependence of the convict classes but expose the free to the corrupting effects of their own tyrannical authority. Despite countervailing fears that the immoral influence of the convicts would pervade society, it seemed best to give men and women the chance to expiate their crimes, rehabilitate themselves and grasp the opportunities of a new world in which past sins might be forgotten. Gradually (by sheer force of numbers as much as moral suasion) emancipists won political concessions: the power to sit on juries, to hold public office and, eventually, to participate in responsible government.

The less definable social barriers proved more resilient. Indeed, once it became clear that emancipists were to be integrated into civic society, the task of delineating social boundaries became at once more pressing and more difficult. Yet the exclusives themselves were self-made men, often inflating their claims to social prestige or, like Major Mudie, masquerading under titles to which they had no claim.[23] In this mixed social world, the refinements, niceties and ordered hierarchies of civil society were always under challenge. British colonies were always places of suspect repute, and colonists were anxious to protect not only their own status but also the reputation of their society.[24]

In early Sydney, military officers made it a general rule 'to visit only those who were accepted at Government House'.[25] Status anxiety, exacerbated by vulnerability, was everywhere apparent, and the governor, as the 'social apex', provided one form of reassurance. Niel Black observed in 1839 that 'those who have just got inside the pale of the better Circles are afraid to be seen taking any notice of a stranger' until he was known and accepted within vice-regal walls.[26] Yet the governor's social authority was never beyond dispute – especially when it diverged from the gentry's social preferences. Governor Macquarie's efforts to draw prominent emancipists into the ranks of acceptable society proved deeply controversial. When John Thomas Bigge conducted an enquiry on behalf of the British government into the workings of convict society, he found that despite the governor's sponsorship, individuals were still shunned by society. As William Charles Wentworth would later put it, the exclusives raised 'an eternal barrier of separation between their offspring and the offspring of the unfortunate convict'.[27]

As the character of immigration diversified, society in the growing colonial cities altered too. Many newcomers found the fluidity of colonial society a welcome change from rigid hierarchies that had constrained them

---

23 McKenzie, *A Swindler's Progress*.
24 Kirsten McKenzie, *Scandal in the Colonies: Sydney and Cape Town, 1820–1850* (Melbourne University Press, 2004), pp. 50–4.
25 Ibid., p. 52.
26 Niel Black, Journal, 26 October 1839, in Mackellar, *Strangers in a Foreign Land*, pp. 57–8.
27 Cited in Peter Cochrane, *Colonial Ambition: Foundations of Australian Democracy* (Melbourne University Press, 2006), p. 4.

in Britain or Europe. Indeed, migration could present a welcome opportunity for reinvention of self and status – but so frequent were the reinventions that sometimes the survival of colonial respectability seemed to require a conspiracy of silence, an agreement not to enquire too closely into the question of origins. Ultimately, in a world in which few cared to expose their pedigrees to close scrutiny, backgrounds were often allowed to sink into comfortable obscurity, and social relations were formed on the basis of what was visible on the surface. A colony's convict origins might be acknowledged in general or abstract terms, but it was the height of bad taste to mention the word 'convict' in association with an individual. The epithet was rarely used, and usually resented. By the 1860s, the capacity of Sydney society to ignore and tacitly condone a shady past was gleefully satirised by outsiders smugly free of the 'convict stain': as in the story told in Melbourne of a man who was received at Government House in Sydney despite having been a convict and 'once sentenced to be hanged' – for 'no one can be considered to be finally *out of society* here, until he's *actually hanged!*'[28]

In the face of pervasive uncertainty about people's origins, the conduct of individuals in their personal and social relations became the best guide to their social acceptability. Honour and decorum seemed to define the degree of colonial civilisation. Yet the rules of 'good form' were always up for negotiation in this disorderly world. The colonists of the pre-1850 era, conscious that their status was precarious, were a touchy lot, swift to defend their reputation for honour, dignity or commercial integrity, swift to resent a slur. Amongst the tiny minority who regarded themselves, or hoped to be regarded, as gentlemen, such disputes might take the form of an 'affair of honour'. The custom of duelling was falling out of favour in Britain, and was strictly speaking against the law – but that did little to hinder a tendency to issue challenges amongst elites and their imitators, or to lodge accusations of cowardice against those who declined. A man who showed reluctance to engage in a duel might be 'placarded' as a coward, or horsewhipped in the street as an act of public humiliation. Such incidents came regularly before the courts of New South Wales and Van Diemen's Land and were especially common among the wild young gentlemen of Port Phillip in the 1830s and 1840s. They contained as much bombast as actual violence; few duels had a fatal outcome.[29] Duelling was nevertheless the despair of judges, who

28 Russell, *Savage or Civilised?* p. 178.
29 Atkinson, *The Europeans in Australia*, vol. 2, p. 111; Paul de Serville, *Port Phillip Gentlemen: and Good Society in Melbourne Before the Gold Rushes* (Oxford University Press, 1980), p. 107.

condemned both the practice and its associated rituals. Again and again they warned both plaintiffs and defendants that their behaviour amounted to a breach of the peace, and that had a duel occurred, and ended in death, all involved – including the seconds – might have been charged with murder. Yet judges were gentlemen too, and though they upheld the code of law in the courts they were not themselves personally immune to involvement in the code of honour.[30]

Questions of pedigree and reputation loomed large in the tiny societies of the first half of the century. By the later decades it was no longer possible for all members of respectable society to know each other personally, or even by name and reputation. Admission to elite circles could be more readily achieved by means of political or professional success, even simply through the accumulation of wealth. Equality of opportunity and of political rights were enshrined in colonial parliaments, with their refusal 'to recreate here a closed system of privilege'.[31]

The most readily available mark of social distinction was to be recognised as a gentleman. Even in England some fluidity in this category was apparent by the nineteenth century; in Australia traditional criteria disappeared altogether, so that anyone who reached a certain level in the occupational hierarchy or who possessed independent means might claim the label. Colonial society, as the historian John Hirst has written, was preoccupied with ranks and titles precisely because these signs of success confirmed upward mobility. It made for both fluidity and competitive anxieties, for where 'new men could not be excluded, the contentions for place and precedence were fearsome'. Even liberal democrats who battled against Old World privilege remained obsessed with titles and honours, which alone offered solidity and certainty amidst social chaos.[32]

One mark of the spread of 'good society' was the ever-growing invitation lists for Government House functions. Though distinctions were still drawn between those who might be invited to private functions by the governor, those who were invited only to large affairs such as the Queen's Birthday Ball, and those who were never invited at all, in practice these careful gradations were difficult to make and even more difficult to sustain. The social columns of the press were littered with outraged remarks about the 'dodges' tried by those anxious to gain admittance – such as sending a gracious acceptance to

30 Russell, *Savage or Civilised?* pp. 133–8.
31 John Hirst, 'Egalitarianism', in S.L. Goldberg and F.B. Smith (eds), *Australian Cultural History* (Cambridge University Press, 1988), p. 59.
32 Ibid., pp. 58–64.

an invitation that had never been sent. They also satirised those who were admitted: bejewelled and overdressed, fawning and fluttering around the governor and his wife, talking too loudly and in unmistakably vulgar accents of their grand acquaintance, and handing over visiting cards that were too large or gave excessively detailed information. A calling card was not intended for self-advertisement, Melbourne's *Argus* sternly reminded its readers.[33] J.F. Archibald's *Bulletin* drew on both British disdain for colonial pretension and the rhetoric of the new labour movement, which seemed about to sweep away distinction and privilege even in the Old World, to develop an irreverent critique of slavish imitations of English social relationships that showed colonial society to be pathetically provincial.[34] The *Bulletin* parodied the 'fat Govt 'Ouse haunter in the nodding bonnet and handbag',[35] because her thirst for social distinction was antithetical to the republican cause. But one of the easiest ways to parody such pretensions was to hint at the light in which they must appear to the governor and his wife, fresh from the aristocratic society of the metropolis. After the New South Wales governor's wife, Lady Jersey, conducted her first reception at Government House one columnist noted the vulgarity of her visitors, and wondered how the governor's wife had 'managed the corners of her mouth…for, unlike most women, Lady Jersey seems to have a keen sense of the comical'.[36]

Advice proliferated about how to conduct oneself in polite society – alongside a flurry of satirical descriptions of status-seeking wives and daughters who anxiously initiated their prosperous but bewildered menfolk into the ways of etiquette. The honest tradesman was stereotypically blunt, unpretentious and irredeemably vulgar. The vulgarity of his wife and daughters took a different form in popular imagination: all ostentatious finery, pretension and petty snobbery, layered across a profound incomprehension of anything approaching true elegance of mind or person. Etiquette books promised to guide such social newcomers towards a better sense of grace and courtesy, tact and hospitality. But the mere fact of relying on such manuals was enough to condemn the 'parvenu'. 'When the Australian pater-vulgaris makes a rise in the world', wrote one satirist at the end of the century, 'his daughters start to teach him etiquette'. She thought that it must be 'an awful thing to try to regulate one's behaviour' by such means; that 'but for his bound and hide,

---

33 Russell, *Savage or Civilised?* pp. 309–10, 306–9.
34 Hirst, 'Egalitarianism', pp. 71–3.
35 *The Bulletin,* 14 March 1891.
36 Ibid.

the torture of the new-rich Australian with a family would be worse than vivisection. But he has bound and hide. God is good to him.'[37]

The impulse to preserve some sense of social merit and order alongside a commitment to opportunity and social mobility contained a fundamental paradox. The masculine world of colonial society could not afford to be exclusive: a myth of egalitarianism was indispensable to its processes of accommodation. In Australian literature, as in its parliaments, the working man was increasingly invested with a new dignity, representing qualities of hard-working respectability against the charade of social distinction.[38] The myth of egalitarianism was sustained by leaving most of the responsibility for maintaining social distinction and social distance to women.[39] The ultimate security for a gentleman who had to endure the hearty blows on the shoulder, the hideous familiarity of self-made men, was to know that his wife would not visit theirs. The penalty for the wives was ridicule: for adhering to social standards and conduct that seemed out of place in this New World, and for so often getting it wrong. But though such mockery was a vital component in the egalitarian myth, it was not altogether sincere. The comportment of a lady – such a preoccupying concern for women, and so readily mocked and trivialised by men – drew a reassuring boundary around the limits of 'good' society for both sexes. It was rendered less visible, but not less vital to social relations, by being relegated to the feminine sphere.

Reorienting 'home'

Colonial 'society' could never be a unified and homogeneous community. The constraints of the environment, distribution of natural resources and the contingencies of history combined to make the south-eastern mainland colonies of Victoria and New South Wales by far the most populous. In each the white population had passed the million mark by 1887, while in the same year that of Western Australia was still less than 50,000.[40] Variations in population and prosperity shaped the character of society in each colony, yet common threads of sociability and tension ran through them all. Men and women, bond and free, immigrants and native-born, English and Irish, rural and urban: all found

---

37 Valerie Desmond, *The Awful Australian* (Melbourne: E.W. Cole, 1911), p. 48.

38 Hirst, 'Egalitarianism', p. 74.

39 Beverley Kingston, 'The Lady and the Australian Girl: Some Thoughts on Nationalism and Class', in Norma Grieve and Ailsa Burns (eds), *Australian Women: New Feminist Perspectives* (Oxford University Press 1986), p. 40; Penny Russell, *A Wish of Distinction: Colonial Gentility and Femininity* (Melbourne University Press, 1994).

40 Australian Bureau of Statistics, *Australian Historical Population Statistics*, 2008, accessed 10 December 2011.

ways of adapting to their circumstances as they formed sociable communities for work and play. All defined the terms of their belonging differently. The elision of differences between these groups could create a tentative sense of colonial identity or even national cohesion, but sociability within groups always carried the shadow of excluded others. The most profound exclusion of all was inherent in the act of colonisation itself: as they struggled to establish a sense of belonging in a new society, colonists remained for the most part heedless of, and indifferent to, the destructive effects of their presence and ill-judged policies upon the homes and communities of Aboriginal Australians.

Immigrant colonists were at once home-leavers and home-makers, the emotional core of their lives and families often split between two places. The attachment to 'Home' could survive through generations, nurtured by parents who encouraged in their children a sentimental sense of belonging to another place. Many held their past lives in close remembrance, maintained contact with relatives and brought up their children to love and respond to the written and visual culture of 'home' – which for most colonists meant Britain. Historians have sometimes interpreted such sentimental attachment as a sign of poor adjustment to colonial life. Russel Ward long ago argued that their attachment to home in Australia rather than Britain distinguished the convicts, the native-born, the Irish and the working class (especially in rural Australia) from an English-born middle class, ensuring in turn that vernacular nationalism in Australia would have a distinctly rough-and-ready, egalitarian cast.[41] As a matter of course, he attributed these sentiments to men rather than women. With this Beverley Kingston agreed, suggesting that women tended to assume that one of their responsibilities as homemakers was to preserve links with family and 'home': acting as a 'link with a past they had never seen, and as a brake on the future they were rushing towards'.[42]

But such dichotomies between the 'future' and the 'past', or between national and colonial loyalties, tend to simplify the complex experience of attachment and longing in nineteenth-century colonial society. Studies of correspondence from convicts and poor Irish, for example, have shown the importance of continuing links to Home and family in all classes.[43] Attachment to 'Home' did not necessarily imply a repudiation of colonial life: rather, it helped to shape its character. Immigrants felt both distance

---

41 Russel Ward, *The Australian Legend* (Oxford University Press, 1958).

42 Kingston, 'The Lady and the Australian Girl', p. 41.

43 David Fitzpatrick, *Oceans of Consolation: Personal Accounts of Irish Migration to Australia* (Melbourne University Press, 1995); Lucy Frost and Hamish Maxwell-Stewart (eds), *Chain Letters: Narrating Convict Lives* (Melbourne University Press, 2001).

and displacement as their intimate relationships with family and kin were stretched almost to breaking point: yet they maintained a 'breathtaking assurance' that home could exist in two places.[44] Amongst the papers of the Scott Mitchells – early pastoral families in New South Wales – are some lines of verse 'supposed to be spoken by an Emigrant family in N.S.W.'. The early stanzas delineate the grief of the migrants, their hearts breaking as child-hood ties are 'burst' by distance, but by the end the poet was celebrating the 'scenes of present bliss' that drowned the 'thoughts of past delight', as the emigrants found home anew in the embrace of immediate family.[45]

Men and women of all classes might find colonial life more tolerable if they could stay in touch with distant loved ones: exchanging news, however slow its passage, and sharing vicariously in grief and joy. Literacy rates were high and growing, and even those unaccustomed to wielding a pen would make the effort to send an occasional letter home in the hope of receiving one in return. But slow communication could be almost paralysing – and sometimes was completely so, with relationships effectively sundered by silence.[46] At the Swan River colony in Western Australia, George Fletcher Moore noticed that his servants rarely wrote – partly because of not knowing when the ships would sail till it was too late, partly because they preferred 'carousing, and singing'. Moore himself found it difficult, when faced with the blank page, to 'do justice to my own feelings or your affections!'[47]

Two surviving letters to his family in England from Richard Corbett, a farmer near Western Port, hint at the difficulties of maintaining connection, perhaps because poorly addressed letters went astray. 'Dear Brother I would pertcler wish to here from som of you once more', he wrote in 1849, 'if you please to faver me with a few lines to let me know how many of you are in the land of the living'.[48] Four years later he reproached his sister for neglect. 'You say you have been expectin to here from me from 49 till this tim', he wrote, but insisted he had written many letters to all his siblings, but had received no answer for years. 'I mad shoor you was all ded or thought I was not worth riting to.'[49] Facility

44 Maggie Mackellar, 'Love, Loss and "Going Home": The Intimate Lives of Victorian Settlers', in Desley Deacon, Penny Russell and Angela Woollacott (eds), *Transnational Ties: Australian Lives in the World* (Canberra: ANU E Press, 2008), pp. 98–9.
45 Quoted in Introduction to Russell (ed.), *For Richer, For Poorer*, pp. 8–9.
46 Atkinson, *The Europeans in Australia* vol. 2, p. 107.
47 Quoted in ibid.
48 Richard Corbett (Kilmor Station, Western Port) to John Corbett (brother), Taunton, Somerset Shire, England, 10 September 1849, State Library of Victoria [SLV], MS 6748 H16135 Box 107/2 a.
49 Richard Corbett to his sister Mrs E. Pope, Tenbury England, 22 May 1853, SLV, MS 6748 H16135 Box 107/2 b.

with a pen did not overcome all the difficulties of correspondence. A West Australian settler, Louisa Clifton, found that the sense of distance imposed 'a barrier to communication not as far as feelings are concerned, only in the verbal expression of them'. In the face of the difficulty of communicating feelings, letters might become the barest exchange of essential family news, though some emigrants set themselves to sketch word pictures of their new lives or altered appearance,[50] or connected to the emotional world of the families by commenting on shared literary tastes.[51]

Though colonists may have shared some common sensations of attachment and loss, social divisions also found strong expression. In the early years the 'native-born' – a term exclusively applied to white settlers born in the colonies – were regarded with curiosity and some contempt by the immigrant population. In the 1840s the native-born were significantly outnumbered by those born elsewhere – and of course were over-represented amongst the children of the colonies. They were 'Currency' lads and lasses, a term first seen in print in 1822, which likened the native-born to colonial currency as compared with British sterling – 'illegal, second rate, of dubious value and to be avoided'.[52] The stigma was never accepted with humility, of course: the term soon took on resonances of native pride. As the demographic balance shifted, jokes at the expense of colonial 'currency' were first turned on their heads and then gave way altogether to colonial contempt for new arrivals. 'You may call it *at home*', growled a police magistrate to a solicitor who had thus referred to Britain in 1854, 'but we Currency Lads call it *abroad* and this is our home'.[53] By 1881 the native-born outnumbered the immigrant population in each colony. Now they scoffed in rhyming slang at the 'Jemmy grant', who was said to lack the 'practical virtues' and 'open manly simplicity' of the native-born, and to cling to European prejudices and 'appearances'.[54] But a 'new chum' did not stay 'new' forever. In Victoria an informal association of 'Old Colonists' flourished, priding themselves on belonging to that generation of immigrants to the Port Phillip District who had arrived before the gold rushes. In 1887 the *Bulletin* famously declared that all *white men* who came to Australia willing

50 See, as one of many examples, John Green's letter to his sister Eliza, 22 July 1853, La Trobe Library, SLV, MS 10619.

51 Atkinson, *The Europeans in Australia*, vol. 2, p. 251.

52 John Molony, *The Native-Born: The First White Australians* (Melbourne University Press 2000), p. 26.

53 Quoted in Ward, *The Australian Legend*, p. 62.

54 See in particular Ward, *The Australian Legend*, pp. 61–8; Inglis, *The Australian Colonists*, p. 17; Bruce Moore, *Speaking our Language: The Story of Australian English* (Oxford University Press, 2008), pp. 57–66; Beverley Kingston, *Oxford History of Australia. Volume 3, 1860–1900: Glad Confident Morning* (Oxford University Press, 1988), p. 113.

to 'leave behind them the memory of the class-distinctions and the religious differences of the old world' were 'Australian'.[55] The implied exclusions were of course as significant as the inclusions. In colonial society 'belonging' was critical to status: but belonging was always a matter of degree.

By the middle of the century about a fifth of the Van Diemen's Land population was of Irish birth and Catholic faith; in Victoria it was perhaps as high as a quarter; in New South Wales, between a quarter and a third.[56] Over-represented amongst the convicts, and again amongst the immigrants who enthusiastically accepted the assisted passages offered by colonial governments, the Irish were easily stereotyped and stigmatised as the Catholic poor, sentimentally – and often loudly – attached to their troubled homeland. The patriotism of the Irish found riotous expression on St Patrick's Day each year – sometimes enjoyed with good cheer, sometimes marked by a bitter intensity of sectarian rivalry. English immigrants were inclined to regard them with suspicion and disdain: as peasants who knew little of the ways of polite society, even as 'Blackguards' who formed a distinctive group among the petty criminals of the colony.[57] But as Patrick O'Farrell reminds us, the 'Irish' were never the singular, homogeneous group of popular imagination. They came from very different Irelands, divided not only by class but also by the shifting phases of Ireland's history experienced by each arriving generation. Some were born Irish and affirmed their heritage with enthusiasm. Some achieved Irishness – among the most active Irish in the colonies were men (and some women) who had arrived as infants, and as adults held vigorously to a culture they had scarcely known. Some had it thrust upon them – and held against them. Others again managed to elude recognition altogether.[58] But with all their complexity, they constituted a visible and potentially dissident group whose very presence thwarted fantasies of a thoroughly 'English' society.

Other groups, though less numerous, exerted their influence on the composition or character of society by virtue of their social status, their propensity to cluster in one place, or their enthusiasm for particular cultural forms. The Scots, far less numerous than the Irish, were also in general more prosperous. As flourishing landholders in Victoria, they brought an element of Calvinist morality and Presbyterian prudence to Victorian elite society – but by virtue

---

55 C.M.H. Clark (ed.), *Select Documents in Australian History, 1851–1900* (Sydney: Angus & Robertson, 1955), pp. 800–1.
56 Inglis, *The Australian Colonists*, p. 88.
57 Ibid., p. 93.
58 Patrick O'Farrell, *The Irish in Australia*, rev. edn (Sydney: UNSW Press, 1993), pp. 5–6.

of their very success, had less influence on the culture of Australian working people.[59] Non-British immigrants also claimed distinctive cultural identities whenever the moment seemed right to do so. When Queen Victoria's second son, Alfred, toured the Australian colonies in 1867–68 he was feted with loyal addresses from self-defined communities. Men dressed in German national costumes serenaded him with German songs in Adelaide, Melbourne and Sydney.[60] The 'Hungarian residents of New South Wales' presented him with an address; so did the Chinese communities of Melbourne, Sydney and several gold towns of Victoria.[61] Such performances of cultural identity simultaneously gave expression to the diversity of colonial society in ways that also implied commitment to loyalty, harmony and good order.

Gender and sociability

Both men and women sought refuge from the isolation of rural life in forms of sociability, but their needs and desires were directed differently. When the editor of the *South Australian Register* had mused with such apparent innocence upon the power of language to shape colonial sentiment, his words enraged one reader. He wrote of women in a state of 'imaginary martyrdom' whose recital of the grievances of colonial life distressed both themselves and their hapless menfolk. He likened them to a 'creaking hinge', their constant complaints sowing marital discord and domestic unhappiness.[62] 'One of the Creaking Hinges' was swift to respond. Women were well prepared for the hardships 'inseparable from the removal to a new country', she declared, and did not complain of them. What did cause discontent was the lack of reward when those initial trials had passed: not the *want* of society, but 'the form which that society has assumed'. A woman might perform the duties of wife, mother, daughter or sister to perfection, 'and yet feel a void if she cannot look beyond her own door for the friends and relaxation which have rendered her own civilized home so dear to her'. Alas, 'the society of Adelaide, with the elements of something better too in its composition, is such as to excite the regret of every reflecting person'. Gossip and scandal-mongering prevailed, only because there was no worthier subject to talk about. 'Give us matter of conversation, of innocent and instructive amusements, gentlemen',

---

59 Ward, *The Australian Legend*, pp. 48–9.
60 Cindy McCreery, 'A British Prince and a Transnational Life: Alfred, Duke of Edinburgh's Visit to Australia, 1867–68' in Deacon et al. (eds), *Transnational Ties*, p. 61.
61 Ibid., p. 66.
62 *South Australian Register*, 31 August 1839.

she urged, 'and you will find us neither discontented nor ungrateful'. The hinge was 'rusty' because women were allowed 'no respite from cattle and sheep, surveys and politics'.[63]

In the early decades bush life was overwhelmingly male dominated. The few white women who ventured to the bush could find life lonely, a condition exacerbated for those of higher birth who tried to preserve a sense of social distinction. On the Macquarie Plains in Van Diemen's Land in 1831, the free settler Elizabeth Fenton found 'not one individual in the neighbourhood I either could or would associate with'.[64] Men of every class lived rough and worked hard, with little by way of organised entertainment. Reading, talking, singing, playing cards, smoking and drinking formed their chief pleasures. Alcohol was a comfort and a social lubricant for men of all classes. As a social ritual governed by minute but stringent laws of etiquette, drinking was integral to gentlemanly culture; in the form of the 'spree', when rural workers blew their pay packets for the season on a single bout of hard drinking, it was also integral to working-class camaraderie. If nothing else, it offered some release from the lonely monotony of sheep, and the accompanying diet of tea, damper and mutton three times a day.

Drink and domesticity made uneasy partners. The letters of Julia Cross, who emigrated to Queensland with her husband and five children in 1855 in the hope of a better life and settled near Ipswich, record how her hopes were dashed and her life rendered both difficult and dangerous when her husband reverted to his former drinking habits. Within ten years George was spending all the money he earned on rum, and would ransack the house for the savings that Julia had been able to put together from her own work doing washing or needlework. The convivial drinking life of men was often an appropriation of the family's limited budget, and a factor contributing to domestic violence. Julia had strategies for dealing with George's drinking fits: 'I have a good big kitchen and when he is mad drunk…I put things away and he kicks and smashes and has it all to himself only we have a peep now and then to see what he is up to.' But she worried about the children, for whom there was only 'curses and black looks', and grieved when all, in turn, left home as soon as they could. Her only recourse was to work, and to save her meagre earnings. Eventually she was able to buy some land in her own name and thus to secure 'the one object of my life in this country to be independent of

---

63 Letter to editor from 'One of the Creaking Hinges', *South Australian Register*, 31 August 1839.
64 Boyce, *Van Diemen's Land*, p. 157.

the man', as she wrote to her mother. It was small compensation for a life of struggle.[65]

One tradition that attracted much remark from the early years of rural settlement was that of obligatory hospitality. Inns were few, far between and often rough and rudimentary: travellers therefore relied on the hospitality of squatters, and by the 1860s 'hospitality was more or less demanded as a right'.[66] Squatters who lived close to the major roadways could find the obligation burdensome – to the point that they might shift to a less conveniently placed dwelling. The ploy was not always successful. When the Tasmanian governor's wife, Jane Franklin, travelled overland from Port Phillip to Sydney, she stayed one night with a family who had already moved once, to a place with less water and amenity, in an effort to escape the road and the incessant demands of travellers, only to find that the travellers – and therefore the road – followed them. Mrs Smith had a reputation for bad temper; Lady Franklin thought this story might go far to explain her 'sulkiness'.[67]

Experiments in closer settlement were hampered by the vagaries of soil and climate. Many farms failed, others were consolidated, and only in some fertile zones did agricultural settlement resemble the 'yeoman ideal' of small farms in close propinquity. The experience of rural Australia for many nineteenth-century settlers was one of relentless loneliness. They countered it with various strategies of sociability. Pastoral families and others with the means to do so would think little of riding 20 miles to attend a dance or a race meeting. The very rareness of such events ensured them a lasting place in cultural memory, perhaps serving to distract from the quiet months between. Farming families, still less mobile, nevertheless considered themselves 'neighbours' with others who lived miles off – and took a corresponding interest in each other's business. News 'flies like wildfire through this place', wrote one woman settled to the west of Melbourne, 'and when I perchance see any of my neighbours, what wonderful tales we have to hear and relate'.[68]

The growing prosperity of the pastoral industry, the establishment of agriculture in some districts, the discovery of gold in others, and the spread

65 Howard Le Couteur, 'Of Intemperance, Class and Gender in Colonial Queensland: A Working-Class Woman's Account of Alcohol Abuse', *History Australia*, 8, 3 (2011): 139–57.
66 Waterhouse, *The Vision Splendid*, p. 118.
67 Penny Russell (ed.), *This Errant Lady: Jane Franklin's Overland Journey to Port Phillip and Sydney, 1839* (Canberra: National Library of Australia, 2002), p. 72.
68 Penelope Selby, quoted in Lucy Frost, *No Place for a Nervous Lady: Voices from the Australian Bush* (Melbourne: McPhee Gribble/Penguin, 1984), p. 164.

of railways connecting rural towns to each other and to the capital cities all gradually transformed the social life of rural Australia. Trains gave new viability to rural enterprise and new life to merging provincial centres. Entertainments were more organised: theatre companies toured the bush, efforts were made to regulate prize fighting and gambling, race meetings and sports competitions were more carefully managed and the conduct of both the players and the crowds of spectators subjected to new rules and boundaries.[69] Temperance campaigns grew in popularity from the 1880s, and in country towns as well as cities concerted efforts were made to bring a more respectable cast to rural entertainments. While the shearers' 'spree' became valorised in cultural mythology, the ritual itself became less common as married selectors and men from the city took over the work of shearing in the late nineteenth century.[70]

The American-founded Woman's Christian Temperance Union galvanised widespread support in the closing decades of the century. Reformers such as Bessie Harrison Lee (who had some unfortunate childhood experience to draw upon) identified alcohol as a central issue in the difficulties of women's domestic life, though these were compounded by a double standard of sexual morality that left men free to indulge their desires, even when to do so brought strife, disease or the hazards of excessive childbearing to the domestic hearth. Temperance and moderation in all things was Lee's recipe for domestic harmony and social progress; but it was a recipe that found little support amongst an increasingly vocal and masculinist culture that celebrated freedom from domestic tyranny as a manly right. While many socialist and radical reformers certainly placed the virtues of family life at the heart of their social visions alongside the manly independence of the worker, such visions had to contend with a leisure culture that was lighter on social conscience, and inclined to see all pressures towards 'respectability' as a middle-class, 'wowserish' imposition upon the freedom of the working man.[71]

By the end of the century, Australia's population was distributed in a way that caused alarm to those who still thought its best prospects of democratic prosperity lay in small-scale farming. Only about one third lived in the 'bush' and another third in provincial towns; the rest clung to the coastal fringe and

---

69 Waterhouse, *The Vision Splendid*, pp. 113–62.
70 Ibid., p. 126.
71 Patricia Grimshaw, 'Bessie Harrison Lee and the Fight for Voluntary Motherhood', in Marilyn Lake and Farley Kelley (eds), *Double Time: Women in Victoria, 150 Years* (Melbourne: Penguin, 1985), pp. 139–47; Marilyn Lake, 'The Politics of Respectability: Identifying the Masculinist Context', *Historical Studies*, 22, 86 (1986): 116–31.

the reassuring urbanity of the capitals. Sydney and Melbourne, in particular, were large, modern industrial cities, but the pace of growth and change was evident in all the capital cities, with the possible exception of Hobart. The expansion of new service industries led to the proliferation of associated occupations: railway clerks, tram conductors, shop assistants and the like. The expansion of commercial centres encouraged new ways of doing business and new forms of recreation: tea rooms and circulating libraries sprang into existence and theatres, operas and concerts proliferated, bringing men and women more often into the centre of town. Men and women of all classes clustered and jostled: larrikin gangs, homeless 'bummers' and loafers, flashily dressed members of the 'demi-monde', simpering dandies, elegantly dressed ladies, and the 'rag, tag and bobtail of bookmakers, and their hangers-on'. Urban life demanded new rules of conduct, to govern relations between strangers in professional and public contexts. Newspapers called for better management of pedestrian behaviour in the busy streets, women deplored the pall of tobacco smoke that hung over the sidewalks, men complained about the women's elaborate 'matinee hats' that obscured their view at the theatre, and everyone complained about the squalling of babies at public entertainments. Municipal by-laws proliferated in the vain attempt to govern public conduct.[72]

Colonial society talked itself into being, in endless self-conscious debate about its character and trajectory.[73] But it was also shaped in more organic, less explicit, less conspicuous ways. It separated individuals from the homes and communities through which they had understood their social identities, and forced them to think anew. And it flung together individuals whose differences of habit, speech and bearing reflected profound differences in upbringing, social awareness and ethical understanding. The vagaries of fortune created shifting social relationships, sometimes bringing men and women of widely different social backgrounds into a semblance of equality, sometimes creating new hierarchies and inequalities, new relationships of dominance and deference. Years of propinquity dulled the mistrust of individuals who had at first looked on each other as strangers. Each new generation inherited more and more complex weavings of lineage and cultural heritage. Gradually they adjusted to the rhythm of seasons and the rigours of climate, the barriers of distance and the new patterns of life that all these factors demanded. Gradually, too, they adjusted to each

72 Russell, *Savage or Civilised?* pp. 270–1.
73 Alan Atkinson, *The Commonwealth of Speech: An Argument about Australia's Past, Present and Future* (Melbourne: Australian Scholarly Publishing, 2002).

other. Distance, difference and competing interests all made it singularly difficult to fashion a new society in the colonies – and yet those very factors also made it imperative to try. As they made the necessary adjustments, colonists found new ways to talk to and of each other, and to understand themselves.

20

Art and literature: a cosmopolitan culture

ROBERT DIXON AND JEANETTE HOORN

The history of art and literature in the Australian colonies, at least in the first half of the nineteenth century, can be understood not as the beginnings of a tradition that led naturally to the nationalist culture of the Federation period, but as a series of attempts to establish forms of subjectivity and sociability, and the cultural institutions associated with them, deriving from late-Georgian and Victorian Britain. These typically looked backwards rather than forwards, and were often unsuccessful in the Australian context. Since the idea of the nation functioned as an absence in these early years,[1] we might begin by asking: what were Australian art and literature like *before* the nation? How and in relation to what kinds of social and intellectual forma-tions can colonial culture best be located?[2]

When Governor Lachlan Macquarie arrived in Sydney in 1810, he appointed Michael Massey Robinson, an emancipated convict, to write com-memorative verses in celebration of the birthdays of King George III and Queen Charlotte. Robinson's odes were read at Government House and pub-lished in the colony's only newspaper, the *Sydney Gazette*. Since the accession of George I it had been incumbent upon all British poets laureate to pre-sent, annually, a New Year's Ode and a Birthday Ode to be performed before the King and court at St James's Palace in London. Robinson's birthday odes were not seen, then, as the commencement of a new national literature, but as a way of modelling the fledgling institutions of colonial society on the protocols of Augustan good taste. His 'ODE for the Queen's Birth-Day, 1816' was about the crossing of the Blue Mountains west of Sydney and the expansion of agriculture across the continent. Robinson created an originary narrative by conjuring a line of explorer-heroes from Aeneas and Columbus,

---

1 Andrew McCann, *Marcus Clarke's Bohemia: Literature and Modernity in Colonial Melbourne* (Melbourne University Press, 2004), p. 7.
2 Philip Mead, 'Nation, Literature, Location', in Peter Pierce (ed.). *The Cambridge History of Australian Literature* (Cambridge University Press, 2009), p. 549.

and locating the beginnings of colonial history in the ancient Mediterranean and Atlantic worlds. These epic associations were then transferred to the more recent history of inland exploration in the New World. The discovery of the Great South Land brought to a close the period of epic adventures on 'the watery World', and Aeneas's descendants now turn their attention to Australia's vast 'Tracts of untravers'd EARTH', 'Where yon Blue Mountains, with tremendous Brow, / Frown on the humbler Vales that wind below'.[3]

Robinson's neoclassicism created a context that was antique rather than future-oriented. Macquarie had come to office worried about his predecessor William Bligh's legacy of civil unrest, and to the extent that he fostered a cult of Augustan leadership, hailing Sydney as 'a second Rome, rising at the antipodes',[4] his intention was to promote Enlightenment ideals of civility in a convict colony troubled by dissent among its fractious military officers. Other voices of dissent could be heard in satirical verse written by convicts, such as Frank the Poet's 'A Convict's Tour to Hell'. In London, meanwhile, the tradition of the laureate odes had long since fallen out of fashion, the publication of Thomas Warton's birthday ode on 4 June 1785 inciting a torrent of abuse.

The early history of Australian literature is also a history of writing that is distinct from the idea of 'literature' as it is generally understood; that is, as a set of novels, poems and plays written by Australian writers about colonial Australian life. By contrast, the word 'literature' was not confined to imaginative writing. As it was understood for much of the nineteenth century – in newspaper advertisements, on library, book sellers' and auctioneers' catalogues, or in the title of G.B. Barton's *Literature in New South Wales* (1866) – 'literature' was a capacious and flexible term that embraced newspapers and magazines, the Greek and Latin classics, voyages and travels, law, history, oratory and theology. Literature was 'a discourse, a means of self-improvement, an exemplary and coded embodiment of certain written conventions and proprieties, and an arena for intellectual disputation'.[5] It encompassed philosophy, criticism, political economy and social commentary. Yet the modern forms of literary subjectivity that came into being in Britain at this time, and the kinds of social networks and sites of literary sociability

---

3 Quoted in Robert Dixon, *The Course of Empire: Neo-classical Culture in New South Wales 1788–1860* (Oxford University Press, 1986), p. 123.
4 Michael Massey Robinson, 'Song for His Majesty's Birth-Day', *Sydney Gazette*, 18 August 1821.
5 Ken Stewart, 'Britain's Australia', in Pierce (ed.), *The Cambridge History of Australian Literature*, p. 32.

that sprang into being with it, largely failed to take root in the Australian colonies, at least during the first half of the nineteenth century. This is partly because social institutions were too thin to support literary life, and partly because colonial society was so strongly materialistic. It is also because of the competing pressures from religion and from more secular and utilitarian modes of nation building and community identity, which were unusually intense in the colonies: hence the failure to create a sustained and continuous literary culture by circles that formed for a limited time, for example, around Louisa Anne Meredith in Tasmania, Nicol Drysdale Stenhouse and Frank Fowler in Sydney, William and Mary Howitt in Port Phillip and Catherine Helen Spence in Adelaide.[6]

One significant institutional development was the evolution of private into public libraries by the second half of the century. While a number of wealthy citizens had amassed significant private libraries by the 1820s, including the explorer John Oxley, the first 'public' library was the Australian Subscription Library in Macquarie Street, Sydney, established in 1826. Its first president was the colonial secretary, Alexander Macleay. The library maintained its stock of books and periodicals by receiving monthly shipments from England, and engaged a full-time librarian, John Fairfax, who later became editor and publisher of the *Sydney Morning Herald*. The Australian Subscription Library charged a fee of three guineas to subscribers, with membership limited by nomination, and was frequently criticised for its exclusiveness. In 1869 the library was purchased by the Legislative Assembly and reconstituted as the Free Public Library of Sydney and then, in 1895, as the Public Library of New South Wales. In Hobart, various reading rooms and book societies had been active since the 1820s, and a Public Library was established there in 1849 with membership also on a subscription basis. Victoria's Public Library opened in 1856.[7]

The idea of a 'national literature'

While a national literature was experienced by the majority as an absence in colonial society, others increasingly anticipated its future growth. That

6 Simon During, 'Out of England: Literary Subjectivity in the Australian Colonies, 1788–1867', in Judith Ryan and Chris Wallace-Crabbe (eds), *Imagining Australia: Literature and Culture in the New New World* (Cambridge, MA: Harvard University Press, 2004), pp. 3–21.

7 George Nadel, *Australia's Colonial Culture: Ideas, Men and Institutions in Mid-Nineteenth Century Eastern Australia* (Melbourne: F.W. Cheshire, 1957), pp. 80–5.

promise was especially strong at the beginning of the 'patriotic decade' of the 1850s, in which transportation of convicts ceased, legislatures were established, colonial constitutions written and self-government realised.[8]

It was precisely to create the means by which a 'national literature' might come into being that the visiting London journalist Frank Fowler launched Sydney's first but short-lived literary journal, *The Month*, which appeared between July 1857 and November 1858 and was modelled on *Blackwood's*. Fowler's various contributions to literary life in Sydney give a good indication of the meaning of literature at this time. Shortly after arriving in December 1855, he gave a series of public 'orations'. Lectures were a major form of literary sociability and were delivered on a wide range of topics, including moral philosophy, theology, history, geography and science, as well as literature in its modern sense.[9] The subjects of Fowler's orations included the Crimean War and a series of 'Literary Portraits' expounding on Edgar Allan Poe, Coleridge and Douglas Jerrold. As a journalist, writing under his own name as well as the pseudonyms 'Cosmopolitan' and 'A Literary Vagabond', Fowler contributed articles and sketches to the Sydney press, especially on political topics.

The main contributors to *The Month* were the circle of writers and men of letters that had formed at the Balmain home of Edinburgh-born lawyer Nicol Drysdale Stenhouse, including James Lionel Michael, Richard Rowe, Edward Reeve, Joseph Sheridan Moore, Daniel Deniehy and Henry Kendall.[10] In the editorial for the February 1858 issue Fowler announced, 'It has been his earnest desire, ever since his arrival in the colony, to establish something like a national literature...by the publication of a free and fearless organ of literary criticism'.[11] Fowler's aspiration for a 'national literature' was something like the development of a set of cultural institutions – centrally, a periodical literature – in which the latest books from both the colonies and Europe would be the occasion, even the provocation, for men of letters to engage critically with ideas in the public sphere from a broadly liberal point of view. Colonial reading habits before the nation, therefore, were not confined to Australian books. Rather, these were read alongside imported books, their reception interacting in quite complex ways. Even at the end of the century, Australians continued to read British periodicals and the novels of Scott, Dickens and

---

8 Ibid., p. 57.
9 Elizabeth Webby, 'Literary Lectures in Early Australia', *Southerly* 40, 3 (1980): 268–83.
10 Ann-Mari Jordens, *The Stenhouse Circle: Literary Life in Mid-Nineteenth Century Sydney* (Melbourne University Press, 1979).
11 Quoted in R.G. Geering, 'Introduction', *Southern Lights and Shadows*, new edn (Sydney University Press, 1975), p. 12.

Trollope alongside the work of local writers, although the colonial reception of canonical Victorian novels such as Dickens' *Great Expectations* was no doubt affected by their thematic associations with contemporary Australian books about settler societies.[12]

It was in the vocation of poet that the idea of a 'national' literature first emerged in something like its modern sense, especially in the second generation of native-born Australians, including Charles Harpur and Henry Kendall. The literary scholar Michael Ackland has argued for the existence of a 'colonial verse tradition', tracing a succession of poets through the nineteenth century who read each others' work and saw themselves as establishing a 'national' poetry.[13] Paradoxically, however, Ackland's account of this tradition is also an argument for its failure to succeed under the difficult material conditions for the production of a local literature: aspiring poets often struggled to achieve book (as distinct from newspaper) publication, and were forced to earn a living by more prosaic means, such as journalism, the law or public service.

The commitment to New World possibilities had already been expressed in the poetry of the first generation of native-born Australians, William Charles Wentworth and Charles Tompson. In the preface to *Australasia* (1823), Wentworth wrote of his compulsion to compete for the chancellor's medal at Cambridge in 1823, when the proposed theme was Australasia, and he described his work patriotically as 'the first fruits of Australian poetry'.[14] Tompson's *Wild Notes, From the Lyre of a Native Minstrel* (1826) openly declared its currency – or nativist – sympathies in its very title. His individual poems, while imitative of English precedents, nevertheless conveyed a sense that for his generation the local landscape was rich in personal associations and linked with nascent republican ideals of individual liberty that were incompatible with the convict system. In 'Blacktown', Thompson expressed an early awareness of frontier conflict and an empathy for the effects of settlement on the Indigenous population that were to recur in the work of the second generation of colonial-born poets. 'Retrospect; or, A Review of My

---

12 Tim Dolin, 'First Steps Toward a History of the Mid-Victorian Novel in Colonial Australia, *Australian Literary Studies*, 22, 3 (2006): 273–93; Elizabeth Webby, 'Not Reading the Nation', *Australian Literary Studies*, 22, 3 (2006): 308–18.

13 Michael Ackland, *That Shining Band: A Study of Australian Colonial Verse Tradition* (Brisbane: UQP, 1994), p. 39.

14 William Charles Wentworth, *Australasia: A Poem Written for the Chancellor's Medal at the Cambridge Commencement, July 1823*, ed. G.A. Wilkes (Sydney University Press, 1982), pp. vii-viii.

Scholastic Days' was a prospect piece in which the 'native' poet reflected upon nature's gift of liberty:

> Nature has giv'n all creatures to be free,
> And Man in embryo pants for liberty;
> ...
> It bids the Negro spurn his galling chain,
> And curse – tho' vainly curse – its unearn'd pain ...[15]

Such implicit sympathies with American republicanism were already evident in Wentworth's *Statistical, Historical, and Political Description of New South Wales* (1819), and his poem *Australasia* was openly critical of convict transportation as inimical to liberty. Wentworth envisaged a future in which New South Wales would take on the imperial responsibilities of a declining Great Britain, becoming 'A new Britannia in another world!'[16] In such passages, the first generation of Australian poets cast themselves as active, individual agents of liberty and of an independent Australian culture to come.

Aboriginal cultural production

Indigenous artists made drawings, paintings and sculptures throughout the Australian continent for many thousands of years before the arrival of Europeans. They produced art works in bark and on stone surfaces, on their own bodies, in the earth and onto the sand that related intimately to rituals such as coming of age, birth and death but also to the hunting of food. They told stories about their ancestors, who created the trees, the rocks and the rivers. Aranda and Warlpiri depicted the kangaroo and the honey ant Dreaming, and Yolngu decorated their spears and shields with barramundi and goanna. Indigenous Australians were clearly the first and, according to Sidney Nolan, the 'best' Australian artists.[17] They sang their culture though the 'songlines' of their country and played its rhythms on the *yerdaki*, or didgeridoo.

Within a short time after the arrival of the First Fleet, objects bearing print travelled along traditional trade routes and were actively assimilated into Aboriginal social life. One of the earliest pieces of Indigenous writing in English is Bennelong's letter to 'Mr and Mrs Phillip', dictated to an unknown scribe at Sydney Cove on 29 August 1796. Bennelong, who was to spend two

15 Charles Tompson, *Wild Notes, From the Lyre of a Native Minstrel* [1826], eds G.A. Wilkes and G.A. Turnbull (Sydney University Press, 1973), p. 5.
16 Wentworth, *Australasia*, p. 21.
17 Sidney Nolan, (Sydney) *Daily Telegraph*, 17, 23 December 1949.

years in England, depicted his more or less successful struggle to 'negotiate a position in two social orders simultaneously'.[18] At Lake Macquarie Mission north of Sydney in the 1830s, the British missionary Lancelot Threlkeld carried out scriptural translation with the assistance of the Awabakal man, Biraban. Threlkeld also wrote translated fragments of Biraban's speech, including a reference to the demise of one of his children in which Biraban 'chose to put his child's death on the written record when the opportunity arose'.[19]

The petitions sent by residents of the Coranderrk Aboriginal Reserve in Victoria to the Board of Protection of Aborigines from the 1860s to the 1880s conveyed the political aims of the Wurundjeri in relation to the ownership of their land. Following the death of Simon Wonga in 1875, William Barak (Beruk) became Coranderrk's *ngurungaeta,* or main speaker, the most senior member of the Wurundjeri clan (of the Woiwurung people) upon whose lands the reserve had been established. Barak dictated his words as clan head to one or more young scribes who had been taught to write at the Coranderrk school. In the 1880s and 1890s he painted surpassingly beautiful images of the Wurundjeri people in a figurative idiom on cardboard and on paper. His pictures were executed in a unique blend of pencil, gouache, charcoal and ochres, showing aspects of the life-ways of his people, often seen in magisterial possum cloaks. Few of these original garments still exist but William Barak's paintings have inspired contemporary Indigenous artists such as Treahna Hamm, who has made a series of possum-skin cloaks of great beauty. Alfred Howitt, the pioneer authority on the culture of Aboriginal people in Victoria, recounts that Barak was not only a painter, but also an artisan, and that he sang the traditional songs of his people. He recorded the dance and theatre of his community in the scenes of corroborees that fill his drawings. Barak befriended the Presbyterian Mrs Ann Fraser Bonn, who supported the many attempts of his community to prevent the closure of the station. She wrote of Barak:

> He had refined tastes, being fond of music and painting...When Barak could get a sheet of drawing paper he made the outside of his chimney his easel, having the canopy of heaven for his studio. His brush and his colours were crude, the colours being pigments extracted from the earth.

18 Penny van Toorn, *Writing Never Arrives Naked: Early Aboriginal Cultures of Writing in Australia* (Canberra: Aboriginal Studies Press, 2006), p. 63.
19 Ibid., p. 46. See also Jeanette Hoorn's account of Joseph Lycett's drawing of the Awabakal in *The Lycett Album: Drawings of Aborigines and Australian Scenery* (Canberra: National Library of Australia, 1990).

Notwithstanding this, some of his pictures are to be seen in the museums of Europe.[20]

Other artists who used similar media include Tommy McRae (Yakaduna or Warra-euea) from the upper Murray, who in the 1860s sometimes made satirical references in his drawings to Europeans, and Mickey of Ulladulla, who described the fishing communities and native animals on the south coast of New South Wales in the 1880s as well as the boats of white settlers.

Public patronage and the emergence of museums, galleries and schools of arts

The need for accurate records for the successful establishment and expansion of the colony at Sydney Cove meant that artists were employed more broadly in the day-to-day running of the colony than were writers, poets or musicians. Naval draftsmen such as William Bradley, George Raper and the group around them, now referred to as the Port Jackson Painters, recorded the development of the colony, the life and appearance of the Eora, Gadigal and Wangal Wangal, the native flora and fauna.[21] They drew the landscape and its people with remarkable verisimilitude, even though generations of nationalist historians and critics tended to diminish these artists' skills in rendering Australian nature accurately.

On occasion, artists recorded conflict between the British and the Indigenous clans. One such event is the spearing of the first governor, Arthur Phillip, at Manly Cove in 1790, depicted in the *The Spearing Quintet,* a set of five watercolours.[22] The naturalist John William Lewin, who had arrived in New South Wales to enhance his collection of botanical specimens, travelled widely in the colonies to gather material for his two books on insects and birds. He was commissioned by Macquarie to draw transparencies as decorations for the Queen's Birthday Balls at Government House in 1811 and 1815, and was a member of the party that accompanied Macquarie's crossing of the Blue Mountains. He also drew illustrations from material gathered during Oxley's expeditions.[23] Macquarie and his wife, Elizabeth, were robust

20 Quoted in Andrew Sayers, *Aboriginal Artists of the Nineteenth Century* (Oxford University Press, 1994), p. 25.
21 Bernard Smith and Alwyne Wheeler (eds), *The Art Of The First Fleet & Other Early Australian Drawings* (Oxford University Press, 1988).
22 Jeanette Hoorn, *Australian Pastoral: The Making of a White Landscape* (Fremantle Arts Centre Press, 2007), pp. 21–31.
23 Richard Neville, *Mr J.W. Lewin, Painter and Naturalist* (Sydney: UNSW Press, 2012).

patrons of the arts, with Elizabeth involved in the design of a number of the colony's major public buildings and of the gardens at Government House.[24]

A number of artists were found among the ranks of the convicts transported to New South Wales and Tasmania, and they too were pressed into service by a series of governors. Thomas Watling was one of the first to paint landscape views of Sydney in oils, answering to the demand for topographic views combined with a picturesque sensibility.[25] Joseph Lycett recorded the development of a free society out of the convict settlement. He was commissioned to produce a set of drawings that were engraved in a folio of views, presenting the land in a positive light that was attractive to potential emigrants and introducing the first pastoral elements into locally produced art works.[26] Thomas Bock drew elegant portraits of the Tasmanian landed gentry. He also painted a portrait of Mathina, the young Palawa child taken from her parents, incarcerated on Flinders Island and adopted by the governor and his wife, Sir John and Jane, Lady Franklin. The picture is probably the first portrait of a 'stolen child' by a European artist.[27]

Augustus Earle and Conrad Martens, both artists on Charles Darwin's expedition on HMS *Beagle*, found employment among the colonial gentry of New South Wales. Earle, who visited Sydney and Hobart in 1825 before his sojourn on the *Beagle* in the period 1831–32, painted portraits of Sydney's colonial ruling class, including two large oils of John Piper and Mrs Piper with her children, which have become iconic images of early British settlers. Martens arrived in Sydney in 1835, having left the *Beagle* in Valparaiso, and established himself as an artist painting views of Sydney and the houses of its citizenry. Both Earle and Martens executed stunning canvasses depicting sublime views of the Blue Mountains landscape in which the achievements of science, the grandeur of nature and the success of the explorers in overcoming a hostile landscape were celebrated.

The 'national' galleries that appeared in the Australian colonies coincided with the flourishing of British galleries and museums as expressions of civic humanism. Following the values and principles of a classical revival, it was the duty of all members of a 'republic of equals' to educate those who were less fortunate about art and its virtues, so that all might become enlightened

24 Elizabeth Ellis, *Rare & Curious: The Secret History of Governor Macquarie's Collectors' Chest* (Melbourne: Miegunyah Press, 2010).

25 Bernard Smith, *European Vision and the South Pacific* [1960] (New Haven: Yale University Press, 1985), pp. 180–4.

26 Jeanette Hoorn, 'Joseph Lycett: The Pastoral Landscape in Early Colonial Australia', *Art Bulletin of Victoria*, 26 (1986): 4–14.

27 Hoorn, *Australian Pastoral*, pp. 65–6.

citizens.[28] The same principles enlivened civic consciousness in Australia, with state museums appearing from the middle of the nineteenth century.

The Lady Franklin Museum, built near Hobart in 1842–43 and the first in Tasmania, was modelled on a Greek temple. Jane Franklin originally had a small museum of classical art in mind that she imagined might hold 'a dozen casts of the Elgin and Vatican marbles', but the views of her husband prevailed and the museum, while holding some art works, specialised in natural history, botany and Tasmanian history.[29] Gothic revival architecture appeared later in the century, dominating ecclesiastical and civic building programs all over the empire, especially in Canada, New Zealand and Australia. The universities of Sydney, Melbourne and Adelaide all followed the international movement, adorning the centres of their campuses with Gothic revival buildings. Those encircling the main quadrangle at the University of Sydney are notable examples of Tudor Gothic.[30] St Paul's Anglican Cathedral in Melbourne was designed by William Butterfield, the celebrated architect of All Saints, Margaret Street in London, and is a brilliant feature in the centre of Australia's most gothic city.

The wealth generated by the gold rushes in Victoria resulted in the transformation of Melbourne into a thriving Victorian city boasting Italianate mansions and grand terraces whose distinctive decorative features became known as 'boom style'. A robust pastoral economy also enabled the opening of Australia's first national gallery in 1861. The art critic James Smith, a firm advocate for the cultural and intellectual life of Victoria, had argued fervently for such a gallery. An active proponent of civic education, he was also involved in the establishment of the Garrick Club, the Shakespeare Society, the Dante Society and Alliance Française.[31] The gallery, museum and library were all under one roof, following the proportions and organisation of the British Museum, with its domed library and reading room at its centre, although the domed reading room was not built until the early twentieth century. The Art Gallery of New South Wales followed nearly 20 years later in 1880, with Adelaide (1881), Hobart (1885), Brisbane (1895) and Perth (1895) all building what became state galleries over the following two decades. Their

---

28 John Barrell, *The Political Theory of Painting from Reynolds to Hazlitt* (New Haven: Yale University Press, 1986), pp. 18–23.

29 Alison Inglis, 'Imperial Perspectives on Art in Nineteenth-Century Australia', in Jaynie Anderson (ed.), *The Cambridge Companion to Australian Art* (Cambridge University Press, 2011), p. 61.

30 Joan Kerr, *Our Great Victorian Architect: Edmund Thomas Blacket 1817–1883* (Sydney: National Trust of Australia, 1983).

31 'James Smith', *Australian Dictionary of Biography*, vol. 6, pp. 145–6.

aims were to collect British art and copies from the classical world as well as to encourage and foster the productions of local artists by acquiring the best examples of their work.[32]

Civic humanism was perhaps most actively fostered through the mechanics' institutes and schools of arts that were established throughout the Australian colonies. Here, useful knowledge and self-improvement in the arts, literature and sciences were made available to all who wished to learn. They were among the most important sites of literary sociability and their conditions of membership were more open and less exclusive than the early public libraries. Founded initially in Scotland, the movement soon spread throughout Britain. The Australian colonies quickly followed, with the establishment of the Hobart Town Mechanics' Institute and Library in 1827 and the Sydney Mechanics' School of Arts in 1833, followed by Melbourne in 1839, Geelong in 1846, Brisbane in 1849, and Perth in 1851.[33] While the taste for reading fiction increased throughout the period, colonial libraries were also well stocked with the leading British literary magazines and reviews, including the *Edinburgh*, the *Quarterly*, the *Westminster*, the *Dublin*, *Blackwood's* and the *Cornhill*.

A classical civilisation in Australia

Classical ideals shaped the colonies' burgeoning cultural institutions. From the mid-1850s, universities were founded with Arts degrees grounded firmly in the received tradition of Greek and Latin languages and literature. The concept of 'classical civilisation' was also the principle behind the art produced for public patronage by the colonies' growing number of artists. The ideals of the pastoral, in which humankind is depicted in an effortless harmony with nature, as well those of the more political georgic, in which leisure was represented as the just reward for hard work, were central framing devices for the representation of Europeans in the Australian landscape. John Glover's painting, *My Harvest Home* (1835), is a celebration of agriculture and the traditions that surround it. The painting boasted of the success of the Europeans in Australia, of their victory over nature, the land and the Aboriginal nations that had been displaced. The picture takes for its subject the gathering-in of the wheat harvest at Glover's farm in Tasmania,

32 Gerard Vaughan, 'The Cross-Cultural Art Museum in Australia', in Anderson (ed.), *The Cambridge Companion to Australian Art*, p. 261.
33 Eileen Chanin, *Book Life: The Life and Times of David Scott Mitchell* (Melbourne: Australian Scholarly Publishing, 2011), pp. 65–6.

Patterdale. According to its inscription, Glover began work on the painting '[t]he day the harvest was all got in'.[34] A loaded cart and the six oxen that pull it, complemented by six farm hands at work in various occupations associated with the harvest, control the composition. There was a resurgence of agricultural subjects in British painting between 1790 and 1830,[35] and when Glover came to paint his harvest picture there were plenty of harvest scenes painted within the georgic mode to provide models.[36]

In the pastoral tradition, by contrast, work is hidden and the landscape appears to be naturally ordered without labour. This became the principal means through which the relationship of Europeans to the land was represented, in the 'homestead portraits' of artists Eugene von Guerard and Conrad Martens, for example, who followed the patronage of squatters to find work.[37] These artists had to adapt the pastoral traditions to the peculiarities of the Australian landscape. While in England, France or Italy, the spaces with which artists had to work were usually relatively confined and enclosed, artists in Australia grappled with vast tracts of land that made up the properties of their patrons.

The principles of civic humanism, motivating the citizens of the Australian colonies towards increasing the greater prosperity of all of the members of its society, were on display in the narratives contained in the paintings, prints and drawings as well as the sculptures that artists produced. Benjamin Duterrau's *The Conciliation* (1840) is a case in point.[38] Like Reynolds, Duterrau gave lectures on the visual arts. He set about creating in Hobart what he believed to be a community of intellectuals, fashioning himself in his public lectures as one of its leaders. He compared the Hobart Mechanic's Institute, where he delivered his lectures during the 1830s and 1840s, to the School of Athens. Using Raphael's painting of the *Stanza de la Signatura,* Duterrau educated the young colony in the principles of civic humanism:

> The object of the Mechanics' Institute is to increase the number of enlightened characters, which not only lessen the number of loose and wanton characters, but will eventually sink them into nothingness. Shame can do

---

34 Inscribed 'My Harvest Home, Van Diemen's Land, Begun March 19 1835'.

35 Michael Rosenthal, *British Landscape Painting* (Oxford: Phaidon, 1982), p. 96.

36 Thomas Gainsborough's *Harvest Wagon* of 1767, the later version of 1784–85, and Francis Wheatley's painting of the same title of 1774 were well known works with which Glover must have been familiar.

37 Candice Bruce, Edward Comstock and Frank McDonald, *Eugene von Guerard 1881–1901: A German Romantic in the Antipodes* (Martinborough: Alister Taylor, 1982).

38 See Paul Paffen, 'A Grand Illusion: Benjamin Duterrau and *The Conciliation*', *Melbourne Art Journal*, 5 (2001): 58–63.

much. 'Tis shame that makes a barbarous savage turn to be a good Christian, when the difference is clearly pointed out to him. The Missionary duty has proved that good effect completely...As the School of Athens has proved much in the great world, so may the school of Hobart Town do much in the little world where our happy community subsist, by honest industry and cheerful contentment.[39]

He conveyed those principles in *The Conciliation*. Here, George Augustus Robinson is depicted in one large embrace with the remaining Tasmanian Aboriginal people, whom he had been appointed to persuade into captivity and exile, eventually on Flinders Island. It is an entirely utopian image: a fantasy of what a truly humanistic society might have achieved had it not initially displaced the Palawa from their lands, incarcerated them and allowed them to die. Two years after the painting was completed, Timmy, the model for the central figure seen shaking Robinson's hand, and his friend Jack, also possibly a model for one of the figures, were executed in Melbourne purportedly for murdering two white men. They were the first men officially executed in Victoria, despite a spirited defence by Redmond Barry, who in 1852 would become a judge of the Supreme Court.[40]

Artists Robert Dowling, Charles Hill and John Michael Crossland took up the displacement of Aboriginal people and the implied debt that Europeans owed to them for the taking of their land and the destruction of their lifeways. In Hill's *The Lesson* (c. 1869) a settler instructs her young daughter in the principles of charity as she offers bread to an Aboriginal woman at their doorstep.

The development of patronage networks

The first exhibitions held in Victoria consisted of British and European art from private collections, but by the 1870s, when the Victorian Academy of the Arts commenced holding annual exhibitions, Australian scenes executed by local artists gradually came to the fore.[41] While the Heidelberg School painters made pastoral subject matter famous in Australia in the 1890s, their

---

39 Benjamin Duterrau, lecture delivered at the Mechanic's Institute, Hobart, 29 June, 1849, reprinted in Bernard Smith (ed.), *Documents on Art and Taste in Australia* (Oxford University Press, 1975), pp. 85–96.

40 Stephen Scheding, *The National Picture* (Sydney: Random House, 2002), p. 208.

41 In 1870, 130 of the 228 pictures that made up the exhibition were Australian landscapes. This represents some three-fifths of the pictures. By 1872 the proportion had increased to two-thirds; *Exhibition of the Victorian Academy of Arts, Catalogues for the Years 1871–1880*.

work had its roots in local painting as well as in the illustrated press. The process of developing the public taste for local landscape was a lengthy one, but as early as the mid-1850s the *Journal of Australasia* urged its readers to buy local work:

> We need no longer decorate our walls with the miserable daubs exported hither from Houndsditch and St Martin's Lane, or with bad copies of good originals in foreign galleries. With the pencils of Guerard, Davies, Chevalier and Gilfillan, at command, the man of taste need no longer hesitate between blank walls, and pictures which are foils to their gilded frames.[42]

While merchants and the urban elite were from the outset important patrons of art in colonial Australia, the role of pastoralists as patrons strengthened as the century progressed. Von Guerard and Martens both travelled into pastoral districts when they could not survive on the patronage provided in Sydney and Melbourne. Martens was experiencing financial problems when he left for the Darling Downs during the 1830s. Von Guerard's position was sufficiently serious for him to resort to selling his pictures by lottery. Von Guerard's patronage came from both urban and rural areas in Victoria. Of his 22 rural patrons almost all were pastoralists, but the merchant F.G. Dalgetty was his best patron.[43]

By the 1870s artists and critics alike were looking for a national iconography in Australian art, and by the 1880s calls were being made for the development of a national school of painting based on the land use and culture of pastoral Australia. The group of artists later known as the Heidelberg School became the best known painters of Australian rural life in which the ideals of the nation were reflected. These centred on 'mateship', labour and the celebration of European power and control over the land. In a lecture published in the *Australasian Critic* in 1890, the American critic Sidney Dickinson addressed the subject, 'What Should Australian Artists Paint?' He encouraged artists to paint 'the mixed life of the city and the characteristic life of the station and the bush', urging them to 'present on canvas the earnestness, rigour, pathos, and heroism of the life that is about them'.[44] He 'hoped that Mr Roberts, Mr McCubbin, and the others who have been impressed with the opportunities for pictorial description which lie in Australian life will not be discouraged either by silent indifference or outspoken criticism'.[45] In this

---

42 *Journal of Australasia and Monthly Magazine*, 2, 7 (1856): 26.
43 Hoorn, *Australian Pastoral*, pp. 139–40.
44 Smith (ed.), *Documents on Art and Taste in Australia*, p. 250.
45 Sidney Dickinson, 'What Should Australian Artists Paint?' *The Australasian Critic*, 1 October 1890.

way, local artists received endorsement to develop a national iconography in which the everyday life of the colony was represented.

Literature, visual culture and the transpacific imaginary

One neglected aspect of nineteenth-century Australian literary and visual culture is the relationship between the colonies and the United States, especially after the discovery of gold. The gold-rush circuit produced what the literary scholar Paul Giles has called a transpacific imaginary, transforming perceptions of Australia's location in space and time from an orientation toward the classical European past to a more modern connection with the United States.[46] If Robinson could describe New South Wales in 1821 as 'a second Rome, rising at the antipodes' and Wentworth in 1823 as 'A new Britannia in another world', in 1840, John Dunmore Lang foresaw 'a second America in the Southern Hemisphere'.[47]

The transpacific imaginary was present in Australian writing as early as Wentworth's own *Statistical, Historical, and Political Description of the Colony of New South Wales* (1819). In his description of the region west of the Blue Mountains, Wentworth wrote: 'Nothing is now wanting to render this great western wilderness the seat of a powerful community, but the discovery of a navigable river communicating with the western coast'.[48] His thinking was influenced by ideas of continental destiny in the United States:

> The vast tide of emigration which is incessantly rolling along the banks of the Mississippi, and of its tributary streams, and the numberless cities, towns, and settlements, that have sprung up as it were by the agency of magic, in what but a few years back was one boundless and uninterrupted wilderness, speak a language not to be mistaken by the most ignorant and prejudiced.[49]

With the discovery of gold in California in 1848, Australian gold seekers were among the first to arrive in what was then a new and isolated part of the United States, for the run across the Pacific made California more

46 Paul Giles, *Transpacific Republicanism: American Transcendentalism, John Dunmore Lang and the Gold-Rush Circuit* (La Trobe University: American Studies Bernard Bailyn Lecture no. 15, 2010), p. 9.
47 John Dunmore Lang, *Religion and Education in America: With Notices of the State and Prospects of American Unitarianism, Popery, and African Colonization* (London: Thomas Ward, 1840), p. 465.
48 William Charles Wentworth, *A Statistical, Historical, and Political Description of the Colony of New South Wales* (London: G. and W.B. Whittaker, 1819), pp. 60–5.
49 Ibid., pp. 86–7.

immediately accessible to Sydney and Hobart than it was to the United States' own eastern ports. Up to 11,000 Australians had made the journey across the Pacific to the Californian goldfields by the end of the 1850s.[50]

This transpacific circuit brought an intensification of exchange, especially in the domain of popular culture. Folk songs and ballads, sheet music, pamphlets, newspapers and periodicals, photographs and engravings began to circulate widely between California and the eastern Australian colonies, and there was a marked increase in the number of touring American musical, theatrical and circus troupes. US companies regarded the voyage out to Sydney and Melbourne as another leg of their West Coast tour, often taking in Honolulu on the outward or return journey.[51] The famous American actors Edwin Booth and Laura Keene toured Australia in 1854, playing both Shakespeare and contemporary plays, often in abbreviated form in the mixed programs that were typical of the era, while the pervasive influence of American vaudeville and minstrel shows in Australia appealed to the colonies' egalitarianism.[52]

The small narrative painting, *Euchre in the Bush* (1867), opens a window onto this prolific exchange of popular visual, literary, musical and stage culture across the Pacific. The painting depicts three men, one British, one Chinese and one Aboriginal, playing cards in a miner's hut on the Victorian goldfields. The artist, Joseph Johnson, explained that 'the incident recalls the lines of American writer Bret Harte's best-known poem, "The Heathen Chinee"', and that 'the three races have been for some time playing a game for life on this continent. The Aboriginal race have very nearly played their last card.'[53] Through their circulation of racial stereotypes – the Chinese, the Irishman, the Negro, the Aborigine, the Māori – these forms of vernacular imagery helped, as Giles observes, 'to consolidate an infrastructure of racial prejudice in Australia, at the same time as opening up the country more generally to the dynamics of liberal individualism'.[54]

As two signature projects of the period demonstrate, the transpacific imaginary continued to have a profound influence on Australian literary and visual culture during the period of mounting nationalist sentiment

---

50 Erika Esau, *Images of the Pacific Rim: Australia and California, 1850–1935* (Sydney: Power Publications, 2010), p. 22; Giles, *Transpacific Republicanism*, p. 5.

51 E. Daniel and Annette Potts, *Young America and Australian Gold: Americans and the Gold Rush of the 1850s* (Brisbane: UQP, 1974).

52 Richard Waterhouse, *From Minstrel Show to Vaudeville: The Australian Popular Stage 1788–1914* (Sydney: UNSW Press, 1990), p. 6.

53 Quoted in Esau, *Images of the Pacific Rim*, p. 71.

54 Giles, *Transpacific Republicanism*, p. 9.

between the centenary of European settlement in 1888 and Federation in 1901. The first was the multi-volume *Picturesque Atlas of Australasia* (1886–88), designed to mark the centenary by the publication of engravings and letter-press description made to the highest standards.[55] This meant assembling a large complement of artists, engravers and printers, most of them from the United States. Founded in Sydney in 1886, the Picturesque Atlas Publishing Company imported three of the finest presses and recruited the leading American illustrators Fredric B. Schell, William T. Smedley and William C. Fitler, who had worked on *Picturesque Canada*. Together they produced the illustrations for the Australian publication, Schell creating the majority of the full-page engraved plates of landscapes and urban scenes. While the artists were American, their visual styles often drew on modern European fashions, including impressionism and *trompe l'oeil* devices. The virtuosic exercises in graphic design assured readers that Australia now possessed printing and artistic capacities on a par with anything coming out of London, New York or even Paris.[56]

The second project was the establishment in 1880 of the 'vicious and electrifying' magazine, the Sydney *Bulletin*.[57] While its founding editor, J.F. Archibald, campaigned for Australian nationalism, he was himself a noted bohemian and Francophile, who changed his Christian names from John Feltham to Jules François, and published contemporary European writing alongside the new generation of Australian writers that the *Bulletin* championed, including Henry Lawson, A.B. ('Banjo') Paterson and Joseph Furphy. The *Bulletin* sought to emulate the work of US publishers and their illustrators, and during the 1880s Archibald and William Traill (who had acquired control of the *Bulletin* in 1892) and William MacLeod travelled to the United States to recruit graphic artists. In 1883 the American artist Livingston Hopkins ('Hop') joined the *Bulletin* staff; he would go on to develop the famous 'little boy from Manly', who became an iconic representation of the young Australian nation as the *Bulletin* envisioned it. Ironically, then, while the *Bulletin* was in certain respects the epitome of the new literary nationalism, it remained at heart a cosmopolitan and even transpacific enterprise.

---

55 See Tony Hughes-D'Aeth, *Paper Nation: The Story of the Picturesque Atlas of Australasia 1886–1888* (Melbourne University Press, 2001).
56 Esau, *Images of the Pacific Rim*, pp. 123–4.
57 Sylvia Lawson, *The Archibald Paradox: A Strange Case of Authorship* (Melbourne: Allen Lane, 1983), p. ix.

Novels, newspapers and theatre

While newspapers and periodicals provided essential work for artists and illustrators, the same was true for writers, especially aspiring novelists. During the 1870s and 1880s, serialisation of fiction in newspapers was one of the major outlets, leading the Melbourne journalist and critic James Smith in 1878 to speak of the 'Grub-street condition' of local literature.[58] Some novels about Australian life were written by British visitors and published in London, such as Henry Kingsley's *The Recollections of Geoffrey Hamlyn* (1859). Some colonial writers went to live in Europe and were published in London, including Rosa Praed, 'Tasma' (the pen name of Jessie Couvreur) and Fergus Hume, who achieved international success with a crime novel set in Melbourne. Those who worked in Australia found overseas publication difficult to achieve, and the local facilities for book publishing were limited. Ada Cambridge's novel about the Melbourne Centennial Exhibition of 1888, *A Woman's Friendship*, was serialised in the *Age* in weekly instalments between August and October 1889, but remained unpublished in book form until 1988. By the 1890s, however, this 'Grub-street' phase had largely passed and Australian writers increasingly found publication in London and New York: Marcus Clarke's *For the Term of His Natural Life*, first serialised in the *Australian Journal* in 1870–72 as *His Natural Life*, was published by George Robertson in Melbourne 1874 and by Bentley in London in 1875; Rolf Boldrewood's *Robbery Under Arms*, serialised in the *Sydney Mail* in 1882–83, was published by Remington in 1888 and again by Macmillan in 1889; and Cambridge's 'A Black Sheep', serialised in the *Age*, was published by Heinemann as *A Marked Man* in 1890. One consequence of this scarcity of colonial novels in book form for much of the nineteenth century is that none was held in private libraries prior to 1850, and it was not until their republication in cheap one-volume 'colonial editions' in the late 1880s and early 1890s that even these famous titles became widely available to Australian readers.[59]

Although there were attempts to establish theatre in Australia from the early 1790s,[60] commercial theatre really began in April 1832, when Governor

---

58 Elizabeth Morrison (ed.), 'Introduction', Ada Cambridge, *A Woman's Friendship* (Sydney: UNSW Press, 1988), p. xvi.

59 Paul Eggert, 'Australian Classics and the Price of Books: The Puzzle of the 1890s', *Journal of the Association for the Study of Australian Literature* (special issue 2008: *The Colonial Present*): 130–57; Graeme Johanson, *A Study of Colonial Editions in Australia 1843–1972* (Wellington: Elibank Press, 2000).

60 See Robert Jordan, *The Convict Theatres of Early Australia 1788–1840* (Sydney: Currency House, 2002).

Richard Bourke granted a licence to Sydney merchant and hotelier Barnett Levy, who opened his purpose-built Theatre Royal in October 1833. For the next hundred years, until the talkies in the late 1920s, live commercial theatre was the major public entertainment industry in Australia.[61] The most successful productions on the nineteenth-century Australian stage were London plays, plus a significant number from the United States.[62] It was typical of dispersed societies in a modernising world that theatre audiences had cosmopolitan tastes: they wanted and expected 'the best'.[63] Before 1900 the 'overtly Australian play' was not central to the repertoire of any troupe, with the exception of 'second-ranking' companies such as the one led by the actor and playwright George Darrell, and even then at least 75 per cent of their repertoire was made up of overseas plays, mostly from London.[64] For this reason, genuinely Australian-written plays representing aspects of Australian life were seldom performed, and when they were they had relatively short runs. Henry Melville's *The Bushrangers; or, Norwood Vale* (1834), for example, had only three performances, James R. McLaughlin's *Arabin; or, The Adventures of a Settler* (1849) and Richard Henry Horne's *The South-Sea Sisters: A Lyric Masque* (1866) had only one performance each, while *Life in Sydney; or, The Ran Dan Club* (1843) by 'A.B.C.', was banned and never performed.[65] The one exception to this general pattern was the company of actor and manager Alfred Dampier, which staged the work of a succession of local playwrights between 1877 and 1903, including adaptations of Boldrewood's *Robbery Under Arms* and Clarke's *For the Term of His Natural Life*.

Bohemia and cosmopolitanism

The sense of belonging to the transnational culture of colonial modernity was perhaps most strongly felt by those associated with the colonial theatre and popular stage, but it was shared by the urban cultural elites.[66] The writer whose career best epitomises this culture of transnational belonging was the Melbourne critic, journalist, playwright and novelist, Marcus Clarke.

61 Richard Fotheringham (ed.), *Australian Plays for the Colonial Stage: 1834–1899* (Brisbane: UQP, 2006), p. xxiii.
62 Ibid., p. lv.
63 Jack Poggi, *Theater in America: The Impact of Economic Forces, 1870–1967* (Ithaca: Cornell University Press, 1968), pp. 87–8.
64 Fotheringham, *Australian Plays for the Colonial Stage*, pp. xl–xli.
65 Ibid., p. lvi.
66 Robert Dixon and Veronica Kelly (eds), *Impact of the Modern: Vernacular Modernities in Australia, 1870s to 1960s* (Sydney University Press, 2009); Veronica Kelly, *The Empire Actors: Stars of Australasian Costume Drama 1890s–1920s* (Sydney: Currency House, 2010).

Instead of longing for a lost sense of Englishness or rehearsing forms of 'Australianness' that had not yet come into being, he embraced the kinds of experiences thrown up by settler colonialism, notably 'cosmopolitanism, dislocation, itinerancy, and vagabondage'.[67]

Clarke recorded the experiences of migrants who shared his sense of dislocation, for at the age of seventeen he was sent to Australia by an uncle after the death of his father. His 1877 essay, 'The Future Australian Race', focused on the role of modern transport in bringing together disparate peoples within the settler colony

> The tendency of that abolition of boundaries which men call civilisation is to destroy individuality. The more railways, ships, wars, and international gatherings we have, the easier is it for men to change skies, to change food, to intermarry, to beget children from strange loins. The 'type' – that is to say, the incarnated result of food, education, and climate, is lost.[68]

Clarke's short story 'Grumbler's Gully' (1873) depicted the goldfields population as lacking either a shared cultural tradition or an investment in nationhood. The people of Grumbler's Gully play the 'latest music', read the 'latest novels' and take a keen interest in all that is new from Europe, and yet

> [a]midst all this, there is no nationality. The Frenchman, German and Englishman all talk confidently about 'going home', and if by chance some old man with married daughters thinks he will die in the colony, he never by any chance expressed a wish to leave his bones in the horribly utilitarian cemetery at Grumbler's Gully.[69]

In addition to the goldfields, Clarke offered the urban space of the colonial city, and especially its Upper and Lower Bohemias, as an epitome of the dislocations of colonialism. Clarke's Melbourne is a dream-like space that imagines itself to be London or Paris, yet this only reveals 'the colonial dilemma': 'the colony reproduces the metropolis, but in the urgency of its desire to do so, it also reveals its own distance from it'.[70]

Australian artists placed the colonial viewing public in a similar proximity to the visual culture of Britain and Europe, uniting them in an appreciation for new developments in the world of art. Bohemia was alive and well in

---

67 McCann, *Marcus Clarke's Bohemia*, p. 7.
68 Marcus Clarke, 'The Future Australian Race' (1877), quoted in McCann, *Marcus Clarke's Bohemia*, p. 1.
69 Marcus Clarke, 'Grumbler's Gully', in *Holiday Peak and Other Tales* (Melbourne: George Robertson, 1873), quoted in McCann, *Marcus Clarke's Bohemia*, pp. 7–8.
70 Ibid., p. 12.

the studios of what was soon to become the nation's cultural capital. Artists, musicians and academics at the University of Melbourne formed a lively enclave that pushed the boundaries of respectability among the city's elite. Bohemia excluded women and involved rowdy nights of drinking in men's-only establishments, and painting camps in the bayside suburbs and the bush. The leaders of Melbourne's artistic bohemia, the Heidelberg artists Tom Roberts, Charles Conder and Arthur Streeton, were joined by Walter Baldwin Spencer, professor of biology at the University of Melbourne, Louis Marshall-Hall, professor of music, and the parliamentarian and educationist, Theodore Fink. Roberts, who was nicknamed 'Bulldog' for his advocacy of Darwin (following Huxley's reputation as Darwin's bulldog), cut a dash around Melbourne in his black and red cape.[71]

These connections between artists and academics were manifested through their commercial as well as social interactions. Baldwin Spencer was one of the first serious collectors of Australian art, purchasing many paintings by Heidelberg School artists over a period of 40 years. When financial problems forced him to sell his collection in 1918, there were 167 pictures by Australian artists listed in a catalogue of 313 works. Spencer was also a noted feminist, surrounding himself with talented female staff at the University of Melbourne and designing his own Christmas cards showing, in irreverent fashion, the three wise men as three wise women. His work on Indigenous people, such as *The Native Tribes of Central Australia* (1899), co-written with F.J. Gillen, remain ground-breaking anthropology. He was among the first to make film and sound recordings of the people of the Western Desert and Cape York.[72]

Streeton, Roberts and Conder had all trained or worked in London and Paris during the decades of the *belle époque*. In their youth, they aligned themselves with impressionist practice in their famous 9 x 5 exhibition (1889), declaring their sympathy with the new French painting. The catalogue of the 9 x 5 Impressions Exhibition quoted Gérôme: 'When you draw, form is the important thing; but in painting the *first* thing to look for is the *general impression* of colour'. Taking up the impressionist dictum they wrote: 'An effect is only momentary...Two half hours are never alike.' Predictably, the exhibition caused a furor among the critics, with James Smith calling it 'a pain to

---

71 Humphrey McQueen, *Tom Roberts* (Sydney: Macmillan, 1996).
72 John Mulvaney, 'Baldwin Spencer: Evolution and Melbourne University', in Jeanette Hoorn (ed.), *Reframing Darwin: Evolution and Art in Australia* (Melbourne: Miegunyah Press, 2009), pp. 80–95.

the eye'.[73] The work shown consisted of small oil sketches of mainly urban subject matter depicting intimate landscapes, figure studies and genre pieces that annoyed most of the public (62 were painted on cigar-box lids) and did not pay the rent. The artists' bread and butter lay in portraiture and large academic paintings.

During the later nineteenth century pastoral painting emerged as a national art. Located within one of the world's centres of pastoral capitalism, Tom Roberts' *Shearing the Rams*, in which splendid young white men divest sheep of their fleece, was heralded as emblematic of Australian national identity. Australian art historians called *Shearing the Rams* a pastoral painting, although it was dominated by an image of labour. At the same time landscapes similar in style to the *en plein air* painting appeared, in which *flânerie* made a strong showing. Two distinctive types of pastoral art emerged, one about the work of colonial life and the other about leisure, but all celebrated the ownership of the land by Europeans.

Correspondence between artists reveals a vigorous homosocial culture among the artistic communities of Melbourne and Sydney in the late nine-teenth century. Some of the most loved landscapes of the Heidelberg School, such as Tom Roberts' *The Sunny South*, are Arcadian spaces in which men enjoy their own company in the outdoors. Cosmopolitan references abound in late nineteenth-century Australian painting. The title *The Sunny South* was itself a reference to the Arcadian experiences of Britons in Italy. Streeton's lauded portrait of the Hawkesbury, *The Purple Noon's Transparent Might* (1896) takes its title from Shelley's 'Stanzas Written in Dejection near Naples': 'The sun is warm, the sky is clear, the waves are dancing fast and bright blue isles and snowy mountains wear/ The purple noon's transparent might'.[74] The title of Streeton's famous early study of the Yarra River, the painting that established his reputation as an important artist and his first to enter a public collection, *Still Glides the Stream and Shall Forever Glide* (1890), comes from Wordsworth's *Sonnets to The River Duddon*: 'Still glides the stream and shall forever glide, the form remains, the function never dies'.[75] Transpacific imaginary was also strong in Australian visual culture, pointing to a close relationship between the imagery contained in the popular illustrated press

---

73 'Thomas Roberts', *Australian Dictionary of Biography*, vol. 11, pp. 409–12.

74 See the discussion in 'Picture and Verse: Europe's Endowment in the Landscape', in Hoorn, *Australian Pastoral*, pp. 183–94.

75 William Wordsworth, 'The River Duddon', in T. Hutchinson (ed.), *Wordsworth: Poetical Works* (Oxford University Press, 1974), pp. 296–301.

of American magazines and those of many paintings.[76] Cosmopolitanism ruled as artists interpreted local subject matter through a range of influences, themselves contributing to the international culture of which they were a part in national and international exhibitions appearing the world over.

In literature, the end of the century marked the decline of a transnationally dispersed, pre-national culture, and the beginning of the modern sense of Australian literature: that is, as a national literature, an expression of the national character or way of life of a people developed through the shared experience of place; as exclusively the 'higher' genres of poetry, the novel and drama; and as an organic tradition of canonical books and authors. This is evident in Melbourne critic Arthur Patchett Martin's *The Beginnings of an Australian Literature* (1898). Martin noted that his survey would be 'in no sense exhaustive', since it would exclude some of 'the more serious and philosophical writers, such as the late Dr Hearn and Professor Pearson'. Charles H. Pearson was the author of *National Life and Character* (1893), an internationally influential study of race and immigration, especially in the United States, and just the kind of work that might once have been considered 'literature'. Instead, Martin promised to deal 'merely with the *belles-lettres*', by which he now meant 'prose-writers and verse-men'.[77] This is the modern sense of literature as it would be understood in the new century, with the emergence of isomorphic connections between literature, land and nation that would come to define the cultural nationalist account: 'When I use the phrase "Australian literature", I mean the works of those few writers who reflect the life, describe the scenery, and reveal the social conditions of Australia'.[78] And finally, Martin's criticism is evaluative and canon forming in the sense that he aspired to name the best works of this new national literature. They were, in the novel, Clarke's *For the Term of His Natural Life*, Kingsley's *The Recollections of Geoffrey Hamlyn*, Boldrewood's *Robbery Under Arms* and, surprisingly perhaps in light of arguments about the marginalisation of previously successful women writers at this time,[79] Rosa Praed's *Policy and Passion*. Martin considered her 'a much more artistic novelist' than Boldrewood, who 'is not by any means a great or original writer, nor is he in any sense a profound or subtle artist in words'.[80] In verse, Martin included Adam Lindsay Gordon's *Bush*

---

76 Leigh Astbury, *City Bushmen: The Heidelberg School and the Rural Mythology* (Oxford University Press, 1985).

77 A. Patchett Martin, *The Beginnings of an Australian Literature* [1898] (Canberra: Mulini Press, 1998), pp. 7–8.

78 Ibid., p. 11.

79 Eggert, 'Australian Classics and the Price of Books'.

80 Martin, *The Beginnings of an Australian Literature*, p. 27.

Ballads and Galloping Rhymes and Banjo Paterson's *The Man from Snow River and Other Verses*.

In Martin's work, therefore, we witness not only 'the beginnings' of Australian literature as a now familiar corpus of canonical texts, but also as a disciplinary formation – as a way of constructing the modern idea of a national literature that would come to prevail throughout the twentieth century and whose naturalness we are only now beginning to question. The appearance of an equivalent account of Australian art had to wait for another 35 years, with William Moore's two-volume history, *The Story of Australian Art*, appearing in 1934.

21

Empire: Australia and 'Greater Britain', 1788–1901

DERYCK M. SCHREUDER

In the Cambridge autumn of 1881, the Regius Professor of History, Sir John Seeley, began a two-part series of lectures to undergraduates on 'The Expansion of England', a topic very different from his usual religious and constitutional themes. Seeley's intention was partly to chide his fellow English historians for not paying sufficient attention to the history of Empire: hence his famous, ironic epigram about the Empire having apparently been acquired 'in a fit of absence of mind'. But more especially he wanted to make a startling assertion about imperial Britain as a state: 'our Empire is not an empire at all in the ordinary sense of the word', as he put it. 'It does not consist of a congress of nations held together by force, but in the main is one nation, as if it were no empire but an ordinary state.'[1] That 'Empire' had increasingly come to mean the settler empire, created through a diaspora of British migrants to major regions like Australasia. It was essentially an 'intimate and momentous union'. Before globalisation, here was a new style of transnational polity: 'I mean the simple fact of the extension of the English name into then other countries of the globe, the foundation of Greater Britain'. In such power lay the future of Britain.

This chapter is about Greater Britain and Australian colonisation, and its standpoint is accordingly global. It is no longer possible to write the history of 'Britain and Australia' as a singular, dialectical relationship, separate from the wider world of modern history. Colonial Australia was the product of several interrelated 'revolutions' – beginning with the geopolitical changes that defined the Western world in the later eighteenth century, together with the American and French revolutions, then extending to transformations brought about by European industrialisation and its effects on international

---

1 J.R. Seeley, *The Expansion of England* [1883] (University of Chicago Press, 1971), pp. 12–13, 38, 44. See also, Bernard Porter, *The Absent-Minded Imperialists* (Oxford University Press, 2004), pp. 9–10; Stefan Collini, *Absent Minds: Intellectuals in Britain* (Oxford University Press, 2006), pp. 70–1.

politics in the following century. A mass migration of Britons ultimately underpinned an 'Anglo-settler revolution', which formed a 'Greater Britain' based on history and ethnicity.[2]

British 'empires' in history

The global phenomenon of the British Empire evolved without a unifying concept – other than that of the crown. It is important to locate Australian colonisation within that pantheon of expansion. There were, in truth, many 'British empires' created through oceanic projections over the *longue durée*.[3] It had grown organically through the centuries – invasions of Ireland, plantations in the Caribbean, convicts and migrants to the thirteen colonies, a vast royal-chartered company in South Asia – together with encrustations of quirky individual initiatives on the coastlines and islands of Africa and the Pacific.

The invasion of Botany Bay in 1788, on the east coast of a landmass later named 'Australia' by Matthew Flinders, admirably captured the manner in which motives and agencies could intermingle. Social policy pressed the case for convict transportation and the utility of a new penal settlement within the British regime of law and order at a time of social disturbance and revolutionary fears at home. Having failed to find appropriate localities in North America and Africa, attention had turned to coastal lands mapped recently by James Cook. Geopolitical imperatives were to be potentially even more important in this bold oceanic gesture. As a global power facing a new world order, the British government was drawn to the idea that a settlement at Sydney Cove could be a master key to open the South Pacific to imperial trade and also to navalism. The presence of the East India Company in South Asia gestured towards further exploitation through a beachhead on the Pacific Rim. And it might even be a vital pre-emptive action against a growing French presence in the South Pacific and the Indies. While historians still remain divided over the exact intentions of the British cabinet, we can say that the architects of Botany Bay were statesmen of geopolitics. Australian colonisation began not least as a bold strategic statement in the South Pacific.[4]

2 James Belich, *Replenishing the Earth: The Settler Revolution and the Rise of the Anglo-World, 1783–1939* (Oxford University Press, 2009). See also Stephen Howe (ed.), *The New Imperial Histories Reader* (London: Routledge, 2010); Sarah Stockwell (ed.), *The British Empire: Themes and Perspectives* (Oxford: Blackwell, 2008); Antoinette Burton, *Empire in Question: Reading, Writing, and Teaching British Imperialism* (Durham: Duke University Press, 2011).
3 John Darwin, 'Britain's Empires', in Stockwell (ed.), *The British Empire*, pp. 1–20.
4 Alan Frost, *Convicts and Empire: A Naval Question, 1776–1811* (Oxford University Press, 1980) and *Botany Bay: The Real Story* (Melbourne: Black Inc., 2011); Alan Atkinson, *The Europeans in Australia: A History. Volume 1, The Beginning* (Oxford University Press, 1997).

The unification of the British Isles – integrating the Celtic regions through the *Act of Union with Scotland* (1707) and the more unilateral *Act of Union with Ireland* (1800) – had developed the concept of 'Britons', and confirmed a national capacity for extra-territorial outreach beyond Europe.[5] The British state rose in power with the other European seaborne empires by asserting power through the *Declaratory Act* of 1766, the *India Act* of 1784 and the *Canada Act* of 1791. The concentration on the North Atlantic economies and societies was soon to be diversified as the British redrew their strategic world maps to encompass the Indian Ocean environments, and then looked further to the east – Australasia and the South Pacific. An older concentration on the singular First Fleet to Botany Bay is better seen as but one of the several naval flotillas that reflected a growing British presence in Asia and the Pacific.[6]

Having lost hold of their transatlantic American colonies, the British soon gained new possessions in the Caribbean and the East at the expense of the French, Dutch, Spanish, Portuguese and Russian overseas empires, while also projecting a new-style, colonial Pacific empire in Australasia (from 1788), and an Indian Ocean presence in southern Africa (from 1814). After the American rebellion (and the loss of the famed thirteen colonies), the British state continued to administer some 26 of its original overseas colonies; while by 1816 that colonial system had grown to 43 overseas formal possessions, including the key territories of New South Wales and Van Diemen's Land. Not only was there to be significant territorial expansion under free trade, but there soon existed British 'spheres of interest' in resource-rich Latin America, in Singapore and through unequal treaties of access to the China trade – not least through the Treaty of Nanking (1842), which delivered the prize of Hong Kong to the empire of the South Pacific. The Australasian colonial project was complementary to these new oceanic outreaches.

'The imperialism of free trade'

Much of this British 'world system' reflected 'soft power', rather than occupation or regime change. Yet 'soft power' was still power. 'The formal empire of rule was but part of the informal empire of trade and influence', as Robinson and Gallagher once famously argued, 'commercially speaking, colonies were the lesser part of the iceberg visible above the water line'.

5 Linda Colley, *Britons: Forging the Nation, 1707–1837* (New Haven: Yale University Press, 1992).
6 Peter J. Marshall, *The Making and Unmaking of Empires: Britain, India, and America c. 1750–1783* (Oxford University Press, 2005).

Here was the embryonic core of their exposition of 'The Imperialism of Free Trade' (1953).[7]

'Formal Empire' became geopolitically necessary when informal methods failed to meet the challenges of changing global conditions. Viscount Palmerston, the representative mid-Victorian prime minister, had long made plain that the primary role of the state itself was to ensure an 'open door' for British free trade and investment. There was also a special place within the empire of free trade for the settler empire. Indeed, in the pointed language of Robinson and Gallagher 'policy makers felt sure that their self-governing colonials, bound with the silken cords of kindred, tradition and self-interest, would continue to be their most loyal and energetic partners in spreading British influence and multiplying British commerce'. Colonies such as those in Australia had 'the supreme virtue of being self-propelling'. It was to prove both good and bad that 'the impetus to expansion was soon coming, not so much from the Metropolis as from the colonial communities themselves'.[8] Empire happened from Sydney and Melbourne, along with London and Liverpool. In the recent analysis of James Belich, Australian colonisation became central to that 'remarkable explosion of the nineteenth century that put the Anglophones on top of the world'.[9]

Empire also begat local empire. Having established British power on the east coast of the Australian mainland, for example, a Pacific 'sub-imperialism' emerged, involving both imperial power and Australian colonial governments.[10] Norfolk Island was momentarily critical to British naval ship-building. Pitcairn Island was seized by mutineers from the *Bounty* in 1790 and ultimately came under the crown. New Zealand itself was proclaimed British from the cantilever of the Australian presence in 1840. Entanglement with the Malaysian polities led to the Straits Settlement, in the form of a crown colony (1867) – later converted, as the Federated Malay States (Perak, Selangor, Negri, Sembilan and Pahang), into a British protectorate. Fiji was importantly added to the Empire as a crown colony in 1874 through the agency of the New South Wales governor (Sir Hercules Robinson), who acted as its first administrator. New Guinea was ultimately partitioned with the German empire; the Gilbert and Ellice Islands became British in 1886, shortly

---

7 J.A. Gallagher and R.E. Robinson, 'The Imperialism of Free Trade', *Economic History Review*, 6, 1 (1953): 1–15; R.E. Robinson and J.A. Gallagher, with Alice Denny, *Africa and the Victorians: The Official Mind of Imperialism* (London: Macmillan, 1961).

8 Robinson and Gallagher, *Africa and the Victorians*, p. 9.

9 Belich, *Replenishing the Earth*, pp. 4, 358.

10 Roger C. Thompson, *Australian Imperialism in the Pacific: The Expansionist Era, 1820–1920* (Melbourne University Press, 1980).

before an Anglo-French condominium was created over the New Hebrides, followed by British protectorates in North Borneo, Sarawak, Brunei and the Cook Islands (1888). British New Guinea became a crown colony the same year, to the exasperated relief of anxious Australian colonial leaders.

However, a dramatic attempt by the Queensland government to annex New Guinea territory in 1883, without express British permission, was disallowed.[11] The Second Berlin Conference of 1889 ultimately fixed European imperial claims in the South Pacific (the first had largely 'partitioned' Africa in 1885). But tensions continued as the British aimed for a greater Empire with smaller fiscal outlay, while the colonists welcomed a bigger imperial presence with minimal Australian costs. The colonies also wanted protected commerce under the British flag. Trading companies such as Burns Philp were eager to exploit the Pacific island resources.[12] Colonial commercial interests looked to their own version of an Australasian 'Anglo Monroe Doctrine' in what they saw as 'their region'.[13]

Anatomy of an imperial 'system'

This imperial system – of which the settler dimension was so distinctive – was indeed unlike any other.[14] There was no grand design. Here was an empire in 'total want of any permanent binding force, or rational system', according to no less than the British imperial supremo, Alfred Lord Milner.[15] But certain expansive elements now stand out.[16] A functional rationale had even evolved: 'by the late nineteenth century, this "project of an empire" (in Adam Smith's phrase) had become a world system. Its component parts assumed increasingly specialised roles. They fitted together in ways that maximised British

11 The Earl of Derby wondered whether they would annex the stars if they could. See Stuart Ward, 'Security: Defending Australia's Empire', in Deryck M. Schreuder and Stuart Ward (eds), *Australia's Empire* (Oxford University Press, 2008), pp. 237–8.

12 Stuart Macintyre, *The Oxford History of Australia. Volume 4, 1901–1942: The Succeeding Age* (Oxford University Press, 1986), pp. 138–9.

13 K. Buckley and K. Klugman, *The Australian Presence in the Pacific: Burns Philp, 1914–46* (Sydney: George Allen & Unwin, 1983); Macintyre, *The Oxford History of Australia*, vol. 4, p. 178.

14 C.A. Bayly, *The Birth of the Modern World, 1780–1914: Global Connections and Comparisons* (Oxford: Blackwell, 2004); John Darwin, *After Tamerlane: The Global History of Empire Since 1405* (London: Allen Lane, 2010).

15 Milner quoted in Peter Burroughs, 'Imperial Institutions and the Government of Empire', in Andrew Porter (ed.), *The Oxford History of the British Empire. Volume 3, The Nineteenth Century* (Oxford University Press, 1999), p. 171.

16 G.S.R. Clark, *An Expanding Society: Britain 1830–1900* (Melbourne University Press, 1967).

power in the world'.[17] Australian colonisation had a very special place within that project.[18] Ideology was also significant. Pressure mounted on older forms of government. If slavery was increasingly seen as an affront to the new sensibilities in an evangelical Age of Atonement, so now mercantilist tariffs were seen to hold back the fructifying powers of new commerce.[19] The Corn Laws became the symbol of transformation. Mercantalism was soon to be dismantled, product by product: 'l'exclusif was dead'.[20] A deluge of legislative reform ultimately created free trading internationalism.[21]

The traction for 'take off' in the 'empire project' was energised by global migration, trade and investments, which much benefitted the settlement empire. A mass of British individuals looked out in hope towards the New World. An expanding kingdom of little over 10 million people at 1815, rising to 37 million at 1900, ultimately saw some 20 million of its citizens migrate to 'Anglo-worlds' by 1900.[22] Indeed, between the end of the Napoleonic wars and the Great War, the Australasian colonies received no fewer than 2,359,961 Britons – being 10.7 per cent of all migrants from the British Isles, out of a grand total of 7,334,827 who settled in the Empire at large.[23] (The United States alone received a larger number – 13,714,007, or 62 per cent of all Anglo-migrants.[24]) The state was moved to intervene in regulating the safety of the migrant movement through the 'Passenger Acts' that scholars see as emblematic of government growth within a laissez-faire state.[25]

Australia was an exemplar of the total process. Slave labour was gone, but the British state still enjoyed a capacity for moving free and 'unfree'

17 John Darwin, The Empire Project: The Rise and Fall of the British World System, 1830–1970 (Cambridge University Press, 2009), p. 25.

18 E.J. Hobsbawm, Industry and Empire: An Economic History of Britain Since 1750 (London: Weidenfeld & Nicolson, 1968), p. 107.

19 Boyd Hilton, The Age of Atonement: The Influence of Evangelicalism on Social and Economic Thought, 1785–1865 (Oxford University Press, 1988).

20 D.K. Fieldhouse, The Colonial Empires: A Comparative Survey from the Eighteenth Century (London: Weidenfeld & Nicolson, 1966), p. 248.

21 K. Theodore Hoppen, The Mid-Victorian Generation, 1846–1886 (Oxford University Press, 1998), pp. 127–41. See also Boyd Hilton, A Mad, Bad and Dangerous People? England 1783–1846 (Oxford University Press, 2006).

22 Eric Richards, Britannia's Children: Emigration from England, Scotland, Wales and Ireland since 1600 (London: Hambledon and London, 2004).

23 Gary B. Magee and Andrew S. Thompson, Empire and Globalisation: Networks of People, Goods and Capital in the British World, c 1850–1940 (Cambridge University Press, 2010), table 3.1, p. 69.

24 Andrew Porter, 'The Empire and the World', in Colin Matthew (ed.), The Nineteenth Century: The British Isles, 1815–1901 (Oxford University Press, 2000), p. 137.

25 Oliver MacDonagh, A Pattern of Government Growth, 1800–60: The Passenger Acts and Their Enforcement (London: MacGibbon and Kee, 1961).

labour around the globe. Chinese people came early to Australia (especially in commerce and mining), while Pacific Islanders came later to work in rural industries. Above all, Australian colonisation itself was underpinned by an extraordinary act of human capital transfer in the form of penal transportation. Paid for by the imperial government, this process of convict 'settlement' formed a major labour and resource base for making a new society. Beyond the journey of the famed First Fleet some 150,000 convicts ultimately came to New South Wales, Van Diemen's Land and Western Australia. Remarkably, the process was only ended in 1867 with the last penal ships sent to Western Australia. The migration of free settlers was supported by individuals, with the support of charities and direct state subsidies (British and colonial). Some of it also relied on funds remitted from the overseas migrant communities themselves – nearly £200 million between 1873 and the Great War, with some 30 per cent from the Empire itself; Australian migration provided a substantial £8.6 million between 1870 and 1913.[26]

Matching the migrant diaspora was the great nineteenth-century movement of British capital: £50 million in 1815, rising to over £1 billion in 1914. A stunning 46 per cent of that outflow ultimately stayed within the Empire, and was deployed to a variety of British possessions – with a preponderance (26.9 per cent) to the economically progressive settler societies. Cain and Hopkins reckon that by the end of the century three times as many exports also went to the settler colonies as to the remainder of the Empire.[27] Australia alone received a quarter of all British manufactured exports in the last decades of the century, while 70 per cent of Australian imports came from Great Britain and 80 per cent of its exports were directed at the British Isles. The tilt towards the settlement Empire was equally as marked in British imports. In the mid-Victorian period some 32.2 per cent came from the colonies (with 5.2 per cent from Australasia); by the Edwardian years that figure had risen to a striking 54.6 percent (with Australasia contributing 32.6 per cent).[28] The British were well on their way to becoming the first global society in history.

26 Magee and Thompson, *Empire and Globalisation*, pp. 97–105, esp. table 3.3.

27 Peter J. Cain and Anthony G. Hopkins, *British Imperialism, 1688–2000*, 2nd edn (London: Longman, 2001), pp. 151–8. See also Magee and Thompson, *Empire and Globalisation*, pp 119–26.

28 W. Schlote, *British Overseas Trade from 1700 to the 1930s* (Oxford University Press, 1952), table 25, pp. 172–3.

The idea of a 'Greater Britain'

Empire as global state was more than a rhetorical flourish.[29] As Seeley himself had shrewdly adjudged, the development of a 'Greater Britain' was an event of enormous historical significance in world affairs.[30] W.E. Gladstone, four-time prime minister, came to perceive his society as 'head servant in the great household of the world'.[31] The future of the British people was also now bound up with their own extra-territoriality. British power had become contingent on a contested global 'geopolitics' – defined recently as not merely 'a defence of a territorial heartland alone, or even exclusively a reaction to international state rivalry', but rather that broader sense of having become 'pre-occupied with borders, resources, flows, territories and identities'.[32] This was especially significant for an empire state on whose problems the sun never set. The Australian colonies may have sat at the edge of Empire but not at the periphery of imperial geopolitical thinking, in which material forces mattered greatly.[33] As Magee and Thompson have shown, 'empire' and 'globalisation' were close cousins.[34] Imperialism was always about forms of power.[35]

The lodestone of the complex story of British globalism was increasingly to be a 'British world', of which Australian settlement was so central. The 'idea' of a Greater Britain had already entered the British mindset well before Seeley's lecture.[36] The young radical British MP, Charles Dilke, could set out in the 1860s on a global tour to explore the British diaspora in a work he indicatively entitled *Greater Britain*. That two-volume travel book was the Victorian bestseller of autumn 1868. Dilke evocatively caught the sense of Australian settlement as a 'New World' in its democratic ethos and politics, its conspicuous prosperity and migrant success, its culture of aspiration and opportunity.

---

29 See Howe (ed.), *The New Imperial Histories Reader*; Stockwell (ed.), *The British Empire*; Burton, *Empire in Question*.
30 On the concept itself, see David Armitage, 'Greater Britain: A Useful Category of Historical Analysis?' *American Historical Review*, 104 (1999): 427–45.
31 W.E. Gladstone, 'Kin Beyond the Sea', *North American Magazine*, 127, 264 (1878): 179–213.
32 Klaus Dodds, *Geopolitics: A Very Short Introduction* (Oxford University Press, 2007), p. 3. See also Ronald Hyam, *Understanding the British Empire* (Cambridge University Press, 2010), pp. 69–154; Darwin, *The Empire Project*, pp. 26–36.
33 J.H. Elliot, 'How They Made the Empire', *New York Review of Books*, 18 August 2011, p. 23.
34 Magee and Thompson, *Empire and Globalisation*, pp. 232–3.
35 Hyam, *Understanding the British Empire*, p. 91.
36 See Duncan Bell, *The Idea of Greater Britain: Empire and the Future of the World Order, 1860–1900* (Princeton University Press, 2007).

He had seen the future and it looked like Australia. Yet it also remained fascinatingly familiar to British eyes: a kind of progressive English provincialism, dominated by emergent middling classes, radical politics and new productive technologies. James Froude repeated much of the same journey a few decades later, and penned *Oceana* in 1885, with its radical call to drop the term 'empire' for the migrant colonies – in favour of 'Commonwealth'. Between the publication of those iconic global travel books, a range of public activists had also begun to address the issue of colonial futures. Ideas of 'empire consolidation', 'empire unity', even 'imperial federation', were now advanced. A young, globe-trotting Lord Rosebery (later British Liberal prime minister) was to flatter Australian audiences in seeing Empire as 'a league of nations', indeed 'a commonwealth of nations'.[37] By 1886 the London *Times* had routinely taken to referring to 'what is now generally called Greater Britain'.[38]

Geopolitics: the coming of a 'new imperialism'

While the nineteenth century is often viewed as the era of 'the long peace' between the end of the Napoleonic wars in 1815 and the Great War in 1914, it is better seen as a long struggle for mastery over the global environment between Great Powers and their empires (Britain, France, Germany); as older polities declined (Spain, Portugal and the Netherlands); and as challenges to ancient monarchies emerged (especially in tsarist Russia and Habsburg Austro-Hungary). There was also the slow collapse of Ottoman rule as part of a smouldering 'Eastern Question', which then threatened European stability, the security of the Mediterranean region, and the sea route to India and the East through the newly built Suez Canal (1869).[39] Australia might have been geographically isolated but the entangling net of geopolitics fell across its polities as the British now vested power in an existing 'Empire' system.[40] Colonies were no longer disparaged as 'millstones' around the neck of the state. From the 1870s British governments indeed evinced a 'new imperialism' – through the Disraelian projection of the British state as essentially

---

37 Nicholas Mansergh, *The Commonwealth Experience* (London: Weidenfeld & Nicolson, 1969) remains important. For recent general histories, see Philippa Levine, *The British Empire: Sunrise to Sunset* (Harlow: Longman Pearson, 2007); Bernard Porter, *The Lion's Share: A Short History of British Imperialism*, 4th edn (Harlow: Longman Pearson, 2004).
38 Quoted in Belich. *Replenishing the Earth*, p. 458.
39 John Clarke, *British Diplomacy and Foreign Policy, 1782–1865: The National Interest* (London: Unwin and Hyman, 1989).
40 John Charmley, *Splendid Isolation? Britain and the Balance of Power, 1875–1914* (London: Sceptre, 1999).

an imperial kingdom and realm. Empire was now celebrated through the *Royal Titles Act* of 1876 – which transformed the monarch into an 'empress of India' – and the major fiscal and strategic commitment to the eastern empire in the purchase of a substantial parcel of Suez Canal shares (no less than 44 per cent of the total).[41]

A spirit of raw expansionism was gathering traction: Anthony Trollope could write about the arrival of an unwelcome 'money imperialism' in *The Way We Live Now*, as early as 1873. J.A. Hobson's famous book, *Imperialism: A Study* (1902), formed a major critique of the dominating doctrine. Political, commercial and patriotic groups also increasingly argued for greater Empire unity – especially through versions of 'imperial federation', aimed at connecting the United Kingdom more closely to a United Empire of British citizens globally, in which Australia was cast as playing a leading role.[42] ('India' was always outside this projection in ethnic nationalism.) The second edition of Dilke's famous book – now significantly retitled *Problems of Greater Britain* (1890) – was devoted to issues of closer unity.

However, the attempt to propagate the panacea of 'imperial federation' divided not only colonists in Australia and elsewhere, but also the imperialists themselves over constitutional structures (what sort of supra-parliament could represent *both* the British Isles and the diversity of the British Empire?). Closer-unity movements within the settlement empire became a mixed blessing: would a federated Australian state not actually rival a 'Federated Greater Britain'? A major reason the several 'Home Rule' bills for Ireland from 1886 proved to be so incendiary was that they also appeared to threaten the integrity of the United Kingdom. The Liberal argument – that Irish Home Rule would merely return to the United Kingdom the proven success of responsible government in the settler colonies like Australia – failed to convince a nervous national populace.

From 1887 the metropolitan state under Tory leadership began to move in the opposite direction. Devolutionary policy was abandoned and the Conservative government looked to consolidate power. This included a greater defence commitment, as well as developing regular Imperial and Defence Conferences with colonial leaders from 1887.[43] Joseph Chamberlain

41 Admirably summarised in Bill Nasson, *Britannia's Empire: Making a British World* (Stroud: Tempus, 2004), p. 131.
42 Andrew S. Thompson, 'The Language of Imperialism and the Meaning of Empire', in Howe, (ed), *The New Imperial Histories Reader*, pp. 306–22.
43 For a succinct account of the Victorian Empire and its challenges, see Porter, 'The Empire and the World', pp. 135–60. See also Andrew S. Thompson, *Imperial Britain: The Empire in British Politics, c. 1880–1932* (Harlow: Longman, 2000).

was to bring the issues of Empire to a dramatic head when he chose to become colonial secretary in the conservative-unionist government (1895–1903), with an avowed imperialist agenda. He was to commit the ultimate apostasy of rejecting a free trading Empire – first in the name of 'fair trade', and then of 'tariff reform'. He advocated a British-style *zollverein* – a closed system of imperial preference at a time of rising international tariff competition. The future, he declared, would be about a contested world of divided resources and territory. Not to assure 'the national interest' through a consolidated Empire was to negate Great Power status.[44] Australia sat squarely within Chamberlain's vision of an interdependent, global imperial state.

Much was now made of the fact that Great Britain's relative share of world production in key commodities was in steady decline: steel stood at 70 per cent in 1850, 40 per cent in 1870 and just on 20 per cent in 1900; coal production began at 80 per cent of world output in 1800, was still at 70 per cent in 1840, but by 1900 it was only some 35 per cent, then 20 per cent in 1911; while the cotton-goods figures were slower to fall (50 per cent in 1830 and remaining at 45 per cent in 1870), they were then suddenly halved, to around 20 per cent by 1900.[45] The modern concept of 'geopolitics' itself first entered international discourse during this era of uncertainty. The geographer Halford Mackinder applied it to the 'condition of England question', with considerable influence and notoriety. He had well caught the growing dual British neuroses – fears over prosperity and class conflict, coupled with the fragility of being a maritime global empire when its rivals in Europe (and the emerging US giant) essentially had the advantage of being consolidated land-base 'empires'. In the analysis of Gerry Kearns' *Geopolitics and Empire*, this hard-edged realpolitik school of thought depicted 'the world structured by geographical realities that Mackinder believed undermined any attempt to build a global order on the basis of legalism and pacifism. Force was unavoidable.'[46]

The new century unsurprisingly found the British at war in South Africa. Over half a million Imperial troops (including 16,000 volunteers in contingents from Australia) were marshalled from across the Empire to fight a

---

44 E.H.H. Green, 'The Political Economy of Empire, 1880–1914', in Porter (ed.), *The Oxford History of the British Empire*, vol. 3, pp. 346–70. See also Travis L. Crosby, *Joseph Chamberlain: A Most Radical Imperialist* (London: I.B. Taurus, 2011).

45 Hobsbawm, *Industry and Empire*, pp. 278–315.

46 Gerry Kearns, *Geopolitics and Empire: The Legacy of Halford Mackinder* (Oxford University Press, 2009), p. 9. See also Ronald Hyam, 'The Primacy of Geopolitics: The Dynamics of British Imperial Policy, 1763–1963', *Journal of Imperial and Commonwealth History*, 27, 2 (1999): 27–52.

protracted guerrilla conflict on the African highveld against a pastoralists' army no larger than the citizenry of Brighton. Ultimately 'methods of barbarism' were involved in victory. Immediately at stake were indeed the British mineral resources and financial investments in South Africa. But more deeply the British 'war aims' were centrally directed at geopolitical issues involving naval guardianship of the sea-lanes to Australia and the East.[47] By 1890 an American admiral, Alfred T. Mahan, had already established the classic doctrine of supreme global sea-power, which he 'lay down as axiomatic for imperial success'.[48]

The crucial Carnarvon Commission (1879–80) had set the benchmark for late-Victorian defence. The Suez Canal was vital from 1869, but it was vulnerable to political and environmental challenges. The southern route – via the Cape – remained critical: 'essential to the retention by Great Britain of her possessions in India, Mauritius, Ceylon, Singapore, China and even Australia'. More trade actually then went via the Cape route (£91 million) than through Suez (£65 million), despite its slightly shorter shipping time.[49] Much of this trade was conducted in improved sailing vessels: steam did not immediately overwhelm the famed clipper ships.

The British merchant marine had expanded with trade and with colonisation as never before in history. The repeal of the *Navigation Acts* in 1849 had opened British ports to non-British shipping and introduced stiff international competition. By the late-nineteenth century Australian harbours were among the busiest in the world (London was first, with Melbourne at eleventh and Sydney fourteenth).[50] Concurrently, the tentacles of copper telegraph cables shrank the oceans and deployed new technologies in linking markets and overseas communities: from 1866 the Atlantic was crossed, followed by deep-ocean cables to India (1870) and, finally, to Africa and Australasia (1872). Technology was starting to shrink space and time. It did more towards creating a 'Greater Britain' than all the imperial Federation propositions.

Military might was also involved, albeit in a way contingent on Empire. By the mid-Victorian period there were 55,000 troops in England and Wales, with a further 25,000 in Ireland. But what allowed the British to be a Great

47 See Darwin, *The Empire Project*, ch. 2.
48 A.P. Thornton, *Doctrines of Imperialism* (London: Wiley, 1965), p. 123; Alfred T. Mahan, *The Influence of Sea Power Upon History, 1660–1783* (London: Sampson Low, 1890).
49 First Report of the Carnarvon Commission, 18 September 1881, The National Archives [TNA], CO 812/38.
50 D.M. Schreuder, 'The Imperial Connection', in Graeme Davison, J.W. McCarty and Ailsa McLeary (eds), *Australians 1888* (Sydney: Fairfax, Syme & Weldon Associates, 1987), p. 416.

Power was its reserve standing army in the Indian Raj: over 200,000 troops, commanded by a British officer corps yet supported by Indian taxes.

With the changing balance of power in Europe itself after 1870, the British began a consolidation of power – the famed 'withdrawal of the garrisons' – but linked this to naval redeployments, and defence agreements with the settlement colonies, such as those in Australasia. The scale of the Royal Navy remained steady at some 154 ships, but between 1875 and 1898 the 'home' fleet was reduced from 52 to fifteen warships, while the Australia 'station' expanded from eleven to sixteen, facilitated by new Anglo-Australian naval agreements. From the 1870s, indeed, the British security agenda included not just strategic security but supplies of key raw materials and foodstuffs from the settlement Empire.

The 'colonial interest' was more narrowly defined. Frontier fears over conflict with Aboriginal clans were as nothing compared with anxiety over rival imperial ambitions, even invasion scares – notably French, Russian and especially Japanese fleets (after its victory over China in 1895). From 1872 the telegraphic cable had given a certain umbilical line of comfort to the mother country. But it was also 22,000 kilometres in length and endangered by earthquakes and omnivorous turtles. Every time the cable broke for any length of time, a degree of fear, even panic emerged. 'Australians, for the moment are as completely cut off from the heart of humanity as if they had been transported to one of the planets', the Melbourne *Age* commented, for example, in June 1888 when the cable broke. In the view of the *Sydney Morning Herald*, 'the risk of isolation that we run at present is very great'. The cable and imperial defence remained critical.[51]

Empire and globalisation

Until the 1870s the British could well feel they had 'history on their side'. They enjoyed forms of relative 'economic hegemony' hitherto unrivalled by any empire.[52] The British share of world production had reached an exceptional 16.6 per cent – with its only rivals being a rising Germany (8.3 per cent) and a late-industrialising France (8.3 per cent). By comparison, the United States only surpassed that figure in the 1970s, while in the 1870s the United States was still an awakening but self-absorbed giant, with Japan's industrialisation

51 Quoted in Schreuder, 'The Imperial Connection', pp. 403–4.
52 See Arvind Subramanian, *Eclipse: Living in the Shadow of China's Economic Dominance* (Washington: Peterson Institute for International Economics, 2011).

on the cusp of major growth.[53] The British had benefitted greatly from what economists today see as the 'gravity model' of growth, with commerce being strongest between nations who combine both greatest productivity and proximity. Britain could obviously exploit Europe and the North Atlantic market economies: by 1900 the British sent 41 per cent of exports to Europe and 10.3 per cent to North America, while Europe provided 42.4 per cent of imports, with 30.9 per cent from North America. But the unequalled British mercantile marine also allowed it to shrink dramatically (if not fully remove) distances in reaching global markets: by 1900 Australia absorbed nearly 10 per cent of British exports and provided 6.8 per cent of its imports.[54] Australia itself received a quarter of all British manufactured exports in the last decades of the century; and within that statistic 70 per cent of Australian imports came from British factories, while over 80 per cent of exports went to the mother country, notably 75 per cent of the wool clip, plus hides and tallow products. Here was the material heart of cultural connection. Since 1882 the Australian colonies had come to absorb an astonishing 25 per cent of all British global capital exports.[55]

Australian ports saw the arrival of more American, French and German vessels, as well as traders from China and Japan, but the overwhelming majority remained British-based. To view their 'cargo manifests' is to witness the unpacking of the British connection itself: here came entire rail systems (engines, rolling stock and iron rails), building materials (roofing, wooden beams and flooring, paint, glass, slate), canned foodstuffs, printed goods, musical instruments, even *objets d'art*. The growth of local production brought a diversification of imports. From the 1880s Australian pastoralists were quick to use the new technologies of cold storage refrigeration and fast steam-shipping to enhance meat exports.

Empire growth indeed demonstrated what economists have identified as 'the magic of diaspora'.[56] The British increasingly did business with systems, communities and cultures that shared modern economic British models – whether in banking and investment, technologies and communications, patents and copyright, professional classes of experts (and their 'Associations'), systems of civil order and civic values in law and public ethics, not to

---

53 *Economist*, 19 November 2011.
54 Schlote, *British Overseas Trade*, pp. 156–7.
55 Geoffrey Bolton, 'Money: Trade, Investment and Economic Nationalism', in Schreuder and Ward (eds), *Australia's Empire*, pp. 211–31; Schreuder, 'The Imperial Connection', pp. 415–19.
56 *Economist*, 19 November 2011.

mention consumption tastes and a desire for betterment, for 'getting on' within free enterprise environments. In short: Anglo people like themselves. In the idiom of Ferguson and Schularick, here was a palpable 'Empire effect' at work.[57] Well before the *Colonial Stock Act* of 1900 regulated the standing of the market, investors had been given a degree of surety through perceptions of 'Britishness' in the business culture of the Australian colonies, reinforced by the flow of financial information about colonial ventures through the new global communication technology. The character of the Australian banking system was also significant. Until the 1850s most banks were British-based financial institutions, and when the local colonial banks emerged they entered a fiscal regulatory environment already set by the British Treasury. Rates of interest on Australian colonial loans in the London financial markets could be more favourable than the cost of money on other international markets.[58] The real danger for Australian colonists was over-borrowing, expenditure on consumables rather than on infrastructure, plus floats of dubious mining portfolios. Those initiatives and choices came from Australians themselves, as individuals and governments. A 'gentlemanly capitalism' has recently been identified in relation to British metropolitan expansionism. It is a theory that needs to be viewed alongside the 'pull factor' of over-eager colonial developers and borrowers.[59]

Bureaucracy, power and colonial democracy

While no single office of state administered or steered such an Empire, the role of the state itself is not to be under-estimated.[60] The imperial domain initially came under ministries of war, trade, foreign relations and treasury, before the surprisingly late (1854) Victorian creation of a separate Colonial Office.[61] With the ending of the East India Company Charter (1857), the Indian Raj had its own minister and ministry. Ireland was also treated separately and was often the subject of political debate. Parliament did not routinely debate

57 Niall Ferguson and M. Schularick, 'The Empire Effect: The Determinants of Country Risk in the First Age of Globalization, 1880–1913', *Journal of Economic History*, 66 (2006): 283–312.
58 See Magee and Thompson, *Empire and Globalisation*, pp. 46–56.
59 Cain and Hopkins, *British Imperialism*, part 2; J.A. Hobson, *Imperialism: A Study* (London: Nisbet, 1902); D.K. Fieldhouse, *Economics and Empire, 1830–1914* (London: Weidenfeld & Nicolson, 1973).
60 Darwin, 'Britain's Empires', p. 20.
61 Henry L. Hall, *The Colonial Office: A History* (London: Longmans, 1937); R.B. Pugh, 'The Colonial Office, 1801–1925', in E.A. Benians et al. (eds), *The Cambridge History of the British Empire, Volume 3* (Cambridge University Press, 1959), pp. 711–68.

'Empire'. Even granting forms of colonial self-rule within the settlement empire – such as the several Australian colonies – were rarely the subject of intense parliamentary scrutiny, debate and divisions. Empire scandals aside, imperial issues only made a substantial entrance onto the national stage in the 1870s, when Disraelian Toryism began to cast state as empire, and when the Gladstonian Liberals set out an alternate vision in the famed Midlothian Campaigns of 1878–9.

For day-to-day oversight of the several British empires, the Secretary of State for the Colonies had considerable delegated powers under the crown. The Colonial Office itself was small in proportion to the vast Empire that it oversaw. But it was not a cipher. The permanent under-secretaries of state were knowledgeable about the complexities of British colonisation, and sometimes held strongly influential views. James Stephen came to be known as 'Mr Over-Secretary' during his long tenure 1836–47, and had an affinity with philanthropic groups that influenced his views on trusteeship and the rights of indigenous subjects; while Sir Robert Herbert took a special interest in the settlement empire, having earlier lived in Australia and been the young premier of the new state of Queensland.[62] There were also specialised 'area desks' within the Colonial Office, where public servants built up a degree of close local knowledge. Australia was sometimes seen more as a geographic expression than a polity; and its six colonial communities were thought to be small, isolated and fragile, belying the colonial radical's notion of 'Happy England Abroad'.[63]

Much of the administration of the Empire was carried out by vice-regal appointees, crown officers appointed to be 'men on the spot'. Executive determinations and patronage underpinned the system. Australia's first 'proconsul', Arthur Phillip, was the shrewd personal choice of the minister of state. Naval and military officers – especially those with an aristocratic connection – were common appointees, as were younger sons of minor aristocracy. 'Outdoor relief for the upper classes', was the radical jibe. After the Napoleonic wars it has been said that the Empire was run by 'Wellington's old sweats'. That changed from mid-century when a professional service gradually evolved, with an unspoken hierarchy of colonial appointments. The self-governing colonies (notably in Australia, New Zealand, Canada and the Cape) were at the top. But colonial seniority still did not give access to the inner workings of royal appointments.

---

62 Detailed in Brian L. Blakely, *The Colonial Office* (Durham: Duke University Press, 1972): 32–41, 152–63.

63 J.J. Eddy, *Britain and the Australian Colonies, 1818–1831: The Technique of Government* (Oxford: Clarendon, 1969).

Mistakes were sometimes made and governors recalled or censured. The most famous instances of policy controversy surrounded the creative (but imperious) Governor Macquarie in New South Wales – which ultimately involved public controversy and the critical 'Report' of Commissioner J.T. Bigge (1822–23) – as well as the unjust recall of Governor Darling in 1831.[64] Tension, controversy and conflict were inherent within the imperial connection. Communication with the Colonial Office from Australia was, until the 1870s, slow and uncertain. Before the telegraph cable it took 75 days for a despatch to reach Whitehall. The proconsuls of Australia were expected to build good relations with colonial leaders and society, and to resolve immediate problems swiftly.[65] But some engaged in activist administrative politics from Government House. Governors sat at the apex of colonial society and were able to use patronage, personal connections and the print media (their speeches were often reported verbatim in the Australian press). They had constitutional powers to dissolve or deny the dissolution of parliaments, together with the capacity to shape the formation of governments and to influence the imperial government itself.[66] The appointment of governors was an enduring issue. Henry Parkes had proposed a 'Council of Australia' to give advice to Her Majesty's Government on various matters including vice-regal appointments. The suggestion was not taken up and conflicts emerged over persons nominated to be Australian vice-regal appointees.

In general, the Victorians ran a liberal empire of devolved authority, and managed influence and power through a range of clients, allies and associates. Anglo-settlers were potentially 'the ideal pre-fabricated collaborators'.[67] Patronage oiled the imperial machine.[68] Relations with the Australian colonial leaders ultimately represented a form of enduring if occasionally stormy imperial marriage partnerships.

---

64 See John Ritchie, *Lachlan Macquarie: A Biography* (Melbourne University Press, 1986); Brian H. Fletcher, *Ralph Darling: A Governor Maligned* (Oxford University Press, 1984).

65 Fieldhouse, *The Colonial Empires*, pp. 242–50. See also John Benyon, 'Overlords of Empire? British "Proconsular Imperialism" in Perspective', *Journal of Imperial and Commonwealth History*, 19 (1991): 164–202.

66 See Mark Francis, *Governors and Settlers: Images of Authority in the British Colonies, 1820–60* (London: Macmillan, 1992); Hall, *The Colonial Office*, pp. 87–114.

67 R.E. Robinson, 'Non-European Foundations of European Imperialism: Sketch for a Theory of Collaboration', in Roger Owen and Bob Sutcliffe (eds), *Studies in the Theory of Imperialism* (London: Longmans, 1972): 117–42.

68 Colin Newbury, *Patronage and Politics in the Victorian Empire: The Personal Governance of Sir Arthur Hamilton Gordon (Lord Stanmore)* (Amherst: Cambria Press, 2010).

Colonial self-government

The Australian experience offers a generic pattern of constitutional change in the settlement empire. 'Crown colony' government still allowed for advisory members. Next came extension of this system by greater (if still qualified) local participation ('representative government'), and then a colonial version of constitutional democracy ('responsible government') – where imperial power was both tempered and enhanced by elected colonial parliaments and cabinet government.[69] Colonies deemed too weak (demographically or economically) were denied such devolved authority: huge Western Australia, with its small white settler population (45,000 colonists by the end of the 1880s), was held back over concerns for its administration of the vast Kimberley region, with its relatively large Aboriginal population. New South Wales and Victoria, on the other hand, were encouraged towards responsibly self-governing arrangements. Social class was another conditioning factor. The imperial authorities embedded upper houses in the devolved Australian constitutional arrangements, with the intention of balancing colonial democracy with the respectable social classes.

Constitutional models were also transferred across the Empire.[70] Australian colonisation was, for example, a beneficiary of earlier political developments in North America. Following '1838' in Canada – involving the Durham Report and 'Rebellion Losses Bill' – it was boldly determined in Whitehall that hereafter governors must work to govern with majority support of their colonial assemblies. The lesson endured. Following the contentious 1888 'Kitt case' in Queensland, for example, the imperial secretary of state (Knutsford) overruled the governor (Musgrave). The Brisbane *Courier Mail* crowed: the outcome 'vindicated the most cherished right of a free people – the right to govern themselves'.[71] Colonial democracy was born painfully. Certain imperial constraints were still 'reserved'. Through the governors, the Colonial Office carefully monitored all colonial legislation. Colonial laws must not be in conflict with British parliamentary legislation, and the *Colonial Laws Validity Act* of 1865 was there to strike down such legislation, notably over 'race' discrimination, while all major defence and treaty decisions remained

---

69 John M. Ward, *Colonial Self-Government: The British Experience, 1759–1856* (London: Macmillan 1976); Peter Burroughs, *Britain and Australia, 1831–1855: A Study in Imperial Relations and Crown Lands Administration* (Oxford: Clarendon, 1967).

70 John W. Cell, *British Colonial Administration in the Mid-Nineteenth Century: The Policy-Making Process* (New Haven: Yale University Press, 1970).

71 The Kitt case is discussed in Schreuder, 'The Imperial Connection', pp. 410–11.

with the crown. The right of legal appeals to the Privy Council endured throughout.

Friction also arose over free trade, or the increasing lack of it, in the settlement empire. Australian colonists wanted to safeguard their own new industries with differential tariffs. The British were not inclined to repeal the sections of the *Australian Colonies Government Act* of 1850 that debarred the levying of such tariffs. But compromise was forced on them, within imperial limits.[72] Free trade remained the gospel of the Empire: but some of its members adhered to their own reading of the concept. Canadian initiatives towards colonial entitlement to levy tariffs forced the hand of the imperial authorities. The Empire ultimately reformed itself.

An Australian 'proconsular' portrait

An excellent biographical exemplification of these themes is found in the career of the Empire's pre-eminent proconsul, Sir Hercules George Robert Robinson, later 'Lord Rosmead of Westmeath and *Tafelberg*', governor of New South Wales during the formative 1870s.[73] Robinson epitomised the new professional career officers who ran Victoria's Empire and was seen by several colonial secretaries as the best of the 'proconsuls'.[74] The younger son of an Anglo-Irish naval family (his father was an admiral in Nelson's navy), Robinson was educated at Sandhurst before family patronage gained him access to employment on the Board of Public Works in Ireland during the crisis years of the Great Famine. He was instrumental in the development of a state paper on revitalising Irish fairs and markets, before the 29-year-old was appointed to West Indian governorships (Montserrat and St Kitts). Successful in dealing with assertive planter society, he was then commissioned to head the administration of vital British dependencies in Asia – as youngest ever governor of Hong Kong (1859), followed by Ceylon (1865). He proved himself as a utilitarian social improver (finance and currency, health and sanitation, education and training, police and corruption), as well as economic moderniser (trade, manufacturing, roads, railways, harbours and currencies).

By the time Robinson was appointed to prestigious vice-regal office in New South Wales (1872–79), he was not only a KCMG, but the very embodiment

---

72 Paul Knaplund, *Gladstone and Britain's Imperial Policy*, 2nd edn (London: Allen & Unwin, 1927), pp. 110–12.

73 There is no biography of Robinson, but see Deryck Schreuder, 'H.G.R. Robinson, Baron Rosmead', in *Oxford Dictionary of National Biography*, 5th edn (Oxford University Press, 2004), pp. 347–50.

74 Blakely, *Colonial Office*, pp. 119, 125.

of the professional imperial bureaucrat, adroit in using his constitutional powers. A settler democracy required a lighter hand, but this did not stop him from involvement in public leadership of the colony, especially at a time of instability in the Parkes–Robertson governments. Beyond colonial cabinets, Robinson energetically pressed the case for major infrastructure investment (especially railways and harbours), education (tertiary as well as secondary), capital investment, rural development and social reform. With a natural taste for county and colonial life, Robinson also shrewdly identified himself with colonial life while Lady Nea Robinson was patron to a great range of charities. Sydney's Government House (expanded in his time, with his own initials carved into the stone) became a centre for 'society' – dinners, celebratory balls and the presentation of debutantes. A keen horse owner, Robinson was closely involved in 'Royal Randwick'. He was delighted that his daughter married at Government House in a wedding gown representing his Randwick racing colours.

When Robinson was suddenly transferred in 1879 to urgent duties in New Zealand, the *Sydney Morning Herald* reflected that while he had been a strongly creative governor, because of his interventionist instincts he would also be remembered as 'Hercules the Troublemaker'. The *Herald* hoped that New Zealand would benefit from lessons he might have learned in New South Wales about colonial democracy. It was a vain hope. After a short tenure in Wellington, Robinson was again hastily dispatched to deal with crises at the Cape. 'Hercules the Troublemaker' was to be crucially involved in the imperial partition of Africa. His key *aide-de-camp* was Captain Graham Bower of Sydney.[75] Together they worked with Cecil John Rhodes to expand the British Empire in tropical Africa.

Colonial nationalisms

By the later nineteenth century travellers had begun to observe an increasingly self-conscious assertiveness among Australian settler citizens.[76] 'Home' was often taken metaphorically to be Great Britain; but they also identified themselves with their new societies.[77] Here were the nascent 'independent

---

75 Deryck Schreuder and Jeff Butler (eds), *Sir Graham Bower's Secret History of the Jameson Raid and the South African Crisis, 1895–1902* (Cape Town: Van Riebeeck Society, 2nd series, 2002).

76 Nasson, *Britannia's Empire*; Carl Bridge and Kent Fedorowich (eds), *The British World: Diaspora, Culture and Identity* (London: Frank Cass, 2003).

77 Stuart Ward, 'Imperial Identities Abroad', in Stockwell (ed.), *The British Empire*, pp. 226–34.

Australian Britons'.[78] Henry Parkes, for example, had migrated to New South Wales as a radical working-class Chartist, and he first projected the future of his new land in utopian terms.[79] But he never lost his sense of Britishness. He turned his back on republicanism, and it seemed appropriate that he should ultimately become 'Sir Henry Parkes, KCMG'. With the majority of his fellow citizens he recognised 'the crimson thread of kinship' that ran through Anglo-migrants, and which accordingly bounded the settler empire. Parkes came to symbolise the symbiotic relationship with the British homeland. He asserted colonial interests with a passion, but he also relished being feted in somewhat triumphal returns to his land of birth. For Parkes there was no incongruity in being the proponent of an Australian Federation and of the British Empire.

At the other end of the social scale, a working man such as Fred Coneybeare of Adelaide – a saddler – kept a diary in which he recorded the daily life of skilled labour, happily mixing pride in his new homeland with loyalty to his monarch. He had become a senior official in his trade union and assisted in organising protests against further Chinese immigration. In his private life he was delighted when Australian cricketers achieved a rare victory over England, and also when South Australians defeated a touring British football team, while still celebrating the annual birthday of Queen Victoria: 'Thursday [24 May, 1888], Queen's Birthday, and *also* my sister Kate...'[80] Revealingly, Australian colonists celebrated both the golden anniversary of Victoria as monarch (1887) and the centenary of Australian settlement in (1888) in close sequence. The Victorian agent-general of the time (Sir Graham Berry) explained to The Royal Colonial Institute in London that 'a feeling of nationality is arising in Australia'; and yet they should not be alarmed – it is 'quite consistent with loyalty to the Crown'.[81]

It was the young Edwardian traveller, Richard Jebb, who first popularised the term 'colonial nationalism' in a travel book of that name (1905) following his own global tour of the Anglo world of settler empire.[82] Australia was critical in shaping his views. The message of his book was essentially to argue that Great Britain had nothing to fear, and everything to gain, from such

---

78 Vividly described in Peter Cochrane, *Colonial Ambition: Foundations of Australian Democracy* (Melbourne University Press, 2006).
79 See Allan Martin, *Henry Parkes: A Biography* (Melbourne University Press, 1980).
80 Quoted in Schreuder, 'The Imperial Connection', p. 425.
81 Barry is quoted in ibid., p. 413.
82 John Eddy and Deryck Schreuder (eds), *The Rise of Colonial Nationalism* (Sydney: Allen & Unwin, 1988), pp. 63–91.

vibrant colonial nationalisms. These were not schizophrenic settlers within a British Empire. They celebrated their dual identity. W.K. Hancock intuitively explained in 1930 the sense of living concurrently in two worlds of 'felt experience': the immediacy of local Australian society, culture and environment, all within a global diaspora of an ethnic Anglo culture.[83] Australians belonged in a supra-state that was the Empire. Their nationalism was also their imperialism.[84] Australian citizenship was informed by a pan-Britannic race nationality. The 'Meaney thesis' on Australian nationalism has been broadly vindicated: 'British race patriotism was dominant until the 1970s'.[85] Hancock himself revealingly remarked that at Federation Australia was 95 per cent British and distrusted the remaining 5 per cent.

The making of Australia's empire ultimately involved a negotiated mutuality of interests.[86] Underlying the Australian accented language of colonial nationalism was the emergence of an identity (and security) that was increasingly 'pan-Britannic' – an idiom first promoted from 1891 by a former Australian colonist, H.M. Hervey. If nationalism rests in an 'imagined community', then Australians saw themselves within that global Britannic polity. An acute sense of ethnic vulnerability came to the Anglo settlers of Australia with the rise of Japanese power and a Chinese presence in the Pacific. Charles Pearson's sensational bestseller of 1893, *National Life and Character: A Forecast* – with its racialised determinism, predicting ultimately dominant oriental societies – hardly placated Australian fears. Rather, 'by pointing to the insecurity of the white man's place in the world', it energised a defensive race nationalism.[87] George Craig's influential *Federal Defence of Australasia* (1897) was dedicated revealingly 'to those noble sons of the British race at Home or in the Colonies, true to kith and kin, and who glory in the name of Anglo-Australians'.[88] By 1914 an Australian prime minister could declare: 'Australia today is as proudly British as Britain itself'.[89] There is still debate

---

83 Jim Davidson, *A Three-Cornered Life: The Historian W. K. Hancock* (Sydney: UNSW Press, 2010).

84 Carl Berger, *The Sense of Power: Studies in the Ideas of Canadian Imperialism, 1867–1914* (University of Toronto Press, 1970).

85 Neville Meaney, 'Britishness and Australian Identity: The Problem of Nationalism in Australian History and Historiography', *Australian Historical Studies*, 32, 116 (2001): 76–90; Neville Meaney, '"In History's Page": Identity and Myth', in Schreuder and Ward (eds), *Australia's Empire*, pp. 363–88.

86 Schreuder and Ward 'Introduction', *Australia's Empire*, pp. 1–24.

87 Marilyn Lake and Henry Reynolds, *Drawing the Global Colour Line: White Men's Countries and the International Challenge of Racial Equality* (Cambridge University Press, 2008), p. 93.

88 Quoted in Ward, 'Security', p. 241.

89 Quoted in Belich, *Replenishing the Earth*, p. 464.

as to how and why this all happened so intensely in Australia. But as Stuart Ward has trenchantly suggested, 'it was only during the late-Victorian atmosphere of looming crisis that colonial identities became securely anchored within a pan-British ethnic framework'.[90]

Australia felix: 'Recessional' or 'resurgent'?

Queen Victoria died at the turn of the new century (22 January 1901) having been on the throne for 64 years. Australians mourned with the rest of the British world. Even before her passing it had become increasingly common to portray Great Britain as a 'weary titan', in the midst of younger and ambitious powers. As poet laureate of the Empire, Rudyard Kipling had penned *Recessional* on the 1897 jubilee of the Queen as an epic tribute to Greater Britain. Where once the British had held 'Dominion over palm and pine', now 'The captains and Kings depart'.

In fact it was a relative 'decline'. The British Empire had enjoyed pre-eminence but never hegemony.[91] Indeed the later-Victorian Empire was already finding strength again, even revival, as the Edwardians saw prosperity return to Great Britain, and as the Australian economy picked up significantly from 1904. The Empire system itself pulsed with growth. The federated state of Australia was to become a great dominion in a British world of migration, trade and security. The Empire faced the Great War in 1914 as far from a spent force in world affairs.[92] A veritable second spring had come to Empire itself with the emergence of the 'Dominions' and of 'Commonwealth'. The new *Australian Federation Act* of 1 January 1901 held out the promise of an Empire-Commonwealth for the twentieth century. Where Canada and South Africa demanded access to imperial decision-making itself, Australia was readier to accept a more qualified partnership. Australian Federation within the Empire had the attraction of the sirens without the foundering rocks. There would be imperial obligations, but also membership of a pan-Britannic community. Being home-grown, Federation would allow the upholding of all the old colonial shibboleths – tariffs, exclusionist immigration policies, state control over resources and industries, even the new wage-arbitration system – without sacrificing Australian autonomy to imperial fealty. There

90 Ward, 'Security', p. 240.
91 For a comparative perspective, see Fareed Zakaria, *The Post-American World* (New York: W.W. Norton, 2008).
92 See J.A. Gallagher, *The Decline, Revival and Fall of the British Empire: The Ford Lectures and Other Essays* (Cambridge University Press, 1982).

was even the notion of a muscular 'New Australian Man' reinvigorating a deracinated British stock. In the words of one modern scholar, 'Australian nationalism was not the repudiation of imperialism but its confident vanguard'.[93] For another, it has provocatively meant a kind of 're-colonisation' of the 'newlands', as 'the balance of power shifted back to the oldlands' within the Empire.[94]

The Australian imperial journey from 1788 to Federation had indeed been remarkable. Seeley's exhortatory vision – of drawing together 'a great homogenous people, one in blood, language, religion and laws, but dispersed over a boundless space' – had once seemed the impossible dream of a global Britannic state. Imperial federation itself had also lamentably failed, along with colonial separatism and Australian republicanism. But, a 'Greater Britain' had risen after all, in which Australia was at the very heart.

93 Darwin, *The Empire Project*, p. 167.
94 Belich, *Replenishing the Earth*, pp. 558–9.

22

Colonial Australia and the
Asia-Pacific region

MARILYN LAKE

A regional perspective

The history of Australia has traditionally been written as though its geographical position in the south-west Pacific, at the edge of Asia and adjacent to Oceania, were largely irrelevant to its historical experience and formation as a nation, as though its history and geography were somehow at odds. In standard national histories, Asia and the Pacific might receive only a paragraph or two and barely rate a mention in the index. Beset by the 'tyranny of distance', located thousands of kilometres from the metropolitan centres of Europe, Australia and New Zealand have been conceptualised as isolated British outposts, 'in most senses', in Geoffrey Blainey's words, 'imitations of Britain'.[1]

The new imperial history together with recent scholarship on the 'British world' has often been motivated by a desire to locate Australia in a transnational context. Yet because of its 'insiderism' (in the historian Antoinette Burton's phrase) it has frequently reinforced an understanding of an Australian history as bounded by 'Britishness', isolated from the countries and cultures of its own region and the non-British world.[2] Recent promotion of the salience of 'British race patriotism' in Australia has, moreover, obscured the strong transpacific identification among radical liberals of the late nineteenth century with the United States.[3] The affective

1 Geoffrey Blainey *The Tyranny of Distance: How Distance Shaped Australia's History*, new edn (Melbourne: Macmillan, 1974), p. 200.
2 See, for example, Carl Bridge and Kent Fedorowich (eds), *The British World: Diaspora, Culture, and Identity* (London: Frank Cass, 2003); Kate Darian-Smith, Patricia Grimshaw and Stuart Macintyre (eds), *Britishness Abroad: Transnational Movements and Imperial Cultures* (Melbourne University Press, 2007).
3 Diane Kirkby, *Alice Henry: The Power of Pen and Voice* (Cambridge University Press, 1991); Marilyn Lake '"The Brightness of Eyes and Quiet Assurance Which Seem to Say American": Alfred Deakin's Identification with Republican Manhood', *Australian Historical Studies*, 38, 129 (2007): 32–51; Marilyn Lake and Vanessa Pratt, '"Blood Brothers": Racial Identification and the Right to Rule', *Australian Journal of Politics and*

solidarity with the white republic found expression in the popular support offered to the Americans in the Spanish–American war and the welcome to the United States naval fleet in 1908, a solidarity encouraged on both sides of the Pacific by Prime Minister Alfred Deakin and President Theodore Roosevelt.

In an essay calling for British imperial historiography to orient itself better to world history, Antoinette Burton has recommended that historians adopt 'an enlarged spatial optic' that recognises the 'multiple imperial presences' across much of the world and the ways in which the British Empire was shaped in dynamic tension with Asian and other empires.[4] Recent historical research in Australia and New Zealand makes clear that Australasian nation-building was shaped in a series of critical encounters with the empires of China and Japan.[5] Australian historiography is thus being transformed by a regional perspective that has begun to illuminate the ways in which many 'connected worlds' – Indigenous, British, Australian, Chinese, Malay, American, Pacific Islander, Japanese and New Zealand – have intersected to shape the colonial and national experience.[6]

The Asia-Pacific was a region whose shores were lapped by one ocean, but whose peoples were divided by imperial and racial hierarchies and relations of exploitation and exclusion. As the Australian colonies grew in population some Pacific Islands were robbed of a majority of their adult men by the labour trade. The introduction of immigration restriction by self-styled 'white men's countries' bore increasingly heavily on Chinese and Indians. During the nineteenth century racial divisions and imperial hierarchies hardened. Within this larger world, the colonies of Australia and New Zealand forged a solidarity expressed in the idea of 'Australasia' to express a sense of

History, 54, 1 (2008): 16–27; Robert Dixon and Nicholas Birns (eds), Reading Across the Pacific: Australia–United States Intellectual Histories (Sydney University Press, 2010).

4 Antoinette Burton 'Getting Outside the Global: Re-Positioning British Imperialism in World History', in Catherine Hall and Keith McClelland (eds), Race, Nation and Empire: Making Histories, 1750 to the Present (Manchester University Press, 2010), pp. 200, 206–7.

5 Brian Moloughney and John Stenhouse, '"Drug-besotten, sin-begotten fiends of filth": New Zealanders and the Oriental Other, 1850–1920', New Zealand Journal of History, 33, 1 (1999): 43–64; Tony Ballantyne, 'Writing Out Asia: Race, Colonialism and Chinese Migration in New Zealand History', in Charles Ferrall, Paul Millar and Keren Smith (eds), East by South: China in the Australasian Imagination (Wellington: Victoria University Press, 2005), pp. 87–109; Marilyn Lake and Henry Reynolds, Drawing the Global Colour Line: White Men's Countries and the Question of Racial Equality (Cambridge University Press, 2008).

6 Ann Curthoys and Marilyn Lake (eds), Connected Worlds: History in Transnational Perspective (Canberra: ANU E Press, 2005).

common ideals and racial identity, although the designation fell into disuse with the emergence of separate nation states in the twentieth century.[7]

In the north of Australia, close to Southeast Asia, multi-national, multi-racial and multi-religious communities – Indigenous, Malay, Indian, European, Chinese and Japanese – were established in which non-whites often composed the majority of the population in towns such as Broome, Cooktown, Townsville and Darwin.[8] It was widely assumed that white men could not work in the tropics, and intense debate ensued as to whether Queensland and the Northern Territory could prosper without importing coloured labour from China, India or the Pacific Islands.

Further north in Singapore the last decades of the nineteenth century saw that British port town transformed into a Chinese settlement, whose demography, culture and labour force influenced in turn the labour and social relations of Darwin.[9] New historical work on regional connections has enriched our view of the entangled nature of the Australian past. No longer cast as an isolated British outpost, colonial Australia is seen to be the site of dynamic, disruptive and sometimes deadly encounters between different peoples and empires that shaped the character of the new Commonwealth of Australia inaugurated in 1901.

Imperial settlement involved more than a binary relationship between settlers and natives, colonisers and colonised, as Tony Ballantyne has noted in an essay on the Asian presence in New Zealand.[10] In a similar argument Regina Ganter has called for recognition of the 'triangulated' dynamic of race relations in the north of Australia that joined Indigenous, European and Asian people in new families, labour networks and communities.[11] Elsewhere in the Australian colonies, British settlers encountered not just different Indigenous communities, whose lives, livelihoods and lands they were taking, but foreigners from many different parts of the world, including the 'Afghan' camel

---

7 Donald Denoon and Philippa Mein Smith with Marivic Wyndham, *A History of Australia, New Zealand and the Pacific* (Oxford: Blackwell, 2000), pp. 30–2.

8 Geoffrey Bolton, *A Thousand Miles Away: A History of North Queensland to 1920* (Canberra: ANU Press, 1963); Henry Reynolds, *North of Capricorn: The Untold Story of Australia's North* (Sydney: Allen & Unwin, 2003); Regina Ganter with Julia Martínez and Gary Lee, *Mixed Relations: Asian–Aboriginal Contact in North Australia* (Perth: UWA Press, 2006).

9 Julia Martínez, 'Ethnic Policy and Practice in Darwin', in Ganter et al., *Mixed Relations*, pp. 122–45; Julia Martínez 'The Evolution of "Malay" Labour Activism, 1870–1947: Protest Among Pearling Crews in Dutch East Indies-Australian Waters', *Transforming Cultures eJournal*, 4, 2, (2009): 85–110; Julia Martínez and Claire Lowrie, 'Colonial Constructions of Masculinity: Transforming Aboriginal Australian Men into "Houseboys"', *Gender and History*, 21, 2 (2009): 305–23.

10 Ballantyne, 'Writing out Asia', p. 88.

11 Ganter et al., *Mixed Relations*, pp. 1–3.

drivers, who were responsible for vital inland transport, and 'Lascar' seamen who often manned coastal trading vessels.[12]

Anglo-Australians were also confronted in the late nineteenth century by the political demands of the subjects and officials of the Chinese and Japanese empires, as, for example in 1887 on the occasion of the visit of Chinese imperial commissioners, General Wong Yung Ho and Commissioner U Tsing, who demanded reciprocal rights and equality of treatment for their imperial subjects living overseas. Their visit coincided with a strong declaration by the leading London-based Chinese diplomat, Marquis Tseng, who called for recognition of the equality of national sovereignties, the equality of peoples and acknowledgment that China enjoyed its own regional sphere of influence equal to that of the Great Powers.[13]

Early histories of Chinese Australians documented a history of racial hostility, harassment and sometimes murder, as occurred at Lambing Flat in New South Wales and on the Buckland River in Victoria. More recent historiography has shifted away from a depiction of beleaguered victims of colonial racism – 'colonial casualties' in Kathryn Cronin's phrase – to emphasise their role as active participants in the colonial enterprise, shaping the social, economic and political life of local communities and commercial and political developments in China itself.[14] Social and cultural histories of the Chinese diaspora – their experience now understood in a transnational frame as members of a global community – have been complemented by new political histories, informed by the writings of Chinese colonists who in a series of booklets, pamphlets, petitions and remonstrances invoked international law and the ethic of cosmopolitanism as well as the universal values of Confucianism and Christianity to demand equality of treatment and recognition of their 'common human rights'.[15]

---

12 Blainey, *The Tyranny of Distance*, pp. 177–9; Christine Stevens, *Tin Mosques and Ghantowns: A History of Afghan Camel Drivers in Australia* (Melbourne University Press, 1989); Frances Steel, *Oceania Under Steam: Sea Transport and the Cultures of Colonialism, c.1870–1914* (Manchester University Press, 2011).

13 John Fitzgerald, *Big White Lie: Chinese Australians in White Australia* (Sydney: UNSW Press, 2007), p. 112.

14 Kathryn Cronin, *Colonial Casualties: Chinese in Early Victoria* (Melbourne University Press, 1982); J.W. Cushman, 'A "Colonial Casualty": The Chinese Community in Australian Historiography', *Asian Studies Association of Australia Review*, 7, 3 (1984): 100–13; Sophie Couchman, John Fitzgerald and Paul McGregor (eds), *After the Rush: Regulation, Participation and Chinese Communities in Australia 1860–1940* (Melbourne: Otherland Press, 2004); John Fitzgerald 'Revolution and Respectability: Chinese Masons in Australian History', in Curthoys and Lake (eds), *Connected Worlds*, pp. 89–110.

15 Fitzgerald, *Big White Lie*, pp. 100–25; Lake and Reynolds, *Drawing the Global Colour Line*, pp. 24–45.

Australian and New Zealand histories have often cast Chinese in the nineteenth-century colonies anachronistically, as already constituted 'national minorities', rather than as subjects of another empire belonging to 'at least two places at once', as both 'natives of China and as citizens of Victoria', as Lowe Kong Meng, Cheok Hong Cheong and Louis Ah Mouy, the authors of *The Chinese Question in Australia*, described themselves.[16] The future was uncertain. The English historian Goldwin Smith, who had migrated to the United States and then Canada, wondered whether the Anglo-Saxon race would continue to rule settler lands. In the case of Australia, it seemed increasingly likely, he ventured, that the vast 'reservoir of industrial population of China' would ultimately 'inherit' the southern continent, where China already had 'a strong foothold'.[17]

It was this vision that disturbed his fellow English historian, Charles Pearson, himself a migrant whose career as a colonial politician and journalist culminated in the 'epoch-making' work of prophecy, *National Life and Character: A Forecast*, which called for defensive action against China in the form of race-based immigration restrictions.[18] It was Pearson's new-found 'Australian point of view', according to a reviewer in the English *Athenaeum*, that allowed him to understand the 'growth of Chinese power'.[19] He saw the world not from 'London or Paris, but Melbourne' and this perspective allowed him fresh insight into the world historic changes going on around him. Living in Melbourne, Pearson was also able to draw on the writings of Chinese colonists. 'With civilisation equally diffused', Pearson predicted, 'the most populous country must ultimately be the most powerful; and the preponderance of China over any rival – even over the United States of America – is likely to be overwhelming'.[20]

A regional perspective makes clear that Australian history has been shaped by its geographical location in formative ways, economic, political, social and cultural. The proclamation of nationhood in 1901 defined the identity of the

---

16 Lowe Kong Meng, Cheok Hong Cheong and Louis Ah Mouy, *The Chinese Question in Australia* (Melbourne: F.F. Bailliere, 1879). On the 'Chinese minority', see Geoffrey Serle, *The Golden Age: A History of the Colony of Victoria 1851–1861* (Melbourne University Press, 1977), ch. 11; Adam McKeown, *Chinese Migrant Networks and Cultural Change: Peru, Chicago, Hawaii, 1900–1936* (University of Chicago Press, 2001), pp. 1–2.
17 Goldwin Smith, *The Political Destiny of Canada* (London: Chapman and Hall, 1878), pp. 41–2.
18 Charles H. Pearson, *National Life and Character: A Forecast* (London: Macmillan, 1893). Lothrop Stoddard referred to Pearson's 'epoch-making book' in *The Rising Tide of Color Against White World-Supremacy* (New York: Charles Scribner's Sons, 1920), p. 29.
19 *Athenaeum*, 4 March 1893, quoted in Lake and Reynolds *Drawing the Global Colour Line*, pp. 91–2.
20 Pearson, *National Life and Character*, p. 30.

new Commonwealth of Australia in terms of the ideal of 'white Australia'. As the first prime minister, Edmund Barton, put it: 'We have decided to make a legislative declaration of our racial identity'.[21] This decision was a response to, and only made sense in terms of, the country's proximity to Asia and the islands of the Pacific, its sense of isolation from Europe, its experience of mass Chinese immigration from the mid-nineteenth century, indentured Pacific Islander labour on Queensland sugar plantations in the late nineteenth century and the continued presence of a mixed-descent Asian, Pacific and Indigenous majority in the north of the continent.

Australia's constitutive identity as an 'anxious nation', in David Walker's phrase, its continuing concern with the arrival of 'boat people' from the north, from the *Afghan* incident of 1888 to the *Tampa* crisis in 2001 and beyond, and its definition of national sovereignty in terms of border protection ('we will decide who comes to this country', as Prime Minister Howard proclaimed in 2001) all gain meaning from the fact of Australia's geographical location.[22] It was as much the perceived peril of proximity to Asia as the imagined tyranny of distance from Europe that defined Australia's colonial experience and shaped the character of its nation building. Raising up walls of protection and determinedly keeping its neighbours at bay, Australia earned a reputation in the early twentieth century as a 'hermit democracy', cutting itself off from international intercourse.[23]

A new nation called for a new national history, as Stuart Macintyre observed in his study of the role of historian Ernest Scott in this enterprise.[24] Its effect, as in all such projects, was to nationalise the past, to recast the regional experience as but a prelude to a narrower, national story; a shift that retrospectively cut off Australia from its formative connections. 'The manifest destiny of Australia', declared David Syme, the editor of the *Age* newspaper, self-consciously employing an 'Americanism' shortly after his return from a trip to California, 'is to colonise and subdue the islands of Melanesia'. When the new Commonwealth of Australia resolved in 1901 to deport Pacific Islanders, who had been recruited to serve the needs of the sugar industry, it also made clear its simultaneous intention to consolidate its rule over them by establishing an island empire in the Pacific.

---

21 Edmund Barton, untitled speech on Federation, Barton papers, NLA MS 51/5/977.
22 David Walker *Anxious Nation: Australia and the Rise of Asia 1850–1939* (Brisbane: UQP, 1999); John Howard, 20 August 2001.
23 'Australian Ideals', *The Times*, 5 September 1908, quoted in Lake and Reynolds, *Drawing the Global Colour Line*, p. 4.
24 Stuart Macintyre, *A History for a Nation: Ernest Scott and the Making of Australian History* (Melbourne University Press, 1994).

Greater Britain or Greater China?

In *The Chinese Question in Australia*, published in 1879, Lowe Kong Meng, Cheok Hong Cheong and Louis Ah Mouy offered a short history of their countrymen's decision to migrate to Victoria in the 1850s. Reports of short distances and the availability of land featured prominently:

> When we heard, about five and twenty years ago, that there was a great continent nearly half as large again as China, and containing only a few hundreds of thousands of civilized people thinly scattered around the coast; and that it was rich in precious metals and very fertile; and that it was only a few weeks' sail from our own country, numbers of Chinese immigrants set out for this land of promise…Australia comprises an area of close upon 3,000,000 square miles and it contains no more than 2,100,000 white people, and a few thousand blacks. [25]

Only recently have Chinese perspectives been integrated into the history of migration, yet by the late 1850s, when their number swelled to 42,000 in Victoria, Chinese immigrants comprised around one in five men in that colony. On the goldfields, Chinese comprised 25 per cent of the diggers in Victoria and up to 60 per cent in New South Wales, where there were fewer miners overall. But although the Australian colonies, like California and Otago in New Zealand proved particularly alluring to gold seekers, they were part of a much larger movement of people through Southeast Asia and around the Pacific during this age of unprecedented global mobility.

The period between 1850 and 1930 was the most intensive period of migration in human history.[26] Although Australian historians have tended to think of the history of migration in terms of European and especially British migration, in global terms Chinese migration during this period was as significant. More than 50 million Chinese embarked for new lands in these decades, about the same number of Europeans and some 30 million Indians.[27] Like most migrants, the Chinese were seeking to make a better life for themselves and their families. Foreign incursions into China provided them with fresh incitements to travel overseas, as Lowe Kong Meng and his co-authors noted. It was the British, they pointed out, who forced their way into China and said in effect: 'We must come in and you shall come out. We will not suffer you to shut yourselves up from the rest of the world.'[28]

25 Lowe Kong Meng et al., *The Chinese Question in Australia*, pp. 5–9.
26 Patrick Manning, *Migration in World History* (New York: Routledge, 2005), p. 149.
27 Ibid.
28 Lowe Kong Meng et al., *The Chinese Question in Australia*, p. 4.

The treaties enacted between the Chinese and British empires following the Opium Wars and subsequent creation of the 'treaty ports' opened up new opportunities for outward migration. Research on the background to Chinese migration has shown that they were driven to leave their homes by poverty, over-population and civil war. Once in the New World, they created a strong global community, linked by native-place associations, cultural heritage, commercial and political networks across North, Central and South America, Southeast Asia and Australasia.[29] They assumed a freedom to travel – living 'both here and there' – sometimes building families in two or three places at once. Against emergent ideas of exclusive nationalism they invoked an ethic of cosmopolitanism.[30]

By the 1860s many thousands of Chinese had settled in the two main urban centres of Melbourne and Sydney, sections of which took on a completely foreign appearance. Chinatown in Little Bourke Street, in Melbourne, where the tea merchant and community leader Lowe Kong Meng established his business, still has many of its original buildings and remains one of the oldest surviving Chinatowns in the world. Walking in the Chinese Quarter of Melbourne in 1868, the novelist Marcus Clarke observed: 'One half of Little Bourke Street is not Melbourne but China. It is as though some *genie* had taken up a handful of houses in the middle of one of the Celestial cities, and flung them down, inhabitants and all, in the antipodes.'[31]

The first race-based immigration restriction legislation in Australia, perhaps in the world, was passed in Victoria in 1855 but was repealed under British pressure in 1863. By the 1870s colonial anxieties were fuelled afresh by the arrival of 13,000 Chinese diggers on the Queensland goldfields and reports from California of the growing Chinese presence there, documented in the widely circulated 1876 report of the US Congressional Joint Committee. Its charges would be repeated many times over in Australia:

> There was danger of the white population in California becoming outnumbered by the Chinese; that they came here under contract, in other words as coolies of a servile class; that they were subject to the jurisdiction of

---

29 Moloughney and Stenhouse, 'Drug-besotten, sin-begotten fiends of filth', pp. 53–4.
30 McKeown, *Chinese Migrant Networks and Cultural Change*, p. 1; Marilyn Lake, 'Lowe Kong Meng Appeals to International Law: Transnational Lives Caught between Empire and Nation', in Desley Deacon et al. (eds), *Transnational Lives* (Basingstoke: Palgrave Macmillan, 2010), pp. 223–7.
31 (Melbourne) *Argus*, 9 March 1868, quoted in Keir Reeves and Benjamin Mountford, 'Sojourning and Settling: Locating Chinese Australian History', in *Dragontails: New Perspectives in Chinese Australian History*, special issue of *Australian Historical Studies*, 42, 1 (2011): 113.

organized companies...that Chinese cheap labor deprived white labor of employment, lowered wages, and kept white immigrants from coming to the state.[32]

In his pioneering comparative study, *Fear and Hatred*, Andrew Markus documented the powerful influence of Californian political discourse on developments in the Australian colonies, where the ascendant labour movement was also mobilising against the employment of Chinese. Australian newspapers employed their own correspondents in San Francisco and regularly received American files and personal accounts from travellers taking the popular San Francisco shipping route.[33]

The late 1870s and early 1880s witnessed mounting agitation about the 'Chinese Question' in Australia: did the continent's future lie with Greater Britain or Greater China?[34] Was Australasia to become part of the 'new China' being built outside Chinese territory?[35] A regional perspective enables historians to better understand the context for this anxiety, as the nineteenth century saw a significant expansion of the Chinese empire into Southeast Asia and the Pacific. 'Demographic revolution fuelled territorial expansion', as historians have noted. The Chinese population doubled during the eighteenth century from 150 to 300 million and increased to over 400 million by the middle of the nineteenth century.[36] Millions moved south to settle in the Malay Peninsula, Sumatra and Sarawak, while Singapore was transformed into a Chinese colony. In 1871 just a few thousand Chinese labourers lived in Singapore. By 1884 the population comprised 86,000 Chinese, 20,000 Malays and 100 white men.[37] Pearson pointed to Chinese colonisation in the Straits Settlements as evidence of 'what the race is capable of'.[38] Just as Goldwin Smith predicted that Australia would become a Chinese possession, the British journalist John Wisker sounded a similar alarm. Australia, he suggested to his readers in 1879, was at a crossroad.[39]

On his arrival in Melbourne, Wisker found a continent preoccupied by the question of 'the coloured man': 'the stock subject of the newspapers,

32 Charles A. Price, *The Great White Walls are Built: Restrictive Immigration to North America and Australasia, 1836–1888* (Canberra: ANU Press, 1974), p. 129.
33 Andrew Markus, *Fear and Hatred: Purifying Australia and California 1850–1901* (Sydney: Hale & Iremonger, 1979).
34 For 'Greater China' see Ronald Skeldon, 'Migration from China', *Journal of International Affairs*, 49, 2 (1996): 434–5; Walker, *Anxious Nation*, pp. 37–43.
35 Moloughney and Stenhouse, '"Drug-besotten, sin-begotten fiends of filth"', p. 53.
36 Ibid., p. 51.
37 Pearson, *National Life and Character*, p. 47.
38 Ibid., p. 29.
39 John Wisker, 'The Coloured Man in Australia', *Fortnightly Review*, 1 July 1879.

the regular topic of public meetings and theme of numerous parliamentary debate'.[40] He noted that there were diverse types of coloured men posing different types of challenges – Aborigines, Pacific Islanders and Asians – but as 'an object of public interest and public dread' the Chinese man had no equal. 'This ubiquitous, all-suffering, all-capable individual – the future possessor of the world in his own opinion – has invaded Australia in thousands'.[41] Wisker referred to the seamen's strike in the southern colonies, aimed at preventing the employment of Chinese on coastal steamships and noted how far nationalist sentiment in Australia had become racialised. 'It was a strike against the yellow man', he wrote. 'Thus it acquired a sacred character; it became an Australian movement, securing universal sympathy, and what was more to the purpose, substantial support.'[42]

There is a large historiography on the enactment of racially discriminatory immigration legislation in Australia, which since Federation has usually been framed as a national narrative focused on the emergence of, and sometimes written to justify, the policy of white Australia. This was Myra Willard's purpose in 1923 when she published her pioneering and prize-winning *History of the White Australia Policy to 1920*, an account framed by a division of the world between 'Western' and 'Eastern' peoples, in which Australians, who belonged to 'one of the most energetic and most advanced Western peoples' had successfully taken possession of 'a continent almost the size of Europe'.[43]

Although presenting a nationalist justification for policies of racial exclusion and the defence of labour standards, Willard was more alert than many later historians to the world context and changing historical forces – the 'stirring among Eastern peoples' – in which Australian nationhood was formed. 'That the development of the Australian Colonies was contemporaneous with the renewed activity in the East', she wrote, 'was of primary moment to these colonies for two reasons – their proximity to Asia and their recent formation'.[44] Willard was also attuned to the political challenge to British imperial authority posed by the Australians' determination to exclude all coloured races regardless of their status as British subjects – 'a principle hitherto almost unrecognised in the Empire' – and a decision with particular implications for Indian subjects, as well as imperial unity, the latter a

---

40 Ibid.
41 Ibid.
42 Ibid.
43 Myra Willard, *History of the White Australia Policy to 1920* (Melbourne University Press, 1923), p. xi.
44 Ibid., p. xi.

matter of increasing concern to the British government, faced with the rise of German power in Europe.[45]

The work of later historians of white Australia took two different directions. On the one hand a new wave of comparative histories showed that immigration restrictions were not confined to Australia, but enacted around the Pacific and across the British Empire. On the other hand, national histories written in the new sociological framework of 'race relations' increasingly stressed the determining role of racial ideas often glossed as social Darwinism.[46] Such studies began to subsume Aboriginal history in the larger story of white Australia, which, as historians of North Queensland made clear, comprised a long history of 'exclusion, exploitation and extermination'.[47]

One effect of the new emphasis on racial ideology in histories of the Chinese in Australia was to deprive them of global presence and historical agency. Thus historians depicted the Chinese in colonial Australia together with other 'Asiatics' with reference to white attitudes as revealed by racist cartoons and diatribes in the press, rather than in terms of their own ambitions and aspirations, as Jennifer Cushman noted in her influential critique of Cronin's Colonial Casualties in 1984.[48] Since then new historical research, both community-based and academic, have documented the full diversity of Chinese lives in the Australian colonies, their economic contribution and their continued presence in Australia after Federation. Unlike Pacific Islanders, who had no state to defend their interests, Chinese Australians were never deported. Many remained politically active, engaging in campaigns for political reform in Australia and China, before and after the revolution of 1911, when they played a significant role raising money and sustaining overseas branches of the Kuomintang.[49]

---

45 Ibid., p. 110.

46 Frank Lewins, 'Race and Ethnic Relations: Sociology and History', in Ann Curthoys and Andrew Markus (eds), Who Are Our Enemies? Racism and the Australian Working Class (Sydney: Hale & Iremonger, 1978), pp. 10–19; Price, The Great White Walls; Markus, Fear and Hatred; Robert A. Huttenback, Racism and Empire: White Settlers and Colored Immigrants in the British Self-Governing Colonies 1830–1910 (Ithaca: Cornell University Press, 1976); Henry Reynolds, 'Racial Thought in Early Colonial Australia', Australian Journal of Politics and History, 20, 1 (1974): 45–53; Cronin, Colonial Casualties.

47 Raymond Evans, Kay Saunders and Kathryn Cronin, Race Relations in Colonial Queensland (Brisbane: UQP, 1975); Andrew Markus, Exclusion, Exploitation and Extermination: Australian Race Relations 1788–1993 (Sydney: Allen & Unwin, 1994).

48 Cushman, 'A "Colonial Casualty'. For a similar critique of New Zealand historiography, see Moloughney and Stenhouse '"Drug-besotten, sin-begotten fiends of filth', pp. 44–5.

49 Paul Jones, 'The View from the Edge: Chinese Australians and China, 1890 to 1949', in Ferrell et al. (eds), East by South, pp. 46–9; Julia Martínez, 'Patriotic Chinese Women: Followers of Sun Yat-sen in Darwin, Australia', in Lee Lai To and Lee Hock Guan

Recent research has established that Chinese in colonial Australia forged a strong tradition of political protest that called for recognition of their human rights in campaigns that linked to international demands for an end to racial discrimination.[50] From the late 1870s, local community leaders argued eloquently and repeatedly for equality of treatment under international law and protested to the British government about the discriminatory and unconstitutional laws passed by colonies they deprecated as 'British dependencies'. Chinese Australians thus participated in a dynamic triangular relationship with colonial political leaders, on the one hand, and British imperial authorities on the other, in which Chinese intervention provoked local leaders into ever-more strident claims of their right to self-government, increasingly theorised as a right to exclude unwanted immigrants.[51] As the Melbourne *Age* put it, to defer to any external authorities, whether Chinese or British, amounted to 'a partial surrender of the right of self-government'.[52]

The Australian colonies passed new immigration restriction laws against the Chinese in 1881 and again in 1888, when they were extended to all Chinese, regardless of whether they were British subjects. New Zealand shared the preoccupation with the threat of the Chinese to their living standards. Its first race-based immigration restriction law was passed in 1881 and further legislation culminated in the *Immigration Restriction Amendment Act* in 1920, which, following Australia's example, declared for a 'White New Zealand'. The determination to institutionalise a white standard of living in Australasia – the goal of their famous 'state experiments' – should be seen, as the New Zealand politician and author of the 1894 *Arbitration Act*, William Pember Reeves, made clear in his book on the subject, not just as a response to conflict between capital and labour, but also to the threat posed by the industrial population of Asia.[53]

Chinese political intervention influenced Australasian political developments in the last decades of the nineteenth century in a number of ways. In repeatedly drawing attention to their long and proud civilisation – often

(eds), *Sun Yat-Sen, Nanyang and the 1911 Revolution* (Singapore: Institute of Southeast Asian Studies, 2011), pp. 200–18.

50 Marilyn Lake, 'Chinese Colonists Assert Their "Common Human Rights": Cosmopolitanism as Subject and Method of History', *Journal of World History*, 21, 3 (2010): 375–92.

51 See the arguments of H.B. Higinbotham in *Chung Teong Toy v. Musgrove, Victorian Law Reports*, vol. 14, 1888.

52 (Melbourne) *Age*, 2 April 1888.

53 William Pember Reeves, *State Experiments in Australia and New Zealand*, 2 vols (London: Grant Richards, 1902), cited in Ballantyne, 'Writing Out Asia', p. 95.

providing lists of 'Chinese Civilization and Attainments' – they prompted Australian political leaders, like their counterparts in New Zealand and California, to redefine the meaning of civilisation on new world terms. No longer a matter of culture, learning and antiquity, civilisation for white men referred to their 'standard of living'. 'The civilization of the white man', declared Samuel Mauger, the federal member for Melbourne Ports and author of *A White Man's World*, 'is a civilization dependent on free white labour'.[54]

This reworking of the meaning of 'civilisation' was clear in H.B. Higgins' arguments in the federal parliament in support of the white Australia policy: 'We do not want men beside us who are not as exacting in their demands on civilization as ourselves'. The future president of the Commonwealth Court of Conciliation and Arbitration, Higgins was a leading supporter of the white Australia policy: he watched its course with the 'deepest anxiety'.[55] Six years later when he presided over the landmark Harvester judgment that determined a 'fair and reasonable' living wage, Higgins used the same language when he defined the average employee as a 'human being living in a civilized community'. The 'first and dominant factor', he repeated, was 'the cost of living as a civilized being'.[56]

Compulsory arbitration schemes – the most distinctive of the state experiments – were introduced across Australasia from the 1890s into the following decade. 'Arbitration became one of the best-known expressions of Australasian identities', wrote Philippa Mein Smith and Donald Denoon, 'claimed simultaneously as distinctively New Zealand and Australian. It was indeed distinctive in that no other settler society adopted it'.[57] The particularities of the arbitration schemes in the Australian colonies and New Zealand were worked out in a process of close interaction.[58] Their peoples enjoyed close relations at the end of the nineteenth century. 'One New Zealander in twenty was Australian-born, much of its finance and external trade was in Australian hands, and since Sydney could be reached by saloon passage for as little as 2 pound 10 shillings, there was a steady traffic across the Tasman of visitors and men seeking work'.[59] One of these

54 Lake and Reynolds, *Drawing the Global Colour Line*, p. 152.
55 *Commonwealth Parliamentary Debates*, vol. 5, p. 6819 (5 November 1901).
56 Harvester judgment quoted in John Rickard, *H.B. Higgins: The Rebel as Judge* (Sydney: Allen & Unwin, 1984), p. 172.
57 Denoon et al., *A History of Australia, New Zealand and the Pacific*, p. 233.
58 Stuart Macintyre and Richard Mitchell (eds), *Foundations of Arbitration: The Origins and Effects of State Compulsory Arbitration 1890–1914* (Oxford University Press, 1989), p. 10.
59 Stuart Macintyre, *The Oxford History of Australia. Volume 4, 1910–1942: The Succeeding Age* (Oxford University Press, 1986), p. 137.

was the teacher Alexander Don, who grew up on the Ballarat goldfields, trained in Chinese language in Canton and took on mission work with the Presbyterian Church in Dunedin, where in 1883 he began to compile the invaluable historical record of Chinese in the south island known as Don's Roll.[60]

Australia and New Zealand shared another world historic experiment in the enfranchisement of women, with New Zealand leading the way in 1893, followed by South Australia in 1894. In 1902 the new Commonwealth of Australia became the first country in the world to extend full political rights to women – the right to stand for election as well as to vote – but this right, as well as the popular Maternity Allowance introduced by the Fisher Labor government in 1912, was restricted to white women, offered in recognition of their status as citizens. No allowance would be paid to women who were 'Asiatics', 'aboriginal natives of Australia, Papua or the islands of the Pacific'. Asians were also barred from naturalisation and denied old-age pensions.

As the number of Chinese in Australia and New Zealand decreased in response to restrictive legislation, a new threat appeared on the horizon. In 1894 the British government entered a Treaty of Commerce and Navigation with Japan, an empire that proved its new military might by waging a successful war against China in the following year. Colonial leaders, meeting in Sydney in 1896 to discuss the rise of the new Asian power in the Pacific, resolved, with the exception of Queensland, not to adhere to the Treaty of Commerce, and to extend exclusion laws to all 'Asiatics'. The new measure was aimed at Japanese, but it would also affect Indians, both groups the British government was keen not to offend. Their respective numbers were small in Australia – just a few thousand – but Australian discrimination against them had larger imperial significance. The Colonial Office immediately made clear its objections.[61]

The issue was placed on the agenda of the colonial conference in London, planned to coincide with the Queen's Jubilee in 1897. There the colonial leaders agreed to the so-called 'Natal formula' that provided for the use of a literacy test to achieve the desired result of racial discrimination, a device that Natal had borrowed from the United States, where a literacy test had

60 Brian Moloughney, Tony Ballantyne and David Hood, 'After Gold: Reconstructing Chinese Communities, 1896–1913', in Henry Johnson and Brian Moloughney (eds), *Asia in the Making of New Zealand* (Auckland University Press, 2006), pp. 58–75.
61 A.T. Yarwood. *Asian Migration to Australia: The Background to Exclusion, 1896–1923* (Melbourne University Press, 1967), pp. 5–18.

been introduced in Mississippi in 1890 to disenfranchise African Americans.[62] The *Immigration Restriction Act* passed by the Australian parliament in 1901 incorporated a dictation test in a 'European' language, despite the strenuous objections made by Chinese and Indian spokesmen and Japanese diplomats in Sydney and London. Invoking their own understanding of civilisation, the Japanese protested against the undeserved 'insult' of being classified with other Asians and Pacific Islanders: 'The Japanese belong to an empire whose standard of civilization is so much higher than that of Kanakas, Negroes, Pacific Islanders, Indians or other Eastern peoples, that to refer to them in the same terms cannot but be regarded as a reproach, which is hardly warranted by the shade of the national complexion'.[63] The Japanese realised, as the Chinese had before them, that the real issue was not civilisation, but colour. The British government, caught in a four-way conflict involving their new Asian ally, British imperial subjects of different races and the white self-governing colonies, gave way to the demands of the white men and imperial unity was, for the moment, preserved.

The white Australia policy rested on several planks. The *Immigration Restriction Act* was joined by the *Post and Telegraph Act,* which aimed to prevent the employment of non-white labour, in particular so-called 'Lascars' on ships carrying Australian mail. The *Pacific Island Labourers' Act* provided for the deportation of Pacific Islanders. In support of the legislation, Higgins again invoked the white standard of living: 'I feel convinced that people who are used to a high standard of life – to good wages and conditions – will not consent to labour alongside men who receive a miserable pittance and who are dealt with very much in the same way as slaves'.[64] Although Pacific Islanders would be expelled from the new Commonwealth, national leaders also asserted their right to rule over them in an Australian island empire.

Greater Australasia

It might seem anomalous that the Australian Constitution gave the new federal government power over 'the relations of the Commonwealth with the Islands of the Pacific', when foreign policy remained the preserve of the

---

62 Marilyn Lake, 'From Mississippi to Melbourne via Natal: The Invention of the Literacy Test as a Technology of Racial Exclusion', in Curthoys and Lake (eds), *Connected Worlds,* pp. 209–30.

63 Consul Eitaki to Prime Minister Barton, in Lake and Reynolds, *Drawing the Global Colour Line,* p. 147.

64 *Commonwealth Parliamentary Debates,* vol. 5, p. 6815 (5 November 1901).

British government. Here was a potential source of conflict involving other European powers, but the clause alerts us to colonial leaders' jealously held belief in Australia's special destiny to rule the Pacific. This vision had been promoted since the 1840s and was registered in the constitution of the Federal Council of Australasia in 1885, when colonists began formally discussing a federated future. The Federal Council at first included New Zealand and Fiji, reflecting the more regional and less continental sense of identity that underpinned these first federating moves.

New Zealand shared Australia's expansionist goals in the Pacific, seeing itself sometimes as a partner in commercial and political enterprise, sometimes as a rival. Auckland and Sydney competed as rival ports, both with claims to trade with Fiji and other island groups. Fiji was incorporated into the British Empire through the dubious 'Cession' of 1874, presided over in Sydney by the governor of New South Wales, Sir Hercules Robinson, and Ratu Seru Cakobau, the former King of Fiji. In the following decade Fiji withdrew from the Federal Council, because, as Governor Charles Mitchell reported to the Colonial Office: 'from a financial point of view he could consent to nothing that would involve any expenditure and from a social point of view he would chiefly represent a race that has nothing in common with the Anglo-Saxon communities of Australasia'.[65]

As Anglo-Saxons, Australians and New Zealanders claimed more than the right of self-government stridently asserted in response to Chinese claims; they also claimed the right to rule over others who were deemed not to enjoy this capacity, most notably the natives of Australia and the Pacific Islands. The Australian record in governing Indigenous peoples, especially the recent ferocity of their violence in Queensland, the Northern Territory and Western Australia, was well known to be shameful, but political leaders hoped to redeem their reputation in the Pacific, which they envisaged as their very own imperial domain, the islands 'our dependencies, in expectancy'.[66] Hoping to cast off their demeaning status as 'dependencies of the British Crown', as they were routinely referred to by the Chinese, Australians wanted to rule dependencies of their own.

In a pioneering study, Roger Thompson remarked that given the longevity and significance of Australian political ambition in the Pacific – and that Australian pressure was primarily 'responsible for the extension of British or Australian rule over the greater part of Melanesia' – it was surprising how

---

65 Steel, *Oceania Under Steam*, p. 36.
66 *Sydney Herald*, 12 July 1832, quoted in Roger C. Thompson, *Australian Imperialism in the Pacific: The Expansionist Era, 1820–1920* (Melbourne University Press, 1980), p. 9.

few Australian historians addressed the subject.[67] The history of Australian imperial ambition remains a largely neglected topic despite the fact that colonial visions of national greatness often included an imperial dimension. 'It is the obvious destiny of these communities', wrote the Melbourne *Age* in 1859, 'to expand not only around the shores of this continent and over the habitable interior, but eastward and northward likewise among the islands of the Pacific and the Indian Ocean'.[68]

Many colonial leaders would have agreed with Alfred Deakin's matter-of-fact statement that the self-governing colonies of Australia expected, in the fullness of time, 'to be masters of the Pacific'.[69] In the colonies of white settlement the imperialist became a democrat and the democrat an imperialist. Deakin had travelled to Fiji as the 23-year-old companion of an Australian investor, and found the governor, Arthur Gordon to be an 'autocratic character' and the Fijians 'good humoured, polite and hospitable'. He was unsure about the prospects for investment: 'everything is very unsettled at present owing to confusions over the land question'.[70] Thirty years later, confusion over the land question in colonial territories continued to confound Deakin, by then prime minister in the government that had assumed control of the new Australian colony of Papua.

If Australian historians have written little about Australian imperial ambition and the way it shaped nation-building, still less interest has been shown in the response and aspirations of the island communities subjected to white rule. Their worlds were disrupted, communities torn apart, resources exploited, populations depleted and lives destroyed by disease, dislocation and despair.[71] A measles epidemic, brought back from New South Wales, destroyed an estimated 25 per cent of the Fijian population in the 1870s. The islands suffered further depopulation as a result of the labour trade. Tracey Banivanua Mar has detailed the systematic violence perpetrated in the islands and in Queensland, where around 60,000 Islanders were transported

---

67 Ibid., pp. 1–2.
68 Ibid., p. 23.
69 Geoffrey Serle, 'The Victorian Government's Campaign for Federation 1883–1889', in A.W. Martin (ed.), *Essays in Australian Federation* (Melbourne University Press, 1968), p. 31.
70 Alfred Deakin to Catherine Deakin, 30 October 1979, Catherine Deakin papers, NLA MS 4913.
71 Brij V. Lal, Doug Munro and Edward D. Beechert (eds), *Plantation Workers: Resistance and Accommodation* (Honolulu: University of Hawai'i Press, 1993); Peter J. Hempenstall and Noel Rutherford, *Protest and Dissent in the Colonial Pacific* (Suva: Institute of Pacific Studies of the University of the South Pacific, 1984).

to work under contract on sugar plantations.[72] She has also identified the role of a colonial discourse on 'Melanesianism' in essentialising Islander identity, robbing them of their status as historical agents and depoliticising Islander resistance: 'Attacks by Islanders on vessels were almost exclusively described as mindless, indiscriminate, and unpredictable explosions to which cannibals were prone'.[73]

Australians had invested in trade in the Pacific since at least the 1830s, when Australian-based missionaries also began work in Tahiti. As the editor of the *Sydney Gazette* put it, 'the Missionary was the merchant's Pioneer'.[74] Sydney became an entrepôt for the South Pacific, supporting trade in copra, sandalwood, *bêche de mer*, seafood, sugar and other products. From the mid-nineteenth century, the Pacific also became a significant site of great power rivalry. When the French overthrew the Tahitian Queen, Pomare, there was outrage in Sydney and further indignation when the French government annexed Caledonia in 1853 and turned it into a dumping ground for convicts. The French also earned the ire of Presbyterian missionaries based in Melbourne, critical of their exploitation of Islander labour on New Caledonian plantations and suspicious of their intentions with regard to the New Hebrides (now Vanuatu).[75]

Australian missionaries were not just effective in bringing the brutal treatment of Islanders to the attention of authorities, they also succeeded in converting many thousands of Pacific Islanders to Christianity, laying the basis of 'the profoundly Christian post-colonial nations of the Pacific' today.[76] Missionaries to the Pacific established churches and theological colleges and appointed local clergy and teachers, who formed new 'transnational' networks between the island groups of Tonga, Samoa, Fiji, New Britain and Papua, that often became the basis of opposition to further land appropriation.

The spread of Christian missions across the Pacific came at a cost. They disrupted established trading networks, undermined traditional political and economic relationships and subverted local culture and custom. Opposition to missionary activity could be met with harsh punishment; Islanders

---

72 Tracey Banivanua Mar, *Violence and Colonial Dialogue: The Australian-Pacific Indentured Labor Trade* (Honolulu: University of Hawai'i Press, 2007).

73 Ibid., p. 28.

74 Thompson, *Australian Imperialism in the Pacific*, p. 10.

75 Dorothy Shineberg, *The People Trade: Pacific Island Laborers and New Caledonia, 1865–1930* (Honolulu: University of Hawai'i Press, 1999).

76 Helen Gardner, *Gathering for God: George Brown in Oceania* (Dunedin: Otago University Press, 2006), p. 12.

suspected of attacking or killing missionaries were subjected to violent retaliatory raids and murderous reprisals. The consequent lawlessness of the Pacific frontier – usually blamed on ruthless labour traders and uncivilised cannibalistic natives – was often invoked by white colonists as a reason for British or Australian annexation.

Missionary expeditions sometimes combined geographical exploration with scientific research, ethnological observation and collecting specimens for museums. Their findings were sought by the emergent professionals in the new discipline of anthropology. The Methodist missionary George Brown, who served in Samoa and New Britain, was in correspondence with cultural evolutionary anthropologist E.B. Tylor, who read Brown's paper on 'Papuans and Polynesians' to the Royal Anthropological Society in London in 1886. Tylor's *Notes and Queries in Anthropology, for the use of Travellers and Residents Among Primitive People* was used by Brown to guide his investigations. Brown's book, *Melanesians and Polynesians: Their Life Histories Described and Compared,* was published in 1910, at the highpoint of racial thinking in Australia.[77]

That white men could not work in north Australia was a long-held assumption. Pacific Islanders had been recruited by planters in Queensland from the Solomons, the New Hebrides, New Guinea, New Caledonia and Fiji from the 1860s, supporting a labour trade that would last until the twentieth century. Queensland plantations generated large profits for sugar companies together with an unsavoury reputation for cruelty, murder, violence and massacre. Official enquiries and newspaper investigations, notably those conducted for the *Age* newspaper by Ernest Morrison, H.B. Higgins' brother-in-law, documented the cruelty and deception involved in the recruitment. Regular attempts were made to regulate the trade and end its worst abuses.

The *Polynesian Labourers Act* was passed in Britain in 1868, but some of the worst violence against Islanders occurred after this date, including the massacre of recruits bound for Fiji on the Melbourne-based ship *Carl*. From 1871 the Queensland government required government agents to sail with each ship and supervise conditions on board. Following more reports of abduction and brutality, a royal commission appointed by the Queensland government in 1885 interviewed 500 Islanders whose evidence helped produce a damning report against the trade. The Liberal Premier, Samuel Griffith, was persuaded to prohibit it, but faced concerted resistance from planters ever-more reliant on Islander labour and fearful about the economic future.

77 Ibid., pp. 105–27.

By the early 1880s, around Mackay for example, 14,600 acres (5,900 hectares) were planted with sugar cane and there were 25 mills.[78] There was also a sugar boom in Cairns, where the companies including Colonial Sugar Refinery (CSR), the Hop Wah and the Melbourne biscuit manufacturers, Thomas Swallow and Francis Derham, established new plantations and built mills, railways and fine homesteads. At the same time, the disease and death rates among the Islander labour force soared. With poor diets and vulnerable to European infectious diseases such as whooping cough, tuberculosis, influenza and dysentery, Islanders suffered terribly.[79] In 1883 one Islander in every twelve working on plantations died, by 1884 one in every seven. In some places the death rate was even higher, reaching 60 per cent on the CSR estate at Goondi.

There has been a long debate in Australian history over how to characterise the process of recruitment – often called 'kidnapping' – and the labour relations on the plantations.[80] The South Sea Islander activist Faith Bandler, whose father was brought from the island of Ambrym in the New Hebrides to work on plantations around Mackay, emphasised its similarity to slavery. Incorporating childhood memories of her father's stories, she also drew on popular histories and the conventions of American slave narratives to depict in novel form her father's terrifying experience of the shipboard journey, his sale on the auction block and the cruel slave drivers who lorded it over their charges on the plantations.[81]

This account and other popular histories of 'kidnapping' were contested by more hard-headed labour historians, who insisted that Islanders were willing recruits who worked as contract labourers. By working with quantitative demographic and economic data, they argued that the labourers entered freely into contracts to work for a fixed period of time and often chose to do so repeatedly, after which they were free to return to their island homes. Many found employment in Queensland, bought houses and built new

---

78 Bolton, *A Thousand Miles Away*, p. 135.

79 Banivanua Mar, *Violence and Colonial Dialogue*, p. 13.

80 Doug Munro, 'Revisionism and its Enemies: Debating the Queensland Labour Trade', *Journal of Pacific History*, 30, 2 (1995): 240–9; Doug Munro, 'The Labor Trade in Melanesians to Queensland: An Historiographic Essay', *Journal of Social History*, 28, 3 (1995): 609–27; Doug Munro, 'Indenture, Deportation, Survival: Recent Books on Australian South Sea Islanders', *Journal of Social History*, 31, 4, (1998): 931–48.

81 Faith Bandler, *Wacvie* (Sydney: Rigby, 1977); Marilyn Lake, *Faith: Faith Bandler, Gentle Activist* (Sydney: Allen & Unwin, 2002), pp. 3–4, 175–7, 187; E.W. Docker, *The Blackbirders: The Recruiting of South Seas Labour for Queensland, 1863–1907* (Sydney: Angus & Robertson, 1970).

families and communities.[82] Although emphasising Islander agency, these accounts were not especially interested in how labourers and their families remembered their experiences, their degrading and often deadly working conditions and the indignity of their lives.[83] As Banivanua Mar has pointed out, the labour trade was not a form of free migration, but an experience shaped by colonial violence. Much of the recent historiography on Pacific Islanders in Australia – or South Sea Islanders as they came to call themselves – has elaborated on the new communities established in Australia and the maintenance of cultural and religious practices through family, religious and political associations.[84]

Australians looked to the Pacific not just to provide a labour supply but also to build new fortunes. Investors in the Melbourne Polynesia Company, envisaged as the 'East India Company of the Pacific', went to Fiji in 1868 to investigate opportunities in cotton and sugar. Private individuals also began to settle there; by 1871 the white population in Fiji reached 2,760. There was pressure on governments to provide security for white settlers. 'Since England can rule India', asked the *Age*, 'why should not Victoria make the experiment of trying to govern Fiji?'[85] There were also calls for annexation in Sydney, the base of the Burns Philp shipping company that prospered from Pacific trade and developed extensive investments in copra plantations, the pearling industry and tourism. In the event, Britain assumed control of Fiji and established a High Commission for the Western Pacific. Soon after, CSR began operations there, employing Islander and increasingly indentured Indian labour to build a powerful monopoly.

To advance their cause in the Pacific, the Victorians regularly spoke of Australia's 'Monroe Doctrine', much to the exasperation of the Colonial Office, which thought it a preposterous conceit. Victorian Premier Graham Berry, an ardent admirer of the United States, suggested in 1877 that 'a kind of Monroe Doctrine should be established that all the islands in this part of the world should be held by the Anglo Saxon race'. This became a rallying cry over the following ten years, promoted by the Australian Natives

---

82 Peter Corris, *Passage, Port and Plantation: A History of Solomon Islander Labour Migration 1870–1914* (Melbourne University Press, 1973); Clive Moore, *Kanaka: A History of Melanesian Mackay* (Port Moresby: University of Papua New Guinea Press, 1985).
83 Lake, *Faith*, pp. 1–4, 175–6, 187.
84 Patricia Mercer and Clive Moore, 'Melanesians in North Queensland: The Retention of Indigenous Religious and Magical Practices', *Journal of Pacific History*, 11, 1 (1976): 66–88; Patricia Mercer, *White Australia Defied: Pacific Island Settlement in North Queensland* (Townsville: James Cook University Press, 1995).
85 Thompson, *Australian Imperialism in the Pacific*, p. 27.

Association in support of their vision of a Greater Australasia in the Western Pacific.[86] 'The islands of Australasia', declared Victorian leader James Service, 'ought to belong to the people of Australasia'.[87] Like the United States, the Australians wanted to keep their region free from European powers, to forestall and resist rival empires so that they might more easily consolidate their own.

The increased visibility of European powers in the Pacific, especially France and Germany, deepened colonial apprehension and spurred on calls for annexation of the different island groups. The lobbying of the Melbourne-based Presbyterian mission was effective in bringing the activities of the French in the New Hebrides and New Caledonia to the attention of Victorian leaders, but the colony was also imbued with larger imperial fervour. Emulating American rhetoric, they wanted to keep 'old-world imperialistic conflicts out of the Pacific' so that Australia might be free to work out its destiny.[88]

Liberal leader Alfred Deakin became outspoken in his assertion of Australian interests in the south-west Pacific, developing what could be called an obsession with preventing the French from gaining control of the New Hebrides, a group of little strategic importance in British eyes. The divergence of interests between the British government as a European power and the self-governing colonies located in the Pacific intensified Australian feelings of anger at not being consulted with regard to issues of foreign policy in their region.

When Deakin discussed Australia's future in 1888 with his new friend, the Harvard philosopher Josiah Royce, the conflict of interests between Australia and Britain dominated the discussion. As Royce reported:

> There will always be a conflict between imperial and colonial interests…This conflict will grow worse in time…Some day a crisis will be reached…Then Australia by that time grown strong, will decline to be ruled by the interests of England in India and a separation will take place.

Royce looked forward to an alliance between the United States and Australia as 'sister republics' and 'co-workers' in the Pacific.[89]

---

86 Gardner, Gathering for God, p. 86
87 Geoffrey Serle, The Rush to be Rich: A History of the Colony of Victoria 1883–1889 (Melbourne University Press, 1974), p. 183.
88 Serle, 'The Victorian Government's Campaign', p. 85.
89 Quoted in Lake, 'The Brightness of Eyes', p. 42.

Just the year before, as he no doubt reported to Royce, Deakin had clashed famously with the British Prime Minister, Lord Salisbury, over French designs on the New Hebrides. In revolutionary language he told the British Prime Minister that:

> the people of Victoria would never consent to any cession of the island on any terms and that the Australian-born who had made this question their own would forever resent the humiliation of [such] a surrender...[90]

Australian ambition in the Pacific regularly brought colonial governments into conflict with the British government, which seemed more mindful of the claims and sensitivities of rival European powers than the complaints and pretensions of the Australasian colonies. Such clashes, like that over Asian immigration, showed how far Australian priorities diverged from Britain's. This was also clear in the case of New Guinea, when fears of German annexation led to the dramatic and unilateral decision by the Queensland government to claim the whole of Eastern New Guinea on behalf of the British Empire in 1883.

The Colonial Office was not amused. Colonial Secretary Lord Derby reported his incredulity when a delegation of agents-general visited him in London to explain their case: they 'came to me with a gigantic scheme of annexation, including not only New Guinea, but the New Hebrides, Samoa & in fact all the South Pacific within about 1,000 to 1,500 miles from the Australian coast'.[91] When Germany made its intentions plain by establishing a Protectorate over north-east New Guinea, however, Britain finally responded to colonial clamour by claiming south-east New Guinea for the British Empire. While some historians have emphasised the play of Australian idealism and imperial ambition in their accounts of these events, others have argued that concern about defence and military security – a dynamic of fear rather than desire – was paramount.[92]

Australia's desire for an island empire would be made very clear, however, as soon as the new federal parliament met in 1901. An unseemly scramble ensued in which Australia and New Zealand competed for the right to rule particular island groups: the Cook Islands, Fiji, the Solomons, Samoa were up for grabs. The Australian government called on the Colonial Office

90 Ibid., p. 44.
91 Stuart Ward, 'Security: Defending Australia's Empire' in Deryck M. Schreuder and Stuart Ward (eds), *Australia's Empire* (Oxford University Press, 2008), pp. 237–8.
92 Ibid., p. 239.

to provide them with a map showing which of the Pacific island groups were already claimed by foreign powers. Fearing further conflict with France or Germany, the Foreign Office was reluctant to oblige, suggesting that the Colonial Office advise the Australians to publish their own map, because it could be 'more easily repudiated if necessary'.[93] At the same time the new Commonwealth signalled its desire to take over the administration of British New Guinea, an ambition not finally realised until 1906.

When the Australians learned that the British had awarded the Cook Islands to New Zealand they were outraged. The Colonial Office was unapologetic, recalling that although Barton had made some 'chaffing remarks' about an 'Island Empire', New Zealand had a stronger claim.[94] Besides New Zealand also had a good record in dealing with native peoples, 'with whom it has succeeded in establishing entirely satisfactory relations'. The setback prompted Barton to remind the British government that in passing the *Constitution Act* it had given statutory authority to the Australian imperial vision:

> For many years past and throughout all the discussions which preceded the establishment of the Commonwealth, the hope was widely and sincerely held, that as time went on, the Federal government would be able to exercise and direct a growing influence over the islands forming part of His Majesty's Dominions in the South Pacific...Ministers desire respectfully to submit that by giving Statutory Authority to the Constitution of the Commonwealth, a tacit recognition has been given by the parliament of the United Kingdom to the power and influence of the Commonwealth in connection with the Islands of the South Seas.

Barton further explained that the Commonwealth was now ready 'to relieve Britain of its duties and responsibilities connected with the immediate control of many scattered islands'.[95]

Self-government was the assumed right of white men. Governing the natives of the Pacific was their burdensome duty, as Rudyard Kipling had only recently reminded the Americans with regard to the Philippines. In carrying this burden Australians had to compete with New Zealanders, who enjoyed a rather better reputation as colonialists. Australians well recognised the fact. 'We know that the treatment of the Aborigines in Australia has been a blot

---

93 Governor-General to Joseph Chamberlain, 13 September 1901, The National Archives [TNA] CO 418/10; Bertram Cox note, 15 November, TNA CO 418/10.
94 Correspondence between Governor-General and Colonial Office, 28 November 1901, TNA CO 418/10/479.
95 Hopetoun to Chamberlain and enclosure, 2 December 1901, TNA CO 418/10/147.

upon Australian history', noted the Labor member of parliament, Charles McDonald, in 1901.[96] In their new colony in New Guinea – renamed Papua – Australians might redeem their reputation. Australian policy in Papua was characterised by an emphasis on protecting indigenous lands and labour from white exploitation.

In 1906, the year in which the Australian government assumed control of Papua, Alfred Deakin writing in his anonymous column in the London *Morning Post*, quoted Richard Seddon, the prime minister of New Zealand and former resident of Victoria, to emphasise the importance of the distinction between ruling and ruled races. 'The British empire', he told his London readers, 'though united in the whole, is, nevertheless divided broadly into two parts, one occupied wholly or mainly by a white ruling race, the other principally occupied by coloured races who are ruled. Australia and New Zealand are determined to keep their place in the first class.'[97]

White Australia was an imperial project as well as a national one, its vision of 'Greater Australasia' the logical expression of its long-held ambition to be 'masters of the Pacific' and leading members of the 'ruling race'. This ambition was shaped by its regional location, many thousands of miles away from Europe, but adjacent to the islands of the South Pacific and close to the rapidly expanding Chinese settlements of Southeast Asia. The definition of its national identity in explicitly racial terms was a response to its location in the world; its assertion of an imperial identity was an attempt to control that world.

96 Roger C. Thompson, *Australia and the Pacific Islands in the Twentieth Century* (Melbourne: Australian Scholarly Publishing, 1998), p. 8.
97 (London) *Morning Post*, 28 May 1906.

23

The Australian colonies in a maritime world

CINDY McCREERY AND KIRSTEN McKENZIE

Assumptions about an impermeable maritime frontier remain enshrined in what is arguably the most famous (and most mocked) line of 'Advance Australia Fair', composed in 1878:'Our home is girt by sea'.[1] As the national anthem since 1984, the song reminds us that Australia is an island continent, the only nation-state to have a major landmass to itself. Yet across the eighteenth and nineteenth centuries the oceans enabled connection as well as separation. Colonial Australia emerged as a society that was bound within developing global networks, connected through the movement of individuals, geostrategic naval decisions, flows of information and trade routes. Such networks, particularly in the north of the continent, created distinct communities that locked Australia into its immediate maritime region. In the period during which the Australian colonies came into being, it was the maritime that structured, enabled and set the terms by which networks of global connection were forged, sustained and broken.

Trade and shipping

Maritime connections between Australia and the wider world long pre-dated the arrival of Europeans on the continent. Voyagers from what would become the Indonesian archipelago crossed the Timor Sea to develop a centuries-long association with the Indigenous people of northern Australia, primarily through the *trepang* industry that harvested marine invertebrates for consumption in Asian markets. The north-western edge of the continent was bound into established regional networks; in terms of geography, culture and commerce, this coast of

---

1 David Campbell, 'Time Girt went Down the Gurgler', (Melbourne) *Herald Sun*, 22 April 2008; Suvendrini Perera, *Australia and the Insular Imagination: Beaches, Borders, Boats, and Bodies* (New York: Palgrave Macmillan, 2009), pp. 9–10.

Australia could perhaps be more accurately envisaged as the furthest shoreline of Southeast Asia.[2]

So, too, Australia's west coast was known to Europeans long before its east coast. The Dutch route to the East Indies took ships up the west coast, and prevailing winds, currents and navigational limitations drove many ashore. Yet the apparently inhospitable landscape discouraged further investigation. Well over a century later, in 1770, armed with superior navigational instruments and new scientific curiosity about the landscape's potential, Lieutenant James Cook managed to land on Australia's east coast. With Cook's arrival, Australia was drawn into Britain's imperial network and assessed according to its strategic objectives. Britain's immediate concern was to pre-empt the territorial claims of its rivals, the Netherlands and France. New South Wales' isolation favoured its selection as the site of a future penal colony, yet commercial possibilities also heightened its appeal. The discovery on Norfolk Island of apparently high-quality flax and timber for naval stores naturally delighted the maritime superpower. A fertile Australia might even furnish a commodity to trade in return for Chinese tea. For the British, then, as for the Macassans, trade with Australia was understood as only a small part of the much larger and lucrative East Asian market. Indeed, the British were in no rush to develop Australia's commercial potential. This was made clear in the instructions issued to New South Wales' first governor, Arthur Phillip, which explicitly banned both colonial boat building and contact with settlements in Asia. These restrictions were not just intended to prevent convict escape. They were also designed to prevent the development of a colonial shipping industry that might infringe on two of the most important, albeit controversial, pillars of contemporary British maritime policy: in the first place, the East India Company's monopoly on trade between the Cape of Good Hope and Cape Horn and, secondly, the *Navigation Acts'* restriction of all trade between Britain and her colonies, and between the colonies, to British or colonial shipping of a minimum of 350 tonnes.[3]

In practice these rules proved both impossible and undesirable to enforce. Despite the prohibition, convicts did escape occasionally by boat: a few made it as far as Batavia (present-day Jakarta). Furthermore, colonial vessels were needed if the community was to survive. When severe food shortages threatened starvation in the first three years, the governor sent the colony's precious remaining ships to buy emergency supplies at Cape Town (1788),

2 C.C. Macknight, *The Voyage to Marege': Macassan Trepangers in Northern Australia* (Melbourne University Press, 1976), p. 128.

3 John Bach, *A Maritime History of Australia* (Melbourne: Thomas Nelson, 1976), p. 46.

Batavia (1790) and Calcutta (1791).[4] Such voyages demonstrated New South Wales' dependence on shipping for its survival, and the fact that the colony's natural trading partners were not far-distant British ports but African and Asian entrepôts, which in turn were linked into regional as well as international trade networks. These early trading voyages revealed the underlying tensions between Britain's commitment to mercantilist policies and the colony's appetite for free trade.

New South Wales carved out a shipping industry in the loopholes afforded by British regulation and in response to colonial needs and opportunities. In 1797, for example, colonists were permitted to build small vessels to develop the new sealing industry in Bass Strait. The East India Company permitted its second-tier 'country' ships to send goods to the Australian colonies. Direct trade with Canton remained strictly off limits, however, until the end of the East India Company's monopoly on trade with China in 1834. Most importantly, because the *Navigation Acts* applied only to British and colonial shipping, the United States and other maritime nations were free to trade between New South Wales and other ports. American whalers helped to establish whaling and sealing in Australian and New Zealand waters, as well as trade with New Zealand, various South Pacific islands and South American republics. Following the end of the Napoleonic wars in 1815, Britain's liberalisation of regulations made it easier for Australian shipping to develop, although in this year American traders were banned from trading in New South Wales. From 1819 the abolition of the 350-tonne-minimum rule for ships trading between Britain and Australia meant that colonial-built ships could participate in this trade. The repeal of the *Navigation Acts* in 1849 further freed the development of colonial Australian shipping.[5] Ships and crews now became truly international – as did the Australian colonies' port communities.[6]

The challenge was to develop an export commodity that could be shipped in the otherwise empty (save for ballast) holds of ships returning from delivering convicts and later emigrants. Until 1820 colonial Australia's main exports were drawn from the sea. Whale oil and sealskins dominated trade, and even after wool became Australia's principal export commodity in the 1830s, maritime activity continued.[7] Despite its lowly origins as a British penal colony, New South Wales continued to develop its maritime links beyond the

---

4 Ibid., pp. 48–9.
5 Ibid., pp. 46–55.
6 Frank Broeze, *Island Nation: A History of Australians and the Sea* (Sydney: Allen & Unwin, 1998), p. 154.
7 Bach, *A Maritime History of Australia*, p. 52.

framework of the British Empire. By the 1830s and 1840s New South Wales was importing tea from China, sugar from Java and Manila, sandalwood from various Pacific islands and, when local shortages occurred, wheat from Chile. In turn New South Wales exported wool, whale oil and sealskins, while Western Australia exported its famous hardwood, jarrah, and horses to India and Mauritius. With the discovery of gold in California in 1848, Newcastle coal was shipped across the Pacific, beginning an important cross-Pacific trade.[8] In the second half of the nineteenth century, as global trade boomed, ships carrying wool, wheat, meat, copper, tin, silver, lead, coal, gold and dairy products connected rural Australia to the world.

With the opening of the Suez Canal in 1869 (and in particular following work to deepen it in 1875), more and bigger ships were able to reach the Australian colonies in record time. Most trade was with Britain, but from the mid-1880s the French Messageries Maritimes line and the German line, Norddeutsche Lloyd, provided direct services to continental Europe.[9] By the 1890s Australia developed direct shipping links with Japan and China. Ships increasingly crossed the Pacific, exporting coal from New South Wales to Chile and Peru, and in turn loading fertilisers (nitrates) for delivery to Europe. Sydney was linked with San Francisco through services provided by partnerships of international shipping firms, such as that between New Zealand's Union Steamship Company and the United States' Oceanic Company.[10] By contrast, competition and increasing costs (steel ships were more expensive than iron, and Australian wage rates were much higher than those earned by foreign crews) meant that relatively few Australian firms were involved in international shipping. At the turn of the century three companies were engaged in shipping between Australia and Calcutta, Singapore and the Pacific islands. By 1913 only one remained, the iconic Burns Philp, whose general cargo ships maintained an important link between Australia and the Pacific islands, as well as New Guinea, well into the twentieth century.

As with steam technology and improved engines at mid-century, Australian trade benefitted enormously from the development of shipboard refrigeration in the second half of the nineteenth century. The Australian colonies were among the first to export refrigerated goods, and by 1896 over 100 ships carried Australian beef, lamb, mutton and dairy products as well as Tasmanian fruit. In 1894 the Sydney Botanic Gardens sent frozen flowers

---

8 Ibid., pp. 63–4.
9 Broeze, *Island Nation*, p. 92.
10 Frances Steel, *Oceania under Steam: Sea Transport and the Cultures of Colonialism, c. 1870–1914* (Manchester University Press, 2011), pp. 30–4.

to Queen Victoria, and the head of the Australia Station, Admiral Cyprian Bridge, sent a case of chilled passionfruit to his wife in London.[11]

Ports

In maritime systems ports provide the necessary interface between land and sea. Geography both helped and hindered their development in colonial Australia. The story of Sydney Harbour's fortuitous discovery is well known. Expecting to share James Cook's enthusiastic response to Botany Bay, Governor Arthur Phillip was instead disappointed by its poor soil, insecure anchorage and lack of fresh water. The search for an alternative site led a few miles north to a gap in the sandstone cliffs, which Cook had noted but not explored. A few days after arriving in New South Wales, the administrator discovered something that the explorer had missed in weeks of studying the Australian coastline. In his first dispatch to the British government Phillip reported proudly: 'we had the satisfaction of finding the finest harbour in the world, in which a thousand sail of the line may ride in the most perfect security'. 'Port Jackson' became the administrative centre of the colony and the heart of its shipping industry. As Frank Broeze writes, 'Sydney *was* Port Jackson'.[12]

Yet Sydney's large, sheltered and deep-water harbour was in many ways the exception that proved the rule. Australia possesses only two other major deep-water harbours, Hobart in Tasmania and Albany in Western Australia, and both sites were developed in the first half of the nineteenth century as colonial ports. Elsewhere shallow rivers, narrow entrances and unsheltered bays complicated port development.[13] When first the pastoral industry and later the discovery of gold brought Europeans to Victoria at mid-century, for example, enormous time, energy and funds had to be expended to connect the shipping in Port Phillip Bay with the centre of Melbourne, located upstream on the Yarra River. The bay's dangerous ocean entrance onto Bass Strait necessitated the placing of markers and pilot boats, and extreme vigilance. Despite significant improvements, many ships were wrecked trying to negotiate entrance to Melbourne. Adelaide's city centre was also laid out some distance from the coast. Brisbane's location, upstream from Moreton Bay, was also problematic. Sand bars and tidal variation made river navigation difficult, particularly for steamships. Until dredging of the Brisbane

11 Bach, *A Maritime History of Australia*, pp. 177, 183.
12 Broeze, *Island Nation*, p. 153.
13 Ibid., p. 148.

River began in 1862, many ships had to unload their goods at Moreton Bay, to be towed on lighters to the town wharves.[14] In Western Australia, many ships avoided Fremantle, at the mouth of the Swan River, due to its dangerous, exposed approach, until the new inner harbour opened in 1897. Only with Fremantle's modernisation was it able to overtake Albany as Western Australia's premier port and provide direct trade with the commercial centre and colonial capital, Perth. While this helped to connect Western Australia with the rest of the continent, it also pulled the colony more firmly into the Indian Ocean network. Fremantle's harbour modernisation was matched by similar port projects in Karachi, Colombo, Madras and Durban.[15]

In northern Australia, Britain sought to profit from pre-colonial maritime networks and to undermine Dutch presence in the region by taking over the *trepang* industry. The Straits Settlements were emerging as profitable trading entrepôts. In the decades immediately following the end of the Napoleonic wars there were hopes that this success could be replicated in northern Australia. Grandiose dreams of a second Singapore were as repetitive as the expensive failures that followed and were abandoned in their turn. Fort Dundas (1824) gave way to Fort Wellington (1827) and Port Essington (1838). None prospered. They became a twentieth-century symbol of European hubris, and the Australian composer Peter Sculthorpe's work for strings, *Port Essington* (1977), is a meditation on the fate of Europeans setting themselves in opposition to the Australian continent.

Ports loomed large in the colonial imagination. Bird's-eye views of Australian port cities, such as those by A.C. Cooke, were popular in late nineteenth-century illustrated newspapers such as the *Australasian Sketcher*, *Illustrated Australian News* and *Illustrated Sydney News*. Special events such as the 1867–68 tour of Prince Alfred aboard HMS *Galatea*, and the centenary of white settlement in 1888 inspired large-format, souvenir editions with detailed port views.[16] *Sydney, A Bird's-eye View from Darling Harbour*, for example, drew viewers' attention not only to the sheer volume and diversity of shipping in the harbour, but also to the range of maritime infrastructure that supports it.[17] Three-masted sailing barques, small paddle-wheel steam ferries and large

---

14 Bach, *A Maritime History of Australia*, p. 42.

15 Broeze, *Island Nation*, p. 149.

16 Cindy McCreery, 'A British Prince and a Transnational Life: Alfred, Duke of Edinburgh's Visit to Australia, 1867–68', in Desley Deacon, Penny Russell and Angela Woollacott (eds), *Transnational Ties: Australian Lives in the World* (Canberra: ANU E Press, 2008), pp. 57–74.

17 *Sydney, A Bird's-Eye View from Darling Harbour*, in Supplement to the Centenary issue, *Illustrated Sydney News*, 1888, reproduced in Paul Ashton and Duncan Waterson, *Sydney Takes Shape: A History in Maps* (Brisbane: Hema Maps, 2000), pp. 42–3.

steamships were shown docked at finger wharves in front of tall warehouses and wool stores, or unloading their goods for transport by rail or road. All roads (and seaways) appeared to lead from Darling Harbour. The number, size and scope of these engravings indicate the great civic pride in Australian capitals as modern, international port cities. Nor were these engravings designed solely for local audiences. In 1879 the *Illustrated Sydney News* praised its large bird's-eye view of Sydney: 'The whole picture is one which we feel sure will be greatly treasured by the public, and largely made use of in sending to distant friends as conveying better than anything yet published, an adequate idea of the extent and beauty of the City of the South'.[18] Absent from such glorified views were people, and in particular the maritime labour that made seaport cities like Sydney possible. As in the engraving, the arduous working conditions and poor-quality, often disease-ridden housing of seamen and wharf labourers remained largely hidden from view. In many Australian cities, distinct working-class maritime precincts such as Balmain, Port Adelaide and Fremantle remained physically separate from elite commercial and residential districts. Where maritime precincts existed closer to city centres, as in The Rocks in Sydney, tensions between residents and officials often led to conflict and, in turn, increased government intervention. In 1900 an outbreak of bubonic plague led to the demolition of hundreds of houses, buildings and wharves; but, helped by the interruption caused by World War I, the neighbourhood endured.[19]

Colonial Australia's maritime identity was defined as much by coastal shipping and small regional ports as by international trade and capital–port cities. Even after the development of railways in the post-gold rush period, it often remained cheaper, more convenient and quicker for people and goods (for example wool, timber, grain, sugar and dairy products) to travel around the continent by sea. As with the mail, coastal trade was well suited to steamships, which could refuel with Australian coal. Just as price wars might shake up international routes, however, so bitter competition sometimes bedevilled coastal runs. Over time the trend was towards consolidation, with usually one company dominating a particular region. Services varied but could be extensive. In the 1860s, for example, the Australasian Steam Navigation Company (ASN) engaged three ships on a weekly service between Melbourne and

---

18 Supplement to the *Illustrated Sydney News*, 2 October 1879, quoted in Ashton and Waterson, *Sydney Takes Shape*, pp. 34–5.

19 Shirley Fitzgerald, *Sydney 1842–1992* (Sydney: Hale & Iremonger, 1992), pp. 215–24; Grace Karskens, *Inside The Rocks: The Archaeology of a Neighbourhood* (Sydney: Hale & Iremonger, 1999), pp. 191–8.

Sydney. Three ASN ships served Curtis Bay and Rockhampton, two went to Brisbane and others sailed to New Zealand as well as coastal New South Wales.[20] The rhythm of coastal steamers arriving and departing from local Queensland ports continued until at least the 1930s.[21] Anxious about competition from foreign shipping, which often benefitted from government subsidy and far lower labour costs, Australian shipowners resisted making what they believed were expensive concessions to their workforce. Working conditions remained both dangerous and precarious for the casual workforce of manual labourers. In response, seamen's unions and a waterside workers' union were established in individual colonies in the early 1870s, and in 1876 the Federated Seamen's Union of Australasia united Australian and New Zealand unions. Of particular concern to seamen was the employment of cheaper foreign crews on Australasian shipping, and in 1878 the crews of the ASN struck against the company's employment of Chinese seamen. Victory here demonstrated not only the growing strength of the union movement within Australia, but also the appeal of a future 'white Australia'.[22] Yet the late nineteenth-century waterfront remained notorious for bitter labour disputes, most notably the 1890 maritime strike, which paralysed shipping in Australian and New Zealand ports and left over 50,000 men out of work during a period of worldwide Depression. When the shipowners (helped by the government and supported by middle-class opinion) eventually broke the strike, maritime labour turned increasingly towards arbitration and political representation to improve working conditions. The founder of the Waterside Workers' Federation, the British-born William Morris Hughes, built a colourful political career upon his passion for protecting Australian labour (and promoting himself), and served as prime minister during World War 1.[23] In the early twentieth century the Commonwealth Arbitration Court, under Justice Henry B. Higgins and the 1906 *Navigation Act* (not implemented until 1921), worked to protect Australian industrial conditions in the maritime industry. Yet disputes continued and left a legacy of mistrust between shipowners and maritime workers.

As Britain's trade with colonial Australia grew, so too did the need for measures to protect shipping and the colonies themselves. The establishment

---

20 Bach, *A Maritime History of Australia*, pp. 120–1.
21 Broeze, *Island Nation*, p. 151.
22 Ann Curthoys, 'Conflict and Consensus', in Ann Curthoys and Andrew Markus (eds), *Who Are Our Enemies? Racism and the Australian Working Class* (Sydney: Hale & Iremonger, 1978), pp. 48–65.
23 Broeze, *Island Nation*, pp. 206–8.

of the Royal Navy's Australia Station in 1859 indicated both Australia's growing commercial and diplomatic significance and Sydney's suitability as the western Pacific's regional naval hub. It also reflected colonial fear of foreign naval powers following the Crimean War. Intermittent scares of Russian and American, and later German and Japanese, warships invading Australian ports gripped colonists and led to calls for better coastal defence.[24] Yet the push to develop colonial naval forces also reflected British Liberals' anxiety about imperial overstretch, and in particular William Gladstone's determination to trim naval budgets.

Boosted by massive growth in both population and wealth following the mid-century discovery of gold, Victoria was well placed to lead the way in colonial naval building. As early as 1856 the colony took delivery of the British-built gunboat *Victoria* to help defend its shores.[25] The *Victoria* became a much-loved symbol of colonial progress and featured frequently in Melbourne newspaper articles as well as in contemporary paintings.[26] New South Wales and the other colonies lagged behind, either unable or unwilling to shoulder what many argued was Britain's burden. In 1865 the *Colonial Defence Act* officially gave individual Australian colonies the power to develop local naval forces and to administer them in colonial waters. Tensions remained, however, particularly over Britain's 1869 naval cuts, which involved a partial shift from port-based to 'blue-water' squadrons. Thanks to the new technology of the telegraph, the argument ran, warships could be directed instantaneously to wherever they were needed. By extension, these warships were no longer needed to guard Australian port cities. To compensate for the reduction in ships on foreign naval stations – including previous reductions, the Australia Station was reduced from twelve to ten ships and from 2,775 to 2,000 men – Britain would send 'flying' squadrons to boost morale in colonial ports.[27] The subsequent visits of Prince Alfred aboard HMS *Galatea* (1867–71), and the 'flying' squadrons in 1869 and 1881 should thus be understood in terms of Britain's wider naval retrenchment policy. Yet colonial newspapers preferred to see them as proof of Britain's

---

24 David Stevens, '1901–1913: The Genesis of the Australian Navy', in David Stevens, (ed.), *The Royal Australian Navy* (Oxford University Press, 2001), pp. 6–7.

25 John Bach, *The Australia Station: A History of the Royal Navy in the South West Pacific, 1821–1913* (Sydney: UNSW Press, 1986), p. 172.

26 Cindy McCreery, 'Defending Our Shores', in *Sea of Dreams: The Lure of Port Phillip Bay 1830–1914* (Mornington Peninsula Regional Gallery, 2011), p. 33.

27 Bach, *The Australia Station*.

continuing concern for Australia. Alfred's status as a 'sailor prince' endeared him to Australian colonists, but the appearance of his ship in Port Phillip Bay was even more reassuring.[28]

Despite the popularity of such visits, a more coherent and long-term defence program was required, and in 1887 the Australian colonies and New Zealand signed a ten-year naval agreement with Britain. In return for five fast cruisers and two torpedo gunboats for the protection of commerce in Australian waters, the Australian colonies agreed to pay an annual sum of £106,000, with New Zealand paying an additional £20,000. This agreement was revised in 1902–03, with the Commonwealth agreeing to pay £200,000 annually in return for an improved squadron and the establishment of a branch of the naval reserve. In 1909, in the wake of the scare caused by the German dreadnought program, New Zealand offered to pay for a British battleship while Australia, like Canada, offered to organise its own navy. The Royal Australian Navy was officially established in 1911. With the onset of World War 1, Australia put its warships under Royal Naval control until the end of hostilities, but the principle of an independent navy was by now finally and firmly established.[29]

Nor did Australia look only to the Royal Navy. The immensely popular 1908 visit of the US Navy's 'Great White Fleet' was the culmination of decades of fleet visits to Australian ports by foreign naval powers, including France, Russia and Japan. So, too, in Hobart, Antarctic exploration fleets received enthusiastic welcomes throughout the nineteenth century, from James Clark Ross's 1839–43 British expedition to the Norwegian-Australian Carsten Borchgrevink's 1898 *Southern Cross* expedition. The latter expedition brought the Tasmanian scientist Louis Bernacchi to the icy continent to collect meteorological and magnetic records. There was an important maritime dimension to this research.[30] It followed a long tradition in which the Australian continent and surrounding seas had served as a laboratory for visiting scientific expeditions, and Royal Naval officers such as Robert FitzRoy and John Lort Stokes of Charles Darwin's ship HMS *Beagle* used observations made in Australian waters to improve the understanding of hydrography.

---

28 (Melbourne) *Argus*, 15 November 1867.
29 Stevens, '1901–1913', pp. 9, 13, 22; Stevens, '1914–1918: World War I', in Stevens (ed.), *Royal Australian Navy*, pp. 30–2.
30 Tom Griffiths, *Slicing the Silence: Voyaging to Antarctica* (Sydney: UNSW Press, 2007), p. 44.

Communication and correspondence

If ship-based research was vital to the advancement of global knowledge, maritime networks equally need to be placed at the centre of our understanding of how knowledge moved across the globe. Even after the coming of the telegraph to the Australian continent in 1872, most information in the colonial period moved along the routes used by ships to convey both people and paper.

One instance of the power of such networks came in 1824, when the convict transport *Minerva* arrived in Sydney with a particularly dramatic juxtaposition of different forms of communication on board. The vessel carried Cape Colony newspapers protesting the illegal transportation by the Cape government of one William Edwards. Also on board was Edwards himself, a firebrand lawyer and self-appointed crusader against government corruption, loud in his own defence. The Sydney press, feeling the pressure of Governor Darling's authoritarian regime, scented blood. Here, they felt, was yet another example of gubernatorial autocracy against a freeborn Englishman. Yet no sooner had the self-described 'patriot' disembarked from the *Minerva* than his presence made a mockery of the press reports that accompanied him. Edwards was soon recognised by several people in Sydney as the escaped convict Alexander Loe Kaye, transported to New South Wales in 1819 for the distinctly unheroic crime of stealing a horse and gig.[31] The incident underlines just how ambiguous the forces of distance and connection were for those living in colonial Australia, and how difficult it was to manipulate or control them. At least until the mineral revolution of the mid-nineteenth century, colonial societies remained small enough to operate as face-to-face communities in which people knew one another's business. Yet they were also linked into global routes of exchange along which multiple forms of communication constantly flowed. Information came to and from the colonies in a variety of forms, from official government correspondence to newspapers and whispered gossip, but it was never disembodied. To understand how these emerging societies were connected to the outside world, we need to track how both individuals and the news they carried with them moved along maritime routes.

The passage to the southern continent was a defining moment in the lives of many colonial Australians. Well over one million free migrants made

---

31 Kirsten McKenzie, 'The Daemon Behind the Curtain: William Edwards and the Theatre of Liberty', *South African Historical Journal*, 61, 3 (2009): 482–504.

the long sea voyage in the nineteenth century. British and Irish migrants predominated, but they were joined by growing numbers of Germans, Scandinavians and Americans, as well as Asians and Pacific Islanders who came largely, but not solely, under the constraints of indenture. The opportunity to turn a profit on both outward (emigrants) and return (wool) cargoes drew more shipowners to enter the Australian trade in the 1830s and 1840s. After a dip during the depression of the 'hungry forties', ship arrivals grew markedly with the discovery of gold in Victoria in 1851. Port Phillip Bay now became the Australian destination of choice for shipping; vessels arrived with immigrants and took away gold. The port struggled to cope with the increased workload until a series of major infrastructure projects were completed. By the late nineteenth century Port Phillip Bay was widely admired as one of the most modern and efficiently administered ports in the British Empire.[32]

At mid-century, as in earlier decades, colonial Australia's maritime development benefitted from American ingenuity as much as a relaxation in British shipping regulations. Sleek, fast, American-style softwood 'clipper' ships (so-called because they moved at a 'good clip') became popular on the Australian run, helped by the repeal of the *Navigation Acts* in 1849 and the 1854 *Merchant Shipping Act,* both of which stimulated British ship designers to create faster sailing ships to compete with foreign shipping.[33] Famous clippers such as the *Marco Polo* entered the colonial imagination and were recorded in paintings by maritime artists such as John Thompson of Melbourne, himself a ship's captain and part of the diaspora of British sea captains who settled in colonial Australian ports. By contrast, Isambard Kingdom Brunel's enormous and technologically advanced SS *Great Britain* also became a familiar sight, delivering immigrants to Melbourne from the early 1850s. The *Great Britain* illustrates the trend towards larger ships on the Australian run and the growing importance of steamships. By the 1870s, with the development of far more efficient (and thus cost-effective) compound engines, steamships began to replace sailing ships in the migrant trade. In following decades the development of triple expansion and later steel engines further reduced the time and fuel consumption of the voyage. Yet sailing ships carrying bulk cargoes such as wool and wheat remained a common sight in Australian ports until World War 1.

32 Bach, *A Maritime History of Australia*, pp. 128–9.
33 Ibid., pp. 56–7.

Emigrant ships grew larger in response to demand for passengers, and after 1850 individual ships regularly carried 300, 400 or even 600 migrants to Australia.[34] The vast majority were working-class people who travelled steerage. Their experience of the voyage differed markedly from that of privileged passengers whose cabins near the top of the ship provided more space, light and air. Steerage passengers were housed below deck in confined and tightly controlled spaces, with single men clustered at the front of the vessel, married couples with young children in the middle and single women sequestered at the rear. Each group lived in a dark, crowded and frequently damp communal dormitory of double wooden bunks arranged around the sides of the ship, with long wooden tables running down the centre. Their time was strictly regulated, particularly that of single women, some of whom complained of being treated like convicts. Despite claims that there was 'no privacy for writing', many emigrants did manage to keep diaries to record their experience of the voyage and their hopes and fears of their new home.[35] Emigrants' experience of the voyage changed with the adoption of the faster but more dangerous 'Great Circle Route' in the 1850s. As the Victorian gold rush fuelled demand for quicker voyages to Australia, maverick ship captains, like the notorious James 'Bully' Forbes, took their ships deep into the Southern Ocean to catch the 'Roaring Forties', the fast and furious westerly winds that pushed ships eastward towards Australia. While voyage times were reduced, the new route meant that most emigrant ships travelled nonstop and out of sight of land.[36] Shipboard journals record emigrants' mixed emotions at first glimpsing the Australian coast: delight at finally seeing land combined with disappointment at the alien appearance of the landscape.[37]

Greater attention to shipboard diet and health, especially following the appointment of surgeon superintendents, improved emigrants' experience of the voyage. Yet as Patricia Jalland's analysis of shipboard diaries indicates, married women, young children and infants travelling steerage to Australia were much more likely to die than steerage men, single women or privileged cabin-class passengers. They perished from infectious disease or starvation

34 Andrew Hassam (ed.), *No Privacy for Writing: Shipboard Diaries 1852–1879* (Melbourne University Press, 1995), p. xviii.
35 Ibid., pp. xviii–xxiv.
36 Andrew Hassam, *Sailing to Australia: Shipboard Diaries by Nineteenth-Century British Emigrants* (Manchester University Press, 1994), p. 8.
37 Ibid., p. 162.

caused by the lack of suitable food for nursing mothers and small children, and were buried at sea with little fuss and often undue haste; evidence of both their low status as passengers and emigrants and their shipboard companions' horror of sea burials.[38] While most emigrants survived (fewer than 1 per cent died on emigrant ships to Queensland, for example), travelling to Australia remained a risky business.[39] Even after the construction in the 1840s and 1850s of lighthouses along the coastline facing Bass Strait, numerous ships wrecked, often with total loss of life.

Not everyone who arrived safely by ship in colonial Australia stayed. Some free migrants as well as former convicts who could raise the fare made return passages to Britain and Ireland. A few convicts, including Loe Kaye, alias Edwards, even managed to escape. More successful was the Irish political prisoner John Mitchel, who sailed from Van Diemen's Land in 1853 to continue his nationalist campaign from the United States. From the mid-nineteenth century the bones of Chinese migrants were carefully shipped from Australia to be reburied in their home villages. So important was this tradition that by the 1890s coffins were placed on ships carrying Chinese passengers and crew in order to ensure that no bodies were lost. Such practices connected colonial Australia's Chinese communities with their counterparts in Hawai'i and California, and drew attention to the ways in which during the mid to late-nineteenth century the Pacific was thought of by some as a 'Chinese lake'.[40]

Even when they were not moving physically across maritime borders, nineteenth-century people put considerable effort into controlling how information about themselves did. They maintained interpersonal networks with great diligence through both private and official correspondence. They guarded their reputations and promoted their interests, not only through such letters but also by means of the local press.

Tracking such networks reminds us how personal this far-flung world was. The number of people involved in imperial administration, for example, was small. This cohort was closely connected, its actions determined by personalities as well as by policy. Those who wielded government power in the Australian colonies were part of a vast but nonetheless intimate web of

38 Pat Jalland, *Australian Ways of Death: A Social and Cultural History* (Oxford University Press, 2002), pp. 16, 18.

39 Helen R. Woolcock, *Rights of Passage: Emigration to Australia in the Nineteenth Century* (London: Tavistock Publications, 1986), p. 329.

40 Michael Williams, 'Departed Friends', *Journal of Chinese Australia*, 2 (October 2006), <www.chaf.lib.latrobe.edu.au/jca/issue02/10Williams.html>, accessed 15 March 2012.

imperial postings.[41] Before becoming governors of New South Wales Richard Bourke had served previously in Ireland and the Cape Colony, and Ralph Darling ran Mauritius. The explorer of inland Australia, Edward John Eyre, went on to become lieutenant-governor of provincial New Zealand and the notorious governor of Jamaica. Lieutenant-Governor George Arthur served in Egypt, Sicily, Jamaica and Honduras before his time in Van Diemen's Land.

Until 1835, when the practice was officially banned, unofficial private correspondence was a central part of government decision-making. Dispatches might announce official decisions and the ostensible reasons for them, but private letters told the real story. Building networks of influence through private correspondence was vital, not only for officials but also for family, business and professional interests. It was equally important for lobby groups such as settler capitalists and humanitarian activists.[42]

In managing this vast web of information, the implications of a maritime system were everywhere, even down to the daily rhythm of an army of clerks. While the British Post Office and Admiralty ran their own packet services to Europe and North America, this was financially impossible for Australia, and mail was carried by ordinary ships' masters. This meant that the regularity of the mail service was linked inextricably with commercial shipping patterns.[43] In the early nineteenth century every overseas dispatch from the Colonial Office in London needed to be hand-copied three times. An original was sent immediately, a second by a later mail to guard against accidents such as shipwreck or piracy and the third copy kept as a record. Lest pity for this endless drudgery be taken too far, by modern standards the Colonial Office clerks during this period kept leisurely hours (11 a.m. to 4 p.m.). The assumption that they needed time outside the office to pursue the social lives of gentlemen was slow to erode. But the arrival and departure of suitable vessels prompted an abrupt change of pace: clerks descended into a vortex of overtime copying, with huge bursts of activity required to make the 8 a.m. mail coach for Falmouth. There was much quarrelling and an endless blame game played out between different government departments over clerks and messengers who took their deadlines down to the wire. Holding up the mail was a dire administrative sin. If correspondence

---

41 David Lambert and Alan Lester (eds), *Colonial Lives Across the British Empire: Imperial Careering in the Long Nineteenth Century* (Cambridge University Press, 2006), p. 21.

42 Zoë Laidlaw, *Colonial Connections 1815–45: Patronage, the Information Revolution and Colonial Government* (Manchester University Press, 2005).

43 Broeze, *Island Nation*, p. 88

was late, or delivered late to the mail coach, it could miss the sailing of the required vessel. Being late by even a few minutes could mean a delay in communication of weeks or even months.[44]

No matter how hard a clerk scribbled at his desk, or how efficiently the official mail was collected and dispatched, before the steamship or the telegraph cable information was at the mercy of the wind and tide. Imperial administration was forced to manage with long delays between instructions and action, between advice sought and given. Between 1788 and 1820 the average length of the passage between England and Australia was cut from 180 to 110–20 days but little further improvement was made until after 1850. Even then the shorter passage was a best-case scenario. Sea travel was uncertain and a correspondent might have to wait up to a year for a reply to a letter sent from Australia to Europe.[45] Officials on the ground had wide discretionary powers; nor was it unknown for them to make strategic use of time delays for their own ends. The allegations of government autocracy that flared up periodically in the eastern Australian colonies before the middle of the nineteenth century were directed at the specifics of a penal administration, yet they were also testament to the logistics of a maritime empire. Even if the wheels of information ground slowly, they did grind exceedingly fine. It might take time, but imperial officials were often startlingly aware of information on the ground. It was entirely in their interests to keep abreast of local gossip in a world in which personal reputation was so closely connected to political influence. Testifying in London before a House of Commons investigation into Governor Darling in 1835, Captain Robert Robison tried to make scandalous insinuations about a Sydney doctor to prove his point about widespread cronyism. He was given short shrift when the committee claimed (with some justification) that it knew far more about the marital troubles in question than he did.[46]

Those seeking to change their identity or pass themselves off as other than what they were eventually found that past lives were likely to catch up with them. The swindler and serial impostor, John Dow, hoped to make use of the social and geographic distance between convict-era New South Wales and the circles of the British aristocracy to pass himself off as Edward, Lord Viscount Lascelles. While he was astute enough to pull off the role for well

---

44 D.M. Young, *The Colonial Office in the Early Nineteenth Century* (London: Longmans, 1961).

45 Broeze, *Island Nation*, pp. 79, 88.

46 Kirsten McKenzie, *Scandal in the Colonies: Sydney and Cape Town, 1820–1850* (Melbourne University Press, 2004), p. 117.

over a year, a cat's cradle of correspondence from disgruntled victims, colonial officials and Lascelles' family agents (combined with a Sydney lawyer's handy copy of *Burke's Peerage*) duly exposed him as the son of a Scottish coal miner.[47] The Australian colonies were frequently held up as a place in which unsavoury characters might reinvent themselves, yet global information networks were often far stronger than allowed for by opportunists.

Just as emigrants and wool provided ideal alternate cargoes for clipper ships on the Australian run, so mail contracts boosted the fortunes of steamships. Until the 1840s all letters to Australia went by private ship, at the discretion of the captain. Although the Admiralty contracted with a private firm in 1843 for a monthly mail service to Sydney, the slowness of the sailing ship led by 1848 to demands for a regular steamship service. Steamships were expensive to run, and the need to refuel at designated coaling stations necessitated a strict itinerary and timetable. Australian colonies recognised the value of being added to existing imperial mail routes, and fought bitterly with one another to establish the most direct route between their capital port city and Britain. Thus colonists in New South Wales favoured the northern route via Torres Strait while Victorians and South Australians preferred the Cape.[48] Debates over the mail route and the thorny issue of colonial subsidy (to recompense shipping companies for the extra expense involved in keeping a regular and reliable service) took up many hours of parliamentary select committees and as many more column inches in colonial newspapers. Despite numerous competitors and various service interruptions, from 1852 the Peninsular & Oriental Steam Navigation Company (P&O) – along with its future partner, the Orient Line – dominated the Australian mail service to Britain via Asia and Suez. Use of the Suez Canal led to quicker voyages, although it was not until 1874 that the Post Office (which had taken over from the Admiralty the authority to contract for seagoing mail services) permitted P&O to use the more expensive canal rather than the adjacent overland route. Melbourne served as the main terminus for the mail route in the 1870s, but a new contract in 1880 gave Sydney that honour. New South Wales and New Zealand collaborated on a transpacific service. By the end of the 1870s a letter from Sydney took approximately 45 days to arrive in London by the Pacific route, via New Zealand and North America, and 48 days by the Suez route via South Asia. By 1901 a letter from London to Melbourne via Suez took only 31-and-a-half days. With the first mail contract involving all the Australian colonies signed

---

47 Kirsten McKenzie, *A Swindler's Progress: Nobles and Convicts in the Age of Liberty* (Sydney: UNSW Press, 2009).

48 Bach, *A Maritime History of Australia*, p. 109.

in 1888, P&O and Orient, still two companies, consolidated their position as the primary providers of mail to the Australian colonies. But there were competitors. By 1911, for example, the Union Steamship Company of New Zealand controlled the Pacific mail route between Australia and Canada.[49] From 1872 Australia was connected to the world not just by ships crossing the oceans but also by telegraphic cables laid beneath. By allowing return communication in minutes or even seconds, rather than weeks or months, the cable drew Australians closer to both the decision-makers in London and trade partners. Conversely, when earthquakes, ocean currents or even whales broke the cable, the ensuing silence reawakened the colonists' fears of their geographical isolation.

Media and maritime communications

By the 1820s those seeking to protect their personal reputations and to influence public opinion could make use of an emergent colonial press. Newspapers were a fundamental medium through which Australia connected to the wider world, making reading a profoundly communal practice; from private subscribers to coffee house readership, to the copies routinely filed in government departments like the Colonial Office in London. From 1834 newspapers could be sent by packet boat from the colonies to Britain and from colony to colony free of postage duty.[50] For much of the nineteenth century, these newspapers were quite literally 'shipping news'. The first page invariably began with notices of vessels arriving and departing, the goods they had brought and the people disembarking. The maritime pervaded the rest of the pages, too, with a constant undercurrent of how the knowledge contained within had reached its destination: 'News. By the *Portland* and *Asia*. (From the *Spectator* of Feb 16th)'[51] Or less helpfully: '*The Guardian*. We have received papers by this vessel down to the date of her sailing from England (10 August), but we can find no news of any interest to our readers than that which we have already published.'[52] So, too, ships' crew used colonial newspapers to search for friends and relations who had left Britain years earlier. In December 1867, for example, the *Sydney Morning Herald* published the following advertisement: 'If this should meet the eye of Ann Sawyer, who

---

49 Ibid., pp. 148–50, 190; Steel, *Oceania Under Steam*, pp. 34–5.
50 Alan Lester, 'British Settler Discourses and the Circuits of Empire', *History Workshop Journal*, 54 (2002): 32.
51 *Sydney Monitor*, 3 July 1833.
52 *Sydney Gazette*, 16 December 1834.

left Maidstone, Kent, about 16 years ago, she is requested to write to Charles Sawyer, H.M.S. *Virago*'.[53]

The importance of the press in thus shaping global public opinion was underscored by the bitter struggle to secure press freedom in Australia and elsewhere. Colonial authorities were fully aware of the power of the press, and wary of giving it sway. Newspapers allowed colonies to benchmark their achievements against one another, to lobby for greater rights and privileges and to protest against unpopular policies. The first independent newspapers of Sydney and Cape Town were founded in the same year (1824) under two governors (Darling in New South Wales, Somerset at the Cape) whose attempts to stamp out press freedom made them notorious both at the time and long since. The *Australian* gave a graphic account of the forcible closure of the *South African Commercial Advertiser*, complete with pointed allusions to its own situation.[54] The practice of reproducing extracts from foreign papers was universal, and newspaper editors routinely linked their own conflicts with autocratic regimes to those taking place in other colonial societies.

Issues big and small were played out through a global network of newspapers, from the individual reputation of a businessman concerned with his oceanic trading networks to such profound questions as the rights of colonised people or the transportation of convicts. In Sydney, Francis Short complained in a libel action of 1826 against the *Sydney Gazette* that the suggestion that he had committed perjury 'might be read in England, at the Cape, and in India' and thus 'it was very improper to insert it, lest those whose eyes it caught might suppose, for the first time in their lives, that Francis Short had been guilty of perjury'.[55] The violence between settlers and Indigenous people enacted on colonial frontiers was mirrored in the ideological warfare conducted between settlers and humanitarian activists in the colonial press of the 1830s. At stake in these paper wars, argues Alan Lester, was the 'definition of Britishness as a globalising phenomenon',[56] with accusations of savagery and assertions of civilisation traded through the press and through interpersonal networks of lobbyists crossing between colonies and from colonies to the London metropole. When the British government unilaterally transported convicts to the Cape and New South Wales in the middle of the nineteenth century, settler protests were followed carefully across the Indian Ocean, with calls of solidarity in the Australian

---

53 *Sydney Morning Herald*, 11 December 1867.
54 (Sydney) *Australian*, 2 December 1824.
55 Ibid., 26 January 1826.
56 Lester, 'British Settler Discourses', p. 31.

colonial press between 'the Southern Colonies' as a community of political interest made up by the Cape, New Zealand and the Australian settlements.[57] Likewise, in 1860 the Municipal Commissioners of Cape Town commented that Prince Alfred's visit appealed to both Dutch and British colonists because it recalled the glorious naval history of both nations.[58]

Maritime networks and Australia's north

By the last third of the nineteenth century, such calls to identity and action were taking on a proto-nationalist tone, one that was overtly pitched in racial language. Yet assumptions about a European nation in the Asia-Pacific were undercut by the regional peculiarities of northern Australia. There, maritime networks combined with geography and labour practices to disrupt received thinking about borders, about the nature of a settlement's 'hinterland' and about the relationship between land and sea.

While the northern coast was the site of the continent's first transoceanic economy during the pre-colonial period, European trade was far slower to establish itself. Until the 1860s maritime surveyors were the most notable European presence in the region, testament to the rise of the Royal Navy's hydrographic service.[59] Mercantile success had to wait until the 1860s, when pearling came to northern Australia, an industry driven by fashion and, more prosaically, by buttons.[60] Pearlers became notorious for kidnapping and enslaving Aboriginal workers and, as the shallow oyster beds were fished out, for forcing them to dive in more and more dangerous conditions. Repeated regulation such as the prohibition on using women divers (1871) and the *Pearl Shell Fishery Regulation Act* of 1873, were easy to evade. By the 1880s the exhaustion of shallow beds forced technological change, and the transition from skin diving to diving suits and air pumps brought about a fundamental shift in the labour force. The pearling industry reached out for workers far across the Indian and Pacific oceans as well as Torres Strait; Burns Philp from New Guinea, Guthrie & Co. from Hong Kong.[61] By the late nineteenth

---

57 *Sydney Morning Herald*, 6 March 1850, 8 March 1850.
58 Loyal Address of the Municipal Commissioners of Cape Town, 1860, quoted in *The Progress of His Royal Highness Prince Alfred Ernest Albert through the Cape Colony, British Kaffraria, the Orange Free State, and Port Natal, in the year 1860* (Cape Town: Saul Solomon & Co., 1861), pp. 7–8.
59 Alan Powell, *Northern Voyagers: Australia's Monsoon Coast in Maritime History* (Melbourne: Australian Scholarly Publishing, 2010), p. 84.
60 Ibid., p. 179.
61 Ibid., p. 186; Ruth Balint, *Troubled Waters: Borders, Boundaries and Possession in the Timor Sea* (Sydney: Allen & Unwin, 2005), p. 24.

century men from the southern Philippines and eastern Indonesia as well as Japan were working as divers and crew members aboard Australian pearl luggers; the industry could not have operated without Asian indentured labour.[62] Towns such as Broome became notorious as much for their polyglot population as for the distinct behaviour of their white populations, for the wealthy pearling masters who dressed in tropical kit (or in batik sarongs for relaxation) and sent their laundry and tailoring to Singapore.[63]

In the same decade that the pearling industry was becoming notorious for kidnapping Aboriginal labour, a practice known as 'blackbirding', the sugar industry of Queensland was driving similar practices across the Pacific. A deadly triumvirate of factors came together in an aggressive new phase of frontier expansion: an Empire-wide disillusionment with the outcomes of humanitarian reform, a more rigid and biological idea of racial difference, and breech-loading rifles that widened the gap between Indigenous and non-Indigenous firepower. In this context Queensland became arguably 'the most savage frontier in all Australia'.[64] It was a frontier that expanded far beyond the shores of the continent and into its maritime surrounds.

The sugar plantations established in northern Queensland from the middle of the 1860s relied on maritime industries and infrastructures. Labourers were first recruited to work in Queensland from the islands of the New Hebrides, now Vanuatu, in 1863, and 60,000 indentured labourers, mainly from Vanuatu and the Solomon Islands, but also other Pacific Islands, arrived over the following 40 years. Plantation owners hired experienced mariners to recruit workers, and the Queensland labour trade built upon existing island trade networks. Many of the same ships that had previously exported *bêche de mer* and sandalwood now exported people, often for considerable profit. Competition was fierce and as existing labour pools dried up ships had to travel to more remote island groups to find recruits. Ships dropped anchor in bays and off beaches, negotiated for and loaded Islanders, then continued to the next village until their holds were full. Sail and steam vessels left northern Queensland ports such as Bundaberg, Mackay and Maryborough, but ships occasionally sailed from Sydney, too. In June 1898, for example, the

---

62 Julia Martínez, 'Indonesians Challenging White Australia: 'Koepangers' in the North Australian Pearl-Shell Industry, 1870s to 1960s', *Indonesia and the Malay World*, 40, 117, (2012): 231–48.

63 Henry Reynolds, *North of Capricorn: The Untold Story of Australia's North* (Sydney: Allen & Unwin, 2003), pp. 126–7.

64 Powell, *Northern Voyagers*, p. 111; Raymond Evans, Kay Saunders and Kathryn Cronin, *Race Relations in Colonial Queensland: A History of Exclusion, Exploitation, and Extermination* [1975] (Brisbane: UQP, 1993).

experienced British sea captain and stubborn defender of the labour trade, W.T. Wawn, sailed the 253-tonne barque *Loongana* (owned by the only firm of Chinese shipowners in Sydney, the On Chong Company) from Sydney to the Gilbert Islands. Aboard was a cargo of mail, timber and other goods – plus 65 Gilbertese, who had completed their labour contract in Queensland.[65] By law ships had to return labourers to their original point of departure, although this practice was not always scrupulously adhered to, particularly in the early years of the trade. While from 1870 Queensland appointed government agents to ensure that recruitment was voluntary and that recruits were well treated aboard ship, the poorly paid agents often proved no match for greedy captains and shipowners. Paid by the number of recruits they landed in Australia, captains all too often flouted regulations limiting the number of recruits according to the tonnage of the ship. Unusually quick return voyages also raised doubts about the 'voluntary' nature of recruitment in the islands.[66]

Kidnapping was common at first, particularly among those Islanders with little knowledge or experience of European trade practices. In the 1970s an elderly Queensland woman, Esther Henaway, recounted to the historian Clive Moore the story of how her father had been captured from a Pacific Island at about the age of 14 and brought to work on the plantations of Queensland. He had been lured onto the ship by deceit, and 'when he knew the boat was going away from shore he said all he could do was to cry. Because his mother and father and all his relations were left behind.' He had seen those who tried to escape over the side summarily shot by the recruiters.[67]

Once labour recruitment became established in certain areas it took on a more voluntary character. As Pacific Islanders gained some understanding of the process, many agreed to work in exchange for desired European goods and for the chance to increase their status in their own society when they returned at the end of their indenture. Offering double wages and a far superior as well as less expensive range of trade goods, Queensland proved a more popular destination for Pacific Island labourers than Fiji and, later, New Caledonia.[68] It provided men with the possibility of financial security on their

---

65 Jane Samson, *Imperial Benevolence: Making British Authority in the Pacific Islands* (Honolulu: University of Hawai'i Press, 1998): 116; W.T. Wawn, *The South Sea Islands and the Queensland Labour Trade: A Record of Voyages and Experiences in the Western Pacific, from 1875 to 1891* [1893] ed. and introd. Peter Corris (Canberra: ANU Press, 1973), p. xxxviii.

66 Peter Corris, *Passage, Port and Plantation: A History of Solomon Islands Labour Migration, 1870–1914* (Melbourne University Press, 1973), p. 277.

67 Clive Moore (ed.), *The Forgotten People: A History of the Australian South Sea Island Community* (Sydney: Australian Broadcasting Commission, 1979), p. 14.

68 Dorothy Shineberg, *The People Trade: Pacific Island Laborers and New Caledonia, 1865–1930* (Honolulu: University of Hawai'i Press, 1999), p. 22.

return; in particular, the opportunity to accumulate bride-wealth without lapsing into debt. Many Islanders signed up voluntarily for the increased wealth and European material goods they could bring back to the islands, especially guns, although this was illegal. Sid Ober described to Clive Moore how his father and uncle had been inspired to sign up as labourers after seeing what the men who came back counted among their possessions: 'we got talking. Mmm…we'll have to have a look at this Queensland.' The two brothers signalled to the recruiting ships and went to the plantations in the 1880s, much to the distress of their families. Sid Ober's father returned with the coveted guns smuggled in calico bundles, and subsequently signed up for a second contract: 'Oh, when you get a bit of Queensland, you sort of get it in your blood. When you see them schooners out at sea in full sail coming in, oh, it gives you the urge. You want to go again. So I came out again.'[69]

Increasing labour demands of the expanding Queensland plantation economy had a significant effect on the intervention of Australia in the Pacific region and the expansion of a seawards frontier for the continent. Some began to see a new destiny for Australia as a power within the southern Pacific region. There was also intense concern about the security of the continent from threats offered by both rival imperial powers and the movement of non-European peoples. This maritime frontier was policed slowly, intermittently and haphazardly by warships based in Sydney. Royal Naval ships were expected to patrol the islands of the south-west Pacific to enforce the provisions of the *Pacific Islanders Protection Act* of 1872, keep an eye on developments in Fiji and also fly the flag in the face of the growing presence of other naval powers, particularly Germany and the United States.[70] As the activities of Commodore James Goodenough demonstrate, some Royal Naval officers took their responsibilities toward protecting Pacific Islanders very seriously indeed. Yet Goodenough's death in 1875 (from tetanus contracted when the Pacific Islanders of Santa Cruz shot him full of arrows) also indicates the limits of naval officers' comprehension of local cultural practices and perspectives.[71] But just as the British flag often followed existing shipping routes, so too shipping routes sometimes followed the flag. Hence after Britain's annexation of Fiji in 1874 – a direct result of Goodenough's humanitarian crusade – the ASN established a service between Fiji and Sydney.

The idea of Australia as a white man's country was firmly entrenched by the late nineteenth century. Yet it was a much more unstable construction

---

69 Moore (ed.), *The Forgotten People*, p. 37.
70 Bach, *The Australia Station*, p. 176.
71 Samson, *Imperial Benevolence*, p. 66.

than the rhetoric suggested. The labour practices of the sugar and pearling industries bound northern Australia into the immediate maritime region. This was in stark contrast to developments to the south in precisely the same period, where methods of quarantine and blockade mobilised the sea as a barrier to sustain the fiction of a 'white' continent.[72] The SS *Ocean* and SS *Brisbane*, both carrying Chinese immigrants, were quarantined in Sydney in the midst of the 1881–82 smallpox epidemic, although the passengers had no proven contact with the disease. Despite the press accusations that the New South Wales government had used the incident to distract attention from its own public health failings, the quarantine of the *Ocean* and the *Brisbane* was mobilised to drum up political opposition to Chinese workers entering Australia.[73]

It was the sea that enabled the pearling and sugar industries, in their labour recruitment as well as, in the former case, in their product. Indenture may have been designed as a system to provide a steady workforce without permanent residence, but reality inevitably undermined such theories. Sugar and pearling in Australia also undercut assumptions about how the borders between land and sea should operate. New communities and cultures emerged that linked the continent into what was in effect its maritime hinterland. As Australians debated Federation, they ignored the fact that there were two very different 'Australias' then in existence. The southern, densely settled and predominantly white part of the continent was deeply hostile to its very different northern counterpart.

The interconnected maritime world of the pearling industry survived Federation, with a 1916 Royal Commission ultimately ruling in favour of the continuation of an Asian (predominantly Japanese but also Indonesian) labour base. Despite the best efforts of the federal government, the pearl shell industry was ultimately killed off not by white Australia but by the plastic button.[74] Some Indonesian workers, however, managed to fight deportation orders and remained in Australia as respected members of northern communities.[75] The transpacific cultural world of the Queensland sugar industry fared even worse. By the 1880s there was a significant proportion of Pacific Islander workers in Queensland who had formed a distinct segment

---

72 Alison Bashford, *Imperial Hygiene: A Critical History of Colonialism, Nationalism and Public Health* (Basingstoke: Palgrave Macmillan, 2004), p. 124.

73 Greg Watters, 'The S.S. Ocean: Dealing with Boat People in the 1880s', *Australian Historical Studies*, 33, 120 (2002): 331–43.

74 John Bailey, *The White Divers of Broome: The True Story of a Fatal Experiment* (Sydney: Pan Macmillan, 2001).

75 Martínez, 'Indonesians Challenging White Australia', pp. 9–10, 13–14.

of a general working class. The reorganisation of the sugar industry into smaller units led to the abandonment of the plantation gang system and the increasing presence of white labour in the cane fields from the 1890s. The Commonwealth *Pacific Islands Labourers Act* was passed in 1901, preparing for the abolition of the Pacific Island labour trade. Despite forming the Pacific Islanders Association to fight their deportation, all but a small proportion of these men and women were forcibly removed by 1907. Many had forged new lives in Australia, and now families were tragically wrenched apart. 'Government he hurry up along we fellow', wrote a man we know only as 'Louie' in a farewell letter to his partner Rosie and their son Herbert in 1906. 'I been ask Government along you, but you no stop alongside me…I sorry I no see my Missus any more.'[76]

Northern towns such as Broome might have been anomalous in the eyes of the south, but they were very much of a piece with their natural, as opposed to their political, geography. They were at one with the cosmopolitan port towns of the region. They looked out to sea and kept a far closer eye on the maritime highways that linked them to similar entrepôts across the Indian and Pacific oceans than they did on the isolating landmass behind.[77] With Federation in 1901 the achievement of unity was cast, in prime minister Edmund Barton's oft-quoted phrase, as 'a nation for a continent and a continent for a nation'. In the process Australia seemingly forgot that it was an island that the sea both isolates and joins to the wider world. The maritime had always been an ambivalent force in Australia's history, a bridge as much as it was a barricade.[78] The sea would now become fundamental to the way in which a new nation could distance itself from its neighbours.

76 Quoted in Reynolds, *North of Capricorn*, p. 181.
77 Balint, *Troubled Waters*, p. 24.
78 Ibid., p. 3.

Further reading

Reference

Australian Dictionary of Biography, 18 vols (Melbourne University Press, 1966–). All entries are available online at <http://adb.anu.edu.au/>.

Australian National Bibliography 1901–1950, 4 vols (Canberra: National Library of Australia, 1988).

J.A. Ferguson, *Bibliography of Australia*, 1784–1900, 7 vols (Canberra: National Library of Australia, 1941–69).

Handbooks

Jaynie Anderson (ed.), *The Cambridge Companion to Australian Art* (Cambridge University Press, 2011).

Barbara Caine (ed.), *Australian Feminism: A Companion* (Oxford University Press, 1998).

Frank Crowley and Peter Spearritt (gen. eds), *Australians: A Historical Library*, 5 vols: *A Historical Atlas, A Historical Dictionary, Events and Places, Historical Statistics, A Guide to Sources* (Sydney: Fairfax, Syme & Weldon Associates, 1987).

Brian Galligan and Winsome Roberts (eds), *The Oxford Companion to Australian Politics* (Oxford University Press, 2007).

John Hirst, Graeme Davison and Stuart Macintyre (eds), *The Oxford Companion to Australian History*, rev. edn (Oxford University Press, 2001).

David Horton (ed.), *The Encyclopaedia of Aboriginal Australia: Aboriginal and Torres Strait Islander History, Society and Culture*, 2 vols (Canberra: Aboriginal Studies Press, 1994).

James Jupp (ed.), *The Australian People: An Encyclopedia of the Nation, Its People and Their Origins*, rev. edn (Cambridge University Press, 2001).

James Jupp (ed.), *The Encyclopedia of Religion in Australia* (Cambridge University Press, 2009).

Alan McCulloch and Susan McCulloch (eds), *The Encyclopedia of Australian Art*, rev. edn (Sydney: Allen & Unwin, 1994).

Peter Pierce (ed.), *The Cambridge History of Australian Literature* (Cambridge University Press, 2009).

Wray Vamplew et al. (eds), *The Oxford Companion to Australian Sport* (Oxford University Press, 1994).

Elizabeth Webby (ed.), *The Cambridge Companion to Australian Literature* (Cambridge University Press, 2000).

William H. Wilde, Joy Hooton and Barry Andrews (eds), *The Oxford Companion to Australian Literature*, 2nd edn (Oxford University Press, 1994).

Records

Historical Records of Australia, 33 vols (Sydney: Library Committee of the Commonwealth Parliament, 1914–25).

Historical Records of Australia, resumed series, 3 vols (Melbourne University Press, 1997–).

Trove, National Library of Australia, online Australian resources: books, images, historic newspapers, maps, music and archives <http://trove.nla.gov.au/>.

General histories

Alan Atkinson, *The Europeans In Australia: A History* (Oxford University Press).

Volume 1, *The Beginning* (1997).

Volume 2, *Democracy* (2004).

Geoffrey Bolton (ed.), *The Oxford History of Australia* (Oxford University Press, vols. 2–5, 1986–92).

Jan Kociumbas, *The Oxford History of Australia. Volume 2, 1770–1860: Possessions* (Oxford University Press, 1995).

Beverley Kingston, *The Oxford History of Australia. Volume 3, 1860–1900: Glad, Confident Morning* (Oxford University Press, 1993).

C.M.H. Clark, *A History of Australia*, 6 vols (Melbourne University Press, 1962–87).

Volume 1, *From the Earliest Times to The Age of Macquarie* (1962).

Volume 2, *New South Wales and Van Diemen's Land 1822–1838* (1968).

Volume 3, *The Beginning of an Australian Civilization 1824–1851* (1973).

Volume 4, *The Earth Abideth for Ever 1851–1888* (1978).

Volume 5, *The People Make Laws 1888–1915* (1981).

Donald Denoon and Philippa Mein Smith with Marivic Wyndham, *A History of Australia, New Zealand and the Pacific* (Malden: Blackwell, 2000).

Alan D. Gilbert and K.S. Inglis (gen. eds), *Australians: A Historical Library*, 5 vols (Sydney: Fairfax, Syme & Weldon Associates, 1987).

D.J. Mulvaney and J. Peter White (eds), *Australians to 1788.*

Alan Atkinson and Marian Aveling (eds), *Australians 1838.*

Graeme Davison, J.W. McCarty and Ailsa McLeary (eds), *Australians 1888.*

Jeffrey Grey, *A Military History of Australia*, 3rd edn (Cambridge University Press, 2008).

Patricia Grimshaw, Marilyn Lake, Ann McGrath and Marian Quartly, *Creating a Nation* (Melbourne: McPhee Gribble, 1994).

Stuart Macintyre, *A Concise History of Australia*, 3rd edn (Cambridge University Press, 2008).

Mark Peel and Christina Twomey, *A History of Australia* (Basingstoke: Palgrave Macmillan, 2011).

John Rickard, *Australia: A Cultural History*, 2nd edn (New York: Longman, 1996).

Part I

Australian prehistory and archaeology

Jane Balme, Iain Davidson, Jo McDonald, Nicola Stern and Peter Veth, 'Symbolic Behaviour and the Peopling of the Southern Arc Route to Australia', *Quaternary International*, 202, 1–2 (2009): 59–68.

Josephine Flood, *Archaeology of the Dreamtime: The Story of Prehistoric Australia and its People* (Adelaide: J.B. Publishing, 2004).

Josephine Flood, *The Original Australians: Story of the Aboriginal People* (Sydney: Allen & Unwin, 2006).

Bill Gammage, *The Biggest Estate on Earth: How Aborigines Made Australia* (Sydney: Allen & Unwin, 2011).

Peter Hiscock, *Archaeology of Ancient Australia* (New York: Routledge, 2008).

Jennifer Isaacs (ed.), *Australian Dreaming: 40,000 Years of Aboriginal History* (Sydney: New Holland Publishers, 2005).

Michelle C. Langley, Christopher Clarkson and Sean Ulm, 'From Small Holes to Grand Narratives: The Impact of Taphonomy and Sample Size on the Modernity Debate in Australia and New Guinea', *Journal of Human Evolution*, 61, 2 (2011): 197–208.

Ian Lilley (ed.), *Archaeology of Oceania: Australia and the Pacific Islands* (Oxford: Blackwell, 2006).

Harry Lourandos, *Continent of Hunter-Gatherers: New Perspectives in Australian Prehistory* (Cambridge University Press, 1997).

Jo McDonald and Peter Veth, 'Information Exchange amongst Hunter-Gatherers of the Western Desert of Australia', in Robert Whallon, William A. Lovis and Robert K. Hitchcock (eds), *Information and its Role in Hunter-Gatherer Bands* (Los Angeles: The Costen Institute of Archaeology Press, 2011), pp. 221–34.

M.J. Morwood, *Visions from the Past: The Archaeology of Australian Aboriginal Art* (Sydney: Allen & Unwin, 2002).

D.J. Mulvaney and Johan Kamminga, *Prehistory of Australia* (Sydney: Allen & Unwin, 1999).

D.J. Mulvaney and J. Peter White (eds), *Australians to 1788* (Sydney: Fairfax, Syme & Weldon Associates, 1987).

Sue O'Connor and Marjorie Sullivan, 'Coastal Archaeology in Australia: Developments and New Directions', *Australian Archaeology*, 39 (1995): 87–96.

Sue O'Connor and Peter Veth (eds), *East of Wallace's Line: Studies of Past and Present Maritime Cultures in the Indo-Pacific Region* (Rotterdam: A.A. Balkema, 2000).

David Andrew Roberts and Iain Davidson, '14 000 BP: On Being Alone: The Isolation of the Tasmanians', in Martin Crotty and David Andrew Roberts (eds), *Turning Points in Australian History* (Sydney: UNSW Press, 2009), pp. 18–31.

Robin Torrence and Anne Clarke (eds), *The Archaeology of Difference: Negotiating Cross-Cultural Engagements in Oceania* (London: Routledge, 2000).

Mike Smith, *Puritjarra Rock Shelter: Final Report of Excavations 1986–1990* (Canberra: National Museum of Australia Press, 2010).

Peter Veth, *Islands in the Interior: The Dynamics of Prehistoric Adaptations within the Arid Zone of Australia* (Ann Arbor: University of Michigan Press, 1993).

Peter Veth, Mike Smith and Peter Hiscock (eds), *Desert Peoples: Archaeological Perspectives* (Malden: Blackwell, 2005).

Peter Veth, Peter Sutton and Margo Neale (eds), *Strangers on the Shore: Early Coastal Contacts in Australia* (Canberra: National Museum of Australia, 2008).

Newcomers and European explorers, c. 1600–1800

Len Collard and Dave Palmer, 'Looking for the Residents of *Terra Australis*: The Importance of Nyungar in Early European Coastal Exploration', in Peter Veth, Peter Sutton and Margo Neale (eds), *Strangers on the Shore: Early Coastal Contacts in Australia* (Canberra: National Museum of Australia, 2008), pp. 181–97.

Ian Donaldson and Tamsin Donaldson (eds), *Seeing the First Australians* (Sydney: Allen & Unwin, 1985).

Bronwen Douglas, 'Seaborne Ethnography and the Natural History of Man', *Journal of Pacific History*, 38, 1 (2003): 3–27.

Colin Dyer, *The French Explorers and the Aboriginal Australians 1772–1839* (Brisbane: UQP, 2005).

William Eisler, *The Furthest Shore: Images of Terra Australis from the Middle Ages to Captain Cook* (Cambridge University Press, 1995).

Jean Fornasiero, Peter Monteath, and John West-Sooby, *Encountering Terra Australis: The Australian Voyages of Nicolas Baudin and Matthew Flinders*, rev. edn (Adelaide: Wakefield Press, 2010).

John Gascoigne, *Joseph Banks and the English Enlightenment: Useful Knowledge and Polite Culture* (Cambridge University Press, 1994).

John Gascoigne (with the assistance of Patricia Curthoys), *The Enlightenment and the Origins of European Australia* (Cambridge University Press, 2005).

Sylvia J. Hallam, 'A View From the Other Side of the Western Frontier: or "I met a man who wasn't there …"', *Aboriginal History*, 7, 2 (1983): 134–56.

Chris Healy, 'Captain Cook: Between Black and White', in Margo Neale and Sylvia Kleinert (eds), *The Oxford Companion to Aboriginal Art and Culture* (Oxford University Press, 2000), pp. 92–5.

Shino Konishi, *The Aboriginal Male in the Enlightenment World* (London: Pickering & Chatto, 2012).

C.C. Macknight, *The Voyage to Marege': Macassan Trepangers in Northern Australia* (Melbourne University Press, 1976).

Adrian Mitchell, *Dampier's Monkey: A Reading of the South Seas Narratives of William Dampier* (Adelaide: Wakefield Press, 2010).

D.J. Mulvaney, *Encounters in Place: Outsiders and Aboriginal Australians, 1606–1985* (Brisbane: UQP, 1989).

Maria Nugent, *Captain Cook Was Here* (Cambridge University Press, 2009).

Michael Pearson, *Great Southern Land: The Maritime Exploration of Terra Australis* (Canberra: Department of the Environment and Heritage, 2005).

N.J.B. Plomley, *The Baudin Expedition and the Tasmanian Aborigines, 1802* (Hobart: Blubber Head Press, 1983).

Günter Schilder, *Australia Unveiled: The Share of the Dutch Navigators in the Discovery of Australia*, trans. Olaf Richter (Amsterdam: Theatrum Orbis Terrarum Ltd, 1976).

Bernard Smith, *European Vision and the South Pacific* [1960] (New Haven: Yale University Press, 1985).

Nicholas Thomas, *Discoveries: The Voyages of Captain Cook* (London: Allen Lane, 2003).

Glyndwr Williams and Alan Frost (eds), *Terra Australis to Australia* (Oxford University Press, 1988).

Eighteenth-century Britain and Botany Bay

Alan Atkinson, *The Europeans In Australia: A History. Volume 1, The Beginning* (Oxford University Press, 1997).

Geoffrey Blainey, *The Tyranny of Distance: How Distance Shaped Australia's History*, rev. edn (Sydney: Macmillan, 2001).

Emma Christopher, 'A "Disgrace to the very Colour": Perceptions of Blackness and Whiteness in the Founding of Sierra Leone and Botany Bay', *Journal of Colonialism and Colonial History*, 9, 3 (2008): online.

Emma Christopher, *A Merciless Place: The Lost Story of Britain's Convict Disaster in Africa and How it Led to the Settlement of Australia* (Sydney: Allen & Unwin, 2010).

K.M. Dallas, *Trading Posts or Penal Colonies: The Commercial Significance of Cook's New Holland Route to the Pacific* (Hobart: Fullers, 1969).

Alan Frost, *Convicts and Empire: A Naval Question, 1776–1811* (Oxford University Press, 1980).

Alan Frost, *Botany Bay Mirages: Illusions of Australia's Convict Beginnings* (Melbourne University Press, 1994).

Alan Frost, *Botany Bay: The Real Story* (Melbourne: Black Inc., 2011).

Mollie Gillen, 'The Botany Bay Decision, 1786: Convicts not Empire', *English Historical Review*, 97 (1982): 740–66.

Ged Martin (ed.), *The Founding of Australia: The Argument about Australia's Origins* (Sydney: Hale & Iremonger, 1978).

Hamish Maxwell-Stewart, 'Convict Transportation from Britain and Ireland 1615–1870', *History Compass*, 8, 11 (2010): 1221–42.

Angus McGillivery, 'Convict Settlers, Seamen's Greens, and Imperial Designs at Port Jackson: A Maritime Perspective of British Settler Agriculture', *Agricultural History*, 78, 3 (2004): 261–88.

David Meredith and Deborah Oxley, 'Condemned to the Colonies: Penal Transportation as the Solution to Britain's Law and Order Problem', *Leidschrift*, 22, 1 (2007): 19–39.

Stephen Nicholas (ed.), *Convict Workers: Reinterpreting Australia's Past* (Cambridge University Press, 1988).

Wifrid Oldham, *Britain's Convicts to the Colonies* (Sydney: Library of Australian History, 1990).

Bob Reece, *The Origins of Irish Convict Transportation to New South Wales* (Basingstoke: Palgrave Macmillan, 2001).

A.G.L. Shaw, *Convicts and the Colonies: A Study of Penal Transportation from Great Britain and Ireland to Australia and Other Parts of the British Empire* (London: Faber & Faber, 1971).

The early colonial presence

Graeme Aplin (ed.), *A Difficult Infant: Sydney Before Macquarie* (Sydney: UNSW Press, 1988).

Alan Atkinson, *The Europeans In Australia: A History. Volume 1, The Beginning* (Oxford University Press, 1997).

Val Attenbrow, *Sydney's Aboriginal Past: Investigating the Archaeological and Historical Records* (Sydney: UNSW Press, 2002).

Tim Bonyhady, *The Colonial Earth* (Melbourne: Miegunyah Press, 2000).

James Boyce, *Van Diemen's Land* (Melbourne: Black Inc., 2008).

James Broadbent and Joy Hughes (eds), *The Age of Macquarie* (Melbourne University Press, 1992).

Inga Clendinnen, *Dancing with Strangers* (Melbourne: Text, 2003).

Joy Damousi, *Depraved and Disorderly: Female Convicts, Sexuality and Gender in Colonial Australia* (Cambridge University Press, 1997).

Kay Daniels, *Convict Women* (Sydney: Allen & Unwin, 1998).

Ross Fitzgerald and Mark Hearn, *Bligh, Macarthur and the Rum Rebellion* (Sydney: Kangaroo Press, 1988).

Brian H. Fletcher, *Landed Enterprise and Penal Society: A History of Farming and Grazing in New South Wales before 1821* (Sydney University Press, 1976).

Lisa Ford, *Settler Sovereignty: Jurisdiction and Indigenous People in America and Australia 1788–1836* (Cambridge, MA: Harvard University Press, 2010).

Alan Frost, *Botany Bay Mirages: Illusions of Australia's Convict Beginnings* (Melbourne University Press, 1994).

D.R. Hainsworth, *The Sydney Traders: Simeon Lord and his Contemporaries, 1788–1821* (Melbourne: Cassell, 1972).

J.B. Hirst, *Convict Society and Its Enemies: A History of Early New South Wales* (Sydney: Allen & Unwin, 1983).

Grace Karskens, *The Rocks: Life in Early Sydney* (Melbourne University Press, 1997).

Grace Karskens, *The Colony: A History of Early Sydney* (Sydney: Allen & Unwin, 2009).

Bruce Kercher, *An Unruly Child: A History of Law in Australia* (Sydney: Allen & Unwin, 1995).

Stephen Nicholas (ed.), *Convict Workers: Reinterpreting Australia's Past* (Cambridge University Press, 1988).

Geoff Raby, *Making Rural Australia: An Economic History of Technical and Institutional Creativity, 1788–1860* (Oxford University Press, 1996).

Henry Reynolds, *A History of Tasmania* (Cambridge University Press, 2011).

John Ritchie, *Lachlan Macquarie: A Biography* (Melbourne University Press, 1986).

Lloyd Robson, *A History of Tasmania. Volume 1, Van Diemen's Land from Earliest Times to 1855* (Oxford University Press, 1983).

Bernard Smith and Alwyne Wheeler (eds), *The Art of the First Fleet & Other Early Australian Drawings* (New Haven: Yale University Press 1988).

Richard Waterhouse, *Private Pleasures, Public Leisure: A History of Australian Popular Culture since 1788* (Melbourne: Longman, 1995).

Expansion, 1820–50

Alison Alexander, *Tasmania's Convicts* (Sydney: Allen & Unwin, 2010).

Alan Atkinson and Marian Aveling (eds), *Australians 1838* (Sydney: Fairfax, Syme & Weldon Associates, 1987).

Bain Attwood, *Possession: Batman's Treaty and the Matter of History* (Melbourne: Miegunyah Press, 2009).

Further reading

Geoffrey Bolton, *Land of Vision and Mirage: Western Australia since 1826* (Perth: UWA Press, 2008).

James Boyce, *1835: The Founding of Melbourne & the Conquest of Australia* (Melbourne: Black Inc., 2011).

N.G. Butlin, *Forming a Colonial Economy: Australia 1810–1850* (Cambridge University Press, 1994).

Lisa Ford, *Settler Sovereignty: Jurisdiction and Indigenous People in America and Australia 1788–1836* (Cambridge, MA: Harvard University Press, 2010).

Robert Foster and Amanda Nettelbeck, *Out of the Silence: The History and Memory of South Australia's Frontier Wars* (Adelaide: Wakefield Press, 2011).

Heather Goodall, *Invasion to Embassy: Land in Aboriginal Politics in New South Wales, 1770–1972* (Sydney: Allen & Unwin, 1996).

J.B. Hirst, *Convict Society and Its Enemies: A History of Early New South Wales* (Sydney: Allen & Unwin, 1983).

Robert Hughes, *The Fatal Shore: A History of the Transportation of Convicts to Australia, 1787–1868* (London: Harvill Press, 1987).

Sharon Morgan, *Land Settlement in Early Tasmania: Creating an Antipodean England* (Cambridge University Press, 1992).

Henry Reynolds, *Frontier: Aborigines, Settlers and Land* (Sydney: Allen & Unwin, 1987).

Eric Richards (ed.), *Flinders History of South Australia. Volume 1, Social History* (Adelaide: Wakefield Press, 1986).

John Ritchie, *Punishment and Profit: The Reports of Commissioner John Bigge on the Colonies of New South Wales and Van Diemen's Land, 1822–1823; Their Origins, Nature and Significance* (Melbourne: Heinemann, 1970).

Michael Roe, *Quest for Authority in Eastern Australia 1835–1851* (Melbourne University Press, 1965).

Lyndall Ryan, 'Settler massacres on the Port Phillip Frontier, 1836–1851', *Journal of Australian Studies*, 34, 3 (2010): 257–73.

Penny Russell, *Savage or Civilised? Manners in Colonial Australia* (Sydney: UNSW Press, 2010).

Michael Sturma, *Vice in a Vicious Society: Crime and Convicts in Mid-Nineteenth Century New South Wales* (Brisbane: UQP, 1983).

Self-government

Geoffrey Bolton, *Land of Vision and Mirage: Western Australia since 1826* (Perth: UWA Press, 2008).

Peter Burroughs, *Britain and Australia 1831–1855: A Study in Imperial Relations and Crown Lands Administration* (Oxford: Clarendon, 1967).

Peter Cochrane, *Colonial Ambition: Foundations of Australian Democracy* (Melbourne University Press, 2006).

Brian de Garis, 'Self-government and the Evolution of Party Politics 1871–1911', in Tom Stannage (ed.), *A New History of Western Australia* (Perth: UWA Press, 1981), pp. 326–51.

Julie Evans, Patricia Grimshaw, David Phillips, and Shurlee Swain, *Equal Subjects, Unequal Rights: Indigenous People in British Settler Colonies, 1830–1910* (Manchester University Press, 2003).

Neville Green, 'From Princes to Paupers: The Struggle for Control of Aborigines in Western Australia 1887–1898', *Early Days*, 11, 4 (1998): 447–62.

John Hirst, *The Strange Birth of Colonial Democracy: New South Wales 1848–1884* (Sydney: Allen & Unwin, 1988).

T.H. Irving, '1850–70', in Frank Crowley (ed.), *A New History of Australia* (Melbourne: Heinemann, 1974), pp. 124–64.

Terry Irving, *The Southern Tree of Liberty: The Democratic Movement in New South Wales before 1856* (Sydney: Federation Press, 2006).

Dean Jaensch (ed.), *The Flinders History of South Australia. Volume 2, Political History* (Adelaide: Wakefield Press, 1986).

Mark McKenna, *The Captive Republic: A History of Republicanism in Australia, 1788–1996* (Cambridge University Press, 1996).

Kirsten McKenzie, *Scandal in the Colonies: Sydney and Cape Town, 1820–1850* (Melbourne University Press, 2004).

A.C.V. Melbourne, 'The Establishment of Responsible Government', in J. Holland Rose, A.P. Newton, E.A. Benians with Ernest Scott (eds), *The Cambridge History of the British Empire*, vol. VII, part 1, *Australia* (Cambridge University Press, 1933), pp. 273–95.

Jessie Mitchell, '"The galling yoke of slavery": Race and Separation in Colonial Port Phillip,' *Journal of Australian Studies*, 33, 2 (2009): 125–37.

Keith Moore, 'English Liberty and People's Rights: The Influence of Heritage in Achieving Self-Government in Queensland', *Queensland History Journal*, 20, 12 (2009): 738–47.

Paul A. Pickering, 'A Wider Field in a New Country: Chartism in Colonial Australia', in Marian Sawer (ed.), *Elections: Full, Free and Fair* (Sydney: Federation Press, 2001), pp. 28–44.

Paul A. Pickering, 'Loyalty and Rebellion in Colonial Politics: The Campaign against Convict Transportation in Australia', in Philip Alfred Buckner and R. Douglas Francis (eds), *Rediscovering the British World* (University of Calgary Press, 2005), pp. 87–107.

Henry Reynolds, *A History of Tasmania* (Cambridge University Press, 2012).

David Andrew Roberts, 'Remembering "Australia's glorious League": The Historiography of Anti-Transportation', *Journal of Australian Colonial History*, 14 (2012): 205–15.

Geoffrey Serle, *The Golden Age: A History of the Colony of Victoria, 1851–1861* (Melbourne University Press, 1963).

John M. Ward, *Colonial Self-Government: The British Experience 1759–1856* (London: Macmillan, 1976).

The gold rushes

Robyn Annear, *Nothing but Gold: The Diggers of 1852* (Melbourne: Text, 1999).

Weston Bate, *Lucky City: The First Generation at Ballarat, 1851–1901* (Melbourne University Press, 1978).

Weston Bate, *Victorian Gold Rushes* (Melbourne: McPhee Gribble/Penguin, 1988).

Ralph W. Birrell, *Staking a Claim: Gold and the Development of Victorian Mining Law* (Melbourne University Press, 1998).

Geoffrey Blainey, *The Rush that Never Ended: A History of Australian Mining*, 5th edn (Melbourne University Press, 2003).

Further reading

David [Fred] Cahir and Ian D. Clark, '"Why Should they Pay Money to the Queen?" Aboriginal Miners and Land Claims', *Journal of Australian Colonial History*, 10, 1 (2008): 115–28.

C.M.H. Clark, *A History of Australia. Volume 4, The Earth Abideth for Ever, 1851–1888* (Melbourne University Press, 1978).

Kathryn Cronin, *Colonial Casualties: Chinese in Early Victoria* (Melbourne University Press, 1982).

Charles Fahey, 'Peopling the Victorian Goldfields: From Boom to Bust, 1851–1901', *Australian Economic History Review*, 50, 2 (2010): 148–61.

Charles Fahey and Alan Mayne, *Gold Tailings: Forgotten History of Family and Community on the Central Victorian Goldfields* (Melbourne: Australian Scholarly Publishing, 2010).

David Goodman, *Gold Seeking: Victoria and California in the 1850s* (Sydney: Allen & Unwin, 1994).

Marilyn Lake and Henry Reynolds, *Drawing the Global Colour Line: White Men's Countries and the Question of Racial Equality* (Melbourne University Press, 2008).

Susan Lawrence, *Dolly's Creek: An Archaeology of a Victorian Goldfields Community* (Melbourne University Press, 2000).

Alan Mayne (ed.), *Eureka: Reappraising an Australian Legend* (Perth: Network Books, 2006).

W.P. Morrell, *The Gold Rushes*, 2nd edn (London: Black, 1968).

June Philipp, *A Poor Man's Diggings: Mining and Community at Bethanga, Victoria, 1875–1912* (Melbourne: Hyland House, 1987).

Daniel Potts and Annette Potts, *Young America and Australian Gold: Americans and the Gold Rush of the 1850s* (Brisbane: UQP, 1974).

Andrew Reeves, Iain McCalman and Alexander Cook (eds), *Gold: Forgotten Histories and Lost Objects of Australia* (Cambridge University Press, 2001).

Keir James Reeves and David Nichols, *Deeper Leads: New Approaches to Victorian Goldfields History* (Ballarat Heritage Services, 2007).

Geoffrey Serle, *The Golden Age: A History of the Colony of Victoria, 1851–1861* (Melbourne University Press, 1963).

Colonial states and civil society, 1860–90

Alan Atkinson, *The Europeans in Australia: A History. Volume 2, Democracy* (Oxford University Press, 2004).

N.G. Butlin, *Investment in Australian Economic Development, 1861–1900* (Canberra: Department of Economic History, Research School of Social Sciences, ANU, 1972).

Graeme Davison, *The Rise and Fall of Marvellous Melbourne*, 2nd edn (Melbourne University Press, 2004).

Graeme Davison, J.W. McCarty and Ailsa McLeary (eds), *Australians 1888* (Sydney: Fairfax, Syme & Weldon Associates, 1987).

David Denholm, *The Colonial Australians* (Melbourne: Penguin Books, 1979).

John Ferry, *Colonial Armidale* (Brisbane: UQP, 1999).

Lionel Frost, *The New Urban Frontier: Urbanisation and City-Building in Australasia and the American West* (Sydney: UNSW Press, 1991).

Robin Gollan, *Radical and Working Class Politics: A Study of Eastern Australia, 1850–1910* (Melbourne University Press, 1960).

Patricia Grimshaw, Ellen McEwen and Chris McConville (eds), *Families in Colonial Australia* (Sydney: Allen & Unwin, 1985).

J.B. Hirst, *Adelaide and the Country 1870–1917: Their Social and Political Relationship* (Melbourne University Press, 1973).

J.B. Hirst, *The Strange Birth of Colonial Democracy: New South Wales 1848–1884* (Sydney: Allen & Unwin, 1988).

H.R. Jackson, *Churches and People in Australia and New Zealand 1860–1930* (Sydney: Allen & Unwin, 1987).

R.V. Jackson, *Australian Economic Development in the Nineteenth Century* (Canberra: ANU Press, 1977).

Beverley Kingston, *The Oxford History of Australia. Volume 3, 1860–1900: Glad Confident Morning* (Oxford University Press, 1988).

Ann Larson, *Growing Up in Melbourne: Family Life in the Late Nineteenth Century* (Canberra: Demography Program, ANU, 1994).

P. Loveday and A.W. Martin, *Parliament, Factions and Parties: The First Thirty Years of Responsible Government in New South Wales, 1856–1889* (Melbourne University Press, 1966).

Stuart Macintyre, *A Colonial Liberalism: The Lost World of Three Victorian Visionaries* (Oxford University Press, 1991).

Henry Reynolds, *North of Capricorn: The Untold Story of Australia's North* (Sydney: Allen & Unwin, 2003).

Geoffrey Serle, *The Rush To Be Rich: A History of the Colony of Victoria, 1883–1889* (Melbourne University Press, 1971).

Marjorie Theobald, *Knowing Women: Origins of Women's Education in Nineteenth-Century Australia* (Cambridge University Press, 1996).

The 1890s

Judith A. Allen, *Rose Scott: Vision and Revision in Feminism* (Oxford University Press, 1994).

Melissa Bellanta, *Larrikins: A History* (Brisbane: UQP, 2012).

Geoffrey Blainey, *The Rush That Never Ended: A History of Australian Mining*, 5th edn (Melbourne University Press, 2003).

E.A. Boehm, *Prosperity and Depression in Australia, 1887–1897* (Oxford: Clarendon, 1971).

John Docker, *The Nervous Nineties: Australian Cultural Life in the 1890s* (Oxford University Press, 1991).

Veronica Kelly, *The Empire Actors: Stars of Australasian Costume Drama 1890s–1920s* (Sydney: Currency House, 2010).

P. Loveday, A.W. Martin and R.S. Parker (eds), *The Emergence of the Australian Party System* (Sydney: Hale & Iremonger, 1977).

Ross McMullin, *The Light on the Hill: The Australian Labor Party, 1891–1991* (Oxford University Press, 1991).

Humphrey McQueen, *A New Britannia: An Argument Concerning the Social Origins of Australian Radicalism and Nationalism*, 4th edn (Brisbane: UQP, 2004).

Susan Magarey, *Passions of the First-Wave Feminists* (Sydney: UNSW Press, 2001).

Susan Magarey, Sue Rowley and Susan Sheridan (eds), *Debutante Nation: Feminism Contests the 1890s* (Sydney: Allen & Unwin, 1993).

John Merritt, *The Making of the AWU* (Oxford University Press, 1986).

John Murphy, *A Decent Provision: Australian Welfare Policy, 1870 to 1949* (Farnham: Ashgate, 2011).

Anne O'Brien, *Poverty's Prison: The Poor in New South Wales 1880–1918* (Melbourne University Press, 1988).

Vance Palmer, *The Legend of the Nineties* (Melbourne University Press, 1954).

Henry Reynolds, *North of Capricorn: The Untold Story of Australia's North* (Sydney: Allen & Unwin, 2003).

John Rickard, *Class and Politics: New South Wales, Victoria and the Early Commonwealth 1890–1910* (Canberra: ANU Press, 1976).

Bruce Scates, *A New Australia: Citizenship, Radicalism and the New Republic* (Cambridge University Press, 1997).

Ken Stewart (ed.), *The 1890s: Australian Literature and Literary Culture* (Brisbane: UQP, 1996).

Luke Trainor, *British Imperialism and Australian Nationalism: Manipulation, Conflict, and Compromise in the Late Nineteenth Century* (Cambridge University Press, 1994).

Richard White, *Inventing Australia: Images and Identity 1688–1980* (Sydney: Allen & Unwin, 1981).

Federation

Scott Bennett (ed.), *The Making of the Commonwealth* (Melbourne: Cassell Australia, 1971).

Scott Bennett (ed.), *Federation* (Melbourne: Cassell Australia, 1975).

Geoffrey Bolton, *Edmund Barton: The One Man for the Job* (Sydney: Allen & Unwin, 2000).

L. F. Crisp, *Federation Fathers* (Melbourne University Press, 1990).

Alfred Deakin, *'And Be One People': Alfred Deakin's Federal Story*, ed. Stuart Macintyre (Melbourne University Press, 1995).

Robert Garran, 'The Federation Movement and the Founding of the Commonwealth', in J. Holland Rose, A.P. Newton, E.A. Benians with Ernest Scott (eds), *The Cambridge History of the British Empire*, vol. VII, part 1, *Australia* (Cambridge University Press, 1933), pp. 425–53.

David Headon and John Williams (eds), *Makers of Miracles: The Cast of the Federation Story* (Melbourne University Press, 2000).

John Hirst, *The Sentimental Nation: The Making of the Australian Commonwealth* (Oxford University Press, 2000).

Helen Irving, *To Constitute a Nation: A Cultural History of Australia's Constitution* (Cambridge University Press, 1997).

Helen Irving, (ed.), *A Woman's Constitution? Gender and History in the Australian Commonwealth* (Sydney: Hale & Iremonger, 1996).

Helen Irving, (ed.), *The Centenary Companion to Australian Federation* (Cambridge University Press, 1999).

J.A. La Nauze, *Alfred Deakin: A Biography*, 2 vols (Melbourne University Press, 1965).

J.A. La Nauze, *The Making of the Australian Constitution* (Melbourne University Press, 1972).

J.A. La Nauze, *No Ordinary Act: Essays on Federation and the Constitution*, eds Helen Irving and Stuart Macintyre (Melbourne University Press, 2001).

W.G. McMinn, *Nationalism and Federalism in Australia* (Oxford University Press, 1994).

A.W. Martin (ed.), *Essays in Australian Federation* (Melbourne University Press, 1969).

A.W. Martin, *Henry Parkes: A Biography* (Melbourne University Press, 1980).

R. Norris, *The Emergent Commonwealth: Australian Federation, Expectations and Fulfilment 1889–1910* (Melbourne University Press, 1975).

Gavin Souter, *Lion and Kangaroo: The Initiation of Australia*, new edn (Melbourne: Text, 2000).

John M. Williams, *The Australian Constitution: A Documentary History* (Melbourne University Press, 2005).

Part II

The environment

Neil Barr and John Cary, *Greening a Brown Land: The Australian Search for Sustainable Land Use* (Melbourne: Macmillan Education Australia, 1992).

Tim Bonyhady, *The Colonial Earth* (Melbourne: Miegunyah Press, 2000).

Geoffrey Bolton, *Spoils and Spoilers: Australians Make Their Environment 1788–1980* (Sydney: Allen & Unwin, 1981).

James Boyce, *Van Diemen's Land* (Melbourne: Black Inc., 2008).

Graeme Davison, 'Australia: The First Suburban Nation?' *Journal of Urban History*, 22, 1 (1995): 40–74.

Thomas R. Dunlap, *Nature and the English Diaspora: Environment and History in the United States, Canada, Australia, and New Zealand* (Cambridge University Press, 1999).

Tim Flannery, *The Future Eaters: An Ecological History of the Australasian Lands and People* (Sydney: New Holland Publishers, 1997).

Lionel Frost, *The New Urban Frontier: Urbanisation and City-Building in Australasia and the American West* (Sydney: UNSW Press, 1991).

Bill Gammage, *The Biggest Estate on Earth: How Aborigines Made Australia* (Sydney: Allen & Unwin, 2011).

Don Garden, *Droughts, Floods & Cyclones: El Niños that Shaped Our Colonial Past* (Melbourne: Australian Scholarly Publishing, 2009).

Tom Griffiths and Libby Robin (eds), *Ecology and Empire: Environmental History of Settler Societies* (Melbourne University Press, 1997).

John Hardy and Alan Frost (eds), *Studies from Terra Australis to Australia* (Canberra: Australian Academy of the Humanities, 1989).

Katie Holmes, Susan K. Martin and Kylie Mirmohamadi, *Reading the Garden: The Settlement of Australia* (Melbourne University Press, 2008).

William J. Lines, *Taming the Great South Land: A History of the Conquest of Nature in Australia* (Sydney: Allen & Unwin, 1991).

D.W. Meinig, *On The Margins Of The Good Earth: The South Australian Wheat Frontier, 1869–1884* [1962] (Adelaide: Rigby, 1970).

J.M. Powell, *Environmental Management in Australia 1788–1914* (Melbourne: Oxford University Press, 1976).

Stephen J. Pyne, *Burning Bush: A Fire History of Australia* (Sydney: Allen & Unwin, 1992).

Eric C. Rolls, *They All Ran Wild: The Animals and Plants that Plague Australia* (Sydney: Angus & Robertson, 1984).

Ian Tyrrell, *True Gardens of the Gods: Californian-Australian Environmental Reform, 1860–1930* (Berkeley: University of California Press, 1999).

Mary E. White, *After the Greening: The Browning of Australia* (Sydney: Kangaroo Press, 1994).

Population and health

W.D. Borrie, *The European Peopling of Australasia: A Demographic History, 1788–1988* (Canberra: Demography Program, ANU, 1994).

Gordon Briscoe and Len Smith, *The Aboriginal Population Revisited: 70,000 Years to the Present* (Canberra: Aboriginal History Incorporated, 2002).

Gordon A. Carmichael, *With This Ring: First Marriage Patterns, Trends and Prospects in Australia* (Canberra: Department of Demography, ANU, 1988).

J.H.L. Cumpston, *Health and Disease in Australia: A History* (Canberra: AGPS, 1989).

Henry Finlay, *To Have But Not To Hold: A History of Attitudes to Marriage and Divorce in Australia 1858–1975* (Sydney: Federation Press, 2005).

Bryan Gandevia and Sheila Simpson, *Tears Often Shed: Child Health and Welfare in Australia from 1788* (Sydney: Pergamon Press, 1978).

J.M. Goldsmid, *The Deadly Legacy: Australian History and Transmissible Disease* (Sydney: UNSW Press, 1988).

Patricia Grimshaw, Chris McConville and Ellen McEwen (eds), *Families in Colonial Australia* (Sydney: Allen & Unwin, 1985).

Neville D. Hicks, *'This Sin and Scandal': Australia's Population Debate, 1891–1911* (Canberra: ANU Press, 1978).

Pat Jalland, *Australian Ways of Death: A Social and Cultural History 1840–1918* (Oxford University Press, 2002).

Elise F. Jones, 'Fertility Decline in Australia and New Zealand, 1861–1936', *Population Index*, 37, 4 (1971): 301–38.

Anne Larson, *Growing Up in Melbourne: Family Life in the Late Nineteenth Century* (Canberra: Demography Program, ANU, 1994).

Milton J. Lewis, *The People's Health: Public Health in Australia, 1788–1950* (Westport: Praeger, 2003).

Janet McCalman, *Sex and Suffering: Women's Health and a Women's Hospital* (Baltimore: Johns Hopkins University Press, 1999).

Peter F. McDonald, *Marriage in Australia: Age at First Marriage and Proportions Marrying, 1860–1971* (Canberra: Department of Demography, ANU, 1974).

R.B. Madgwick, *Immigration into Eastern Australia, 1788–1851*, new edn (Sydney University Press, 1969).

Patricia Quiggin, *No Rising Generation: Women & Fertility in Late Nineteenth-Century Australia* (Canberra: Department of Demography, ANU, 1988).

F.B. Smith, *Illness in Colonial Australia* (Melbourne: Australian Scholarly Publishing, 2011).

Graeme D. Snooks, *Portrait of the Family Within the Total Economy: A Study in Longrun Dynamics, Australia 1788–1990* (Cambridge University Press, 1994).

Wray Vamplew (ed.) *Australians: Historical Statistics* (Sydney: Fairfax, Syme & Weldon Associates, 1987).

The economy

James Belich, *Replenishing the Earth: The Settler Revolution and the Rise of the Anglo-World, 1783–1939* (Oxford University Press, 2009).

Geoffrey Blainey, *The Tyranny of Distance: How Distance Shaped Australia's History* (Melbourne: Sun Books, 1966).

E.A. Boehm, *Prosperity and Depression in Australia, 1887–1897* (Oxford: Clarendon, 1971).

N.G. Butlin, *Investment in Australian Economic Development 1861–1900* (Cambridge University Press, 1964).

N.G. Butlin, *Economics and the Dreamtime: A Hypothetical History* (Cambridge University Press, 1993).

N.G. Butlin, *Forming a Colonial Economy: Australia 1810–1850* (Cambridge University Press, 1994).

S.J. Butlin, *Foundations of the Australian Monetary System 1788–1851* (Sydney University Press, 1953).

Graeme Davison, *The Rise and Fall of Marvellous Melbourne*, 2nd edn (Melbourne University Press, 2004).

Charles Fahey, '"A Splendid Place for a Home": A Long History of the Australian Family Farm 1830–2000', in Alan Mayne and Stephen Atkinson (eds), *Outside Country: Histories of Inland Australia* (Adelaide: Wakefield Press, 2011), pp. 231–66.

Shirley Fitzgerald, *Rising Damp: Sydney 1870–90* (Melbourne: Oxford University Press, 1987).

Lionel Frost, 'The Contribution of the Urban Sector to Australian Economic Development Before 1914', *Australian Economic History Review*, 38, 1 (1998): 42–73.

J. W. McCarty, 'Australian Capital Cities in the Nineteenth Century', *Australian Economic History Review*, 10, 2 (1970): 107–37.

Ian W. McLean, 'Recovery from Depression: Australia in an Argentine Mirror 1895–1913', *Australian Economic History Review*, 46, 3 (2006): 215–41.

Ian W. McLean, *Why Australia Prospered: The Shifting Sources of Economic Growth* (Princeton University Press, 2013).

Rodney Maddock and Ian McLean, 'Supply-Side Shocks: The Case of Australian Gold', *Journal of Economic History*, 44, 4 (1984): 1047–67.

D.W. Meinig, *On the Margins of the Good Earth: The South Australian Wheat Frontier, 1869–1884* [1962] (Adelaide: Rigby, 1970).

Stephen Nicholas (ed.), *Convict Workers: Reinterpreting Australia's Past* (Cambridge University Press, 1988).

Geoff Raby, *Making Rural Australia: An Economic History of Technical and Institutional Creativity, 1788–1860* (Oxford University Press, 1996).

Simon Ville, *The Rural Entrepreneurs: A History of the Stock and Station Agent Industry in Australia and New Zealand* (Cambridge University Press, 2000).

Michael Williams, *The Making of the South Australian Landscape: A Study in the Historical Geography of Australia* (London: Academic Press, 1974).

Indigenous history and settler relations

Warwick Anderson, *The Cultivation of Whiteness: Science, Health and Racial Destiny in Australia* (Melbourne University Press, 2002).

Bain Attwood and S.G. Foster (eds), *Frontier Conflict: The Australian Experience* (Canberra: National Museum of Australia, 2003).

Bain Attwood and Andrew Markus, *The Struggle for Aboriginal Rights: A Documentary History* (Sydney: Allen & Unwin, 1999).

James Boyce, *Van Diemen's Land* (Melbourne: Black Inc. Press, 2008).

James Boyce, *1835: The Founding of Melbourne & the Conquest of Australia* (Melbourne: Black Inc., 2011).

Richard Broome, *Aboriginal Australians: A History Since 1788*, rev. edn (Sydney: Allen & Unwin, 2010).

Robert Foster, Rick Hosking and Amanda Nettelbeck, *Fatal Collisions: The South Australian Frontier and the Violence of Memory* (Adelaide: Wakefield Press, 2001).

Regina Ganter with Julia Martínez and Gary Lee, *Mixed Relations: Asian–Aboriginal Contact in Northern Australia* (Perth: UWA Press, 2006).

Heather Goodall, *Invasion to Embassy: Land in Aboriginal Politics in New South Wales, 1770–1992*, rev. edn (Sydney University Press, 2008).

Ann McGrath, *'Born in the Cattle': Aborigines in Cattle Country* (Sydney: Allen & Unwin, 1987).

Andrew Markus, *Australian Race Relations, 1788–1993* (Sydney: Allen & Unwin, 1994).

Dawn May, *Aboriginal Labour and the Cattle Industry: Queensland from White Settlement to the Present* (Cambridge University Press, 1994).

Aileen Moreton-Robinson (ed.), *Whitening Race: Essays in Social and Cultural Criticism* (Canberra: Aboriginal Studies Press, 2004).

Henry Reynolds, *North of Capricorn: The Untold Story of Australia's North* (Sydney: Allen & Unwin, 2003).

Henry Reynolds, *Fate Of A Free People: The Classic Account of the Tasmanian Wars*, new edn (Melbourne: Penguin, 2004).

Lynette Russell (ed.), *Colonial Frontiers: Indigenous-European Encounters in Settler Societies* (Manchester University Press, 2001).

Lyndall Ryan, *Tasmanian Aborigines: A History Since 1803* (Sydney: Allen & Unwin, 2012).

Nonie Sharp, *Stars of Tagai: The Torres Strait Islanders* (Canberra: Aboriginal Studies Press, 1993).

Peta Stephenson, *The Outsiders Within: Telling Australia's Indigenous-Asian Story* (Sydney University Press, 2007).

Education

A.G. Austin, *Australian Education, 1788–1900: Church, State and Public Education in Colonial Australia* (Melbourne: Pitman, 1961).

Alan Barcan, *A History of Australian Education* (Oxford University Press, 1980).

Craig Campbell, *Toward the State High School in Australia: Social Histories of State Secondary Schooling in Victoria, Tasmania, and South Australia, 1850–1925* (Sydney: Australian and New Zealand History of Education Society, 1999).

P.C. Candy and J. Laurent, *Pioneering Culture: Mechanics' Institutes and Schools of Art in Australia* (Adelaide: Auslib Press, 1994).

John F. Cleverley, *The First Generation: School and Society in Early Australia* (Sydney University Press, 1971).

J.J. Fletcher, *Clean, Clad and Courteous: A History of Aboriginal Education in New South Wales* (Sydney: J. Fletcher, 1989).

Ronald Fogarty, *Catholic Education in Australia 1806–1950*, 2 vols (Melbourne University Press, 1959).

W.J. Gardner, *Colonial Cap and Gown: Studies in the Mid-Victorian Universities of Australasia* (Christchurch: University of Canterbury, 1979).

Denis Grundy, *Secular, Compulsory and Free: The Education Act of 1872* (Melbourne University Press, 1972).

Julia Horne and Geoffrey Sherington, 'Extending the Educational Franchise: The Social Contract of Australia's Public Universities, 1850–1890', *Paedagogica Historica*, 46, 1–2 (2010): 207–27.

R.J.W. Selleck, *Frank Tate: A Biography* (Melbourne University Press, 1982).

Geoffrey Sherington, 'Religious School Systems', in James Jupp (ed.), *The Encyclopedia of Religion in Australia* (Cambridge University Press, 2009), pp. 668–76.

Geoffrey Sherington and Craig Campbell, 'Middle Class Formations and the Emergence of National Schooling', in Kim Tolley (ed.), *Transformations in Schooling Historical and Comparative Perspectives* (Basingstoke: Palgrave Macmillan, 2007), pp. 15–40.

Geoffrey Sherington and Julia Horne, 'Empire, State and Public Purpose in the Founding of Universities and Colleges in the Antipodes', *History of Education Review*, 39, 2 (2010): 36–51.

Geoffrey Sherington, R.C. Petersen and Ian Brice, *Learning to Lead: A History of Girls' and Boys' Corporate Secondary Schools in Australia* (Sydney: Allen & Unwin, 1987).

Andrew Spaull and Martin Sullivan, *A History of the Queensland Teachers' Union* (Sydney: Allen & Unwin, 1989).

Marjorie Theobald, *Knowing Women: Origins of Women's Education in Nineteenth-Century Australia* (Cambridge University Press, 1996).

Marjorie R. Theobald, and R.J.W. Selleck (eds), *Family, School and State in Australian History* (Sydney: Allen & Unwin, 1990).

Clifford Turney, *William Wilkins: His Life and Work: A Saga of Nineteenth-Century Education* (Sydney: Hale & Iremonger, 1992).

Law

Judith A. Allen, *Sex & Secrets: Crimes Involving Australian Women since 1880* (Oxford University Press, 1990).

A.R. Buck, *The Making of Australian Property Law* (Sydney: Federation Press, 2006).

Paula J. Byrne, *Criminal Law and Colonial Subject: New South Wales, 1810–1830* (Cambridge University Press, 1993).

Alex C. Castles, *An Australian Legal History* (Sydney: Law Book Co., 1982).

Alastair Davidson, *The Invisible State: The Formation of the Australian State 1788–1901* (Cambridge University Press, 1991).

Paul D. Finn, *Law and Government in Colonial Australia* (Oxford University Press, 1987).

Mark Finnane, *Police and Government: Histories of Policing in Australia* (Oxford University Press, 1994).

Hilary Golder, *Divorce in 19th Century New South Wales* (Sydney: UNSW Press, 1985).

Hilary Golder, *High and Responsible Office: A History of the NSW Magistracy* (Sydney University Press, 1991).

Robert Haldane, *The People's Force: A History of the Victoria Police* (Melbourne University Press, 1986).

J.B. Hirst, *Convict Society and its Enemies: A History of Early New South Wales* (Sydney: Allen & Unwin, 1983).

J.B. Hirst, *The Strange Birth of Colonial Democracy: New South Wales 1848–1884* (Sydney: Allen & Unwin, 1988).

Bruce Kercher, *An Unruly Child: A History of Law In Australia.* (Sydney: Allen & Unwin, 1995).

Diane Kirkby (ed.), *Sex, Power and Justice: Historical Perspectives of Law in Australia* (Oxford University Press, 1995).

B.H. McPherson, *The Supreme Court of Queensland, 1859–1960: History, Jurisdiction, Procedure* (Sydney: Butterworths, 1989).

David Neal, *The Rule of Law in a Penal Colony: Law and Power in Early New South Wales* (Cambridge University Press, 1991).

Jonathan Richards, *The Secret War: A True History of Queensland's Native Police* (Brisbane: UQP, 2008).

Susan West, *Bushranging and the Policing of Rural Banditry in New South Wales, 1860–1880* (Melbourne: Australian Scholarly Publishing, 2009).

Dean Wilson, *The Beat: Policing A Victorian City* (Melbourne Publishing Group, 2006).

G.D. Woods, *A History of Criminal Law In New South Wales: The Colonial Period, 1788–1900* (Sydney: Federation Press, 2002).

Religion

Bain Attwood, *The Making of the Aborigines* (Sydney: Allen & Unwin, 1989).

Ian Breward, *A History of Australian Churches* (Sydney: Allen & Unwin, 1993).

K.J. Cable, 'Protestant Problems in New South Wales in the Mid-Nineteenth Century', *Journal of Religious History*, 3, 2 (1964–5): 119–36.

Edmund Campion, *Australian Catholics* (Melbourne: Viking, 1987).

Hilary M. Carey, *Believing in Australia: A Cultural History of Religions* (Sydney: Allen & Unwin, 1996).

Richard Ely, *Unto God and Caesar: Religious Issues in the Emerging Commonwealth 1891–1906* (Melbourne University Press, 1976).

Allan M. Grocott, *Convicts, Clergymen and Churches: Attitudes of Convicts and Ex-convicts towards the Churches and Clergy in New South Wales from 1788–1851* (Sydney University Press, 1980).

John Harris, *One Blood: 200 years of Aboriginal Encounter with Christianity* (Sydney: Albatross Books, 1990).

David Hilliard, *Godliness and Good Order: A History of the Anglican Church in South Australia* (Adelaide: Wakefield Press, 1986).

Michael Hogan, *The Sectarian Strand: Religion in Australian History* (Melbourne: Penguin, 1987).

H.R. Jackson, *Churches and People in Australia and New Zealand 1860–1930* (Sydney: Allen & Unwin, 1987).

Further reading

Stephen Judd and Kenneth Cable, *Sydney Anglicans: A History of the Diocese* (Sydney: Anglican Information Office, 1987).

Bruce Kaye (ed.), *Anglicanism in Australia* (Melbourne University Press, 2002).

Robert Kenny, *The Lamb Enters the Dreaming: Nathanael Pepper and the Ruptured World* (Melbourne: Scribe, 2007).

Anne O'Brien, *God's Willing Workers: Women and Religion in Australia* (Sydney: UNSW Press, 2005).

Patrick O'Farrell, *The Catholic Church and Community*, rev. edn (Sydney: UNSW Press, 1985).

Walter Phillips, 'Religious Profession and Practice in New South Wales, 1850–1901: The Statistical Evidence', *Historical Studies*, 15, 59 (1972): 378–400.

Walter Phillips, *Defending a Christian Country: Churchmen and Society in New South Wales in the 1880s and After* (Brisbane: UQP, 1981).

Jill Roe, *Beyond Belief: Theosophy in Australia 1879–1939* (Sydney: UNSW Press, 1986).

Malcolm Wood, *Presbyterians in Colonial Victoria* (Melbourne: Australian Scholarly Publishing, 2008).

Science, technology and exploration

Geoffrey Badger, *Explorers of Australia* (Sydney: Kangaroo Press, 1981).

Gordon Clark (ed.), *Technology in Australia 1788–1988* (Melbourne: Australian Academy of Technological Sciences and Engineering, 1988).

Colin Finney, *To Sail Beyond the Sunset: Natural History in Australia 1699–1829* (Adelaide: Rigby, 1984).

Colin Finney, *Paradise Revealed: Natural History in Nineteenth-Century Australia* (Melbourne: Museum of Victoria, 1993).

Katherine Foxhall, *Health, Medicine and the Sea: Australian Voyages, c. 1815–60* (Manchester University Press, 2012).

Tom Frame, *Evolution in the Antipodes: Charles Darwin and Australia* (Sydney: UNSW Press, 2009).

John Gascoigne (with the assistance of Patricia Curthoys), *The Enlightenment and the Origins of European Australia* (Cambridge University Press, 2005).

Raymond Haynes, Roslynn Haynes, David Malin and Richard McGee, *Explorers of the Southern Sky: A History of Australian Astronomy* (Cambridge University Press, 1996).

R.W. Home (ed.), *Australian Science in the Making* (Cambridge University Press, 1988).

R.W. Home, *Science as a German Export to Nineteenth Century Australia* (London: Sir Robert Menzies Centre for Australian Studies, 1995).

Roy MacLeod (ed.), *The Commonwealth of Science: ANZAAS and the Scientific Enterprise in Australasia, 1888–1988* (Oxford University Press, 1988).

Roy MacLeod, *Archibald Liversidge, FRS: Imperial Science under the Southern Cross* (Sydney University Press, 2009).

Roy MacLeod and Philip F. Rehbock (eds), *Darwin's Laboratory: Evolutionary Theory and Natural History in the Pacific* (Honolulu: University of Hawai'i Press, 1994).

Sara Maroske, '"The whole great continent as a present": Nineteenth-century Australian Women Workers in Science', in Farley Kelly (ed.), *On the Edge of Discovery* (Melbourne: Text, 1993), pp. 13–34.

Further reading

Ann Moyal, *A Bright & Savage Land: Scientists in Colonial Australia* (Sydney: Collins, 1986).

F.B. Smith, *Illness in Colonial Australia* (Melbourne: Australian Scholarly Publishing, 2011).

Jan Todd, *Colonial Technology: Science and the Transfer of Innovation to Australia* (Cambridge University Press, 1995).

Ian Tyrrell, *True Gardens of the Gods: Californian-Australian Environmental Reform, 1860–1930* (Berkeley: University of California Press, 1999).

David Walker and Jürgen Tampke (eds), *From Berlin to the Burdekin: The German Contribution to the Development of Australian Science, Exploration and the Arts* (Sydney: UNSW Press, 1991).

Colonial society and gender

Katrina Alford, *Production or Reproduction? An Economic History of Women in Australia, 1788–1850* (Oxford University Press, 1984).

Judith A. Allen, *Rose Scott: Vision and Revision in Australian Feminism* (Oxford University Press, 1994).

Martin Crotty, *Making the Australian Male: Middle-Class Masculinity 1870–1920* (Melbourne University Press, 2001).

Joy Damousi, *Depraved and Disorderly: Female Convicts, Sexuality and Gender in Colonial Australia* (Cambridge University Press, 1997).

Patricia Grimshaw, Marilyn Lake, Ann McGrath and Marian Quartly, *Creating a Nation* (Melbourne: Penguin, 1994).

Patricia Grimshaw, Chris McConville and Ellen McEwen (eds), *Families in Colonial Australia* (Sydney: Allen & Unwin, 1985).

Jan Kociumbas, *Australian Childhood: A History* (Sydney: Allen & Unwin, 1997).

Marilyn Lake, 'The Politics of Respectability: Identifying the Masculinist Context', *Historical Studies*, 22, 86 (1986): 116–31.

Marilyn Lake, *Getting Equal: The History of Australian Feminism* (Sydney: Allen & Unwin, 1999).

Kirsten McKenzie, *Scandal in the Colonies: Sydney and Cape Town, 1820–1850* (Melbourne University Press, 2004).

Susan Magarey, *Passions of the First Wave Feminists* (Sydney: UNSW Press, 2001).

Susan Magarey, *Unbridling the Tongues of Women: A Biography of Catherine Helen Spence*, rev. edn (University of Adelaide Press, 2010).

Susan Magarey, Sue Rowley and Susan Sheridan (eds), *Debutante Nation: Feminism Contests the 1890s* (Sydney: Allen & Unwin, 1993).

Pat Quiggin, *No Rising Generation: Women & Fertility in Late Nineteenth Century Australia* (Canberra: Department of Demography, ANU, 1988).

Kirsty Reid, *Gender, Crime and Empire: Convicts, Settlers and the State in Early Colonial Australia* (Manchester University Press, 2007).

Penny Russell, *A Wish of Distinction: Colonial Gentility and Femininity* (Melbourne University Press, 1994).

Penny Russell, *Savage or Civilised? Manners in Colonial Australia* (Sydney: UNSW Press, 2010).

Kay Saunders and Raymond Evans (eds), *Gender Relations in Australia: Domination and Negotiation* (Sydney: Harcourt Brace Jovanovich, 1992).

Linda Young, *Middle Class Culture in the Nineteenth Century: America, Australia and Britain* (New York: Palgrave Macmillan, 2002).

Art and literature

Michael Ackland, *That Shining Band: A Study of Australian Colonial Verse Tradition* (Brisbane: UQP, 1994).

Candice Bruce, Edward Comstock and Frank McDonald, *Eugene von Guérard 1881–1901: A German Romantic in the Antipodes* (Martinborough: Alistair Taylor, 1982).

Robert Dixon, *The Course of Empire: Neo-Classical Culture in New South Wales 1788–1860* (Oxford University Press, 1986).

Richard Fotheringham (ed.), *Australian Plays for the Colonial Stage: 1834–1899* (Brisbane: UQP, 2006).

Jeanette Hoorn, *The Lycett Album: Drawings of Aborigines and Australian Scenery* (Canberra: Australian National Library of Australia, 1990).

Jeanette Hoorn, *Australian Pastoral: The Making of a White Landscape* (Fremantle Arts Centre Press, 2007).

Graeme Johanson, *A Study of Colonial Editions in Australia 1843–1972* (Wellington, NZ: Elibank Press, 2000).

Robert Jordan, *The Convict Theatres of Early Australia 1788–1840* (Sydney: Currency House, 2002).

Joan Kerr, *Our Great Victorian Architect: Edmund Thomas Blacket, 1817–1883* (Sydney: National Trust of Australia, 1983).

Sylvia Lawson, *The Archibald Paradox: A Strange Case of Authorship* (Melbourne: Allen Lane, 1983).

Andrew McCann, *Marcus Clarke's Bohemia: Literature and Modernity in Colonial Melbourne* (Melbourne University Press, 2004).

John McDonald, *Art of Australia. Volume 1, Exploration to Federation* (Sydney: Pan Macmillan, 2008).

Humphrey McQueen, *Tom Roberts* (Sydney: Macmillan, 1996).

Howard Morphy, *Ancestral Connections: Art and an Aboriginal System of Knowledge* (University of Chicago Press, 1991).

Andrew Sayers, *Australian Art* (Oxford University Press, 2001).

Bernard Smith, *European Vision and the South Pacific* [1960] (New Haven: Yale University Press, 1985).

Bernard Smith and Alwyne Wheeler (eds), *The Art of the First Fleet & Other Early Australian Drawings* (Oxford University Press, 1988).

Ken Stewart, 'Journalism and the World of the Writer: The Production of Australian Literature, 1855–1915', in Laurie Hergenhan (ed.), *The Penguin New Literary History of Australia* (Melbourne: Penguin, 1988), pp. 174–93.

Lurline Stuart, *James Smith: The Making of a Colonial Culture* (Sydney: Allen & Unwin, 1989).

Australia and Greater Britain

Christopher A. Bayly, *The Birth of the Modern World, 1780–1940* (Oxford: Blackwell, 2004).

James Belich, *Replenishing the Earth: The Settler Revolution and the Rise of the Anglo-World, 1783–1939* (Oxford University Press, 2009).

Duncan Bell, *The Idea of Greater Britain* (Princeton University Press, 2007).

Peter Burroughs, *Britain and Australia 1831–1855: A Study in Imperial Relations and Crown Lands Administration* (Oxford: Clarendon, 1967).

Peter Cochrane, *Colonial Ambition: Foundations of Australian Democracy* (Melbourne University Press, 2006).

John Darwin, *The Empire Project: The Rise and Fall of the British World System, 1830–1970* (Cambridge University Press, 2009).

Charles Dilke, *Greater Britain*, ed. with introduction by Geoffrey Blainey [1868] (Sydney: Methuen Haynes, 1985).

John Eddy and Deryck M. Schreuder (eds), *The Rise of Colonial Nationalism: Australia, New Zealand, Canada and South Africa First Assert their Nationalities, 1880–1914* (Sydney: Allen & Unwin, 1988).

David Fitzpatrick, *Oceans of Consolation: Personal Accounts of Irish Migration to Australia* (Melbourne University Press, 1994).

Alan Frost, *Convicts and Empire: A Naval Question, 1776–1811* (Oxford University Press, 1980).

Alan Frost, *The Global Reach of Empire: Britain's Maritime Expansion in the Indian and Pacific Oceans 1764–1815* (Melbourne: Miegunyah Press, 2003).

Zoë Laidlaw, *Colonial Connections, 1815–45: Patronage, the Information Revolution and Colonial Government* (Manchester University Press, 2005).

Gary B. Magee and Andrew S. Thompson, *Empire and Globalisation: Networks of People, Goods and Capital in the British World, c. 1850–1914* (Cambridge University Press, 2010).

Neville Meaney, 'Britishness and Australian Identity: The Problem of Nationalism in Australian History and Historiography', *Australian Historical Studies*, 32, 116 (2001): 76–90.

Eric Richards, *Britannia's Children: Emigration from England, Scotland, Wales and Ireland Since 1600* (London: Hambledon and London, 2004).

Deryck M. Schreuder and Stuart Ward (eds), *Australia's Empire* (Oxford University Press, 2008).

Roger Thompson, *Australian Imperialism in the Pacific: The Expansionist Era, 1820–1920* (Melbourne University Press, 1980).

Luke Trainor, *British Imperialism and Australian Nationalism: Manipulation, Conflict, and Compromise in the Late Nineteenth Century* (Cambridge University Press, 1994).

John Manning Ward, *Colonial Self-Government: The British Experience, 1759–1856* (London: Macmillan, 1976).

Helen R. Woolcock, *Rights of Passage: Emigration to Australia in the Nineteenth Century* (London: Tavistock Publications, 1986).

Colonial Australia in the Asia-Pacific region

Tracey Banivanua Mar, *Violence and Colonial Dialogue: The Australian-Pacific Indentured Labor Trade* (Honolulu: University of Hawai'i Press, 2007).

Ann Curthoys and Marilyn Lake (eds), *Connected Worlds: History in Transnational Perspective* (Canberra: ANU E Press, 2005).

Donald Denoon and Philippa Mein Smith with Marivic Wyndham, *A History of Australia, New Zealand and the Pacific* (Oxford: Blackwell, 2000).

Charles Ferrall, Paul Millar and Keren Smith (eds), *East by South: China in the Australasian Imagination* (Wellington: Victoria University Press, 2005).

John Fitzgerald, *Big White Lie: Chinese Australians in White Australia* (Sydney: UNSW Press, 2007).

Regina Ganter with Julia Martínez and Gary Lee, *Mixed Relations: Asian–Aboriginal Contact in North Australia* (Perth: UWA Press, 2006).

Helen Gardner, *Gathering for God: George Brown in Oceania* (Dunedin: Otago University Press, 2006).

Henry Johnson and Brian Moloughney (eds), *Asia in the Making of New Zealand* (Auckland University Press, 2006).

Marilyn Lake and Henry Reynolds, *Drawing the Global Colour Line: White Men's Countries and the International Challenge of Racial Equality* (Melbourne University Press, 2008).

Andrew Markus, *Fear and Hatred: Purifying Australia and California 1850–1901* (Sydney: Hale & Iremonger, 1979).

Clive Moore, *Kanaka: A History of Melanesian Mackay* (Port Moresby: University of Papua New Guinea Press, 1985).

Charles A. Price, *The Great White Walls Are Built: Restrictive Immigration to North America and Australasia, 1836–1888* (Canberra: ANU Press, 1974).

Geoffrey Serle, *The Rush to be Rich: A History of the Colony of Victoria, 1883–1889* (Melbourne University Press, 1974).

Frances Steel, *Oceania Under Steam: Sea Transport and the Cultures of Colonialism, c.1870–1914* (Manchester University Press, 2011).

Roger C. Thompson, *Australian Imperialism in the Pacific: The Expansionist Era, 1820–1920* (Melbourne University Press, 1980).

Roger C. Thompson, *Australia and the Pacific Islands in the Twentieth Century* (Melbourne: Australian Scholarly Publishing, 1998).

David Walker, *Anxious Nation: Australia and the Rise of Asia 1850–1939* (Brisbane: UQP, 1999).

A.T. Yarwood, *Asian Migration to Australia: The Background to Exclusion, 1896–1923* (Melbourne University Press, 1967).

Colonial Australia in a maritime world

John Bach, *A Maritime History of Australia* (Melbourne: Thomas Nelson, 1976).

John Bach, *The Australia Station: A History of the Royal Navy in the South West Pacific, 1821–1913* (Sydney: UNSW Press, 1986).

Ruth Balint, *Troubled Waters: Borders, Boundaries and Possession in the Timor Sea* (Sydney: Allen & Unwin, 2005).

Alison Bashford, *Imperial Hygiene: A Critical History of Colonialism, Nationalism and Public Health* (Basingstoke: Palgrave Macmillan, 2004).

Frank Broeze, *Island Nation: A History of Australians and the Sea* (Sydney: Allen & Unwin, 1998).

Penelope Edmonds, *Urbanizing Frontiers: Indigenous Peoples and Settlers in 19th-Century Pacific Rim Cities* (Vancouver: University of British Columbia Press, 2010).

Heather Goodall, Devleena Ghosh and Lindi Renier Todd, 'Jumping Ship: Indians, Aborigines and Australians across the Indian Ocean', *Transforming Cultures eJournal*, 3, 1 (2008): 44–74

Further reading

Andrew Hassam, *Sailing to Australia: Shipboard Diaries by Nineteenth-Century British Emigrants* (Manchester University Press, 1994).

Cindy McCreery, 'A British Prince and a Transnational Life: Alfred, Duke of Edinburgh's Visit to Australia, 1867–8', in Desley Deacon, Penny Russell and Angela Woollacott (eds), *Transnational Ties: Australian Lives in the World* (Canberra: ANU E Press, 2008), pp. 57–74.

Kirsten McKenzie, *Scandal in the Colonies: Sydney and Cape Town, 1820–1850* (Melbourne University Press, 2004).

Kirsten McKenzie, *A Swindler's Progress: Nobles and Convicts in the Age of Liberty* (Sydney: UNSW Press, 2009).

Tamson Pietsch, 'A British Sea: Making Sense of Global Space in the Late Nineteenth Century', *Journal of Global History*, 5, 3 (2010): 423–46.

Alan Powell, *Northern Voyagers: Australia's Monsoon Coast in Maritime History* (Melbourne: Australian Scholarly Publishing, 2010).

Jane Samson, *Imperial Benevolence: Making British Authority in the Pacific Islands* (Honolulu: University of Hawai'i Press, 1998).

Anna Shnukal, Guy Ramsay and Yuriko Nagata (eds) *Navigating Boundaries: The Asian Diaspora in Torres Strait* (Canberra: Pandanus Books, 2004).

Frances Steel, *Oceania under Steam: Sea Transport and the Cultures of Colonialism, c. 1870–1914* (Manchester University Press, 2011).

David Stevens (ed.), *The Royal Australian Navy. The Australian Centenary History of Defence*, vol. 3 (Oxford University Press, 2001).

Chronology

c. 50,000 BP	Humans arrive on northern coastline of Australian continent
c. 26,000 BP	Evidence of first Indigenous Australian pigment rock art
c. 14,000 BP	Rising sea levels separate Tas. and mainland Australia
8,000–6,000 BP	Torres Strait Islands form as sea level rises
1606	Willem Janszoon lands near Cape York, north-east Australia
1616	Dirk Hartog lands on west coast at Shark Bay
1642	Abel Tasman lands on east coast of Tas., names Van Diemen's Land
c. 1660	'Indonesian' *trepangers* commence trade along north coast
1688	William Dampier lands at King Sound on west coast
1770	James Cook explores east coast, lands at Botany Bay
1772	Marc-Joseph Marion-Dufresne lands at Marion Bay, VDL
1776	*Hulk Act* passed in Britain; decommissioned warships used as prisons
1777	James Cook lands at Adventure Bay, VDL
1788	Governor Arthur Phillip and First Fleet land at Botany Bay (18 January)
1788	Phillip sails to Port Jackson; colony of NSW established; French ships under La Pérouse enter Botany Bay (26 January)
1788	Norfolk Island founded as penal colony by Philip Gidley King
1788	First conflict with Aboriginal people at Rushcutter's Bay
1789	Smallpox spreads among Aboriginal people around Port Jackson
1789	William Dawes attempts to cross Blue Mountains
1789	Phillip captures Bennelong and Colebee
1790	Spearing of Governor Phillip near Manly, by Wileemarin
1790	First circumnavigation of Australia by Henry Lidgbird Ball aboard HMS Supply
1791	Sealing and whaling commences
1791	Parramatta named by Governor Phillip
1792	Assignment system for convicts commences
1793	Free settlers arrive aboard Bellona
1793	Bruny D'Entrecasteaux explores VDL
1794	George Shaw first writer to use 'Australia' to describe entire continent

1794	Hawkesbury River valley settled by ex-convicts
1795	John Hunter appointed governor of NSW
1797	Merino sheep introduced
1798	George Bass sails through Bass Strait
1800	Philip Gidley King appointed governor of NSW
1801	Ticket-of-leave system introduced
1801–3	Nicolas Baudin's *Géographe* and *Naturaliste* circumnavigate Australia
1801–3	Matthew Flinders explores coastline and circumnavigates Australia
1803	David Collins attempts penal settlement at Port Phillip Bay
1803	British settlement in VDL (Risdon Cove)
1803	New England whalers arrive in Australia
1803	First newspaper, *Sydney Gazette*, published by George Howe
1804	David Collins founds Hobart Town, appointed lieutenant-governor of VDL
1804	Castle Hill rising suppressed by NSW Corps
1804	Newcastle convict station founded
1805	Norfolk Island penal colony abandoned
1805	William Bligh appointed governor of NSW
1806	Launceston founded, VDL
1808	Bligh deposed by NSW Corps
1810	*Derwent Star* first newspaper published in VDL
1810	Lachlan Macquarie appointed governor of NSW
1813	East India Company trade monopoly revoked
1813	Thomas Davey appointed lieutenant-governor of VDL
1813	Crossing of Blue Mountains by Blaxland, Wentworth and Lawson
1813	Benevolent Society of NSW established
1813	Mission established in New Zealand by Samuel Marsden
1815	Macquarie establishes Native Institution, Parramatta
1815	Bathurst established, first inland town (NSW)
1816	NSW Botanical Gardens established
1817	William Sorell appointed lieutenant-governor of VDL
1817	Bank of New South Wales established
1819	Hyde Park convict barracks opens in Sydney
1819–21	John Thomas Bigge conducts Commission of Inquiry into colonial affairs; reports published 1822–23
1820	Catholic Church officially recognised
1821	Sir Thomas Brisbane appointed governor of NSW
1821	Port Macquarie penal station established, NSW
1822	Macquarie Harbour penal station established, VDL
1822	Astronomical Observatory established at Parramatta
1823	*New South Wales Act* (UK) establishes Legislative Council (NSW) and Supreme Courts (NSW and VDL)
1824	Martial law declared by Governor Brisbane against the Wiradjuri, around Bathurst
1824	Sir Frances Forbes appointed first chief justice of NSW
1824	George Arthur appointed lieutenant-governor of VDL
1824	Moreton Bay penal colony founded (later Brisbane)

1824	Hume and Hovell travel overland from Sydney to Port Phillip
1824	Australian Agricultural Company established
1824	Fort Dundas established on Melville Island, north coast; (abandoned, 1829)
1825	Lancelot Threlkeld's mission granted 10,000 acres at Port Macquarie, NSW
1825	Ralph Darling appointed governor of NSW
1825	Norfolk Island resettled as penal colony
1825	Separation of VDL from NSW
1826	Executive Council for VDL formed
1826	Military outpost at King George Sound (later Albany)
1827	Colonial Museum founded (later Australian Museum), Sydney
1827	James Stirling explores Swan River, WA
1827	Fort Wellington established on north coast (abandoned 1829)
1828	Martial law declared, VDL
1828	*Australian Courts Act* declares English statute and common law to apply to colonies
1829	Governor Darling proclaims the limits of settlement in NSW
1829	*Western Australia Act* (UK) proclaims new colony; James Stirling appointed lieutenant-governor
1830	Charles Sturt discovers the junction between the Murray and Darling rivers
1830	The 'Black Line', VDL
1830	Port Arthur penal settlement opens, VDL
1831	Sir Richard Bourke appointed governor of NSW
1831	Emigration Commissioners appointed in London
1834	*South Australia Act* (UK) based on Wakefield's scheme of 'systematic colonisation'
1834	Armed conflict between Stirling and Aboriginal people at Pinjarra, Swan River
1835	Batman's Treaty with Wurundjeri, Port Phillip; revoked by Governor Bourke
1836–7	*Church Acts* (NSW) provide financial aid to the four principal denominations
1836	John Hindmarsh appointed governor of SA
1836	Adelaide founded; province of South Australia established
1837	Sir John Franklin appointed lieutenant-governor of VDL
1838	Sir George Gipps appointed governor of NSW
1838	Killing of Aboriginal people at Myall Creek, NSW
1838	Molesworth select committee recommends abolition of convict transportation to NSW
1838	Troops stationed at Port Essington on north coast (abandoned 1849)
1839	John Hutt appointed governor of WA
1839	Charles Joseph La Trobe appointed superintendent of Port Phillip District

1839	George Augustus Robinson appointed Chief Protector of Aborigines (Port Phillip District)
1839	Port Darwin, NT, named
1839	New Zealand incorporated into NSW
1840	Convict transportation to NSW ends
1840	Beginning of six-year depression, wool market collapses
1841	New Zealand becomes separate crown colony
1841	George Grey appointed governor of SA
1842	*South Australia Government Act* passed
1842	Representative government granted to NSW
1843	Sir John Eardley-Wilmot appointed lieutenant-governor of VDL
1844	Charles Sturt expedition discredits theory of inland sea
1845	Frederick Holt Robe appointed lieutenant-governor of SA
1845	First steamer arrives, WA
1846	Andrew Clarke appointed governor of WA
1846	Sir Charles FitzRoy appointed governor of NSW
1847	Sir William Denison appointed lieutenant-governor of VDL
1848	*National Education Board Act* (NSW) leads to establishment of public elementary schools
1848	Order in Council abolishing transportation of convicts to NSW revoked
1848	Chinese arrive in Sydney from Hong Kong; employed as shepherds
1849	Anti-Transportation League formed in Launceston, VDL
1849	Caroline Chisholm forms Family Colonisation Loan Society (London) to promote emigration
1849	Repeal of *Navigation Act* ends British monopoly of trade with colonies
1850	First convict transportation to WA
1850	Port Phillip District separated from NSW and renamed colony of Victoria
1850	University of Sydney established
1851	Australasian Anti-Transportation League established
1851	Charles La Trobe appointed lieutenant-governor of Vic.
1851	Gold discovered near Bathurst, NSW, and Clunes, Vic.
1851	Black Thursday bushfires (Vic.)
1853	Convict transportation ends, VDL
1853	University of Melbourne established
1853	Melbourne Public Library established (later State Library of Victoria)
1854	First steam railway opens, Melbourne
1854	Sir Charles Hotham appointed lieutenant-governor of Vic.
1854	First southern hemisphere telegraph line opened, Vic.
1854	Eureka Rebellion (December 3)
1854	Sir William Denison appointed governor-general of Australian colonies
1855	*Immigration Act* (Vic.) limits Chinese immigration; repealed 1865
1855	Eight-hour working day granted to Sydney stonemasons
1855	Steam railway between Sydney and Parramatta

1855	Colonial Sugar Refining Company established in Sydney
1856	Responsible government for NSW, Vic., Tasmania
1856	Norfolk Island abandoned as penal settlement
1856	Secret ballot first used
1856	Eight-hour working day for Victorian stonemasons
1857	Male suffrage, Vic.
1857	SA gains responsible government
1857	Chinese restriction legislation (SA); repealed 1861
1858	Male suffrage, NSW
1858	Sydney, Melbourne and Adelaide linked by telegraph
1859	Queensland separated from NSW, and gains responsible government
1859	First trade union representative elected to parliament, Vic.
1860	Troops despatched from NSW to Māori wars in NZ
1860	Nicholson's *Land Acts* release crown land in Vic; allows small holders to select crown land on credit.
1860–1	Burke and Wills expedition, Melbourne to Gulf of Carpentaria
1861	Anti-Chinese riots at Lambing Flat goldfields, NSW
1861	First English cricket team arrives in Melbourne
1861	Robertson's *Land Acts* release crown land, NSW
1861	First stock exchange opens, Melbourne
1861	*Chinese Immigrants Regulation and Restriction Act* (NSW); repealed 1867
1861	Victorian Acclimatisation Society established, Melbourne, to introduce European plants and animals
1863	First Intercolonial Conference, Melbourne
1863	SA administers Northern Territory
1863	Coranderrk mission established, Vic.
1863	Pacific Islander labourers first brought to Queensland
1865	*Felons Apprehension Act* (NSW)
1865	Goyder's 'line of rainfall' sets limit to agriculture in SA
1865	*Colonial Laws Validity Act* (UK)
1866	*Public Schools Act* (NSW) funds and regulates public and church schools
1867	Alfred, Duke of Edinburgh begins tour of the colonies
1868	*Polynesian Labourers Act* (Qld)
1868	Aboriginal cricket team tours England
1868	Transportation of convicts to WA ends
1869	Palmerston (Darwin from 1911) founded
1869	*Aboriginal Protection Act* (Vic.)
1870	Representative government granted to WA
1870	British troops withdrawn from Australian colonies
1871	Australian Natives Association formed, Melbourne
1872	*Pacific Islanders Protection Act* (UK)
1872	*Education Act* (Vic), first comprehensive system of compulsory primary education
1872	Overland telegraph line completed, Port Augusta in SA to Port Darwin, NT

1872–75	First Parkes ministry (NSW)
1874	Fiji Islands under NSW sovereignty
1874	University of Adelaide established, first university to admit women
1875	First Berry ministry, Vic.
1877	Port Arthur penal settlement closed
1877	First cricket test match between England and Australia
1877	*Chinese Immigrants Regulation Act* (Qld)
1879	Intercolonial Trade Union Conference, Sydney, passes eight-hour day resolution
1879	The National Park (Sydney) declared (Royal National Park from 1955)
1880	*The Bulletin* first published, Sydney
1880	Ned Kelly tried and executed, Melbourne
1880	*Public Instruction Act* (NSW)
1881	First Australia-wide census
1881	*Act to Restrict the Influx of Chinese into NSW*
1883	Aborigines Protection Board established in NSW
1883	Attempted annexation of Papua by Queensland; disallowed by UK
1883	Intercolonial Convention (Sydney) agrees to establish Federal Council
1883	Burns, Philp & Co. established; trading commences between Australia, New Guinea and the Pacific
1884	Imperial Federation League formed
1884	Victorian Women's Suffrage Society formed
1884	British protectorate over Papua declared
1885	Federal Council of Australasia established
1885	Broken Hill Proprietary (BHP) mining company founded
1886	*Aboriginal Protection Act* (WA)
1886	*Act to Regulate and Restrict Chinese Immigration* (WA)
1887	*Chinese Immigration Act* (Tas.)
1887	First Colonial Conference, London (later Imperial Conference)
1887	Peak of Melbourne's land boom
1887	Visit of the Chinese Imperial Commissioners to Sydney
1888	Attack on Chinese, Brisbane
1888	Intercolonial Conference in Sydney decides to legislate uniform restrictions on Chinese immigration
1888	*Chinese Immigration Restriction Act* (SA)
1888	Women's Suffrage League of South Australia formed
1889	*Chinese Immigration Restriction Act* (WA)
1890	Responsible government, WA
1890	Australasian Federal Conference, Melbourne
1890	University of Tasmania established
1890	Maritime strike
1890–1	Labor electoral leagues established, NSW, Qld, SA, Vic.
1891	Shearers' strike, Qld
1891	National Australasian Convention, Sydney
1892	Broken Hill miners' strike

1892	Gold discovery, Coolgardie, WA
1893	Gold rush to Kalgoorlie, WA
1893	Banking and building society crisis
1894	Shearers' strike, Qld
1894	SA women gain right to vote
1896	*Coloured Races Restriction and Regulation Act* (NSW)
1896	*State Children Relief Act* (NSW) allowance for destitute single mothers (mainly widows)
1897	*Protection Act* (Qld) creates reserves for Aboriginal people, managed by Aboriginal Protectors
1897	Jandamarra killed in the Kimberley (WA), ending six years' fighting against pastoral expansion
1897	Second Australasian Federal Convention, Adelaide and Sydney sessions
1898	Final session of Australasian Federal Convention, Melbourne
1898	First referendum on Federation; fails in NSW
1898	*Immigration Restriction Act* (NSW)
1899	Colonial Australian contingents depart for Anglo-Boer War
1899	Second referendum on Federation approved by NSW, Qld, SA, Tas. Vic.
1899	First Labor government formed, Qld
1899	Female suffrage, WA
1900	Male suffrage, Tas.
1900	WA referendum on Federation succeeds
1900	Old-age pensions and compulsory arbitration scheme, NSW
1900	*Commonwealth of Australia Constitution Act* (UK)
1900	Earl of Hopetoun appointed first governor-general of Australia
1901	Commonwealth of Australia inaugurated (January 1)

Index

Note: Page references in bold indicate map, figure or table

Index

Index

Index

Printed in Great Britain
by Amazon

66326647R00383